REFERENCE SERIES

Encyclopedia of U.S. Air Force Aircraft and Missile Systems

Volume II

Post-World War II Bombers 1945–1973

Marcelle Size Knaack

OFFICE OF AIR FORCE HISTORY
UNITED STATES AIR FORCE
WASHINGTON, D.C., 1988

Library of Congress Cataloging-in-Publication Data

Knaack, Marcelle, date.
    Encyclopedia of US Air Force aircraft and missile
systems.

    Vol. 2 has title: Encyclopedia of U.S. Air Force
aircraft and missile systems.
    Includes bibliographies and index.
    Contents: v. 1. Post-World War II fighters,
1945-1973 -- v. 2. Post-World War II bombers, 1945-1973.
    1. Airplanes, Military--United States. 2. Guided
missiles. 3. United States. Air Force. I. United
States. Air Force. Office of Air Force History.
II. Title. III. Title: Encyclopedia of U.S. Air Force
aircraft and missile systems.
UG1243.K53   358.4'3'0973   77-22377
ISBN 0-912799-59-5

For sale by the Superintendent of Documents, U.S. Government Printing Office
Washington, D.C. 20402

United States Air Force
Historical Advisory Committee

(As of August 1, 1988)

Alfred D. Chandler
Harvard University

Charles R. Hamm
Lieutenant General, USAF
Superintendent, USAF Academy

Mrs. Anne Foreman
The General Counsel, USAF

Ralph E. Havens
Lieutenant General, USAF
Commander, Air University

Norman A. Graebner
The University of Virginia

John H. Morrow, Jr.
The University of Tennessee at
   Knoxville
(*Chairman*)

Dominick Graham
University of New Brunswick,
   Canada

Thomas M. Ryan, Jr.
General, USAF (Retired)

Ira D. Gruber
Rice University

Gerhard L. Weinberg
The University of North Carolina,
   at Chapel Hill

The Author

MARCELLE SIZE KNAACK rejoined the Office of Air Force History in 1970, after serving on two occasions as Deputy Chief Historian of the United States Air Forces in Europe. She became a senior historian in 1980. Born and educated in France, Mrs. Knaack graduated from the College d'Artois and attended the University of Lille, where her interest focused on foreign policy and international relations. Her first book was *Post-World War II Fighters, 1945–1973,* Vol I, *Encyclopedia of U.S. Air Force Aircraft and Missile Systems* (Office of Air Force History, 1978).

Foreword

The second in a series of encyclopedias of U.S. Air Force aircraft and missile systems, this volume covers the development and fielding of bomber aircraft between 1945 and 1973, commencing with the Convair B–36 Peacemaker and ending with the development of the Rockwell International B–1A. Marcelle Knaack's detailed and comprehensive discussion of each bomber type provides a wealth of technical material painstakingly extracted from official Air Force sources. The researcher will find the information readily available and easy to use.

Equally critical to our understanding of bomber development, however, is the author's treatment of the policy issues and the technological decisions that molded each bomber program. During the postwar years, the nation's emerging nuclear capabilities placed new emphasis on developing bombers capable of delivering the atomic weapon. Subsequent military needs in Korea and Southeast Asia, however, required a return to conventional weapons. New technologies continually spawned modifications in the weapons systems. And throughout, the Air Force adapted developmental programs and modified production aircraft to fit new roles, from strategic reconnaissance to tactical operations for the Southeast Asia theater.

These pages contain essential data for a wide spectrum of audiences inside and outside the U.S. Air Force. Mrs. Knaack's exacting research and her ability to translate difficult and often conflicting documentation into clear and concise capsule histories will enable planners and those engaged in the research and development of aircraft to benefit from the Air Force's experience. As she points out, the success of the postwar bomber program has been the result of the Air Force's willingness to consider several different developmental pathways simultaneously, to modify existing aircraft as technology permits, and above all, to assume continually the development risks required to keep the service at the forefront of technology.

Richard H. Kohn
Chief, Office of Air Force History

Preface

This reference volume compiles basic information on all Air Force strategic, tactical, and experimental bombers developed or produced between World War II and 1973. The book begins with the Convair B-36 Peacemaker, the first long-range, strategic atomic carrier, and closes with the development of the Rockwell International B-1A. The main narrative covers eight bomber types, most of which weathered some 30 years of world crises and two wars—the conflicts in Korea and Southeast Asia. Included is the premier B-52 Stratofortress, due to remain a prime asset of the Strategic Air Command through the 1980s.

The volume's first appendix considers the Douglas B-26 Invader and the Boeing B-29 Superfortress, aircraft of World War II vintage which made important contributions in subsequent years. Appendix II, Experimental and Prototype Bombers, deals with 10 aircraft, including the controversial Northrop XB-35 and YB-49; the ill-fated North American XB-70A; and the Advanced Manned Strategic Aircraft (AMSA), redesignated as the B-1A in April 1969.

The origin of each bomber is traced as well as, whenever applicable, its most significant development, production, and operational problems. Also noted are production decision dates, program changes, test results, procurement methods, production totals, delivery rates, prominent milestones, and brief descriptions of special features of new aircraft versions and configurations. Selected technical data and operational characteristics are provided at the end of each section.

This volume follows the pattern established in *Post-World War II Fighters, 1945-1973,* Vol I, *Encyclopedia of U.S. Air Force Aircraft and Missile Systems* (Office of Air Force History, 1978). Like the first encyclopedia, the bomber volume does not provide complete consistency of data. This is particularly understandable in the bombers' case because every program was highly individual and far more complex than the fighter programs. Nevertheless, as the specific bomber programs evolved, their respective *raison d'être* and the planned interlacing of the various programs became obvious.

One cannot anticipate history's ultimate assessment of the Air Force's achievements through the mid-1970s. The passage of time seldom worked in favor of the young service. Caution did not always pay off: when at long last operational, the B–36 was obsolete. Conversely, rising world tensions prompted the hurried production of unsuitable B–47s, which had to be reworked. The threat, never ceasing to exist, assumed many guises. In the rapidly changing environment, the very factors that fueled the growth of specific weapon systems could also alter their intrinsic modes of operation. A case in point is the B–52. Singled out for the atomic role, these bombers in 1972 found themselves flying conventional bombing missions against military targets in the Hanoi and Haiphong areas of North Vietnam.

This volume's sketchy compendium of data does not do justice to the Air Force, which met extraordinary challenges from the start. At the end of World War II, the operational forces were sharply reduced, then increased, only to be cut again. Besides hindering planning, such changes disrupted the aircraft industry and made it far more difficult to procure, given the many variables, the best weapon systems possible, in timely fashion. Money was continually in short supply. New administrations might shift the emphasis afforded to certain weapons—whether missiles or manned aircraft—but the tight budgets remained a constant limitation. Undoubtedly, the Air Force made mistakes. Yet, the service did place a premium on getting the greatest return from each dollar spent. The knowledge gained from canceled experimental programs was quickly put to other uses. Old aircraft were stripped and sold. Valuable surplus equipment and still serviceable engines were carefully retained, and savings routinely ensured.

In the early and mid-sixties, recurring world crises and the high cost of new weapon systems and space programs added urgency to the demand for cost-efficiency. Moreover, as the tempo of activities rose in Southeast Asia, the Air Force's task grew even more difficult. Improvisation and versatility became the order of the day. Refurbished aircraft and their heroic crews soon proved their worth; and the Air Force again met its commitments. Above all, the Air Force's greatest achievement was its success in coping with revolutionary technological developments. This is not to say, as 1973 came to an end, that technology had reached a plateau. Scientific progress was not likely to stop. Still, the foreseeable future appeared to be more settled, concentrating on the refinement process. The pioneering spirit of the three turbulent decades following World War II was giving way to a new equilibrium.

This volume is based essentially on U.S. Air Force sources, and I alone am responsible for the many omissions, and possible distortions, in this compilation.

Marcelle Size Knaack

Acknowledgments

The author wishes to express her appreciation to Maj. Gen. John W. Huston, USAF, Ret., formerly Chief, Office of Air Force History, who effectively supported this project from the beginning; to Dr. Richard H. Kohn, the present Chief, his Deputy, Col. Fred Shiner, and to Herman S. Wolk, Chief of the General Histories Branch, for their advice, encouragement, and unfailing assistance throughout the entire task.

The author owes a considerable debt to John Bohn, Command Historian of the Strategic Air Command, and his staff; to Robert J. Smith, formerly Command Historian of the Air Force Logistics Command and now Command Historian of Tactical Air Command; to Dr. Richard Hallion, formerly Chief of the Air Force Flight Test Center's History Office, now Director, Special Staff Office of the Air Force Systems Command's Aeronautical Systems Division, and his staff; to Albert E. Misenko, Chief Historian of the Aeronautical Systems Division, and his staff; to R. Cargill Hall, Chief, Research Division of the USAF Historical Research Center, who generously shared his thorough knowledge of the B–58 intricacies; and to colleagues in the Office of Air Force History: Capt. RitaVictoria DeArmond, Dr. Michael H. Gorn, Maj. John F. Kreis, Lt. Col. Vance O. Mitchell, Dr. Walton Moody, Dr. Daniel Mortensen, Senior Historian Bernard C. Nalty, Jack Neufeld, currently Chief of the Air Staff History Branch, and Dr. George Watson. Special mention is due to Lt. Col. Michael F. Loughran, Deputy Division Chief, Strategic Offensive Forces Division, Directorate of Plans, Headquarters, USAF, for his invaluable assistance during the security and policy review process.

Grateful acknowledgment also goes to Dr. Sylvia Fries, Director, History Office, National Aeronautics and Space Administration, for her review of the entire manuscript and very important contributions, especially her participation in the final panel which approved the manuscript for publication.

Finally, the author owes a special debt to some other colleagues at the Office of Air Force History: Dr. Alfred M. Beck, Chief of the Editorial Branch; Anne E. Johnson, who edited the volume and monitored the publishing process with enthusiasm and dedication; and SSgt. Glenn B.

Reynolds and Sgt. Rosalyn L. Culbertson, who patiently typed the original manuscript.

Marcelle Size Knaack

Contents

B–57 Canberra

B–58 Hustler

B/RB–66 Destroyer

Post–World War II Bombers

B-36 Peacemaker

Consolidated Vultee Aircraft (CONVAIR) Corporation

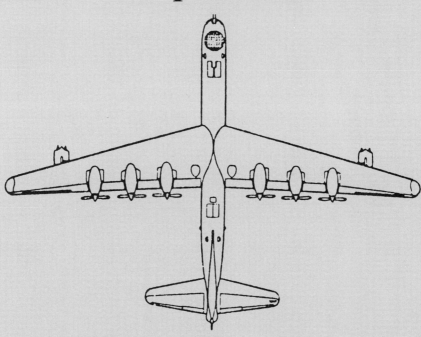

B–36 PEACEMAKER
CONVAIR

Manufacturer's Model 36

Overview

The development of the B–36 was triggered by Nazi Germany's aggression and subsequently by the Japanese attack on Pearl Harbor. The Army Air Forces (AAF) required a long-range bomber to carry the war to the enemy. Despite the sense of urgency, the B–36 program progressed slowly. Existing technology failed to satisfy the military requirements of 1941, early wartime demands exceeded materials, and weapons more readily available received the highest priority during the war.

Military setbacks in 1942 led the AAF to concentrate on the Boeing B–29 (under production order since September 1941) at the expense of the B–36. However, growing concern in the spring of 1943, as China appeared near collapse, reversed the situation. Believing the B–36 might be the only bomber capable of attacking the Japanese homeland, the AAF called for 100 production model B–36s. Meanwhile, the contractor continued to struggle with various development troubles, serious engine problems, and significant weight increases. In mid-1944, engine problems reached a climax. Still, Convair's request for consideration of another engine was ignored because of the cost, time involved, and technical unknowns. In any case, the military position was no longer critical after the capture of Pacific bases and the deployment of the B–29, which would ultimately devastate Japan's home islands.

Yet, the B–36 did survive in the postwar environment. The United States Air Force (established as an independent service in September 1947) needed a long-range aircraft to carry the atomic bomb, and to further its claim on the atomic mission.

As the cold war intensified, deterrence through fear of atomic retaliation became the linchpin of American national security policy. Until air-refuelable, jet-powered bombers were operational, only the B–36, with its vast bombload capacity, could strike the Soviet Union, America's previous ally and now potential adversary. No matter the cost in effort or money, the B–36 had to be made to work. Just the same, the B–36 required technical innovations that were beyond the state-of-the-art. The experimental flight of August 1946, nearly 6 years after signature of the development contract, confirmed that the new bomber was underpowered. Improvement of the original R–4360 engine yielded little relief, and Convair's attempts to fit the engine with a variable discharge turbine failed. In 1949, the engine problem was somewhat alleviated by mounting turbojets under each of the B–36's wings. Still, throughout its entire operational career, the B–36 heavy bomber remained too slow, a shortcoming that increased its vulnerability and necessitated the protection of escort fighters.

In the early fifties, after modification of the landing gear, correction of the electrical system, and elimination of fuel tank leakages, the first B–36 remained highly troublesome. Other production models were not faring much better: the gunnery system was operationally unsuitable, the defensive armament was poor, and its fire-control system was barely adequate. At long last, in 1954, so-called "Featherweight" B–36s came into being. Whether new or reworked production models, the Featherweights proved fairly problem-free. The B–36s were also used for reconnaissance and served effectively. Perhaps the aircraft's most important contribution, though impossible to measure, lay in deterring a general war during the difficult years of its active life.

Basic Development   1941

Development of a long-range bomber was spurred by Nazi Germany's spectacular campaigns at the outset of World War II.[1] Even though the scheduled invasion of the British Isles had been postponed, they seemed far from secure in the fall of 1940. The loss of Britain would leave the United States without European allies and with no bases outside the Western Hemisphere. The Air Corps[2] therefore needed a long-range bomber that could carry the war to any enemy from this continent. The early successes of the German offensive against Russia in June 1941 further deepened America's concern.

---

[1] It took Hitler just 20 days to crush the Polish army in September 1939 and but a few weeks for the German forces to speed across the Low Countries and France in 1940. (The western campaign started on 10 May; the French surrendered on 22 June).

[2] The Army Air Forces was not formally established until 20 June 1941.

Requests for Proposals   11 April 1941

The Air Corps opened a design competition for a truly intercontinental bomber—a fast, high-altitude airplane with a heavy bombload and unprecedented range. Invitations for preliminary design studies were sent to the Consolidated Aircraft Corporation[3] and to the Boeing Aircraft Company on 11 April. Northrop Aircraft, Incorporated was contacted on 27 May, when it was also asked for further design studies on a "flying wing" bomber having a range of 8,000 miles at 25,000 feet, with 1 ton of bombs.[4] Not long afterwards the Douglas Aircraft Company took part in the long-range bomber competition.[5] Solicited much later, the Glenn L. Martin Company declined the invitation due to a shortage of engineering personnel.[6]

Revised Military Characteristics   19 August 1941

The preliminary characteristics set forth in the Air Corps requests for proposals of April 1941 called for a bomber with a 450-mile-per-hour top speed at 25,000 feet, a 275-mile-per-hour cruising speed, a service ceiling of 45,000 feet, and an overall range of 12,000 miles at 25,000 feet. These characteristics were revised during a conference on 19 August attended by Robert A. Lovett, Assistant Secretary of War for Air, Maj. Gen. George H. Brett, Chief of the Air Corps, and ranking officers of the Air Staff. Since the conference's main purpose was to accelerate the bomber project, the conferees decided to scale down their requirements. But their revision was

---

[3] The Consolidated Aircraft Corporation and Vultee Aircraft, Inc., merged on 17 March 1943. The new Consolidated Vultee Aircraft (Convair) Corporation became the Convair Division of the General Dynamics Corporation on 29 April 1954.

[4] Until the early 1950s, the range and speed of aircraft were usually shown in statute miles. Afterwards, the Air Force began to measure speed in knots and range in nautical miles. Speed records, however, continued to be in miles per hour and distances were expressed in kilometers. (A knot—nautical mile per hour—is 1.1516 times swifter than a statute mile per hour. A nautical mile represents around 6,080 feet and is 800 feet more than the statute mile.)

[5] Douglas Aircraft had been given a contract on 19 April 1941 to check if the Allison 3420 engine could be used in bombardment type aircraft—clearly a closely related project. Douglas had also been working for several years on the XB-19—just recently flown and the largest aircraft ever built in the United States. The Air Corps planned to use the XB-19 as a flying laboratory to gather information that would help the design and construction of future giant aircraft.

[6] The Glenn Martin Company had been engaged in a new bomber (the XB-33, under contract since June 1941), before becoming involved in the Northrop "flying wing" program. In addition, by 1943 the company had been approached by the Navy for participation in a new production project.

still a tall order—a minimum overall range of 10,000 miles, and an effective combat radius of 4,000 miles with a 10,000-pound bombload.[7] This was about 4 times the combat radius of the Boeing B–17, the AAF's newest and best bomber. The conferees further specified that the future intercontinental bomber should have a cruising speed between 240 and 300 miles per hour, and a 40,000-foot service ceiling (5,000 feet less than originally requested).

Contractor Selection   3 October 1941

After a review of preliminary data from Boeing, Consolidated, and Douglas, the Materiel Division of the Air Corps suggested prompt action on the Consolidated study, which covered several long-range bomber designs, both 4- and 6-engine pusher and pusher-tractor types.[8] This endorsement of Consolidated was in no way a rejection of either Boeing or Douglas services.[9] Yet, it proved to be a turning point in the intercontinental bomber program.

Development Decision   16 October 1941

The decision was made by Maj. Gen. Henry H. Arnold, Chief of the new Army Air Forces, on the recommendation of Brig. Gen. George C. Kenney, Commanding Officer of the Air Corps Experimental Division and

---

[7] Although the word "range" is often qualified, in this context it indicates how far an aircraft can fly under given operating conditions from the moment of takeoff to the time when its fuel supply is exhausted, as in "the aircraft's range was 7,000 miles, enough to fly nonstop from San Francisco to London." The "combat radius" is the radius of action for any given airplane on a combat mission with a specified load and flight plan. The "radius of action" differs from "range" in that the aircraft is always considered to return to the point at which it takes off. It is like the radius of a circle, and represents the maximum distance at which a given airplane can operate, under given conditions, from the center of the circle and still return to the center. This distance, under combat conditions, is considerably less than one-half the distance that the aircraft can fly under noncombat conditions.

[8] Consolidated, after specializing for many years in seagoing aircraft, reentered the landplane field early in 1940, with development of the B–24 Liberator. Keenly aware of the Air Corps's interest in large bombers with extended ranges, the company at this time had begun work on a number of design possibilities.

[9] Douglas Aircraft stated in late 1941 that it did not desire to undertake an "out-and-out 10,000-mile airplane project." It proposed instead the development of Model 423, a 6,000-mile bomber, which was rejected. As for Boeing, the AAF believed as late as April 1942 that the company was "overly conservative" and had not yet "really tackled the [long-range] airplane design with the necessary degree of enthusiasm." Two Boeing bomber designs (Models 384 and 385) submitted in September were never developed.

Engineering School at Wright Field, Ohio. General Kenney's recommendation rested on a detailed proposal (drawings and bid were submitted by Consolidated on 6 October), which asked for $15 million plus a fixed-fee of $800,000 for research and development, mockup, tooling, and production of 2 experimental long-range bombers (Model 35). Delivery of the first airplane would be 30 months after approval of the contract; that of the second, 6 months later. Consolidated also stipulated that the project could not be "entangled with red tape" and constantly changing directives.

Initial Contract Date   15 November 1941

The initial contract (W535 ac–22352) of 15 November 1941 met Consolidated's terms. On 22 November, 7 days after the contract's approval, Wright Field Engineering Division concluded that the 6-engine rather than the 4-engine design should be adopted. This posed no problem, since it had been one of the options offered by Consolidated. On 10 December,[10] Model 35 was redesignated Model 36 to avoid confusion with the Northrop "flying wing," by then known as the B–35. There was yet no sign of the difficulties soon to come.

Mockup Inspection   20 July 1942

After more than 6 months had been spent in refining the chosen design, exerting every effort to control weight, reduce drag, and eliminate the various developmental kinks of a new airplane, the B–36 mockup was inspected. Controversy generated by the inspection nearly caused cancellation of the experimental program. The Mockup Committee wanted to reduce firepower and crew to make the B–36 meet its 10,000-mile range requirement. But some members argued that such changes would render the airplane tactically useless and in fact superfluous, since the Experimental Engineering Division already had a "flying laboratory" (XB–19). If these reductions were necessary, the AAF should stop the project and channel the manpower into more productive bomber programs. The Mockup Committee eventually agreed to delete "less necessary" items of equipment from the aircraft. This reduced weight and saved the future B–36—at least temporarily.

---

[10] Three days after the Japanese attack on Pearl Harbor. The United States declared war on Japan on 8 December 1941; on the 11th, Germany and Italy declared war on the United States. The U.S. war declaration was made on the same date.

Development Slippage   1942–1943

A month after inspection of the B–36 mockup, Consolidated suggested shifting the XB–36 project from San Diego, California, to its new government-leased plant in Fort Worth, Texas. Even though the move was completed in September 1942, less than 30 days after being approved by the AAF, development was set back several months. Innumerable problems remained to be solved, but Consolidated asked the AAF to place a contract for a production quantity of the new aircraft. The contractor claimed that 2 years could be pared from the development cycle if preliminary work on production B–36s started without waiting for completion of the experimental planes. Consolidated's request was ill-timed. Military setbacks during 1942, especially in the Pacific, plus the fact that even under the best circumstances the B–36 could not soon become operational, prevented the AAF from diverting scarce resources for its production.

Another Consolidated request in the summer of 1942 fared somewhat better. The AAF agreed to development of a cargo configuration of the XB–36, provided that 1 of the 2 experimental bombers was produced at least 3 months ahead of the cargo plane (referred to as the XC–99). Consolidated actually wanted the XC–99 to test the engines, landing gear, and flight characteristics of the forthcoming XB–36s. The contractor also believed the XC–99 could be ready to fly much sooner than either of the 2 XB–36s because armament and other military gear would be left out. The AAF conditions were accepted, however, and a $4.6 million contract was approved by year's end.[11]

Production Go-Ahead   19 June 1943

While engineers kept on wrestling with weight increases and various developmental troubles,[12] war problems suddenly boosted the importance of the B–36. Military setbacks that had hampered the program in 1942 assumed a new dimension in the spring of 1943 as China appeared near collapse. The

---

[11] The proposed C–99 could have carried 400 fully equipped troops or more than 100,000 pounds of cargo, but only a single XC–99 was built. It was delivered in 1949 and remained in the inventory until 1957.

[12] The B–36's twin tail was to be deleted in favor of a single vertical one. This would decrease weight by 3,850 pounds, stabilize direction, and lower drag. The modification was approved on 10 October 1943, when the initial development contract (W535 ac–22352) was amended by Change Order No. 7. This change order (previous ones were insignificant) also allowed the contractor a 120-day delay in delivery. So at best the AAF would not get its first XB–36 until September 1944.

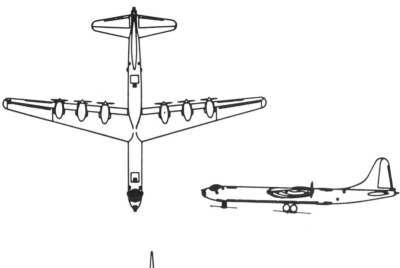

A flight engineer at his station in the CONVAIR XB–36.

B-17 and the B-24 had insufficient range to operate over the vast distances of the Pacific. The Boeing B-29 was in the early stage of production, but was experiencing more problems than usual.[13] The parallel development of the Convair B-32 (Consolidated until mid-March), generally considered by AAF as an "insurance plane," in case the B-29 failed, did not progress as well as hoped for. The B-32 seemed much less promising than the B-29, on which higher priorities had been concentrated. Moreover, even if production delays could be overcome, neither of these planes could reach Japan, for battles had to be won before the Mariana Islands could become a base for B-29 or B-32 operations. Speeding up B-36 development might provide a way, possibly the only one, for attacking the Japanese homeland and at least would immediately bolster Chinese morale.[14] Therefore, on 19 June General Arnold[15] directed procurement of 100 B-36s. The order, however, would be cut back or canceled in the event of excessive production difficulties. The AAF letter of intent for 100 B-36s was signed by Convair on 23 July.

New Setbacks   1943-1944

In spite of its elevated status, the B-36 program made scant progress. Essential wind tunnel tests of the new design were postponed until the spring of 1944, because other projects had retained higher priorities and no alternate testing facilities were available. Meanwhile, besides usual engineering difficulties, Convair was greatly concerned over the growing weight of the Pratt & Whitney X-Wasp engine selected for the experimental B-36. In Convair's opinion, tying the XB-36 to a single engine design was a mistake. Yet, further study of the Lycoming BX liquid-cooled engine (noted for lower fuel consumption) had been discontinued on the belief that development of the BX engine would demand manpower, materiel, and facilities that could not be spared. The AAF also insisted that development of a new engine would only delay "expeditious prosecution" of the B-36 design. In any case,

---

[13] Appendix I, pp 482, 484.

[14] The war in the Pacific dominated the discussion at the "Trident" conference of President Roosevelt and Prime Minister Churchill in May 1943—Lt. Gen. Joseph W. Stilwell and Maj. Gen. Claire L. Chennault both confirming that the situation in China was desperate. Ensuing talks between Secretary of War Henry L. Stimson, Assistant Secretary of War Robert P. Patterson, and high-ranking officers of the AAF, led Secretary Stimson to waive customary procurement procedures and to authorize the AAF to order B-36 production without awaiting completion and testing of the 2 experimental planes then under contract.

[15] General Arnold became Commanding General of the AAF in March 1942 and was promoted to 4-star general 1 year later.

before much of anything could be done, the B–36 was relegated to a secondary position. This time, the Convair B–32 had to come first.[16]

Definitive Production Contract   19 August 1944

The letter of intent of 23 July 1943,[17] supplemented by Letter Contract W33–038 ac–7 on 23 August 1943, gave way 1 year later to a definitive contract. This $160 million contract (including a $6 million fixed fee and the cost of all spare parts and engineering data) continued to cover the production of 100 B–36s, but no longer carried any priority rating. Delivery schedules, however, were unchanged. The first B–36 was due in August 1945; the last, in October 1946.[18]

Program Reappraisal   1945

With victory in sight,[19] war contracts were scrutinized for cancellation or drastic cutback. Aircraft production was actually cut by 30 percent on 25 May, a reduction of 17,000 planes over an 18-month period. The review left the B–36 contract untouched. There was no question that a long-range bomber was needed. The proof was in the terrible price paid in lives and materiel to win advanced bases in the Pacific. The atomic bomb, unlikely to remain an American monopoly, was another strategic justification. Inasmuch as U.S. retaliation would have to be quick, there would be no time for conquering faraway bases. And, realistically, a long-range bomber could be the best war deterrent for the immediate future. From the economic standpoint, the B–36 also looked good. It out-performed the B–29 and the

---

[16] The military situation in the Pacific improved materially by mid-1944. The Marianas campaign neared its successful conclusion, and the forthcoming use of bases on Saipan, Tinian, and Guam urgently called for medium-range bombers. Production troubles with the B–29 were almost solved, and it was now left to Convair to accelerate the B–32 program. B–36 work would continue, but only as a safety measure.

[17] The U.S. Government was not liable should a letter of intent be canceled. This was not so for the more often-used letter contract which obligated funds.

[18] Not surprisingly, these delivery dates were subsequently changed, as was the $160 million contract— increased by $61 million on 26 August 1946, when Change Order No. 10 was approved.

[19] The German surrender was officially ratified in Berlin on 8 May 1945; Japan surrendered unconditionally on 14 August, but the Japanese Emperor did not sign the Potsdam requirements for surrender until 2 September.

B–35 "flying wing" for long-range missions and was cheaper by half to operate than the B–29 in terms of cost per ton per mile. On 6 August 1945, General Arnold approved the Air Staff recommendation to keep the B–36 production contract intact.[20]

Unrelenting Problems   1945–1946

While the fate of the B–36 program vacillated with changing wartime priorities, the aircraft's development remained painfully slow. By 1945 Convair still worried over the weight of the R–4360–25 engine—Pratt & Whitney's third version of the original X–Wasp. Adding nose guns required extensive rearrangement of the forward crew compartment. A mockup of the new nose section had been approved in late 1944 and would become a prototype nose for the second XB–36. Yet, the radio and radar equipment in the new nose would augment gross weight by at least 3,500 pounds—more, if the antenna of the AN/APQ–7 radar could not be installed in the leading edge of the wing. This and the 2,304-pound increase for the 6 new engines could present a serious problem. Nor was it easy to select wheels for the aircraft's landing gear. The rationale for dual main wheels was simplified maintenance without a need for special tools. The single-wheel type had other merits. These arguments ended in mid–1945 when Maj. Gen. Edward M. Powers, Assistant Chief of Air Staff for Materiel, Maintenance, and Distribution, recommended that a new landing gear be devised to distribute the aircraft weight more evenly, thus reducing the need for specially built runways.[21]

Meanwhile, faulty workmanship and use of substandard materials were discovered in the experimental B–36. AAF inspectors also noted the dearth of qualified workers at the beginning of the project and the failure of the airfoil contour of the aircraft wing to conform to specifications. In fairness to Convair, substituting materials was a generally accepted practice in urgently awaited experimental planes. As for other discrepancies, the contractor was not altogether to blame but promised to correct them promptly. Progress was made, but labor strikes at the Fort Worth plant in

---

[20] Lt. Gen. Hoyt S. Vandenberg, then Assistant Chief of Air Staff for Operations, Commitments, and Requirements, advocated formation of 4 "Very Heavy" groups equipped with B–36s to constitute an "effective, mobile task force for our postwar air force." General Vandenberg's recommendation was embodied in the AAF's postwar 70-group program. This program remained a constant, though unreachable goal until the start of the Korean War.

[21] The four-wheel truck-type gear eventually adopted was 1,500 pounds lighter than the one previously considered. It also enabled the B–36 to use any airfield suitable for the B–29.

October 1945 and in February 1946, a normal part of postwar adjustment, delayed the program for several months. On 25 March General Powers indicated that the structural limitations of the forthcoming XB–36 might make it useless, other than as a test vehicle for the initial flight.

First Flight   8 August 1946

In spite of every effort, the all-metal, semimonocoque XB–36 did not fly until almost 6 years after signature of the development contract. The initial 37-minute flight of 8 August was deemed successful, but the wing flap actuating system and the aircraft's overall performance fell below the original expectations. Besides its known structural limitations, the XB–36 had an already obsolete single-wheel landing gear, carried only a minimum of components, and lacked the nose armament designed for the second XB–36. Still, a beginning had been made. After being grounded in late 1946 for modification, the XB–36 was test-flown for 160 hours by pilots of the Air Materiel Command (AMC).[22] The plane was then sent to the contractor for further testing,[23] and the United States Air Force (USAF)[24] retrieved it in mid–1948. As predicted by General Powers, the experimental B–36 had limited operational value and was used by the Strategic Air Command (SAC)[25] for training.

Third Program Review   December 1946

On 12 December 1946, General Kenney, who had been promoted to 4-star general in March 1945 and headed SAC since April 1946, suggested reducing the procurement contract for 100 B–36s to a few service-test

---

[22] The lineage of AMC reflected the many reorganizations following the establishment on 17 July 1944 as the AAF Materiel and Services Command (Temporary), the parent organization. On 31 August 1944, the Materiel and Services Command (Temporary) became the AAF Air Technical Service Command, which became the Air Technical Service Command on 1 July 1945. AMC was created on 9 March 1946, and on 1 April 1961, it became Air Force Logistics Command.

[23] Convair pilots made 53 test flights with the XB–36 (Serial Number 42–13570), logging a total of 117 flying hours.

[24] The United States Air Force was established on 26 July 1947, when the National Security Act of 1947 became law. It began functioning as a separate service, coequal with Army and Navy, on 18 September 1947.

[25] The Strategic Air Command was established by the Army Air Forces on 21 March 1946.

aircraft. After studying available performance estimates on the B–36, the SAC Commander believed it to be inferior to the forthcoming B–50,[26] a Boeing development of the famed B–29. The B–50 and the B–36 were to become the only 2-piston-powered bombers produced in the postwar era of jet bombers. Among the B–36 shortcomings cited by General Kenney were a useful range of only 6,500 miles, insufficient speed, and lack of protection for the bomber's gasoline load. Neither the Air Staff nor Lt. Gen. Nathan F. Twining, Air Materiel Command Commanding General, agreed with General Kenney.

General Twining said that the B–36 could not be judged from the XB–36, which had just entered testing. All new airplanes encountered developmental problems, as exemplified by the B–17 and other successful aircraft. Moreover, many improvements could soon be expected, and the B–36 was the only suitable aircraft far enough along to serve as an interim long-range atomic carrier until the B–52 arrived.[27] Gen. Carl Spaatz, the AAF's new Commander, wholly agreed with General Twining. Thus once more, the B–36 contract was retained in full.

Engine and Other Improvements   December 1946–July 1947

Even though the B–36 program seemed to undergo one crisis after another, engineers kept on forging ahead. By mid-1947 Convair was confident that the 4-wheel landing gear would be ready for the first B–36 production model (B–36A). And while this B–36A and 21 others would retain the R–4360–25 engine of the XB–36, conversion of this engine had been approved in December 1946. The new water-injection R–4360–41 engine with its 3,500 horsepower (500 more than the –25 engine) would allow ensuing productions (B–36Bs) to take off within a shorter runway distance. It would also yield slightly better performance at both high and cruising speeds. Nevertheless, more improvements appeared in order. Hence, an even more powerful version of the R–4360 engine, fitted with a variable

---

[26] Known as the B–29D in July 1945, when 200 were ordered. This number was almost immediately reduced to 60. The future B–29D was redesignated B–50 in December because the many design changes resulted in a nearly new airplane. Except for the B–36, the B–50 was the only piston-powered bomber produced in the postwar era of jet bombers.

[27] General Twining also argued that the normal desire for the best could be deceiving. Keeping pace with the speed of technological advances was a tricky business. The Boeing B–52, then in the design stage, would probably become a better plane than the B–36, but a promising development could not be abandoned every time a better one appeared on the horizon.

discharge turbine (VDT), was under development.[28] Convair claimed that the VDT engine (also proposed for the B-50) would give the B-36 a top speed of 410 miles per hour, a 45,000-foot service ceiling, and a 10,000-mile range with a 10,000-pound bombload. To offset the cost of adapting the VDT engine to the B-36, Convair suggested financing the airframe modification for 1 prototype B-36 with the VDT engine by slashing 3 B-36s from the current procurement contract. This was approved by the Commanding General, AAF, in July 1947. Although Convair hoped additional VDT-equipped B-36s (B-36Cs) would be ordered if the prototype proved successful, a decision on this matter was deferred.

Fourth B-36 Reappraisal   August 1947

The creation of an independent Air Force obviously meant more authority and greater responsibility in the choice of basic weapon systems. General Vandenberg, Deputy Chief of Air Staff,[29] therefore wasted no time in forming the USAF Aircraft and Weapons Board. Through this forum, senior officers would recommend the weapons that would best support long-range plans for the Air Force's development and gradual buildup. The board first met on 19 August and, because of the advent of the atomic bomb, the role of strategic bombing and the means of accomplishing such missions took precedence. The B-36 was the only bomber that could launch an immediate atomic counterattack without first acquiring overseas bases. Although vulnerable to enemy fighters because of its fairly low speed, the B-36 did offer an important advantage: its great range would promote the crew's chances of completing their mission. On the other hand, future supplies of atomic bombs were expected to be sparse. Hence, plans had to cover the possible use of conventional bombs.[30]

The board members differed on how to solve these complex problems. Some considered the B-36 obsolete and favored buying fast jet bombers—an obvious gamble since these would have insufficient range and would not be available for years. Others wanted to increase the B-36's speed with the new

---

[28] Convair also offered in February 1947 to install 8 Curtiss-Wright T-35 gas turbine engines in one B-36. The installation was expected to cost less than $1.5 million and to be completed by April 1948. The proposal was turned down. The T-35 engine was too far in the future for the B-36, and the Curtiss-Wright delivery estimates were overly optimistic.

[29] General Vandenberg became Vice Chief of Staff of the United States Air Force, with 4-star rank, on 1 October 1947.

[30] Large stocks of wartime B-29s were still in the inventory for economic reasons, although the Superfortress's range was inadequate without overseas bases.

B-36 Peacemaker at Eglin AFB, Florida, September 1950.

VDT engine and also use it as an all-purpose bomber. Still others preferred the B-50, because it was faster than the B-36 and could attain even greater range and speed with the addition of VDT engines. After prolonged discussion, a consensus emerged to retain the B-36 as a special purpose bomber. This special purpose B-36 would eventually be replaced by the B-52,[31] if the latter proved satisfactory and no better means for delivering the atomic bomb came on the scene. Since the endorsed B-36 would be for specialized use, there were several reasons for not installing the VDT engine in a prototype B-36. No additional B-36 procurement would be needed. And even though the promised improvements were tempting, any retrofit with VDT engines would delay completion of the 100 B-36s on order and run up costs. General Spaatz[32] promptly approved the board's recommendations and the VDT-equipped B-36 prototype was canceled on 22 August.

Unsolved Dilemma   1947

Concern with weapon selection left many problems unanswered. Limited B-36 procurement was one solution; finding some use for the

---

[31] At best not to be expected before 1953.

[32] In September 1947 General Spaatz was appointed by President Truman as the first Chief of Staff of the new United States Air Force.

government-owned Fort Worth plant, soon to be idle, was another problem. The Air Force could not stand by as Convair's dejected B–36 work force sought and probably secured more stable employment before completion of the B–36 program.[33] There were further complications. Funds had been appropriated during the war for the 100 B–36s, but any amount unspent by the end of June 1948 would have to be reappropriated by a Congress that might be of a different mind. Production speedup was one solution. If Convair turned out 6 aircraft every month, the hundredth B–36 would be delivered in January 1949. This would leave but 7 months of production (July 1948–January 1949) for which new funds would have to be provided. Chiefly because of shortages of government-furnished equipment, accelerating production proved impossible.[34] This was just as well since it would have hastened the end of the Fort Worth activities. But the monthly production rate of 4 B–36s, as later endorsed, carried another pitfall—post-

---

[33] In mid–1948 the Air Force convinced Northrop that production of the future RB–49 (a development of the experimental YB–49 "flying wing") should be sub-contracted to Convair. To begin with, this would keep the Fort Worth plant in operation upon completion of the B–36 program. Of perhaps greater import, this cooperation would blend Northrop's engineering skill and Convair's experience in quantity production of large aircraft. Cancellation of the RB–49 project in January 1949 wiped out all this planning, although Northrop received a go-ahead from Air Materiel Command for completion of a YRB–49 prototype, which was extensively flight-tested.

[34] Production was also slipping (and more delay later occurred) because of defective propellers, landing gear door problems, corroded hinges, unsatisfactory magnesium castings, deficiencies in turret installations, and occasional malfunctions of the constant speed drive. Meanwhile, the government was spending $150,000 a day to keep the plant operating.

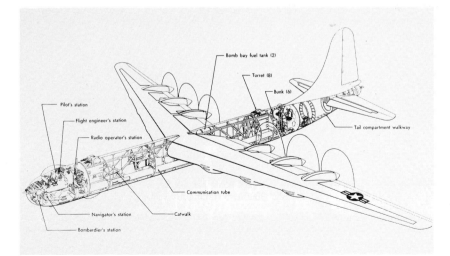

poning delivery of the last B–36 to November 1949. This would extend by 10 months the production time for which Convair would have to plan with no assurance that money would ever be available to complete the program.[35] Aware of the contractor's predicament, the Air Force in late December 1947 promised to request a reappropriation of B–36 funds when Congress reconvened in early 1948.

First B–36A Delivery   30 August 1947

This B–36A and the next 12 productions were known for a while as YB–36As. All, save the first one, eventually reverted to the B–36A designation (some even before leaving the production line). The exception was earmarked for static tests.[36] This decision had been made in mid–1946, after a convincing argument by General Twining. The general admitted that much might be known about a given structure, but deemed it wise to static test one to destruction.[37] He said, "Experience has shown that we would have been unable to use our bombers efficiently had we not had this policy in effect in the past. The B–17, originally designed for a gross weight of 37,000 pounds, fought the war flying universally at 64,000 pounds. This could never have been done without accurate knowledge of the strength of the component parts."

Contractor New Proposal   4 September 1947

The post–World War II years spelled trouble for the aircraft industry. Competition was fierce, and no contractors could afford to forego any significant prospects. Cancellation of the VDT-equipped B–36 prototype,

---

[35] Convair was responsible for payment of work under subcontracts. Payments incurred before the expiration of a prime contract (30 June 1948 in the B–36's case) could be recovered, but the contractor's capital would remain tied up during the long drawn-out process of going through the Court of Claims. The other alternative (and one the Air Force certainly did not want) was for Convair to throttle down the flow of supplies, trim plant operations, and lay off workers until the financial future of the B–36 program was straightened out.

[36] Hence, the plane could dispense with various items of still hard-to-get or highly unreliable equipment. Completion of the true productions was another story. Delivery of a second B–36 slipped another 8 months, and the last B–36A (of 22 finally produced) did not reach the Air Force until September 1948.

[37] Static testing is the testing of an aircraft, missile, or other device in a stationary or hold-down position, either to verify structural design criteria, structural integrity, and the effects of limit loads, or to measure the thrust of a rocket engine or motor.

therefore, did not deter Convair from reopening the project a few weeks later. The contractor this time proposed to offset the cost of installing VDT engines in the last 34 of the 100 B–36s under contract by simply reducing the contract's total to 95. No extra money would have to be found, other than enough to cover necessary government-furnished equipment. Convair further offered to produce the new B–36s (B–36Cs) without delaying the current contract by more than 6 months (November 1949–May 1950). The possibility of retrofitting the remaining B–36A and B–36B aircraft was suggested, inasmuch as both types were much nearer completion. Afforded immediate attention, the Convair proposal of September 1947 was approved on 5 December, except for retrofitting the 61 B–36s, which could be dealt with later. SAC alone totally disagreed, having lost faith in the B–36 as a long-range bomber. As a whole, SAC officials generally believed the relatively slow aircraft could better serve in such tasks as sea-search and reconnaissance. For these purposes, General Kenney emphasized, the extra speed promised by the VDT engines was of no real importance. As it turned out, mating the VDT engine with the B–36 failed completely.[38] The project died in early 1948, but not without repercussion.

First Flight (YB–36)   4 December 1947

This plane (Serial No. 42–13571), the second of the 2 experimental B–36s ordered by the AAF, had been chosen as the production prototype on 7 April 1945.[39] It was equipped with few components, but featured the many configuration changes so far approved.[40] Convair was expected to retain the YB–36 for 6 to 12 months to test its configuration and identify future production line changes. During its third flight on 19 December 1947, the YB–36 reached an altitude of more than 40,000 feet—a rewarding event at the time. Nevertheless, it stayed with Convair much longer than anticipated and was not accepted by the Air Force until 31 May 1949. The aircraft reached SAC in October, but was returned to Convair 1 year later (October

---

[38] There was nothing wrong with the engine itself (it was the basic R–4360 used in other B–36s), nor with the variable turbine that boosted the engine power. The problem stemmed from the cooling requirements (generated by the aircraft's high-operating altitude), which degraded the engine's rated performance.

[39] Following approval of Change Order No. 11 to the initial contract of November 1941. This order also relegated complete performance tests to the second B–36A production (temporarily designated YB–36A and due to be fully equipped).

[40] Included were new landing gear, bubble canopy (for better vision), reversible pitch props, nose guns, and redesigned forward crew compartment.

1950) to be fitted for reconnaissance. The YB–36's operational life ended after 2,050 flying hours.[41] In the spring of 1957, it was placed in the Air Force Museum at Wright-Patterson AFB, Ohio.

Fifth Near-Cancellation   April–June 1948

When it became obvious that a faster B–36 (equipped with VDT engines and due to be known as the B–36C) could not be obtained, the Air Force once more thought of canceling the entire B–36 program. Yet, various factors had to be considered. Twenty-two of the basic and relatively slow B–36s were nearly completed, and a great deal of money had already been spent on the controversial program. The Air Force, therefore, decided to postpone any decisions. It instructed the Air Materiel Command to waive the modification of several shop-completed B–36s that had been awaiting adjustments, and to expedite their delivery. This would allow Convair to speed up the aircraft's flight test program, as consistently recommended by the Air Force. In addition, new yardsticks were established to compare the basic B–36's performance with that of other bombers under similar conditions. The new yardsticks measured the 4 most important and inter-dependent characteristics of any given bomber— speed, range, altitude, and load capacity.

Test results, although not spectacular, favored the basic B–36. They showed that the slow B–36 surpassed the B–50 in cruising speed at long range, had a higher altitude, larger load capacity, and a far greater combat radius than the B–50 or B–54—a B–50 variant then being considered, but canceled in 1949. It now seemed that the B–36 might become a much better plane than had been expected. If so, any hasty reduction of the contract might wreck the program just as it was about to pay off. The beginning of the Russian blockade of West Berlin on 18 June 1948 spared the Air Force further indecision. On the 25th, Air Force Secretary W. Stuart Symington and other top USAF officials, deeply concerned by the Soviets' aggressive-ness, unanimously agreed to stay with the B–36.[42] The proposed VDT-

---

[41] Thirty-six Convair test flights accounted for 97½ hours; Air Force pilots flew the remainder.

[42] The Berlin blockade of June 1948 came at the time the administration decided to give high priority to building an atomic deterrent force. The crisis increased the decision's urgency, and the concurrent cancellation of any important military program would have been psycho-logically unsound. Finally, the B–36 was the only intercontinental bomber available, and its shortcomings, whatever they were, were not that obvious. These facts undoubtedly prompted General Kenney to join in the decision, even though a month before he had still recommended that the B–36 production be halted.

equipped B–36C (34 of them) would revert to the B–36B configuration, assuring the Air Force of getting 95[43] of the 100 B–36s under contract since June 1943.

Initial Delivery   18 June 1948

This B–36A, officially accepted by the Air Force in May 1948, was delivered on 18 June to the Air Force Proving Ground Command[44] to undergo extensive testing. It was a true production aircraft, whereas the first B–36A (accepted in August 1947 and permanently designated as the YB–36A) had few components, was stripped of its engines, and never went past static testing.

Enters Service   26 June 1948

SAC's 7th Bomb Wing at Carswell AFB, Texas, received the first 5 B–36As.[45] These and ensuing B–36A deliveries were unarmed and were used mainly for training and crew conversion. They did not join the operational forces until converted to the reconnaissance configuration.

Total B–36As Accepted   22

Included in this total was the first B–36A (YB–36A) that had been earmarked for static tests.

---

[43] There could be no B–36Cs, but the 5-aircraft reduction remained necessary to meet the price rise and to pay for the ill-fated VDT engine installation.

[44] At Eglin AFB, Fla.

[45] By that time, the very heavy bomber designation, previously applied to the B–36, had been dropped. The change dated back to 18 September 1947 (the same day the United States Air Force started functioning as a separate service), when all USAF bombers had been reclassified into 3 categories. In effect, range, rather than weight, had become the primary classification factor. Hence, bombers with an operating radius of more than 2,500 miles were categorized as heavy; those with an operating radius between 1,000 and 2,500 miles were medium bombers, and all those with operating radius of less than 1,000 miles were designated as light bombers. Under these provisions, the B–36 and B–52 became heavy bombers; the B–29, B–50, B–47, and B–58, medium bombers; and the B–45, B–57, and B–66, light bombers.

Acceptance Rates   1947–1949

The Air Force accepted the first B–36A (YB–36A) in August 1947 and 20 other B–36s in 1948—1 in May, 5 in June, 5 in July, 4 in August, and 5 in September. The twenty-second and last B–36A was accepted in February 1949.

End of Production   September 1948

Five months before the last acceptance.

Flyaway Cost Per Production Aircraft $2.5 million

This prorated figure reflected the original contract cost for 100 B–36s, as amended on 26 August 1946. It did not include the post-production cost of reconfiguring each B–36A for reconnaissance.

Subsequent Model Series   B–36B

Other Configurations   RB–36E

All RB–36Es were converted B–36As. The YB–36, first flown 4 December 1947, was fitted for reconnaissance in lieu of the YB–36A, bringing the RB–36E total to 22. During the reconfiguration, the B–36A's 6 R–4360–25 engines were replaced by 6 R–4360–41s—the more powerful engines already installed in the B–36Bs. Equipped with cameras like the K–17C, K–22A, K–38, and K–40, the RB–36E also received some of the B–36B's more advanced electronics. The E-model featured equipment vital to its intrinsic missions—all-purpose strategic reconnaissance, day-and-night mapping and charting, as well as bomb damage assessment. Its normal crew was 22, which included 5 gunners to man the 16 M–24A1 20-millimeter guns.

Phaseout   1950–1951

Convair began adapting the B–36A to the reconnaissance configuration in early 1950. The B-36A's phaseout was fairly fast, the Air Force taking delivery of the last RB-36E in July 1951.

Milestones   30 June 1948

A B-36A dropped 72,000 pounds of bombs during a test flight on 30 June, demonstrating the aircraft's vast capacity.

B-36B

Previous Model Series   B-36A

New Features

In the B-36B, R-4360-41 engines with fluid injection supplanted the B-36A's R-4360-25s. The B-36B also offered better and more electronics equipment, including the AN/APQ-24 bombing-navigation radar (substituted for the B-36A's APG-23A). The B-36B could carry 86,000 pounds of bombs (a 14,000-pound increase). Of greater importance, it could carry atomic bombs weighing perhaps as much as 43,000 pounds.[46] Eighteen of the B-36Bs could handle remote-controlled VB-13 "Tarzon" bombs (2 per bomber).

First Flight   8 July 1948

The plane, flown by Convair, performed well—far better than expected. Several later tests by Convair and AMC pilots showed more rewarding results. On 5 December 1948, a long-range mission of 4,275 miles was flown at high altitude. Save for climb and descent, an average cruising speed of 303 miles per hour was maintained during the entire 14-hour flight at 40,000 feet. This was surpassed during a similar mission on 12 December, when the average speed rose to 319 miles per hour. Then on 29 January 1949, a B-36B dropped two 43,000-pound bombs on a practice target, the first from 35,000 and the second from 40,000 feet.

---

[46] The bombs were 364 inches long and had a diameter of some 54 inches. To carry these bombs internally, bomb bays needed to be rearranged. Although approved in 1945 as the "Grand Slam Installation," this modification did not reach the production line until all B-36As had been built. There were good reasons for the delay. When B-36 production first started, the high secrecy given to the atomic bomb kept the necessary engineering specifications from reaching the contractor. The Air Force at the time did not know how many atomic bombs were available, and lacked other data on which to base firm carrier requirements. The B-36As could have been retrofitted to carry the crucial weapons, but the modifications appeared senseless since these early bombers were highly deficient.

Enters Operational Service   November 1948

The B–36Bs joined the B–36As of SAC's 7th Bomb Group at Carswell AFB in November 1948. On 7–8 December, one of these new B–36s flew a nonstop, round-trip, simulated bombing mission from Carswell to Hawaii. On the way back, the aircraft's 10,000-pound bombload was dumped a short distance from Hawaii. The distance flown in 35½ hours exceeded 8,000 miles.[47] Yet, because many "bugs" had to beworked out, the B–36 did not become truly operational until several years later. In 1951, many B–36s were available and, if called upon, were capable of accomplishing their long-range, high-altitude bombing mission, with either conventional or special weapons. However, the aircraft were in a constant state of flux, either being reconfigured or awaiting modification. In reality, full operational capability was not achieved before 1952.

Additional Procurement   1949

The Air Force possessed 59 groups in the fall of 1948, when the B–36 was just entering the SAC inventory. The soundness of the postwar 70-group objective had been confirmed,[48] and a 66-group force seemed possible within a near future. Hence President Truman's decision to hold the 1949 defense budget to a ceiling of $11 billion had been a drastic blow.[49] The job of rebuilding the Air Force had to be done all over again, and this time from the opposite direction. The problem was no longer how to procure additional airplanes for 70 groups, but how to whittle current forces to 48 groups with the least possible harm to national security. Canceling the aircraft already on order, with minimum loss to the government, was the other difficult task facing the Air Force in early 1949. The B–36 actually gained from the crisis. The Air Force canceled the purchase of various bombers,

---

[47] A B–50, another of SAC's newly assigned bombers, made the flight over a much longer route of 9,870 miles in 41 hours and 40 minutes, receiving 3 inflight refuelings from KB–29 tankers.

[48] A Civilian Air Policy Commission (headed by Thomas K. Finletter) was established by the President in 1947. At the same time, a Joint Congressional Aviation Policy Board was formed. Both thoroughly investigated the weaknesses of the Air Force as it began functioning as a separate service. The 2 reports (published on 1 January and 1 March 1948 respectively) recommended orderly but prompt expansion of the forces towards a minimum goal of 70 groups.

[49] The $14 billion budget was to be parceled almost equally among the 3 military services. This prompted Secretary Symington to compare it to throwing a piece of meat into a lion's den and letting the animals fight over it—a remark fully justified by later events.

fighters, and transports in mid-January. At the time, however, it endorsed the urgent procurement of additional B–36s,[50] as recommended by Gen. Curtis E. LeMay, SAC's Commanding General since October 1948. A second augmentation of the program was approved in the spring, when RB–54s were canceled in favor of still more B/RB–36s, as again recommended by General LeMay.[51] The President authorized the recertification and release of funds for the first increase on 8 April; for the second, on 4 May.

Sixth and Last Near-Cancellation   1949

Curtailment of the defense budget brought interservice disagreements to a boil. The Air Force and the Navy had long recognized that whichever service possessed the atomic mission would eventually receive a larger share of the budget. Thus, they had grown more and more wary of each other's strategic programs. Meanwhile, the B–36 atomic carrier had been the target of much criticism, even though few people had seen it—let alone flown it.[52] In early 1949, the B–36's censure grew ominous and could not be brushed aside. An anonymous document began making the rounds in press, congressional, and aircraft-industry circles charging that corruption had entered into the selection, and that the aircraft's performance did not live up to Air Force claims. In August, a second unsigned paper accused the Air Force of having greatly exaggerated the importance of strategic air warfare. The charges of corruption and favoritism were investigated by the Armed

---

[50] The Air Force proposed to spend $172 million (of some $270 million released by the cancellation of other aircraft) to buy 39 additional B–36s and to improve or reconfigure those already under contract. This was in line with General LeMay's testimony before the Board of Senior Officers hastily convened on 29 December 1948 by General Vandenberg, who had replaced General Spaatz as Chief of Staff of the Air Force on 30 April 1948. General LeMay insisted that the safest course called for an increase of 2 groups of B–36 heavy bombers (at the expense of 2 medium bomb groups), plus 1 strategic reconnaissance group of B–36s (in lieu of RB–49s).

[51] General LeMay was sure that the B–36 could do everything as well as, and in most cases better than, the B–54. The big B–36 required more parking apron space, but this was not a serious problem. Its maintenance so far had been surprisingly easy. Therefore, it was not impossible to raise the 18-aircraft authorization of every B/RB–36 group to the 30-aircraft level of each medium bomb group. This would slash personnel costs and boost SAC's offensive power. A larger B–36 fleet, General LeMay asserted, together with the approved stepped-up production of Boeing's forthcoming B–47, was the best strategic way to face the near future.

[52] The B–36 had been accused of being as slow as the ancient B–24 and far more vulnerable. Some critics claimed that under the most favorable conditions it would take up to 12 hours to ready the aircraft for flight. Others, with obvious relish, wrote that the connecting tunnel between the B–36's pressurized cabins was too small for a fat sergeant.

Services Committee of the House of Representatives and quickly proven false. On 25 August the investigation closed, after completely clearing the Air Force. However, hearings on the B–36 resumed in October. Briefly stated, the committee had to decide, at least for the time being, whether the nation should rely on massive retaliation with intercontinental bombers in case of attack, or depend upon the Navy's fleet and air arm to defend the North American continent. Even though there were doubts about the B–36's ability to evade fighters, the Air Force emerged triumphantly from the October debates. Yet, the argument between the 2 services over roles and missions was far from settled.[53]

Initial Deficiencies   1949–1950

In contrast to the B–36As, the B–36Bs were equipped from the start

---

[53] August 1949 amendments to the National Security Act of 1947 had enlarged and strengthened the Office of the Secretary of Defense and severely weakened the authority of the service secretaries. Interservice rivalry nevertheless persisted.

The front section of a B–36, which accommodated the navigator, bombadier, radar operator, and nose gunner.

with remote retraction turrets and 20-millimeter guns. Unfortunately, this was no asset. The B–36Bs in their original configuration would be long gone before either the turrets or guns worked properly.[54] Also, the R–4360–41 engines of the B–36Bs demanded extra fuel tanks. Even though the new bomb-bay tanks were supposedly self-sealing, their leaks lasted throughout the B–36B's short life.

Other Problems   1949–1950

Many of the B–36B's initial troubles resembled those of any other new aircraft. Minor adjustments were needed and— as so often the case—parts shortages were acute. Although the Air Force frowned on cannibalization as never affording a lasting solution, stripping parts from one B–36 to keep another flying became fairly common. Shortages of equipment, such as empennage stands, dollies, jacks, and related items, hampered maintenance. Because there was no money for new equipment, maintenance crews utilized as well as they could some of the tools used for the old B–29s. Personnel turnover further hampered progress. All these problems persisted through 1950.

Post-Production Conversions   1950–1951

Even though the B–36's performance since mid–1948 kept on exceeding early expectations, the aircraft's relatively slow speed continued to cause concern. Tests had shown that altitude was very important in protecting a bomber.[55] Nonetheless, a bomber putting on a burst of speed over a target

---

[54] The B–36's defensive armament system, furnished by the government, was designed and built by General Electric according to Air Materiel Command specifications. At first, obvious gun and turret defects postponed the system's installation. Then, lack of ammunition, also government-furnished, delayed testing until mid–1949. And, obviously, the guns had to be air-fired before remaining deficiencies could be found and corrected. As the Eighth Air Force Commander bluntly put it in February 1950: "There is no use driving a B–36 around carrying a lot of guns that don't work."

[55] Locating, intercepting, and shooting down a bomber flying at 40,000 feet was not easy, even if the bomber's speed was no faster than that of the B–36B with its 3,500-horsepower engines. General Kenney had long been disenchanted with the B–36, but admitted in an October 1948 interview, "How are you going to shoot down a bomber at night flying at 40,000 feet with a solid overcast?" Most likely, General Kenney's words could be challenged. During World War II, the Luftwaffe had caused heavy attrition of the Royal Air Force's Bomber Command over the night sky in Europe. On the other hand, it should be noted that General Kenney's interview was conducted on the eve of the Armed Services Committee investigation of the B–36. The Air Force could hardly belittle an aircraft which had acquired a symbolic dimension in the Air Force's and Navy's dispute over the atomic mission.

or while under attack increased its chances of survival. This could have been achieved with the substitution of VDT engines, had this project not failed. A step-up in speed could also be gained, Convair insisted, by mounting 2 General Electric turbojet engines under each of the B-36's wings. These engines could be cut in to boost the power of the B-36's regular ones. Using the proven twin jets already selected for the future B-47 would trim development and testing, while raising the B-36's top speed over the target from 376 to 435 miles per hour. Unlike the extensive changes needed to install the VDT engines, only minor modifications of the aircraft would be required to mount wing nacelles. In fact, Convair was confident that a prototype B-36 with jet-assist engines would be ready to fly less than 4 months after Air Force approval.

The Air Force did not question the merits of the jet pod installation proposed by Convair as early as October 1948. Approval was delayed because of the budgetary restrictions looming in December 1948 and the decision a month before to convert some B-36s for reconnaissance. A prototype B-36 with jet pods was not authorized until 14 January 1949—far too late to allow changes on the B-36B assembly line. Hence, B-36Bs that had barely become operational had to leave the inventory to be equipped with jet pods. But the modification was simple, and most of them soon rejoined the SAC forces as B-36Ds. Eight of the aircraft were also brought up to the reconnaissance configuration, becoming RB-36Ds.

Total B-36Bs Accepted   62

Convair actually built 73 B-36Bs, but the Air Force directed modification of 11 prior to formal acceptance. Four of the 11 appeared on USAF rolls as B-36Ds, and 7 as RB-36Ds.[56]

Acceptance Rates

The Air Force accepted 31 B-36Bs in fiscal year (FY) 1949; 30 in FY 50, and a last one in September 1950 (FY 51).

End of Production   September 1950

With delivery of the sixty-second B-36B.

---

[56] Convair kept on listing the planes as B-36Bs. Consequently, the Convair B/RB-36D production totals never did match the USAF B/RB-36D acceptances. These discrepancies resulted from different accounting methods and proved of no real importance.

Flyaway Cost Per Production Aircraft $2.5 million

As in the B–36A's case, this was a prorated figure based on the estimated procurement costs of 100 B–36s. The price the Air Force paid to bring the B–36B to the B–36D configuration as well as other post-production modification expenses were not included.

Subsequent Model Series   B–36D

Phaseout   1951

The B–36B phaseout was fast, almost as quick as that of the B–36A. Twenty-five B–36Bs were already undergoing conversion during the first half of 1951.

B–36D

Previous Model Series   B–36B

New Features

The B–36D featured 2 pairs of J47–GE–19 turbojets (in pods, beneath the wings) to assist the basic 6 R–4360–41 engines; K–3A bombing and navigation system (in lieu of B–36B's APG–24 radar)[57] to allow a single crew member to act as radar operator and bombardier; AN/APG–32 radar (instead of APG–3) to control the tail turret; and higher takeoff and landing weights (370,000 and 357,000 pounds, respectively).[58] The aircraft was fitted with snap-action bomb-bay doors, as opposed to the sliding type of the preceding B–36As and Bs. The new bomb-bay doors opened and closed in 2 seconds.

First Flight (YB–36D)   26 March 1949

Flown even sooner than Convair expected, the prototype B–36D was a converted B–36B. It differed notably from ensuing B–36Ds by carrying in its pods 4 Allison J35 jet-assist engines, in place of the later standard J47–GE–19s.

First Flight (Production Aircraft)   11 July 1949

The first true B–36D flew on 11 July 1949, but the Air Force did not accept any of these aircraft for another year.

---

[57] The K–1—not the K–3A—at first equipped most B–36Ds (new productions as well as converted B–36Bs). This K–1 system was little more than a refined APQ–24. It likewise had its share of problems, chief among them the random failure of vacuum tubes. In fact, soon after the B–36s entered the inventory, more than 25 percent of their aborts were due to radar deficiencies.

[58] Forty thousand more takeoff pounds than the B–36B and a 29,000-pound landing weight increase.

Enters Operational Service   1950

The first B-36Ds accepted by the Air Force in August 1950 went to Eglin AFB for testing, but SAC received some of the new productions much later. By December, the command's operational bombers included 38 B-36s—several B-36Ds and about 24 B-36Bs (soon to be brought up to the D configuration). The aircraft equipped units of the Eighth Air Force's 7th Bombardment Wing.

Overseas Deployments   1951

Except for the sole B-36 simulated bombing mission to Hawaii in December 1948, no B-36s were flown overseas before 1951. Then on 16 January, 6 B-36Ds went to the United Kingdom, landing at Lakenheath Royal Air Force Station, having staged through Limestone AFB, Maine. The flight returned to Carswell on 20 January. A similar flight was made to French Morocco on 3 December, when 6 B-36s of the 11th Bombardment Wing touched down at Sidi Slimane, having flown nonstop from Carswell.

Remaining Deficiencies   1951

Despite 2 years of engineering test flights and high priority modifications, many of the problems in early productions remained unsolved.[59] Undoubtedly, progress was being made through gradual changes and carefully devised fixes. The aircraft were nearly combat ready by 1951, but far from perfect. In October, for example, the B-36's gunnery system remained operationally unsuitable. In fact, SAC viewed the "gunnery and defensive armament as the weakest link in the present B-36 capability."

Operational Improvements   1952–1953

Improved containers and better sealants reduced fuel tank leakages.

---

[59] An early major B-36 problem was the recurring leaks in the aircraft's fuel system. The unreliable electrical system and the dangerous flight conditions that could result were also of deep concern through the end of 1949. Engine troubles were still frequent in 1950, compounded by the fact that an engine malfunctioning at a given altitude could check out in perfect order on the ground. Hence, the Air Force on 15 September approved a SAC request for "immediate procurement and installation of airborne ignition analyzers together with necessary spares and supporting equipment for all B-36, B-50, and C-124 type aircraft assigned to this command."

Changes in the electrical system had pared fire hazards during ground refueling operations. Landing gear and bulkhead failures were almost totally corrected. Nevertheless, the Air Force was not satisfied. In April 1952 it ordered a series of gunnery missions for both B–36 and RB–36 aircraft. Known as Far Away, this test was completed in July. It showed that malfunction of the B–36's defensive armament system was due in part to poor maintenance and gunnery crew errors.[60] This prompted Test Fire, a field service exercise begun in September by a RB–36 squadron of the 28th Strategic Reconnaissance Wing. Test Fire ended in December, having attained its main purpose of helping to standardize maintenance and operational procedures.

As anticipated by the Air Force, Test Fire also confirmed the overall conclusion of Fire Away that the B–36's defensive armament was nearly as bad as ever. Various pieces of equipment needed to be redesigned and the fire-control system was barely adequate. In light of this, Hitmore was launched in early 1953. This third project pooled the efforts of the Air Force, General Electric, and Convair (the prime contractor). It required the modification of 6 B–36s to further assess the actual airborne accuracy of the fire-control system. In addition, these planes made separate test flights to gauge the operational efficiency of the gunnery system. The Hitmore results proved encouraging. By mid-year no critical problems had been uncovered. The B–36's defensive armament could be made to work well, after numerous but minor modifications.

Special Modifications   1954

Several B–36Ds received the special modifications initially applied to a number of the B–36Js (sixth and last of the B–36 model series). Approved in February 1954, the modification contract extended over 11 months. The first modified B–36D, flown in June by Convair, was returned to the Air Force the same month. The modified B–36Ds were identified as Featherweight B–36D-111s. Like other featherweight B–36s, they were to be used for high-altitude operations. Hence, they had been stripped of all armament except the tail turret. Convair had also removed all non-essential flying and crew comfort equipment from the modified planes. To shed even more

---

[60] The problem of caring for new and highly sophisticated equipment came as no surprise to the Air Force. In early 1949, the Sperry Company had opened a school to train personnel in proper maintenance of the K radar system. SAC, however, was reluctant to let its few trained radar men attend the 8-month course, and it was just as hard to recruit qualified students.

weight, the Featherweights carried a 13-man crew, 2 fewer than the standard B–36D.

Total B–36Ds Accepted   26

Just 26 B–36Ds came off the production lines,[61] but modification of most of the B–36Bs accepted by the Air Force gave SAC a sizeable B–36D contingent.

Acceptance Rates

Except for 1 B–36D received in fiscal year 1952 (August 1951), all B–36Ds were accepted by the Air Force in FY 51—5 in August 1950, 5 in September, 1 in October, 2 in November, 1 in December, 3 in January 1951, 6 in March, and 2 in April.

End of Production   June 1951

Production ended in June and the Air Force accepted its twenty-sixth B–36D in August.

Flyaway Cost Per Production Aircraft $4.1 million

Airframe, $2,530,112; engines (installed), $589,899; propellers, $184,218; electronics, $55,974; ordnance, $30,241; armament, $747,681.

Subsequent Model Series   B–36F

Other Configurations RB–36D, GRB–36D, and RB–36D–111

Phaseout   1956–1957

In December 1956, SAC's operational inventory counted 250 B/RB–36s of

---

[61] Including 4 planes accounted for by Convair as B–36Bs.

one kind or another. Only 11 B-36Ds remained, after some 6 years of service. It was merely a matter of months before the last of the Ds would be gone.

Milestones   1953

In August and September, B-36s of the 92d Heavy Bomb Wing completed the first mass flight to the Far East, visiting bases in Japan, Okinawa, and Guam. Nicknamed Operation Big Stick, this 3-day exercise came shortly after the end of hostilities in Korea and demonstrated U.S. determination to try every means possible to keep peace in the Far East. On 15 and 16 October, the 92d Heavy Bomb Wing left Fairchild AFB, Washington,[62] bound for Andersen AFB in Guam and 90 days of training. This was the first time an entire B-36 wing was deployed to an overseas base.

Two airmen at work on a portion of a B-36 bomb bay.

---

[62] Fairchild's severe winter climate adversely affected the 92d Wing's combat readiness. The B-36Ds were still prone to fuel cell leaks, and their usual staging from Fairchild to even colder areas made matters worse. The wing had not yet been able to trade its Ds for either Hs or Js that promised better fuel cell sealant.

RB–36D

New Features

The RB–36D carried cameras (similar to those on the RB–36Es) and electronics, as required by the aircraft's principal missions—all-purpose strategic reconnaissance, day and night mapping, charting, and bomb damage assessment. The RB–36D carried a crew of 22; the B–36D, a crew of 15.

Basic Development   1949

Development of the RB–36D coincided with that of the jet pod-equipped B–36B—later identified as the B–36D. As in the bomber's case, General LeMay strongly influenced the procurement decision that soon followed.[63] He had commanded the B–29 strikes against Japan in World War II, and one of his first actions upon taking charge of the Strategic Air Command was to insist on a quick supply of strategic reconnaissance planes. Speedy conversion of the B–36As and delivery of the RB–36Es ahead of the RB–36Ds attested to the urgency of the SAC Commander's request.

First Flight   18 December 1949

The RB–36D was first flown less than 6 months after the first true B–36D, and only 6 more months passed before the Air Force began accepting some of the reconnaissance aircraft.

---

[63] Only 3 strategic reconnaissance candidates remained in November 1948, when the Board of Senior Officers met to review the Air Force's needs for long-range reconnaissance aircraft. The jet pod-equipped B–36 emerged as the board's first choice. The B–47 was second, as also favored by the SAC Commander. The B–54, officially canceled within several months, was third and last. The RB–49, once a strong contender, was not even discussed. Its fate had been sealed during the summer, when problems had arisen in testing the B–49—Northrop's latest tactical configuration of the unconventional B–35 "flying wing." Moreover, development of the RB–49 would have been time-consuming and expensive, 2 commodities the Air Force could not afford.

Enters Operational Service   June 1951

Due to severe materiel shortages, the new RB–36Ds did not become operationally ready until nearly half a year after delivery to SAC.

Problems and Improvements   1951–1953

Being virtually alike, the B/RB–36Ds shared the same problems and received similar improvements.

Special Modifications   1954

As in the B–36's case, some RB–36Ds were changed to the featherweight configuration. These RB–36D–IIIs retained a large crew, 19 instead of 22. The Convair modification contract extended from February 1954 to the following November. The first modified RB–36D–III was flown in August, and returned to the Air Force in the same month.

Total RB–36Ds Accepted   24

The Air Force carried these 24 aircraft as RB–36D productions. In contrast, 8 of them initially appeared on the contractors' records as B–36Bs.[64]

Acceptance Rates

The Air Force took delivery of 3 RB–36Ds in June 1950. It accepted the other 21 in FY 51—between July 1950 and May 1951. The Air Force never acquired more than 3 RB–36Ds in 1 month.

End of Production   May 1951

Delivery of the 24th RB–36D spelled the end of this aircraft's production.

---

[64] The fine line between Convair and USAF ledgers was of no consequence—it did not affect costs nor the aircraft's operational capability.

Flyaway Cost Per Production Aircraft

The RB–36D carried the $4.1 million price tag of the B–36D.

Subsequent Model Series   B–36F

Other Configurations   GRB–36D–111/RF–84F

The GRB–36D/RF–84 combination, better known as the FICON (*fi*ghter *con*veyor) or carrier-parasite program, came into being in the early fifties. The RB–36s were becoming more and more vulnerable, and no new form of defense was readily available. The Air Force therefore looked to the past for solutions. As a result, it planned in 1951 to put a parasite RF–84 in the RB–36's bomb bay.[65] The parasite plane would be released about 800 or 1,000 miles from the target and within a relatively safe area. The pilot of the RF–84 would continue on to the target, obtain high- or low-level photography as desired, then return to the mother aircraft. An alternate FICON mission would be long-range, high-speed bombing. No real problems arose, but it took longer than thought to bring the FICON project to fruition.

Flown in January 1952, the FICON composite prototype comprised a modified, standard RB–36D and a straight-wing Republic F–84E Thunderjet. Extensive flight tests soon demonstrated the FICON concept was practical. The parasite's straight wings posed no great difficulties. Sweeping down the tail of a forthcoming F–84 prototype (YF–84F) would enable it to fit in the RB–36 bomb bay. Elimination of the YF–84F's tail flutter by using faired bomb-bay doors removed the last stumbling block.

Contracts awarded Convair and Republic in the fall of 1953 called for modifying 10 RB–36Ds and 25 RF–84Fs, respectively. This was far below the

---

[65] A carrier-parasite combination had been tried before for somewhat different purposes. It had long been known that heavily laden bombers could not cope with interceptors. Studies undertaken in 1944 to afford some protection to the then yet-to-be flown B–36 envisioned a pilotless, remote control, fast fighter that could be carried to the battle area in one of the bomb bays of the huge long-range bomber. However, this was given up in favor of a pilot-operated fighter that would be more maneuverable in facing repeated attacks. The tiny, folding-wing XF–85 Goblin which ensued was developed by the McDonnell Aircraft Corporation in late 1945 and first flown in August 1948. Because no B–36s were readily available, it was test-dropped from a B–29. The project, however, never went past the experimental stage. The Goblin production was abandoned for a number of technical and financial reasons, but danger was the primary obstacle. The Air Force believed the odds of retrieving a fighter in the midst of a raging battle were poor. Moreover, if the bomber was shot down before the fighter was launched, both crews would be lost. Finally, if the bomber was destroyed after the launching, the short-range Goblin would also be doomed.

number of aircraft SAC had in mind—30 RB-36s and 75 RF-84s. Still, modification of only 35 was to take time. To begin with, the carrier RB-36Ds turned out to be featherweight configurations of the big reconnaissance bomber, and none of these were available before 1954. Furthermore, the reconfigured planes had to be modified to carry the additional mechanisms for stowing, aerial servicing, releasing and retrieving the F-84F parasites.[66] Specifically, this meant that each carrier was equipped with a straight beam extended down from the bottom of the airframe. Each modified parasite featured a retractable probe, mounted on the forward top fuselage section to ease hook-up. Actually, the technical operation of FICON was simple. Carriers and parasites could fly out of different bases. The parasite could be picked up in midair enroute to the target area, or by ground hook-up prior to takeoff. Night operations were also possible. The first GRB-36D-111 carrier was delivered in February 1955, 6 months ahead of the first parasite RF-84F (subsequently identified as the RF-84K). The FICON B-36s served with SAC's 99th Heavy Strategic Reconnaissance Wing.

Phaseout   1956–1957

The RB-36D followed the B-36D's phaseout pattern. That of the FICON aircraft was much the same.[67]

---

[66] The FICON carriers retained all their ferret electronic countermeasures components, which were relocated aft of the bomb bays. New APX-29 rendezvous equipment was added.

[67] By mid-1957, SAC's strategic and reconnaissance fighters, the RF-84Ks included, were on their way out.

B–36F

Previous Model Series   **B–36D**

New Features

The only telling difference between the B–36F and the preceding B–36D lay in the substitution of more powerful engines—R–4360–53s in lieu of R–4360–41 engines.

First Flight (YB–36F)   **18 November 1950**

The prototype B–36F and B–36F production models were equipped from the start with six 3,800-horsepower R–4360–53 engines. Each generated 300 more horsepower than a B–36D engine, but still failed to bring the B–36F's performance up to par.[68]

Enters Operational Service   **1951**

The Air Force accepted a first B–36F in March 1951 and a few more in the months that followed. No B–36Fs reached SAC until August.

Operational Problems   **1951–1952**

The B–36F's R–4360–53 piston engines were not wholly satisfactory because of excessive torque pressure as well as ground air cooling and

---

[68] Production plans early in 1951 projected a normal growth in the B–36 employment through use of even more powerful engines. Adoption of the Pratt & Whitney R–4360–57 reciprocating engines would stretch the combat radius of a B–36 with a 10,000-pound bomb load from 3,360 to 4,200 nautical miles. It would also jump the bomber's average speed from 186 to 300 knots. These plans were dropped in August 1952, when the Air Force decided that no more B–36s would be built other than those now in production. The announcement coincided with USAF statement that Boeing's all-jet, 8-engine B–52 would replace the B–36 heavy bomber, and that Boeing had been awarded a letter contract to build 70 of the new bombers.

combustion problems. Pratt & Whitney, Convair, and the Air Materiel Command joined forces to solve these deficiencies quickly.

Post-Production Modifications   1954

As in the case of other B-36 model series, a number of the new B-36Fs were brought up to the configuration introduced by the Featherweight B-36J-111. Approval of the Convair modification contract in February 1954 was followed by delivery of the first B-36F-111 in May. The B-36F featherweight modifications were completed in December, on schedule.

Total B-36Fs Accepted   34

Among the 34 B-36Fs bought by the Air Force was the B-36F prototype, later completed as a true production model.

Acceptance Rates

The Air Force took delivery of the first 4 B-36Fs toward the end of fiscal year 1951—1 in March 1951, 1 in May, and 2 in June. The other 30 B-36Fs were accepted in FY 52—2 in July 1951, 5 in August, 4 in September, 8 in October, 6 in November, 4 in December, and 1 in January 1952.

End of Production   October 1951

The Air Force did not get its last B-36Fs until several months after production was over.

Flyaway Cost Per Production Aircraft $4.1 million

The B-36F carried the price tag of the B-36D. Airframe, engines, electronics, all cost the same.

Subsequent Model Series   B-36H

Other Configurations   RB-36F and YB-60

RB-36F: The Air Force ordered and took delivery of 24 long-range reconnaissance versions of the B–36F. The first 4 RB–36Fs were accepted in fiscal year 1951 (all in May); the 20 others in FY 52 (between August and December 1951). Cost records listed both the B–36F and the RB–36F at $4.1 million each.

YB–60: This B–36 configuration never went past testing. First known as the YB–36G, this apparent successor to the B–36F, was redesignated YB–60 in mid-1951 because it so obviously differed from the B–36. At the same time, Convair's plans to bring existing B–36s to the G configuration were given up. The swept-wing, pure-jet YB–60, with its new needle-nose radome and new type of auxiliary power system, soon found itself competing with the future B–52. Both used the same jet engines (Pratt & Whitney J57–P–3s), but in comparison the YB–60's performance test results proved disappointing, and the program was canceled in January 1953. The cost of building and testing the 2 B–60 prototypes (accepted in the fall of 1951) ran around $15 million.

Phaseout   1958–1959

In mid-1958, 46 RB–36s remained in the active inventory. SAC identified 19 of them as RB–36Fs. No B–36Fs were listed, although USAF rolls still reflected 32 B–36s. Total phaseout was imminent in any case.

Items of Special Interest   1954–1955

On 16 June 1954, SAC's 4 RB–36-equipped heavy strategic reconnaissance wings were given a primary mission of bombing. They did limited reconnaissance as a secondary mission. Then on 1 October 1955, the RB–36 reconnaissance wings were redesignated heavy bombardment wings, while retaining a latent reconnaissance capability.

B-36H

Previous Model Series   **B-36F**

New Features

The B-36H had a rearranged crew compartment and additional twin tail radomes to store the components of the AN/APG-41A radar.[69]

First Flight (YB-36H)   November 1950

The B-36H and B-36F prototypes were first flown at almost the same time. Yet, B-36H deliveries did not start until December 1951, when the Air Force already had most of its 34 B-36Fs. The B-36H's marked improvement over the F accounted for the delay between production. The Air Force bought 156 B/RB-36Hs—more than double the production total of any other B-36.

Enters Operational Service   1952

Once underway the production flow of B/RB-36Hs was steady, averaging 8 aircraft per month during 1952, and 6 monthly between January and September 1953.

Operational Problems   1952

By 1952, engineering on the B-36 was little more than correction of rather minor deficiencies showing up in service. The B-36H (like the B-36F) had 6 R-4360-53 engines, but the early troubles of these new engines were virtually under control. Other problems arose, however. During a few months in 1952, all B-36s were restricted to an altitude of 25,000 feet after

---

[69] The AN/APG-41A was far superior to the AN/APG-32 gun-laying radar employed by the preceding B-36Ds and B-36Fs.

an RB–36 accident at 33,000 feet was traced to a faulty bulkhead. This restriction remained in effect until all deficient bulkheads were discovered and replaced.

The B–36's original propeller blades carried flight restrictions that hampered performance. A new blade, made by a special flash-welding process, could be used freely except for landing and takeoff. This blade weighed an extra 20 pounds, but its greater efficiency promised to compensate for the loss in aircraft range. A batch of 1,175 was ordered for prompt installation.

Grounding   1952

In March, defective landing gears caused a series of accidents. After 2 crashes, the Air Force grounded all B–36s except the first 152. This meant that almost all of the last half of B/RB–36F productions and some 30 B/RB–36Hs already accepted by the Air Force could not be flown. Investigations from the start had blamed the aircraft's landing gear pivot shaft. Since a heavier bar could be devised and serve until a permanent alteration could be made, the grounding orders were soon lifted.

Post–Production Modifications   1954

Some B–36Hs and B–36H reconnaissance versions were reconfigured by Convair in 1954. They were returned to SAC in the same year as B/RB–36H–111s, having undergone the same stripping and overall modification as other featherweight B/RB–36s. No troubles were met with during the fulfillment of the B/RB–36H or other featherweight modification contracts. The crew of each aircraft so modified was cut. For high-altitude operations, B–36s carried only a crew of 13 (a decrease of 2); RB–36s, a crew of 19 (a decrease of 3).

Total B–36Hs Accepted   83

Acceptance Rates

The Air Force accepted 32 B–36Hs in fiscal year 1952—7 in December 1951, 5 in January 1952, 3 in February, 5 in March, and 4 in each of the next 3 months. It received 43 B–36Hs in FY 53—4 in July 1952, 4 in August, 7 in September, 3 in October, 4 in November, 2 in December, 4 in January 1953, and 3 during each of the next 5 months. The last 8 B–36Hs were accepted in FY 54—3 in July 1953, 3 in August, and 2 in September.

End of Production   July 1953

All B–36Hs, including the last one built, had been accepted by the end of September.

Flyaway Cost Per Production Aircraft $4.1 million

In round figures, the B–36H and B–36F prices were alike. In reality, the B–36H cost an additional $11,321. Airframe costs were much lower, but the price of the engines showed a steep increase. Armament, electronics, and propeller cost also had gone up. The new costs were: airframe, $2,077,785; engines (installed), $874,526; propellers, $214,186; electronics, $80,272; ordnance, $30,241; armament, $872,436.

Subsequent Model Series   B–36J

Other Configurations   RB–36H and B–36H (Tanker)

RB–36H: The Air Force bought 73 long-range reconnaissance versions of the B–36H. Twenty-three were accepted in FY 52 (all during the first 6 months of 1952); 42 others in FY 53 (between July 1952 and June 1953). The last 8 were delivered in FY 54 (3 in July 1953, 3 in August, and 2 in September). The RB–36H price matched that of the B–36H and did not include the featherweight modification costs of 1954.

B–36H (Tanker): Searching for a tanker that could refuel jet aircraft at higher altitudes and higher speeds, SAC in early 1952 became interested in a readily convertible B–36 bomber-tanker. The Air Force therefore asked Convair to equip one B–36 with a probe and drogue refueling system. The modification contract was approved in February 1952 and the work was completed in May. Testing, postponed to the end of the month because of the late delivery of one B–47 receiver aircraft, was satisfactory enough. Yet, no other tests took place until January 1953, after a new and vastly

The NB-36H—modified to be a test bed for a nuclear reactor.

improved British-made probe and drogue refueling system was installed.[70] The converted B-36H tanker subsequently flown could refuel one or more receiver aircraft. The 9-crewmember tanker could be returned to its standard bomber configuration in some 12 hours. But the B-36's bomber commitments never really allowed SAC to exploit these features.

Phaseout   1956–1959

Conversion of SAC's heavy bomb wings to B-52 aircraft began in June 1956, with the B-36H-equipped 42d Wing at Loring AFB, Maine.[71] Nonetheless, like the final B-36Js, the much-improved B-36Hs were among the last to go.

---

[70] The British had developed refueling techniques to the point where they were actually in use on commercial airplanes, and the Air Staff in late 1947 had already begun to consider adapting the British technique to combat aircraft refueling. This would allow short-range but relatively speedy bombers of the B-50 type to get to a distant and heavily defended target with the atomic bomb—a task allocated to the B-36, but especially hazardous due to that long-range bomber's slow speed.

[71] The 93d Bomb Wing at Castle AFB, Calif., fully equipped with B-52s in April 1956, had been a B-47 outfit prior to conversion.

Other Uses

One B–36 was modified by Convair in 1952 to carry guided air missiles (GAMs), specifically the GAM–63 Rascal,[72] under development by the Bell Aircraft Corporation since 1946. A mockup inspection of the B–36/Rascal prototype disclosed no major obstacles, and 11 other B–36s were programmed to be modified as director aircraft (DB–36s) for the new missiles.[73] Several factors soon dictated changes in USAF plans. The principal ones were ongoing Rascal difficulties, imposition of new technical requirements, and reorientation of the program to achieve the best aircraft/missile operational combination. Although testing with the DB–36 would go on for awhile, the Air Staff decided in mid-1955 that it definitely wanted the B–47, not the B–36,[74] to carry the Bell rocket-powered GAM–63. Time lessened the decision's importance, the Rascal program being canceled in November 1958.[75]

1955–1957

One B–36H (Serial No. 51–5712) never reached SAC. The Air Force reserved it for special tests that might lead to the design of the world's first atomic-powered plane. The future nuclear-propelled B–36 (temporarily labeled the X–6) did not materialize. Even so, the modified and redesignated B–36H (NB–36H) saw extensive duty as a nuclear-reactor test bed. Forty-seven test flights were made, yielding valuable data on the effects of radiation upon airframe and components. The NB–36H had undergone various modifications prior to testing. The most important one added a crew compartment to the fuselage nose section. This shielded all crew members from radioactive rays, when the nuclear reactor in the aft bomb bay operated. Composed of lead and rubber, this compartment completely surrounded the crew. Only the pilot and copilot could see out through the

---

[72] The name Rascal derived from the guidance system used during the missile's dive on the target. This system was called a *Ra*dar *Sca*nning *L*ink, and the word Rascal was formed by combining the underlined letters of the 3 words.

[73] Such aircraft as the B–29, B–50, B–47, and even the B–52 were considered or modified as Rascal carriers, either for experimental or operational use.

[74] Most of the DB–36 modification contract was canceled. Convair completed only 3 aircraft and reimbursed $1.6 million to the Air Force.

[75] At a top speed of Mach 2.95, the Rascal could carry a 3,000-pound nuclear warhead 90 nautical miles. Still, it remained unreliable and was overtaken by technological progress.

foot-thick, leaded-glass windshield. A closed-circuit television system enabled the crew to see the reactor as well as other parts of the aircraft.

Milestones   6 April 1955

A B–36 launched a guided missile with an atomic warhead from 42,000 feet. The explosion took place 6 miles above Yucca Flat, Nevada. It was the highest known altitude of any nuclear blast at the time.

B–36J

Previous Model Series   B–36H

New Features

The B–36J had 2 additional tanks, 1 on the outer panel of each wing, allowing an extra fuel load of 2,770 gallons. It also had a much stronger landing gear, permitting a gross takeoff weight of 410,000 pounds.[76]

First Flight (YB–36J)   July 1953

The prototype flight was swiftly followed by the September flight of the first B–36J production model. The latter was immediately accepted by the Air Force.

Enter Operational Service

SAC received its full contingent of B–36Js in less than a year.

Production Modifications   1954

The last 14 B–36Js entered the operational inventory as lightweight B–36J–111s. In contrast to other B–36 featherweights (modified after production), Convair made all necessary changes before completing the aircraft. This delayed delivery for a month (too short to disrupt SAC's plans) and saved more than $100,000.

---

[76] This had long been a SAC goal. The Air Force and Convair as early as 1952 discussed how to increase the takeoff weight of available B–36s without compromising safety—USAF engineers arguing that the structural integrity of some of the aircraft's new components was unknown. Takeoff weight was raised to 370,000 pounds in June 1952. But still cautious, the Air Force's authorization covered only B–36s that already had somewhat stronger landing gears.

Operational Problems   1953–1958

SAC had no critical problems with the B–36Js. For that matter, the entire B–36 fleet showed improvement, largely because of Project SAM-SAC. This program, initiated in 1953, required the cyclic reconditioning of all operational B–36s (215 as of September 1954) and constantly tied-up 25 aircraft in depots. Yet, the intensive maintenance paid off for both the older B–36s and the latest and final B–36Js. In the same vein, the crew-to-aircraft ratio (too low for many years) began to improve as the number of combat-ready crews grew steadily.

Other Improvements   1953–1958

The B–36 was certain to be entirely outmoded by mid-1955.[77] Until then, however, it remained SAC's primary atomic bomb carrier and perhaps the Nation's major deterrent to Soviet aggression. Meanwhile, the Air Force found ways to keep enhancing its effectiveness. Ever resourceful, the service set up the Quick Engine Change Program, which combined an engine and accessories in a power package that could be field-installed in no time. Applied to other aircraft as well, the change program for B–36s ran from 1953 until September 1957. Another ingenious and long-lasting project was Big-Kel (devised by the San Antonio Air Materiel Area at Kelly AFB, Texas), which replenished the flyaway kits of B–36 spares utilized in SAC wing rotation overseas.

Planning Changes   1957–1958

Defense funds cutbacks in fiscal year 1958 compelled the Air Force to alter plans for every USAF program at every echelon. SAC did not escape the crisis. The B–52 procurement was stretched out and the B–36 service-life extended. Although the worldwide flying hours of the 2 bombers were reduced, these changes were fraught with complications. To begin with, phasing out the giant B–36s was a large undertaking. Because it could "find no other use for them," the Air Force had ordered the $1 billion fleet

---

[77] Phaseout of the B–36 was settled before 1953. All kinds of technological advances called for it. Withdrawing B–36s from the inventory would also make it possible to do away with the strategic fighters that were to accompany the cumbersome bombers on most of their missions.

scrapped.[78] Still, the B–36s were to remain first-line strategic bombers up to their final day. As a rule, B–36s flew from their last operation straight to the Arizona storage base for reclamation and destruction.[79] The shortage of B–52s forced the withdrawal of B–36s from several reclamation contracts. By then, the Air Force had made it a practice to support the B–36s still in service with components from out-of-service planes. Moreover, to conserve the most in money and manpower, only required items were saved and unneeded reclamations were avoided. Hence, the reactivated B–36s obviously posed problems.

Total B–36Js Accepted   33

Acceptance Rates

The Air Force accepted 28 B–36Js in fiscal year 1954—2 in September 1953 and 2 in October, 3 each month from November 1953 through March 1954, none in April, 4 in May, and 5 in June. Five more B–36Js were accepted in FY 55—4 in July 1954 and 1 in August.

End of Production   August 1954

The Air Force received the last B–36J on 10 August and delivered it 4 days later to the 42d Heavy Bomb Wing at Loring AFB.

Flyaway Cost Per Production Aircraft $3.6 million

The B–36J cost half a million dollars less than the preceding

---

[78] The scrapping of the first 200 B–36s was due to yield a return of $93.5 million, but the Air Force recouped much more. Various configurations of the B–36's basic R-4360 engines equipped other USAF aircraft (KC-97s, B-50s, C-119s, and C-124s) and $22,000 worth of parts (mainly, crankshafts and cylinders) was removed from each B-36 engine. This was no small savings because 4,000 engines (1,200 of the early R-4360-41s and 2,800 of the more powerful -53s) became surplus as a result of the B-36 phaseout.

[79] B-36s began arriving at Davis-Monthan in February 1956. Reclamation and destruction were handled by the Mar-Pak Corporation, Painesville, Ohio. Mar-Pak had reclaimed 161 B-36s by December 1957 and processed the last B-36 in April 1959.

B–36H—airframe, $1,969,271; engines (installed), $639,651; propellers, $214,186; electronics, $77,691; ordnance, $32,036; armament, $707,379.

Subsequent Model Series   None

Other Configurations   None

Phaseout   1958–1959

In December 1958, only 22 B–36s (all B–36Js) remained in the operational inventory. Symbol of global airpower during the early days of the United States Air Force, the B–36 Peacemaker neared its end. On 12 February 1959, the last of SAC's giant bombers and the final B–36J built by Convair left Biggs AFB, Texas, where it had seen duty with the 95th Heavy Bomb Wing. The plane (Serial No. 52–2827) was flown to Amon Carter Field in Fort Worth and put on display as a permanent memorial.

Milestones   12 February 1959

Retirement of the last B–36 marked the beginning of a new era—SAC's becoming an all-jet bomber force on that day.

Program Recap

The Air Force accepted a grand total of 385 B-36s (prototype, test, and reconnaissance aircraft among them). As recorded by the Comptroller of the Air Force, the program consisted of 1 XB-36, 1 YB-36, 22 B-36As, 62 B-36Bs, 26 B-36Ds, 34 B-36Fs, 83 B-36Hs, 33 B-36Js, 24 RB-36Ds, 24 RB-36Fs, 73 RB-36Hs, and 2 swept-wing, all-jet B-36 prototypes (known for a while as YB-36Gs but redesignated and flown as YB-60s). Be that as it may, these listings were far afield from most operational counts. Modifications and reconfigurations sharply altered the B-36 program. The Air Force accepted only 26 true B-36D productions, but conversion of the B-36Bs gave SAC another 50 B-36Ds. Similarly, the B-36A reconfiguration gave the reconnaissance forces 22 RB-36Es, not reflected in production data. Pinning a price on the B-36 was not so involved. Some true productions, like the B-36Hs, ran as high as $4.15 million, but early B-36s were far cheaper. The Air Force estimated the entire program (research, development, prototypes, and production) at $1.4 billion. Prorated, this came to $3.6 million per aircraft. Omitted from every unit cost, however, were the expenses incurred for all engineering changes and modifications, added on after approval of a basic contract.

TECHNICAL AND BASIC MISSION PERFORMANCE DATA

B/RB-36 AIRCRAFT

	B-36A	B-36B	RB-36E	B-36D	B-36D-111	B-36F	B-36H	B-36J	B-36J-111
Manufacturer (Airframe)	Consolidated Vultee Aircraft Corp. Fort Worth, Tex.								
(Engines)	The Pratt & Whitney Aircraft Division of United Aircraft Corporation, East Hartford 8, Conn., and The General Electric Co., Schenectady, N.Y.								
Nomenclature	Strategic Heavy Bomber and Reconnaissance Aircraft.								
Popular Name	Peacemaker								
Length/Span (ft)	162.1/230	162.1/230	162.1/230	162.1/230	162.1/230	162.1/230	162.1/230	162.1/230	162.1/230
Wing Area (sq ft)	4,772	4,772	4,772	4,772	4,772	4,772	4,772	4,772	4,772
Weights (lb)									
Empty	135,020	140,640	164,238	161,371	161,264	167,646	168,487	171,035	166,165
Combat	212,800	227,700	238,300	250,300	244,400	254,300	253,900	266,100	262,500
Max Takeoff[a]	311,000	328,000	370,000	370,000	370,000	370,000	370,000	410,000	410,000
Engine: Number, Rated Power per Engine & Designation	(6) 3,000-hp R-4360-25	(6) 3,500-hp R-4360-41	(6) 3,500-hp R-4360-41 & (4) 5,010-lb st J47-GE-19	(6) 3,500-hp R-4360-41 & (5) 5,010-lb st J47-GE-19	(6) 3,500-hp R-4360-41 & (5) 5,010-lb st J47-GE-19	(6) 3,800-hp R-4360-53 & (4) 5,010-lb st J47-GE-19	(6) 3,800-hp R-4360-53 & (4) 5,010-lb st J47-GE-19	(6) 3,800-hp R-4360-53 & (4) 5,010-lb st J47-GE-19	(6) 3,800-hp R-4360-53 & (4) 5,010-lb st J47-GE-19
Takeoff Ground Run (ft)									
at Sea Level	6,000	6,030	4,400	4,400	4,400	3,990	3,990	5,290	5,290
Over 50-ft Obstacle	8,000	8,520	5,685	5,685	5,685	5,110	5,110	6,820	6,820
Rate of Climb (fpm) at Sea Level	502	500	970	960	970	920	920	720	780
Combat Rate of Climb (fpm) at Sea Level	1,447	1,510	2,140	2,210	2,330	2,060	2,060	1,920	1,995

	1	2	3	4	5	6	7	8	9
Service Ceiling (ft) (100 fpm Rate of Climb to Altitude)	—	28,500	32,200	33,100	33,400	33,000	33,000	27,400	28,500
Combat Ceiling (ft) (500 fpm Rate of Climb, Max Power, to Altitude)	—	38,800	40,000	40,700	41,300	40,900	40,800	39,900	39,500
Average Cruise Speed (kn)	189	176	190	193	192	204	203	198	197
Max Speed at Optimum Altitude (kn/ft)	300/31,600	331/34,500	348/36,500	353/36,200	363/37,300	363/37,100	361/36,700	357/36,400	363/37,500
Combat Radius (nm)	3,370	3,740	3,057	3,065	3,260	2,807	2,705	2,955	3,465
Total Mission Time (hr)	35.6	42.43	31.7	31.5	33.7	26.7	26.4	29.4	34.6
Armament	16 20-mm guns	16 20-mm guns	16 20-mm M24A1 guns	16 20-mm M24A1 guns	16 20-mm M24A1 guns	16 20-mm M24A1 guns	16 20-mm M24A1 guns	16 20-mm M24A1 guns	2 20-mm M24A1 guns
Crew	15	15	22	15	13	15	15	15	13
Max Bombload[b] (lb)	72,000	72,000	None[c]	72,000	72,000	72,000	72,000	72,000	72,000

Abbreviations			
fpm	= feet per minute	mm	= millimeter
hp	= horsepower	nm	= nautical miles
kn	= knots	st	= static thrust
max	= maximum		

[a] Limited by the strength of the aircraft's main landing gear. The maximum takeoff gross weight of a number of B-36Bs was restricted to 278,000 pounds. B-36s with higher takeoff weights (370,000 pounds or more) were equipped with stronger landing gears (modified after production) or new landing gears (installed on the production line).

[b] The basic mission bombload was 10,000 pounds. Bombloads could be made of various combinations—WW II box fins, interim conical fins, and so-called new series. Except for the B-36As, all B-36s could carry bombloads of 86,000 pounds (e.g., two 43,000-lb bombs), when their gross weight did not exceed 357,500 pounds.

[c] Like other B-36s in the reconnaissance configuration, the RB-36E was equipped with 23 cameras (mostly K-22As, K-17Cs, and K-38s) and carried 80 T-86 photo flashes.

Basic Mission Note

All basic mission performance data were based on maximum power, except as otherwise indicated.

Combat Radius Formula:

B–36A—Not applicable, since this model was used mainly for training and crew transition.

B–36B—Warmed up, took off, climbed on course with normal power to 10,000 feet, cruised at long-range speeds at altitudes for best range (10,000 feet minimum). Climbed to arrive at 25,000 feet, 30 minutes prior to target. Cruised long-range speeds for 15 minutes, conducted 15-minute normal-power bomb-run, dropped bombs, conducted 5-minute evasive action plus 10-minute escape at normal power. Returned to base at altitudes for best range using long-range cruise-climb technique. Range-free allowances included 10-minute normal-power fuel consumption for warm-up and take-off, 5-minute evasive action at normal-power fuel consumption, and 5 percent initial fuel for landing and endurance reserves.

B–36D—Warmed up, took off, and climbed on course to 5,000 feet at normal power; cruised out at long-range speeds to point of cruise-climb operation. Began climb to combat altitude, using long-range climb powers, to arrive at cruise ceiling 500 nautical miles from target. Cruised at long-range speeds at combat altitude, using best engine (reciprocating-jet) combinations; 15 minutes from target, conducted 10-minute engine normal-power bomb-run, dropped bombs, and conducted 2-minute evasive action and 8-minute escape from target at normal power. After leaving target area, cruised back at long-range speeds, using best engine combinations, until 500 nautical miles from target. Descended to optimum cruise altitude and cruise-climbed back to base. Range-free allowances included 10-minute normal-power fuel consumption for reciprocating engines and 5-minute normal-power fuel consumption for jet engines for starting and take-off, 2-minute normal-power fuel consumption at combat altitude for evasive action, 30-minute fuel consumption for long-range speeds at sea level (reciprocating engines only), plus 5 percent of initial fuel load for landing and endurance reserves.

B–36D–111—Same as B–36D.

B-36F, B-36H, B-36J, and B-36J-111—Same as B-36D and B-36D-111, except also dropped chaff.

RB-36E—Same as B-36D and B-36D-111, except "conducted 10-engine normal-power photo-run" (instead of bomb-run), and "dropped flash bombs" (instead of bombs).

B–45 Tornado

North American Aviation, Incorporated

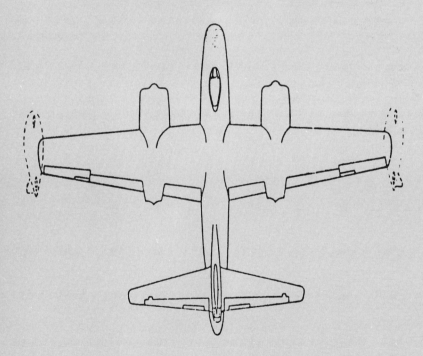

B-45 Tornado
North American

Manufacturer's Model 130

Overview

In 1943, aware of Nazi Germany's advances in the field of jet propulsion, the Army Air Forces (AAF) asked the General Electric Company to devise a more powerful engine than its prospective axial turboprop. This was a tall order, but it eventually brought about the production of the J35 and J47 turbojets. In 1944, 1 year after the jet engine requirements were established, the War Department requested the aircraft industry to submit proposals for various jet bombers, with gross weights ranging from 80,000 to more than 200,000 pounds. This was another challenge, and only 4 contractors answered the call.

Pressed for time, the AAF in 1946 decided to skip the usual contractor competition, review the designs, and choose among the proposed aircraft that could be obtained first. The multi-jet engine B-45, larger and more conventional than its immediate competitor, won the round, with the understanding that if a less readily available bomber was to prove superior enough to supplant it (which the Boeing XB-47 did), that aircraft would also be purchased.

Testing of the XB-45 prompted pre-production changes. North American Aviation, Incorporated, redesigned the nose panel, increased the aircraft's stabilizer area, and lengthened the tailplane by nearly 7 feet. In August 1948, 22 of the 90 B-45s, ordered less than 2 years before, reached the newly independent Air Force. However, the B-45's increased weight, excessive takeoff distance, and numerous structural and mechanical defects generated scant enthusiasm.

Meanwhile, the B-47's future production had become certain, and in mid-1948 the Air Staff actually began to question the B-45's intrinsic value as well as its potential use. Soon afterwards, as President Truman's budgetary axe slashed Air Force expenditures, the programmed production of B–45s was reduced to a grand total of 142, a decrease of 51 aircraft.

Although continuously plagued by engine problems, component malfunctions, lack of spare parts, and numerous minor flaws, the B–45 regained importance. Like all bombers produced after the end of World War II, the B–45 was designed to carry both conventional and atomic bombs. In mid-1950, when U.S. military commitments to the Korean War reemphasized the vulnerability of the North Atlantic Treaty Organization forces in Europe to Soviet attack, the Air Force made an important decision. Since the U.S. planned to produce large quantities of small atomic and thermonuclear weapons in the near future, the use of such weapons, heretofore a prerogative of the strategic forces, would be expanded to the tactical forces, particularly in Europe.

The program that ensued, under the code name of Backbreaker, entailed difficult aircraft modifications because several distinct atomic bomb types were involved and large amounts of new electronics support equipment had to be fitted in place of the standard components. In addition, the 40 B–45s allocated to the Backbreaker program also had to be equipped with a new defensive system and extra fuel tanks. Despite the magnitude of the modification project, plus recurring engine problems, atomic-capable B–45s began reaching the United Kingdom in May 1952, and deployment of the 40 aircraft was completed in mid-June, barely 30 days behind the Air Staff deadline.

All told, and in spite of its many valuable secondary functions, the B–45 did not achieve great glory. The entire contingent, Backbreaker and reconnaissance models included, was phased out by 1959. Yet, the B–45 retained a place in aviation history as the Air Force's first jet bomber and as the first atomic carrier of the tactical forces.

Basic Development   1944

Like the trouble-plagued but eventually successful and long-lasting B–47, the B–45 officially originated in 1944, when the War Department called for bids and proposals on an entire family of jet bombers, with gross weights ranging from 80,000 to more than 200,000 pounds. These were ambitious requirements considering the kind of airplanes being planned at the time in the United States and elsewhere. Yet, the emergence of unrealistic requirements was a common practice that would endure for decades.[1]

---

[1] From experience, government officials most likely rationalized that inflating the requirements was the only way to get at least the minimum acceptable. Late in 1948, engineers

Unofficially, the roots of both the B-45 and B-47 aircraft could be traced to 1943, when the Army Air Forces, aware of Nazi Germany's advances in the field of jet propulsion, asked the General Electric Company to design something better than the TG-100 axial-flow turboprop engine that was being developed for the Consolidated-Vultee's 2 experimental P-81 escort fighters (the mass production of which did not materialize). The AAF's demands were met with General Electric's development of the 4,000-pound-thrust TG-180 and the TG-190 engines,[2] of which various models were to power subsequent bomber and fighter aircraft. For its part, North American began to attempt satisfying the AAF's requirements for a jet bomber with a design for an easy-to-build airframe, conventional in concept and straightforward in its aerodynamic form. Model 130, as the design was labelled in early 1944, was a mid-wing monoplane with dihedral tailplane and a retractable landing gear. North American planned to propel its new bomber with 4 jet units, grouped in horizontal pairs, 1 pair on each side of the fuselage outboard of the tailplane.

Initial Procurement   September 1944

The AAF initiated the procurement of the future B-45 with Letter Contract AC-5126. This document, issued on 8 September 1944, called for the development and testing of 3 experimental B-45s,[3] all of which were to be based on North American design 130. In time, as production of the

---

of the Air Materiel Command began to point out the pitfalls of this practice. But their concern did not prevail. In 1952, many in the Air Staff also recommended caution and their efforts achieved some degree of success. Nevertheless, as the "weapon system concept" gained momentum, it became evident that the Air Force believed increasingly that mission objectives had to come first and that technology could be made to satisfy such objectives. (For details, see B-58, p 354 and pp 373-374).

[2] The TG-180, eventually built in large quantities by the Allison Division of the General Motors Corporation, became the J35; the TG-190, continuously produced by the General Electric Company, became the J47.

[3] The basic terminology of military aircraft underwent little change throughout the years. For the United States Air Force (as well as the preceding Army Air Forces), an experimental aircraft is a vehicle in a developmental or experimental stage, which is not established as a standard vehicle for service use. The experimental aircraft may be built to try out an idea, or to try for certain capabilities or characteristics. It may embody a new principle or a new application of an old principle. The status of such aircraft is indicated by the prefix, or classification letter X. In contrast, the prototype aircraft is a preproduction vehicle procured for evaluation and test of a specific design. The prototype status is indicated by the letter Y. This prefix symbol is acquired by the first complete and working aircraft made of a given model or model series, intended to serve as the pattern or guide for subsequently produced members of the same class.

aircraft appeared probable, North American altered the overall configuration of 1 of its 3 XB–45s. The selected vehicle was actually completed as a tactical model and, although seldom referred to as YB–45, assumed the role of a standard prototype.

Production Decision   2 August 1946

The AAF originally intended to schedule a formal competition between the various contractors working on projects to satisfy the War Department's requirements of 1944. In 1946, since the early production of a jet bomber seemed highly desirable, the AAF decided to forgo the planned competition. Instead, available designs would be reviewed to determine which model could be obtained first. Four contractors were involved: North American, working on the XB–45; the Boeing Airplane Company, engrossed in the development of the swept-wing, 6-jet XB–47; the Consolidated Vultee Aircraft Corporation (Convair), engaged in the XB–46; and the Glenn L. Martin Company, builder of the XB–48.[4] But while the XB–45 and XB–46 were nearing completion and flights of these aircraft were scheduled for 1947, the XB–47 and XB–48 in 1946 were still in the early stages of development, and 2 years might elapse before the end of their fabrication and initial flight testing. Pressed for time, the AAF opted to appraise the XB–45 and XB–46 immediately and to postpone consideration of the XB–47 and XB–48 until they flew. Then, if either the XB–47 or the XB–48 proved superior enough to supplant the new bomber being produced (which the XB–47 did) that aircraft would be bought.[5] On 2 August 1946, the AAF

---

[4] The military characteristics, issued by the AAF on 17 November 1944 (see B–47, pp 101–102) and embodied by the 4 projects, were specific but not restrictive. The B–45 and B–47 aircraft, the only 2 programs that went beyond the experimental stage, stemmed from the same requirements but ended having very little in common. Both were ordered as "medium" bombers, but in contrast to the B–47, which retained its medium bomber designation, the B–45 became a light bomber. The fact that the B–45, weighing 47,000 pounds and having a combat radius of 764 nautical miles, was finally listed as "light" also showed how swiftly concepts changed. Five years before, the World War II B–17G Flying Fortress, which weighed 37,672 pounds and had a combat radius of 873 nautical miles, was considered "heavy."

[5] The AAF anticipated that the B–47's performance characteristics would exceed those of the B–45, but realistically believed that the swept-wing, underslung engine nacelles, bicycle-type landing gear, and other experimental features of the Boeing design would require an extended period of development. The XB–48, although more conventional than the XB–47, featured a 3-engine installation in each wing and would incorporate the bicycle-type landing gear of the B–47. The XB–48 might prove to be superior to the XB–45, but any potential production of the Martin design remained several years away.

endorsed the immediate production of the B-45.[6] Several factors accounted for the selection. First, the AAF concluded that the XB-46's projected performance most likely would be inferior to that of the XB-45. Second, the XB-46's fuselage was not configured to hold all required radar equipment. Finally, since the XB-45's design only departed slightly from proven configurations, it was the most logical choice prior to testing of the experimental model. The AAF's decision of 2 August prompted within 1 week the negotiation and signature of Contract AC-15569, which called for an initial lot of 96 B-45As (North American Model N-147), plus a flying static test version of the experimental type (NA Model N-130). The cost of the contract was $73.9 million.

First Flight (XB-45)   17 March 1947

On 17 March 1947, the first of the 3 experimental B-45s made its initial flight. The 1-hour flight, from Muroc Army Airfield, California, was conducted under stringent speed restrictions because the aircraft's landing gear doors did not close properly when the landing gear was retracted. This problem could have been avoided by installing new and available landing gear uplocks, but this time-consuming installation was postponed.[7] Nevertheless, the XB-45's demonstration was impressive. No large multi-engine jet bomber had ever been flown before.[8] And, of primary importance from the manufacturer's standpoint, even though a B-45 production order had already been secured, the XB-45 flight preceded that of the still potentially competitive XB-46.

Initial Testing   March 1947–August 1948

The Air Materiel Command planned an extensive test program for the

---

[6] The decision did not specifically spell the end of the XB-46, but it was a poor omen. Already reduced to only 1 plane, the experimental B-46 program actually lingered until August 1947, when the AAF terminated the whole venture.

[7] As soon as World War II ended, most manufacturers had to compete fiercely for the few, limited orders. This was reason enough for North American not to delay the XB-45's flight.

[8] Douglas's experimental twin-jet B-43, an outgrowth of the company's XB-42 Mixmaster, flew almost 1 year before the XB-45, but the XB-43 was very small and the 2 could not be compared. In the same vein, 2 German developments appearing in 1944 presented no true challenge. One of them, the Arado Ar-234, introduced by the Luftwaffe as a jet-bomber, was so tiny that it rightly belonged to the fighter category. The Junkers Ju 287 only flew as a prototype designed to test a radical wing, Germany's nearing collapse presumably preventing completion of the aircraft.

3 experimental airplanes developed by North American; each of the 3 was to be instrumented for a specialized phase of the program.[9] The testing, however, was marred at the start by an accident that killed 2 of North American's crack test pilots and destroyed their aircraft. This accident was attributed to an engine explosion, but other contributing factors later came to light. These accounted for most of the changes specified in the B-45's production articles. Meanwhile, flight testing of the remaining XB-45s went on. Air Force pilots did not participate extensively in the initial tests. They flew only about 19 hours, while the contractor logged more than 165 flight hours on the 2 surviving aircraft. This total was accumulated in 131 flights, conducted before the Air Force took delivery of the planes. The Air Force accepted 1 XB-45 on 30 July 1948; the other, on 31 August. The acceptances were conditional because the pressurization systems of both planes did not function.

Other Experimental Testing   1948–1950

After North American fixed the pressurization of the XB-45 cabins, additional tests were undertaken. Air Force pilots flew a total of 181 hours in 1 XB-45 between August 1948 and June 1949, when an accident damaged the aircraft beyond economical repair. The remaining XB-45, although constructed to serve as a prototype, had limited testing value due to an initial shortage of government-furnished equipment. Still, the Air Force put another 82 hours of flying time on the plane. A USAF flight test crew delivered the airplane to Wright-Patterson AFB, Ohio, where equipment was installed for bombing tests at Muroc AFB, California. Unfortunately, the YB-45 proved to be an unsatisfactory test vehicle because it required excessive maintenance. Only 1 mission was accomplished between 3 August and 18 November 1949, and that mission was to evaluate the long-awaited components. The airplane was used for high-speed parachute drops after November 1949, but on 15 May 1950, it was transferred to the Air Training Command to serve as a ground trainer.

Pre-Production Changes   1947–1948

As might be expected, the crash of an XB-45 precipitated a thorough

---

[9] In the late fifties, the various testing phases to which all aircraft were submitted were supplanted by testing categories. However, the changes affected the testing program's terminology more than its scope. (For specific information, see B-52, pp 224–225).

Close-up of 2 of the 4 jet engines that powered the XB–45.

An XB–45 undergoes a taxi test at Muroc Army Airfield, California.

investigation. As suspected, special wind tunnel tests confirmed that the aircraft's insufficient stabilizing area had contributed directly to the accident. The lack of ejection seats, moreover, had practically eliminated the pilot and co-pilot's chances for survival. As a result, 2 ejection seats were installed in the other experimental planes, while an advanced ejection system was being devised for the forthcoming production aircraft. In addition, future B–45s would be equipped with wind deflectors, placed in front of the escape doors from which the other 2 crew members (bombardier-navigator and tail gunner) would have to bail out in case of an emergency. North American also altered the structural configuration of the production vehicle. Most noticeable was a redesign of the nose panel. Finally, the aircraft's stabilizer area was increased, and the tailplane was lengthened from 36 to almost 43 feet.

B–45A

Manufacturer's Model NA–147

New Features

The B–45A differed from the experimental B–45s in featuring improved ejection-type seats for the pilot and co-pilot and safer emergency escape hatches for the bombardier-navigator and tail gunner. Communication equipment, emergency flight controls, and instruments, installed at the co-pilot's station, also were new. Other improvements included the E–4 automatic pilot, a bombing-navigation radar, and A–1 fire-control system, all of which were provided as standard equipment. Some of the B–45As were equipped with the AN/APQ–24[10] bombing-navigation radar system and such sophisticated electronic countermeasures components as the AN/APT–5; other B–45As only provided for the easy retrofit of this equipment. The first B–45As featured versions of the Allison-built J35 jet engines (in most cases, 4 J35–A–11s), but later aircraft were fitted from the start with the higher-thrust jets developed by the General Electric Company, either 2 J47–GE–7s or 2 J47–GE–13s, and 2 J47–GE–9s or 2 J47–E–15s.

First Flight (Production Aircraft)   February 1948

The initial production model of the XB–45 flew in February 1948, less than a year after the first flight of the experimental aircraft.

First Production Deliveries   April 1948

The Air Force began taking delivery of the initial batch of B–45As, 22 of them, in April 1948. These aircraft were identified as B–45A–1s to distinguish them from the subsequent 74 B–45As, known as B–45A–5s. Among other improvements, the B–45A–5s were equipped with more powerful

---

[10] The AN/APQ–24 bombing-navigation radar system made its operational debut with the Convair B–36B.

J47 engines. As soon as possible, the Air Force assigned 2 B–45A–1s to an accelerated service test program, which was already progressing well by mid-July. Under this program, each of the 2 planes accumulated 150 hours of rigorous testing under day and night operating conditions—test results actually accounting for some of the improvements featured by the B–45A–5s. Three additional B–45A–1s were deployed to Muroc AFB[11] to serve as transition trainers in support of the accelerated service test program. In effect, most of the early B–45As were relegated to the training task and became known as TB–45A–1s. In later years, however, priorities were to dictate that a few TB–45s be brought up to the combat configuration.

Unexpected Problems   1948

From the start, the introduction of the B–45 was hindered by a misunderstanding about the number of USAF pilots who were to be "checked out" in the aircraft at Muroc AFB by personnel of North American Aviation. In June 1948, delays in production made matters worse for the 47th Bombardment Wing, which was earmarked as first recipient of the new multi-jet bombers. Late in the year, the pioneer wing's training problems were aggravated by shortages of several months' standing in ground handling equipment and special maintenance tools. Structural or mechanical defects in a number of the few available B–45s did not help.

Program Uncertainty   Mid-1948

Although available records do not disclose any serious consideration of canceling the entire B–45 production, the program apparently ran into

---

[11]Among the base's predecessors was the Materiel Command Flight Test Base (ca 1942), which was redesignated Muroc Flight Test Base in 1944. In 1946, the Muroc Flight Test Base on the north end of Muroc Dry Lake and the Bombing and Gunnery Crew Training Base on the south end of the dry lake were merged into a single flight test center at Muroc Army Airfield under the jurisdiction of the Air Materiel Command. Muroc Army Airfield was redesignated Muroc AFB in February 1948 and became Edwards AFB 1 year later in honor of Captain Glen W. Edwards, a USAF pilot killed on 5 June 1948 while testing a prototype jet bomber of the Northrop Aviation's unconventional B–49 "flying wing." Officially dedicated on 27 January 1950, Edwards AFB remained under the Air Materiel Command until April 1951, when the Air Research and Development Command, established as a new major air command in January 1950, assumed jurisdiction. The Air Research and Development Command activated the Air Force Flight Test Center at Edwards AFB on 25 June 1951. The installations, as well as the research and development functions previously assigned to Air Materiel Command, were retained by Air Research and Development Command until 1961, when the newly formed Air Force Systems Command took over.

trouble even before any of the aircraft became truly operational.[12] As early as June 1948, at a meeting held in the office of General Hoyt S. Vandenberg, Air Force Chief of Staff since 30 April, doubts were expressed as to the B–45's value and its future utilization. It was decided (a decision evidently later rescinded) that no contract beyond the current one would be let, that production would go on as planned up to the 119th article, and that the funds already made available for a new contract would be used for another purpose.[13] One group would be equipped with the operational type, the initial 90 aircraft; the remaining aircraft would be placed in storage to cover the group's eventual losses. At the time, officials of the Tactical Air Command (TAC) were asked whether or not they liked the Northrop B–49 prototype, which had an empty weight of 88,000 pounds, almost twice that of the B–45. Shortly afterward, Gen. Muir S. Fairchild, USAF Vice Chief of Staff since 27 May, asked the Aircraft and Weapons Board[14] to determine if

---

[12] Some B–45 records were destroyed; others provided a surprising amount of conflicting information. Throughout the years, Air Force historians in attempting to answer certain B–45 queries could only point out that early systems were acquired in many different ways and that variances in methods of documentation complicated matters. For instance, the date on which the B–45 reached an initial operational capability (IOC) could not be ascertained. Other historical data such as the B–45's first production delivery, total USAF testing hours, and the identification of the XB–45 initially destroyed, remained unclear. North American Aviation provided its testing hour total, but the figures did not agree with those obtained from Air Force sources. The most striking examples of the inadequacy of old records undoubtedly pertained to test data—not only on the B–45 bomber, but on other early aircraft as well. This was understandable to some degree because Air Force tests were accomplished at numerous bases and for a great variety of purposes. In any case, all dates and information supplied on the B–45 are based upon documentary evidence. Bits and pieces included in the B–45 coverage are provided in the belief that they may be significant to users.

[13] Obviously, the quantity of B–45s first ordered had been increased, but the contract amendment's date as well as other details are no longer known. A second contract (AC–18000) had been issued in February 1947, either on the 7th or 17th day of that month. This contract dealt with another version of the B–45 (see p 88), but the information also is sketchy. Reportedly, a third contract (W33–038 AC–21702) came into being in June 1948, when the Air Force as a whole showed scant enthusiasm for the aircraft, only to be canceled on an unknown later date.

[14] The Aircraft and Weapons Board was established in August 1947. It made recommendations on problems submitted by the Air Staff and the commands. Composed of the Deputy Chiefs of Staff and major air commanders, the board proved too cumbersome and in December 1948 was replaced by the USAF Board of Senior Officers which included the Vice Chief of Staff, Deputy Chief of Staff for Operations, Deputy Chief of Staff for Materiel, and the Commanding General, Air Materiel Command. The dormant Aircraft and Weapons Board was discontinued in the fall of 1949. However, the establishment of the Air Council in April 1951 was accompanied by the formation of 4 additional boards: the Force Estimates Board; Budget Advisory Board; Military Construction Board; and a new USAF Aircraft and Weapons Board which replaced the Senior Officers Board. The reactivated Aircraft and Weapons Board lasted for over a decade. (For details, see Herman Wolk, *Planning and Organizing the Postwar Air Force*).

the weight of the various types of aircraft earmarked for or already in production could be reduced. Several conferences ensued, special attention being devoted to the B–45, with some board members suggesting that elimination of the co-pilot position, of the AB/ARC–18 liaison set installed in that position, and of the B–45's tail bumper would take 700 pounds off the aircraft's empty weight. There were other suggestions, some of them equally haphazard. Col. William W. Momyer,[15] who represented TAC at these conferences, discovered that the Air Staff labored under the false impression that TAC did not consider the B–45 suitable for bombardment operations, a conclusion probably based upon previous studies by the command on the aircraft's excessive take-off distances. In the early fall of 1948, by which time 190 B–45s were tentatively scheduled for production, the program's future still remained uncertain. Headquarters USAF wanted to know if TAC needed a reconnaissance aircraft, and if so would a reconfigured B–45 be satisfactory? If this should be the case, all B–45s would be converted to the reconnaissance role. TAC's answers came promptly. Indeed the command needed a new reconnaissance aircraft, but a reconnaissance version of the B–45 would not fulfill its requirements. TAC believed the Air Force would accrue more benefits by equipping 2 groups with the B–45 in order to determine the tactics and limitations of jet bombers. The merits of TAC's recommendations became academic, as budgetary restrictions and other unexpected developments altered all planning.

Enters Operational Service   November 1948

B–45A–5s began reaching squadrons of TAC's 47th Bombardment Wing at Barksdale AFB, Louisiana, in the fall of 1948. Despite slippages, 96 B–45As were completed by March 1950. Unfortunately, during the intervening months financial problems had already begun to take their toll on the B–45 program.

Program Reduction   1948–1949

The budgetary axe that slashed the fiscal year 1949 defense expenditures did not leave the B–45 program unscathed. According to plans, 5 light bomb

---

[15] Twenty years later, immediately after serving in Southeast Asia as Deputy Commander for Air Operations, Military Assistance Command, Vietnam, and simultaneously as Commander, Seventh Air Force, General Momyer, now a full general, assumed command of Tactical Air Command.

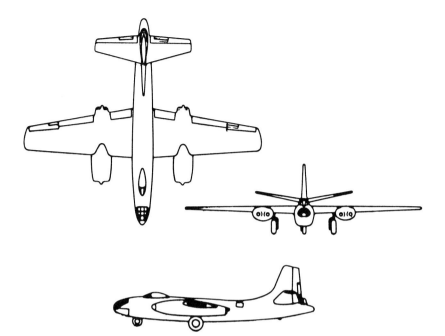

The B–45A, first flown in February 1948.

groups and 3 light tactical reconnaissance squadrons were included in the Air Force's goal of 70 groups.[16] The reduced Air Force program dictated by continued financial restrictions and, more specifically, by President Truman's budget for fiscal year 1950 brought into focus the Air Force's dilemma. The shrunken B–45 program called for only 1 light bomb group and 1 night tactical reconnaissance squadron, which meant that the procurement of the aircraft had to be scaled-down or that a substantial number of the aircraft would have to be placed in storage upon acceptance from the factory. Neither solution was attractive, but the Aircraft and Weapons Board quickly decided to cancel 51 of the 190 aircraft on order. Over $100 million would be released for crucial programs, and sufficient B–45s would be left to equip 1 light bomb group, 1 tactical reconnaissance squadron, plus a much-needed high-speed tow target squadron. Moreover, there would still be extra B–45s to take care of attrition throughout the aircraft's first-line life.[17]

Other Planning Changes   1948–1949

Five light bomb groups were included in the 70-group force planned by the Air Force. In reprogramming available forces to meet the 48-group composition and deployment imposed by current funding limitations, only 1 light bomb group was authorized. This group, the Air Force tentatively decided, would be allocated to the Far East Air Forces (FEAF) and would be equipped with B–45s. Specifically, the Air Force intended to inactivate Barksdale's 47th Group and to replace the B–26s of FEAF's 3d Light Bomb Group, at Yokota Air Base in Japan, with the B–45s of the defunct group. Maintenance personnel of the 47th also would be transferred to Yokota so that FEAF would benefit from the B–45 "know how" gained by the aircraft's first recipient. But even logical and simple plans could go astray. Available and in-coming B–45s could not carry sufficient fuel to fly to Hawaii, and equipping the aircraft with additional fuel tanks, a probable

---

[16] See B–36, pp 25–26.

[17] The first-line life of an aircraft cannot be predetermined, only predicted. As a rule, an aircraft remains "first-line" as long as it is "operational," "modern," and "capable of being used to perform critical and essential Air Force missions." Conversely, an aircraft becomes "second line," when its limitations for combat or other military use have been formally recognized. However, second-line aircraft may be called for first-line duty under certain circumstances—in emergency, and in services for which first-line aircraft are not available.

feature of future B-45 models, was at the time impossible.[18] Of course, it might have been practical to move the B-45s to Japan by sea. If a minimum of 10 feet could have been removed from each of the aircraft's wings, a rather impractical expedient, 3 B-45s could be deck-loaded on a Liberty or Victory ship, for a transport fee of approximately $4,000 per aircraft. The use of other sea transports might also have proved possible, but further investigation came to a halt. Early in 1949, the Deputy Chief of Staff for Materiel stated that the overseas deployment of B-45s was out of the question for the time being as well as the immediate future. To begin with, the B-45s were not truly operational. They had no fire-control or bombing equipment, and a suitable bomb sight was yet to be developed for the aircraft. Structural weaknesses, such as cracked forgings, had been uncovered in some of the few B-45s already available. And until corrected, such deficiencies certainly precluded any deployment abroad. Still another impediment arose. As reported by Air Materiel Command (AMC), the new J47 engine due to equip most of the B-45s suffered from serious problems. The engine had to be inspected thoroughly after 7½ hours of flying time; if found still serviceable, it could only be flown an additional 7½ hours before requiring a complete overhaul. Lack of money prevented the purchase of sufficient spare engines to ensure that, if deployed overseas, the B-45s could be kept flying. AMC anticipated difficulties, even for those aircraft that remained in the U.S., not far from the depots where the engines had to be inspected and overhauled. By mid-year, the home-based B-45s were expected to need 900 spare engines, none of which would be available. The shortage was compounded by the fact that F-86 requirements for J47s had first priority.[19] Little relief could be expected, AMC concluded, until jet engines could be used for almost 100 hours between overhauls. At best, this meant that no jet aircraft could be stationed out of the country for another year.

---

[18] B-45A-1s, equipped with J35 engines, had a ferry range of 2,120 miles and a take-off weight of 86,341 pounds that included 5,800 gallons of internal fuel. Almost half of the fuel was contained in two 1,200-gallon bomb-bay tanks and no additional fuel space was available. Incoming B-45-5s, equipped with J47 engines, had a similar take-off weight and a negligible range increase of 30 nautical miles. Obviously, General Fairchild's interest in weight reduction retained its validity, but there were no simple solutions. Ferry ranges were computed on the basis that the aircraft's wing tip tanks and bomb-bay tanks were retained when empty. If an increase of the weight figure was desired by a using agency, a reliable rule of thumb up to 1,000 pounds, Air Materiel Command engineers pointed out, was that every extra pound of weight induced a range decrease of 0.025 nautical miles. A corresponding small increase in range could be achieved by weight reduction.

[19] The 1-engine F-86 Sabres, also produced by North American, began entering operational service in 1949, but did not go overseas before December 1950.

Deficiencies and Malfunctions   1949–1950

Difficulties encountered by B–45 units, while impairing further the training of jet pilots, posed serious operational problems. The B–45's flaws varied in importance, but were numerous. High speeds affected the Gyrosyn compass[20] and the E–4 automatic pilot, when the aircraft's bomb-bay doors were open. The emergency brake, which was tied to the B–45's main hydraulic system, was unreliable. Because of poorly designed bomb racks, the bomb shackles became unhooked during certain maneuvers. The B–45's airspeed indicator was inaccurate, and the aircraft's fuel pressure gauges were both difficult to read and erratic. Another safety hazard derived from the engines which, when first started, often caught fire because the aspirator system worked improperly. The temperature gauge of the aircraft's tail pipe, moreover, was so poorly calibrated that it could not indicate the temperatures experienced at high altitudes.

Special problems, with many ramifications, stemmed from the B–45's AN/APQ–24 bombing-navigation radar system, and the fact that hardly any B–45s had already received such equipment did not minimize present or future difficulties. Malfunctions of the pressurization pump limited the altitude at which the APQ–24's receiver and transmitter component could operate. The modulator component of the system was not pressurized at all and likewise limited the APQ–24's utility. In addition, the faulty position of the radar antenna affected the coverage of targets as soon as the APQ–24 had to operate at an altitude of 40,000 feet. In fact, the radar system's overall location left a great deal to be desired, a shortcoming shared by several other components. When utilizing the APQ–24, the B–45 observer had to manipulate 2 mileage control dials, placed to his right and about 1 foot behind his back, while observing the radar scope directly in front of him. The layout of the B–45's radar system was not any better from a maintenance standpoint. The Air Force still lacked sufficient qualified personnel for maintenance and repair, and it took 8 hours just to remove and replace the APQ–24's modulator, one of the system's numerous troublesome links. Contributing to the dismal maintenance situation were shortages of spare parts, special tools, and ground handling equipment as well as engine hoists, power units, and aero stands.

---

[20] The trade name for a compass that consisted of a directional gyro synchronized with the horizontal component of the earth's magnetic field by means of a flux gate—the flux gate detecting the direction of the lines of force and transmitting the information electrically to a procession device.

Decision on Nuclear Capability   1950

Prior to 1949, the Air Force did not consider seriously the tactical employment of atomic weapons apart from their use for strategic air warfare. The most important reason was the AAF and Air Force's allegiance to the primacy of strategic air warfare per se.[21] Another factor was the belief that atomic weapons, because of their great cost and the scarcity of fissionable material, would remain relatively few in number. When the

---

[21] After the German surrender, AAF leaders declared their long-held theory of strategic bombing had been proved— that massive bombing of selected vital targets in a nation's interior could cripple its war-making capabilities and seriously weaken the people's will to resist. Critics argued that strategic bombing had failed to achieve its objectives, that its cost was excessive, and that tactical air power had made the greater contribution to Allied victory. Despite the controversy, it soon became obvious that Boeing's spectacular B-17 Flying Fortresses and subsequent B-29 Superfortresses had a greater impact on U.S. policy than the best known World War II fighters.

The cockpit of the B-45 Tornado, specially designed so the pilot could view all indicators at a glance.

development and large quantity production of small nuclear weapons became probable, the Air Force earmarked such weapons again for strategic use, especially as warheads for proposed guided missiles. Nevertheless, the Weapons Systems Evaluation Group conducted a study on the use of the atomic bomb on tactical targets, after evaluating the effect of the bomb on such targets as troops, aircraft, and ships massed for offensive operations, as well as naval bases, airfields, naval task forces, and heavily fortified positions. Concluded in November 1949, the study found nuclear bombs to be effective on all targets. Although informal in nature, the Weapon Systems Evaluation Group's study was noted by the Air Staff. Yet no action was taken until mid-1950, when the outbreak of the Korean War underlined the weakness of the North Atlantic Treaty Organization forces, should the Russians decide to seize the opportunity to attack in Europe. From then on events moved promptly. The lion's share of the atomic responsibilities, including the retardation mission that normally would fall under the tactical sphere of activities, was retained by the Strategic Air Command (SAC),[22] but the use of atomic or thermonuclear weapons would become Air Force-wide. On 14 November 1950, the Air Staff directed TAC[23] to develop tactics and techniques for the utilization of atomic weapons in tactical air operations. The directive received further impetus in January 1951, when an Air Staff program was outlined to ensure that TAC would become atomic-capable as soon as feasible. The B–45 was tremendously affected by the new planning. Already established as the Air Force's first multi-jet bomber, the B–45 also became the first light bomber fitted for atomic delivery.[24]

Immediate Setback   1950

Ordered in the wake of World War II as a SAC medium bomber, the B–45 was designed to carry the A-bomb.[25] But the secrecy surrounding the production of the first atomic weapons created difficulties for which neither the contractor nor the AAF could be blamed. Because of faulty informa-

---

[22] The retardation mission consisted of bombing operations to slow or stop the advances of ground forces. The latter rightly belonged to the fleeting target category, and SAC did not retain the retardation mission permanently.

[23] TAC, part of the Continental Air Command since December 1948, regained major command status on 1 December 1950.

[24] The deterrent impact of the B–45 remained unknown. Moreover, the aircraft represented but a tiny segment of the Air Force's early atomic armada.

[25] For details, see B–47, pp 111–112.

tion, the B–45 from the start could not have been used as an atomic carrier without significant internal modifications, the principal obstacle being a large spar extending laterally across the aircraft's bomb bay. However, the problem had become moot quickly, the small, short-range B–45 being reclassified as a light bomber in September 1947 and reallocated to TAC.[26] Ironically, the decision to extend the use of atomic weaponry to all combat forces meant that most of the B–45s acquired by TAC would no longer remain under the command's direct control. It also meant that TAC, now due to develop tactical operational techniques with the new weaponry, would have to do so with too few aircraft. In the meantime, the Air Force faced other problems. While the post–World War II achievements in the atomic field had been spectacular, and safer and lighter atomic bombs entered the stockpile much sooner than expected, intensive secrecy again had accompanied the new developments. Hence, as in the case of the old atomic bomb, the B–45 would be unable to carry any of the new weapons without first undergoing extensive modification.

Special Modifications   1950–1952

The special modification program, spurred by the Air Force's decision of mid-1950, was not allowed to linger. In December 1950, 5 months after tentatively earmarking 60 B–45s for atomic duty,[27] the Air Staff directed AMC to modify a first lot of 9 aircraft to carry the small bombs for which designs were then available. This initial project would allow suitability tests by the Special Weapons Command,[28] and give TAC at least a few test aircraft to undertake its new tasks. As a beginning, 5 of the 9 aircraft would be equipped with the scarce AN/APQ–24 system; the remaining 4, with the AN/APN–3 Shoran navigation and bombing system, plus the visual M9C Norden bomb sight. North American would bring the 9 light bombers to the required special weapons configuration for a total cost of $512,000. In mid-1951, the program for operational use of the B–45 in potential atomic operations was established. The aircraft in this program were nicknamed

---

[26] See B–36, p 21.

[27] Enough for 3 squadrons of 16 aircraft each, plus 12 attrition aircraft. This total, reduced to 40 aircraft in mid-1951, was re-increased in mid-1952, when 15 other B–45s were added to the special modification program.

[28] A separate command of short duration. Established in December 1949, the Special Weapons Command was redesignated Air Force Special Weapons Center and assigned to Air Research and Development Command in April 1952, losing major command status at that time.

Backbreaker and included, in addition to the B–45 light bombers, 100 of the many F–84 fighter-bombers built by the Republic Aviation Corporation.[29] Moreover, the program was accorded a priority second only to a concurrent and closely related modification program involving various SAC bombers. In the early fall of 1951, the program received further impetus. The Air Staff confirmed that modified B–45s, equipment, and allied support had to be supplied to enable units of the 47th Bombardment Wing in the United Kingdom to achieve an operational atomic capability by 1 April 1952. In addition to the first lot of 9 aircraft, the program would count 32 B–45s, the latter aircraft's modification cost being set at $4 million.[30] The Air Staff wanted 16 of the planes to be ready by 15 February 1952; the remainder, by 1 April. These were ambitious plans. Remodeling the B–45 aircraft to the Backbreaker configurations was an extensive operation. Equipment had to be installed in the aircraft for carrying 3 distinct bomb types, and this necessitated some structural modifications to the bomb bay.[31] Then too, a large amount of advanced electronics support equipment had to be added, in place of the standard equipment. Also, the aircraft had to be fitted with a new defensive system and extra fuel tanks. North American and the Air Materiel Command's San Bernardino Air Materiel Area, in San Bernardino, California, shared modification responsibilities for the B–45 Backbreaker program. In early 1952, the 9 B–45s, already brought to a limited Backbreaker configuration by AMC and North American, were sent by TAC to San Bernardino for completion of the modifications. Complete reconfiguration of the other 32 B–45As also took place at the San Bernardino Air Materiel Area during the first 3 months of 1952, with North American furnishing all necessary kits. That the work was done without significant delay was noteworthy, for all parties had to overcome serious difficulties. Much of the electronic and support components required for the Backbreaker configuration, being new and of advanced designs, were in very short supply. The requirement for the AN/APQ–24 radar was in direct competition with a SAC special program. Also, the few available AN/APQ–24 sets had to be adapted to the special weapons configuration. Shoran sets, as well, were not readily available, and a quantity had to be diverted from Far East Air Forces' and TAC's B–26 programs. There were other challenges. Some of the new equipment could not be installed before

---

[29] The aircraft were modified F–84Es, identified as F–84Gs.

[30] One B–45A was destroyed by fire in February 1952 and not replaced, thus reducing the total from 41 to 40. Of the $4 million allocated to the project, some of the funds came from other Tactical Air Command projects which had to be canceled.

[31] Special cradles were provided for the 3 types of bombs; and special hoisting equipment was required for loading each type of bomb on the Backbreaker B–45.

connecting parts were manufactured. In addition, some needed components simply did not exist. For example, the bomb scoring device, which consisted of a series of switches and relays, was actually manufactured at San Bernardino. The Air Materiel Area also made parts for the A–6 chaff dispenser, including a removable chute for easier maintenance. In the same vein, a special fuel flow totalizer was produced by North American, which likewise manufactured special tie-in equipment for the AN/APG–30 radar and the rest of the Backbreaker B–45's tail defense system. Finally, the Fletcher Aviation Corporation of Pasadena, California, produced the extra fuel tanks, while AMC's Middletown Air Materiel Area in Middletown, Ohio, built the special slings that had to be used to carry some of the new bombs.

Overseas Deployment   1952

Atomic-capable B–45As began reaching the United Kingdom on 1 May 1952, and deployment of the 40 aircraft was completed on 12 June. This

Tornadoes of the 47th Bombardment Group, Langley AFB, are prepared for deployment to the United Kingdom, July 1952.

schedule fell about 30 days behind the Air Staff deadline, but was a remarkable achievement considering the project's magnitude. Not only had the Backbreaker modifications proven exacting, but the Air Force had to cope with various engine problems. As reported by the General Electric Company field representatives servicing the 47th Bombardment Group throughout most of 1951 the J47s powering the Backbreaker aircraft shared some of the flaws of the aircraft's initial engines. Turbine buckets of the new J47s ruptured like those of the Allison J35s. Tail cones fractured just as easily when the J47s functioned improperly. Oil leaks appeared, which meant that the engines had to be removed for repairs and test runs. The Air Force did not expect any new engine to be problem-free from the start, but the urgency surrounding the Backbreaker program made these difficulties more significant. Besides, TAC had to take care of many other tasks. The B-45 deployment called for a somewhat more integrated atomic weapons support system than that used by SAC. TAC had immediately envisioned a concept that actually emphasized the mobility, flexibility, and speed characteristic of tactical air operations. While the TAC concept and the demands it necessarily entailed were not all approved, the Air Staff had endorsed the salient points of the command's proposal. As a result, after being activated on 31 August 1951, the 1st Tactical Support Squadron moved to Europe in the spring of 1952. Once overseas, the support squadron was attached to the 47th Bombardment Wing,[32] now a Third Air Force unit of the United States Air Forces in Europe. Like the Backbreaker modification program, the logistic organization and supply system devised by TAC had required much work. Still the system soon was accused of being unwieldy, wasteful of personnel, and unsuited to the support of delivery operations from widely dispersed bases. Modified during the ensuing year, TAC's revised atomic weapons support system was expected to allow greater dispersion in weapon storage and to provide the flexibility essential for varied theater requirements.

New Modifications and Retrofit   1952–1953

In July 1952, the Air Force decided to increase the number of atomic B-45 aircraft by 15. The endorsed configuration was to be that of the Backbreaker aircraft, plus improvements. In short, some electronic changes were needed, the Backbreaker aircraft's tail defense system had to be upgraded, and the fuel flow totalizer, which had been required for the first

---

[32] TAC's 47th Wing was at Langley AFB, Virginia, in early 1952. The B-45 overseas deployment prompted the wing's relocation to Royal Air Force Station Sculthorpe, England.

40 Backbreaker B-45s but had not been installed because of production delays, was to be added. Another important change, perhaps the most important, called for relocation of the supports required by a specific type of atomic bomb. The supports had to be moved into the forward bay to allow the installation of a 1,200-gallon fuel tank in the rear bay, since theextra fuel would give the aircraft a range increase of almost 300 nautical miles.

In September 1952, after conferring with North American, the Air Force decided on the improved Backbreaker configuration and established a program for procurement and installation of the necessary kits. The Air Force allocated $2.2 million for modification of the 15 additional B-45s, and $3 million for retrofit of the first 40 Backbreaker aircraft. Logically, the San Bernardino Air Materiel Area was to take care of the new modifications and would also provide all necessary kits for the Backbreaker retrofit, which would be done in the field. Although less involved than the original Backbreaker modifications, the new program slipped. During the second half of 1952 the Air Materiel Command was in the process of decentralizing responsibilities from its headquarters to the various air materiel areas. Hence, delays occurred in processing engineering data and purchase requests which, in turn, retarded kit preparation and delivery by North American.

Contractual problems, too, occurred at North American, as the contractor was no longer tooled for the B-45 and was working to capacity on other products. As a result, kit deliveries did not start until July 1953, pushing installation back 4 months. In September 1953, the Air Force added 3 B-45s to the modification program, but as 2 of the original aircraft had been deleted and 1 had crashed, the total still remained at 15. Because no more B-45As were available, 3 of the subsequent models in the B-45 series were modified, postponing the program's completion to March 1954.

Remaining Shortcomings   1953–1954

While the Backbreaker modifications and retrofit enabled the B-45s to handle several types of small atomic bombs, the modified aircraft were not fitted to deliver the special atomic bombs needed for the retardation mission.[34] In 1953, because of the increasing availability of atomic weapons, the Air Force thought of relieving SAC from the retardation responsibility. However, the matter again was dropped, since no tactical aircraft would be able to satisfy the retardation requirements until the Douglas B/RB-66s

---

[34] The retardation mission covered the slowing down of enemy troop movements or lines of supply by air interdiction, in this case, tactical bombing.

entered the TAC inventory, a prospect several years away.[35] Other possibilities were entertained in 1953 and 1954. Quantum technological jumps made it likely that small thermonuclear weapons would be obtainable sooner than anticipated. Since modified B-45s and a whole family of fighter-bombers could now carry some of the small atomic bombs, modified B-45s and other aircraft presumably could also be made to deliver, within their range limitations, thermonuclear weapons of similar weight and dimensions. Such possibilities, as sound as they later proved to be, in the B-45's case did not go past the theoretical stage.

End of Production   March 1950

The B-45A production ended in March 1950, when the Air Force took delivery of the last aircraft.

Total B-45As Accepted   96

The Air Force accepted its 96 B-45As over a period of 24 months, the first deliveries being made in April 1948.

Flyaway Cost Per Production Aircraft $1.1 million

The $73.9 million procurement contract of 1946 provided for 96 B-45As, which would put the aircraft's unit cost below $800,000. However, the basic cost of each B-45A was finally set at $1,080,603—airframe, $682,915; engines (installed), $189,741; electronics, $81,907; ordnance, $552; armament (and others), $125,488. The same price tag was assigned to every model of the B/RB-45.[36]

---

[35] Although the A3D, from which the B/RB-66 derived, served well in the tactical role for the Navy, the Air Force bought it without illusions, knowing the Douglas aircraft could not become the tactical bomber truly needed by the Tactical Air Command (TAC). Similarly, the B-57 was ordered for TAC in 1951 as an interim recourse. The Martin B-57, a night intruder bomber primarily, was first earmarked for atomic operations only because the number of B-45s was limited. And as with other post–World War II planes, the alternate use of reconnaissance models of the B-57 and B-66 as atomic bombers also was being planned. In any case, not only did production of the B-57 and B-66 slip but the 2 programs proved troublesome, which hardly lessened TAC's predicament.

[36] The B/RB-45's identical unit price represented an average reached regardless of contractor or fiscal year procurement and did not reflect engineering change and modification

Subsequent Model Series   **B/RB–45C**

Other Configurations   **B–45B and TB–45A**

B–45B—A basic B–45 offering new radar and fire-control systems. This projected variant did not reach production.

TB–45A—Some of the early B–45As, bare of most components and equipped with Allison engines until re-fitted with more powerful J47s, were used to teach pilots the tricky new skill of jet flying. Occasionally referred to as TB–45As, a few of them were brought up to the Backbreaker configuration.

Phaseout   **1958**

In January 1958, less than 50 B–45s remained in the Air Force's operational inventory. These multi-jet bombers, the first ever assigned to a combat unit, belonged to the 47th Bomb Wing (Tactical) which, 10 years before, had also been the first to fly them. However, the wing's conversion to Douglas-built B–66s was underway, spelling the B–45's end. By July 1958, the obsolescent B–45s had left Sculthorpe Air Station for other bases in Europe and North Africa, where they were briefly used for fire fighting training. Late in the summer of 1958, a few B–45s stood under the hot Spanish sun at Moron Air Base, where they were to be junked and sold for scrap.

Other Uses

One B–45A, designated JB–45A,[37] served as an engine test bed for a

---

costs subsequent to approval of basic contract. As was often the case, the Air Force endorsed this price formula because of fluctuations of costs and cost arrangements during the production period of the entire program.

[37] The classification letter J, like the classification letters X and Y (see p 63) symbolizes the special status of a vehicle, be it an aircraft, a ship, or a missile. The letter or prefix symbol J shows that the vehicle is assigned to a special test program. This program may be conducted in-house, or may require a formal loan contract usually referred to as bailment contract. In either case, whatever modifications are made to accommodate testing are temporary. Upon test completion, the vehicle is returned to its original configuration, or returned to standard operational configuration. The same status prefix symbols, or classification letters, are used by all services of the Department of Defense.

Westinghouse development. The B–45 light bomber was also tentatively earmarked for a special duty. Believing that utilization rather than aircraft design and construction determined whether a plane was a tactical or a strategic tool, TAC thought the B–45 might be used for close air support operations. There were good reasons for the command's investigation. Sufficient close support of ground forces could not be mustered from the tactical units available in early 1950. Moreover, the bombardment classification of an aircraft in no way obviated the aircraft's potential close air support role. Still, the project was killed in infancy. To begin with, the B–45 was not rugged enough to accomplish the necessary ground attack maneuvers. In addition, modification costs to equip the aircraft properly would be quite high. Finally, the extra equipment would compromise the B–45's capability for level bombing.

B/RB-45C

Manufacturer's Model NA-153

Previous Model Series   B-45A

New Features

Few new features separated the B-45C from the B-45A. The B-45C was equipped for air refueling[38] and fitted from the start with wing tip tanks.[39] The RB-45C also looked like the B-45A, except for a small bump on the tip of the aircraft's nose, where a forward oblique camera was enclosed. The RB-45C in addition featured a water injection system for increased take-off thrust that utilized two 214-gallon droppable tanks suspended beneath the nacelles by means of assisted take-off suspension hooks. If preferable, the RB-45C could make use of 2 droppable assisted take-off rockets located on the underside of the nacelles. The RB-45C included sweeping internal changes. Five stations were provided, and these stations could mount 10 different types of cameras. However, the crew could not move to the aft camera compartment when the RB-45C was flying; in-flight access to the bomb bays was possible, but only if the bomb bays were empty, the bomb-bay doors were closed, and the pressurized compartments were depressurized.

Basic Development   1947 and 1949

North American began working on the B-45C design on 22 September 1947, 2 months after the AAF had endorsed the aircraft's production.

---

[38] The air refueling arrangement consisted of a boom receptacle located on the top of the fuselage, about midway, and of a single-point refueling receptacle on the left side aft of the bomb bays.

[39] The B-45C was often flown with 1,200-gallon wing tip tanks; when full, each fuel tank weighed some 7,500 pounds.

Design of the RB–45C was initiated in January 1949, when the entire B–45 program was significantly reduced.[40]

Production Decision   1947 and 1949

The Air Force decided to buy a sizable fleet of B–45Cs on 3 July 1947 and signed the necessary document (Contract AC–18000) in October of the same year. But after only 10 B–45Cs were completed, numerous change orders were issued that drastically altered the October contract. Procurement was limited to the 10 B–45Cs already built, plus 33 airframes that were to be modified on the production lines to serve as photo-mapping and reconnaissance aircraft.[41] As it turned out, the RB–45C order marked the end of the B–45 production run.

First Flights   1949 and 1950

The B–45C first flew on 3 May 1949; the RB–45C in April 1950.

Enters Operational Service   1950–1951

The Air Force started taking delivery of the B–45C in May 1949 and of the RB–45C in June 1950. Even though a few of the aircraft were deployed overseas in late 1950, no B/RB–45C unit reached an initial operational capability (IOC) before 1951. The RB–45Cs were earmarked for SAC, primarily. The command's inventory reached a peak of 38 aircraft in 1951, some B–45s being included in this total. However, no B/RB–45 aircraft remained on the SAC rolls in 1953. Yet, this did not spell the RB–45's end.

---

[40] The additional production of 2 B–45Cs and 49 RB–45Cs (Manufacturer's Model NA–162), under contract since 17 June 1948, was canceled either in late 1948 or early 1949. Although money was a factor, the Air Force's belief that a reconnaissance version of the B–47 would be superior to the best RB–45 nailed the cancellation.

[41] Lt. Gen. Curtis E. LeMay replaced Gen. George C. Kenney as Commander of the Strategic Air Command on 19 October 1948. SAC's new Commanding General had commanded the B–29 strikes against Japan during World War II and lost no time in re-emphasizing to Air Force officials at the highest level the importance of reconnaissance. In fact, every bomber produced after World War II had a genuine reconnaissance counterpart, or could be used for reconnaissance. In the latter case, it might take but a few hours to prepare a given aircraft for the reconnaissance role, or to bring back the reconnaissance bomber to its original configuration. Sometimes the 2 versions of 1 aircraft were assigned to the same unit.

Like the B–45As, the aircraft served other Air Force commands for several more years.

War Commitments   1950–1951

The B/RB–45s were not officially committed to the Korean War,[42] but 3 TAC B/RB–45s reached the Far East in the fall of 1950. The small detachment, TAC personnel and civilian technical representatives included, departed for Japan in late September for the express purpose of measuring the reconnaissance capability of a configuration which had not yet been given the most telling of all tests, that of actual combat. Arrival of the RB–45s was well timed, as the RB–29s of the 91st Strategic Reconnaissance Squadron were no longer able to perform with impunity the special missions ordered by Far East Air Forces or the targeting and bomb-damage assessment photography desired by its Bomber Command. Eager to maintain its reconnaissance capability in the face of the Soviet-built MiG jets, Bomber Command on 31 January 1951 took control of the RB–45 detachment and attached it to the 91st Squadron. The RB–45 crews managed to outrun and outmaneuver the MiGs for several months. Yet, on 9 April 1951, 1 of the too few RB–45s barely escaped a numerically far superior enemy. In the ensuing months, while the RB–29s were no longer allowed to enter northwestern Korea, even with escort, the RB–45s could still go into the MiG-infested area if they had jet fighter escort. However, after another harrowing experience on 9 November 1951, the RB–45s also were restricted by Far East Air Forces from entering the sensitive areas of northwestern Korea in daylight. In January 1952, the 91st Squadron was directed to convert to night operations, but testing soon showed that the squadron's RB–45s could not be used for night photography because the aircraft buffeted too badly when its forward bomb bay was opened to drop flash bombs. In any case, deficiencies confirmed soon after the RB–45s had reached Japan,[43] plus the many commitments levied on the 33 aircraft, had foretold the eventual end of the RB–45's Korean experience.

End of Production   1950 and 1951

Production of the B–45C was completed on 13 April 1950, that of the RB–45C in October 1951, when the last aircraft were delivered.

---

[42] The B/RB–45s were not shown on the Air Force listing of aircraft which participated in any fashion in the 3-year conflict.

[43] The 91st Strategic Reconnaissance Squadron thought the RB–45s were so unsafe for ditching that a Japan-based rescue plane held a station orbit over the Sea of Japan each time these planes crossed to Korea.

Total B/RB–45Cs Accepted   43

The Air Force accepted 10 B–45Cs and 33 RB–45Cs between May 1949 and October 1951.

Flyaway Cost Per Production Aircraft $1.1 million

The Air Force prorated the basic cost of the entire program. Consequently, the B/RB–45Cs carried the price tag of the B–45As.

Subsequent Model Series   None

Other Configurations   TB–45s

Some B–45s, after undergoing in-production modifications, assumed a training role usually assigned to elderly, surplus aircraft. This unusual project took shape early in 1949, when Secretary of the Air Force W. Stuart Symington informed Secretary of Defense James V. Forrestal that future technological trends in aircraft and weapons development called for various types of special training. Even though the procurement of aircraft had been cut, in line with President Truman's fiscal policy, steps had to be taken to keep improving the striking power of the Air Force within the approved 48-group structure. Hence, Mr. Symington recommended and Mr. Forrestal approved the conversion of 16 B–45Cs for tow target duty in order to teach anti-aircraft gunners high-speed, high-altitude firing. The B–45C conversion project, accomplished by North American, was allocated $1.6 million. Broken down, this meant that the modification of each aircraft cost about $80,000 and that $20,000 covered the spare components required by every plane. Targets and reels were supplied from current Air Force stocks. But as Mr. Symington had pointed out, there was no exact troop basis for the computation of tow target requirements. The 16 TB–45Cs proved insufficient for antiaircraft gunnery practice, so a few early B–45As were also converted as tow target airplanes. Unfortunately, the low thrust of the Allison J35 engines of the first B–45As prevented the additional conversions from performing well, and the TB–45A association with the tow target program was of short duration.

Phaseout   1958

The B/RB–45C phaseout followed the B–45A pattern. In mid-1959, only 1 RB–45C remained in the Air Force inventory.

Other Uses   JB–45C and DB–45s

In early 1950, the Air Force considered using some B–45s as aerial tankers for F–84s carrying special weapons. TAC wanted to know in particular the speed at which refueling, by means of the probe and drogue system, could best be accomplished. The command also asked how much extra fuel could be carried by the B–45, taking into consideration the weight of refueling gear and tanks. Although no actions were taken following these investigations, the Air Force determined that Republic F–84s could operate with a B–45 "Mother" aircraft as a "cell." The most serious handicap would be the necessity for lights during night formation. Without lights, night formation could be conducted with reasonable safety only under bright moonlight. It was also determined that, as a tanker, 1 B–45 aircraft could service 4 planes as well as 2, with the exception that the fuel available for each fighter would be proportionally reduced.

JB–45C. One B–45C, designated JB–45C after its temporary reconfiguration, served as engine test bed for Pratt & Whitney J57 and J75 engines.

DB–45. One B–45C and another unspecified B–45 model, designated DB–45s after conversion, were used as director aircraft in connection with the development of guided weapons.

Milestones   1950 and 1952

The first air-to-air refueling of a jet aircraft was accomplished in 1950,

The RB–45C (left) was the first jet aircraft to be refueled in the air in this country. The tanker (right) is a KB–29A. 1950.

with a SAC RB–45C and a Boeing KB–29B tanker. On 29 July 1952, a 91st Strategic Reconnaissance Wing RB–45C (Serial Number 48–042), a SAC aircraft commanded by Maj. Louis H. Carrington, made the first nonstop, trans-Pacific flight from Elmendorf AFB, Alaska, to Yokota AB, Japan. This flight, made possible by 2 KB–29 inflight refuelings, earned Major Carrington and his 2-man crew the Mackay Trophy for 1952.

Program Recap

The Air Force accepted a grand total of 142 B–45s—XB–45s and reconnaissance versions included. Precisely, the B–45 program counted 3 experimental airplanes (one of which completed as preproduction article and sometimes referred to as prototype), 96 B–45As (some of them singled out as B–45A–5s because of in-production improvements), 10 B–45Cs, and 33 RB–45Cs. The entire small contingent (51 aircraft less than originally ordered) was produced by North American Aviation, Incorporated, of Inglewood, California, with most of the aircraft actually being built in a former Douglas facility at Long Beach, California.

TECHNICAL AND BASIC MISSION PERFORMANCE DATA

B/RB-45 AIRCRAFT

Manufacturer (Airframe) North American Aviation, Inc., Inglewood, Calif.
Manufacturer (Engines) The General Electric Co., Schenectady, N.Y.
Nomenclature Light Tactical Bomber and Day or Night Photo-reconnaissance Aircraft.
Popular Name Tornado

	B-45A	B-45A (Backbreaker)	B-45C	RB-45C
Length/Span (ft)	75.3/89	75.3/89	75.3/89	75.9/89
Wing Area (sq ft)	1,175	1,175	1,175	1,175
Weights (lb)				
Empty	45,694	47,022	48,969	50,687
Combat	58,548	67,820	73,715	73,200
Takeoff[a]	91,775	92,745	112,965	110,721
Engine: Number, Rated Power per Engine & Designation	(2) 5,500-lb st J47–GE–7 or –13 & (2) 5,000-lb st J47–GE–9 or –15	(2) 5,500-lb st J47–GE–7 or –13 & (2) 5,000-lb st J47–GE–9 or –15	(2) 5,000-lb st J47–GE–7 or –13 & (2) 5,000-lb st J47–GE–9 or –15	(2) 5,000-lb st J47–GE–7 or –13 & (2) 5,000-lb st J47–GE–9 or –15
Takeoff Ground Run (ft)				
at Sea Level	3,400	4,950	6,900	6,100
Over 50-ft Obstacle	4,930	7,570	8,960	8,070
Rate of Climb (fpm) at Sea Level	4,050	2,950	2,500	2,700
Combat Rate of Climb (fpm) at Sea Level	5,950	4,300	4,550	1,020

Service Ceiling (ft) at Combat Weight (100 fpm Rate of Climb, to Altitude)	46,400	1,700	41,250	41,500
Combat Ceiling (ft) (500 fpm Rate of Climb, Max Power, to Altitude)	32,800	8,000	37,550	37,800
Average Cruise Speed (kn)	408	401	405	404
Maximum Speed at Optimum Altitude (kn/ft)	496/3,500	492/Sea Level	498/Sea Level	495/4,000
Basic Speed at Altitude (kn/ft)	438/35,000	434/35,000	436/35,000	436/35,000
Combat Radius (nm)	463	764	876	916
Total Mission Time (hr)	2.4	3.9	4.47	4.6
Armament	2 .50-cal machine guns in tail turret	2 .50-cal M3 guns in tail turret	2 .50-cal machine guns in tail turret	2 M-7 .50-cal machine guns in tail turret
Crew	4	4	4	4
Maximum Bombload (lb)**	22,000 (1 Grand Slam) (1 12,000-lb Tall Boy) (2 4,000-lb general purpose bombs) (4 2,000-lb gp; 14 1,000-lb gp; 27 500-lb gp; & 16^b 500-lb gp)	22,000 (1 Grand Slam) (27 100-lb M38A2 special bombs)	22,000 (1 Grand Slam) (1 12,000-lb Tall Boy) (2 4,000-lb general purpose bombs) (4 2,000-lb gp; 14 1,000-lb gp; 27 500-lb gp; &16^b 500-lb gp)	25 M-122 Photo Flash, 188-lb each; Cameras, in various stations, 12 (3 K-17Cs, 1 K-38, 1 K-37, 1 T-11, 1 S-7A, 1 K-22, 2 K-37s, 2 K-38s)

Abbreviations

cal	= caliber	kn	= knots
fpm	= feet per minute	nm	= nautical miles
gp	= general purpose	st	= static thrust

a Limited by space.
b Loading allowed for 1 bomb-bay tank.

Basic Mission Note

All basic mission's performance data is based on maximum power. B–45 Backbreaker and B/RB–45C's combat radius formula: took off and climbed on course at maximum power to cruise ceiling, the latter being defined as that altitude at which the aircraft had the performance potential of making a 300-foot-per-minute rate of climb using normal thrust at momentary weight. Cruised at long-range power at cruise ceiling; 15 minutes prior to target, power was increased to normal power and bomb run was made to target. Dropped bombs, conducted 2-minute evasive action followed by an 8-minute normal power run out from target. Continued flight to base at long-range speeds at cruise ceiling. Under nacelle tanks and droppable bombing tanks were dropped when empty.

B–47 Stratojet
Boeing
Airplane Company

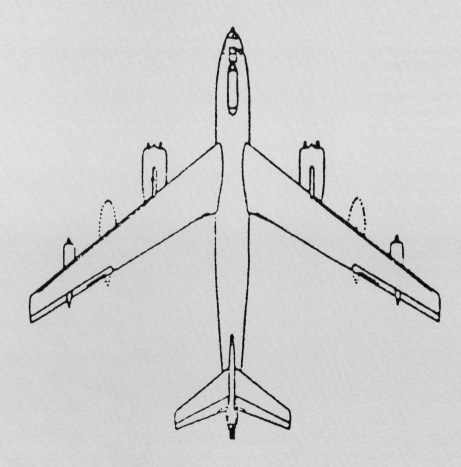

B-47 Stratojet
Boeing

Manufacturer's Model 450

Weapon System 100A

Overview

The B-47's production was spurred in 1944 by the War Department's demand for jet bombers. In contrast to the B-45, and other concurrent proposals, the B-47 design, as finally approved, included radically new features. Foremost were the aircraft's thin swept wings which, coupled with 6 externally mounted jet engines, promised a startling, high-speed bomber, probably capable of carrying out effective operations for the foreseeable future despite an enemy's fighter air defense. Undoubtedly, the B-47 lived up to expectations. More than 2,000 production models were bought, and some B-47 versions, true production models or post-production reconfigurations, remained in the operational inventory for nearly 2 decades. Yet few aircraft programs witnessed as much development, production, and post-production turbulence as the B-47 did. To begin with, there were arguments about cost and plant location and after 1947, complaints by Boeing that the newly independent Air Force had laid additional requirements that changed the concept of the overall program. Also, the secrecy which shrouded the development of atomic weapons, long after the atomic attacks on Japan, increased the difficulty of preparing the B-47 to handle every new type of special weapon—a problem shared by the B-36 and B-45. Ensuing events only compounded the initial disarray.

As it had for the B-36, the Truman Administration's stringent financial restrictions worked in favor of the B-47. Pressed for money, the Air Force decided to buy more B-47s instead of purchasing additional B-50s or future B-54s, since neither one of those rather expensive bombers had any growth potential. Hence, even though the B-47 was yet to fly, the initial production order of 1948 was increased in mid-1949. The subsequent Korean War, rising world tensions, and mounting urgency to build an atomic deterrent force raised the tempo of the B-47 program. In December 1950, the Air Force foresaw a monthly production of 150 B-47s, but still recommended changes, making it almost impossible to settle on an acceptable type. Other factors made matters worse.

The B-47 was the first USAF bomber to receive a weapon system designation, a move prompted by the Air Force recognition that the rising complexity of weapons no longer permitted the isolated and compartmented development of equipment and components which, when put together in a structural shell, formed an aircraft or missile. However, this was as far as the B-47 benefited from the new developmental philosophy. The Boeing airframe was built without adequate consideration for its many crucial components. In turn, the components, subcontracted or furnished by the government, were behind schedule and when provided, did not match the sophistication of the high-performance B-47.

In 1951 alone, the Air Force took delivery of 204 B-47Bs, none of which were suitable for combat. The aircraft's canopy was unsafe; the B-47B had no ejection seats (a deficiency shared by 200 successive B-47s); the bombing and navigation system was unreliable; a new tail defense system was needed; and the jet engines were creating unique development problems such as fuel boil-off at high altitudes, which reduced the aircraft's range—already shorter than anticipated. In sum, the hasty production of an aircraft as revolutionary as the B-47 proved to be costly, generating extensive, unavoidable modification projects like Baby Grand, Turn Around, High Noon, and Ebb Tide. Yet once accomplished, the B-47 modifications worked.

Finally deployed overseas in mid-1953, the B-47s totally replaced the obsolete, atomic-carrier B-50s by the end of 1955, when new B-47 production models were delivered that could carry larger fuel loads and thus had greater range. After the B-47 demonstrated that it was rugged enough for low-altitude bombing, some of the aircraft were again modified to satisfy a new set of requirements levied in 1955. These modifications also worked, and in 1957, the Air Force publicly demonstrated its new low-altitude, strategic bombing tactics, an achievement marking the beginning of an era in aeronautics.

Despite its convoluted start, the B-47 program proved successful. The aircraft served in various roles and was involved in many experimental projects, some connected to the development of more sophisticated atomic weapons, like Brass Ring, or with the development of air refueling or other endeavors of great significance to the Air Force. Strategic Air Command's last B-47s went into storage in early 1966, while a few converted B-47 bombers and reconnaissance models kept on paying their way for several more years, remaining on the Air Force rolls until the end of the 1960s.

Basic Development   1943

Development of the B-47 can be traced back to June 1943, when an informal Army Air Forces (AAF) request led several aircraft manufacturers to begin design studies of multi-jet aircraft that could be used for fast photographic reconnaissance or medium bomber missions.[1] General Electric's successful development of an axial flow jet engine, easier to install in wing nacelles than previous jet types, came at the same time. This undoubtedly was important. Boeing and several other companies quickly included the new engine in their planning. But more crucial to the aircraft's development was Boeing's use at war's end of captured German research data on the design of swept-back wings. This led in 1947 to the sensational XB-47.

Design Competition   1944

The informal requirements of 1943 became official on 17 November 1944. The AAF issued military characteristics for a jet-propelled medium bomber with a range of 3,500 miles, a service ceiling of 45,000 feet, an average speed of 450 miles per hour, and a top speed of 550. Besides the Boeing Airplane Company of Seattle, Washington, the other firms—North American Aviation, Incorporated, Convair, and the Glenn L. Martin Company—entered the design competition prompted by these requirements. The Boeing entry (Model 432), designated the XB-47 by the AAF, was a straight-wing design resembling a B-29 with much thinner wings and carrying 4 of the new General Electric axial flow jet engines. To overcome problems experienced with the engine pod-nacelles of a previous design, Boeing had buried the new engines inside the fuselage of Model 432. All

---

[1] Requirements had to be readied and money had to be found before a formal announcement could be made. Yet the procedure followed in June 1943 was not unusual and could only benefit the AAF. In this case, it might also have had the distinct advantage of keeping Boeing engineers busy and preventing them from drifting to Navy projects upon completion of their work on the development of a long-range bomber. The AAF already knew that Convair had pretty well clinched the long-range bomber program (a B-36 production order had just been issued) and that the concurrent procurement of a similar bomber was out of the question. (Boeing did not receive a study-contract for its "long-range" XB-52 until mid-1946.)

designs submitted by the other companies featured wing nacelles for housing the jet engines.[2]

Letter Contract   1 February 1945

This letter contract authorized Boeing to spend up to $150,000 (against an estimated $1.5 million set aside for development) in a Phase I (wind tunnel) study of Model 432, Boeing's first entry in the recently opened medium bomber competition. The model nevertheless was rejected on the grounds that the location of the engines could be unsafe. The AAF actually thought that Boeing engineers should do more research in the basic jet problems associated with high-speed bombers. To achieve superiority in the air would require a new concept superior to any of the current bomber designs. Early in September, Boeing revised the original configuration of Model 432 and proposed its first swept-wing bomber design. Labeled Model 448 (the AAF designation remained XB-47), the new aircraft featured a thin wing swept back and 2 more engines—a total of 6 engines. The AAF liked the wing configuration of Model 448, but still insisted that housing engines inside a fuselage created a fire-hazard. Besides, externally mounted engines were easier to maintain and replace, which could add years to the service life of an aircraft. Boeing's hasty return to the drawing board resulted in Model 450, which carried 6 jet engines hung under the wings in pods—2 pairs in strut-mounted inboard nacelles and single units attached directly under the wing, at a distance of 8 feet from the wing tip. The AAF promptly approved Model 450 in October 1945.

Development Decision   December 1945

In December, a technical instruction authorized contractual negotiations for the development of 2 experimental aircraft. The AAF endorsed Boeing's proposal to build and test 2 flyable XB-47's for $9,357,800, counting the $1.5 million that had been set aside for development of the straight wing design (Model 432) initially submitted by Boeing. The proposed planes would be bare of any tactical equipment, but necessary space would be provided. The subsequent discovery that more equipment space was needed and that some structural changes had to be made raised

---

[2] Letter contracts for development and mockups of the 3 designs were awarded in the fall of 1944, resulting in the North American XB-45, Convair XB-46, and Martin XB-48. Of these, only the North American XB-45 went into production.

Boeing's original quotation to $9,441,407. This figure also was approved, after the Wright Field price control experts concluded that the XB–47's cost of $95 per airframe-pound was reasonable and considerably lower than the corresponding costs of the XB–45 and XB–48 bombers. Nonetheless, the letter contract of February 1945 was not officially amended until 17 April 1946 (after completion of the XB–47 mockup).

Mockup Inspection   April 1946

The XB–47 mockup was completed, inspected, and approved in the spring of 1946. Army Air Forces personnel attending the XB–47 mockup seemed impressed. Just the same, the Mockup Committee suggested major changes in the nose compartment, pilot and co-pilot seating, and landing gear arrangement. The Chief of the AAF Requirements Division cautioned that any additional weight would cut down the speed of the XB–47, thus defeating the purpose for which the plane was designed.

Development Slippage   April 1946–September 1947

Even though the XB–47 mockup had been well received, development of the experimental plane took longer than expected. Actual work began in June 1946, but progress was hampered by problems with the aircraft landing gear,[3] control surfaces, as well as bottlenecks in power plant installations. The initial lack of overtime pay for the Boeing personnel did not help. All told, a 6-month slippage occurred.

Definitive Development Contract   10 July 1947

It took a year and a half to complete the contractual negotiations initiated by the technical instruction of December 1945. The definitive fixed-price contract (W33–038 ac–8429) of July 1947 called for 2 stripped XB–47s, spare parts, mockups of the completed airplane and fuselage, wing tunnel tests, and research data at a total cost of almost $9.7 million—about $25,000 more than the cost of the amended letter contract of April 1946,

---

[3] The XB–47's thin swept wing eliminated any possibility of suspending a landing gear or retracting one into it. The problem was solved, however, with the installation of a tandem gear, fairly similar to the type previously tested on a Martin B–26. The new arrangement had an additional advantage: reducing the XB–47's weight by 1,500 pounds.

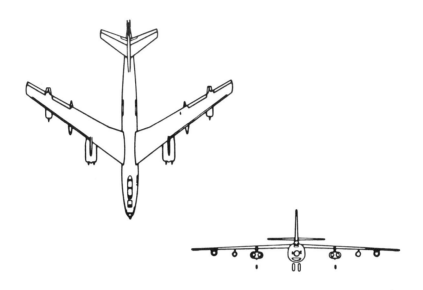

First large American jet featuring swept wings—the XB–47.

which the fixed-price contract superseded. Moreover, the AAF estimated that post-test flight changes most likely would raise the aggregate cost of the contract to more than $10.5 million—a prediction that did materialize. By February 1950, numerous change orders had brought total costs near the $12 million mark.

XB–47 Roll-out   12 September 1947

The first XB–47 rolled out of the Seattle factory in the same month that the United States Air Force was established. The plane was even more startling than the spectacular B–17 Flying Fortress had been 12 years before. The swept wing had already been used experimentally by the Bell Aircraft Corporation on 2 modified P–63 Kingcobras and by North American on the XP–86, first flown in October 1947, but this was the first time the design appeared on a large American jet.

First Flight (XB–47)   17 December 1947

The experimental B–47 was flown from Seattle to nearby Moses Lake AFB, Washington, to begin a series of extensive flight tests. Bad weather delayed the flight until 17 December—44 years to the day after the Wright brothers' first manned flight at Kitty Hawk, North Carolina.

Testing   1948–1954

The Air Force flew the first XB–47 (Serial No. 46–065) for about 83 hours, including nearly 38 hours of Phase II flight tests that were accomplished between 8 July and 15 August 1948. The contractor tested the XB–47 during most of the aircraft's 6 years of life, accumulating more than 330 hours of test flights in the process. In 1954, having been stripped of wings and engines, the experimental B–47 was cut in 2 and exhibited at Palm Beach AFB, Florida.

Appraisal   1948

The Boeing pilots that first flew the XB–47 liked it. After completion of the first phase of testing, a Boeing pilot remarked, "The plane still is doing much better than anyone had a right to expect. We're still exploring one thing at a time, but every door we've kicked open so far has had good things inside." Just the same, the XB–47's overall performance proved disappointing. Its maximum altitude was 2,500 feet below the 40,000-foot ceiling proposed by Boeing and 7,500 feet lower than originally required by the AAF. Its speed was also slower than expected. In fact, in mid-1949 the XB–47 exchanged its six J35-GE–7/9 engines for the larger 5,200-pound thrust J47-GE–3s that equipped the second XB–47 from the start.

Acceptances   1948

The Air Force accepted the first XB–47 conditionally (minus certain equipment to be installed later by Boeing) on 29 November 1948. The second XB–47, first flown in mid-1948, was accepted the following month, under the same conditions. The Air Force took delivery of the experimental planes in December 1948, but lent them to the contractor in subsequent years. Like its predecessor, the second XB–47 was extensively tested. Boeing logged almost 100 hours of test flights; the Air Force, over 237.

B-47A

Manufacturer's Model 450-10-9

Production Decision   September 1948

The Air Force began to plan for the procurement of B-47 productions in December 1947—at about the same time the experimental version first flew—and planning in the following months centered on the production of 54 B-47s (13 B-47As and 41 B-47Bs). A serious misunderstanding arose during the ensuing negotiations. The Air Force assumed $35 million would pay for 10 aircraft and enough tooling for the production of an additional 44. Boeing thought tooling and plant expenses to build 54 B-47s would reach $31 million, without counting the actual cost of each plane. In any case, when Boeing received an official production go-ahead in September 1948, it was only authorized to proceed with the engineering, planning, tool design, procurement of tool materials, and placing of subcontracts for 10 B-47s, in an amount not to exceed $35 million. Moreover, production would not take place in Seattle, as Boeing wished, but at a government-owned plant in Wichita, Kansas—a shift that accounted in part for the slippage that later occurred.

Production Letter Contract   22 November 1948

This letter contract (W33–038 ac–22413) covered a first order of 10 B-47As for $28 million and the future procurement of 3 additional B-47As and 41 B-47Bs, at a cost still to be negotiated. In keeping with routine procurement practices, the letter contract of November 1948 was amended more than once. First, the 3 additional B-47As were canceled; then on 28 February 1949, the number of B-47Bs on order was raised from 41 to 55.[4]

---

[4] The Air Force had interrupted Boeing's testing earlier in the month and flown the first XB-47 to Andrews AFB, Maryland, where it was shown to members of the House Armed Services Committee. The 3-hour flight from Moses Lake AFB, Washington, on 8 February 1949 averaged 602.2 miles per hour over a 2,289-mile course and set an unofficial transcontinental speed record. Evidently, the XB-47 was capable of reaching great speeds, but the Air Force still considered its combat speed too slow.

The Air Force also ordered the design and construction of a ground test rig for the prototype jet-assisted take-off system that it believed future B–47s would need.

Program Reappraisal   1949

As in the case of the B–36, President Truman's decision in late 1948 to hold down defense expenditures worked in favor of the B–47. Pressed for money, the Air Force had to evaluate carefully its limited options. It finally decided to buy more B–47s, an aircraft that General LeMay, also a strong supporter of the B–36, much preferred to the B–50 or future B–54 (almost immediately canceled). The B–47 program increase was reflected in a June 1949 amendment of the basic production letter contract of November 1948. This noteworthy amendment (No. 8) authorized the expenditure or obligation of about $60 million (twice the original amount) for the purchase of 15 B–47s (10 B–47As, plus 5 B–47Bs) and follow-on procurement of 97 B–47Bs (not yet priced). Amendment No. 8 also covered the modification of the 2 XB–47s for use as partial prototypes of production aircraft. Production deliveries were scheduled for the period April 1950 through December 1951.

Definitive Production Contract   14 November 1949

It took months of hard bargaining to arrive at a fair price for the B–47Bs covered by the letter contract of November 1948, as amended in June 1949. The definitive $208.7 million contract (W33–038 ac–22413) of November 1949 was actually a compromise. The Air Force settled for 87 B–47Bs (15 less than planned during the preceding June), and Boeing's fixed fee was reduced. The contract still required that the B–47B be developed according to the new specifications that had been issued in September 1948. These called for single-point refueling (through 1 opening), tactical type assisted take-off (ATO) installation, external fuel tanks, increased gross weight (202,000 pounds after in-flight refueling), the K–2 bombing and navigational system (also earmarked for the B–47A), and an unmanned radar-controlled tail turret—all of which would require some redesign of the wing, body and landing gear. Delivery schedules, however, remained unaltered. The 10 B–47As were due between April and November 1950; the 87 B–47Bs, between December 1950 and December 1951.

First Flight   25 June 1950

Even though deliveries had been scheduled to start in March 1950,

Boeing did not fly the first B–47A until 25 June. It took another year to deliver all 10 B–47As on order to the Air Force.

Testing[5]   1950–1951

Continued flight testing of the B–47A and of the first XB–47 revealed that neither plane was safe, mainly because both were underpowered. Also, critical braking problems occurred following refused takeoffs, and after gross weight landings on wet runways. In addition, after refused landings, go-arounds were hazardous owing to the jet engines' poor acceleration. The answer lay in equipping B–47 productions with higher thrust engines and drogue parachutes that would act as in-flight air brakes. But these remedies were not yet available. Modifications of subsequent B–47As yielded sufficient improvements, but not without considerable delay. Yet none of the changes recommended by a March 1950 USAF engineering inspection reached any of the B–47As.[6]

Enters Service   May 1951

The B–47A entered service at MacDill AFB, Florida, with the 306th Bombardment Wing, Medium. The 306th had been told to prepare for the combat crew training of its own aircrews well in advance of the receipt of its first new plane, also that the 306th aircrews in turn would train the crews of other future B–47 wings. The arrangement, considered temporary since late 1950 when the B–47 program was almost doubled, lasted through December 1951. The Air Training Command then took over most of the training task, which in time proved even more complex than anticipated.

---

[5] Runways of adequate length were available at Wichita, Kansas. Hence in line with the change of production location, testing was shifted from Seattle in the fall of 1949. Moses Lake AFB was transferred to the Continental Air Command at about the same time.

[6] Many factors accounted for the production slippage that plagued the B–47 program from the start. The XB–47's flight to Andrews in February 1947 set back Boeing tests for several weeks. Relocation from Seattle to Wichita took time. Modification of the second XB–47 in August 1950 and allocation of the aircraft to Operation Greenhouse (a Pacific atomic test scheduled for 1951) was another testing handicap. Still, Boeing claimed that the principal reason for the B–47A production delay was that the concept of both the B–47A configuration and the overall B–47 program had been changed by the Air Force in September 1948 (when the production decision was made). The Air Force, on the other hand, pointed out that the requirements of 1948 barely affected the B–47As. Also, the engineering changes requested in March 1950 were to be made on a "no delay" basis on the B–47Bs and had no bearing on the B–47As.

Subsequent Model Series   B–47B

Other Uses   1951–1952

None of the B–47As saw operational duty. Never considered as true production aircraft, the B–47As were unarmed and at first practically bare of components; upon delivery, only 4 of the 10 were equipped with the K–2 Bombing-Navigational System. One of their few advantages probably lay in their crew ejection seats, a controversial feature deleted from the first B–47B lots.[7] In addition to their training role, the B–47As were used in extensive tests. Some stayed with the Air Proving Ground Command. Two were designated to try out the A–2 and A–5 fire-control systems.

---

[7] Boeing had problems from the start with B–47 ejection seat equipment. Canopy ejection technology in the early planes was reconsidered after an XB–47 accident in which the pilot was killed. Boeing then proposed an additional escape hatch and bail-out spoiler (much like the one eventually featured by the B–47B).

B–47B

Manufacturer's Model 450–11–10

Previous Model Series   B–47A

New Features

The B–47B differed from the B–47A in many ways. It carried J47–GE–23 engines (6 of them) and solid fuel rockets for assisted take-off. It had a Nesa[8] glass windshield with rain repellant (in lieu of impractical windshield wipers); hydraulic boost on all control surfaces; a spoiler door (at the aircraft's main entrance) to ease in-flight escape, plus a single-point ground and air-to-air refueling receptacle. Finally, it featured a 2-gun tail turret controlled by radar sight; a B–4 fire-control system; K–4A bombing-navigational system; AN/APS–54 warning radar, and many other improved electronic components, including AN/APT–5A electronic countermeasure devices.

Initial Design September 1948

Design of the B–47B started 5 years after Boeing began work on a multi-jet aircraft for photoreconnaissance and bombing missions with conventional weapons. The informal photographic reconnaissance requirements of 1943 were dropped the following year, when the need for a new medium bomber was clearly established. But by the time Boeing received a production go-ahead, circumstances had changed. The Air Force now wanted its new jet bomber to carry atomic weapons as well as conventional bombs.[9] In

---

[8] Trade name of glass coated with a transparent chemical conductor of electricity. Nesa glass, therefore, was easily kept free of ice.

[9] The mounting urgency to build an atomic deterrent force despite the lack of funds posed grave problems in the fall of 1948. While the B–36 program was no longer in jeopardy, other programs had to be canceled or drastically reduced. Faced with far-reaching decisions, the Air Force opted for the faster production of a more versatile and atomic-capable B–47. This approach was not new. Back in 1946, the AAF had decided that all new planes capable of

addition, the photo-reconnaissance requirements of several years past were revitalized.

Developmental Problems   1948–1952

Deficiencies identified in the XB–47 and subsequent B–47As complicated the B–47B's development. It was one matter to devise fixes for a handful of B–47As, but far more difficult and time-consuming to come up with definite production line modifications. In any case, there were other deep-seated problems that later became obvious. The B–47 was the first USAF bomber to receive a weapon system designation, which meant in theory that all systems to equip and maintain the plane were designed exclusively for the B–47. In effect, however, the Boeing airframe was developed without adequate consideration for such crucial components as engines and bombing systems. Then, too, rising world tensions and the outbreak of the Korean War led to the hasty production of the B–47, before quality and performance were assured. Even though the B–47B was yet to be flown, the Air Force as early as December 1950 foresaw 149 aircraft per month coming off the assembly line. As in World War II, new contractors were selected to pool production.[10] This haste in the long run hampered both development and production. By August 1950, the Air Force had recommended some 2,000 changes, making it almost impossible to settle on an acceptable production type. Meanwhile, Boeing had begun to step up production. By mid-1951, B–47Bs were flowing in ever-increasing numbers from the Wichita line but had to await the modifications and equipment that would make them suitable for combat.[11]

---

carrying bombs as heavy as the atomic bomb should be able to carry the A-bomb itself. Yet, long after the atomic attacks against Japan, the secrecy shrouding the bomb persisted. As in the B–36's case, this would be of no help to B–47 development.

[10] Douglas Aircraft Co., was awarded a production letter contract in December 1950; Lockheed Aircraft Corp., soon afterwards. This would allow production to start without awaiting the definitive contracts that were signed in October 1952. The Air Force's determination to solve unexpected B–47B problems promptly changed this planning. As a result, neither the Douglas plant at Tulsa, Okla., nor the Lockheed facilities at Marietta, Ga., started production before 1953.

[11] Despite an overall production slippage of nearly a full year, components subcontracted by Boeing as well as government-furnished equipment and parts were still behind schedule. General LeMay was adamant in pointing out that failure to develop component systems in phase with production of the new bomber was an indication of bankruptcy in USAF procurement policy. The SAC Commander also thought that the USAF Armament Laboratory was not capable of satisfying the Air Force's needs.

A Stratojet on a jet-assisted take-off, Wright-Patterson AFB, Ohio.

Front and rear cockpits of a B–47, canopy removed.

By mid-1952, the B-47 development was still under way. Requirements kept expanding, special mission modifications were requested, and the Air Force again considered various redesigns of the aircraft's propulsion system.

Testing   1948–1954

In view of the B-47's sweeping new features, it was envisioned from the start that development and testing would be involved as well as lengthy.[12] The XB-47's early flight tests quickly confirmed this expectation. Hence, the Air Force on 7 April 1950 endorsed an unusual operational suitability test, known as Project WIBAC (Wichita Boeing Aircraft Company). This meant that before the B-47 could be delivered to SAC's operational units, the aircraft and its equipment would be thoroughly tested at Wichita by Air Proving Ground Command and SAC personnel.[13] Besides, WIBAC promised to provide statistics on parts consumption, parts failures, and engine life. Guiding data on service testing, maintenance procedures, base facilities, and training needs were also part of the deal. The ambitious WIBAC task soon proved overwhelming. While no B-47Bs had reached WIBAC by mid-1951, the project was already in trouble. In August, WIBAC requested review of the whole B-47 program—production, allocation, requirements, and operational deficiencies.

First Flight (Production Aircraft)   February 1951

The Air Force accepted this plane in March and 87 similar productions within a year.[14] Testing by WIBAC in late July 1951 verified that the new B-47Bs could not possibly meet the Strategic Air Command's require-

---

[12] The development and test phase, mostly completed in mid-1953 (after some 50,000 flight-test hours), exceeded the original time estimate by almost 4 years.

[13] Early WIBAC appraisals of the B-47 gave the Air Force something to think about. In mid-1951, SAC observers liked the airplane, but noted that the airframe and engines were much more advanced than the component systems. Moreover, designers and manufacturers of component parts, as well as the numerous subcontractors producing such items as relays, fuel selector valves, booster pumps, and the like, were not in tune with the sophisticated designs necessary for such a high-performance aircraft. As a result, Boeing was forced to fit the B-47 with the same type of equipment that had caused so much difficulty in the B-29s and B-50s.

[14] The 88 planes, like the B-47As, featured 6 J47-GE-11 engines until re-fitted with the more powerful J47-GE-23s that equipped subsequent B-47Bs.

ments.[15] In September, USAF test pilots pointed out that the plane's weight gain, from 125,000 to 202,000 pounds, had badly affected its flying qualities, making it unstable at high altitude and generally hard to maneuver.

Modification Planning   October 1951

The impasse reported by WIBAC led to a conference in October 1951, attended by many top Air Force generals. Most conferees seemed to believe that WIBAC, and more specifically the office of the B–47 project officer, had been given an impossible job. Opinions differed, however, on how some of the difficulties encountered could have been avoided or at least reduced. Maj. Gen. Bryan L. Boatner, Commanding General of the Air Proving Ground, thought better results could have been secured had Air Research and Development Command and Air Materiel Command (AMC) contributed technical personnel and stationed them permanently at WIBAC as Strategic Air Command (SAC) and Air Proving Ground did. Lt. Gen. Earle E. Partridge, who headed the research and development command, commented that the concentration of all B–47 tests at Wichita had been a mistake. Generals Partridge and Boatner agreed that the B–47 was a very complicated piece of equipment and that the production problems were the greatest ever experienced. Then, General Twining (Vice Chief of Staff since October 1950) said that the B–47 problem fell to the Air Staff and that it would be solved. To this end, a so-called refinement program was set to begin in early 1952 at the USAF Grand Central Plant in Tucson, Arizona. The minimum modifications to make the B–47 combat ready were lined up, SAC alone suggesting close to 50. Maj. Gen. Thomas S. Power, SAC's Vice Commander, pointed out that his command was more familiar than most with the bomber's deficiencies. He announced that an engineering operational program in the 306th Wing would get under way in early 1952. This program, General Power stated, should help significantly in speeding up progress.

Additional Procurement   1951–1952

Advanced procurement plans were finalized in November 1951—on the heels of the October conference—by a definitive contract for 445 additional

---

[15] The first SAC B–47B (Serial No. 50–008) was flown on 23 October 1951 from Wichita to MacDill by Col. Michael N. W. McCoy, Commander of the 306th Wing. Even though the plane was not combat ready, a beginning had been made and this was celebrated on 19 November, when the aircraft was named "The Real McCoy." Six more B–47Bs programmed for the 306th during that month were refused because of serious deficiencies, but a total of 12 were accepted before the end of the year.

productions. This number was reduced to 395 in March 1952, after more realistic production schedules were endorsed.[16] Nonetheless, new procurement soon followed. Fifty-two RB–47s and 510 B–47Bs were ordered in June 1952, and 3 other production contracts were issued during the year—1 in September called for 540 B–47Bs; 1 in October, for 70 RB–47s; and 1 in December, for another 193 B–47Bs. As it turned out, the Air Force reduced the number of B/RB–47s (1,760 aircraft) ordered in 1952, and most of these aircraft came off the production line as B–47Es.

Basic Safety Deficiencies   1951–1952

Explosive decompression tests in 1951 proved the B–47's original canopy unsafe for high altitude combat operations. A sectionalized canopy was the answer, but would not be available for some time. Another major problem was the lack of ejection seats in the B–47B. SAC long believed that ejection-type seats were the safest method of egress from high-speed aircraft. Boeing studies on the subject had shown it would be impossible to get out of an uncontrolled B–47 without ejection seats. Escaping under controlled flight conditions would even be hazardous without them. Although the 10 B–47As had ejection seats, these were operationally marginal. Therefore, in the interest of saving weight—at least until the B–47 reached a 4,000-nautical mile range—a group of senior officers (including some from SAC) had decided to dispense with the seats. SAC's ensuing objections were to no avail, but its request in mid-1950 for reinstatement of the seats was finally approved. Still it became obvious in December 1951 that ejection seats would not be incorporated in production for quite a while.[17] As many as 400 B–47s would not have any, and this was far more than SAC had been

---

[16] As the B–47 bomb bay was designed to carry atomic bombs, no additional framework installation was required. Bomb racks, sway braces, hoists, and other equipment items were attached from the start to the airframe, specifically to the bomb-bay fuel tank floor. Just the same, production and operational difficulties with the aircraft itself prompted a further cutback in the B–47B's atomic capability in April 1952. The Air Force decided at the time that the first 89 B–47Bs would not be required to carry any atomic bombs, and that the next 80 aircraft would only be expected to handle 2 specific types of bombs. While some of this early planning changed, a directive that all subsequent B–47Bs would be able to carry low-density atomic bombs could not be satisfied. Despite all efforts, the high-speed B–47s proved unable to release subject bombs at altitudes below 30,000 feet.

[17] Providing satisfactory ejection seats for the B–47's 3-man crew entailed the relocation of important pieces of equipment. Air Material Command estimated this might require as many as 26,000 engineering manhours. In addition, much more was involved to ensure crew safety. In fact, high-speed testing of the approved seats (upward for pilot and co-pilot; downward for the navigator) was still going on in December 1952.

prepared to accept. Since retrofit of the aircraft then seemed economically impossible, the only alternative was to settle for the next best means of egress. To begin with, this called for development of a redesigned dinghy.[18]

Other First Shortcomings   1951–1952

The K–2 bombing and navigation system, like the early K–1 of many B–36s, was unreliable and hard to maintain.[19] By mid-1952 the K–2 had been made to work somehow, but still needed improvement even after additional modifications had brought about its redesignation as the K–4. The Emerson A–2 tail defense system, earmarked for the B–47,[20] was canceled before the end of the year in favor of the General Electric A–5. The decision, based on Project WIBAC's recommendation, proved sound but posed an immediate problem. No A–5 fire-control systems were available and none were to be expected much before 1953. In the meantime, it was mandatory for SAC that a makeshift system be devised. Retrofit of early B–47s with a 2-gun turret and an N–6 optical sight was the chosen solution. This would at least give the aircraft some kind of defense. Although contrary to plans, the extra modification was included in the refinement program that had been endorsed during the conference of October 1951. Not surprisingly, further pioneer difficulties were

---

[18] It was difficult to maneuver from the crew positions to the escape hatch with the present dinghy attached to the parachute harness. Yet, in an emergency, there seldom was time to attach the raft after leaving one's seat.

[19] The 1,600-pound K–2 counted 41 major components, totaling some 370 vacuum tubes and close to 20,000 separate parts. Since the B–47 was compact, the K–2 equipment had been scattered throughout the aircraft. Many of the system's parts were outside of the plane's pressurized area. Hence, no inflight maintenance was possible and high abort rates were to be expected. Maintenance on the ground was nearly as difficult. Pre-flight checking took too long—8 hours, compared to 1 hour for checking almost the same system on the B–36.

[20] Development of the system could be traced back to 1946, when the XB–47 was first reviewed by the AMC's armament laboratory—the same laboratory General LeMay still took to task in 1951. Engineers believed that the Emerson-built tail turret, referred to as the A–1 fire-control system and intended for the North American B–45, could be fitted into the B–47 without altering the turret's basic mechanism. With Boeing's concurrence, the Air Force in June 1948 asked Emerson to design for the B–47 a turret gunner cab similar to that of the B–45, but providing sufficient comfort for missions of long duration. The project quickly became so complicated that it was given up. A remote controlled system that would be operated by one of the flight crew members appeared more feasible. This gave way to the A–2 fire-control system, a system eliminating the need for a tail gunner. This A–2 was due to provide accurate defensive fire for protection of the B–47 and to perform, although not simultaneously, both search and track. The A–2, after being fitted into the tail of a B–29, was successfully tested under Project Hornet. Moreover, in theory, the A–2 was superior to the APG–32 built by the General Electric Company for the B–36. In practice, however, while major APG–32 problems could be solved, the A–2's basic suitability for the B–47 remained too questionable to warrant its retention.

encountered. One was fuel boil off and fuel purging, found more critical in jet bombers. The B–47 was designed for maximum speed and range at a high altitude, and the sooner it reached that altitude, the better. Yet, at high altitudes fuel boil and loss of fuel occurred, reducing the aircraft's range which, in any case, remained far shorter than required in early 1944. Development of JP–4 fuel, after numerous experiments, appeared to solve much of the problem, but production quantities would not be available until January 1952. Again, purging fuel tanks required the use of dry ice, which would be difficult to purchase in areas where the B–47s were expected to operate, especially when the aircraft would be operating overseas. Development of portable dry ice manufacturing equipment was a partial answer. A new exhaust gas purging system, being devised by AMC, would be more dependable and less hazardous. It would require no additional maintenance and provide greater and longer protection for more fuel volume than the dry ice system. This was all for the best but, as with every new system, the AMC development would take time.

Slippage Impact   1951–1952

There were extenuating circumstances for the topsy-turvy B–47 program. As Maj. Gen. Albert Boyd, the Wright Air Development Center's Commander, explained in 1952:

> There is a limit to what we can do, or for that matter, what anyone can do, toward developing a radically new airplane in record time, and we, no more than anyone else, are capable of pulling a rabbit out of our hats or cranking out a new aircraft that meets all the desires of the operating activities.

Yet, the impact of the B–47 slippage was serious from the start. To prepare for, operate, and maintain a weapon system as revolutionary as the B–47 presented a tremendous challenge.

SAC confronted numerous problems,[21] some of them crucial. To begin

---

[21] Bases had to be prepared for the B–47, particularly by lengthening runways. Since the aircraft's range did not meet requirements, air refueling was a necessity. This complicated matters. Extra troop housing, maintenance facilities, equipment and supply were needed to support B–47 squadrons and their accompanying KC–97 tankers. Training problems came to the fore. Even the first 90 B–47s, finally earmarked for Air Training Command, were fitted with receptacles to teach both B–47 and KC–97 trainees the ticklish air-refueling mating of a fast jet and a slow tanker. Briefly stated, the all-jet B–47, with its crew of 3, played havoc with SAC personnel policies. Large numbers of people became excess, whereas hundreds of others were needed to fill specialties peculiar to jet aircraft. All kinds of mechanics and supervisors had to be retrained for the B–47. Moreover, SAC and other USAF commands never had used pilot-observers. Since the B–47 demanded quadruple-rated aircrewmen, ATC had to turn pilots into proficient navigators, bombardiers, and radar operators.

with, the production delay meant that conversion plans had to be shuffled many times over.[22] Then, slippage of the refinement program, which now appeared unavoidable, would further dilute the command's readiness. Each month lost forced SAC to be ready to fight with even more outmoded B–29s and B–50s. To make it worse, everyone knew that when at long last available, the modified B–47Bs would give SAC only a basic combat aircraft and that considerable modifications were still to come.

Refinement Program   1952–1953

The program, due to begin in January 1952, involved the modification of 310 B–47Bs.[23] SAC expected its first modified planes in July and a monthly input of 75 by year's end. This was optimistic. As predicted by AMC, the Grand Central Depot of Tucson could not possibly handle such a workload without greatly expanding facilities and manpower. This would take time and money, and neither could really be spared. The Air Force found a way out of its new dilemma. Boeing agreed to modify 90 of the aircraft (for about $10 million) and Douglas was also asked to help.[24] The original modification schedule nevertheless slipped. First, it proved difficult to assemble the necessary modification kits. Then, there were not enough kits. In September 1952, SAC's few B–47s were grounded because of serious fuel cell leakages. This again slowed the refinement program, since it obviously required an extra inspection of the aircraft being modified.

---

[22] SAC was told in 1949 to get ready for the early conversion of certain units to B–47 aircraft. It learned in September that 108 B–47s would be forthcoming during the years 1950 and 1951. In the spring of 1950, when, as some put it, if the Air Force was in the "jam," it was because of the B–47, SAC refused to get into further trouble programming for conversions too far in advance of aircraft delivery dates. The command chose to go ahead with the 306th and 305th conversions, but to postpone deciding which other wings would convert to B–47s and in what order. Meanwhile, SAC had inherited a new problem. After both air and ground crew training had been rushed, SAC wondered how to keep crew proficiency when it had no planes to fly or to look after. Of small consolation, no such overages existed in the K system and armament category where, besides technical factors, personnel training lagged for lack of tools, test equipment, and parts.

[23] Instead of 400, the first 90 aircraft went to Air Training Command as they were. The command later received 90 other B–47s. These planes had been through the refinement program, but their modification did not include the addition of the interim B–4 fire-control system that was fitted in every B–47 modified for SAC.

[24] Douglas agreed to modify 8 aircraft per month in Tulsa. Boeing promised to fix the planes in Tucson, but saturation of the existing facilities changed this planning. To keep its commitment, Boeing shifted the work to Wichita. The contractor was actually able to modify 40 of the planes directly on the assembly line.

Yet, despite its shaky start, the program fulfilled its requirements. SAC received its first batch of modified B–47s in October—a 3-month slippage that was to prove of slight importance. The last modified B–47s flowed from the Douglas modification center in October 1953.

Enters Operational Service   Fall of 1952

As a beginning, SAC received 8 modified B–47Bs in October 1952, 23 in November, 34 in December, and 13 in January 1953. The aircraft immediately went to the 306th and 305th Wings.

Production Improvement   1952–1953

Back in late 1951, mechanical failures and a myriad of minor obstacles had caused the B–47 production to slip again. Yet, in the face of persistent shortages of contractor-furnished equipment and government-furnished parts, production took a turn for the better in the spring of 1952. The improvement soon gained momentum. By mid-1953, production was running smoothly and Boeing was rolling out new configurations (B/RB–47Es). Just getting started, Douglas, Tulsa, had already built 10 B–47Bs; Lockheed, Marietta, 7. In addition, two projects were in progress since January 1953. The first and most important one was Baby Grand. It was conducted by Boeing and would add the A–5 fire-control system in 54 new B–47s (units 400–454). The other, Field Goal, was in the hands of Douglas. It would improve 86 (units 1–86) of the 90 unmodified B–47s, first allocated to Air Training Command.

Standardization Decision   April 1953

Even though all modifications covered by the refinement program were incorporated into the production line of the 410st and subsequent B–47's, much remained to be done. Despite the Baby Grand modification, these aircraft, as well as the modified B–47Bs, did not meet the Air Force's expectations. There were other problems. In the hope of improving performance quickly, complex engineering changes had been introduced into the production line at approximately every fifth aircraft. This had essentially resulted in making the aircraft's maintenance far more difficult and its logistical support almost nightmarish. A standardization conference was held at Wichita in April 1953. There, Boeing's 731st B–47 production, a

B–47E referred to as WIBAC Unit 731, was established as the SAC standardization bomber.[25] In the same month, Headquarters USAF approved Turn Around, an AMC modification plan that would bring 114 new B–47s (units 617–730) to the 731st configuration. The Turn Around plan was clever. The Air Force would conditionally accept the 114 aircraft, but leave them at the Boeing plant for modification. The same procedure could be followed on other occasions. In this first case, it would save more than $7 million by eliminating the costly process of bringing back 114 aircraft for modernization after delivery. Turn Around, however, did not address the problem presented by in-service B–47s. This was to be covered by High Noon, a major modification and IRAN (inspect and repair as necessary) maintenance program, approved before the end of May.

Overseas Deployment   June 1953

SAC was always the first to seek further B–47 improvement. In the meantime, however, the command intended to make ample use of its newly assigned planes. After testing exhaustively in early 1953 the modified B–47B under simulated combat conditions, SAC decided the 306th (its first fully equipped wing) was ready for a 90-day rotational training mission to England. The 306th's deployment originated at MacDill and involved equal flights of 15 B–47s on 3, 4, and 5 June. Establishing a precedent that would be followed many times in the future, the B–47s staged through Limestone AFB, Maine, where they remained overnight before going on the next day. They landed at Fairford Royal Air Force Station on the 4th, 5th, and 6th of June. The 306th Air Refueling Squadron's KC–97s,[26] crammed with support personnel and equipment, deployed on the same dates as the B–47s.[27] They stopped overnight

---

[25] In June the Air Council reaffirmed the April decision and officially endorsed Boeing's WIBAC Unit 731 as the "improved combat configuration." It took the other 2 contractors little more than a year to follow suit. Douglas Unit 125, delivered in September 1954, and Lockheed Unit 128, delivered 1 month before, were the same as WIBAC Unit 731.

[26] MacDill's 306th Air Refueling Squadron was the first unit to begin equipping with the KC–97 tanker. Its first aircraft, a KC–97E, was delivered on 14 July 1951. Outfitted with a flying boom and loaded with fuel tanks, the 4-engine, propeller-driven KC–97 could fly fast enough to match the minimum speed of the B–47. It transformed the B–47 into an intercontinental bomber. Each KC–97 squadron was authorized 20 aircraft.

[27] As far as SAC was concerned, proper support of the B–47s was of prime importance. In this regard, past production slippage had alleviated anticipated problems. Lagging supply programs had been able to pull abreast, and in some cases exceed wing requirements. For instance, the 306th had on hand nearly 90 percent of its equipment items by the end of 1951. Later, Snowtime, a project conceived by SAC, minimized supply difficulties. Snowtime required storage in only 1 depot (Rome, Griffiss AFB, N.Y.) of parts and equipment that would

Two B–47Bs, equipped with 6 J47–GE–23 engines.

at Ernest Harmon AFB, Newfoundland, and then flew on to Mildenhall Royal Air Force Station. Maintaining 1 or more bomb wings in the United Kingdom was nothing new. B–29 and B–50 wings had been rotating there since 1948. Just the same, the 306th rotational deployment was a milestone. Although a handful of specially modified B–45s had arrived in England in 1952, the move of the 306th there was the first routine deployment of a fully operational jet bomber wing. Moreover, the policy of maintaining at least 1 B–47 wing in England at all times would continue until early 1958.[28]

Aircraft Retrofit   1953–1957

Although modified B–47Bs were indispensable either at home or overseas, the Air Force did not lose sight of its April 1953 standardization

---

be needed at B–47 bases at the time of conversion. Sea Weed, a similar project for the overseas B–47 bases, after a tough debut, also helped.

[28] Once started, the deployments were uninterrupted. When the 306th's 90-day rotation was over, the 305th was ready. By the time the 305th's tour was nearing its end, the 22d Bomb Wing had completed the transition to B–47s and was poised for departure.

122

decision. Yet, SAC operational priorities made it necessary to adjust the High Noon program that was due to modernize the bulk of the early airplanes. As finally approved in June 1953, 165 (units 235–399) of SAC's 289 modified B–47s would first go to High Noon.[29] To the maximum extent possible, the rest of the early planes, including those remaining in SAC's inventory, would also be brought to the 731st configuration. This would be done under Ebb Tide,[30] now organized as High Noon's second phase, but would not affect the AMC's 2-year IRAN maintenance program that had been attached to High Noon from the start.

The High Noon contract was assigned to Boeing. The choice was logical since the first 399 B–47s had all been assembled by Boeing from Boeing parts. Moreover, AMC was confident Boeing could do the work better, faster and cheaper than anyone else. High Noon was essentially a retrofit kit installation. Nevertheless, it was a complicated task, calling for removal, rebuilding, and reinstallation of many component-systems, as well as major revisions of the aircraft nose and cockpit. B–47s earmarked for High Noon began arriving at WIBAC in June 1954, and 36 of them had entered the modification line by February 1955. The first renovated B–47 emerged from its "face lifting" operation on 2 March. It featured ejection seats for all crew members, a bombing-navigation system with improved reliability,[31] water-alcohol injection for thrust augmentation, an expanded rack for rocket-bottle take-off assist units, a modified bomb bay that could house the single-sling, high-density, thermonuclear bomb as well as more general purpose bombs, a reinforced landing gear for increased take-off weight (202,000 pounds), the A–5 fire-control system (in place of the B–4), the AN/ARC–21 long range-liaison radio,[32] and better electronic countermeasures equipment. There were no major problems during the High Noon modification of SAC's 165 B–47Bs. The Boeing contract met its early 1956 completion date and was immediately replaced by Ebb Tide, which also took

---

[29] High Noon was the code name assigned to the major modification and maintenance program, approved in May 1953.

[30] Ebb Tide was another code name, the use of which, like that of High Noon, simplified matters when dealing with a complicated standardization project of exceptional scope.

[31] This was still the K system, but it had become more dependable as a result of Reliable, a separate modification project that had also simplified its installation and maintenance.

[32] The problem of obtaining a satisfactory high frequency radio dated back to 1950 and remained of great concern to General LeMay in 1954. Because the AN/ARC–21 long-range liaison radio was not available and its production continued to slip, 13 SAC wings used the Collins 18S–4. The command, however, did not relish having more aircraft fitted with this interim equipment. Fortunately, Project Big Eva, an accelerated test of the AN/ARC/21, concluded in February 1955 that the set perfomed creditably and would not require new maintenance skills.

place in Wichita. Ebb Tide addressed itself to the first 324 B–47s built by Boeing.[33] Of these, 66, selected from units 135–234, would undergo the same transformation as the High Noon planes and return to SAC in the configuration of WIBAC Unit 731. Another 108 of the early productions, out of units 1–134, would be modernized for Air Training Command.[34] In the process, they would exchange their J47-23 engines for the more powerful J47-25s of the other B–47Bs. Finally, 30 planes would be brought to the High Noon standard and be converted to director aircraft (DB–47Bs) for the forthcoming Rascal missiles.[35]

Total B–47Bs Accepted   397

Ten of these aircraft were built by Douglas, 8 by Lockheed, and all others by Boeing.

Acceptance Rates

The Air Force accepted 2 B–47Bs in fiscal year 1951 (1 each in April and May 1951); 204 in FY 52; 190 in FY 53, and a last one in FY 54 (July 1953).

End of Production   June 1953

The Air Force took delivery of the plane the following month.

Flyaway Cost per Production Aircraft $2.44 million

Airframe, $1,767,094; engines (installed), $283,082; electronics, $43,835; ordnance, $5,336; armament, $350,109.

---

[33] The program did not cover all the aircraft. Only specific lots, or about two-thirds of the 324 planes, went to Ebb Tide.

[34] The Air Training Command planes, subsequently known as TB–47s, closely resembled SAC's B–47s, but they carried no defensive armament or electronic countermeasures equipment. They could not be air-refueled and could not drop bombs. Also, take-off and range were unimproved.

[35] The DB–47Bs would carry the missiles to within 90 nautical miles of the target before launching and guiding them.

Subsequent Model Series   **B–47E**

Other Configurations   **RB–47B and YRB–47B**

Design of the RB–47B was started in March 1951. Based on experience, the aircraft's first flight was expected 2 years later. The Air Force at the time also figured that delivery of the new reconnaissance planes could well begin in mid-1953. Yet, in March 1952, the many problems associated with the bomber configuration implied that the reconnaissance B–47 the Air Force had in mind was a long way off. In fact, it was decided shortly before October 1952 that the plane would feature the scarce A–5 fire-control system and the still experimental J47–GE–25 engines. The aircraft, therefore, most likely would not be completed until 1954 and when available, it would have little in common with the basic B–47B. Closely resembling the new E-model, it would come to be known as the RB–47E.

While this marked the production demise of the RB–47B (which never appeared on the Air Force's financial accounts), so-called RB–47Bs and YRB–47Bs came into being to fill SAC's reconnaissance vacuum of the early fifties. These planes, however, were nothing more than converted B–47Bs, equipped with special reconnaissance pods.[36] The Boeing-developed, 8-camera pod could easily be installed in the forward bomb bay, but only provided daylight photographic coverage. The 91st Strategic Reconnaissance Wing (Medium) received its first YRB–47 in April 1953; the 26th, 3 months later. Most of the 90 converted reconnaissance planes were subsequently used as crew trainers for operational RB–47Es.

Phaseout   **1957**

In effect, the B–47Bs ceased to exist in 1957. By then, most of these aircraft had been brought up to the 731st's configuration or, as in the TB–47's case, sufficiently transformed to acquire new designation.

Other Uses   **DB–47A and QB–47B**

As General Boyd later pointed out, multiple demands were pinned on the B–47 from the start. Because it was the fastest bomber, the Air Force

---

[36] The RB–47Bs were pre-1953 conversions carrying, in principle, a dual bomber-reconnaissance mission. The YRB–47Bs were later conversions, more specifically intended for training.

called on it for Brass Ring,[37] a project concerning the delivery of thermo-nuclear weapons by unmanned aircraft. The Brass Ring project, spurred around 1949, was immersed in secrecy and of such importance that it was designated as "Special" by the highest authorities. Yet, Brass Ring was handicapped even before it began. In the late forties, technology was taking giant steps, but these steps went in many highly complex and expensive directions. Meanwhile, there was just a trickle of cooperation between the Atomic Energy Commission, which was building the atomic bombs, and the Air Force, which had to carry them. Early in 1950, as the Air Force looked for better ways to deliver the A-bomb, the forthcoming thermonuclear device (the hydrogen, or H-bomb) changed future carrier requirements. At first glance, it appeared that only a guided missile could handle the new weapon.[38] However, the time element—2½ years for a completely operational system—ruled out all missiles the Air Force had under development. The sole alternative seemed to be an aircraft that could assume the guise of a drone or missile. There were not many planes which could meet the required criteria. The aircraft had to be inexpensive, dependable, hardly vulnerable to enemy counter-actions, easily stabilized for automatic control, and quickly available. Only 3 candidates, the B–36, B–47, and B–49,[39] satisfied the basic load and range requirements. Of those, the B–47 was the best despite its high cost. The big B–36 was even more expensive and much too slow. The single point in favor of the B–49, should it ever reach production, was that its high-altitude performance would decrease its vulnerability. Hence, there was little dissension over selection of the B–47 as the H-bomb's first carrier. The Air Force made up its mind quickly.[40] It decided early in 1950 that 1 of the 10 B–47As (finally expected in by 1951) would be returned to Boeing and be converted into a director aircraft (DB–47A). Boeing also agreed on 27 September to modify 2 future B–47Bs

---

[37] This name was not officially adopted until April 1951.

[38] The H-bomb was expected to produce a lethal area so great that, were it released in a normal manner, the carrier would not survive the explosive effects.

[39] The prototype B–49 represented Northrop's effort to establish a tactical use for a turbojet-powered version of its experimental B–35 "flying wing." The Air Force halted testing of the YB–49 in February 1950 and of its reconnaissance counterpart 2 years later.

[40] The Air Force, nevertheless, made it clear that any B–47 alterations had to be viewed as just one phase of a much larger program. In short, all delivery methods of possible merit had to be weighed. There were good reasons for such reservations. Lt. Gen. Kenneth B. Wolfe, Air Force Deputy Chief of Staff for Materiel, was not alone in believing that a piloted aircraft should be able to drop the new weapon and withdraw in comparative safety. As far as the B–47 was concerned, General Wolfe insisted, thrust could be added to increase the aircraft's turning speed. Moreover, there should be some way to slow down the H-bomb's rate of fall to enhance the carrier's margin of safety. Time soon proved the wisdom of these arguments.

to missile carrier (MB-47) or drone (QB-47) configurations.[41] Still, the project remained full of uncertainties. The Brass Ring MB-47 might become a true missile and dive towards its target. It might also be equipped with a mechanism to trigger the bomb free, as in a normal bombing run, while another gadget would ensure the missile's self-destruction shortly after the bomb release. Little information was available regarding the weight and size of the future H-bomb. All the Air Force knew was its new "emergency" carrier would have to cover more than 4,000 nautical miles with a load that would have to be dropped within a narrow radius of the target. So most likely, the Brass Ring MB-47 would have to be air-refueled several times. In any case, it would be manned until the last refueling operation. The crew would then bail out over friendly territory and the deserted MB-47 would go on towards its targets through automatic control by air director, stellar tracker, and auto-navigation. The scheme was sound, but getting a fully automatic, non-jammable guidance and bombing system to deliver the new weapon with accuracy would not be easy. It became obvious by 1952 that neither the North American nor Sperry guidance systems could be ready for the Brass Ring operational date, even though the latter had been slipped to July 1954.[42] The problem was so serious that the Air Force had begun to envision a director aircraft "mothering" a B-47 drone all the way to the target. Although the director-drone version could be made to work without a complex autonavigator,[43] it presented other difficulties. To begin with, B-47Bs would have to be modified as directors, since the DB-47A's range was too short for a full-scale Brass Ring mission with an unmanned H-bomb carrier. By mid-1952, however, Brass Ring was in far deeper trouble. General Wolfe's predictions had come true: Brass Ring was not the only way to

---

[41] In accordance with the terms of the contractual agreement, Boeing subcontracted 3 major items to other companies. Under these arrangements, North American Aviation, Inc., (involved in an autonavigation development that had been started by the Hughes Aircraft Company) became responsible for the principal guidance system for Brass Ring. The Sperry Gyroscope Company was to supply the automatic flight control system; the Collins Radio Company, guidance equipment. If needed, the Sperry autonavigator—the alternate to North American's—would be supplied as government-furnished equipment.

[42] Continued development of North American's autonavigator was canceled in mid-1952, after costing the government some $850,000. Sperry's work was stopped, as part of Brass Ring, but allowed to resume for a different project. There was ample justification for the decision. In 1953, no other autonavigator had reached as advanced a stage as Sperry's. Also, $2.3 million had already been spent, and not much more was needed to get a finished product.

[43] The lack of a satisfactory autonavigator precluded testing of the original Brass Ring setup. The director-drone combination fared better. The first flight of the carrier, utilizing remote flight control and stabilization equipment, was made on 7 May 1952. By 30 June, both the B-47 drone aircraft and its director, with but part of the required equipment, had flown several test runs with rewarding results.

handle the new thermonuclear device.[44] For instance, testing had shown that a B–36 could deliver a parachute-equipped H-bomb about as accurately as a conventional bomb. Moreover, whether a B–36 or B–47 carried out the operation, the degree of safety would be more than adequate.[45] Against this background, Brass Ring's advantages faded. The acquisition of friendly bases in Europe, Asia, and Africa diminished the importance of range. Availability, a primary Brass Ring plus, also lost merit since the program was slipping. Forecast costs, swelling from $4.9 million in 1950 to $10.3 million in 1952, sealed Brass Ring's fate. The program was officially canceled on 1 April 1953. Despite an appeal by the Wright Air Development Center,[46] the Air Staff's decision stood firm.

DB–47B

The Air Force early in 1952 definitely considered using some bomber types to carry, launch, and guide air-to-surface missiles.[47] This would allow the destruction of enemy targets miles away from the carrier's utmost range. Most importantly, it would prevent the exposure of bombers and crews to hostile ground fire. The Bell Aircraft Corporation's Rascal (GAM–63) was the chosen missile. It was a 20,000-pounder (including an atomic warhead of some 3,000 pounds), with a range of 100 nautical miles. Under development since 1949,[48] the Rascal was earmarked for the Convair B–36, for the B–60

---

[44] Various delivery methods were investigated several months before the first full-scale thermonuclear explosion of November 1952. (The explosion took place at Eniwetok, an atoll of the Marshall Islands, designated by the Atomic Energy in 1947 Commission as permanent mid-Pacific proving ground for atomic weapons.)

[45] B–36s became the first bombers capable of handling thermonuclear weapons. Necessary modifications were accomplished under the code names of SAM-SAC and Featherweight. B–47s were modified soon afterwards as part of High Noon. Thermonuclear-capable B–47s could easily be reconverted in the field to carry the initial atomic weapons.

[46] The Wright Air Development Center was convinced that the $5.9 million spent on Brass Ring was worthwhile. As an emergency carrier of the thermonuclear bomb, the Brass Ring role might be eroded, but the program had many ramifications. The director-drone technique remained a crucial element of strategic air power. An additional $2.5 million would have provided 2 B–47 carriers, 1 B–47A director (with their associated equipment), plus engineering and hardware for 3 B–47B directors.

[47] This separate project came up shortly before Brass Ring took a turn for the worse. The Air Force had already learned much from the ill-fated program and this knowledge quickly served many other developmental endeavors.

[48] The Rascal's origin actually went back to 1 April 1946, when the AAF fathered Project MX-776, which called for a subsonic air-to-surface pilotless parasite bomber carrying a substantial warhead over a distance of 300 miles. After 18 months of study, Bell concluded that

(a jet-powered version of the B–36, built and flown but never placed in production), and for the Boeing B–47 and B–52. In March 1952, the candidate list was reduced to the B–36 and B–47, with the latter's modification assigned first priority. In spite of SAC's dislike of the Air Staff decision, Boeing before year's end was given a letter contract covering the modification of 2 B–47Bs into prototype Rascal carriers. In addition, following testing of the YDB–47s, 17 B–47Bs were to be converted to the DB–47B configuration finally approved. Not prone to give up easily, SAC began to urge that it be allowed to substitute B–50s for the B–47s. In the fall of 1953, after its latest appeal was turned down, SAC again pointed out that equipping the B–47 with the Rascal degraded the aircraft's performance, enough to make the combination of doubtful value. Moreover, it probably would never work well, since guidance of the missile added more complex electronic circuits to the already electronically complicated B–47. Then, too, modification costs (nearing $1 million per B–47 carrier) seemed out of line in view of the missile's current stage of development. Finally, SAC considered it unwise to commit strike aircraft and to train personnel before the Rascal problems were resolved and the missile's worth proved.[49]

The command did not win its case, but recurring Rascal slippages were to work in its favor. After completion of 1 mockup and 2 DB–47 prototypes, the letter contract of 1952 stayed in limbo until March 1955. The definitive contract then signed gave Boeing $3.7 million for completion of the work originally scheduled, bringing the conversion cost of each plane slightly below SAC's first estimate. In June 1955, the Air Force decided the B–47 alone would carry the rocket-powered Rascal, and the B–36 modification contract was canceled. Thirty B–47Bs, earmarked for Ebb Tide, now would also be converted and would emerge from Ebb Tide as DB–47s. Yet, despite a successful first Rascal launch from a YDB–47E carrier in July of the same year, the entire project seemed to falter. Technical problems continued to plague the GAM–63 missile (System 112L), and money was short. The Air Staff informed the Air Materiel Command in early 1956 that production

---

a rocket power plant was not feasible for a 300-mile missile of the size contemplated. Even though the range requirement was pared to 100 nautical miles, other problems quickly surfaced, spurring development of a test vehicle that would be similar, but much smaller and cheaper than originally specified. This became the Shrike, a missile of canard configuration that was powered by 2 liquid rocket motors. The Shrike eventually boasted a cruising speed of Mach 2 and a range of some 50 nautical miles. First fired on 12 December 1951, it contributed much to the development of the Rascal, which was initially flight tested at Holloman AFB, N. M., on 30 September 1952. The 2 missiles, however, soon parted company.

[49] SAC's misgivings were not solely confined to the B–47. The command surmised that of all the B–36s, the H might not be the one best suited to carry the Rascal. As in the past, SAC insisted that the B–52s be kept out of the Rascal program. On this point, the command succeeded.

requirements for DB–47Es would be limited to 2 airplanes—Boeing Units 928 and 929. In May 1957, it was announced that the operational inventory would get 1 instead of 2 DB–47/GAM–63 squadrons. This was still too much, SAC reiterated, because the Rascal would be outmoded by improved Soviet defenses by the time it became operational. Nonetheless, at year's end, crews of the command's 321st Bomb Wing were engaged in Rascal training. Meanwhile, other factors, including persisting fund shortages, seemed to justify SAC's steadfast opinion. Rascal facilities at Pinecastle AFB, Florida, from where the wing's 445th Bombing Squadron would operate, were yet to be built early in 1958. In August, a review of the last 6 months of Rascal testing revealed a gloomy picture. Out of 64 scheduled launches, only 1 was a complete success, more than half were canceled, and most of the others were failures. The Air Staff officially ended the Rascal program on 29 November 1958,[50] after finally agreeing that ensuing savings could be put to better use.

KB–47G and KB–47F

Early in 1953, 2 47Bs were converted for trials with the British-developed probe and drogue refueling system. The resulting tanker was designated KB–47G; the receiving aircraft, KB–47F. The first air refueling between jet-powered aircraft occurred in September. Despite this success, the project remained just an experiment. From the inception of the B–47 program, SAC had recognized the necessity of developing in-flight refueling for the new but fairly short-ranged plane. The command nevertheless insisted that it made more sense to use cargo aircraft as tankers than to convert expensive and critically needed strike B–47s for this role. SAC also realized the drawbacks of using cargo aircraft. The propeller-driven KC–97 picked for the task could not climb to the B–47's best altitude. This forced the bomber down to the tanker's level, wasting both time and fuel. The B–47 had a tendency to stall at slow speed, a problem which persisted for several years. To keep the bomber from stalling during refueling, the slower KC–97 at times had to begin a shallow dive to gain momentum—a nerve-racking procedure when the 2 aircraft were linked by the refueling boom. The experiment of 1953 was revived in mid-1956, not on SAC's behalf but because the KB–50s of the Tactical Air Command lacked both the altitude and speed to air-refuel new tactical fighters of the Century series. The Air Force on 23 July authorized development of a KB–47 2-drogue prototype tanker and also tried to equip the basic B–50 tanker with 2 auxiliary jet

---

[50] AMC was directed on 18 November to dispose of the 78 experimental and 58 production Rascals accepted by the Air Force.

engines. The KB–50 modification soon exceeded expectations. For that matter, work on the new KB–47 prototype also went well, except for one problem—money. By October, Boeing's initial estimate of the KB–47's price had doubled, reaching $2.7 million in April 1957. The cost was too high for a tanker never meant to be more than an interim solution. After making sure than not even Air Research and Development Command had a special need for a 2-drogue KB–47, the Air Force stopped work on the unfinished prototype and canceled the entire program on 11 July 1957.

XB–47D

Design of the XB–47D was initiated in February 1951, and 2 months later Boeing received a contract for the conversion of 2 B–47Bs. The Air Force pinned some hopes on gaining a high speed, long-range turboprop jet bomber from the project, but this was not its primary goal. The XB–47D was essentially developed to test a jet engine-prop combination and to provide data on the installation of turboprops in swept-wing aircraft.

The XB–47D closely resembled a B–47B, retaining the outboard J 47–GE–23 jet engines, while a single Curtiss-Wright YT49–W–1 engine,[51] a turboprop version of the J65 Sapphire, occupied each of the inboard nacelles (in place of the paired J–47s). A successful technical inspection in January 1952 made it seem likely that an early 1953 first flight was possible. This, however, did not materialize. To begin with the Curtiss-Wright prototype engine, with its 4-bladed propellers 15 feet in diameter, failed to pass the 50-hour qualification run. The Air Force then estimated that it would take another year before testing could resume. Continuing troubles with the engine-prop combination and shortages of government-furnished equipment delayed further progress. The first XB–47D was not flown until 26 August 1955; the second, not until 15 February 1956. Even though both aircraft accumulated a good many flying hours, no prototypes were ordered. Having served its basic purposes, the program never went beyond the experimental stage.

YB–47C

The B–47C, normally due to follow the B–47B, did not reach produc- tion. In contrast to the XB–47D, this plane was definitely intended to answer

---

[51] The prototype T–49 was a 1-spool engine; the final article, designated T–47, a 2-spool system.

SAC's requirement for an "ultimate" B-47—a bomber and reconnaissance plane having a combat radius of over 2,000 miles without air refueling. The Air Force hoped that the B-47B (Boeing's 88th production) set aside for the experiment would be ready for flight testing in late 1951. When the thrust of the selected new engines (Allison-built J35s) proved insufficient, more powerful ones had to be found. It was finally decided that the new version, now known as the YB-56, would be powered by 4 Allison J71-A-5 turbojets (still in the prototype stage). The Air Force also considered replacing some of the steel and aluminum in the airframe with titanium and magnesium (lighter materials, just as strong, but far more expensive), and of stripping the plane of its normal bombload in favor of reconnaissance equipment for a future RB-56A. The YB-56 reverted to its YB-47C designation as yet another engine later came into consideration. This final effort signaled the aircraft's doom because the engine in question was the Pratt and Whitney YJ57, yet to be available and already earmarked for the B-52. Because the prototype still lacked suitable engines and its cost could top $8.7 million, the Air Force stopped further work in December 1952. Cancellation of the YB-47C marked the end of the proposed YB-47Z—an improved version of the YB-47C, featuring side-by-side pilot seating and space for a fourth crewman. The projected RB-56As also fell by the wayside.

A specially modified Stratojet—the XB-47D—was used to test the Curtiss-Wright YT49 turboprop engine.

B–47E

Manufacturer's Model 450–157–35

Previous Model Series   B–47B

New Features

Boeing's 400th production included crew ejection seats in a revised nose section, more powerful J47–GE–25 engines,[52] and the General Electric A–5 fire-control system. This configuration, first classified as an Air Force standard, was designated B–47E. A modified landing gear allowing heavier takeoff weight appeared on the 521st and subsequent B–47Es. This configuration was labeled B–47E–II. A far stronger landing gear was incorporated in the 862d B–47 production. This last configuration of the B–47E model series was identified as the B–47E–IV. The armament of all B–47Es was changed to two 20-mm cannons, and the 18-unit internal jet-assisted take off system of early B–47Es was soon replaced by a jettisonable rack containing 33 units, each with a 1,000-pound thrust. Increasingly more efficient components equipped the B–47E and B–47E–II aircraft. Still, many later acquired the improved MA–7A bombing radar, AN/APS–54 warning radar, AN/APG–32 gun-laying radar, and other highly sophisticated electronic devices first carried by the B–47E–IV.[53] The under surfaces and lower portion of the fuselage of most B–47Es were painted a glossy white to reflect the heat from nuclear blasts.[54]

First Flight (Production Aircraft)   30 January 1953

The Air Force accepted this plane in February and took delivery of 127 similar productions before mid-year.

---

[52] Already refitted in several B–47Bs.

[53] In later years, a number of B–47E–IV bombers featured the improved MD–4 fire-control system instead of the A–5.

[54] This reflective paint was applied retroactively to some B–47Bs.

Enters Operational Service   April 1953

The B–47E first went to SAC's 303d Medium Bomb Wing, at Davis-Monthan AFB. The 22d Wing at March AFB, California, upon transfer of its early B–47Bs to Air Training Command, would be next to receive the B–47E. The new planes fell far below the improved combat configuration (WIBAC Unit 731) endorsed by the Air Force in the same month. Yet, strides were being made. Besides the added safety of ejection seats, the B–47E from the start featured an approach chute to increase drag, a brake chute to decrease landing roll, and an antiskid braking device. The discarded B–4 fire-control system could at best spray fire in the general direction of an enemy, but the new A–5 could automatically detect pursuing aircraft, track them by means of radar, and correct the firing of its two 20-mm cannons.

Program Change   September 1953

Early in 1953, just as the B–47 program was being revitalized, it seemed new and much bigger problems were on the way. President Eisenhower's defense and fiscal policies did affect the Air Force's development and procurement plans. In September, the 143-wing program was reduced to an interim 120 wings. As anticipated, the B–47 did not emerge from the crisis unscathed. Yet, all things considered, it fared well. Peak procurement, once expected to reach almost 2,200,[55] was cut by 140. But a further reduction of 200 aircraft, considered in October, was avoided. Instead the Air Force instituted a 20-month stretchout of production, pending full-scale rolling of the B–52 lines. In contrast to the B–36 program—so often on the verge of collapse—no significant attempt was ever made to cancel the B–47 production.

Force Conversion   1953–1956

The production improvement, achieved with the B–47B in 1953, did not falter. Once underway, B–47E deliveries stayed on schedule. By December, SAC had 8 B–47 Medium Bomb Wings; 1 other wing was partially equipped; 5 more had no B–47s assigned, but were scheduled to receive the

---

[55] Ten contracts—7 negotiated and 3 pending—had projected total B–47 procurement to be 2,190. Naturally, as design prime contractor, Boeing had the major portion of the business—4 contracts versus Douglas's 1 and Lockheed's 2. The 3 companies similarly farmed out 50 percent of the B–47 parts to various subcontractors scattered throughout the country.

134

new aircraft. In December 1954,[56] three months after total retirement of the B–29 bombers, the inventory counted 17 fully equipped B–47 wings. Marking the beginning of an all-jet medium bomb force in SAC, the last propeller-driven bombers (B–50s of the 97th Wing) were phased out in July 1955. Six months later, 22 medium bomb wings had received their B–47 contingents, and another 5 wings were getting ready for the new bombers. Conversion of the SAC forces did not necessarily mean that the B–47s were totally free of problems. Nevertheless, it only took until December 1956[57] for SAC to accumulate 27 combat-ready B–47 wings, a phenomenal increase from 12 wings in July of the same year.

Flying training   1953–1956

In addition to materiel failures and component shortages, training problems limited the combat readiness of SAC's B–47 wings. Some argued that the B–47—be it the earliest B–47A or the latest B–47E—was not inherently hard to fly. Others more realistically emphasized that the flying techniques for the new jet aircraft differed vastly from those for conventional bombers. By 1954, the B–47 had the lowest major accident rate per 100,000 flying hours of any jet aircraft. Still, 55 percent of the B–47 accidents were traced to human error—43 percent to pilots, and 12 percent to maintenance crews. First the size of the crew was unusually small for this type of aircraft—3 men performing the functions of pilot, copilot/gunner, and bombardier/navigator. And although the 10 or 12 crewmembers of a B–29 worked with 130 instruments, the B–47's 3-man crew confronted more than 300 gauges, dials, switches, levers, and the like. Moreover, as a true expert noted, the B–47 was relatively difficult to land and terribly unforgiving of mistakes or inattention. Although often admired, respected, cursed, or even feared, the B–47 was almost never loved.[58] Even so, training progressed. In June 1954, Boeing indoctrination teams began keeping crews up to date on the B–47's limitations and stresses, and teaching techniques that would assure maximum performance under safe conditions. This new program was received with such enthusiasm that it was promptly expanded.

---

[56] The 3 contractors achieved monthly peak production in 1954—Boeing rolled out 29 planes in September; Douglas, 11 in March, and Lockheed, 13 in May.

[57] SAC at the time had 1,204 combat-ready B–47 crews and 1,306 B–47 aircraft assigned.

[58] These observations were made in 1975 by Brig. Gen. Earl C. Peck, Chief of the Office of Air Force History. He knew the B–47 well, having achieved the unusual tour-de-force of saving his B–47 on take-off despite the crucial loss of one of the plane's 6 engines. Promoted to 2-star rank in 1976, General Peck became SAC's Deputy Chief of Staff for Operations in April 1977.

The radar-controlled tail turret of the B–47E featured twin 20-mm cannon.

A Boeing B–47E, with its reconfigured nose section.

Heavyweight Modifications   1955–1959

The Air Force received its first B–47E–IV in February 1955. The reinforced landing gear of this "heavyweight" production and subsequent ones permitted heavier take-off weights, a significant achievement in the Air Force's quest for range extension.[59] The B–47E–IV had a take-off weight of 230,000 pounds—precisely 28,000 pounds more than previously permissible. Since the additional weight was largely allotted to fuel load, the B–47E–IV had a combat radius of 2,050 nautical miles. This was almost twice the distance demonstrated 5 years before by the initial B–47s and about 300 nautical miles farther than earlier B–47Es, already equipped with somewhat stronger landing gears.[60] The Air Force decided in March 1955 that in the next 4 years all active B–47s would be brought up to the heavyweight configuration. The modifications consisted of changing the aft landing gear and adding an emergency elevator boost system to ensure safe flights in spite of the increased weight. The forthcoming post-production changes were priced at $9.2 million, but the Air Force deemed them well worth the cost.

New Operational Requirements   1955–1956

About the time the much improved heavyweight B–47E–IV entered the inventory, more requirements were levied on the aircraft. Early in 1955,[61] after initial escape-maneuver tests had convinced SAC that the B–47 might be rugged enough for low-level bombing, the command requested a

---

[59] This had been a tricky undertaking from the start. Normally, range extension meant weight reduction. Yet, back in 1952, while some engineers tried to reduce the aircraft's weight, others needed to add equipment to improve mission performance. The solution at the time appeared to rest on better engines and lighter airframe materials, as proposed for the B–47C. When this did not succeed, SAC suggested modification of the B–47's tandem landing gear.

[60] The B–47E–II, the first range-extended B–47, reached the Air Force in August 1953, after being also brought up to the improved combat configuration that had been endorsed earlier in the year. After flight-testing the stability of the modified plane, the Air Force flew it to find out if still higher gross weight take-offs could be possible. This paved the way for the heavyweight B–47E–IV.

[61] The year started auspiciously. The B–47E–IV was available, and the first B–47 for thermonuclear weapons had been delivered in January. Although the production-line modification of the aircraft had been made without awaiting the results of a concurrent flight test, the Air Force was not overly concerned. Most of the essential equipment had been installed on the aircraft, and only minor changes would be needed to ready it for combat. Justifying the Air Force's confidence, more than 1,100 B–47s could handle the new thermonuclear bombs by the end of April 1956.

further immediate check. There were many potential benefits. High-speed B–47s, flying at low-level, would be less vulnerable—more difficult for enemy radars to track and less likely to be intercepted by fighter aircraft, ground fire, or surface-to-air missiles. Increasingly sophisticated enemy defenses would be double-tasked, facing both high- and low-level attacks. The Air Staff swiftly endorsed SAC's request, but testing came to an abrupt halt after the loss of a low-flying B–47 over Bermuda. Low-level flight tests were not resumed until Boeing and the Air Research and Development Command assured Air Proving Ground Command that the B–47's structural integrity was not in doubt. In June a 6,000-pound dummy bomb was successfully released during a 2.6G-pullup from level flight, and an 8,850-pound practice bomb was properly dropped from a 2.5G-pullup in another flight. In both instances, release took place during the early portion of an Immelmann turn and the low-altitude bombing system functioned respectably.[62] In December 1955, SAC asked that 150 B–47s be modified by Boeing for low-level flight. This was authorized in May 1956.[63] At the time, however, the Air Staff reserved approval of the same modification for other B–47s, even though SAC pointed out that AMC might do the work as part of the aircraft's IRAN program.

Special Training   1955–1959

The B–47's low-level flying task entailed special training requirements. These had been anticipated by SAC in Hairclipper, a training program begun in December 1955. Adverse weather, excessive maintenance requirements due to low-level flying, and personnel losses to other training programs combined to hamper progress. Unexpected and serious LABS deficiencies in the low-altitude bombing systems, as well as several accidents in December

---

[62] Development of the low-altitude bombing system dated back to 1952, and the low-level bombing tactic was not new. SAC's fighter-bomber pilots had been trained to fly at low-level and the command's F–84s had been modified for this purpose. But this did not really create a precedent. One could hardly compare the 200,000-pound (design loaded weight) B–47 with aircraft of the F–84 type. The B–47's thin wings covered a span of more than 116 feet. Empty, the B–47E weighed almost 80,000 pounds. In contrast, the F–84 had a wing span of about 36 feet and its empty weight was under 12,000 pounds.

[63] One year later, the Air Force made public its revolutionary strategic bombing tactic. Use of the B–47 for "toss bombing" was revealed at Eglin AFB in May 1957, during aerial firepower demonstrations before a joint civilian orientation group. (In a toss-bombing attack, the plane entered the run at low altitude, pulled up sharply into a half loop with a half roll on top, and released the weapon at a predetermined point in the climb. The bomb continued upward in a high arc, falling on the target at a considerable distance from its point of release. Meanwhile, the maneuver allowed the airplane to reverse its direction and gave it more time to speed away from the target.)

1957, were the final blows. General Power, SAC's Commander in Chief since 1 July 1957,[64] officially discontinued Hairclipper on 5 March 1958. Yet, demise of the training program did not signify the end of low-level flying. Pop Up, a related training program that took advantage of concurrent advances in weapons developments, fared better.[65] Interrupted in April 1958, when fatigue cracks in the wing structure of some B–47s led to severe flying restrictions, Pop Up resumed in September after the aircraft had been thoroughly checked. Going strong in 1959, this program had practically reached its training goal by year's end.

Structural Modifications   1958–1959

The discovery of fatigue cracks in the B–47's wings and a rash of new flying accidents in early 1958 triggered an immense inspection and repair program. Nicknamed Milk Bottle and started in May 1958, the program involved all 3 manufacturers, although AMC manpower and facilities carried the largest load. More likely to suffer fatigue because of extensive low-level flying training, B–47s of the 306th and 22d Bomb Wings were the first to enter the Milk Bottle program—receiving an interim fix in advance of the permanent repair being devised by Boeing. The interim fix called for a major inspection of suspect areas. After disassembly to reveal the affected structures, each bolt hole was reamed oversized. A boroscope and dye penetrant were used to locate possible cracks. If any were found, the holes were reamed again. The same kind of procedure was used on the milk bottle fittings. B–47s with no further problems—457 of them—were returned to service after receiving the interim fix, which generally required about 1,700 manhours per bomber. Optimistically, as it turned out, Boeing estimated these planes would last about 400 hours before requiring further modifications. The so-called "ultimate" or permanent Milk Bottle repairs were far more involved, leading to no less than 9 technical orders. Briefly stated, the repairs covered primarily the splice that joined outer and inner wing panels; the area where the lower wing skin met the fuselage and, finally, the milk bottle pin (for which the program was named) and surrounding forging located on the forward part of the fuselage, near the navigator's escape hatch. The entire endeavor proved time consuming as well as expensive—

---

[64] General Power succeeded General LeMay, who became Air Force Vice Chief of Staff in July 1957.

[65] The Pop Up tactic also put much less stress on the B–47's flexible wings than low-altitude toss-bombing. In the Pop Up maneuver, the aircraft swept in at low-level, pulled up to high altitude, released its weapon, then dove steeply to escape enemy radars.

fund obligations reaching $15 million by mid-year. But there were results. By the end of July, 1,230 B–47s had been through Milk Bottle, and 895 of them had already been returned to operational units. Considering its magnitude, Milk Bottle proceeded remarkably well, with most of the fleet modified by October. When the program ended in June 1959, only a few of the interim-repaired aircraft still needed work, which could be done during the regular inspect-and-repair-as-necessary cycle. While Milk Bottle did not solve all problems, it put safety back into the workhorse B–47, an aircraft badly needed at the time.

Unsolved Problems   1958–1959

The engineering fixes devised by Boeing for Milk Bottle showed that it was possible to identify the parts in an aircraft that were most likely to fail, but left many questions unanswered. No one could explain why primary structures in the B–47 were affected by maneuvers that the aircraft was designed to perform. General Power saw no use in turning to other aircraft unless SAC was assured they would survive low-level flying. General Power insisted that despite Boeing's evaluation of the B–47's structural life since 1956, not enough was known about aircraft service span. General LeMay agreed that weapon system producers had to give the Air Force more information on operation and its effect on metal fatigue. In addition, the Air Force and aircraft industry needed to combine their efforts. They had to expand existing programs to collect statistical maneuver-loads data, to conduct cyclic testing, and to develop better instrumentation and analytical techniques.[66] The knowledge to be gained, General LeMay thought, together with judicious application of engineering skills and maintenance funds would prevent the early retirement of aircraft, an extremely expensive alternative.[67] Yet, in any aircraft's life cycle, there was a point beyond which further repair became uneconomical. Perhaps, General LeMay noted, all that could be done to keep the aged B–47 combat ready was to correct anticipated problems.

Final Assessment   1958–1959

Devising the Milk Bottle repairs was just a beginning. While the repairs

---

[66] Wright Air Development Center was already considering the B–47's fatigue problem in May 1958 and was flight-testing a Douglas B–66 light bomber to learn more about low-altitude turbulence. Moreover, closely related projects were either in being or soon to start.

[67] Some 15 years later, low-flying B–52s continued to attest to the concept's value.

were underway, Boeing had to develop a broad structural-integrity program to determine the modification's impact on the B–47's service life. Moreover, any other potential problem areas had to be uncovered. The collapse of Boeing's cyclic test aircraft in August 1958 revealed for instance that the B–47's upper longerons—the beams running lengthwise along the fuselage—were susceptible to fatigue when the aircraft approached 2,000 hours of flying time.[68] Similar cyclic tests by Douglas and the National Aeronautics and Space Administration (NASA) did not disclose any serious deficiency until December, when NASA ceased testing after a fracture appeared near one of the B–47's wing stations. Boeing tests continued until January 1959, without duplicating NASA's discovery. But when Douglas stopped in February, after almost 10,000 test hours, its B–47 had also developed a 20-inch crack. If the cyclic testing of the late fifties truly simulated flight conditions, NASA and Douglas's findings were relatively important, since SAC's B–47s had never been individually tagged for 10,000 flying hours. In any event, there were gaps in other crucial research. The low-altitude flying program, using oscillograph recorders to track the stresses and strains of lower levels on the B–47, was far from complete. Still a decision had to be made without delay, if only to justify the purchase of other aircraft. In mid–1959, the Air Force cautiously assigned the B–47 a life expectancy of 3,300 hours.[69]

Other Setbacks   1959–1960

SAC initially wanted 1,000 B–47s modified for low-level flying. This meant fitting the aircraft with absolute altimeters, terrain clearance devices,[70] and doppler radars—the type of new equipment that would require extensive testing and lots of money. In 1959, it became evident that the B–47 would survive the Milk Bottle crisis only to face other severe problems. Because of development testing slippages and the money-saving phaseout of some B–47 wings, SAC scaled down its low-altitude requirements by half. The command did stress, however, the urgency of modifying the 500 B–47s now earmarked for low-level flying. SAC again pointed out

---

[68] This led to further inspections, the identification of 11 B–47s with defective longerons, and the Air Material Command's eventual modification of all the aircrafts' support beams.

[69] Implied was the requirement for regular rigid inspections. In addition, the Wright Air Development Center admitted that this figure was based on technical consideration only. It could change, because service life did not reflect economic or operational factors.

[70] The kind SAC needed to fly low at night or during periods of reduced visibility did not even exist in 1956.

that the aircraft lacked missile penetration aids and was marginally suited for high altitude strikes. Against improved enemy defenses, the B–47 would be obsolete in 1963 if not properly equipped for low-level flight. The Air Staff did not question SAC's justifications, but fund shortages dictated harsh decisions. Hence, in lieu of 500, only 350 B–47s would be modified for low-level flying, and the aircraft would receive simpler and much less costly equipment than asked for by SAC.[71] Obviously, the end of the B–47 was in sight.

Total B–47Es Accepted   1,341

Boeing built 691 of the 1,341 B–47Es; Douglas, 264; and Lockheed, 386.

Acceptance Rates   1953–1957

The Air Force accepted 128 B–47Es in FY 53, 405 in FY 54, 408 in FY 55, 280 in FY 56, and 120 in FY 57.

Flyaway Cost Per Production Aircraft $1.9 million

Airframe, $1,293,420; engines (installed), $262,805; electronics, $53,733; ordnance, $6,298; armament, $253,411.

Average Cost Per Flying Hour $794.00

Average Maintenance Cost Per Flying Hour $361.00

End of Production   1957

The final B–47E (Serial No. 53–6244) was delivered on 18 February to

---

[71] The Air Force had canceled in late 1958 the B–47's use of the GAM–72 Quail, a short-range decoy missile, mainly because of dollar limitations. Procurement of the GAM–67 Crossbow had already been dropped, and modification of the B–47 to protect it from infrared missiles was abandoned in mid-1959.

the 100th Bomb Wing at Pease AFB, New Hampshire. The famous "Bloody Hundreth" of World War II was the 29th and last SAC wing to be equipped with B–47s.[72]

Subsequent Model Series   RB–47E

Other Configurations   EB–47E, EB–47L, ETB–47E
                                  QB–47E and WB–47E

EB–47Es—Several B–47Es were fitted with additional electronic countermeasures equipment, primarily jammers. These EB–47Es, sometimes referred to as E–47Es, normally called for a crew of 5; otherwise, they were identical to the B–47E bombers which they were expected to accompany.[73] The EB–47Es fulfilled many different tasks. Some of the aircraft carried a special electronic countermeasures equipment rack in the bomb bay. Known as Blue Cradle EB–47Es, they only required a 3-man crew.

EB–47Ls—A number of B–47Es received communications relay equipment to allow them to serve as airborne relay stations for command post aircraft and ground communications systems. The EB–47Ls, requiring a 3-man crew, were replaced in the mid-sixties by more modern aircraft.

ETB–47E—After 1959 some B–47Es were used for training. As in the TB–47B's case, the converted ETB–47E featured a fourth crew seat for the instructor.

QB–47E—In this configuration, all armament items and non-essential equipment were removed from the B/RB–47E. Unmanned and radio-controlled, the aircraft served as missile targets. These QB–47Es were considered as nonexpendable, because of their $1.9 million unit cost, and the guided missiles used against them were programmed to make near misses. A few 3-crew QB–47Es featured telemetric and scoring devices.

WB–47E—Converted B–47Es featured nose-mounted cameras that recorded cloud formations. WB–47Es also differed from the B–47Es by carrying air-sampling and data-recording equipment in place of nuclear weapons.

Adaptation of the B–47 bomber to the weather role dated back to 1956.

---

[72] One of these wings, the 93d, had converted to B–52s in 1955.

[73] The prefix letter "E" is assigned to any aircraft equipped with special electronics for employment in a variety of related roles, such as electronic countermeasures or airborne early warning radar.

It followed General Precision Laboratories' successful modification of a SAC B–47B—a project prompted by Congress as a result of the disastrous 1954 hurricane season. The Air Weather Service of the Military Air Transport Service[74] used the modified B–47B to penetrate hurricanes and to perform other weather duties. In November 1958, the aircraft also began to help checking the accuracy of the weather satellite Tiros II. The WB–47B logged 126.5 hours of flying time before retirement in 1963, when more efficient WB–47Es became available. The weather service received the first of 34 WB–47Es on 20 March 1963. These former B–47Es, no longer needed by SAC, were modified by Lockheed at its Marietta plant. The WB–47Es began to be replaced by WC–130 and WC–135 aircraft in 1965, but total phaseout took another 3 years. The last WB–47E—the final operational B–47 in the Air Force's inventory—was delivered to Davis-Monthan AFB on 31 October 1969.

Phaseout   1957–1966

Delivery of the last B–47E coincided with the beginning of the aircraft's phaseout. Both occurred in 1957, shortly after the 93d Bomb Wing started exchanging its B–47s for more modern B–52s. The Air Force, nevertheless, expected the B–47 to be around for many years. The aircraft's accelerated retirement, as directed by President John F. Kennedy in March 1961, was delayed on 28 July by the onset of the Berlin crisis of 1961-1962. In the following years, B–47s were gradually committed to the Davis-Monthan storage facility, but it took Fast Fly, a project initiated in October 1965, to hasten the demise of the elderly plane.[75] SAC's last 2 B–47s went to storage on 11 February 1966.[76]

Item of Special Interest   December 1956

Spurred by the Suez crisis of 1956, SAC demonstrated its potential ability to launch a large striking force on short notice. Within a 2-week period in early December, more than 1,000 B–47s flew nonstop, simulated

---

[74] The Military Air Transport Service was established on 1 June 1948. It became the Military Airlift Command on 1 January 1966.

[75] SAC's last KC–97s were retired on 21 December 1965.

[76] Some RB–47s remained with the 55th Strategic Reconnaissance Wing, but not for long. However, several B–47 conversions saw many more years of duty.

combat missions, averaging 8,000 miles each (a total of 8 million miles) over the American continent and Arctic regions. Commenting on the spectacular mass flights, General Twining, Air Force's Chief of Staff since 30 June 1953, said the operation showed that the ability to deliver nuclear bombs had clearly taken the profit out of war.[77]

Record Flights   1957–1959

25 January 1957—A B–47 flew 4,700 miles from March AFB, California, to Hanscom Field, Massachusetts, in 3 hours and 47 minutes, averaging 710 miles per hour.

14 August 1957—A 321st Bomb Wing B–47 under the command of Brig. Gen. James V. Edmundson, SAC Deputy of Operations, made a record nonstop flight from Andersen AFB, Guam, to Sidi Slimane Air Base, French Morocco, a distance of 11,450 miles in 22 hours and 50 minutes. The flight required 4 refuelings by KC–97 tankers.

30 November 1959—A B–47, assigned to the Wright Air Development Center, broke previous time-and-distance records by staying aloft 3 days, 8 hours and 36 minutes and covering 39,000 miles.

Other Uses

1954—The Air Force set aside 17 B–47Es, already equipped with the necessary alternators, to test the new MA–2 bombing system earmarked for the forthcoming B–52s. The decision's purpose was 2-fold. To begin with, it would speed up testing of the MA–2. Of equal importance, the relatively large number of aircraft involved would allow the training of a cadre of MA–2 technicians. And this, in turn, would provide skilled personnel for SAC's B–52 units much sooner than otherwise possible.

1968-on—As SAC's EB–47Es neared retirement, the United States Navy acquired 2 of the planes and Douglas began modifying them in mid-1968. In addition to their Blue Cradle equipment, these 2 EB–47Es

---

[77] The United States exploded its first "droppable" hydrogen bomb in the Marshall Islands on 1 March 1954. A second U.S. thermonuclear device was successfully tested on the 20th. The tests (part of Operation Castle, an Atomic Energy Commission endeavor) confirmed that it was possible to make light-weight, high-yield thermonuclear weapons. This technical advance obviously would make aerial bombing easier. (It also had an immediate impact on the Convair surface-to-surface Atlas missile. The Atlas's restrictive performance characteristics were loosened to the point where only the "state of the art" bound the missile's continued development.)

received more passive and active electronic systems. Long-range external wing tanks were replaced with a variety of pods filled with electronic countermeasures gear. More chaff dispensers were also added. The modified EB-47Es were redesignated SMS-2 and SMS-3 as they became part of the Navy's Surface Missile System, where they were expected to be used for almost 10 years to sharpen the electronic countermeasures skills of the Fleet. The 2 were due to be retired in the late seventies and to join some other 20 B-47s on display around the country.

RB-47E

Manufacturer's Model 450-158-36

Weapon System 100L

New Features

The RB-47E differed outwardly from the B-47E in that its nose was 34 inches longer. An air-conditioned compartment in the aircraft's redesigned nose housed cameras and other sensitive equipment. Included were an optical viewfinder, photocell-operated shutters actuated by flash lighting for night photography, and intervalometers for photographs of large areas at regularly spaced intervals. The RB-47E had no bombing equipment, but the 20-millimeter tail armament and A-5 fire-control system of the B-47E were retained. A photographer/navigator replaced the bombardier in the aircraft's 3-man crew. The RB-47E also featured the internal jet-assisted take-off system of the earliest B-47Es.

First Flight (Production Aircraft)   3 July 1953

The RB-47E flew sooner than expected. Nonetheless, the problems and delays anticipated by the Air Force in March 1952 (when many B-47Bs were modified for reconnaissance) did occur. It took almost another 2 years for the RB-47E to become a real asset.

Initial Shortcoming   1953-1955

An initial RB-47E was assigned to an operational unit in November 1953. This plane featured an interim camera control system that was also due to equip temporarily the next 134 RB-47Es. The sophisticated Universal Camera Control System,[78] designed by the Air Force's Photographic

---

[78] The Universal Camera Control System provided for the simultaneous automatic operation of cameras. It also controlled shutter speeds, aperture settings, and image compensation according to ground speed, light, and altitude preset data.

Reconnaissance Laboratory, already tested on the RB–47B, and earmarked for the entire RB–47E contingent, would first appear on the 136th RB–47E. Problems with the interim camera control system soon altered the USAF plans. Because of the system's repeated failures, the Air Proving Ground Command recommended early in 1954 that further operational suitability tests of the available RB–47Es be canceled. No meaningful testing could be conducted, Air Proving Ground Command stated, without a RB–47E equipped with the universal system. This fell in line with General LeMay's thinking. The SAC Commander had already advised Maj. Gen. Clarence S. Irvine, AMC Deputy Commander for Production, that the day-and-night photo capability of the reconnaissance B–47E was unsatisfactory, be it at low or high altitude. General Irvine was quick to point out that minor improvements had been made to the interim camera control system. He willingly admitted, however, that the RB–47E's problems would not be entirely solved prior to the October delivery of the first Universal Camera Control System-equipped RB–47E production. Further discussion of the matter ended in May 1954, when the Air Staff decided that the first 135 RB–47Es would receive a simplified camera control system. This seemed to indicate that the aircraft would not undergo retrofit as originally planned and that SAC would be saddled with 2 RB–47E configurations. Although the Air Staff reversed its decision later in the month, this did not mean that all difficulties were over. Shortages of government-furnished equipment, chiefly of Universal Camera Control Systems, continued to hinder the program. The Air Force nearly reached its production total of RB–47Es by mid-1955, but many of the aircraft were not fully equipped. Yet phaseout of the 91st Strategic Reconnaissance Wing—recipient of the earliest RB–47Es—was only 2 years away.

End of Production   August 1955

The Air Force took delivery of the 4 last RB–47Es in August 1955.

Total RB–47Es Accepted   255

Acceptance Rates

The Air Force accepted 97 RB–47Es in FY 54, 139 in FY 55, and 19 in FY 56.

Flyaway Cost Per Production Aircraft $2.05 Million

Airframe, $1,409,441; engines (installed), $258,159; electronics, $49,163; ordnance, $6,303; armament and special equipment, $333,847.

Average Cost Per Flying Hour $794.00

Average Maintenance Cost per Flying Hour $361.00

Subsequent Model Series RB–47H

Other Configurations RB–47K

On 5 November 1954, the Air Force officially agreed that 15 of SAC's RB–47Es would be fitted with special equipment for both weather and photo-reconnaissance operations at low and high altitudes. These new configurations, featuring high-resolution and side-looking radars, were designated RB–47Ks.[79] The first RB–47K was delivered in December 1955, as scheduled. In essence, the aircraft was an airborne weather information gathering system. SAC wanted the RB–47K to sense, compile, record, and make inflight radio transmissions of weather data. All these tasks were to be done automatically. The RB–47K was also expected to determine the size of clouds as well as to wind speed and direction. This was a large order, and severe equipment problems remained after mid-1956, when the 55th Strategic Reconnaissance Wing reached an initial operational capability. The 55th Wing's 15 RB–47Ks were flown all over the world to provide weather data for SAC and to sample fallouts from foreign nuclear blasts. They were phased out in the early sixties, when some of the last and more efficient B–47Es were modified to assume the weather role.

---

[79] USAF delivery ledgers did not list the RB–47Ks because the 15 aircraft were conditionally accepted as RB–47Es, but Boeing accomplished the complex modification before the aircraft left the Wichita plant. This saved time and money. The entire work was done in 5 months and cost less than $5 million.

Phaseout   **1957–1967**

The RB–47E phaseout followed the B–47E's pattern, and the first RB–47E (Serial No. 51–5272) was sent to storage at Davis-Monthan AFB on 14 October 1957. Nevertheless, a number of reconnaissance B–47s (mostly RB–47Hs) kept on serving SAC for another decade.

RB-47H

Manufacturer's Model 450-172-51

Previous Model Series   RB-47E

New Features

A separate pressurized compartment in the area formerly occupied by the short bomb bay housed the aircraft's new electronic reconnaissance and electronic countermeasures equipment as well as 3 operators—bringing the RB-47H's crew to a total of 6.

Basic Development   June 1951

General requirements for electronic countermeasures were established in mid-1951. A detailed configuration was made firm in 1952 because, as Lt. Gen. Laurence C. Craigie, Deputy Chief of Staff for Development, put it, "losses to the potential enemy air defense system would be very high," unless the B-47 possessed the capability to counter them. As initially set up, the Air Force's electronic countermeasures program reflected postwar technological advancements as well as state-of-the-art limits. Five phases were planned. Phases I through IV would provide successively more effective self-protection equipment, such as transmitters and chaff for jamming enemy signals. Phase V would install a 2-man pod in the B-47's bomb bay for escort protection. This beginning, as modest as it might seem, would not come easily. Yet, the urgency was great. On 29 December 1952, General Twining, Air Force Vice Chief of Staff, wrote Boeing's President, William M. Allen, to urge that "the necessary engineering leading to an effective capability be accomplished as speedily as possible." SAC, nonetheless, kept on believing that procuring the desired B-47, specially equipped for electronic countermeasures would take several years. In any case, other requirements needed to be addressed.[80]

---

[80] As previously indicated, most of these requirements were fulfilled between 1953 and 1955. As of 1956, 978 B-47s incorporated basic electronic countermeasures devices. Others carried so-called Phase 2, Phase 3, or Phase 4 equipment. Twelve reconnaissance RB-47s featured the removable Phase V, 2-man capsule, initially requested.

On 25 June 1953, General Power, SAC's Vice Commander, stressed that the command actually needed more advanced technology than promised by Phase V. In short, a so-called Phase VII electronic reconnaissance apparatus had to be permanently installed in a number of B–47s in place of the planned 2-man pod. These electronic B–47s would ferret out enemy radar defenses and would replace the RB–50s, RB–36s, and modified B–29s which lacked the speed to do such work.

Program Changes   1953–1955

As requested by SAC, the RB–47H program was amended. The RB–47H's initial 2-man pod was replaced by a permanent pressurized compartment that enclosed equipment and 3 additional crew members—then referred to as electronic countermeasures observers. In 1955, the number of aircraft in the program was brought to 35—a 5-aircraft increase.

Enters Operational Service   1955–1956

The first RB–47H reached the 55th Strategic Reconnaissance Wing, Forbes AFB, Kansas, on 9 August 1955, after considerable slippage due to production difficulties. Although most of the RB–47Hs had been received by the end of 1956, the 55th Wing still had problems. Besides its operational commitments, the 55th was responsible for "organizing and training a force capable of immediate and sustained strategic electronic reconnaissance and air-to-air refueling on short notice in any part of the world, utilizing the latest technical knowledge, equipment, and techniques." Combat crew training was delayed from the start by the aircraft's late deliveries. Faulty engines in the first available RB–47Hs and the fuel leaks of subsequent aircraft likewise hampered training. Excessive noise in the aircraft's pressurized compartment did not help either. By the end of 1956, many of these problems had been ironed out, but none of the RB–47Hs was fully and effectively equipped.

Post-Production Modifications   1956–1957

The absence of an automatic electronic direction finder was the RB–47H's most crucial deficiency. Two pioneer productions of the required direction finder finally became available in December 1956. Each was immediately installed by Douglas (at the company's Tulsa plant), and the 2 newly equipped RB–47Hs reached the 55th Wing in January 1957. As could be expected, the many relatively untested components in these direction finders caused more problems. Their seriousness resulted in the establishment of a joint military and civilian committee to assist testing and operation.[81] Additional direction finders were received in March and the RB–47H's first modification program began. Basically, it called for the installation of 1 automatic electronic direction finder in each RB–47H. Numerous related adjustments were necessary, however. Just the same, the work was done promptly, on base, by Douglas personnel.

Total RB–47Hs Accepted   35

Boeing built the 35 planes.

Acceptance Rates   1956–1957

The Air Force accepted 30 RB–47Hs in FY 56 and 5 more during the following fiscal year—the last 2 in January 1957.

Flyaway Cost Per Production Aircraft[82] $2.1 million

Airframe, $1,588,723; engines (installed), $273,449; electronics, $54,877; ordnance, $8,271; armament, $201,597.

Average Cost Per Flying Hour $794.00

Average Maintenance Cost Per Flying Hour $389.00

---

[81] Members of this committee included representatives from the Boeing Aircraft Company, the Federal Telecommunications Laboratory, the Strategic Air Command, the Wright Air Development Center, and the Oklahoma Air Materiel Area. Within a month, the committee's work led to the selection of proper test equipment, the development of appropriate maintenance procedures, and the design and manufacture of an oscilloscope calibration instrument to reduce maintenance time.

[82] As noted earlier, the flyaway cost of any production aircraft never included the engineering and modification cost incurred after approval of a basic contract.

End of Production   1957

The Air Force took delivery of its last 2 RB–47Hs in January.

Major Retrofit   1960–1962

Although the RB–47H's post-production modifications of 1957 were satisfactory and the aircraft was practically unique, SAC had to keep pace with incessant technological advances. New requirements and the development of more sophisticated equipment soon required a reconfiguration of the RB–47H's special compartment. A mockup inspection in September 1959 was followed in August 1960 by the first flight of a refitted RB–47H. The plane, besides its 6 radar sets, carried some of the most modern electronics. The RB–47H prototype of 1960 was put together by Boeing, but other RB–47Hs were retrofitted in Tulsa by Douglas. The first reconfigured aircraft was returned to the 55th Wing in November 1961.[83]

Subsequent Model Series   None

Other Configurations   EB–47H/ERB–47H

The EB–47H, for a time designated ERB–47H, was an RB–47H that carried special electronic "ferret" equipment. As such, the 3 planes so modified by Boeing before the end of 1957 were able to detect, locate, record, and analyze electromagnetic radiations.

Phaseout   29 December 1967

On 29 December, SAC's last B–47 type aircraft, an RB–47H (Serial No. 53–4296) of the 55th Wing, was flown to Davis-Monthan AFB for storage. Completion of the RB–47H phaseout came exactly 20 years after the initial flight of the experimental B–47.

---

[83] Seventeen months before, an RB–47H flying over the Bering Sea had been shot down by Soviet fighters. This RB–47H loss closely followed the U–2 incident of May 1960.

154

Program Recap

The Air Force accepted a grand total of 2,041 B–47s (including the first 2 experimental planes and the prototype of a never-produced configuration). Specifically, the B–47 program comprised 2 XB–47s, 10 B–47As (mostly used for testing), 397 B–47Bs, 1 YB–47C, 1,341 B–47Es, 255 RB–47Es, and 35 RB–47Hs. All other B–47s in the Air Force's opertional inventory, be they weather reconnaissance aircraft (WB–47Es), ETB–47E combat crew trainer, QB–47 drones, or others, were acquired through post-production reconfigurations.

TECHNICAL AND BASIC MISSION PERFORMANCE DATA

B/RB–47 AIRCRAFT

Manufacturer (Airframe)	Boeing Airplane Co., Seattle, Wash.; Douglas Aircraft Co., Tulsa, Okla.; Lockheed Aircraft Corp., Marietta, Ga.			
(Engines)	The General Electric Co., Schenectady, N.Y.			
Nomenclature	Strategic Medium Bomber and Reconnaissance Aircraft			
Popular Name	Stratojet			

	B–47A	B–47B	B–47E–IV	RB–47H
Length/Span	106.8/116	106.8/116	107.116	108.7/116.3
Wing Area (sq ft)	1,428	1,428	1,428	1,428
Weights (lb)				
Empty	73,240	78,102	79,074	89,230[a]
Combat	106,060	122,650	133,030	139,000[a]
Takeoff[b]	157,000	185,000	230,000	195,133
Engine: Number, Rated Power per Engine & Designation	(6) 5,200-lb st J47–GE–11	(6) 5,910-lb st J47–GE–23	(6) 7,200-lb st J47–GE–25 or 25A	(6) 7,200-lb st J47–GE–25
Takeoff Ground Run (ft)				
At Sea Level	6,000	9,100	10,400	7,800
At Sea Level with Assisted Take-Off	Not Applicable	7,200	7,350	
Over 50-ft Obstacle	7,210	10,650	12,000	9,300
Over 50-ft Obstacle with Assisted Take-Off	Not Applicable	8,650	8,800	
Rate of Climb (fpm)				
at Sea Level	3,375	2,560	1,850	2,500
Combat Rate of Climb (fpm) at Sea Level	6,200 (mil power)	4,775 (max power)	4,350 (max power)	3,700
Service Ceiling (ft) (100 fpm Rate of Climb to Altitude)	38,100	33,900	29,500	31,500
Combat Ceiling (ft) (500 fpm Rate of Climb to Altitude	44,300	40,800	39,300	37,600
Average Cruise Speed (kn)	424	433	435	424
Max Speed at Optimum Altitude (kn/ft)	521/8,800	528/16,300	528/16,300	516/15,000
Combat Radius (nm)	1,350	1,704	2,050	1,520
Total Mission Time (hr)	6.45	8.27	9.42	6.4
Armament	None	2.50-cal guns	2 20-mm M24A1 guns	2 20-mm M24A1 guns
Crew	3	3	3	6
Max Bombload[c] (lb)	22,000	25,000	25,000	845[d]

---

[a] Pod and strut included.

[b] Limited by the strength of the aircraft's landing gear.

[c] Bombloads could be made of various combinations—World War II box fins, interim conical fins, and so-called new series. The B–47B was also capable of carrying one 25,000-pound general-purpose bomb.

[d] Instead of bombs, the RB–47H carried cameras and 845 pounds of chaff.

BASIC MISSION NOTE

All basic mission performance data based on maximum power, except as otherwise indicated.

Combat Radius Formula:

B–47A—Not applicable, since this model was used mostly for testing.

RB–47H—Not available.

B–47B—Took off and climbed on course to optimum cruise altitude at normal power. Cruised out at long-range speeds, increasing altitude with decreasing airplane weight. Climbed to reach cruise ceiling 15 minutes from target. Ran-in to target at normal power, dropped bombs, conducted 2-minute evasive action and 8-minute escape from target at normal power. Cruised back to home base at long-range speeds, increasing altitude with decreasing airplane weight. Range-free allowances included 5-minute normal-power fuel consumption for starting engines and take-off, 2-minute normal-power fuel consumption at combat altitude for evasive action, and 30 minutes of maximum endurance (4 engines) fuel consumption at sea level plus 5 percent of initial fuel load for landing reserve.

B–47E–IV—Took off and climbed on course to initial cruising altitude. Cruised at long-range speeds and altitudes, dropping external tanks when empty. Climbed to cruise ceiling and conducted a 15-minute level-flight bomb run at normal-rated thrust. Dropped bombload and chaff and conducted a 2-minute evasive action and 8-minute escape at normal-rated thrust. Returned to base at long-range speeds and altitudes. Range-free allowances were: fuel for 5 minutes at normal-rated thrust at sea level for take-off allowance, 2 minutes at normal-rated thrust at combat altitude for evasive action, and 30 minutes at maximum endurance airspeeds at sea level plus 5 percent of initial fuel loads for landing reserve.

B–50 Superfortress

Boeing
Airplane Company

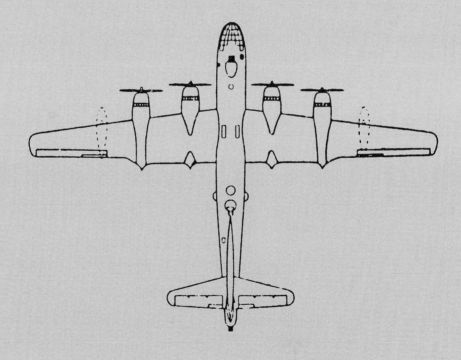

B–50 Superfortress
Boeing

Manufacturer's Model 345-2

Overview

The B–50's development was approved in 1944, when the aircraft was known as the B–29D. Still in the midst of war, the Army Air Forces (AAF) wanted a significantly improved B–29 that could carry heavy loads of conventional weapons faster and farther. As World War II ended, the production of thousands of B–29s was canceled. The B–29D survived, but its purpose was changed. Redesignated as the B–50 in December 1945, the improved bomber was now earmarked for the atomic role. The decision was prompted by the uncertain fate of Convair B–36, the first long-range, heavy bomber produced as an atomic carrier. Of course, some of the B–29s that had been modified to carry the atomic bomb remained available, and surplus B–29s were being reconfigured for the atomic task. Just the same, the B–29s of war vintage were nearly obsolete. Hence, they would have to be replaced by a more efficient, atomic-capable bomber pending availability of the intercontinental B–36 or of another bomber truly suitable for the delivery of atomic weaponry.

While the short-range B–50 was immediately recognized as a stopgap measure, the magnitude of the aircraft's development problems proved unexpected. The B–50's first difficulties stemmed from its bomb bay which, like that of the B–29, was too small to house the new bomb and its required components. The fast development of special weapons created more complications, since the individual components of every single type of bomb had to be relocated within the bomb bay's narrow confines.

In keeping with the usual vicissitudes accompanying the development of any new or improved aircraft, the B–50 soon exhibited engine malfunctions. Then, cracking of the metal skin on the trailing edge of the wings and flaps dictated extensive modifications. And while these problems were being resolved, new requirements were levied on the aircraft. In 1949, as the proposed RB–36 remained a long way off, and because of the older RB–29's deficiencies in speed, range, and altitude, some B–50s had to be fitted for the reconnaissance role. To make matters worse, fuel tank overflows, leaking fuel check valves, failures of the engine turbo-chargers, generator defects, and the like continued to plague every B–50 version.

Meanwhile, contrary to plans, most B–50s came off the production lines without the receiver end of the new air-to-air refueling system being developed by Boeing. Additional, and successful, modifications therefore ensued. Nevertheless, the Strategic Air Command (SAC) had no illusions. The B–50, along with the B–36 (first delivered in June 1948), would be obsolete in 1951. That the B–50 did not start leaving the SAC inventory before 1953 was due to the production problems and many modifications of its replacement: the subsonic B–47.

Basic Development   1939

As an outgrowth of the B–29, the B–50 can be traced back to July 1939, when Boeing Airplance Company introduced Model 334A, the B–29's first direct ancestor.[1] Specifically, however, the B–50 bomber stemmed from a B–29 conversion, initiated in 1944.[2]

Initial Procurement   February 1940

Requirements for the B–29 Superfortress, from which the B–29D (later known as the B–50) derived, were issued in February 1940, when the Army Air Corps asked the aircraft industry to submit designs for a "Hemisphere Defense Weapon." Boeing Model 345 (a further development of Model 334A) was adjudged best of all proposals for bombers with very-long-range

---

[1] Model 334A was actually started in March 1938, when the Army Air Corps asked Boeing to design a pressurized version of its B–17 Flying Fortress. Development of the new pressurized model with tricycle undercarriage was hampered by the Army's lack of money in pre-war years. But Boeing, being aware of the Air Corps' interest, went ahead with the project and managed, still without government funds, to build a mockup of the more refined Model 334A.

[2] The single Boeing Model Number 345 was used for all production versions of the B–29, which in 1942 was the heaviest aeroplane in the world to go into production. The B–29B was the highest designation assigned to a production B–29 model. The B–29C designation was intended for a B–29, earmarked to test new developments of the R–3350 engines, but the project did not materialize. All higher designations identified the purposes of the basic aircraft's various reconfigurations.

characteristics, and the company was authorized in September 1940 to produce the first very heavy bomber to incorporate pressure-cabin installations and other radical changes in design and armament. Development of an improved version of the famed B-29 began in 1944, as a so-called Phase II evolution of the basic design. No specific requirements ensued, but the main intent was to equip the improved bomber with the new Pratt & Whitney R-4360 Wasps and to do away with existing and often troublesome versions of the Curtiss-Wright R-3350 radial engines. The B-29A assigned to the Phase II development project, once reconfigured with the new Wasp engines, was flown by Boeing as the YB-44 prototype. The AAF approved within a few months a production version of the YB-44, which was then designated as the B-29D, and ordered 200 production models of the improved bomber in July 1945.

Procurement Reduction   December 1945

Japan's surrender on 14 August, 3 months after the defeat of Nazi Germany, prompted the cancellation of military procurement. In the process, the 200 B-29Ds on order since July 1945 were reduced to 60 in December of the same year.

New Designation   December 1945

The B-29D became the B-50 in December 1945. Officially, the aircraft's new designation was justified by the changes separating the B-29D from its predecessors. However, according to Peter M. Bowers, a well-known authority on Boeing aircraft, "the redesignation was an outright military ruse to win appropriations for the procurement of an aeroplane that by its designation appeared to be merely a later version of an existing model that was being canceled wholesale, with many existing examples being put into dead storage."[3]

In any case, the former B-29D featured many changes. The redesignated aircraft, built with a stronger but lighter grade of aluminum, had larger flaps, a higher vertical tail (that could be folded down to ease storage in standard size hangars), a hydraulic rudder boost, nose wheel steering, a more efficient undercarriage retracting mechanism, and a new electrical

---

[3] Restoration of peace, as precarious as it already appeared to be, prevented the production of nearly 5,000 B-29s (still on order in September 1945), and thousands of operational B-29s became surplus—at least, temporarily.

device to remove the ice from the pilot's windows. The new aircraft's wings and empennage also could be thermally de-iced. Finally, the 4 higher-thrust Pratt & Whitney R–4360 engines that replaced the standard B–29's R–3350s gave a power increase of 59 percent, and electrically controlled, reversible-pitch propellers allowed the use of engine power as an aid to braking on short or wet runways. There was also some rearrangement of the crew. Yet, no matter what designation, there was no doubt that the piston-powered B–29D/B–50 would seem antiquated in the post-war era of jet bombers.[4]

Program Change   1945–1947

The AAF began to plan for an atomic strike force in the first few months of peace that followed the end of World War II. It ordered that 19 additional B–29s be reconfigured as atomic carriers in July 1946,[5] six months after the improved B–29D had become the B–50. Most likely, the AAF already planned that the redesignated bombers would first supplement the reconfigured B–29s and then replace them until a better atomic carrier became available. But the AAF at the time was not in a particularly strong position to press for what it believed to be essential.[6] Hence, the true purpose of the B–50 program did not become official until the spring of 1947.

Production Decision   24 May 1947

The decision to produce the B–50A, first model of the B–50 series, was confirmed on 24 May 1947, nearly 2 years after the aircraft's initial procurement had been authorized.

Procurement Data   1946–1949

Official records revealed that 60 B–29s were authorized for procurement

---

[4] See B–36, pp 11–12.

[5] Modification of the B–29 aircraft to carry the first atomic bombs began early in 1944. Less than half of the 46 modified B–29s remained operational by November 1946. Unlike the first modifications, which were handmade, improvement of the additional B–29s would consist essentially of a standard installation.

[6] The AAF was still subordinate to the War Department prior to its recognition as a separate department within the National Military Establishment in September 1947.

The Boeing B–50, an improved version of the B–29 adapted to carry atomic weapons.

in fiscal year (FY) 1946; 73 B–50s in FY 47; 82 in FY 48, and 132 in FY 49. Production of the last B–50 type, a trainer, as decided on 4 May 1951, did not entail any new procurement, only the amendment of an order previously increased for a different model. This order involved an extra 24 aircraft, the quantity eventually built in the trainer configuration. Procurement logs did not reflect such transactions, but the lack of specific procurement data, contract identifications, exact dates, and the like was not unusual.[7] The aircraft's historical documentation in the immediate post–World War II period often proved meager. In the B–50's case, however, the paucity of details was most likely due to the secrecy which shrouded the project from the start. Nevertheless, the B–50 program's production total was accurately recorded. This total reached 370 aircraft, including the first 60 planes ordered as B–29Ds, but excluding 1 prototype, taken out of the FY 47 procurement order, built in 1949, and paid for with development funds.

Testing   1947–1957

Officially, there were no experimental or prototype B–50s. In actuality, 7 of the 79 B–50As produced by Boeing were allocated to testing.[8] The first B–50A, Serial No. 46–002, initially flew on 25 June 1947, was accepted by the Air Force on 16 October and delivered on the 31st. The airplane was salvaged at Eglin AFB, Florida, on 12 July 1957, after being finally used to verify a stellar monitoring inertial bombing system. Little remains known of the first aircraft's use during the interim 10 years. It was flown a grand total of 769 hours, of which Boeing logged 324 hours and 13 minutes in 176 flights. The aircraft was also lent to the Bell Aircraft Corporation, which flew it 69 times for a total of 199 hours. The test aircraft then stayed with the A. C. Spark Plug Company of Detroit, Michigan, for almost 2 years, from 26 February 1954 to January 1956. During this time, more than 156 hours were accumulated in 43 flights. Air Force pilots flew the remaining 89 hours, and available reports revealed that Air Materiel Command (AMC) made 4 flights of about 6 hours at the Boeing plant before the aircraft's delivery in October 1947. The first B–50A accepted by the Air Force was reclassified as an EB–50A in March 1949, a classification assigned to any aircraft being modified for the electronic countermeasures role or other related purposes. The aircraft retained this classification until January 1956, when it became

---

[7] See B–45, p 71.

[8] Numerous other B–50s underwent many tests, but in contrast to the 7 aircraft specifically earmarked for testing, they eventually became part of the operational forces.

known as a JB–50A, indicating that the aircraft was then used for the testing of special instrumentation.

The second B–50A, Serial No. 46–003, accepted by the Air Force also in October, followed its predecessor's path. It was designated EB–50A in November 1947, 1 month after being formally accepted, sent back to Boeing in October 1949, returned to the Air Force on 15 February 1950, and again lent to Boeing in June of the same year. The second EB–50A continued to be tested at the Boeing plant until January 1952, but was retained by the Air Force from then on. The rest of the airplane's operational life was given over to testing, by both Air Research and Development Command and AMC. Most of this was done at Aberdeen, Maryland, where the aircraft was involved in a fatal crash on 24 November 1952. Available records indicate that Air Force pilots only flew the plane 59 times.[9] Five of the other B–50As, earmarked for testing from the start, were obviously used to devise the special modifications required by the upgraded and highly classified atomic program. Basic testing data, therefore was also highly classified and strictly disseminated. An extra and vastly improved B–50A[10] was entirely confined to testing in order to develop the canceled B–54.

Production Slippage   1947–1948

The AAF thought that some B–50s would be available in September 1947, and that 36 of the aircraft would be immediately delivered to the Air Materiel Command for atomic modification. It was also believed the programmed modifications would be easier to accomplish than the latest performed on the B–29s, because part of the work would have already been done in production. These estimates proved wrong. Slow delivery of the B–50 postponed the beginning of the modification program to 1 February 1948, and the time spent modifying each B–50 jumped from an estimated 3,500 to some 6,000 manhours. In retrospect, however, there seems to have been scant ground for criticism. The B–50 modification program, together with that of the B–29, promised all along to be complex. As it turned out, the project became far more involved than anticipated.

Special Modifications   1948–1949

As an improved version of the B–29, the modifications of the B–50 were

---

[9] This figure was obtained from test reports on record at the Air Force Flight Test Center and the Federal Records Center at St. Louis, Mo.

[10] Air Force ledgers excluded the plane from the B–50A total. This was the aircraft that was logged as a prototype and paid for with development funds.

of necessity closely interlaced with those performed on the basic aircraft. For the same reason, aware that the B–50's performance would be only slightly better than that of the B–29, the Air Staff by late 1949 had ceased to contemplate large-scale production of the plane.[11] The B–50 was to be a stopgap, to be used until an aircraft more suitable for the delivery of atomic weapons became available. Its extended operational life in this role was dictated by circumstances, not by choice. Therefore, additional, unanticipated modifications became necessary and proved costly.

As directed by the Joint Chiefs of Staff in January 1948—when the B–36 program appeared once again on the verge of collapse[12] and only 3 B–50s had been delivered—the large-scale atomic project to improve SAC's operating capability called for numerous separate projects. Modification of bombers to carry new atomic bombs was the primary requirement, but other required changes were important. The bombers needed a greater range, which meant that they would have to be modified for in-flight refueling and tankers would be needed. In addition, the bombers would have to fly in the worst climate, which also meant that most of them would have to be winterized. Finally, the Joint Chiefs' project required that several bombers be fitted with electronics that could withstand the cold weather of the arctic, and that other significant modifications be made to various types of aircraft in order to make sure that the atomic carriers would be given the best chances of survival.[13]

Inevitably, estimates of modification costs proved highly unrealistic. To make matters worse, the many extra modifications directed by the Joint Chiefs of Staff took place when money was particularly scarce.[14] For example, in August 1948 lack of funds nearly stopped the B–50 modifications being done at the Boeing-Wichita Plant. Moreover, as time went by

---

[11] The Strategic Air Command at the time was increasingly concerned by the long-term problem of developing an atomic carrier of great effectiveness. The command had already admitted that the B–50 (along with the B–36) would become obsolescent after 1951, and that no practical means existed to extend the B–50's life (as well as that of the B–29) beyond 1955. The initial production slippage, various deficiencies, and limited speed of the subsonic B–47, due to supplant the B–50, were serious. SAC's predicament was compounded by the arguments clouding the development of the B–52, which the command believed was the aircraft best suited not only to take over the B–36's task but also to assume most facets of the overall atomic mission.

[12] See B–36, pp 20–21.

[13] There were delays, but these goals were reached. Reactivated B–29s were modified as refueling tankers; reactivated B–29s and incoming B–50s were modified for reconnaissance; F–80 and F–84 escorts were prepared to provide the required protection, and new C–97 transports were bought to support the bombers.

[14] See B–36, pp 25–26.

and a variety of more sophisticated bombs entered the stockpile, the program's complexity grew and new modifications were needed. Obviously, overall costs also rose.

Meanwhile, three-fourths of the additional bombers earmarked by the Joint Chiefs to carry new atomic bombs had received the necessary primary modifications by 15 December 1948. In addition, except for 15 B-50As, all modified bombers had received new standard electronics. Every one of the 72 B-50As involved in the project had been winterized; 57 of them had been fitted for air refueling, and 15 had been given arctic electronics. Production difficulties, program changes, and funding uncertainties delayed some of the modifications. But, save for a few minor exceptions, the Air Force met the Joint Chiefs' extended completion deadline of 15 February 1949.[15]

As usual, modification of the B-50As and of other aircraft connected with the project was split into 2 phases. The contractor, Boeing in the B-50's case, installed all items that became an integral part of the bomber, while removable parts were furnished as "kits" to Strategic Air Command units which then completed the installation.[16]

Enters Operational Service   1948–1949

B-50A deliveries to SAC's 43d Bombardment Wing, at Davis-Monthan AFB, Arizona, began in June 1948,[17] and by the end of the year 34 B-50As were on hand. Nevertheless, a true initial operational capability was not gained until 1949. Problems of all sorts contributed to the delay. In June 1948, the 43d Wing had only 25 percent of the parts required for the new aircraft, and most of the available parts consisted of bolts, nuts, and gaskets. Even though about 25 percent of the B-50A parts were interchangeable with B-29 parts, and some others could be manufactured locally, the wing considered its parts shortages intolerable. Expedients, such as pilot pickup of parts either from the factory or from AMC depots, would "not be feasible with a large number of aircraft." In addition, since only 60 percent

---

[15] Besides the B-50As, B-29s, B-36s, F-80s, and C-97s were included in the first modification package directed by the Joint Chiefs of Staff. The overall cost was high. It took $35.5 million to rejuvenate, modify, or adapt a grand total of 227 aircraft.

[16] Certain classified portions of the bombers' new configurations were assembled by the Sacramento Air Materiel Area of the Air Materiel Command into special kits, designated "X" kits. These kits also were installed in the field by personnel of the Strategic Air Command.

[17] A single B-50A (Serial #46-017) reached the 43d Wing on 20 February 1948. The plane was flown from Seattle, Washington, by a 43d Wing crew, who had been checked out in the B-50 aircraft at Eglin Field, Fla.

of all special tools and equipment had reached the wing, much time and many manhours were lost in getting any work done. In late 1948, the overall situation was getting worse.

Other Early Problems   1948–1949

Because of its atomic bombing mission, the 43d Bombardment Wing was accorded various prerogatives: war-strength manning was one of them.[18] The percentage of effective manning was 97.8 percent for officers and airmen by the end of 1948. In addition, the wing's personnel overages could not be used to fill lower priority requirements which ensured that, once the wing acquired its full complement of aircraft and was brought to complete war strength, such personnel would take over the additional assignments. Meanwhile, however, the wing was particularly short of electronics, air control, and photo interpretation officers. Among the airmen, there were shortages of airplane electrical mechanics, airplane and engine electrical accessories repairmen, and camera technicians.

As early as February 1948, 3 Boeing representatives had come to Davis-Monthan and organized classes to teach personnel how to service in-coming B–50As. Operation of a B–50 Mobile Training Unit had actually started in March—regular squadron maintenance slowing down appreciably in the months that followed because of the time maintenance crews had to devote to learning how to take care of the new aircraft. Also, in keeping with the global concept of the upgraded atomic forces, the maintenance of aircraft operating in extreme cold weather had received major attention from the start. Much time was therefore spent preparing and sometimes slightly modifying the aircraft before they left the United States for less clement environments. Also time-consuming was the training of personnel this preparation entailed.

As extensive as these preparations were, the rotation of B–50 bombers overseas, initiated in November with the deployment of 5 aircraft, disclosed unsuspected problems. Once in Alaska, 1 of the B–50As crashed, the other 4 being grounded until the cause of the crash was determined. Although no definite conclusions were reached, the congealing of oil in the small-sized tubing of the aircraft's manifold pressure regulator appeared to be the correct assumption, and modified regulators, successfully tested by AMC,

---

[18] The same privilege was given to the 509th Bombardment Wing, entirely equipped with B–29s, but remained meaningless throughout the forties, because the Air Force did not have any extra personnel resources. Hence, the 509th had to function with a limited peacetime manning until additional qualified manpower could be provided.

were installed in all B–50s. Also, in keeping with the usual vicissitudes accompanying the introduction of any new aircraft, the B–50As soon exhibited engine malfunctions. In addition, faulty constant speed drive alternators significantly increased the heavy workload of maintenance crews. But progress was made, and the B–50A's performance steadily improved during 1949.

Special Training   1948–1950

Although generally satisfied with the B–50A's initial improvements, SAC knew that forthcoming modifications, program changes, and the reconfigurations usually dictated by such changes, would create new difficulties. These problems could become insurmountable if skilled personnel remained at a premium. The command, therefore, in early 1948 began to plan an extensive cross-training program.[19] As established, the program required that all bombardiers be trained as radar operators, while all radar operators were to master the difficult bombardment skill. Moreover, all pilots were to be trained as loran operators; all navigators, as radar operators; all co-pilots, as flight engineers; all flight engineers, as crew chiefs, and all crew chiefs, as assistant flight engineers.

"Precision bombing" also occupied a place in the overall training program outlined by the Strategic Air Command. In the late forties, because of the limited supply of atomic bombs, "precision bombing" was scrutinized by the highest Air Force authorities. In July 1948, as the SAC training program was just beginning to take shape, the Air Staff underlined the importance of "precision bombing" by pointing out that ". . . each bomb must be employed as though we had a rifle with but one (1) cartridge per man and very few men, thereby placing all the emphasis on the single 'shot' where decisive results will be dependent upon the accuracy with which these few 'shots' are placed." Even though the supply of bombs increased as time passed, the Air Force continued to emphasize bombing accuracy.

Old and New Deficiencies   1948–1950

In November 1948, as a few B–50As were already available and an all out effort was being made to upgrade SAC's atomic striking power, Lt. Gen.

---

[19] The cross-training program included many pre–World War II practices, some of which were poorly received by SAC's rated personnel. Hence, as finally established, the program proved to be of short duration.

Curtis E. LeMay, in charge of the command since October, took a dim view of the overall program.[20] "I am shocked," he wrote to Gen. Hoyt S. Vandenberg,[21] "by the deficiencies of air bases and forward airfields earmarked for the new forces . . . . as we are responsible for dropping the atomic bomb, I maintain that to be unable to dispatch aircraft into and out of these fields at night during marginal weather is ridiculous." Most places, General LeMay pointed out, were without even elementary operational facilities such as suitable control towers, radio aids, night lighting, crash and fire fighting equipment, and the like. In short, regardless of the severe shortages of funds, a minimum of construction money had to be found, and this project was to receive top priority until more permanent improvements could be made. Closely related to the necessary upgrading of the special bases was the development of standardized procedures to prevent the disaster of an accidental atomic detonation. The SAC Commander's demands could not all be satisfied with dispatch, but progress was made in all cases. And of primary importance, the achievements realized did sustain the test of time.[22]

Meanwhile, as base facilities were being improved and strict safety procedures were devised, new problems began to plague the B–50As. At the end of 1949, the planes were prohibited from flying above 20,000 feet, because of turbosupercharger deficiencies. Then, cracking of the metal skin on the trailing edge of the wings and flaps dictated unexpected modifications. Later on, failure of the rudder hinge bearing caused the temporary grounding of every B–50A. To complicate matters, while these problems were being worked out, new requirements were levied on the aircraft.

---

[20] In the process, SAC's new Commander did not overlook some of the cross-training program's weaknesses. While retaining several of the pre-war practices, General LeMay focused his attention on the morale problem within SAC and made training more realistic and worthwhile. In order to familiarize personnel with operating conditions outside the United States, SAC units were deployed on a rotational schedule for limited periods of time to selected oversea bases. Accuracy of high altitude bombing was substantially improved. Combat crew proficiency was raised through the system of "lead-crew" training which had proved so successful during World War II. In 1949, a lead-crew school was established at Walker AFB, New Mexico. Being a lead-crew member enhanced promotion chances and, in later years, became the basis for immediate advancement to higher rank.

[21] General Vandenberg succeeded Gen. Carl Spaatz as USAF Chief of Staff on 30 April 1948.

[22] SAC's nuclear safety record, based on procedures promoted by General LeMay, remained remarkably good in view of the difficulties associated with any type of atomic operations. Nevertheless, accidents occurred. One, in January 1966, when 2 aircraft collided and crashed near Palomares, Spain, generated a great deal of adverse publicity. (See B–52, p 279).

Additional Modifications

Despite its substantial cost—$35.5 million—the modification ordered by the Joint Chiefs of Staff in January 1948 turned out to be a mere preamble. Growing international tension heightened the urgency of the whole endeavor. Hence, on 16 October 1948, the Air Staff directed a new round of special modifications for 1949.[23] Once again, the Air Materiel Command was instructed to give the highest priority to the project, a priority that even the outbreak of the Korean War would not affect.

Even though the entire modification project was carefully outlined, changes occurred. At first, 15 B-50As that did not have air refueling capability were to be fitted with receivers and other necessary equipment. A directive in early 1949 changed this in favor of equipping these 15, plus 5 more B-50A atomic carriers, for a reconnaissance role. As foreseen, this was about the extent of the B-50A's involvement in the second portion of the atomic project. Additional modifications were reserved for subsequent versions of the B-50As and for different aircraft—mostly B-29s, but also some C-97 transports, and new B-36Bs. Later on, however, as the B-47 program faltered, new requirements arose that directly affected the B-50As.

In January 1952, Sacramento area teams began working on the B-50As to allow 50 of them to carry 2 new types of atomic bombs, and Boeing undertook the preparation of the necessary kits. But the B-47's shortcomings created workloads of staggering proportions for both the Air Force and the contractor. For example, 180 additional B-29s left from World War II had to be reactivated and modified for the atomic task.[24] Although Boeing

---

[23] The Air Staff passed on its requirements to the Air Materiel Command, which also dealt with the various contractors, but the highest governmental levels were again involved. In fact, in fiscal year 1949 the President personally approved the release of $35 million (the sum had nothing to do with the $35.5 million previously spent and was added to the only $2 million so far available) to carry the Joint Chiefs of Staff's atomic modification project one step farther. Nevertheless, the Air Force was not a mere agent; its responsibilities kept on growing as the complexities of the modifications increased. The Air Force's task acquired a new dimension in mid-1948, when its resources were needed for the Berlin airlift, which was thus in direct competition with the crucial atomic project.

[24] The Air Materiel Area assigned the work of reconditioning and rehabilitating the 180 B-29s to the Grand Central Aircraft Company of Tucson, Arizona. This sudden modernization program proved difficult. The bomb-bay doors of the reactivated aircraft had to be modified to the B-50's pneumatic type. Bombsights, radars (AN/APQ-7s, AN/APQ-13s or -23s, according to availability), and other components had to be added even though, when reconfigured, the 180 B-29s would still be inferior to other B-29 atomic carriers. Upon completion of the contracted modifications, the aircraft went back to AMC, which was still responsible for the installation of all kits. To speed matters, 2 air materiel areas (Sacramento and Oklahoma City) became involved, but new problems arose, Boeing bearing the brunt of most of them. Under the pressures of World War II, the Bell Aircraft Corporation, the Glenn L. Martin Company, and other contractors besides Boeing, each had been involved in the

was placed on a 24-hour day, 7-day week schedule to supply B–50A and B–29 kits, established deadlines could not be met. The modifications to the B–50As, due to be completed in May, slipped several months. Still, the last B–50A, a straggler, was finished before November 1952.

End of Production   January 1949

Production of the B–50A ended in January 1949 with delivery of the last 3 aircraft.

Total B–50As Accepted   79

The Air Force accepted a total of 79 B–50As within a 16-month period.

Acceptance Rates

The Air Force accepted 30 B–50As in FY 48 (starting in October 1947 and ending in June 1948), and 49 B–50As in FY 49 (from July 1948 through January 1949).

Flyaway Cost Per Production Aircraft $1.14 million

The B–50A's unit cost was set at $1,144,296—airframe, $684,894; engines (installed), $193,503; propellers, $65,496; electronics, $71,369; ordnance, $5,524; armament (and others), $123,060. Except for the program's last model, the TB–50H, every B/RB–50 version was assigned the same price tag.[25]

---

fabrication of the aircraft. The 180 B–29s therefore differed from each other in various respects, which meant that special kits had to be developed to fit every configuration. Boeing's difficulties snowballed as each kind of kit required separate prototyping and separate engineering approval. In the long run, slippages in kit deliveries postponed completion of the new B–29 project to the fall of 1953, a 6-month delay.

[25] The identical unit price of most B–50s represented an average reached regardless of contractor or fiscal year procurement. This average unit cost did not include the engineering change and modification costs incurred after approval of a basic contract. The Air Force often endorsed such price formulae because of the fluctuations of costs and cost arrangements during the production period of many programs, aircraft, missiles, and other weapon systems alike.

Subsequent Model Series   **B/RB-50B**

Other Configurations   TB-50A

As indicated by the prefix letter T, the TB-50As were B-50As that had been modified as bombing-navigation trainers. Eleven B-50As, equipped with the hose-type inflight refueling system, underwent such conversion, and were primarily used for training crews of the B-36, even though this aircraft could not be refueled in the air. Like most B-50s, the redesignated TB-50As, after undergoing further modifications,[26] ended their service life as KB-50J tankers.

Phaseout   1954–1964

The B-50As began phasing out of SAC in mid-1954, when the 93d Bombardment Wing started receiving eagerly awaited B-47s. But retirement from SAC did not mean that the B-50A's operational life was over. Under one designation or another, many of the B-50 aircraft remained in the Air Force's active inventory for about another decade.[27]

Milestones   2 March 1949

On 2 March, Lucky Lady II,[28] a B-50A (Serial No. 46–010) of the 43d Bomb Group, completed the first nonstop round-the-world flight, having covered 23,452 miles in 94 hours and 1 minute. Carswell AFB, Texas, was the point of departure and return. Lucky Lady II was refueled 4 times in the air (over the Azores, Saudi Arabia, the Philippines, and Hawaii) by KB-29 tankers of the 43d Air Refueling Squadron.[29] For this flight, the B-50A crew

---

[26] A difficult modification since the aircraft had to be stripped of all armament (tail guns excepted), and large single tanks had to be installed in the bomb bay.

[27] Available records showed that once released by SAC, 134 B-50s were modified for the tanker role. Some of these aircraft remained in the operational inventory until 1964; other B-50s, after reconfiguration, served the Air Weather Service until almost the end of 1965.

[28] The original Lucky Lady was a wartime B-29, which participated the previous year in a similar but unsuccessful round-the-world flight.

[29] The 43d and 509th Air Refueling Squadrons were the first air refueling units in the United States Air Force. Beginning in late 1948, the 2 squadrons were equipped with World War

of 14, commanded by Capt. James Gallagher, received numerous awards and decorations. Foremost among these were the Mackay Trophy, given annually by the National Aeronautic Association for the outstanding flight of the year, and the Air Age Trophy, an Air Force Association award given each year in recognition of the air age. The Air Age Trophy was later renamed the Hoyt S. Vandenberg Trophy in honor of the second U.S. Air Force Chief of Staff.

II B-29s that had been modified to carry and dispense fuel in the air through the use of trailing hoses and grapnel hooks, a refueling system developed by the British. These modified B-29s were known as KB-29M tankers.

Pilot and co-pilot stations in a Boeing B-50.

B/RB-50B

Manufacturer's Model 345-2

Previous Model Series   B-50A

New Features

An increase in gross weight, from 168,480 to 170,400 pounds, a new type of fuel cell, and a few minor improvements were the basic differences between the B-50B and the preceding B-50A. The B-50B, however, was immediately reconfigured for the reconnaissance role. In this capacity, the RB-50B featured 4 camera stations (numbering a total of 9 cameras), weather reconnaissance instruments, and extra crew members housed in a capsule that was located in the aircraft's rear bomb bay. In addition, the RB-50B carried fittings for two 700-U.S. gallon underwing fuel tanks.

Planning Changes   1948-1949

The Air Force had planned to use its next lot of 45 B-50s as atomic carriers. It also expected that the forthcoming aircraft, identified as B-50Bs, would be capable of carrying both the Mark 3 and Mark 4 bombs.[30] However, neither plans nor expectations materialized. Indeed, besides the 45 non-atomic capable B-50Bs, 35 subsequent B-50 models would also fail to incorporate from the start the B-50A's initial post-production improvements. Meanwhile, the older RB-29's deficiencies in speed, range, and altitude prompted the Air Force to endorse the immediate reconfiguration of its 45 new B-50Bs. The decision did not reflect the Air Force's preferences. Ideally, reconnaissance aircraft should be superior in performance to the bomber type dependent upon their information. But limited funds had not permitted the development of such a specialized aircraft, and the proposed

---

[30] The 81st B-50 was to be the starting point for the necessary production line modifications. (The first 79 B-50s were B-50As; the 80th B-50 was set aside and used as a prototype.)

RB–36B remained a long way off. Acquisition of the RB–50B, therefore, appeared to be the best as well as the only alternative. Although all 45 aircraft were re-fitted for the reconnaissance role, the Air Force's financial ledgers kept on carrying the planes as B–50Bs.

First Flight   January 1949

The first B–50B, initially flown early in January 1949, was accepted by the Air Force on the 18th. Within a short period, 14 B–50Bs were delivered to SAC, the first of the 14 being received by the command on 31 January. This aircraft (Serial No. 47-119) was immediately sent to the Boeing Wichita plant for modification as reconnaissance aircraft, marking the beginning of the B–50B fleet's reconfiguration.

Reconfiguration Task   1949–1951

Adapting the B–50B to the reconnaissance role became a fairly involved project for a number of reasons. At first, the Air Force thought of exempting 15 B–50Bs from the proposed modifications. Then, because of new requirements, the Air Force decided to reconfigure all the B–50Bs and further, to fit them for a variety of reconnaissance purposes. Eventually, 3 different types of reconnaissance B–50Bs came into being. Although identified from the start as RB–50Es, RB–50Fs, and RB–50Gs, the reconfigured B–50Bs were not formally redesignated until 16 April 1951.

The RB–50E, first of the 3 types, was returned from the Wichita plant in May 1950. The Air Force acquired 14 RB–50Es, all of them in just a few months. Earmarked for photographic reconnaissance and observation missions, the RB–50E normally required a crew of 10. According to the type of mission being flown, the left-side gunner served as weather observer, or as in-flight refueling operator. When at this station, at altitudes above 10,000 feet, the left gunner had to use oxygen and wear heated clothing. As in the case of the original B–29,[31] compartments for the other crew members were pressurized and featured heating and ventilating equipment. The RB–50E's defensive armament, like that of other B–50 models, also dated back to the B–29. The only difference was that the number of .50 caliber machine guns had been increased from 10 to 13, all of which were still housed in 5

---

[31] The B–29 was the first military aircraft in the world to have pressurized compartments for all members of the crew, including the tail gunner.

electrically operated turrets. The turrets were controlled remotely from the sighting stations.

The RB–50F, the second reconfigured version, was returned from Wichita in July 1950. The Air Force received 14 RB–50Fs, Boeing completing the required modifications in January 1951. The RB–50F closely resembled the RB–50E, but was equipped with the Shoran[32] radar system for the specific purpose of conducting mapping, charting, and geodetic surveys. However, the Shoran radar prevented the RB–50F from making use of its defensive armament, which was identical to that of the RB–50E. To give the weapon system additional versatility, the Shoran radar and associated components were housed in removable kits. Deletion of the kits and a simple adjustment restored the RB–50F's defensive power. Therefore, if needed, the 2 aircraft types could be used for the same basic reconnaissance missions.

The RB–50G, the third and last reconnaissance version derived from the B–50B, entered SAC's inventory between June and October 1951. The 15 reconfigured aircraft (Manufacturer's Model 345-30-25) differed significantly from the RB–50E and RB–50F. Electronic reconnaissance was the principal mission of the RB–50G. The aircraft featured 6 electronic countermeasures stations, an addition which had necessitated a number of internal structural changes. Some external modifications had also been necessary to accommodate the radomes and antennae of the aircraft's new radar equipment. Finally, during the reconfiguration process, the 16-crew member RB–50G had been fitted with the improved nose of the B–50D, the production model which actually followed the B–50B. In contrast to the RB–50F, the RB–50G could use its defensive armament while operating its new radars and electronic countermeasures equipment.

Other Modifications   1949–1950

Reconfiguration of the RB–50s did not necessarily eliminate some of the B-model's flaws. As a result, several modifications were accomplished either before, during, or after the basic aircraft had been adapted to the reconnaissance role. Problems of various importance were identified,[33]

---

[32] Shoran was originally developed as a *Sho*rt *Ra*nge *N*avigational aid to bombing to enable a bomber to strike its target when the target was not visible from the aircraft. This method, first applied in a primitive fashion during World War II, proved very effective within certain limitations. These parameters were primarily the restricted range of the electronic signal from aircraft to ground and return, and later on the frequent lack of a single geodetic survey control system in the region containing the Shoran ground station sites and the targets.

[33] All of the B/RB–50B shortcomings were retained by the subsequent B–50D, and the same corrective measures were applied to this later model.

Looking in a port of a re-configured RB-50B, one could see the lens cone of a hand-operated reconnaissance camera. This aircraft featured 9 such camera stations.

some of them as soon as the aircraft reentered the Boeing plant. Leaks from fuel cells were an unexpected dilemma—probably attributable to the aircraft's thin, light-weight fuel cells.[34] The B-50A, equipped with heavy-weight fuel cells, had not encountered such difficulties. While AMC wrestled with the problem, interim measures were taken, including the tightening of cell interconnect bolts and replacement of defective tanks. In October, instead of improving, the fuel cell problem became worse, "a considerable increase in fuel tanks leaks [being] attributed to the arrival of cool weather." By year's end, AMC decided to replace the defective cells of the B-50B and all subsequent B-50s with a new type of fuel cell, as soon as it became available.[35] Meanwhile, there were other problems. Like the previous B-50As, the new aircraft experienced fuel tank overflows, leaks in

---

[34] The main fuel cells in the B-50 were located within the wing. Looking forward from the pilot's position there were as many as 17 cells to the left and the same number to his right. On most models only 11 cells were utilized in the right wing and 11 in the left wing.

[35] The B-50D deliveries were actually stopped, pending availability of the new fuel cells.

fuel check valves, failures of the engine turbochargers, warped turbos and warped turbo bucket wheels, generator defects, and the like. In addition, since all B-50 airframes were basically alike, the B/RB-50s shared the B-50A's trailing wing problems. This was not a new experience. Several years before, cracks had also appeared in the metal skin at both forward and trailing edge of the upper side of the B-29's wing assembly. In all cases, stress beyond metal strength had been the most probable cause.[36] The permanent solution, finally endorsed in 1949, was to use heavier metal in the fabrication of future wing flaps. This was a simple enough solution, but not quickly implemented.

Program Reduction   1949

Cancellation of the B-50 program was not seriously considered before the aircraft entered the inventory in substantial numbers, but the program was drastically altered in 1949. An early B-50A, set aside to serve as prototype for the model due to follow the B-50B, did not fare well. Initially known as the YB-50C, this aircraft was expected to feature a longer fuselage, a single bomb bay, larger wings, and 4 new R-4360-43 turbo-compound engines.[37] The YB-50C's take-off weight was tentatively set at 207,000 pounds, a significant 50,000-pound increase over the weight of most B-50 models. By November 1948, the B-50C mockup had been completed, inspection of the prototype was scheduled for May 1949, and 43 production aircraft (14 B-50C and 29 RB-50Cs) were already on order. In late 1948, because of the many changes embodied in its design, the future B-50C became the B-54, the original quantity of aircraft under contract remaining unchanged.[38] The new designation, however, did not help the aircraft's prospects.

President Truman's curtailment of the fiscal year 1949 defense budget forced the Air Force to make some difficult adjustments. While the B-54's high price was known, the cost effectiveness of the aircraft was not clear. Yet for good reasons, neither Secretary of the Air Force W. Stuart Symington nor General Vandenberg wished to give up the new aircraft. No B-54s had been produced, but work was underway by the manufacturer and sub-

---

[36] Responsible for 2 recent B-50A accidents.

[37] The Pratt & Whitney development was usually referred to as the VDT (variable discharge turbine) engine (for details, see B-36, pp 14-15 and p 19).

[38] In addition, the next two annual procurement programs provided for 43 and 58 other B/RB-54s, respectively.

contractors. Therefore, the program's cancellation would entail some financial loss and disturb the industry. On the other hand, certain facts could not be overlooked. Whether known as B–50C or B–54, the aircraft had no growth potential; its design represented Boeing's effort to extract the last ounce of performance out of the final development of the basic B–29. Actually, the B–54 configuration provided an undesirable outrigger landing gear requiring wider taxiways than existed at operating bases; jet engines could not be added without designing entirely new wings; and the new K–1 bombing system could not be installed without sacrificing a belly turret or without a drastic alteration of the aircraft's fuselage. Finally, and of great importance, General LeMay[39] wanted no part of the B–54.

On 21 February 1949, while appearing before the Board of Senior Officers,[40] General LeMay again strongly reiterated that the B–54 program should be canceled in favor of additional B–36s, since development of the B–36 with jet pods indicated superior performance in speed, altitude, and range. Pending quantity production of the B–52, the SAC Commander stated, the B–36 provided the best capability to carry out his command's primary mission, a mission vital to national security.

Although Secretary Symington and General Vandenberg did not question General LeMay's expertise, both remained reluctant to terminate the procurement of the B–54. The crux of the problem was that canceling the B–54s and getting more B–36s would alter the medium/heavy bomber group-combination, included in the program recently approved by the Joint Chiefs of Staff. As an alternative, Secretary Symington then suggested substituting less costly B–50s for the B–54s. But the SAC Commander quickly pointed out that the substitution, even if acceptable on the basis of economy, would still be a very bad solution. Instead, General LeMay testified, if all programmed B–54s could not be replaced by B–36s, the best course of action would be to secure extra B–47s, as soon as possible. After weighing and balancing all factors involved, the Board of Senior Officers concluded that production of the B–47 should be accelerated and additional B–36s bought. The board's recommendations were approved by Mr. Symington and General Vandenberg in April 1949, marking the end of the B–54 program.

---

[39] General LeMay was promoted to full general on 29 October 1951.

[40] The board's members, convened to review the composition of the 48-Group Program imposed by President Truman's budgetary restrictions, included Gen. Muir S. Fairchild, Vice Chief of Staff, Gen. Joseph T. McNarney, Commanding General of the Air Materiel Command, Lt. Gen. H. A. Craig, Deputy Chief of Staff for Materiel, and Lt. Gen. Lauris Norstad, Deputy Chief of Staff for Plans and Operations.

End of Production   1949

The B–50B production ended in April 1949, with the delivery of 7 aircraft.

Total B–50Bs Accepted   45

The Air Force accepted its 45 B–50Bs within a period of 4 months. All but 1 of the 45 aircraft became RB–50s.

Acceptance Rates

The Air Force accepted 9 B–50Bs in January 1949, 14 in February, 15 in March, and the last 7 in April.

Flyaway Cost Per Production Aircraft   1.14 Million

Like the B–50A, the B–50B's unit cost was averaged at $1,144,296. This amount did not include reconfiguration costs, estimated in September 1948 at $217,000 per aircraft.

Subsequent Model Series   B–50D

Other Configurations   EB–50B

One of the first B–50Bs accepted by the Air Force was immediately returned to Boeing, where it was flown experimentally with a track-type nose and main landing gear. As indicated by its "E" designation, the aircraft was also equipped with various electronic devices, while on loan from the Air Force.

Phaseout   1954

The RB–50s began leaving SAC's operational inventory in 1954, when modern but still troublesome RB–47s finally became available. SAC had 40 RB–50s in 1951, a peak total reduced to 12 in 1954 and 1955, with the last aircraft leaving the command in December 1956. However, in contrast to the B–50A, phaseout from SAC did not signify the end of the RB–50's primary role. In 1954, although reassigned from the command, several RB–50s, their Shoran equipment greatly improved,[41] still performed photo-mapping missions; in 1957, a few RB–50Es and RB–50Gs continued to be utilized by the Air Force Security Service. However, these were exceptional cases, and the RB–50's primary career came to a close before the end of the decade.

---

[41] The initial Shoran had been refined and had become known as the Hiran, an abbreviation for *Hi*gh Precision Sho*ran*.

B-50D

Manufacturer's Model 345-9-6

Previous Model Series   B-50B

New Features

Externally, the B-50D differed from the B-50A and B-50B only in that it had an all-plastic nose and provisions for droppable wing tanks. Otherwise, the B-50D bomber greatly resembled the B-50A.[42] A different type of equipment for in-flight refueling, larger fuel capacity, more efficient radar, fewer crew members (10 instead of 11, and sometimes only 8), plus other minor improvements completed the list of changes separating the 2 bombers.

First Flight   May 1949

Initially flown in May 1949, the first B-50D was accepted by the Air Force on 14 June. Deliveries to SAC began 10 days later, with the arrival of 1 B-50D (Serial No. 47-167).

Enters Operational Service   Mid-1949

The B-50Ds entered operational service with SAC in mid-1949, but within 3 months the new planes presented so many major maintenance problems that the command decided to refuse further deliveries and to return those B-50Ds presently assigned whenever possible to the Air Materiel Command. Some 50 B-50Ds were involved, most of which were grounded for extended periods of time during the remainder of 1949 and the first 6 months of 1950, because their main fuel cells, inverters, turbosuper-

---

[42] The B-50D's actual predecessor was the B-50B. In practice, since the B-50B was immediately reconfigured for the reconnaissance role, the 2 aircraft could not be compared.

chargers, alternators, generators, and even wing trailing edges carried flaws of one kind or another. As was usually the case, these problems were resolved, but the solution took time, a commodity the Air Force could then ill afford.

Other Initial Shortcomings   1949–1950

Disappointingly, most B–50Ds came out of production without the "receiver-end" of the new flying boom air-to-air refueling system then being developed by Boeing. Yet, adoption of a refueling system had been planned all along.[43] The experimental refueling program, approved by the end of 1947, provided for modification of a prototype tanker and bomber-receiver which, once satisfactorily tested, would be rushed to SAC for the training of crews. Refueling in the air had been carried out as early as 1923, but only the Flight Refueling, Ltd., a British company formed in the 1930s, was manufacturing the necessary equipment. The Air Force in March 1948 had given Flight Refueling a contract to supply 40 complete sets of tanker-bomber refueling equipment, together with technical assistance by British engineers, necessary tools, and installation drawings.[44] The Air Force was willing to pay a high price—in excess of $1.2 million—for a temporary solution to the air refueling problem. Despite the British system's merits and potential for improvement, the Air Force expected that it would soon be supplanted by the Boeing type, which primarily consisted of substituting a mechanical boom for the hose of the British contraption. Boeing's progress however was slower than anticipated. As a result, neither the "receiver-end" nor the feeding apparatus of the new equipment could possibly be installed during the production of a majority of

---

[43] The Air Force was well aware that the Strategic Air Command's entire atomic capability would rest in the short-range B–29 and B–50 medium bombers until the intercontinental B–36 entered the inventory. This meant, for a few years at least, dependence on carefully selected overseas bases. It also underlined the urgency of the air refueling program. And even though the B–36 was finally considered fully operational in 1951, the number of available aircraft was often limited since the new intercontinental bombers were constantly involved in some of the special atomic project's many modifications. In any case, be it in support of atomic, conventional, or other Air Force missions, air refueling remained a vital capability and top Air Force priority.

[44] The first installation of the British system, employing hose connections and gravity feed, was completed in May 1948. Flight-testing prompted a few modifications, but by September 24 B–29s had been modified, 12 as tankers and 12 as receiver aircraft, and were delivered to SAC. The British hose system permitted the transfer of 2,600 gallons of fuel at a rate of 90 to 100 gallons per minute, thus increasing the receiver aircraft's combat radius by perhaps as much as 40 percent. Still unsatisfied, the Air Materiel Command was already working on the development of a force feed technique to increase the flow of fuel to 200 gallons per minute.

A Strategic Air Command crew was briefed before a mission in a B-50D bomber.

the B-50Ds.[45] This led to several retrofits. The most urgent one entailed giving the aircraft the necessary receivers, since the B-50Ds would serve as atomic carriers until replaced by the B-47s.

Atomic Modifications   1949–1951

As pointed out by the Air Staff in late 1948, the urgency of the second phase of atomic modifications could not be overstated. Many of the additional requirements were specifically addressed to the new B-50Ds. However, the aircraft's participation in the special atomic project started poorly. First, the B-50D deliveries did not begin on time, delaying signifi-

---

[45] Slippage of the flying boom air-to-air refueling system altered many plans. Forty of 92 B-29s, earmarked for the tanker role, were to receive the new system but were fitted with the British hose type instead. All 92 aircraft were designated KB-29Ms. A later directive of the large-scale atomic project assigned another 116 B-29s, withdrawn from storage, to the refueling task. This time, the aircraft were fitted with the American system, but Boeing did not start the modification before August 1950 and only completed it in 1951. These aircraft, identified as KB-29Ps, were mainly used to air-refuel the B-50D atomic carriers. Soon afterward, Boeing undertook to bring another 185 reactivated B-29s to the KB-29P configuration.

cantly the aircraft's post-production modifications. Then, in addition to their imperfections and because of a misunderstanding between Boeing and the Air Force, the first B–50Ds delivered to SAC had not been adapted on the production line to carry both the Mark 3 and Mark 4 bombs,[46] a production feature of all subsequent B–50Ds. This serious omission created more work and delays, because Boeing had to prepare special kits[47] to be installed by personnel of the 93d and 509th Bombardment Wings, the new aircraft's first recipients.

Meanwhile, incredibly rapid technological developments were beginning to complicate the exacting atomic project requirements of January 1948. On the surface, converting a bomber aircraft to an atomic weapon carrier appeared simple. The basic components needed were relatively few in number. The installation consisted of a shackle or bomb rack capable of suspending and releasing the bomb, sway braces to hold the bomb in place during flight, and a limited number of pieces of equipment bracketed to the airplane and connected by cable to the bomb mechanism. Included were arming controls, the capsule insertion gear, and the T-boxes[48] that controlled, tested, and monitored the bomb. In addition, a pair of hoists, attached to the bomb-bay frame lifted the bomb into place. Ironically, the "simple" conversion proved difficult for several reasons. First, the B–50 was a development of the B–29, an aircraft never intended to carry an atomic payload. The B–29/B–50 bomb bay was too small to house the required components and new bombs. Procurement and development of the B–50 occurred in an era when in-house secrecy almost totally enshrouded spectacular atomic advances. The rapid development of more efficient bombs created additional problems, since every single new type of bomb required that associated components be relocated within the narrow confines of the B–29 and B–50 bomb bay.

Faced with uninterrupted modification crises, the Air Force in March 1950 issued military characteristics for the development of a so-called "universal system," which could hoist, suspend, and release most types of atomic weapons and be easily fitted in the bomb bay of all atomic carriers.

---

[46] The Mark 3 was first available in 1948; the Mark 4, in mid-1949.

[47] These kits, called the "auxiliary bombing system," only were to be installed "when and if needed." This qualification, however, did not reduce SAC's extra workload, since field personnel still had to learn how to install the kits.

[48] The T-boxes housed specialized electronics components used for the monitoring, control, and testing of the circuits and equipment that played a role in the atomic operation. As a rule, a T-box (also popularly known as "Black-box" because of the black-color) denotes any unit, as a bombsight, robot pilot, or piece of electronic equipment that may be put into, or removed from, a radar set, an aircraft, or the like, as a single package. Such units are used for ready maintenance.

After many conferences, the requirements were revised, scaled down, and finally dropped in the B–29 and B–50's cases, again because the bomb bay of those aircraft did not provide the necessary space.[49] In the same year, as the new Mark 4 bombs became plentiful, the Air Force ascertained that these bombs, although more efficient than the preceding Mark 3s,[50] were not very satisfactory. Instead the Air Force believed in the necessity of developing a faster-detonating, lighter, safer, and easier-to-handle bomb. From then on, events moved swiftly, with not one, but several new types of bombs entering the atomic stockpile before 1953.[51]

Acquiring several new types of bombs presented a significant advantage for the Air Force, however, ensuring that the bombs could be handled efficiently was a challenge of great magnitude. Tremendous problems soon emerged. First, it appeared that adapting 1 squadron of B–50Ds (15 aircraft) to carry the most advanced of the new bombs would be impossible without destroying the aircraft's capability to handle other types of atomic bombs.[52] Then, the urgent modification of 180 B–50Ds (and 69 B–29s) to prepare these aircraft for the bomb that immediately followed the Mark 4, acquired top priority. A third new type of bomb, fully available before delivery of the most advanced one, also called for prompt and difficult modifications. Finally, and perhaps fortunately, a fourth new type was eliminated from consideration in the B–29 and B–50 bombers, because the bomb was too long to be fitted in the short bomb bay of these aircraft. Meanwhile, the B–50D's many modifications were further complicated by the on-going installation of an improved bombing-navigation radar system, the AN/APQ–24.[53]

---

[49] First installed in the large bomb bay of a B–36 in March 1952, the universal system became a standard feature of the intercontinental bombers. The installation of a fairly similar configuration of the system was seriously contemplated for the B–47, but did not materialize.

[50] The Mark 3s were all phased out by early 1951.

[51] Improved versions of those new bombs became available in 1954 and 1955, by which time better coordination between the Air Force and the Atomic Energy Commission had minimized the physical changes required for aircraft to carry new type bombs. And later on, as thermonuclear weapons came into being, the costly chore of transforming bombers into atomic carriers was eliminated.

[52] In June 1951, the Air Staff endorsed SAC's request to extend the new requirement to 16 B–47Bs and 12 B–36Ds. The Air Staff also directed that if the new bombs could not be carried by the aircraft without hampering their other capabilities, then specifically designed kits would be delivered to SAC, so that the command would be prepared either way. Modification of the 15 B–50Ds, or development of the necessary kits, would retain precedence over any similar work for the B–47s and B–36s.

[53] The B–36B was the first recipient of the new AN/APQ–24 and this radar was not authorized for other B–50 bombers or for the older B–29s, which retained the Norden optical sights. In any case, the APQ–24 also proved to be unsatisfactory because of lack of security, high rate of malfunction, and inadaptability during bad weather.

Completion and Appraisal   1952–1953

Adaptation of the B–50D to the atomic carrier role followed the B–50A's pattern. Boeing worked overtime, extra AMC teams were deployed to the SAC bases, and special care was exercised to make sure that SAC's overall atomic capability was not severely strained by the incessant modifications.[54] For example, only the first 4 aircraft of every B–50D wing were modified to carry the most sophisticated atomic bomb of the period, and the modifications,[55] started in January 1952, were completed in May. Similarly, the adaptation of 180 B–50Ds, to accommodate the Mark 4's immediate successor, was carefully scheduled, 4 groups of 45 aircraft undergoing changes at different times. There were some occasional schedule overlaps and several serious delays. Boeing modification of 80 B–50Ds in late 1951 slipped several months, and another B–50D modification, due to be completed by June 1952, was delayed for lack of the necessary kits. In some instances, however, the bombers' modifications were so successfully organized that the B–50Ds were able to handle a new type of bomb as soon as it became readily available.

In March 1953, several months after new requirements had been formulated, the Mark 4 bombs were removed from the atomic stockpile. By late 1953, just as the modifications prompted by the new requirements were being completed, SAC began to replace some of its B–29 and B–50 bombers with new B–47s. These substitutions had long been planned, although the B–47 deliveries were late. Still, some believed that the long modification lead time had more or less nullified the usefulness of the older B–29 and B–50 aircraft.

Criticism of the atomic modification project was not new. Back in 1951, harrassed AMC personnel complained that the magnitude of the modification task was reaching such proportions that the very existence of the weapons system, through which the atomic bombs were to be employed, was being jeopardized.[56] In June 1951, Maj. P. C. Calhoun, an AMC project officer appearing before the Special Weapons Development Board, expressed the same opinion. "These modifications are necessary," Major Calhoun emphasized, "but if the USAF tactical capability is to be maintained, weapon systems programs must be better planned, better phased,

---

[54] The same careful timing was extended to the modification of the B–29, B–36, and subsequent B–47 bombers.

[55] As anticipated by the Air Force, the aircraft ended being fitted with a number of permanent parts (so-called Parts A), and special kits were provided.

[56] In addition to the many modification programs, numerous retrofit programs were necessary to add new or improved equipment or to correct deficiencies in installed equipments.

and better executed." In short, the Air Materiel Command as a whole deplored the atomic project's short deadlines, interim solutions, and costly crash programs. Moreover, in continually "butchering" the bombers lay the danger of seriously impairing their operational characteristics. AMC's criticism was valid, but the Air Force had no easy solutions. Counterbalancing these drawbacks, and perhaps too quickly overlooked, the fact remained that the B-29 and B-50 wings comprised a large portion of SAC's atomic arsenal until the end of 1953, when their conversion to B-47s began.

End of Production   1950

The Air Force acceptance of the last 2 B-50Ds in December 1950 marked the end of the aircraft's production.

Total B-50Ds Accepted   222

The Air Force accepted its 222 B-50Ds over a period of 19 months.

Acceptance Rates

The Air Force accepted 15 B-50Ds in FY 49, all during the month of June 1949; 160 in FY 50; and 47 in FY 51, starting in July 1950 and ending in December. A peak number of B-50Ds, 29 of them, was accepted in FY 50, during the month of December 1949.

Flyaway Cost Per Production Aircraft $1.14 Million

The B-50D carried the unit price tag of the B-50A and B-50B. It was set at $1,144,296.

Subsequent Model Series   TB-50H

Other Configurations   DB-50D, KB-50, KB-50J,
                                            TB-50D, WB-50D

DB-50D—Early in 1951, 1 B-50 was modified as a director aircraft, identified as DB-50D, and used to launch the Bell rocket-powered GAM-63

Rascal missile.[57] By August, Air Force planning provided for the activation, sometime in 1953, of 2 squadrons of Rascal carriers, one of B-36s and another of B-50Ds, the latter squadron being programmed to operate from oversea bases because of the B-50's limited range. Adaptation of the B-50D to the DB-50D configuration was to begin in June 1952, ahead of the B-36 modification. However, Rascal deficiencies, as well as other considerations, altered these plans. The DB-50D continued flight testing the new missile until 1955, but activation of both the DB-50D and DB-36 squadrons was canceled.

KB-50—The Air Force planned all along that a total of 134 B-50s,[58] made up of B-50As, RB-50s, and B-50Ds, when no longer needed by the SAC atomic forces, would be converted to tankers. The proposed aircraft, referred to as KB-50s, would feature extensively reinforced outer wing panels, as well as the necessary equipment to air refuel simultaneously 3 fighter-type aircraft by the probe and drogue method. The modifications, assigned to the Hayes Aircraft Corporation, also included deletion of the B-50's defensive armament and replacement of the basic aircraft's aft tail section. Although the completion date of the Hayes modifications was tentatively set for December 1957, the project (ordered in the mid-fifties) proceeded so well that it was ended ahead of time. A first KB-50 flew in December 1955 and was accepted by the Air Force in January 1956, the tankers from then on steadily entering the operational inventory of the Tactical Air Command (TAC). By November 1957, TAC's KB-29s, which the KB-50s replaced, had all been phased out. By year's end, all of the command's aerial refueling squadrons had their full complement of KB-50s. TAC had nothing but praise for the new tankers. The KB-50s presented no serious problems, and their reliability was such that the command considered asking for more of them. Extra KB-50s would come "cheap," TAC calculated, if additional numbers of B-50s were merely added on to the Hayes modification line. Nevertheless, the recommendation remained in limbo, which was just as well since the modification line had already been closed and the superior KB-50J was on its way.

KB-50J—The Air Force tentatively endorsed the KB-50J program in mid-1956, because it believed the KB-50s of TAC's aerial tanker fleet no longer had both the speed and altitude to refuel modern jet aircraft effectively.[59] The KB-50J, first flown in April 1957, was still powered by 4

---

[57] See B-36, pp 46–47.

[58] Some records indicated 136 B-50s were involved, a discrepancy probably due to the fact that 2 B-50s, used as prototypes for the forthcoming reconfigurations, were included in the higher total but excluded from the Air Force's operational accounts.

[59] See B-47, pp 130–131.

Pratt & Whitney R–4360–35 piston radial engines, but featured in addition two 5,200-pound thrust General Electric J47–23 turbojet engines that were installed in pods, suspended from pylons at the former locations of the KB–50's auxiliary wing tanks.

Flight testing of the KB–50J, immediately started in April 1957, was completed in December, with rewarding results. The aircraft had made successful hook-ups and transfers of fuel to several types of tactical aircraft at higher altitudes, greater gross weights, and higher airspeeds than possible with the KB–50. The J-model's slightly shorter refueling range was more than compensated by its superior performance. Its jet engines decreased takeoff distance by 30 percent and the time to climb to refueling altitude by 60 percent. Of utmost importance, in contrast to the KB–50, the KB–50J could maintain satisfactory refueling speeds in level flight at altitudes which did not unduly penalize the receiver aircraft. The Air Force, therefore, decided that a great many KB–50s would be brought to the KB–50J configuration. However, only the most modern KB–50s (former B–50Ds) would be eligible for the retrofit. The first such aircraft, withdrawn from Tactical Air Command's 429th Air Refueling Squadron in September 1957, was modified in 4 months' time and returned to the operating forces on 16 January 1958. Reminiscent of the careful procedure applied to the atomic modifications, the KB–50 retrofit was strictly scheduled to make sure that TAC's refueling capability was not seriously impaired. As the Hayes Aircraft Corporation gained more experience, it took 20 fewer days to modify each of the aircraft, and the retrofit project proceeded smoothly.

The Air Force had over 100 KB–50Js by 1959, but its operational requirements had already begun to change. Hence, TAC quickly pointed out that while the KB–50Js were not expected to present major maintenance or

A GAM-63 Rascal missile was attached to a specially modified DB-50D before firing.

supply problems from the start, the retrofitted aircraft should be considered as "interim" refuelers. Tankers were critical to the successful accomplishment of nonstop overseas deployment of the forces, the command insisted, and the often-modified, 12-year-old KB–50J, despite its many merits, was not a high-performance aircraft. In short, TAC wanted to acquire a contingent of the new KC–135, a Boeing tanker assigned to the Strategic Air Command. Still, budget limitations were a problem. Each KC–135 cost about $3.5 million, while the KB–50J's unit price was set at $1.27 million.[60] Although 2 squadrons of KC–135s were eventually programmed to reach TAC in mid-1953, this planning did not materialize. In 1960, the Air Force announced that SAC would get more KC–135s and would serve as the single Air Force manager for tanker support. The decision was to take effect in late 1964 or early 1965. Meanwhile, TAC would retain its KB–50s.

Contrary to anticipation, the elderly KB–50Js began to deteriorate almost as soon as available. In 1959, TAC had to resort to cannibalization to fix some of the retrofitted tankers because tail hose depressor actuators were not readily available. Late in the year, both the Pacific Air Forces and TAC faced more serious difficulties. The inner liner of the KB–50 fuel cells, all of which had been manufactured in 1949 and 1950, began to crack, allowing self-sealing compound to infiltrate the tanker's fuel system. TAC recommended that the defective heavy, self-sealing fuel cells be replaced with new lightweight, bladder-type cells, but the command was overruled by AMC on the grounds that the cost involved could not be amortized over the remaining useful life of the aircraft. In July 1960, Hayes started exchanging all KB–50 fuel cells for new similar ones or for cells that had been removed from B–50s in storage at Davis-Monthan AFB, Arizona. The exchange proved satisfactory, but TAC encountered other problems. Landing gear malfunctions plagued the aircraft, and all sorts of old-age deficiencies began to develop. As a rule, TAC maintenance personnel had to expend every month more than 2,000 manhours of overtime per squadron in order to meet operational commitments, while by-passing certain items vital to the continued KB–50J use. These neglected tasks, including depot overhaul of quick engine change kits, had been expected to sustain the tankers until their scheduled phaseout was completed. The KB–50 inventory was substantially reduced as the aircraft's retirement became closer. In 1964, a few KB–50s saw action in Southeast Asia, but this proved to be the aircraft's last operational commitment.

TB–50D—As in the B–50A's case, 11 B–50Ds were brought up to the

---

[60] This figure included the B–50D's basic cost, leaving some $130,000 for the bomber's adaptation to the KB–50 and KB–50J configurations.

trainer configuration, redesignated TB–50Ds, and used for various support duties, including the training of B–36 crews.

WB–50D—Extensive corrosion of the WB–29s prompted the Air Force to decide in 1953 that some B–50Ds, as they became surplus, would be adapted for the weather role and immediately returned to SAC. There these aircraft accomplished "special weather reconnaissance" missions for the 97th Bomb Wing until April 1955, when all WB–50Ds were earmarked for the Air Weather Service.[61] Meanwhile, a much larger reconfiguration program was also approved. In June 1954, the Air Force confirmed that the weather service's WB–29s would be replaced by modified B–50Ds. The modification contract, assigned to the Lockheed Aircraft Corporation, included 78 B–50Ds and specified a completion deadline of November 1955.

Although the new WB–50Ds would represent only be a partial and temporary solution to the range and altitude problems of the deteriorating

---

[61] The aircraft's withdrawal from SAC left the command with no special weather reconnaissance capability until the end of the year, when the first RB–47K weather aircraft was delivered.

Two student navigator-bombardier-radar operators aboard a TB–50D trainer aircraft.

WB-29s, the Air Weather Service eagerly awaited the forthcoming aircraft. While deficient in overall performance, the modified planes would feature improved equipment and instrumentation of special importance to the weather mission. The APM-82 Automatic Navigator, for example, was a radar navigation device capable of measuring drift and ground speed under all conditions, except a calm and glassy sea. Also included were the ANQ-7 Temperature Humidity Indicator, the ML-313 Psychometer, improved altimeters, and flight indicators. However, the new equipment proved more difficult to install than anticipated, and Lockheed could not meet established modification schedules. The first modified aircraft, or prototype WB-50D, flew on 20 August 1955, and the first production model was delivered to the Air Weather Service in November, when the whole modification program should have been completed. Still, once available, the WB-50Ds performed far better and for a much longer period of time than expected. Like other modified versions of the B-50Ds, the reconfigured aircraft did not avoid some of the problems caused by their near obsolecence. In 1960, after several fuel cells failed in flight, 28 WB-50Ds were grounded. As in the KB-50's case, most WB-50Ds were subsequently retrofitted with new or surplus fuel cells. The modification was well justified, 40 WB-50Ds remaining in the weather service inventory in March 1963. The aircraft's phaseout began shortly thereafter, but the last WB-50D (Serial No. 49-310) was not retired before the fall of 1965.[62]

Phaseout   1953–1955

Some of SAC's 5 wings of atomic-capable B-50s began to exchange their aircraft for new B-47 medium bombers in the last months of 1953, and once underway the delayed conversion proved fairly steady. SAC still possessed 2 wings of B-50s in early 1955, but not for long. The last B-50D (Serial No. 49-330), assigned to the 97th Bomb Wing, Biggs AFB, Texas, was phased out of the atomic forces on 20 October. However, the B-50D retirement from SAC did not spell the end of the aircraft's active life. Like other B-50s, many reconfigured B-50Ds served the Air Force for another 10 years.

---

[62] This aircraft was flown to Davis-Monthan AFB, Ariz., for storage. Later it was displayed at the Smithsonian Institution.

TB–50H

Manufacturer's Model 345–31–26

Previous Model Series   B–50D

New Features

The TB–50H trainer differed significantly from the B–50D, and other models in the series. First, the TB–50H featured 2 astrodomes, which facilitated training by making it possible for crewmen to trade positions during flight. Also, in another departure from combat aircraft, the trainer had no drop tanks, could not be air-refueled, and carried no defensive armament. The TB–50H was designed to teach B–47 crews how to use the K-system of radar navigation and bombing[63] and to train specialized engineers, multi-engine pilots, bombardiers, navigators, and observers. The trainer normally carried a crew of 12, consisting of pilot, co-pilot, engineer, bombardier, navigator instructor, left navigator trainee, right navigator trainee, right scanner, K-system trainee, K-system instructor, radio operator, and left radar trainee. The TB–50H's rear bomb bay was packed with electronic gear, but the aircraft was lighter and therefore slightly faster than the B–50D.[64]

Production Decision   1951

In the spring of 1951, the Air Force decided to cancel the production of the last 24 B–50Ds, ordering instead an equivalent number of B–50 trainers. The decision, confirmed in April 1951, when the B–50 procurement contract was amended, became official on 4 May. The Air Force at the time also decided that the new trainers, directly developed from the B–50D, would be known as TB–50Hs.

---

[63] See B–47, p 117 and p 119.

[64] The TB–50H's basic weight was 82,726 pounds, and its normal take-off weight was 146,756 pounds; the B–50D's corresponding weights were 84,714 and 158,250 pounds, respectively. The TB–50H's maximum speed at the optimum altitude of 31,000 feet was 363 knots, 20 knots faster than the B–50D at 30,000 feet.

First Flight (Production Aircraft)   1952

The first TB–50H was flown in April 1952. Within a few months, several of the aircraft reached the Air Training Command.

Enters Operational Service   August 1952

The TB–50Hs entered operational service in August 1952 at Mather AFB, California. They were assigned to the 3536th Observer Training Squadron of Air Training Command's 3535th Observer Training Wing. As intended, the TB–50Hs were used primarily to train B–47 crews. The last of the 24 TB–50Hs arrived at Mather AFB in March 1953.

End of Production   1953

Delivery of one last aircraft in February 1953 marked the end of the TB–50H production, as well as the termination of the entire B–50 program's production run.

Total TB–50Hs Accepted   24

All 24 aircraft were accepted during fiscal year 1953.

Acceptance Rates

The Air Force accepted 2 TB–50Hs in August 1952, 3 in September, 7 in October, 3 in November, 7 in December, and the final 2 aircraft in 1953, one in January and one in February.

Flyaway Cost Per Production Aircraft $1.48 million

The TB–50H's unit cost was recorded at $1,485,571—airframe, $993,100; engines (installed), $203,232; electronics, $68,392; ordnance, $8,790; others (propellers, included), $212,057.[65]

---

[65] About $350,000 over the average unit price of other B–50s.

Subsequent Model Series   **None**

Other Configurations   **KB-50K**

When no longer needed for training, the TB-50Hs were brought up to the KB-50J configuration and identified as KB-50Ks. The KB-50J and KB-50K tankers were identical, except for their origin, which accounted for their different designations. The first KB-50K flew in December 1957, and was accepted by the Air Force in January 1958. All modifications, including the addition of the 2 jet engines, were also accomplished by the Hayes Aircraft Corporation and were completed in less than a year. The KB-50Ks, like most KB-50Js, were assigned to the Tactical Air Command and were still being flown in the early sixties.

Phaseout   **June 1955**

The TB-50Hs were phased out of Air Training Command in June 1955, but once reconfigured as KB-50Ks the aircraft served the Air Force for nearly another 10 years.

Program Recap

The Air Force bought 370 B-50 production models and 1 B-50 prototype. Specifically, the B-50 program comprised 79 B-50As, 1 YB-50C (prototype of an improved B-50A), 45 B-50Bs, 222 B-50Ds, and 24 TB-50Hs. Other B-50s, such as the RB-50s, KB-50s, and WB-50s, stemmed from extensive modifications. Such modifications were done either on the production lines after conclusion of the basic contract, or years after the aircraft had been utilized in its intended configuration.

The Air Force added jet engines to a number of B-50s, but others, still only piston-powered and conspicuous in the jet era that followed the end of World War II, remained in the active inventory much longer than expected. For example, some of the B-50As, which were operational in June 1948, continued flying as WB-50s in 1964, acquiring in the process a service life of a quarter of a century.

TECHNICAL AND BASIC MISSION PERFORMANCE DATA

B/RB-50 AND KB-50 AIRCRAFT

Manufacturer (Airframe)	Boeing Airplane Co., Renton, Wash.
Manufacturer (Engine)	The Pratt & Whitney Aircraft Division, United Aircraft Corp., East Hartford, Conn., and The General Electric Co., Schenectady, N.Y.
Nomenclature	Medium Strategic Bomber, Reconnaissance Aircraft, and Flight-Refueling Tanker
Popular Name	Superfortress

	B-50A	B-50D	RB-50G	KB-50
Length/Span (ft)	99.0/141.2	99.0/141.2	99.0/141.2	99.0/141.2
Wing Area (sq ft)	1,720	1,720	1,720	1,720
Weights (lb)				
Empty (basic)	85,155	84,714	88,438	90,270
Combat	120,500	121,850	129,209	107,511
Takeoff (max normal)	158,250[a]	158,250[a]	150,250[a]	173,000[b]
Takeoff (max overload)	168,480[c]	173,000[b]	170,400[c]	Not Applicable
Engine: Number, Rated Power per Engine & Designation	(4) 3,500-lb st R-4360-35 & (1) G.E. Turbo Superch CH-7-B1	(4) 3,500-lb st R-4360-35 & (1) G.E. Turbo Superch CH-7-B1	(4) 3,500-lb st R-4360-35 & (1) G.E. Turbo Superch CH-7-B1	(4) 3,500-lb st R-4360-35 & (1) G.E. Turbo Superch CH-7-B1
Takeoff Ground Run (ft)				
At Sea Level	5,940	6,420	6,150	6,350
Over 50-ft Obstacle	7,425	8,025	7,620	7,940
Rate of Climb (fpm) At Sea Level	675	620	630	608
Combat Max Rate of Climb (fpm) at Sea Level (Max Power)	2,260	2,200	1,680	2,210
Service Ceiling (ft) (100 fpm Rate of Climb to Altitude)	26,550	24,000	23,800	23,250
Service Ceiling (ft) at Combat Weight (100 fpm Rate of Climb to Altitude)	37,300	36,900	37,150	39,800

Combat Ceiling (ft) (500 fpm Rate of Climb, Max Power, to Altitude)	36,000	35,650		
Average Speed (kn)	212	212	227	209
Maximum Speed at Optimum Altitude (kn/ft) Max Power	344/30,000	343/30,000	339/29,700 (Opt)	351/30,600 (334 kn with hoses & drogues extended)
Basic Speed at Altitude (kn/ft) Max Power	337/25,000	337/25,000	333/25,000	287/5,000
Combat Radius (nm)	1,905	2,082	2,116	1,000
Total Mission Time (hr)	17.70	19.53	18.69	10.8
Armament	13 .50-cal machine guns (counting 3 in tail turret)	13 .50-cal machine guns (counting 3 in tail turret)	13 .50-cal Colt-Browning M-3 machine guns (counting 3 in tail turret)	None
Crew	11[d]	8[e]	16[f]	6[g]
Maximum Load (lb)	28,000[h] bombs	28,000[h] bombs	10 Cameras (4 K-38s with 36-in lens, or 2 K-38s with 24-in lens; 1 L-22A or K-17; 1 A-6 Motion Picture; 3 K-17Cs; 1 T-11, 6-in lens).	13,821 gal. of fuel (self-sealing wing tanks)

[a] Limited by performance.
[b] Limited by strength.
[c] Limited by space.
[d] Pilot, co-pilot, engineer, navigator-radar operator-bombardier, bombardier-navigator-radar operator, radio-electronic countermeasure operator, left-side gunner, right-side gunner, top gunner, tail gunner, and extra crew member.
[e] Pilot, co-pilot, engineer, radio-electronic countermeasures operator, left-side gunner, right-side gunner, top gunner, and tail gunner.
[f] Pilot, co-pilot, navigator, engineer, nose gunner, top gunner, left-side gunner, right-side gunner-radio operator, radar operator, tail gunner, and 6 electronic countermeasures operators.
[g] Pilot, co-pilot, engineer, radar-navigator, and 2 refueling operators.
[h] 20,000 pounds, internally; 8,000 pounds, externally.

Abbreviations

cal = caliber
fpm = feet per minute
GE = General Electric
kn = knots
max = maximum
min = minimum
nm = nautical miles

Basic Mission Note

All above basic mission's performance data are based on normal power, except as otherwise noted.

B–50A and B–50D's Combat Radius Formula: Warmed up, took off, climbed on course to 5,000 feet (at normal power), cruised at long-range speeds at altitude for best range but not less than 5,000 feet, climbed on course to reach cruising ceiling 500 nautical miles from target, cruised in level flight to target, conducted 15-minute (normal-power) bomb run, dropped bomb when carried, conducted 2 minutes of evasive action at combat altitude (no distance credit) and an 8-minute run-out from target area (with normal power), cruised at long-range speeds at combat altitude for 50 nautical miles, cruised back to base at long-range speeds at not less than 5,000 feet for best range.

RB–50G's Combat Radius Formula: Took off and climbed on course to 5,000 feet (at normal power), cruised out at long-range speeds. Dropped external and bomb-bay tanks when empty. Climbed to arrive at cruise altitude 500 nautical miles from target. Cruised toward target at long-range speeds, 15 minutes from target conducted normal-power bomb run, conducted 2 minutes of evasive action and 8 minutes of escape from target at normal power. After leaving target area, cruised back at long-range speeds until 500 nautical miles from target, descended to 25,000 feet and cruised back to base at long-range speeds. Climbed to arrive at refuel altitude (cruise ceiling) immediately prior to rendezvous (1 hour at long-range speeds for rendezvous and hook-up, no distance credit), transferred fuel at the rate of 980 gallons per minute while proceeding toward bomber target at normal-rated power, disengaged and returned to base at refueling altitude and long-range speeds. (Mission was planned so that radius at the end of transfer was 1,000 nautical miles.)

B-52 Stratofortress

Boeing
Airplane Company

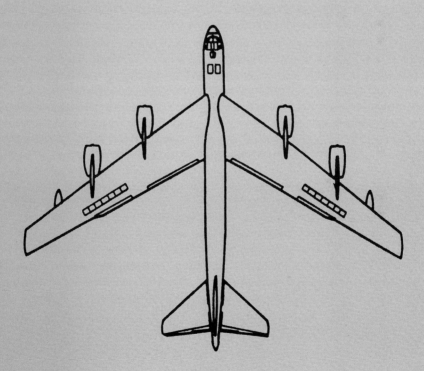

B-52 Stratofortress
Boeing

Manufacturer's Model 464

Weapon System 101

Overview

Most post-World War II bombers evolved from military requirements issued in the early or mid-forties, but none were produced as initially envisioned. Geopolitical factors accounted for the programs; the military threat, varying in degrees of intensity through the years, never ceased to exist. While these factors justified the development of new weapons, technology dictated their eventual configurations. Strategic concepts fell in between, influenced by circumstances as well as the state-of-the-art. Thus the B-36, earmarked in 1941 as a long-range bomber, capable of bearing heavy loads of conventional bombs, matured as the first long-range atomic carrier. The impact of technology was far more spectacular in the case of the B-52, affecting the development of one of history's most successful weapon systems, and the concepts which spelled the long-lasting bomber's many forms of employment.

As called for in 1945, the B-52 was to have an operating radius of 4,340 nautical miles, a speed of 260 knots at altitude of 43,000 feet, and a bombload capacity of 10,000 pounds. Although jet propulsion had already been adopted for the smaller B-45 and B-47 then under development, the high fuel consumption associated with jet engines ruled against their use in long-range aircraft. But what was true in 1945, no longer applied several years later. After floundering through a series of changing requirements and revised studies, the B-52 project became active in 1948. Air Force officials decided that progress in the development of turbojets should make it possible to equip the new long-range bomber with such engines. The decision, however, was not unanimous. Money was short, B–52 substitutes were proposed, and it took the deteriorating international situation caused by the Korean conflict to ensure production of the jet-powered B–52—the initial procurement contract being signed in February 1951.

While technological improvements received top priority when new weapons were designed, untried technology was a tricky business. Hovering over the B–52 weapon system was the specter of the B–47's initial deficiencies. As a result, the B–52 was designed, built, and developed as an integrated package. Components and parts were thoroughly tested before being installed in the new bomber. Changes were integrated on the production lines, giving birth to new models in the series, a fairly common occurrence. Yet, in contrast to the usual pattern, B–52 testing only suggested improvements, and at no time uncovered serious flaws in any of the aircraft. In fact, Maj. Gen. Albert Boyd, Commander of the Wright Air Development Center, and one of the Air Force's foremost test pilots, said that the B–52's first true production model was the finest airplane yet built.

Initially flown in December 1954, the B–52's performance was truly impressive. The new bomber could reach a speed of 546 knots, twice more than called for in 1945, and could carry a load of 43,000 pounds, an increase of about 30,000 pounds. Still, most of the early B–52s were phased out by 1970, due to Secretary of Defense Robert S. McNamara's mid-sixties decision to decrease the strategic bomber force. However, the later B–52G and H-models, and even some of the earlier B–52Ds, were expected to see unrestricted service into the 1980s.

By mid-1973, the B–52s had already compiled impressive records. Many of the aircraft had played important roles during the Vietnam War. Modified B–52Ds, referred to as Big Belly, dropped aerial mines in the North Vietnamese harbors and river inlets in May 1972. In December of the same year, B–52Ds and B–52Gs began to bomb military targets in the Hanoi and Haiphong areas of North Vietnam, where they encountered the most awesome defenses. Although the B–52s were often used for purposes they had not been intended to fulfill, after decades of hard work they remained one of the Strategic Air Command's best assets.

Basic Development 1946

Officially, the B–52's development was initiated in June 1946. However, the basic configuration finally approved bore little resemblance to the original Boeing proposal. In reality, the aircraft's genealogical roots reached back to June 1945, when the Army Air Forces (AAF) directed Air Materiel Command (AMC) to formalize military characteristics for new postwar bombers, as prompted by ". . . the need for this country to be capable of carrying out the strategic mission without dependence upon advanced and intermediate bases controlled by other countries . . . ." The timing of the AAF directive of June 1945 was worthy of note. Although total victory in World War II seemed imminent, the directive obviously reflected growing pessimism over the future of international relations and increasing concern with the experimental B–35 and the problem-ridden B–36, both yet to be flown.

Military Characteristics   23 November 1945

The first in a series of military characteristics for heavy bombardment aircraft was issued in November 1945. This initial document called for a bomber with an operating radius of 5,000 miles (4,340 nautical miles) and a speed of 300 miles per hour (260 knots)[1] at 34,000 feet, carrying a crew of 5, plus an undetermined number of 20-millimeter cannon operators, a 6-man relief crew, as well as a 10,000-pound bombload. Maximum armor protection was another prerequisite.

Request for Proposals   13 February 1946

A design directive, allowing maximum design latitude, was distributed to the aircraft industry with invitations to bid on the military characteristics of November 1945. Three manufacturers—Boeing Airplane Company, Glenn L. Martin Company, and the Consolidated Vultee Aircraft Corporation—submitted cost quotations and preliminary design data close to requirements.

Letter Contract   28 June 1946

The AAF concluded that Model 462, the Boeing proposal for a straight-wing aircraft grossing 360,000 pounds[2] and powered by 6 Wright T-35 gas turbine engines with 6 propellers, promised the best performance per dollar cost. The proposed aircraft, with its 3,110-mile radius, fell short

---

[1] The range and speed of aircraft were shown in statute miles until the late 1940s; in some cases, until the early 1950s. Afterwards, speed was measured in knots; range, in nautical miles.

[2] Gross weight is the total weight of an airplane fully loaded; take-off weight is the actual gross weight of an airplane at take-off; the main factor limiting an airplane's maximum take-off weight is structural strength.

in range, but experience showed such a deficiency could be alleviated during the course of development. Hence, on 5 June Boeing was informed that it was the competition's winner and in mid-month Model 462, which closely resembled the much lighter B-29, became the XB-52.[3] Because money, never sufficient from the users' point of view, appeared particularly scarce at the time, the letter contract awarded to Boeing on 28 June covered only the initial development (Phase I[4]) of Model 462. Specifically, Letter Contract W-33-03A-ac-15065 asked for a full-scale mockup of the intercontinental XB-52, plus preliminary design engineering, construction of a power plant test rig, gunfire testing, structural testing, and the supplying of engineering data. Boeing could spend not more than $1.7 million on this Phase I work. And while the letter contract allowed the eventual continuation into a second phase, money was not mentioned.

Initial Reappraisal   October 1946

Despite the apparent urgency of the new bomber project, the military characteristics of November 1945 did not prevail long. In October 1946, less than 3 months after Boeing's receipt of a letter contract, discussions began that essentially reflected the AAF's unanimous concern over the "monstrous size" of the proposed XB-52 (Model 462). Maj. Gen. Earle E. Partridge, Assistant Chief of Air Staff for Operations, flatly stated that the XB-52 design failed to meet requirements. Boeing thereupon came up with a different proposal. This was Model 464, a much lighter (230,000 pounds), 4-engine version of the previous 6-engine design. Maj. Gen. Laurence C. Craigie, Chief of the AAF's Engineering Division, recommended adoption of the 4-engine XB-52, but many changes were yet to come. Indicative of the period's difficult times, new and sometimes unrealistic requirements later followed that nearly spelled the program's end.

Program Changes   1946-1947

In November 1946, General LeMay, then Deputy Chief of Air Staff for Research and Development, while noting that the 230,000-pound XB-52

---

[3] The next available bomber designation; Martin's Model 234 (a development of the contractor's winning attack design submitted in February 1946 as the XA-45) being already earmarked as the future (and later canceled) B-51 light bomber.

[4] A "phase" was a stage in the planned development of a program considered in respect both to (a) the nature of the tasks undertaken and (b) the timing.

had merits, stressed that besides extra range the future B–52 should have a higher cruising speed, something in the vicinity of 400 miles per hour. Boeing's ensuing suggestion that a 300,000-pound plane (60,000 pounds less than Model 462) might be the answer became academic, or so it seemed. In December, the AAF asked Boeing to provide design studies for a 12,000-mile range, 4-engine general purpose bomber, capable of carrying the atomic bomb. A 400-mile per hour tactical speed was required, and a gross weight of 480,000 pounds was again authorized. Fully aware of the existing limits of technology and because its first turboprop bomber had fallen far short on range, Boeing gave the AAF 2 very-heavy bomber designs—Models 464–16 and 464–17. Both appeared fairly similar and were to be powered by 4 T–35 turboprop engines of higher horsepower than those earmarked for the earlier 464 version. There was a clear difference, however. The special mission 464–16 model would carry only a 10,000-pound bombload; the general purpose 464–17 model, up to 90,000. While perhaps attractive in theory, the AAF categorically rejected the simultaneous development of 2 new bombers because this would be financially reckless. What it really wanted was an aircraft that could either carry many conventional bombs or be stripped for long-range, special missions. After careful evaluation, the AAF opted for Model 464–17.

Revised Military Characteristics   June 1947

The military characteristics of November 1945 were officially superseded in June 1947. The new characteristics called for a heavy bomber offering the improved performances that had been in the definition process for about 8 months. Except for range, the 464–17 XB–52, as proposed, met requirements. Its degree of success, however, would largely depend on the much improved T–35 engine promised by Wright. Moreover, a new problem had begun to surface. The requirements painstakingly established since October 1946 no longer seemed adequate.

New Setbacks   Mid-1947

The latest XB–52 (Model 464–17) appeared satisfactory, but only temporarily. This came as no great surprise. General LeMay long believed that, even if all went well, this XB–52 would be too large and too costly—possibly limiting procurement to 100 aircraft. General Craigie was also highly critical. In his opinion, the new XB–52 would offer little improvement over Convair's B–36G.[5] And, quite likely, the XB–52 would be obsolete before completion. Soon there was talk of scrapping the whole venture, but General LeMay favored caution. The XB–52 project should be given a 6-month "grace" period pending final decision concerning its future. This was in line with the AAF's thinking. Thus, after the shelving of Model 464–17, Boeing continued to search for means to improve the airplane. The company swiftly drew up a series of preliminary configurations (Models 464–23, 464–25, and 464–27), which finally culminated in Model 464–29. Even though the weight remained the same, high speed increased slightly to 455 miles per hour, and the operating radius jumped to 5,000 statute miles. Still, Model 464–29 was not to be the final answer.

Further Reappraisal   July–December 1947

While Boeing was told to continue development of the XB–52, AMC was reminded that no actual construction could be started without express consent of the AAF's Commanding General. The command was also directed to explore every possible means for delivering the atomic bomb. The use of subsonic pilotless aircraft was given priority, but one-way manned flights were not excluded.[6] In late September, the Aircraft and Weapons Board of the now independent United States Air Force convened a Heavy Bombardment Committee to obtain "a fresh evaluation of the long-range bomber program." In other words, committee members were directed "to study methods for aerial delivery and individual and mass atomic attacks against any potential aggressor nation from bases within the continental limits of the United States." The Heavy Bombardment Committee concluded decisively that speed and altitude were the basic qualities required of a bomber due to carry the A-bomb. This was particularly true when the bomber reached the combat zone. Up to that point, the plane could actually cruise at lower altitude. By the same token, the all-important range could well be extended by air refueling in the non-combat theater. The committee ended its work by preparing preliminary military characteristics that essentially asked for a special-purpose bomber (in lieu of a general-purpose weapon) with an 8,000-mile range and a 550-mile-per-hour cruising speed. More changes ensued, but the committee's recommendations had an

---

[5] See B–36, p 42.

[6] The Air Force pursued some of those early projects. Like Brass Ring, spurred by the advent of the hydrogen bomb, none materialized as originally conceived.

immediate impact. Boeing's latest 450-mile-per-hour XB–52 (Model 464–29), obviously too slow to survive in combat, no longer had a chance.

New Military Characteristics   8 December 1947

The military characteristics of June 1947 were officially superseded on 8 December. The new set, as approved by General Vandenberg, Vice Chief of Staff, General Kenney, Commander of Strategic Air Command (SAC), and Gen. Joseph T. McNarney, who now headed the Air Materiel Command, closely resembled the proposal submitted by the Heavy Bombardment Committee. The most telling difference was that the bomber's required cruising speed was reduced—a change endorsed after studies by the AMC and Rand[7] pointed out that the desired 8,000-mile range could be attained only at a speed not in excess of 500 miles per hour.

Near-Cancellation   1947–1948

With the approval of new characteristics, the question arose within the Air Staff whether the Boeing contract should be amended or canceled in favor of a new design competition. The idea of a new competition was tempting. A better bomber might be obtained by again tapping all the engineering brains in the industry. Also, as previously noted by General LeMay, many companies which had failed to bid on the original project were of a different mind now that a large part of the Air Force production funds appeared slated for the future B–52. The Air Materiel Command did not agree with the Air Staff. AMC claimed that Boeing was the best-qualified heavy bomber contractor, that a new competition would consume much valuable time, and that some $4 million would be wasted if the Boeing development contract was nullified. For good reasons, the AMC arguments failed to convince the Air Staff. First, Boeing already had a large share of the Air Force business, and amending the company's contract might cause political repercussions or a public accusation of favoritism. Secondly, if Boeing was truly the best contractor, it would win the competition handily,

---

[7] Rand (for research and development) was the code name applied to numerous studies by the Douglas Aircraft Company—a project initiated by the AAF in 1946. In 1948, a grant from the Ford Foundation brought about a reorganization of the project. It became the Rand Corporation, a non-governmental, nonprofit organization dedicated to research for the welfare and national security of the United States. Research by the corporation was conducted with its own funds or with funds supplied by government agencies. The Rand Corporation is located in Santa Monica, Calif., but maintains offices in Washington, D.C.

and little delay would occur because the company had already worked on the XB–52 preliminary design. Therefore, on 11 December 1947, following verbal approval by Under Secretary of the Air Force Arthur S. Barrows, Lt. Gen. Howard A. Craig, Deputy Chief of Staff for Materiel, directed AMC to cancel the Boeing contract. However, the case was not closed. Before the directive could be executed, Boeing's President, Mr. William M. Allen, protested vigorously to Secretary of the Air Force Stuart Symington that the decision was unsound. The Boeing letter stressed that the proposed cancellation and renewal of XB–52 competition would be "a serious injustice to the contractor . . . and provide a 'second chance' to others who would profit from Boeing's progress." The letter also underlined that the company had passed up other projects after entering the heavy bombardment competition in the spring of 1946. Since then, some of its ablest talent had been dedicated to the project. Finally, the bulk of the other Air Force production contracts held by Boeing would be completed before the B–52 production could begin. In all fairness, the Air Force had to admit that many of Boeing's arguments were valid. Thus, it might be best to avoid any rash decision.

Other Alternatives   1948

In January 1948, Mr. Symington replied to Boeing, giving a keen analysis of the problem facing the Air Force.[8] He considered the heavy bombardment project to be of the greatest importance, and believed the new bomber would play a dominant role in any future war. "For this reason," he emphasized, "the USAF must be assured of the best possible design and configuration. There could be no compromise on this provision." The Secretary said that much scientific progress had been made since the original competition. The technique of air-to-air refueling had been perfected to the point where it should be possible to develop an airplane with the top speed and cruising speed of a medium bomber and with only a slightly higher gross weight. This aircraft should certainly be lighter than previously proposed versions of the XB–52. Another possibility (insufficiently considered, according to the Air Staff) was the flying wing design. Rand studies had noted that this configuration offered definite advantages when applied to long-range, high-speed aircraft. Mr. Symington concluded that, until all avenues had been thoroughly explored, no final decision could be made on the original Boeing contract.

---

[8] Concurrent difficulties with the B–36 did not help. This program once again appeared on the verge of collapse—another major decision soon confronting the Secretary.

Go-Ahead Decision   March 1948

In February 1948, after acknowledging the merits of the flying wing being tested by the Northrop Corporation, Boeing noted some of the inherent disadvantages of this type of configuration. Foremost were marginal stability and control. Boeing willingly emphasized that research and experiment with the all-wing aircraft should not be discouraged. But the proposed B–52 had more flexibility for radar and armament installation and none of the "flying wing's" problems. Consequently, the conventional aircraft should be given first developmental priority, "so that the Air Force should not be left without an effective bomber." From its own investigation, AMC's Engineering Division contended that the XB–52 development should be continued. The Air Staff also began to favor the XB–52, believing it to have a higher probability of success and to be easier to maintain than any potential version of the "flying wing." Thus, in March 1948, the Secretary of the Air Force informed Boeing that its present contract would be modified to develop a bomber meeting the military characteristics of December 1947, as already or subsequently revised. In April Boeing presented a complete Phase II proposal for the design, development, construction, and testing of 2 XB–52s (Model 464–35). Although estimated to cost about $30 million, this Phase II proposal received the Air Force's endorsement in July.

Additional Revisions   1948

During 1948, several revisions were made to the military characteristics of December 1947. The first occurred in March, 2 months after Boeing submitted for the first time Model 464–35—a bomber having the desired range and speed but weighing only between 285,000 and 300,000 pounds. A second revision specified a 360,000-pound plane, with an average cruising speed of 445 miles per hour and a range of 11,635 miles. A final revision on 15 December defined a 280,000-pound bomber that could carry 10,000 pounds of bombs and 19,875 gallons of fuel for 6,909 miles, at a maximum speed of 513 miles per hour at a 35,000-foot altitude. None of the 3 revisions affected the December 1947 requirements for a 5-man crew and tail armament only. But more changes occurred over time and the B–52s eventually carried a crew of 6, as a rule.

Contractual Arrangements   September 1947–November 1948

Boeing's original contract, as initiated by the letter contract of June

1946, was approved on 2 September 1947. By then the contract already reached $4.6 million—$1.7 million for Phase I, the initial development commitment, plus $2.9 million for Phase II, an extension of the Phase I work directed by the existing letter contract. The Phase II funds were provided per supplemental agreement on 13 June 1947. Of necessity, these funds were shuffled around. For a while, the Phase II funds were due to finance the Phase I development of Model 464-17. However, this model's cancellation prompted a second change, the $2.9 million Phase II funds now being earmarked for the Phase II development of yet another configuration—Model 464-35. Meanwhile, as approved by Under Secretary Barrows, an additional $563,766 was allocated on 7 April 1948 for the Phase I development of the same model (464-35), bringing the Phase I investment to a total of $2.3 million. But completion of the Phase II development would prove to be considerably more expensive. In mid-1948, as a result of the revised characteristics of December 1947, the Phase II cost of developing, building, and testing 2 XB-52s (Model 464-35) was estimated at $28.3 million. This did not include $1 million for contractor-selected spare parts or $4.8 million for engineering design improvements and the installation of tactical equipment in the 2 experimental planes. Even spread over several years, the research and development budget could not possibly sustain such expense without jeopardizing other essential projects. Some expedient had to be found. On 17 November 1948, the Air Force approved another supplemental agreement to the definitive contract of September 1947. This time, the agreement shifted $6.8 million of procurement funds to support the first 2 years of the XB-52 development.

Radical Change   1948

In the spring of 1948, after floundering for about 2 years through a series of changing requirements and revised Phase I studies, the XB-52 project finally seemed on its way. Although the Air Force still made it clear that the XB-52 development program must result in the most advanced design possible, Boeing actually prepared to build 2 experimental, turboprop-equipped articles of Model 464-35, its latest bomber proposal. But the plans once again were altered—with more drastic changes yet to come—by recent progress in the development of turbojet engines. The turbojet concept was not new. As early as June 1945, during discussions over the characteristics for strategic bombers, AAF officers had pushed for the development of jet engines suitable for bombers. However, the fuel consumption of jet engines was then so high that this kind of propulsion was discarded in view of the ranges required of the strategic bombers. In 1948 the technological situation was totally different. The Air Force asked Boeing in

May 1948 if it could incorporate jet engines in the proposed XB–52. This resulted in still another XB–52 version (Model 464–40), featuring the Westinghouse J40 engine and a minimum of changes to the turboprop XB–52 under construction. The Air Force received Boeing's preliminary study of its jet-propelled Model 464–40 in late July.

New Controversy   1948

Shortly after Boeing's Model 464–40 was submitted to the Air Force, a new debate arose. In October, General Craig expressed his dislike for the proposal, believing that improvement in heavy bombardment aircraft would come only when the bomber configuration was changed and stating that "unless supersonic propellers become a reality, future aircraft of this class will be powered by turbojet engines, however neither of these developments are sufficiently near at hand that the turboprop step can be eliminated." The Deputy Chief of Staff for Materiel's pessimism proved unwarranted, as Boeing engineers within days of his remarks devised the very solution which led to the development of the remarkable B–52. Still, Boeing did not reap success without toil. On 21 October, after arriving at Wright Field to confer on their XB–52 turboprop aircraft (Model 464–35), Boeing engineering executives were informed by AMC officials that a drastic reappraisal of the XB–52 project seemed in order. In short, AMC wanted a preliminary study of an entirely new airplane which would be powered by Pratt and Whitney Aircraft Division's new J57 turbojet engines. According to popular newspaper accounts, the Boeing representatives retired to a Dayton hotel room over the weekend. Drawing on the experience gained in the B–47 program, they worked around the clock and on Monday morning, 25 October 1948, presented the requested proposal—a 33-page report plus a hand-carved model of their new design—Model 464–49. Perhaps the feat was not as spectacular as it appeared. As exemplified by Model 464–40, Boeing had been considering for quite a while the possible use of jet power plants in bombers far heavier than the B–47. In any case, the Boeing engineers liked Model 464–49, an airplane having 35-degree swept wings, 8 engines slung in pairs on 4 pylons under the wing, and an overall configuration that departed from the B–29 and B–50 for the newer B–47 body style. They were confident that additional range could be gained with "only reasonable increase in weight," and that the new jet engines would provide improved altitude and speed performances. Besides, jet engines would eliminate the many unsolved problems of propeller aerodynamics and control, and probably extend the airplane's operational life. Finally, this jet version of the XB–52 could be available almost as quickly as the turboprop already under development.

Program Reendorsement   1949

The Board of Senior Officers[9] was favorably impressed by most of the operational accomplishments expected of the new 330,000-pound model. When equipped with J57 turbojets (yet to be available), the swept-wing XB-52 promised to reach a top speed of 496 knots (572 miles per hour); to fly 6,947 nautical miles at an average speed of 452 knots (520 miles per hour) without refueling; and to be capable of delivering a 10,000-pound bombload at a comfortable altitude of 45,000 feet. After a final evaluation in January 1949, the board decided to continue development, "with the Boeing Aircraft Company," of the XB-52 as a turbojet in lieu of the turboprop-powered aircraft. This would be done under the same contract, and Boeing was so informed on 26 January. Meanwhile, favorable opinions did not prevail in all quarters. The stringent economy drive directed by President Truman in late 1948 endangered the costly B-52 development program. Concerted attempts were made to equate performance and cost data with present and "soon-to-be" outdated aircraft. In February, the Deputy Chief of Staff for Materiel's Directorate of Research and Development came to the program's rescue. Officials pointed out that the major difference between the B-36 and the proposed B-52 was timing. The B-36 seemed to be the solution to the strategic bombardment problem as it appeared in 1942; the future B-52, as it appeared in 1949. Under existing state-of-the-art limitations, vigorous development of the turbojet B-52 afforded the Air Force its only hope for carrying out the strategic air mission, specifically the delivery of the atomic bomb, should it become necessary over the next 5 years. Surely, the Air Force would be remiss if it failed to develop a successor to the B-36. While the arguments of the Research and Development Directorate were persuasive, a new threat surfaced. In the spring of 1949, the Fairchild Aircraft Corporation forwarded a design proposal for the development of an unconventional strategic bomber.[10] The Board of Senior Officers again reviewed the Boeing airplane's potential growth and agreed to continued development of Model 464-49. However, Fairchild's unconventional design did not disappear, and other contractors soon submitted proposals that further imperiled the new program.

---

[9] Established in December 1948, the USAF Board of Senior Officers included the Vice Chief of Staff, the Deputy Chief of Staff for Operations, the Deputy of Staff for Materiel, and the Commanding General, AMC. This board replaced the USAF Aircraft and Weapons Board, which was composed of all Deputy Chiefs of Staff and major air commanders and had proved too cumbersome. The dormant board was discontinued in the fall of 1949.

[10] The Fairchild proposal aircraft, a fuel-carrying wing, indeed appeared revolutionary. It used a railroad flatcar as a launcher. The intent was to provide maximum initial speed and altitude so that the aircraft would conserve fuel and attain sufficient range.

Mockup Inspections

Like the many model configurations considered at one time or another, all mockup inspections scheduled prior to 1948 were canceled. Moreover, the few finally conducted in January 1948 only covered nose sections, where arrangement of the reduced crew presented difficulties. As for Boeing's latest turboprop XB–52 (Model 464–35), although its mockup was essentially complete by October 1948, all work was halted before any formal inspection could be made. Thus, the swept-wing turbojet XB–52 was the first to merit a full-fledged mockup inspection. This was accomplished at the Boeing Seattle plant and lasted from 26 to 29 April 1949. The inspection board of USAF personnel found no special faults with the mockup but noted in its report that the experimental XB–52, with its J40–6 engines, would not match the B–36's 4,000-nautical-mile radius. The board also indicated that expedited development, as well as significant improvement of the J57 turbojet might assure B–52 aircraft of a 4,000-nautical mile combat radius, but this could not be expected before 1954. In any case, the importance of meeting such a requirement had been emphasized to the contractor. The Air Staff approved the board's report on 1 October, with significant reservations. This was obvious when Gen. Muir S. Fairchild, Vice Chief of Staff since 27 May 1948, carefully underlined that the XB–52 mockup report was approved to expedite potential future production, but that such approval "does not include acceptance of any production article not meeting specified range requirements."

Last Near-Cancellation

General Fairchild's "tentative approval" of the XB–52 mockup inspection report was viewed by many as a practical "cancellation of the program as it now exists." Since the J57 engine, in its present developmental stage, would only give the B–52 a combat radius of about 2,700 nautical miles, the bomber would never materialize unless some "mechanical dodge" was devised to extend range. Maj. Gen. Orville R. Cook, the AMC Director of Procurement and Industrial Planning, favored a review of the program and perhaps a revision of the military characteristics and scheduling of another design competition. General LeMay,[11] in command of SAC since October 1948, believed that the solution lay in engine development, that it was unnecessary to accept inferior performance in either speed or range, and

---

[11] Promoted to full general on 29 October 1951, General LeMay headed SAC until mid-1957.

that a conference on the B–52 airplane was urgently required. Meanwhile, Boeing kept busy. Accelerated engineering and development tests were conducted to solve problems of aero-elasticity, vibration, and control that resulted from the higher wing sweep, greater speeds, and thinner wing. In November 1949, convinced that inadequate range seriously jeopardized the future of its new bomber (Model 464–49), Boeing offered a heavier B–52 (Model 464–67). This 390,000-pound B–52, Boeing said, would have a radius of 3,785 nautical miles for production aircraft anticipated in 1953 and 4,185 nautical miles for a B–52 in 1957. Increased combat radius could be obtained in time and with additional expenditure of money. Boeing concluded that the heavier XB–52 was as technically advanced in aircraft design as possible. The contractor's efforts to safeguard the B–52 program did not go unnoticed. By year's end, SAC officials generally agreed that the contractor had made appreciable progress toward satisfactory development of the airplane. Soon afterwards, the conference suggested by General LeMay took place. However, the meeting's conferees at Headquarters USAF on 26 January 1950 faced a difficult task. Once more, substitutes were proposed for the B–52. Included were new proposals by the Douglas and Republic Aircraft Companies, Fairchild Aircraft Corporation's unusual design, the swept-wing B–36G (later known as the YB–60), a Rand turboprop airplane, 2 new designs of the B–47, and several missile aircraft. Even though General LeMay took a firm stand in favor of the B–52 as the aircraft which would best meet the requirements of the strategic mission, the conference ended before any decision could be reached. But SAC's Commander-in-Chief was not easily deterred. In February, the Air Staff requested from AMC all performance data and tentative production dates of the various combat vehicles recently considered. In the same month, however, General LeMay asked the Board of Senior Officers to accept Boeing Model 464–67 in lieu of Model 464–49. Approved by the board on 24 March 1950, this change eventually led to the production decision General LeMay so badly wanted.

Production Decision   January 1951

Although there were no more direct attempts to sidetrack the B–52 development once Model 464–67 was endorsed, the future of the production program remained uncertain. Some substitutes seemed to regain momentum, with the swept-wing B–36 and long-range B–47Z coming to the fore. SAC opposed both, believing the new B–36 would have lower cruising and target speeds than a future B–52 and that the 3-man crew B–47Z would retain inherent limitations for intercontinental operations. A comparative study of the B–52 and the advanced B–47, SAC officials stated, showed that the B-52 was superior in performance. The B-52's extra crewmen would materially reduce the serious fatigue problems stemming from long missions. Also, electronic countermeasures equipment could be fitted in the larger B-52, thereby ensuring protection against future surface-to-air and air-to-air guided missiles. In spite of such arguments, the Air Staff had made no definite commitment by the fall of 1950, compelling General LeMay to become directly involved once again. And whereas World War II had prompted production of the B-36, another war helped the B-52. General LeMay was quick to point out that the international situation during the Korean conflict was deteriorating rapidly; that SAC's forward operating bases were becoming more vulnerable to enemy attack; and that increasing as well as modernizing SAC's intercontinental bombardment forces should receive priority consideration. Referring again to the B-52, General LeMay said: "Perhaps even more important is the concurrent requirement for the development of a long-range, high-performance aircraft, such as the RB-52, capable of operating alone over highly defended enemy areas in the performance of the reconnaissance mission." Finally convinced, the Board of Senior Officers concurred that the B-52 would be the production successor to the B-36. Also, since the B-52 was not a radical departure from existing stages of aircraft development, procurement could start before completion of the XB-52 testing. General Vandenberg, Chief of Staff since 30 April 1948, approved the board's recommendations on 9 January 1951; Thomas K. Finletter, the new Secretary of the Air Force, on the 24th.

Initial Production Plans   1951–1952

Letter Contract AF33(038)–21096, signed on 14 February 1951 by Boeing and the Air Force, was the first document authorizing production. It covered long lead time items and the production of 13 B-52As, the first of which was tentatively scheduled for delivery in April 1953. The letter contract of 1951 was finalized on 7 November 1952 by a cost-plus-fixed-fee contract. As originally agreed, Boeing's fixed fee remained set at 6 percent of the contract costs. In the interim, there were changes and many more were to follow. An amendment to the first letter contract provided for 17 reconnaissance pods—detachable capsules to be fitted in the early bombers. In July 1951, the Air Staff directed AMC to acquire 4 more B-52s—presumably to match the number of aircraft to the total of reconnaissance pods ordered. The additional planes were to be paid for, like their predecessors, with fiscal year (FY) 1952 funds, but would come from a second Boeing plant—yet to be selected. The directive, however, was soon rescinded, and in October the Air Staff informed AMC that all B-52 production aircraft would be in a reconnaissance configuration. In September 1952, the Air Force gave Boeing a second letter contract—AF33(600)–22119—that called for 43 RB–52s. But none of these early plans materialized due to technical improvements and budgetary restrictions. Ironically, the Korean War, which first worked in favor of the production program, slowed down progress because the industrial situation was confused following the unexpected outbreak of hostilities. Meanwhile, development of the 2 experimental B–52s gradually moved on.

Development Difficulties   1950–1952

As far as General LeMay was concerned, it was difficult enough to persuade the Air Staff to approve Model 464–67, but even more challenging to avoid the frustrating series of events that had marked the B–47 development. The reconnaissance requirements finally stipulated in early 1951 especially complicated matters. Boeing had known for a long while of the Air Force's reconnaissance ambitions.[12] There was nevertheless considerable disagreement between the Air Staff and SAC. Headquarters USAF thought photography should be the RB–52's main mission and that any equipment compromising this function should be excluded. On the other hand, SAC believed the airplane should have a full complement of electronic reconnaissance (or ferret) equipment for operation at night or in bad weather. Furthermore, only a minimum of cameras should be carried to give "local" photographic coverage when light conditions permitted. At any rate, preliminary designs for an experimental RB–52 were completed by mid-1950, but in August Boeing embarked on another approach. The contractor suggested forsaking the RB–52 because it would be simpler and much cheaper to install in the B–52's bomb bays a multi-purpose pod housing reconnaissance equipment. This multi-purpose pod could be replaced by a photo pod or a ferret pod, as needed. At this point, AMC agreed

---

[12] Development of a special, long-range reconnaissance airplane, the so-called X or RX–16, became a topic of primary interest soon after the end of World War II. Yet, by 1949 ideas about the equipment required to accomplish the strategic reconnaissance mission remained in constant flux. There was also increasing concern that the cost of building a specific airplane for reconnaissance would be "staggering to the national economy." The Air Force therefore dropped the RX–16 project. It began instead to consider modifying bomber aircraft for the reconnaissance role. A first step toward this goal, the Air Materiel Command stressed, was to determine the type of data needed, then decide on the equipment best fitted to gather such data. The Air Force nevertheless believed that manned aircraft such as the B–36 and B–52 would be required for reconnaissance duty well into the 1960's. There were concurrent talks about parasite aircraft and guided missiles which most likely would some day perform reconnaissance functions.

that the proposal was sound, but cautioned Boeing that the B–52's bombing capabilities could not be jeopardized to satisfy reconnaissance objectives. In response, SAC proposed in June 1951 a reconnaissance B–52, capable of conversion to the bomber configuration. This could be done, according to SAC, by removing the reconnaissance pod and adding bomb racks in its place. An August conference, attended by representatives from the Air Staff, Air Research and Development Command, SAC, AMC, and the Air Weather Service seemed to settle a controversy that centered essentially on priorities. In short, should the aircraft be primarily a bomber with a secondary reconnaissance role, or vice versa? The conferees voted for a B–52 bomber that could be converted to the reconnaissance configuration and returned to its original configuration, as necessary. This "convertibility," the conferees decided, should allow personnel "at the wing level in the field" to do the transformation in a reasonable time. But the lull in the controversy did not last. As already noted, the Air Staff directed in October 1951 that all aircraft "will be of the RB–52 configuration as there is no requirement for a B–52." The directive was misleading since the aircraft would retain conversion features for bombardment operations. In actuality, the Air Staff's decision was a belated approval of SAC's most recent planning. Just the same, the discussions, delays, and production orders of 1952, along with subsequent deletions, did not as a whole expedite the experimental program.

Other Development Problems   1951–1952

Besides the reconnaissance requirements of 1951, various circumstances affected the B–52's development. Early in the year, General LeMay told Boeing that the tandem-seating arrangement featured by the XB–52 mockup was poor. Since it allowed little room for flight instruments, small panel instruments would have to be used, and this had proven unsatisfactory in all types of aircraft. In addition, the tandem arrangment reduced the copilot's role to a flight engineer operating emergency flight controls— obviously limiting his assistance to the pilot. In a plane as important and costly as the B–52, safety was a top priority. General LeMay believed that side-by-side seating of the pilot and copilot would ensure closer coordination between the two, which in some cases might prove vital. The issue of tandem versus side-by-side seating was settled in August. The Air Staff agreed that significant operational advantages would be gained by adopting the side-by-side arrangement. Some slight confusion nevertheless ensued. First, a few of the early B–52 productions would retain the tandem seating configuration; then, only the experimental planes would not be changed. This was decided after Boeing pointed out that the lack of additional facilities made some production delay inevitable. The production time lost could be put to good use, the contractor felt, by incorporating a side-by-side cockpit from the start. This would save SAC the trouble of operating and maintaining 2 B-52 configurations and cut production costs by almost $17 million. There were other protracted discussions. SAC continued to strive for near-perfection, insisting that even greater range was desired to secure better operational flexibility in the dispersal of the B-52 force. Based on earlier experience, SAC also thought that space should be provided in the aircraft to carry the greater bombloads and large missiles anticipated in the future. Finally, there were several arguments about which engines should be used. For instance, SAC asked that an advanced engine, the General Electric X-24A, be made available without delay to permit the B-52 to realize its full potential. But this engine's production was not scheduled until 1957, and no plans were made to phase such an engine into the B-52 program.

First Flight (YB-52)   15 April 1952

Contrary to usual practices, the prototype B-52 took to the air several months ahead of the experimental B-52.[13] Lagging deliveries of engines[14] and pneumatic systems retarded the XB-52's first flight, but the main delay came from an engineering decision to change the aircraft's rear wing spar—a structural modification directly incorporated in the YB-52. In any case, the prototype's flight also slipped 1 month because General Electric did not deliver the pneumatic systems until 1952. Yet, the YB-52's 15 April flight proved well worth the wait. Taking off from Boeing's Renton Field, Seattle, Washington, the plane flew for 2 hours and 51 minutes before landing at nearby Larson AFB. Enthusiastic reports flowed in from engineers, observers, the pilots and, naturally, from the contractor. Pilots of the escort planes which accompanied the YB-52 on its flight reported that its performance was excellent and commented that its slow approach and landing speed were particularly remarkable. At touchdown, the drag parachute was deployed for testing only, as very little braking was required. Of course, there were a

---

[13] Boeing's original contract called for 2 XB-52s, bare of certain expensive tactical equipment. In mid-1949, Boeing suggested that such equipment be installed in the second XB-52. The contractor justified the costly installation by pointing out that the resultant airplane could serve as production prototype. The Air Force agreed and the second XB-52 became the YB-52.

[14] The Air Force Power Plant Laboratory insisted from the start that Pratt and Whitney had to supply Boeing with prototypes of the J57-P-3 engines for both the X and YB-52s. It believed that since those engines would equip the B-52s, they should also go into the experimental versions of the plane. This would allow Pratt and Whitney to "debug" the engines during the flight test program, while Boeing was "debugging" the airframe.

few minor problems. One of the quadricycle landing gears retracted improperly, the liquid oxygen system failed (due in part to the crew's unfamiliarity with it), and 1 of the engine oil valves leaked, causing a trail of puffy white smoke rings throughout the flight. A second flight on 20 April was even more successful. Remaining below 15,000-foot altitude because of restrictions on engine operation, the YB-52 attained a speed of 350 miles per hour. The restrictions were anticipated. Pratt and Whitney had encountered difficulty in pushing the experimental J57 through the 50-hour qualification run—succeeding only in August 1951, on the third qualification attempt. Whatever the cause, these early problems were swiftly corrected. By October 1952, the YB-52 had flown some 50 hours and had reached speeds of Mach 0.84 without full power at altitudes above 50,000 feet. The Air Force officially accepted the prototype on 31 March 1953 but let Boeing keep it for further testing. The contractor flight-tested the plane for a total of 738 hours, accumulated in 345 flights.[15] The YB-52 remained on loan to Boeing until January 1958, but the contractor kept it in storage during most of 1957. On 27 January 1958, the aircraft was donated to the Air Force Museum, Wright-Patterson AFB, Ohio.

First Flight (XB-52)   2 October 1952

Although the experimental B-52 rolled out of the factory on 29 November 1951,[16] it did not fly until almost 1 year later—after significant modifications. The Air Force took possession of the XB-52 on 15 October 1952 (13 days after the aircraft's 2-hour first flight), but did not formally accept it until 1953. Because of its late start, the XB-52 barely participated in the contractor's Phase I testing, flying only 6 flights for a total of 11:15 hours. For the same reason, the Phase II flight test program, which was the Air Force's responsibility, began behind schedule. It was entirely conducted on the XB-52 between 3 November 1952 and 15 March 1953—reflecting an additional slippage of almost 2 months because of inclement weather in the Seattle area. Phase II tests revealed a number of deficiencies. The XB-52's engines surged and might shut down if normal throttle accelerations were

---

[15] Actually, USAF pilots flew the YB-52 8 times for 27 hours from Edwards AFB, Calif., between 5 June and 18 July 1953. Because the plane was on loan to Boeing, flights and flying hours were included in the contractor's totals.

[16] The XB-52 was moved to the flight test hangar under concealing tarpaulins during the night. According to the press, the great secrecy surrounding the whole event was dictated by the Air Force as a means of testing the effectiveness of its latest security policies. Yet, in view of Boeing's competitors and the many proposals still floating around, one could reasonably assume that the contractor was also eager to keep its new plane out of sight.

attempted at high altitude and low engine inlet temperatures. The brake system could not stop the aircraft within the distances guaranteed by Boeing. The XB–52 tended to pitch up and roll to the right just before stalling. Also, during landing roll, the experimental plane required twice the normal distance to stop. There were also problems with the tires, which tended to blow out when cross winds shoved the aircraft to one side. Completion of the Phase II tests prompted the XB–52's return to Boeing—the aircraft remaining on loan to the contractor for several years. In late March 1953 the plane began to undergo Phase III flight tests, but was soon grounded for major rework and did not resume flying until mid–1954. It nevertheless took part in the overall flight test program, finally accounting for 24 flights and a total of 46 flying hours. Boeing returned the XB–52 to the Air Force in early 1957, and in March the plane was assigned to the Wright Air Development Center at Wright-Patterson, to serve as a test-bed. After 893 hours of flight, 2 J75 engines were installed on the outboard struts, the XB–52 becoming a 6-engine airplane since the 4 inboard J57 engines remained. Modifications to the nacelles and installation of the new engines took time, immobilizing the airplane for almost a year.

Testing Program   1952–1962

Perhaps no aircraft would ever be as thoroughly tested as the B–52, nor did such a long-lasting program often start with so many controversies. The Air Force at first wanted to evaluate the aircraft at Edwards AFB's Flight Test Center. Boeing immediately disagreed, insisting that flying time at Seattle was rarely affected by bad weather and that excessive delays and expenses would occur in correcting defects discovered during testing, if the airplanes were not flown from the Boeing field. The Air Materiel Command somewhat reluctantly sided with Boeing in the belief that B–52 testing at Edwards AFB, under the auspices of the Flight Test Center, might lead to costly post-production modifications—a B–47 episode the Air Force did not care to repeat. The Air Research and Development Command, however, advocated testing the B–52 at the Flight Test Center, since that facility was responsible for the task. Although impressed by the research and development command's logic, AMC pointed out that conducted tests at Edwards would require perhaps an extra $20 million. Air Research and Development Command conceded, "partially as a result of the AMC's uncompromising refusal to provide the necessary additional funds." In 1953, contrary to Boeing's claims, the Seattle weather began to hold back testing. In February, after considering the extended Phase II[17] flying period and the hazards of operating in and to Seattle's metropolitan area, the Air Force directed a change in the test site. Initially, Larson AFB was chosen; subsequently, Fairchild AFB (also in the state of Washington) became the test base, with some of the later tests to be flown from Edwards. Meanwhile, other changes were underway, with more anticipated for the future. To begin with, the testing program acquired several extra B-52s. While the Phase I and II tests were conducted with only the X and YB-52s, the contractor's Phase III testing required 6 B-52s besides the YB-52. In the interim, the Air Force accepted 3 B-52As (the only ones built of 13 ordered) and returned the 3 planes to Boeing for Phase IV testing. Phase IV tests began with the third B-52A production (Serial No. 52-003) on 25 January 1955 and ran through the end of November. These tests had two main purposes. The contractor wanted to spot-check the stability data obtained during the Phase II tests of the reworked XB-52, and to compare the performance of the more powerful J57-P-29 engine against that of the J57-P-1W (first installed in the B-52A). The third B-52A, by itself, accounted for more than 288 hours of Phase IV testing accomplished in 60 flights. As expected, the J57-P-29-equipped B-52A demonstrated superior takeoff and climb performances.

Phase VI functional development testing also took place in 1955, ahead of the Phase V tests, which were delayed because of equipment shortages. The Phase VI tests, conducted at Edwards AFB, started on 3 March and made use of 2 B-52Bs (Serial No 52-005 and 52-006). They ended on 6 September, 2 months earlier than forecast, after 157 flights totaling 984 hours. Phase VI was designed to subject the entire strategic bomber weapon

---

[17] The Air Force used the word "phase" to identify definite facets of the testing program. Phase I testing determined contractor compliance and consisted of some 20 hours of flight testing, during which the aircraft was held at about 80 percent of its design limits. Phase II testing was essentially similar to Phase I, but was done by Air Force rather than by contractor pilots. Phase III testing, called contractor development testing, ironed out most of the "bugs" thus far discovered and incorporated most of the modifications suggested by test pilots. In Phase IV, performance and stability testing, the entire performance range was investigated during some 200 hours of flight. Phase V, all-weather testing, as a rule took place at Wright Air Development Center and Eglin AFB. Phase VI tested functional development, using production models. Pilots of the scheduled using agency tested every part of the weapon system. Usually, this phase made use of 3 to 6 aircraft, each of which flew approximately 150 hours. Phase VII, called "operational suitability," was also performed by pilots of the using agencies. Phase VIII, termed unit operational employment testing, was also accomplished by pilots of the using commands, under the supervision of the Air Proving Ground Command. In the late fifties, there were some superficial changes, affecting the testing program's terminology more than its scope. Three categories supplanted the many pre-1960 phases. Categories I and II were essentially similar to Phases I and II; Category III, and its numerous special tests, covered all other former phases. Obviously, testing had to be flexible to serve its purpose. Often, some tests were extended, while others were scheduled out of order. But the testing program's thoroughness remained constant.

system to the demands of an accelerated program (a speed-up of production being actually recommended on 20 June 1955). One of the primary objectives was to determine the system's durability, maintenance manpower requirements, parts consumption, and compatibility of all support equipment. Completion of the Phase VI tests proved that the B–52 (Weapon System 101) was capable of performing its mission. Each B–52 subsystem had been carefully evaluated, with many improvements being requested. This in no way detracted from the B–52's intrinsic excellence, but attested to the importance of such testing during a period of great technological innovation.

Completion of the Phase VI tests, although a basic milestone, did not spell the end of testing. At least 1 of every B–52 model series was extensively tested, with no less than 1,500 Phase II and III test hours programmed for the last one—the B–52H, still being tested in 1962. Final tabulations showed that 13 B–52 productions were used in the overall testing program. Several of these planes were involved in accidents, and 2 were destroyed. But time would vindicate testing costs and efforts.

Research and Development Costs   1952

The research and development work done over some 5 years, plus the price and early testing of the X and YB–52s totalled about $100 million—1.5 percent of the entire program cost. In the early fifties, this was a shocking sum. Yet, the investment soon paid dividends. No major changes appeared until the last 2 models in the series (B–52G and B–52H), and even though the configuration of the early B–52s remained relatively unaltered, they too were to prove invaluable to the strategic force. In retrospect, the Air Force had to admit that money was seldom so well spent.

B–52A

Manufacturer's Model 464-201-0

New Features

The B–52A differed in several major respects from the prototype B–52. It looked more like an older type of bomber because of its enlarged nose that provided side-by-side pilot seating. To accommodate additional equipment, the forward compartment was extended 21 inches. Other improvements consisted of a 4-gun, .50-caliber tail turret, electronic countermeasures equipment, a chaff dispensing system, and J57–P–1W engines. The engines were fitted for water injection, 360 gallons of water being carried in a rear fuselage tank. Although the A-model was capable of "flying boom" flight refueling, its unrefueled range was increased by providing two 1,000-gallon auxiliary fuel tanks supplementing the normal 35,600-gallon fuel load.

Production Slippage   April 1953–June 1954

Restricted to testing, the B–52As were nevertheless considered as the first B–52 productions. While they were also 14 months behind schedule, extenuating circumstances abounded. As early as 1950, Boeing urged AMC to prepare for production, claiming that 1 year in lead time could be gained by securing tooling, materials, and other items without delay. "I can say in all honesty," Boeing's Vice President wrote, "that I believe the $13 million investment would be the cheapest insurance premium our Government ever paid." That the Air Force did not leap into action made sense at the time, since alternative aircraft remained under consideration. Later, when the XB–52 materialized, the aircraft appeared so complicated that even the contractor doubted that a B–29-type of mass production could be applied to the B–52. Comparing the 2 bombers, Boeing's President was quoted as saying, would be like comparing a kiddie-car and a Cadillac. In fact, designing the B–29 had required 153,000 engineering hours; the B–52, 3,000,000. In any case, it would take until August 1952, long after the

YB–52 flew, to get the rival YB–60 out of potential production;[18] several more months for SAC to dispose of the B–47Z competitor,[19] and until mid-1953 for the B–52 program to get truly under way.

Other Delaying Factors   1951–1954

Had the Air Force endorsed Boeing's early request for tooling, it is questionable whether this would have made much difference. Because of the Korean conflict, the tooling industry was unable to meet the demands of the aircraft manufacturers. Another related problem prevailed, however. After World War II, many trained aircraft personnel of necessity migrated to other jobs. These people had to be regrouped and retrained. And, with industry booming nationwide as a result of the Korean War, military procurement began to compete with commercial production. Although Boeing selected subcontractors in the spring of 1951,[20] (immediately following the production letter contract for 13 B–52As), the low priority assigned to the B–52 by the Air Staff was a formidable handicap.[21] Even more serious, according to

---

[18] The YB–52 made its first flight on 15 April 1952; the YB–60, on the 18th—Convair flying its modified B–36 only 14 days after receipt of the prototype's eighth engine. The initial scarcity of J57 engines (also used by North American F–100 Super Sabres) presented problems. The worried Boeing contractor was being troublesome and kept on reminding the Air Force that the company had been led to believe that it would receive priority allocations of the new engines—particularly over Convair. The issue, however, did not reach serious proportions. The Air Force lost interest in the YB–60 in August 1952, after the aircraft's performance flaws tarnished its first bright prospects. The B–60 project was officially canceled in January 1953, the 2 experimental planes being scrapped in July 1954.

[19] Boeing B–47Z, also earmarked to receive J57 engines, was the last stumbling block to large-scale B–52 production. SAC won the debate in late 1952, after preparing a convincing new study of the problems at hand. To begin with, the B–47Z had a limited growth potential, but the B–52 was in its comparative infancy. The B–52 could carry more atomic weapons than the B–47Z. The latter, because of its weight limitations, would be less suitable to deliver hydrogen bombs. With almost uncanny vision, the SAC study concluded that it would be a serious mistake not to procure an adequate B–52 force.

[20] Boeing used 2 main criteria for its selection—availability of labor and wartime experience. The major subcontractors eventually picked were the A. O. Smith Co., of Toledo, Ohio, for landing gears; the Kaiser Manufacturing Co., of Richmond, Calif., for profile milling items; the Rohr Aircraft Corporation of Chula Vista, Calif., for drop tanks, power pods, and tail compartments; the Briggs Manufacturing Co., of Detroit, Mich., for rudders, elevators, vertical fin flaps, ailerons, spoilers, and outboard wings; and the A. O. Smith Co., of Rochester, N.Y., for weldments.

[21] At its inception, the program was assigned "S" priority position #63 which was exceedingly low and augured poorly for the successful accomplishment of stated production schedules (1 aircraft per month, at first; 4, later). It was not until September 1952 that the

an Air Force team that analyzed the situation, was "a general inability to adequately plan for the magnitude and complexity of the program." In summary, the protracted B-52 development was caused on one hand by revolutionary changes in aircraft design and propulsion; on the other, by uncertainty within the Air Force as to how far and in what direction it could go in utilizing these changes. As to the early production delays, the program's low priority was an obvious factor. Another cause, the Air Force believed, were defects in the overall organization originally set up by Boeing. Finally, production slipped to allow incorporation of mandatory changes that were identified during the early testing phases of the X and YB-52s.

Program Increase   August 1953

The procurement plans of 1951-1952 underwent many changes. In keeping with almost traditional patterns, the B-52's early production was shaped by deletions, additions, and reconfigurations. The letter contract of February 1951 was amended on 9 June 1952—several months before the definitive contract was signed. Consequently, although 13 B-52As had been initially ordered, only 3 were built. As was usually the case, the second model in the aircraft series bore the brunt of the changes. Against this routine background, important events unfolded. The Air Force, during the first half of 1953, finally endorsed a sizeable B-52 program. Made official in August 1953, the decision called for 282 aircraft—enough to equip 7 SAC wings. Since the Air Force wanted Boeing to deliver the aircraft between October 1956 and December 1958, another plant would be needed. Actually, an additional plant had been approved in mid-1951 and canceled within a few weeks. But this time, the decision stood firm. Harold Talbott, who had succeeded Mr. Finletter as Secretary of the Air Force on 4 February 1953, announced the action on 28 September. Boeing's second facility, established at Wichita, Kansas, eventually surpassed the Seattle plant in B-52 production.

B-52A Roll-Out   18 March 1954

The Air Force chose to honor its new bomber months before it flew, with a factory roll-out ceremony attended by Gen. Nathan F. Twining, Air Force Chief of Staff since 30 June 1953. Addressing the several thousand

---

priority level was raised to #27, but by this time slippages had occurred that were not recoverable.

people assembled at Boeing's Seattle plant, General Twining said: "The long rifle was the great weapon of its day. . . . Today this B–52 is the long rifle of the air age." The very existence of these global jet giants, General Twining stressed, would be a powerful deterrent against attack, for the Stratofortresses were designed to deliver devastating blows deep behind any aggressive frontier.

First Flight (Production Aircraft)   5 August 1954

The Air Force accepted the initial B–52A (Serial No. 52–001) in June 1954—2 months before the aircraft's first flight—and returned it immediately to Boeing for use in the test program. For the same purpose, the other 2 B–52As were also loaned to Boeing as soon as accepted.

Total B–52As Accepted

The Air Force accepted 3 B–52As—the total built by Boeing. The 10 other B–52As, ordered in early 1951, were completed as B–52Bs.

Acceptance Rates

All 3 B–52As were accepted in 1954, 1 each in June, August, and September.

End of Production   1954

B–52A production ended in September, with delivery of the third plane.

Flyaway Cost Per Production Aircraft $28.38 million[22]

Airframe, $26,433,518; engines (installed), $2,848,120; electronics, $50,761; ordnance, $9,193; armament, $47,874.

---

[22] Somewhat cheaper than the X and YB–52s, but not much. Air Force records carried the production B–52As at such seemingly fantastic prices because the aircraft were essentially experimental, with much of the initial tooling and new development costs charged against them.

The first B–52A was "rolled out" of the Boeing Seattle plant in March 1954.

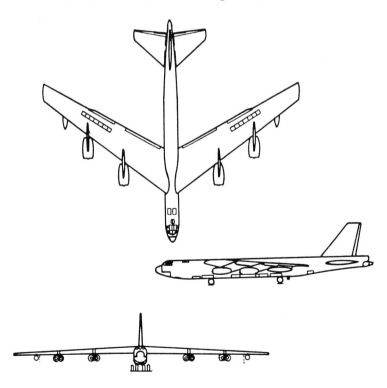

Subsequent Model Series   B–52B

Other Configurations   NB–52A[23]

The last B–52A (Serial No 52-003) was redesignated NB–52A in 1959, after being modified to carry the North American rocket-powered X–15. The origin of the X–15 project dated back to the mid-1950s, when the United States became deeply interested in the space age and manned space flight. The program was a joint venture by the National Advisory Committee for Aeronautics,[24] the Air Force, and the Navy, with the X–15 conceived as a means to obtain technical data on hypersonic aeronautics. As it turned out, the immediate beneficiary of the X–15 flights was the manned space program, and the X–15 established itself as a most successful research aircraft. But the NB–52A's mother ship role, although less spectacular, was important and later a second B–52 became involved. For its part, the B–52A had to undergo extensive as well as permanent modifications by North American and USAF technicians. Specifically, a 6- by 8-foot section was cut out of the B–52's right wing flap to make room for the X–15's wedge tail. A pylon to mate the X–15 to the NB–52 was installed between the bomber's inboard engines and the fuselage. Lines and wires that held the X–15 below the NB–52 passed through this pylon. Large liquid oxygen tanks were placed in the B–52's bomb bays for topping off the X–15's liquid oxygen system prior to separation. A closed circuit television system was added so that the B–52 crew could carefully watch the X–15 and its pilot prior to launch. Finally, there was an elaborate launch control system to make sure that the X–15 was released at precisely the right instant. Captive flights to check out the X–15 and X–15/B–52 combination began at Edwards AFB on 10 March 1959. On 8 June, the first true flight occurred, but the rocket was not lit and the X–15 was flown as a glider. The first rocket-powered flight came in

---

[23] The letter N was a prefix used by the Air Force to denote that an airplane (bomber, fighter, and other aircraft alike) was assigned to a special test program and that the aircraft had been so drastically changed that it would be beyond practical or economical limits to bring it back to its original or to standard operational configuration. Besides the familiar X and Y, 3 other so-called classification letters were used as status prefix symbols: namely, the letter G, which denoted an aircraft permanently grounded, utilized for ground instruction and training; J, temporarily reconfigured for special tests; and Z, in planning or predevelopment stage. As of late 1973, all 3 services of the Department of Defense still applied this medium to identify the status of their aircraft.

[24] The National Advisory Committee for Aeronautics, a federal agency established by Congress in 1915, did research for the benefit of commercial and military aviation. The advisory committee was absorbed by the National Aeronautics and Space Administration in the fall of 1958, becoming in the process the organizational core of the newly created agency.

September, with the NB–52A eventually participating in 59 of the 199 X–15 flights conducted before the program's end in 1968.

Phaseout   1960

The B–52A phaseout began in 1960, when the first of the 3 aircraft was retired after being test flown from Edwards AFB at take-off weights up to 415,000 pounds.

B–52B

Manufacturer's Model 464–201–3

New Features

Increased gross weight (420,000 instead of 405,000 pounds), the MA–6A bombing navigation system, and more powerful engines were the main differences between the B–52B and the preceding B–52A. Also, in contrast to the B–52As, some of the B–52Bs could be fitted with "capsule" equipment for reconnaissance duties.[25] In the latter case, the 6-man crew B–52B became an 8-man RB–52B crew.

Configuration Planning   February 1951

Boeing started working on the B–52B design in February 1951, concurrent with signature of the first production document.

Design Improvements   1951–1954

Because the aircraft design was derived from the B–47, the B–52B (as well as the fairly similar B–52A) benefited from the start from hard-earned experience. Always hovering over the program was the specter of the B–47's initial deficiencies and delays. Both the contractor and the Air Force seemed determined that the B–52 would not endure such problems. Characteristics of the intensive B–52 development were 670 days of testing in the Boeing wind tunnel, supplemented by 130 days of aerodynamic and aeroelastic testing in other facilities. In essence, Boeing personnel designed, built, and developed the B–52 as a well-knit, integrated packaged system. Parts were thoroughly tested before being installed in the new bomber. Improvements suggested by the YB–52's early flight tests appeared on B–52B production lines. That these changes were few remained worthy of note. Test reports were generally pessimistic, concerning themselves with every aerodynamic

---

[25] The result of another policy reversal. See pp 235–236.

fault, however serious or minor, suspected or real. In 1953, more often than not, the published account of a B–52 test flight included the unusual statement that "no airplane malfunctions were reported." But the B–52B development was lengthy. Moreover, several B–52Bs, although earmarked for SAC, were diverted to the test program before joining the operational forces. The B–52B's early participation in complex flight tests soon pinpointed desirable production improvements—giving way in turn to new models in the series. Nevertheless, the airplane was considered to be outstanding, and the praise of Maj. Gen. Albert Boyd, the Wright Air Development Center's Commander, would long be remembered. General Boyd, who was also one of the Air Force's foremost test pilots, in May 1954 said that the B–52 was the finest airplane yet built. In a lighter mood, the general told his staff that someone should try to discover how "we accidentally developed an airplane that flies so beautifully."

Procurement Changes   1952–1955

Letter Contract AF33(600)–22119 of September 1952, which called for 43 RB–52Bs, gave way to a definitive contract that was signed on 15 April 1953. In May 1954, an amendment to this contract reduced the number of RB–52Bs by 10 (leaving 33 RB–52Bs on order) and directed construction of the canceled planes in the configuration of the next model series (RB–52C). The May 1954 amendment also added 25 other RB–52Cs on the 15 April 1953 contract. Hence, even though a sizeable B–52 program had been approved in mid-1953, Boeing in May 1954 had only 88 airplanes under contract—3 B–52As, 17 RB–52Bs (per definitive contract AF33(038)–21096 of November 1952), 33 RB–52Bs, and 35 RB–52Cs. Moreover, forthcoming procurement would not affect the current program—the first new order in August actually calling for still another B–52 model. Just the same, the modest program so far endorsed was not immune to further changes. Of significance, from the early procurement standpoint, was an Air Force decision, made official on 7 January 1955, that flatly reversed the Air Staff directive of October 1951. It gave the B–52 first priority as a bomber and once again relegated the aircraft's reconnaissance potential to a secondary role.[26] As a result of the new decision, the 50 RB–52Bs and 35 RB–52Cs

---

[26] The January 1955 decision coincided with a procurement order for several specialized reconnaissance versions of the Martin B–57 Canberra. These planes would all go to the Strategic Air Command, sometime in early 1956. In the ensuing years, SAC also got a contingent of high-altitude, reconnaissance U–2s, developed by Lockheed and first flown in 1955.

were redesignated B–52Bs and B–52Cs, respectively. Besides, as finally built, 23 of the 50 B–52Bs could not be used for reconnaissance.

Production Slippages   1953–1954

As planned in early 1951, B–52 deliveries were due to start in April 1953. A 15-month slippage soon occurred, because of the Korean War and its many implications. Revised production schedules set up in June 1952 called for the B–52Bs to be delivered between April and December 1954, but additional procurement (finalized in April 1953) extended deliveries to April 1956. Meanwhile, the Air Force accepted 2 B–52Bs in 1954—1 in August and 1 in September. However, scheduled deliveries were suspended for 90 days, while Boeing engineers sought to correct cracking in the landing gear trunnion forgings. This second loss of time was never recouped, the last B–52B reaching the Air Force in August 1956—3 months behind schedule. Yet, once the Air Force decided to go ahead with large-scale procurement, the bulk of the production program went forward with few delays.

First Flight (Production Aircraft)   December 1954

Boeing first flew the B–52B in December 1954. Like the B–52A (and subsequent models in the series), the B–52B Stratofortress was impressive. The new aircraft had twice the wingspan and nearly 3 times the wing area of the B–17, and its 8 engines delivered 10 times the power of the B–29. The B–52B's tail fin stood as tall as a 4-story building, while the bomber's length of almost 157 feet spanned over half the length of a football field. The B–52B's wingspan of 185 feet represented a greater distance than that travelled by Orville Wright in his historic first flight at Kitty Hawk, North Carolina.

Enters Operational Service   29 June 1955

SAC assigned its first B–52, a B–52B (Serial No 52–8711) that could be converted for reconnaissance, to the 93d Heavy Bomb Wing, at Castle AFB, California. The 93d, a former medium bomb wing flying late model B–47s, used its new aircraft for crew transition training. SAC had planned from the start that the B–52s would be integrated into B–36 units on a 1-for-1 replacement basis—with retired B–36s being salvaged. Also, units would be converted 1 squadron at a time to facilitate B–52 operations and to prevent problems likely to arise in the assignment of maintenance equipment.

Combat ready on 12 March 1956, the 93d Wing regressed to a nonready status 2 months later, when it was authorized 15 additional B-52s. The wing was again fully operational on 26 June 1957, after crew training had become its primary mission.[27] Most of the B-52Bs produced were assigned to the 93d. A few early B-52Bs were first earmarked for testing, but they too ended with the heavy bomb wing.

Initial Problems   1955

Uncertain B-52 delivery schedules precluded proper budget planning, affecting in turn crew training, maintenance scheduling, and stocking of spare parts. There were shortages of ground support equipment, dual bomb racks, crew kits, electronic countermeasure components and training items. Delayed construction of maintenance facilities, the lack of warehouse space to store flyaway kits, as well as shortages of operational facilties for squadron briefings and other functions were serious handicaps. In addition, the failure of B-52 ramps and taxiways together with runway deterioration interfered with operations. These initial problems, practically resolved at Castle AFB by the end of 1955,[28] were to prove far more severe at many of SAC's future B-52 bases.

Early Deficiencies   1955-1956

Fuel leaks, icing of the fuel system, imperfect water injection pumps, faulty alternators and, above all, deficient bombing and fire-control systems were the main troubles of the early B-52Bs. However, these deficiencies as a whole were not as severe as those usually encountered by a new bomber,

---

[27] The Air Training Command had no B-52 school, and SAC's new bombers had to become operational as soon as possible. The best way to solve the problem was for SAC to handle the training of B-52 crews with a combat crew training squadron. This did not create a precedent, the same procedure having been used in SAC's B-36 training program at Carswell AFB, Tex. The 4017th Combat Crew Training Squadron was established at Castle AFB on 8 January 1955, as an integral part of the 93d Wing. When the B-52 training task became too great for 1 squadron, the wing's 3 other squadrons took over flight training, with the 4017th assuming ground instruction and the administrative phase of the program. As a rule, the training program consisted of 5 weeks of intensive ground school and 4 weeks of flight training, totaling between 35 and 50 hours in the air.

[28] Castle AFB's parking ramp and runways were strengthened to handle 450,000-pound loads (the forthcoming B-52C's expected take-off weight). The width of the taxi strips was increased 175 feet. In October 1955, postflight B-52 docks, as well as operations and engineering buildings were under construction. A large hangar had been completed.

and far less distressing than those experienced by the B–47 at the same stage of its career. In any case, most of the B–52B's initial problems were not entirely unexpected. Air Research and Development Command and Air Materiel Command had been insisting for months that the aircraft should be perfected before delivery. Strategic Air Command, in contrast, steadfastly objected to further postponement,[29] believing the aircraft should be accepted and modified at a later date—which they were. SAC's objections to more delay were not inconsistent. General LeMay continued to press for the best weapon system for his force. But after approval of a configuration as nearly perfect as possible, the SAC Commander thought too many immediate improvements, refinements, or additional requirements could well be self-defeating. As late as February 1955, SAC protested against "unneccessary changes;" pointed out that operational units would benefit from "more standardization" in the B–52s; and asked to participate in the coordination of all engineering change proposals. While AMC, which was assigned executive responsibility for the new bomber, did not wish to concede any of its engineering prerogatives, SAC did get its way. Some 170 engineering change proposals suggested for the first 20 B–52s were reduced to 60 by the end of March.

Other Temporary Flaws 1955–1956

In October 1955, Boeing engineers had yet to solve the problem of cabin temperatures. The pilots, sitting high in the nose, were comfortable at a given heating setting. However, observer and navigator, sitting with their feet against the bottom of the fuselage, with the metal sometimes reaching 20 degrees below zero, suffered from the cold—the wearing of winter underwear, heavy clothing, and thick flying boots hardly helping.[30] Conversely, if enough heat was turned on to keep the observer and navigator warm, the pilots became overheated. Pilots also criticized the new bomber's high-frequency communications system. First installed in the B–47, the AN/ARC–21 long-range radio was proving even less reliable in the B–52.

---

[29] Most in the Air Force seemed to agree that production should wait until research and development had worked most of the kinks out of any new aircraft. Yet different opinions cluttered the key issue of determining at what point an article was ready for full-scale production. One might conclude that SAC, ill-equipped at the time for its awesome responsibilities, wondered how much caution and time it could reasonably afford.

[30] The problem was compounded by another factor for which the B–52 could not be blamed. The development of personal equipment lagged years behind airframe and engine. Crew MC–1 spacesuits, parachutes, and other paraphernalia were uncomfortable. Crew fatigue from flying the new bomber was often insignificant, compared to that caused by wearing all this survival equipment.

Engine Problems   1955–1956

The J57 engines of the B–52 at first presented a serious problem. The principal difficulty persisting in mid–1955, when the aircraft started reaching SAC, was that none of the various J57s performed adequately with water injection, a process due to augment the engine's thrust at takeoff. The YB–52's J57–P–3 engine had been discarded after many modifications failed to keep it from shutting down at high altitude, regardless of speed. In addition, the power-poor and therefore temporary P–3 could not use water.[31] Equally frustrating were concurrent difficulties with other models of the J57, which left the P–1W as the only fully-qualified engine, even though its performance was substandard. Although fitted for water injection, this model had to be used as a dry engine. For lack of anything better, about one-half of the B–52B fleet was fitted with P–1Ws. The J57–P–9W, slated to succeed the P–1, ran into trouble. It was a lighter engine, incorporating titanium components. Unfortunately, the titanium compressor blades cracked as a result of both forging defects and of substandard metal containing too much hydrogen. A return to steel parts, at a weight penalty of 250 pounds, produced the J57–P–29W[32] and J57–P–29WA engines, which equipped most other B–52Bs. However, by mid-1956 the titanium problems had been solved and the P–19W, a higher-thrust version of the titanium-component P–9W, appeared on the last 5 B–52Bs.

Grounding   1956

The Air Force surmised that the first fatal B–52 accident in February 1956 was caused by a faulty alternator. Twenty B–52Bs, carrying the suspect equipment, were immediately grounded. In addition, the Air Force stopped further B–52 deliveries. In mid-May, after Boeing seemed reasonably convinced that the alternator problem was solved, more aircraft were accepted. However, the alternator problem later resurfaced. The B–52Bs were again temporarily grounded in July, this time because of fuel system

---

[31] Even before the B–52 was built engineers recognized that a serious thrust problem would show up during a fully loaded takeoff, particularly on days when runway temperatures approached 100 degrees Fahrenheit. For a while, it seemed jet assisted takeoff units would be needed to provide reserve auxiliary thrust. The Air Force canceled such a project in April 1954, following Pratt and Whitney's successful development of a water injection system that promised to rectify the thrust deficiency. The unexpected difficulties that followed were serious, but not insurmountable.

[32] The rate of water that could be injected in the P–29W engine was only half that of the P–29WA. Subsequent modifications brought the P–29W to the P–29WA's standard.

and hydraulic pack deficiencies. Although this latest grounding did not last long, the 93d Wing's training program suffered. In mid-year, no combat-ready crews were available for the 42d Heavy Bomb Wing's new B-52s.

Support Achievements   1955–1956

The lessons learned during the B-47 conversion program were put to good use in preventing many B-52 maintenance and supply problems. Specialists associated with jet engines, the repair of fuel tanks, and the maintenance of all kinds of systems (bombing, navigation, hydraulics, electrical, and the like), were dispatched to Air Training Command for schooling on B-52 components, their education proving easier than their original transition from propeller-type aircraft to the jet-powered B-47. Other steps were taken to avoid, or at least to minimize, potential difficulties. After 2 years of bickering with SAC, AMC finally consented to establish special holding accounts at various supply depots for ground support equipment. The "Z" accounts, as they were known by 1955, had two distinct advantages. First, they segregated the various equipment needed by the B-52. Secondly they ensured that the 800 or so B-52 line items, which they eventually comprised, would be used exclusively in support of such aircraft. Once the "Z" accounts were established, SAC made certain that all available support items were in place, whether at Castle or elsewhere, prior to the arrival of any B-52. Yet, the Air Staff agreed with SAC that much more would be necessary to thwart other possible support problems of the B-47 type. As a result, in the summer of 1955 the Air Staff asked AMC to study how to speed up the repair of future malfunctions reported by operational units. The Air Staff's request and ensuing discussions between AMC and SAC representatives gave way to Sky Speed, a program organized by AMC's Oklahoma Air Materiel Area. And, before long, Sky Speed set up 1 contractor maintenance team of 50 people at every B-52 base. The Sky Speed teams did not participate, even indirectly, in the important modification projects subsequently done at the Boeing-Wichita plant. Nor did they take over the depot workload of the San Antonio Air Materiel Area, which was responsible for the B-52 inspect and repair as necessary (IRAN) program. However, the teams did reduce the time B-52s spent at the depot by doing much of the work that would ordinarily await the IRAN cycle. The maintenance teams practically kept the aircraft flying, because they immediately corrected noted safety deficiencies, installed fixes, and performed a great many other technical chores. As a rule, it took an average of 1 week for a B-52 to go through a Sky Speed routine checkup, and each B-52 received at least 1 checkup per year.[33]

---

[33] By 1958, Sky Speed had reaped such success that a similar program was being devised for SAC's KC-135s.

Post-Production Modifications   1956–1958

Sunflower, a modernization project handled by Boeing, brought 7 early B–52Bs to the configuration of the next model in the series (B–52C). Started in the summer of 1956 at the Wichita plant, the project involved the installation of approximately 150 kits. Sunflower took time to accomplish; the last modified B–52B was not returned to SAC until December 1957. B–52Bs underwent many other modifications. They participated in such projects as Harvest Moon, Blue Band, and Quickclip, all of which were first initiated for the benefit of subsequent B–52 models.

End of Production   1956

The Air Force took delivery of the last B–52B in August.

Total B–52Bs Accepted   50

The Air Force accepted 50 B–52Bs, 27 of which qualified as RB–52Bs.

Acceptance Rates

The Air Force accepted 13 B–52Bs in fiscal year 1955 (the first one in August 1954); 35 in FY 56, and the last 2 in FY 57 (1 each in July and August 1956).

Flyaway Cost Per Production Aircraft $14.43 million

Airframe, $11,328,398; engines (installed), $2,547,472; electronics, $61,198; ordnance, $11,520; armament, $482,284.[34]

Subsequent Model Series   B–52C

---

[34] Cost breakouts were sometimes undeterminable and occasionally misleading. For instance, contractor-furnished equipment such as electronics might be included in the airframe's cost, instead of being broken out to its proper category. Similarly, the costs of some components and subsystems were often lumped under armament, a category carried on Air Force records as "other, including armament."

Other Configurations   RB–52B and NB–52B

RB–52B—Development of the RB–52B, once briefly referred to as the RX–16,[35] dated back to the early part of 1951. The reconnaissance model featured multi-purpose pods[36] carried in the aircraft's bomb bay. Initially, 17 pods were ordered, solely as flight test articles. The pods were pressurized and equipped with downward ejection seats for the 2-man crew. For search operations, the multi-purpose pod contained 1 radar receiver (AN/APR–14) at the low frequency reconnaissance electronic station, and 2 radar receivers (AN/APR–9) at the high frequency station. Each station had 2 pulse analyzers (AN/APA–11A), with which to process the collected data. The pod also housed 3 panoramic receivers (AN/ARR–88), and all electronic signals were recorded on an AN/ANQ–1A wire recorder. Photographic equipment consisted of 4 K–38 cameras at the multi-camera station, and 1 camera (either a T–11 or K–36) at the vertical camera station. For mapping purposes, the pod had 3 T–11 cartographic cameras. A December 1951 mockup inspection of the multi-purpose pod went well, no major changes being requested. SAC wanted a special electronic reconnaissance (or ferret) pod but this project did not encounter the same success. Work at Boeing progressed smoothly. Air Research and Development Command ascertained that 1 ferret pod-equipped aircraft could gather in a single flight all the electronic reconnaissance data formerly obtained by 3 conventional RB–52s. Nevertheless, the Air Staff canceled the project in December 1952, and a second SAC request in 1954 for a separate ferret pod did not fare any better. By 1955, however, the original multi-purpose pods had become "general purpose capsules," carrying the latest search, analysis, and direction-finding devices. While the more modern capsules might not satisfy all of SAC's requirements, they constituted clever, if temporary, cost-saving expedients. The capsule, which could be winched in and out of the bomb-bay, added only 300 pounds to the weight of the basic aircraft. Finally, the capsule's installation was so simple that it took just 4 hours to convert a B–52 to the reconnaissance configuration. First flown at Seattle on 25 January 1955 (actually, several months ahead of latest schedules), capsule-equipped B–52Bs began reaching SAC's 93d Heavy Bombardment Wing on 29 June. Phaseout of the 27 RB–52Bs followed the B–52B's pattern.

---

[35] The X–16 or RX–16 designation, first applied to a post–World War II reconnaissance project, was reserved for the test version of high-altitude aircraft and was never permanently used.

[36] A pod is a compartment or container, often streamlined, attached or incorporated into the outer configuration of an airplane or rocket vehicle. The term is usually qualified. For example, a wing pod is a streamlined nacelle slung beneath an airplane's wing, especially for the installation of a jet engine or engines, while a pod gun was a housing for a machine gun.

NB-52B—After undergoing permanent modifications similar to those made on the last B-52A, the eighth B-52 production was redesignated NB-52B. In this configuration, the new bomber was credited with 140 of the 199 X-15 flights resulting from the NB-52/X-15 combination.[37] The NB-52B also participated in many other important projects, including the lifting body research aircraft program sponsored by the Air Force and the National Aeronautics and Space Administration (NASA). Started in 1966, the program's test flights were still going on in late 1973, with Martin-Marietta's needle-nosed X-24 soon to be tested with the NB-52B. The permanently modified B-52B was also used to test solid rocket boosters for the space shuttle. Moreover, as a mother ship, it was expected to play an active role in the remotely piloted research vehicle program, another joint project of the Air Force and NASA. The NB-52B, like the A-model, carried the price tag of the bomber from which it derived. In each case, however, an additional $2 million was spent to fit the basic aircraft for its many experimental tasks.

Phaseout   1965–1966

In March 1965, SAC began retiring B-52Bs that had reached the end of their structural service life, some of the planes going to the Air Training Command for ground crew training. The first B-52B (Serial No 52-8711), received by SAC 10 years earlier, deserved special treatment. On 29 September, it was donated to the Aerospace Museum at Offutt AFB, Nebraska, for permanent display. The remainder of SAC's 2 B-52B squadrons were earmarked for accelerated phaseout in early 1966, and by the end of June all B-52Bs had been sent to storage at Davis-Monthan AFB, Arizona.

Milestones   May 1956

On 21 May, an Air Research and Development Command B-52B, flying at 50,000-foot altitude above the Pacific Ocean, dropped a hydrogen bomb over the Bikini Atoll. It was the first time a B-52 was used as a carrier and drop plane for the powerful thermonuclear weapon.

---

[37] After being dropped from the wing of the NB-52B mothership, the X-15 flew to altitudes of more than 250,000 feet and reached speeds exceeding Mach 6, with air friction heating its skin to 1,100 degrees Fahrenheit.

Items of Special Interest   November 1956

On 24 and 25 November, in a spectacular operation called Quick Kick, 4 B–52Bs of the 93d Wing joined 4 B–52Cs of the 42d Bomb Wing for a nonstop flight around the perimeter of North America. The most publicized individual flight was that of a 93d Wing B–52, which originated at Castle AFB and terminated at Baltimore, Maryland, covering some 13,500 nautical miles in 31 hours and 30 minutes. SAC promptly pointed out that the flight would have been impossible without 4 flight refuelings by KC–97 tankers. Also, flying time could have been reduced by 5 or 6 hours with the refueling help of a higher, faster flying all-jet tanker, such as the KC–135 then being developed by Boeing.[38]

January 1957

From 16 to 18 January, in another spectacular operation called Power Flite, 3 B–52Bs of the 93d Bomb Wing made a nonstop, round-the-world flight. With the help of several KC–97 inflight refuelings, the lead plane, Lucky Lady III, and its 2 companions completed the 24,325-mile flight in 45 hours and 19 minutes, less than one-half the time required on the Lucky Lady II flight—the first-ever nonstop round-the-world flight, accomplished in February 1949 by a B–50A that was refueled by KB–29M tankers. The National Aeronautic Association subsequently recognized Operation Power Flite as the outstanding flight of 1957 and named the 93d Wing as recipient of the Mackay Trophy.

---

[38] SAC's 93d Air Refueling Squadron at Castle AFB received the command's first all-jet tanker on 28 June 1957. The acquisition of KC–135s meant a great deal to SAC. Mating the new tanker and the B–52 would pay high dividends. It would reduce refueling time and increase safety, the latter remaining a constant goal of the command. Specifically, with a KC–135, the refueling rendezvous could be conducted at the bomber's normal speed and altitude. In contrast, using a KC–97, the B–52 had to slow down and descend to lower altitudes than normal to accomplish the hookup—an exacting exercise.

B–52C

Manufacturer's Model 464–201–6

Previous Model Series B–52B

New Features

Increased gross weight (450,000 instead of 420,000 pounds), larger underwing drop tanks, improved water injection system, and white thermal reflecting paint on the under surfaces were the B–52C's main new features.

Configuration Planning December 1953

As a product of the evolutionary process, the B–52C design did not take shape until December 1953.

First Flight (Production Aircraft) March 1956

Less than 30 months elapsed between design and first flight.

Enters Operational Service 1956

All B–52Cs went to the 42d Bomb Wing at Loring AFB, Maine. The 42d received its first B–52C on 16 June 1956, but did not become combat ready until the end of the year.

Avionics Problems 1956–1957

The B–52 (like the B–47) carried only a tail turret for defensive armament. Providing a suitable fire-control system for the aircraft was particularly important, but proved to be a problem from the start. The A–3 system that equipped the B–52A and a few B–52Bs, was capable of both optical and automatic tracking and search, but because of deficiencies, it was replaced by the MD–5. Installed in most B–52Bs, the MD–5 fire-control system did not live up to expectations. Hence, a theoretically perfected A–3, after reappearing on the last 7 B–52Bs, was fitted in every B–52C. Still unsatisfactory, the A–3 was supplanted by the MD–9 in subsequent B–52 models. The bombing-navigation system was another difficulty of the B–52 program. Moreover, the problem promised to be fairly constant, since any progress was likely to be counteracted by enemy technical developments. The problem of bombing navigation was not new. It had plagued Convair's B–36 and still hampered Boeing's B–47. Actually, the Air Force and various contractors had been wrestling for years with the difficulties associated with accuracy, a primary requirement of any bombing system, multiplied many times in importance by the high cost of nuclear weapons. Simply stated, the bombing-navigation system of the atomic age called for greater instrumental accuracy, increased automatic operation to reduce human error, and immunity from more sophisticated defenses. Two main systems remained under consideration as late as 1953:[39] the K-series bombing-navigation system, which relied essentially on radar and optics, and the MA–2 or Bomb Director for High Speed Aircraft system. The MA–2 combined an optical bombsight, a radar presentation of target, and an automatic computer, together with radar modifications designed for use in high-speed aircraft. The MA–2 appeared ideally suited for both the B–47 and the B–52, but SAC did not believe that the system would be tested sufficiently even by the end of 1955. And while the Strategic Air Command was willing to overlook certain minor deficiencies, it stood firm on the issue that no bombing system that had not been tested or fully approved would be installed in any of its bombers. When the B–52s started reaching the Air Force, neither the K–2 or K–4 bombing-navigation systems of most B–47s, nor the B–36's K–3A had proven satisfactory. For lack of any better system, the K–3A was fitted in some early B–52Bs. However, at altitudes above 35,000 feet, the K–3A became almost useless—loss of definition and poor resolution preventing target identification. The Philco Corporation came to the rescue with a "black box" that increased the K–3A's power output by 50 percent. Yet, this development was merely an expedient, rather than the beginning of a new and improved system. It gave way to the MA–6A bombing-navigation system, a modernized K–3A which was installed in all remaining B–52Bs. Meanwhile, after being rushed through intensified flight tests, the MA–2 kept acting up. In mid-1955, the system still did not perform as well as

---

[39] The XB–52, YB–52, and B–52As actually came off production without any bombing-navigation system.

expected and its autopilot was particularly deficient. Nevertheless, progress was being made. A vastly improved system, the AN/ASB–15, initially equipped the B–52Cs. However, technical refinements did not cease, and most B–52Cs were retrofitted with the AN/ASQ–48 bombing-navigation system.

Other Problems   1956–1957

In mid-1956, the Air Force and the Thompson Products Company were still working on a permanent fix for the faulty alternators that had been responsible for the fatal crash of a B–52B. A new Thompson model, in use by 1957, was much better but still troublesome. Problems occurred because of defects in the alternator drive's lubricating system, which used grease instead of oil. This was expected to be corrected before the end of the year. Another B–52 malfunction, detected in March 1957, had to do with the trunnion fittings of the main gear. Defective fittings were found in nearly all B–52Cs.

Post-Production Modifications   1958–1962

A special project, Harvest Moon, increased the B–52C's combat potential to that of the next model in the series. Otherwise, as in the B–52B's case, B–52C post-production modifications were parts of large programs that concerned themselves with the overall improvement of the entire B–52 fleet. None of those programs was initiated for the sake of the small contingent of B–52Cs.

End of Production   1956

All B–52Cs were built in 1956, the last 5 reaching the Air Force in December.

Total B–52Cs Accepted   35

The Air Force received 35 B–52Cs, the total finally ordered. All B–52Cs could readily be converted to RB–52Cs.

Acceptance Rates

The Air Force accepted 5 B–52Cs in FY 56; 30 in FY 57. Actually, 1 B–52C was accepted in February 1956; the rest, between June and December.

Flyaway Cost Per Production Aircraft $7.24 million

Airframe, $5,359,017; engines (installed), $1,513,220; electronics, $71,397; ordnance, $10,983; armament (and others) $293,346.[40]

Subsequent Model Series B–52D

Other Configurations RB–52C

The 35 B–52Cs, like some of the B–52Bs, could easily be fitted for reconnaissance. The RB–52Cs were superior to the RB–52Bs, since they were powered from the start by higher-thrust engines—8 J57-P-29Ws. The RB–52Cs also benefited from the other improvements first introduced by the B–52C. Of special importance to the reconnaissance role was the extra fuel carried by the C-model, which significantly extended the aircraft's unrefueled range.

Phaseout 1971

All B–52Cs were phased out of the active forces in 1971. A B–52C (Serial No 53–402) of the 22d Bomb Wing at March AFB, California, was the last one to be retired. The aircraft reached the storage facility at Davis-Monthan AFB on 29 September, only 3 months later than planned some 5 years before.[41]

---

[40] Increased production meant lower unit costs. First beneficiary was the B–52C, acquired at half of the B–52B's price.

[41] In December 1965, a few months after the first B–52Bs started leaving the operational inventory, Robert S. McNamara, Secretary of Defense from 21 January 1961 to 29 February 1968, announced another phaseout program that would further reduce SAC's bomber force. Basically, this program called for the mid-1971 retirement of all Convair B–58s, of the B–52Cs, and of several subsequent B–52 models. Secretary McNamara in December 1965 also stated that 210 General Dynamics FB–111s would be purchased to replace SAC's phased-out bombers. The forthcoming strategic FB–111, closely related to the once highly controversial TFX, was a modified version of the F–111. As such, information on the FB–111 was included in Volume I, *Post–World War II Fighters, 1945–1973*, published by the Office of Air Force History. However, some of the controversies generated by the FB–111 procurement are covered in this volume, in connection with the B–70, AMSA (Advanced Manned Strategic Aircraft), and B–1A projects. See Appendix II, pp 559–593.

View of a B–52 instrument panel.

A Boeing B–52C in flight, its under surfaces coated with white thermal reflective paint.

B–52D

Manufacturer's Model 464–201–7

Previous Model Series   **B–52C**

New Features

In contrast to the B–52C, easily convertible to the reconnaissance configuration, the B–52D was equipped exclusively for long-range bombing operations. This was initially the most telling difference between the two. Like some of the B–52Bs, the preceding B–52Cs, and subsequent B–52 models, the B–52Ds could carry the newly developed thermonuclear weapons, all necessary modifications being incorporated on the production lines.

Configuration Planning   **December 1953**

As in the case of the B–52C that it so closely resembled, the B–52D's design was initiated in December 1953.

Additional Procurement   **1954–1956**

The B–52D marked the beginning of the B–52 large-scale production. It reflected the mid-1953 decision to raise procurement and Secretary Talbott's final endorsement of a second production plant. The B–52D program also benefited from ensuing program increases, and the "D" became the second most-produced B–52 model. The aircraft were ordered under 4 separate contracts. The first, AF33(600)–28223, finalized on 31 August 1954, covered 50 aircraft; the second, AF33(600)–31267, signed on 26 October 1955, involved 51 B–52Ds and 26 B–52Es—the next model in the series. Like preceding B–52s, the new planes were to be built at the Boeing Seattle plant. The other 2 contracts, AF33(600)–26235 and AF33(600)–31155, finalized on 29 November 1954 and 31 January 1956 respectively, totaled 69 B–52Ds and 14 B–52Es—all to come from Boeing's new production facilities in Wichita, Kansas. The 4 contracts, as well as those that covered other B–52Es and subsequent B–52Fs, were of the fixed price type, with redeterminable incentives.[42]

First Flight (Production Aircraft)   4 June 1956

The Air Force accepted the initial B–52D, a Wichita production, in June 1956, on the heels of the aircraft's first flight. The new Seattle-built B–52D, first flown on 28 September, joined the testing program immediately.

Enters Operational Service   December 1956

The new B–52Ds did not reach SAC before the fall of 1956. The first few went to the 42d Bomb Wing, at Loring AFB, replacing the wing's initial B–52Cs. Before the end of December, several B–52Ds had also begun to reach another SAC wing, the 93d. However, while the B–52 inventory at the time already counted almost 100 B–52s (40 B–52Bs, 32 B–52Cs, and 25 B–52Ds), combat-ready crews lagged behind, with only 16 in the 42d Wing and 26 in the 93d. But the command did quickly resolve this problem. Less than 2 years later, SAC had 402 combat-ready crews for 380 B–52s.

Operational Problems   1957–1962

B–52Ds encountered the same initial problems as preceding and subsequent models. They were hampered by fuel leaks, icing of the fuel system, and malfunctions of the water injection pumps. After much frustration, the cause of the pump's failure was uncovered. It was simply due to the fact that the water pumps kept operating when the water tanks were empty. The installation of water sensors was the answer. This was done by Sky Speed teams as part of the water injection system's overall improvement program, which was completed by the spring of 1959. Other problems, however, took longer to solve.[43]

---

[42] In 1962, when production ended, 16 definitive contracts had been concluded. In addition, the B–52 program was tagged with at least 25 miscellaneous contracts for special studies, special flight tests, the procurement of mobile training units, of flight simulators, and of other related items.

[43] See B–52F, pp 266–267.

Other Problems   1957-1959

As B-52Ds were becoming more plentiful, B-52Es and B-52Fs were also reaching SAC. Concurrently, the command's base facilities kept deteriorating. The eagerly awaited B-52s put stresses on runways that had been designed for the lighter B-47s or the slower B-36s. SAC's problems were further compounded by the large size of the first B-52 wings, generally composed of 45 bombers and 15 or 20 tankers, all situated on 1 overcrowded base.[44] In mid-1958, paving projects started at 9 of 13 bases which, the command pointed out, needed immediate attention. Paving costs alone were estimated at $25 million. Congress also approved $232 million under the fiscal year 1959 military construction program to cover projects programmed by SAC, but an additional $210 million was denied. While few of the requested alert facilities were affected, drastic cuts were made in other SAC construction projects. Strangely enough, the facilities shortage was alleviated somewhat by another problem. In the late fifties, as the Russian missile threat became more pronounced and warning time shrank, SAC bases presented increasingly attractive targets. The only immediate solution was to break up these large concentrations of aircraft and scatter them over more bases.[45] Existing B-52 wings therefore were broken up into 3 equal-size units of 15 aircraft each. Two units would normally be relocated at bases of other commands, which was not an ideal arrangement since runway deficiencies, as well as other difficulties, would be sure to materialize. In essence, after 1958 each dispersed B-52 squadron became a strategic wing, usually accompanied by an air refueling squadron of 10 to 15 aircraft. The same principle would be followed in organizing and equipping the still growing B-52 force.

"Big Four" Modification Package   1959-1963

Concurrent with the increasing Russian missile threat and the beginning of the B-52 dispersal program, a new difficulty came to light. Namely, there was no longer any doubt that the Soviet Union had developed formidable defenses against high altitude bombers. Of some consolation, enemy defenses were known to be far less reliable and potentially successful against low flying aircraft. Undeterred by the fact that its new B-52s had been

---

[44] The early and mid-fifties expansion of the bomber force compelled some of the SAC bases to support as many as 90 B-47s and 40 KC-97 tankers.

[45] In the B-47's case, dispersal was a long-range program. It would be accomplished primarily through the phaseout of wings in the late fifties and early sixties.

designed for high-altitude bombing, SAC wasted no time in planning the best way to face its new challenge. To begin with, all B–52s, except for the early B–52Bs, would have to be capable of penetrating enemy defenses at an altitude of 500 feet or lower, in any kind of weather, and without impairing the bomber's inherent high speed at high altitude. Two other necessary steps were to equip all B–52s, modified for low level, with Hound Dog missiles and Quail decoys, so far due to be carried only by the latest B–52s. SAC's fourth requirement was to add an AN/ALQ–27 electronic countermeasure (ECM) system in every modified B–52. This system, the command believed, would allow the B–52 to automatically counter ground-to-air and air-to-air missiles, airborne and ground fire-control systems, as well as the early warning and ground control interception radars of the enemy. Although the requirements outlined by SAC would involve significant modifications and the addition of complex and costly components, they were approved by Headquarters USAF in November 1959. There was an immediate exception, however. The AN/ALQ–27 production was canceled. The command had wanted 572 B–52s fitted with the new AN/ALQ–27, which promised to integrate all ECM functions into one major subsystem, but this modification alone would cost over $1 billion. The Air Staff chose instead a quick reaction capability (QRC)/ECM combination of black boxes that would cost much less. The B–52H (last of the B–52 model series) would feature this equipment from the start, and it would be retrofitted in other B–52s. However, deletion of the AN/ALQ–27 was not to be the program's only setback. Although eventually successful, the "Big Four" low-level modification—also identified as modification 1000—had to overcome numerous difficulties. First was the lack of money. In early 1960, the Air Staff constantly reiterated that a maximum effort was necessary to eliminate complexities and expensive components that promised only incremental improvements. Meanwhile, low-level modification costs had increased from $192 million in November 1959 to $241 million in March 1960. By July, the cost had risen to $265 million. In August, funds were withheld by the Air Staff pending assurance from the Oklahoma City Air Materiel Area that the work would be completed within the $265 million fund ceiling. At the same time, SAC again emphasized that basic requirements should not be compromised just to keep rising costs down. In any case, technical problems also multiplied. At first sight, the low-level modifications appeared straightforward. They called for improvement of the aircraft's bombing-navigation system, modification of the Doppler radar, and the addition of a terrain clearance radar. Low-altitude altimeters also had to be acquired, and each aircraft had to be equipped to carry its newly allocated missiles. The project was actually far more complicated than it seemed, because it covered different B–52 models. In other words, modifications had to be tailored to fit specific configurations. Airframes had to be strengthened, and they also slightly differed from model to model. As a result, low-level modification costs for each B–52C and B–52D aircraft[46] were almost twice as much as for any other B–52. Finally, development of special terrain clearance radars proved more difficult than anticipated. Nevertheless, most low-level modifications were completed by the end of September 1963. Some ECM improvements, due to be accomplished during the aircraft's regular inspect and repair as necessary program, took longer.[47]

Structural Fatigue   1960–On

The phenomenon of fatigue was yet to be fully understood by 1960, but a great deal had been learned from the B–47's structural problems. For instance, it was well established that takeoffs and landings formed one of the primary sources of fatigue damage. In this case, the B–52, with its wing fuel loads, promised to be especially vulnerable. Moreover, there were other known causes of fatigue: atmospheric gusts, maneuver loads, downwash turbulence from tankers during refueling, taxi, buffet, sonic noise, and stress corrosion. Although flying the B–52 at low level was absolutely necessary, SAC knew there would be a price to pay.

The extent of the damage could not be fully predicted, but gusts at 800 feet were 200 times more frequent than at 30,000 feet. At best, it was believed that low-level maneuvers and gust loads would speed the B–52's structural deterioration by a minimum quotient of 8. Justifying the Air Staff's as well as SAC's opinion, Boeing cyclic testing of a B–52F soon showed that numerous manhours would have to be spent on every B–52F in order to alleviate stress in critical areas of the aircraft. Even though the B–52F contingent was not large, strictly mandatory modifications would total at least $15 million. Meanwhile, following the cyclic tests of a B–52G in early 1960, numerous structural fixes were ordered for the entire B–52 fleet, the B–52Bs included. These modifications, soon carried out as the

---

[46] Extra structural modifications accounted for some of the additional expenditure. Another factor was upgrading of the aircraft's initial MA–6A bombing and navigation system, finally replaced in 1964 by the ASQ–48. In any case, the whole project was complex, and modifying the ASQ–38 bombing navigational system of subsequent B–52 models also proved costly.

[47] The ECM improvements were programmed to take place in several phases. Phase I was an emergency modification that provided the necessary minimum ECM equipment to cope with the enemy's radar and surface-to-air missile threat. Phase II was essentially an ECM retrofit that was included in the "Big Four" package. The components installed during Phase II were either equal to or nearly as sophisticated as those introduced by Phase III. The best available ECM equipment, comparing favorably to the deleted AN/ALQ–27, was fitted in Phase III and also featured in the B–52H. Except for the first 18, all B–52Hs were equipped in production for all-weather and low-level flying.

Hi-Stress Program, initially consisted of 2 phases. The Phase I High Stress fixes were scheduled when the aircraft approached 2,000 flying hours;[48] Phase II, when it was nearing 2,500.[49] The Hi-Stress Program was not to interfere with the "Big Four" modification package; it was not allowed to fall behind schedule and was practically completed by the end of 1962. Concurrently, because of the results of the B–52F cyclic tests, an unanticipated third phase was started. The High Stress Phase III consisted of inspecting and repairing, as necessary, wing cracks in all early B–52s. Sky Speed teams and personnel of the Oklahoma and the San Antonio Air Materiel Areas again took care of most of the work. But these modifications, as thorough as they were, only marked a beginning. In the mid-sixties, the B–52 remained SAC's primary bomber and modifications were necessary to offset structural weaknesses caused by aging.[50] In the early seventies,

---

[48] Phase I counted 9 fixes. The main ones consisted of strengthening the fuselage bulkhead and aileron bay area. Other important fixes were the reinforcement of boost pump access panels and wing foot splice plate.

[49] Phase II called for modification of the upper wing panel splice inboard of inboard engine pods, reinforcement of lower wing panel supporting inboard and outboard pods, reinforcement of upper wing surface fuel probe access doors, and strengthening of a bottom portion of the fuselage bulkhead. Some work was to be done also on the upper wing panel splice, 8 feet inboard of the outboard engine pods.

[50] An engineering change proposal (ECP 1128), approved in 1964, was scheduled for completion in June 1966. It called for various structural improvements, including replacement

The D-model was equipped solely for bombing missions.

similar projects would be undertaken either to beef up or to modernize selected models of the elderly B–52s.

Big Belly Modifications   December 1965

Less than 6 months after the B–52s became involved in the Vietnam War (B–52Fs were the first to go), the Air Force initiated a special modification program to allow the B–52Ds to carry more bombs. Referred to as Big Belly, the modification program left the outside of the aircraft intact. Modified B–52Ds could still carry twenty-four 500-pound or 750-pound bombs externally, but the internal changes were significant. Reconfiguration of the B–52D bomb bay allowed the aircraft to carry 84, instead of twenty-seven 500-pound bombs, or 42, instead of twenty-seven 750-pounders, for a maximum bomb load of about 60,000 pounds—22,000 pounds more than the B–52F.

Overseas Deployment   April 1966

B–52Ds of the 28th and 484th Bomb Wings, deployed to Guam in April 1966, immediately began to replace SAC's B–52Fs in the Vietnam conflict. All B–52Ds committed to Southeast Asia had been modified to carry more bombs than the planes they relieved. In the spring of 1967 modified B–52Ds began also to operate out of U Tapao Airfield in Thailand. From there, the aircraft would complete their mission without inflight refueling, which was necessary when operating from Guam. This saved both time and money.

Additional Training   1968

Because of the war, SAC established on 15 April 1968 a Replacement Training Unit within the 93d Bomb Wing's 4017th Combat Crew Training Squadron at Castle AFB. The unit's purpose was to cross-train every B–52 crew, from the B–52E through the B–52H model, in the operation of B–52D aircraft. After 2 weeks of training, the crews were used to augment the cadre units in Southeast Asia. This spread out combat duties more equitably among the entire B–52 force and provided the crews needed to meet the increased bombing effort.

---

of the vertical fin spar and skin. It would enable most of the B–52s to resume unrestricted operations, but was expected to cost $230 million.

Other Structural Modifications   1966–1968

When a single B–52, set aside for static testing, was subjected to final destruction back in February 1955, its wings accepted 97 percent of the ultimate up-bending load before failing—an entirely satisfactory outcome for the configuration tested. However, since that time, the B–52 had flown many hours and far more years than expected. Furthermore, many of the hours accumulated by the 10-year-old bomber had been flown at low-level, which put a great deal of extra stress on an aircraft structure, originally intended for high-altitude bombing. Therefore, the structural modifications, approved in the mid-sixties as a result of engineering change proposal 1243, came as no surprise. Started in December 1966, this modification program ensured selected B–52s of an additional 2,000 hours of service life. All Big Belly B–52Ds, reconfigured with high-density bomb bays, were automatically earmarked for the work. The others were chosen according to a very straightforward formula. Namely, B–52C, D, or F models qualified if they were nearing their flying maximum of unrestricted "E" hours and had not been tabbed for upcoming phaseout.[51] The modification program was completed during the second half of 1968, at a cost of approximately $16 million, after replacing fatigued structural parts in the most critical wing areas of the involved planes.

Special Modifications   1969–1971

Because they had already been fitted to carry heavier bombloads, a number of B–52Ds were earmarked for another round of modifications. The changes this time would allow the aircraft to carry extra aerial mines. As requested by Deputy Secretary of Defense David Packard in December 1968, the project had been thoroughly reviewed, the Air Force concluding that the suggested modification of later B–52 models would be less efficient and more costly—$6.9 million instead of $6.3 million. Although the Air Force's selection was approved by the Office of the Secretary of Defense in mid-1969, the B–52D special modifications were only completed in the fall of 1971.[52] Not too soon, it seemed, for President Richard M. Nixon ordered the mining of North Vietnam's harbors and river inlets on 8 May 1972.

---

[51] The "E" hour was an equivalent used to indicate the fatigue damage accrued in the wing structure of all B–52C, B–52D, and B–52F bombers.

[52] It also took time to finalize logistics agreements with the Navy for procurement, modification, storage, and delivery of mines.

Southeast Asian Losses   1966–1973

The Vietnam conflict cost SAC 22 B–52Ds. Surface-to-air missiles and other ground defenses accounted for 12 of the losses. Ten B–52Ds were lost in operational accidents of one kind or another.

End of Production   1957

The B–52D production ended in late 1957, the last 6 productions being accepted by the Air Force in November.

Total B–52Ds Accepted   170

The Air Force accepted 101 B–52Ds from Seattle; 69 from Wichita.

Acceptance Rates

Only 1 B–52D was accepted in FY 56 (June 1956); 92 in FY 57 (between July 1956 and June 1957); and 77 in FY 58 (all in calendar year 1957).

Flyaway Cost Per Production Aircraft $6.58 million

Airframe, $4,654,494; engines (installed), $1,291,415; electronics, $68,613; ordnance, $17,928; armament (and others), $548,353.[53]

Subsequent Model Series   B–52E

Other Configurations   None

Initial Phaseout   1973–1974

In accordance with Secretary McNamara's mid-sixties decision to cut

---

[53] Another price decrease, almost $700,000 below the B–52C's cost.

down the strategic bomber force by mid-1971, SAC inactivated 3 squadrons of B–52D and B–52E aircraft during the early part of 1967. This action, however, did not spell the immediate retirement of the aircraft that had been attached to the inactivated units. Badly needed elsewhere, the Big Belly B–52Ds were immediately used to bolster the resources of the B–52D wings committed to Southeast Asia. The B–52Ds actually outlived 2 subsequent B–52 models. In 1973, a partial retirement of the B–52D fleet was planned. Based on the age and condition of their airframe, 45 B–52Ds were earmarked for phaseout by September 1974.

Operational Status   Mid-1973

In mid-1973, SAC forces still counted about 130 B–52Ds. Some of these aircraft were on their way out—45 by the fall of 1974 and a few others soon afterward. But 80 B–52Ds were expected to see unrestricted service into the 1980s. The Air Force was negotiating a contract with Boeing for the Wichita fabrication of kits and the reworking of wings that would be installed on the 80 B–52Ds, during the aircraft's regular depot maintenance. The cost of extending the B–52D's operational life seemed high, over $200 million for 80 planes, but the Air Force believed it had no alternative.[54] As approved by the Office of the Secretary of Defense on 30 November 1972, the modification, identified as engineering change proposal (ECP) 1581, promised to be extensive. It included redesign and replacement of the lower wing skin, to make it similar to the B–52G wing, and in the process Boeing was to use a more fatigue resistant alloy. The wing center panel was also to be redesigned and replaced. Finally, ECP 1581 called for new upper longerons and some new fuselage side skins. Also, the pressure bulkhead in the B–52D nose would be changed. Already delayed for lack of money, ECP 1581 had been programmed to take at least 2 years.

Record Flights   26 September 1958

Two B–52Ds of the 28th Bomb Wing, Ellsworth AFB, South Dakota, established world speed records over 2 different routes. One B–52D flew at 560.705 miles per hour for 10,000 kilometers in a closed circuit without payloads; the other, at 597.675 miles per hour for 5,000 kilometers, also in a closed circuit without payloads.

---

[54] As explained by Secretary of Defense Elliot L. Richardson to the Senate Armed Services Committee, without the hi-density B–52Ds, the Strategic Air Command's conventional bombing capability would be at the expense of its other missions.

B–52E

Manufacturer's Model 464–259

Previous Model Series   B–52D

New Features

As rolled out of either the Seattle or Wichita plant, the B–52E hardly differed from the B–52D. It was equipped with more reliable electronics, and the more accurate AN/ASQ–38 bombing navigational system replaced the B–52D's final AN/ASQ–48. The relocation of some equipment and a slight redesign of the navigator-bombardier station increased crew comfort and provided better access to instruments and greater maintenance ease. Other dissimilarities between the 2 models grew from post-production modifications.

Configuration Planning   December 1953

As an improved B–52D, the B–52E development dated back to the end of 1953.

Program Increases   1954–1956

The beginning of large-scale production, the opening of the Wichita plant, and the 7-wing program endorsed in late 1953 did not satisfy General LeMay. The program's long-range increase to 408 aircraft, as approved in March 1954, remained short of his command's requirements. On 20 June 1955, the Air Force Council recommended that the B–52 program be raised to 576 and that production be accelerated. Secretary Talbott approved the council's recommendation, but pointed out that money remained the limiting factor and only 399 aircraft would be produced on an accelerated basis, beginning in mid-1955. The further increase to 576, the Secretary indicated, would depend entirely on the amount of funds obligated in the coming 2 years.[55] In September 1955, on the

---

[55] On 15 August 1955, Donald A. Quarles replaced Harold Talbott as Secretary of the Air Force.

assumption that money would indeed be forthcoming, SAC began to plan the equipping of 11 bombardment wings, each with 45 B–52s. Five command support B–52s would be added to each wing once every unit had been converted as programmed. In the spring of 1956, the Subcommittee on the Air Force of the Senate Armed Services Committee undertook a review of American airpower. Asked for his opinion, General LeMay again urged that the B–52 production be increased. In December, the President's budget set the B–52 program at 11 wings, and reprogrammed procurement to acquire 53 additional B–52Es, starting in mid-1957, when fiscal year 1958 funds would become available.

Additional Procurement   1955–1956

The B–52E procurement was covered by 4 definitive contracts, funded in fiscal years 1956 and 1957. The first one, AF33(600)–31267, concluded on 26 October 1955, was essentially a B–52D contract to which 26 B–52Es were attached. The second, AF33(600)–32863, signed on 2 July 1956, counted 16 B–52Es and 44 further improved productions (B–52Fs). All such aircraft were to be built in Seattle. The other 2 contracts, AF33(600)–31155 of 10 August 1955 and AF33(600)–32864 of 2 July 1956, also involved other B–52s (either D or F models), but covered 14 and 44 B–52Es, respectively. All would come from the new Wichita plant.

First Flight (Production Aircraft)   October 1957

The Seattle-built B–52E was first flown on 3 October 1957, 3 weeks ahead of its Wichita counterpart.

Enters Operational Service   December 1957

A few B–52Es began reaching the Strategic Air Command in December 1957.

Initial Operational Problems   1958–1964

Besides sharing the initial deficiencies of other B–52s, the B–52E introduced a new problem. The aircraft's new ASQ–38 bombing-navigation system at first was not as accurate as had been anticipated. It was difficult to maintain, and replacement parts were in short supply. The ASQ–38

261

problems at first appeared relatively minor, but grew in importance as soon as the B–52E entered the Big Four modification program. Moreover, since the same bombing-navigation system would be installed in all subsequent B–52s, extensive engineering changes were initiated to improve low-level terrain avoidance for the long term. The modifications promised to be time-consuming and costly, and they gave way to a special project, Jolly Well, which exchanged major parts of the ASQ–38 and replaced the terrain computer—another critical component of the overall system. Jolly Well was completed in 1964, after successful modification of the ASQ–38 of 480 B–52s—B–52E, F, G, and H models.

End of Production   1958

The B–52E production ended before mid-1958, the last 3 aircraft being accepted by the Air Force in June.

Total B–52Es Accepted   100

Of the 100 B–52Es accepted by the Air Force, 58 came from Wichita which thus began to assume production leadership over Seattle.

Acceptance Rates

All B–52Es were accepted in FY 58, between October 1957 and June 1958.

Flyaway Cost Per Production Aircraft $5.94 million

Airframe, $3,700,750; engines (installed), $1,256,516; electronics, $54,933; ordnance, $4,626; armament (and others), $931,665.[56]

Average Maintenance Cost Per Flying Hour $925.00

---

[56] The B–52E cost less than any other B–52. Although production kept on increasing, the price of ensuing models did not go down. On the contrary, in-production structural improvements, better engines, more sophisticated components, and other technological pluses boosted costs.

Subsequent Model Series

Other Configurations

The second B–52E built (Serial No. 56–632) was assigned from the start to major test programs. It was used for prototyping landing gears, engines, and other major B–52 sub-systems, test results contributing significantly to the improvements featured by subsequent B–52 models. Also, the B–52E test plane underwent permanent modifications in order to participate in highly specialized development projects. Small swept winglets were attached alongside the nose of the reconfigured bomber—NB–52E. A long probe extended from the nose of the modified plane and the NB–52E wings displayed nearly twice the normal amount of controlling surfaces. In addition, traditional mechanical and hydraulic linkages to move the control surfaces were replaced by electronic and electrical systems. Internally, the NB–52E was loaded with a multitude of special electronic measuring systems. The aircraft was first used to develop an electronic flutter and buffeting suppression system. This would decrease the fatigue and stress of aircrews flying at low level. The N configuration participated in another project, known by the acronym LAMS—Load Alleviation and Mode Stabilization. During the LAMS flights, sensors noted gusts and activated the control surfaces to cut down on fatigue damage to the aircraft. In mid-1973, the NB–52E flew 10 knots (11.5 mph) faster than the speed at which flutter normally would disintegrate the aircraft. This was made possible by the aircraft's winglets (canards), which reduced 30 percent of the vertical and 50 percent of the horizontal vibrations caused by air gusts. The NB–52E's contributions were significant, but its cost was relatively low—$6.02 million. Over the years, barely more than $500,000 had been spent to bring the aircraft to its permanent testing configuration. In 1973 its career was nearing its end; the Air Force planned to retire the NB–52E in mid-1974.

Beginning of Phaseout 1967–1973

The Secretary of Defense's decision to reduce SAC's bomber fleet by mid-1971 affected the B–52Es more than it did the B–52Ds. While the B–52Ds of units inactivated in 1967 went to other operational wings, excess B–52Es were designated non-operational active aircraft. This meant that the aircraft were stored with operational units, maintained in a serviceable condition, and periodically flown. However, no additional crews or maintenance personnel were authorized for these planes. A few B–52Es were permanently retired in 1967, but only because they had reached the end of their operational life by accumulating a specified number of flying hours under conditions of structural stress. This phaseout pattern was retained in the following years. In mid-1973, the Air Force still carried 48 B–52Es in its inventory, but they were not part of the active operational forces.

B-52F

Manufacturer's Model 464-260

Previous Model Series   B-52E

New Features

New J57-43 engines took the place of the B-52E's J57-P-19s or P-29s. Alternators, attached to the left-hand unit of each pair of the J57-P-43W engines replaced the air-driven turbines and alternators in the B-52E's fuselage. The B-52F's only other new feature was a more efficient water injection system.

Configuration Planning   November 1954

Continued improvements of the J57 engine series prompted the November 1954 initiation of the B-52F design. Incorporation of the J57-P-43W engines had to entail some changes. A slight modification of the wing structure also had to be planned in order to install 2 additional wing tanks, which would give the B-52F's injection system an increased water capacity—the system's main overall advancement.

Contractual Arrangements   1956

B-52F procurement was accomplished by 2 B-52E contracts—AF33(600)-32863 and AF33(600)-32834. One contract called for 44 Seattle B-52Fs; the other, for 45 B-52Fs from Wichita.

First Flight (Production Aircraft)   May 1958

The Seattle-built B-52F first flew on 6 May; the Wichita-built model, on 14 May.

Production Slippages   1958

Whether from Seattle or Wichita, B–52F deliveries lagged a few months behind schedule because authorized overtime for Boeing personnel was curtailed. Fiscal limitations, imposed by the Office of the Secretary of Defense in late 1957,[57] were the cause.

Enters Operational Service   1958

B–52Fs did not start reaching the Strategic Air Command until June 1958. By the end of the month, SAC's 93d Bomb Wing counted 6 B–52Fs.

Initial Problems   1954–1959

Fuel leaks, occurring in the B–52Fs and preceding B–52s, proved difficult to stop. The problem manifested itself from the start. Marman clamps, the flexible fuel couplets interconnecting fuel lines between tanks, broke down on several occasions during the first few weeks of B–52 operation. This caused fuel gushers that obviously created serious flying hazards. Blue Band, a September 1957 project, put new clamps (CF–14s) in all B–52s. Depot assistance field teams did the retrofit well, but Blue Band did not work. The CF–14 aluminum clamps soon showed signs of stress corrosion and were likely to fail after 100 days of service. Highly concerned, the Air Force and Boeing began replacing the aluminum clamps with a Boeing-developed stainless steel strap clamp, the CF–17. Hard Shell, a high-priority retrofit program, put CF–17 clamps in all in-service B–52s. Completed in January 1958, the Hard Shell retrofit was not a fool-proof solution. B–52 operations were again restricted, as several CF–17 clamps ruptured, this time because of deficient latch pins. CF–17A couplings, CF–17 clamps that had been modified to strengthen their latch pins, were used to correct the problem. But neither Boeing nor the Air Force put too much credence on the new modification. This gave way to Quickclip, a new retrofit project started in mid-1958. All B–52s went through Quickclip, which installed a safety strap around the modified clamps. Several cases of broken latch pins were reported before the end of 1958. However, the safety straps prevented the fuel from leaking out, which was Quickclip's whole

---

[57] Charles E. Wilson was sworn in as Secretary of Defense on 28 January 1953, and served until 8 October 1957. He was succeeded by Neil H. McElroy, who resigned on 1 December 1959.

purpose. Additional B-52Fs, entering the inventory after the fall of 1958, therefore were also fitted with Quickclip safety straps.

Other Fuel System Problems   1954-1962

Fuel system icing posed another initial and long-lasting B-52 problem which had been shared for several years by other jet aircraft. However, little was known about its cause and effect. A B-52 accident in 1958 brought the problem to a climax, while providing a few definite findings. In many previous crashes, icing of the fuel system had been recognized as a probable cause of accident, but the ice had melted in ensuing fires, leaving no concrete evidence. This time, the Air Force could ascertain that icing of the fuel system strut filters and fuel pump screens had caused the engine to flame out and lose thrust. As a remedial step, B-52s were immediately fitted with filters and screens which promised to be less susceptible to icing. The Air Force in addition initiated new fuel draining procedures and directed use of the driest fuel available. A new fuel booster transfer valve came under development during the same period. The B-52 accident of 1958 also speeded research on fuel additives that would prevent the formation of ice in fuel system components. The Air Force, Boeing, and fuel vendors participated in the intensified research program. Nevertheless, progress was likely to be slow. In the meantime, the only meaningful solution was to put fuel heaters in every B-52 and to do so as quickly as possible. Despite troubles encountered during the thermal shock and vibration tests of the heaters, this retrofit project proceeded according to schedule in late 1959. Concurrently, however, a new problem arose. The fuel additive program, after going on unabated, came to a sudden stop because the additives were damaging the fuel cell's inner coating. But this latest problem was resolved in due time. In October 1962, jet fuel additives had proven so successful in eliminating icing problems that SAC was disconnecting the fuel heaters on its latest B-52s (B-52Hs).

Overall Improvement   1962-1964

The B-52F, after participating in the High Stress and Big Four modification programs, was further improved. Again the improvement covered all B-52s, even the early B-52Bs. It consisted of installing the equipment necessary to detect and locate actual and incipient malfunctions in the bombing-navigation and autopilot systems. This equipment was known as MADREC, an acronym for Malfunction Detection and

Recording.[58] The requirement for MADREC had been established in 1961, and its installation was part of a long-range program. The first stage involved the B–52B, B–52C, and B–52D bombers and was completed by mid-1963. The second stage was directed at the more complicated ASQ-38 bombing-navigation system of the B–52E, B–52F, and subsequent B–52s. In essence, the program was closely associated with the Big Four package. MADREC equipment would play an important role in monitoring the Hound Dog missiles that were carried by almost every B–52, as a result of Big Four. The program neared completion by 1965.

Special Modifications   1964–1965

The revised strategy of the early sixties, calling for a greater non-nuclear retaliatory force, did not leave the B–52 untouched. In June 1964, the Air Staff approved the modification of 28 B–52Fs under a project known as South Bay. Completed in October of the same year, the modification program allowed selected B–52Fs to carry twenty-four 750-pound bombs externally—almost doubling the aircraft's original conventional bombload. In June 1965, as the tempo of activities in Southeast Asia began to escalate, Secretary of Defense McNamara requested that 46 other B–52Fs receive similar modifications. Referred to as Sun Bath, the project this time carried a 1-month deadline. Some problems arose. Multiple ejection racks, beams, kits, and supporting aerospace ground equipment were in short supply. To fulfill its many commitments, Air Force Logistics Command's Oklahoma Air Materiel Area, the project's prime coordinator, had to borrow assets from war reserve materiel and from units of the Tactical Air Command. Just the same, Sun Bath was completed 1 week ahead of schedule.

Southeast Asian Deployments   1965

The first B–52 bombers that entered the war in Southeast Asia were B–52Fs. On 18 June 1965, the initial Arc Light bombing mission was carried out from Guam by 27 B–52Fs of the 7th and 320th Bomb Wings. B–52Fs were the only SAC bombers committed to the Vietnam conflict throughout 1965. Even though all deployed B–52Fs had received ahead of time the

---

[58] B–47Es were also due to be fitted with MADREC equipment.

South Bay or Sun Bath modifications to increase their bombload to 38,250 pounds, they were replaced before mid-1966 by modified B-52Ds.

Southeast Asian Losses   1965

B-52F participation in Southeast Asian operations accounted for the loss of 2 of the planes. The 2 collided in mid-air on 18 June 1965, on their way to the first Arc Light mission.

End of Production   1958

Production of the B-52F, the last model of the B-52 series built in Seattle, ended in November 1958. The Seattle plant, after manufacturing nearly one-half of the B-52F productions, transferred all B-52 engineering responsibility to Wichita.

Total B-52Fs Accepted   89

The Air Force accepted 44 B-52Fs from Seattle; 45 from Wichita.

Acceptance Rates

The Air Force accepted 10 B-52Fs in FY 58 (all in June 1958), and 79 in FY 59 (between July 1958 and February 1959).

Flyaway Cost Per Production Aircraft $6.48 million

Airframe, $3,772,247; engines (installed), $1,787,191; electronics, $60,111; ordnance, $3,016; armament (and others), $862,839.

Average Maintenance Cost Per Flying Hour $1,025.00

Subsequent Model Series   B-52G

Other Configurations   None

Beginning of Phaseout   **1971–1973**

Although the 93d Bomb Wing retained every one of its B–52Fs, 1971 marked the beginning of the aircraft's phaseout.[59] Retired planes went to Davis-Monthan for storage. In mid-1973, the Air Force still possessed 62 B–52Fs. Thirty-six of these aircraft were in the inactive inventory. Other B–52Fs were used for training.

---

[59] The Air Force retired a few B–52Fs in 1967. As in the B–52E's case, these planes were retired only because they had exceeded their service life criteria.

B-52G

Manufacturer's Model 464-253

Previous Model Series   B-52F

New Features

Besides an increase in gross weight (488,000 instead of 450,000 pounds), major configuration changes characterized the B-52G. A principal distinction was the "wet wing," as it was often called, which contained integral fuel tanks that significantly increased the aircraft's unrefueled range. The B-52G retained the B-52F's new J57-P-43W, but the engine's water injection system was improved in duration by the installation of a single 12,000-gallon tank in the forward fuselage. There were many other changes, some of them quite noticeable. The nose radome was enlarged, the size of the vertical fin reduced, the tail cone modified, and the ailerons eliminated. The B-52G's redesigned wings supported 700-gallon fixed external fuel tanks that replaced the 3,000-gallon auxiliary wing tanks, carried by several preceding B-52 models. While retaining the AN/ASQ-38 bombing navigational system, the B-52G featured the new AN/ASG-15 fire-control system, improved electronic countermeasures technology, a powered stability augmentation system, and emergency ejection seats for the entire crew, including the gunner who was moved to a rearward-facing seat, next to the electronic countermeasures operator.[60] Finally, in addition to its standard bombload, most B-52Gs were in production equipped to carry 2 Hound Dog missiles,[61] 1 on a pylon under each wing between the inboard

---

[60] The location of the bombardier and radar navigator was unchanged. They sat forward facing behind and below pilot and co-pilot. Prior to the B-52G, B-52s and their normal crew of 6 only had 5 ejection seats, none for the gunner.

[61] The North American AGM-28 (formerly GAM-77) Hound Dog was an air-to-surface missile powered by a single Pratt & Whitney J52 turbojet. The AGM-28 was equipped with an inertial guidance system and a nuclear warhead. Launched at high altitude and supersonic speed, the AGM-28 could reach a target 500 nautical miles away; at low altitude and subsonic speed, the distance was reduced to 200 nautical miles.

nacelles and the fuselage. Four Quail decoy missiles could also be fitted in the bomb bay.[62]

Basic Development   1955–1956

The B–52G design was officially initiated in June 1956. Yet the roots of the new aircraft can be traced back to January 1955, when Convair's delta-wing B–58 appeared to be heading for trouble. The Air Force's indecision about the future of the costly, high-risk B–58 program meant that the next decade might not bring new bombers to replace or supplement SAC's B–52s. Development of a much more potent version of the original B–52, Air Research and Development Command stated, would prevent a possible technical obsolescence of the strategic force in the 1960s. As envisioned in May 1955, the new aircraft would be a B–52 fuselage with a redesigned wing, J75 engines, and a number of detailed changes. General LeMay at first was unenthusiastic about the proposal, which brought to mind the Lockheed F–84F and its many early production problems.

While conceding that the Boeing bomber should be improved "as much as possible" during production, General LeMay argued that the B–52 production schedule should not be disrupted. Although he came to favor the "super B–52" somewhat later, General LeMay noted that if "true meaningful improvement" was to result, the B–52 production schedule would inevitably be slowed down. As urgent as it seemed, the B–52G design did not start until June 1956. Delays in providing $1.2 million for Boeing to complete the necessary study was a factor; another was the Air Staff's continued concern about the B–58 and resulting procrastination in formally approving the Boeing project.

Development Engineering Inspection   16–18 June 1956

Once the Air Force finally decided to endorse the B–52 model improvement, events moved quickly. In July, the Air Staff shifted $8.8 million to the project, funds which, in any case, had been allocated to support engineering changes. In the same month, Boeing held an initial development engineering

---

[62] The McDonnell ADM–20 (formerly GAM–72) Quail was a small delta-wing drone, equipped with 1 General Electric J85 turbojet engine. It had a range of several hundred nautical miles, could match the B–52's performance, and accomplish at least 2 turns and 1 speed change. It contained electronic devices that made it look like a B–52 on enemy radar scopes. The Quail was unique among air-launched missiles in that it was the only decoy missile in the United States Air Force.

inspection at its Seattle plant. The purpose of the inspection was to determine the new configuration of the crew compartment. While the Air Force found no specific faults with the arrangements set up by Boeing, it pointed out that many questions remained unanswered. On 15 August, the contractor submitted for review a model improvement program that was more comprehensive. The Air Staff approved the revised program on 29 August, but specified that its implementation would be only on a "minimum sustaining basis" until more was known about the B–58 program. Possible forthcoming fiscal limitations were another reason for curtailing program's implementation.

Mockup Inspection   October 1956

The Air Force inspected and approved the crew compartment's mockup for the improved B–52 toward the end of October. The new configuration, based on the so-called "battle-station" concept, placed the defensive crew (the ECM operator and gunner) facing aft on the upper deck, the offensive team (bombing-navigation system operators) facing forward on the lower deck, and the pilot and co-pilot (still sitting side-by-side) facing forward on the flight deck.

Production Slowdown   1957

The impact of unforeseen events, international as well as domestic, often played havoc with the best plans. In 1955, B–58 problems worked in favor of producing an improved B–52 (B–52G). In April 1956, the Air Force wanted the B–52 production increased to a monthly rate of 20. In December, the President set the B–52 program at 11 wings and procurement was revamped to provide a greater quantity of improved B–52s (B–52Es). Money from the next fiscal year (FY 58) would cover the procurement changes, and faster production would take place as soon as practicable. But the progress was short-lived. In early 1957, Secretary of Defense Wilson made it known that B–52 monthly production rates would be held at 15. There were several compelling reasons for the Secretary's decision. As explained by Secretary of the Air Force Quarles, progress was being made on the B–58 development, and Mr. Wilson had already indicated that the B–58 would not only merit some production effort, but would definitely get it in due time. Moreover, a slower B–52 output might give the Air Force a larger number of further improved models, this time perhaps fewer B–52Es and more B–52Fs. Other factors bearing on the decision were revised intelligence estimates, particularly the latest information on Soviet Bison and Bear bomber production

Roll-out of the first G-model Stratofortress at Boeing's Wichita plant, July 1958.

rates, which seemed to have slowed down. Those, as Mr. Quarles pointed out in Secretary Wilson's words, were "a little different, and it looked like we had more time to do an orderly job." Finally, it was Secretary Wilson's belief that "in many cases we get cheaper production by phasing it out over a longer period of time and getting more expert people to work on it." The Air Force had few grounds for argument, even though SAC pointed out that the endorsed lower production rates would delay its conversion program by almost 1 year. As expected, the decision stood.

Contractual Arrangements 1957–1959

Reflecting the evolutionary production process, preceding B–52s were acquired through contracts that covered a variety of models. As a culmination of this process as well as continued developmental efforts, the B–52G was purchased under different conditions. Three procurement contracts were issued—AF33(600)–35992, funded in FY 57; AF33(600)–34670, in FY 58, and AF33(600)–37481, in FY 59. All 3 contracts involved B–52Gs only. The first one, a cost-plus-incentive fee contract with a sliding percentage of 6 percent, was initiated by letter contract on 29 August 1957 and finalized on 15 May 1958. It purchased 53 aircraft. The second and largest one was a fixed-price-incentive-firm (FPIF) contract for 101 B–52Gs. It was started by a letter contract on 14 June 1957, and also finalized on 15 May 1958.[63] The third and last B–52G contract, begun by letter contract on 5 September 1958, was concluded on 28 April 1959. It was a straightforward fixed-price-incentive (FPI) contract for 39 aircraft.

Enters Operational Service   1959

The B–52G entered service with the 5th Bomb Wing at Travis AFB, California. The wing received its first B–52G (Serial No. 47-6478) on 13 February, one day after SAC's last B–36 bomber was retired and the command became an all-jet bomber force. In May 1959, the 42d Bomb Wing also started getting B–52Gs. By the end of June, 41 of the new bombers had been received by SAC. The early B–52Gs and 13 more could not carry the Hound Dog missiles.[64] A post-production modification, completed in 1962, accomplished necessary alterations and fitted the 54 aircraft with the equipment required to support as well as fire the new weapons.

Special Tests   1960

B–52Gs, of necessity, played an important role in the Category III testing of both the Hound Dog and Quail missiles. A B–52G crew of the 4135th Strategic Wing accomplished the first SAC launch of a Hound Dog on 29 February 1960. On 8 June, a B–52G crew of the same wing repeated the performance with a Quail decoy. By the end of 1961, a respectable supply of the new missiles—225 Hound Dogs and 400 Quails—had already reached the SAC inventory. However, although the new AGM–28 Hound Dogs had become an important part of the B–52's striking power, the missiles were still highly unreliable.[65]

---

[63] The May 1958 contract, as initiated in June 1957, evolved from the President's budget of December 1956, which set the B–52 program at 11 wings and a total of 603 aircraft. The last B–52G contract, started by letter contract in September 1958, and the subsequent procurement of B–52Hs (the last model) were not part of the 11-wing program. They could be viewed as added bonuses, prompted by new dissatisfaction with the B–58 program, concurrent fiscal limitations, and the B–58's high price.

[64] Boeing could not be faulted for the omission. Because of the complexity and high cost of the Big Four modification package, refinement of the many changes under consideration consumed most of 1959. The Air Staff did not decide until the end of that year which B–52 models would be equipped, either in production or through retrofit, to carry the new missiles.

[65] In contrast, the ADM–20 Quail's performance was excellent. In 1963, all Quail decoys were modified for low-level flying. This relatively simple modification added a barometric switch for terrain avoidance and altered the missile's wiring system.

Structural Modifications   1961–1964

Intensive structural testing, conducted by Boeing and the Air Force in 1960, again confirmed that hard usage shortened the structural life of the B–52 aircraft. The B–52Gs and B–52Hs differed significantly from predecessor models, but design changes incorporated in the new bombers made them even more susceptible to fatigue damage. Briefly stated, the changes had been made to extend the aircraft's range, which essentially meant that while the B–52G and B–52H bombers were lighter than preceding B–52s, their fuel loads had been increased. Moreover, the overall decrease in structural weight had been achieved primarily by using an aluminum alloy in the aircraft's wings. While testing did not question the intrinsic strength of the wing, it pinpointed areas of fatigue. No one could forecast accurately when the wing failures would happen, but low-level flying and the structural strains that occurred during air refueling were expected to speed up fatigue considerably.[66] The anticipated problem appeared serious enough for SAC to impose stringent flying restrictions on the new aircraft, pending approval of necessary modifications. In May 1961, the Air Staff endorsed a $219

---

[66] It was estimated that under fairly similar circumstances, the operating stress placed on the new wing was approximately 60 percent higher than the stress inflicted on the wing of preceding B–52s.

A GAM-77 Hound Dog missile was launched from under a B-52's wing over Eglin AFB, Florida.

million modification program for all B-52G and B-52H wing structures.[67] The program provided for Boeing to retrofit the modified wings during the airplanes' regular IRAN schedule, except for the last 18 B-52Hs, which would get their modified wings on the Wichita production lines. Started in February 1962, the program was completed by September 1964, as scheduled.

Other Structural Improvements   1964-1972

While ECP 1050 had strengthened the wings of the B-52Gs and B-52Hs by September 1964, as already noted, ECP 1128, a major engineering change proposal approved in the same year for the entire B-52 fleet, had just begun.[68] Concurrently, MADREC, a previously described improvement program that also covered most B-52s, was in progress. In addition, various modifications, addressed to specific B-52 models, were either underway or about to start. In spite of such projects, the Air Force believed that major efforts would still be required in the ensuing years to keep extending the structural life of the critically needed B-52G and B-52H bombers. Hence, the Air Staff in October 1967 approved ECP 1195, an engineering change studied by SAC since 1965. Eventually known as the B-52 Stability Augmentation and Flight Control program, the $69 million modifications installed a number of new devices in the bombers. Necessary kits, contracted for in December 1967, began reaching the Air Force in mid-1969, and their installation required 2 years. Meanwhile, ECP 1185, due to cost about $50 million and actually initiated in May 1966, had started to replace their aircraft's fuselage side skin, crown skin fasteners, and upper longerons. Completion of these latest engineering changes, accomplished as usual during the aircraft's regular IRAN schedule, was expected to ensure the structural safety of the B-52G and B-52H airframes through the 1980s.

Special Modifications   1970-1975

In line with current plants to retain the B-52Gs and B-52Hs for years

---

[67] The wing structural improvement program, carried out as ECP 1050, replaced the wing box beam with a modified wing box that used thicker aluminum. It also installed stronger steel taper lock fasteners in lieu of the existing titanium fasteners; it added brackets and clamps to the wing skins, added wing panel stiffeners, and made at least a dozen other changes. Finally, a new protective coating was applied to the interior structure of the wing integral fuel tanks.

[68] Shortly before the beginning of ECP 1128, the Air Force had directed that the tail section of all B-52s be reinforced in order to withstand turbulence during low-level penetration tactics. Started in September 1963, this engineering modification (ECP 1124-2) was due to spread over several years.

to come, the Air Force in 1970 decided to equip these bombers with the Boeing-developed AGM–69A nuclear-tipped short-range attack missile (SRAM).[69] Required modifications and the addition of necessary equipment, such as wing pylons, launch gear, rotary launchers, and new avionics would be accomplished by 2 air materiel areas. Oklahoma City would modify all B–52Gs; San Antonio, all B–52Hs. This long-term, $400 million retrofit program began on 15 October 1971, when 1 B–52G entered the Oklahoma City modification center. In March 1972, a SRAM-equipped B–52G was delivered to the 42d Bomb Wing at Loring AFB, Maine. The 42d became SRAM-operational in August, the first of 19 wings programmed to acquire the versatile missiles.[70] Each modified B–52G and H bomber could carry up to 20 SRAMs, 12 externally and 8 inside the rear of the bomb bay.

Southeast Asian Deployment   1972

As SAC strove to preserve the might of its primary bombers, the war in Southeast Asia continued unabated. Since 1965, when the B–52Fs had first arrived in Southeast Asia, B–52 conventional bombing operations had increased from year to year. The purpose of the bombing was not always the same, the theaters of operation also varied, but the task always grew. B–52Gs did not enter the war before mid-1972; yet, their short-lived participation did not prove easy. On 18 December, as ordered by President Nixon, B–52Gs and the older B–52Ds began to bomb military targets in the Hanoi and Haiphong areas of North Vietnam. The bombing operation, nicknamed Linebacker II, ended on 29 December, after a Christmas pause of 24 hours.[71] In this attack on Haiphong and Hanoi, the B–52s encountered awesome defenses. In 11 days, 15 B–52s were shot down by surface-to-air missiles.

---

[69] The 2,300-pound AGM–69A SRAM measured 14 feet in length and 18 inches in diameter. The internally guided, solid-propellant missile could be flown at supersonic or subsonic speeds and set to follow either a high-altitude semi-ballistic trajectory or a low-altitude profile. It could strike targets ahead of the launch aircraft or turn in flight to hit installations to the side or behind the bomber.

[70] SAC's 2 wings of FB–111As would also be equipped with the new missiles, at an estimated cost of $43 million.

[71] SAC B–52s terminated over 8 years of conventional bombing operations in Southeast Asia on 15 August 1973, when all U.S. bombing of targets in Cambodia ceased.

Southeast Asian Losses   1972

SAC lost 7 B–52Gs in Southeast Asia, all of them during 1972.[72] Six of the planes were hit by enemy surface-to-air missiles over North Vietnam, with 4 of them going down around Hanoi and the other 2 crashing in Thailand. The seventh B–52G loss was only indirectly caused by the war. The plane, after taking off from Andersen AFB, Guam, crashed into the ocean, presumably because of materiel failure.

Modernization   1972–On

Ensuring the durability of an airframe was a difficult and costly problem; a worse one, on both counts, was to cope with the enemy's technological developments. In the early seventies, many improvements in electronic countermeasures, initially limited to the Southeast Asia-committed B–52Ds, were extended to the B–52Gs and B–52Hs. These various projects centered essentially on the installation of more efficient jammers to ease the penetration of enemy defenses. One project, Rivet Rambler, was a 2-phase modification accomplished on all B–52Ds by 1971 and specifically directed against the SA–2 radars. In 1973 the Rivet Rambler modification of the B–52G and H bombers was almost completed, but the resulting improvements soon would be nearing obsolescence. Because of the experience gained in Southeast Asia, particularly as a result of the Linebacker II strikes against heavily defended targets, SAC wanted more than ever to equip the B–52Gs and B–52Hs with truly advanced ECM transmitters and jammers. An improved warning system was also needed: one that could detect threats from surface-to-air missiles, anti-aircraft artillery, and airborne interceptors. The Air Staff had already endorsed most of SAC's new requirements. Modification 2525, due to provide more efficient airborne early warning countermeasures, had been approved in June 1971; modification 2519, known as Rivet Ace and due to upgrade the aircraft's

---

[72] Two B–52Gs had been lost years before in highly publicized accidents. The first occurred on 17 January 1966, when a B–52G collided with a KC–135 tanker during a high-altitude refueling operation and both aircraft crashed near Palomares, Spain. The release of some radioactive material required removal of some 1,400 tons of slightly contaminated soil and vegetation to the the United States for disposal. A lost nuclear weapon, finally located by a U.S. Navy submarine about 5 miles from the shore and approximately 2,500 feet under water, was recovered intact on 7 April. Then, on 22 January 1968, a B–52G with 4 nuclear weapons aboard crashed and burned on the ice of North Star Bay, while attempting an emergency landing at nearby Thule Air Base, Greenland. An extensive clean-up operation to remove all possible traces of radioactive material was completed on 13 September.

radar warning receivers, was approved in December of the same year. However, none of these projects would start before mid-1973, and all were scheduled to take several years. There were many reasons for the implementation delays. Technical difficulties had to be worked out, unexpected requirements were likely to materialize, and new components had to be tested for quality as well as compatibility within any given avionics system. An example was Rivet Ace. Within the span of 2 short years, this fairly unsophisticated modification had become a very ambitious endeavor. In mid-1973, although the transformed modification project was about to start, serious problems remained. Components, due to be added to the aircraft's radar warning receivers, had been tested with success, but the system's new surface-to-air missile detection equipment was still defective. Meanwhile, other projects fared well. B–52s were being modified to carry the SRAM, as scheduled, even though a new modification was being done simultaneously. This additional project would give the aircraft an electro-optical viewing system, which made use of forward-looking infrared and low-light-level television sensors. The new system would make low-level flying much easier, and a B–52H, modified by the San Antonio Air Materiel Area, had already been returned to operational duty by mid-1973. Another improvement considered in mid-1973 consisted of fitting the B–52's bombing and navigation system with automated offset units. Such devices, SAC believed, would ease significantly the synchronized bombing of several targets.

End of Production   1961

B–52G production ended in early 1961. The Air Force accepted the last 2 aircraft in February.

Total B–52Gs Accepted   193

The B–52G was the major production model of the B–52 series. All 193 aircraft were built at the Wichita plant.

Acceptance Rates

Fifty B–52Gs were accepted in FY 59 (between October 1958 and June 1959); 106 in FY 60 (between July 1959 and June 1960); 37 in FY 61 (between July 1960 and February 1961).

Front view of a B–52, show-ing the television sensors of the new electro-optical viewing system developed to enhance low-level flight.

Flyaway Cost Per Production Aircraft $7.69 million

Airframe, $5,351,819; engines (installed), $1,427,611; electronics, $66,374; ordnance, $6,809; armament (and others), $840,000.

Average Maintenance Cost Per Flying Hour $1,025.00

Subsequent Model Series   B–52H

Other Configurations   None

Operational Status   Mid-1973

The Air Force in July 1973 retained 175 of 193 B–52Gs, purchased almost 15 years before. These efficient bombers were undergoing modification, with more changes to come in the future.

Record Flight   1960

On 14 December 1960, a B–52G of the 5th Bomb Wing, Travis AFB, California, completed a world record-breaking flight of 10,078.84 miles without refueling. The flight lasted 19 hours and 44 minutes. The previous closed course record, established in 1947 by a B–29, covered only 8,854 miles.

B-52H

Manufacturer's Model 264-261

Previous Model Series   B-52G

New Features

The B-52H did not differ outwardly from the B-52G, except for the shape of its nacelles, slightly altered because of the new engine's larger inlets. Internally, however, there were several important changes. The B-52H featured Pratt and Whitney's 17,000-pound thrust TF-33-P-3 turbofan engines (without water injection system), new engine-driven generators, ECM equipment improved up to the state of the art, and an enhanced fire-control system—the AN/ASG-21. This new system operated a Gatling gun-type of multi-barrel cannon in a remote-controlled tail mounting for rear defense.[73] The AN/ASG-21 also controlled forward-firing penetration rocket launchers. In addition, the B-52H had better cabin arrangements for low-level penetration flights and was equipped to carry the never-to-be GAM-87 Skybolts.[74]

Configuration Planning   January 1959

An outgrowth of the B-52G, the B-52H design was initiated in January 1959, 1 month before SAC received its first B-52G. Although no great innovations resulted, some airframe changes had to be made to take care of the new model's special features. The B-52H was due from the start to incorporate the TF-33 turbofan engine, a modified J57 already adopted by

---

[73] The Gatling gun, the world's first practical machine gun, dated back to the Civil War. The B-52H's ultra-modern version of this 100-year-old weapon was hydraulically operated and electronically controlled. The 6-barreled gun could spew out a stream of 20-mm shells at the rate of 4,000 rounds per minute.

[74] Instead of Skybolts, the B-52Hs carried decoys and missiles identical to those of the B-52Gs.

commercial jet transports. The new aircraft was also designed to carry 4 Douglas GAM–87A Skybolts, which would be a marked improvement over previous B–52s. Had the Skybolt survived, it would have characterized the B–52H as the first manned bomber capable of serving as a flying platform for launching 2-stage solid propellant ballistic missiles with a range of 1,150 miles, fitted with nuclear warheads.

Final Procurement   1959–1962

Like the B–52Gs, the B–52Hs were bought under individual contracts. Two FPI contracts—AF33(600)-38778, funded in FY 60, and AF33(600)-41961, funded in FY 61—accounted for the entire B–52H lot. The first procurement, initiated by letter contract on 2 February 1959, was finalized the following year, on 6 May 1960. It covered 62 B–52Hs. The second B–52H contract was started by a letter contract on 28 July 1960, but was not finalized until the latter part of 1962. There were good reasons for the delay. This was the end of the B–52 procurement and the contract only purchased 40 more B–52Hs. The Air Force could not be sure this would be enough.[75]

First Flight (Prototype)   10 July 1960

The YB–52H's first flight was entirely successful. Ensuing flight tests showed that the new TF–33 turbofan engines would allow the new plane to surpass the B–52G's range. Take-off would also be improved and require about 500 feet less ground roll than the B–52G.

First Flight (Production Aircraft)   6 March 1961

The Air Force accepted the first B–52H in the same month the plane initially flew, but left it with Boeing for testing. By the end of June 1961, B–52H flight tests had confirmed that the TF–33–P–3 engines were working even better than expected. Moreover, even though the new Emerson ASG–21

---

[75] These were difficult times. In September 1962, an Air Force recommendation to expand the North American XB-70 program into a full-scale weapon system development was rejected by Secretary of Defense McNamara. In December, President John F. Kennedy confirmed that further development of the Skybolt, an air-to-surface ballistic missile earmarked for the B-52H, was definitely canceled.

fire-control system and the Sunstrand 120 KVA constant speed alternator drive needed perfecting, they both were tactically operable.

Enters Operational Service   Mid-1961

The B-52H entered operational service with the 379th Bomb Wing, at Wurtsmith AFB, Michigan. The first plane (Serial #60-001) was received by the 379th on 9 May. By the end of June, 20 B-52Hs were in operation. In contrast to all other B-52Hs, 18 of those early planes had not been equipped during production for all-weather, low-level flying. However, modifications accomplished between April and September 1962 brought them up to standard.

Engine Problems   1961-1964

While both the B-52F and B-52G had failed to live up to original range estimates, the B-52H's new TF-33-P-3 turbofan engines gave the aircraft a better range increase than anticipated. Moreover, as indicated by recent B-52H flight tests, some of the new engine's problems appeared to be solved, and remaining malfunctions were being worked out. Yet, despite several engineering fixes, the TF-33 in late 1961 still created difficulties. Throttle creep, hang or slow start, flameout, and uneven throttle alignment were some of the most frequent troubles. In addition, the engine consumed too much oil, turbine blades failed and inlet cases often cracked. By mid-1962, even though most of these early problems had been corrected, Hot Fan, a depot maintenance and overhaul project, was underway. This $15 million modernization effort, involving the accomplishment of 35 technical orders, had 2 essential purposes. The Air Force wanted the TF-33 to be more reliable, and it did not want the engine to fail before 600 hours of operation. Curtailed by the Cuban Missile Crisis of October 1962, when all B-52s stood on alert, Hot Fan was not resumed until January 1963. However, the Oklahoma City Air Materiel Area accelerated its overhaul schedule, and although Hot Fan covered 894 TF-33 engines, the project was practically completed before the end of 1964.

Other Early Difficulties   August 1962

B-52Hs were still being assigned to SAC when a serious and ill-timed problem came to light. In August 1962, again shortly before the Cuban

The ASQ–21 Gatling gun,
mounted in the B–52H's tail,
provided remote-controlled
defense.

A Boeing B–52H, equipped with 4 Douglas GAM Skybolt ballistic missiles.

Missile Crisis, 2 of the B–52Hs at Homestead AFB, Florida, developed cracks where wings and fuselage joined. Boeing and the Air Force focused attention on the taper lock fasteners, which under high stress and in the B–52's operational environment were susceptible to corrosion. They soon determined that the "primary contributing cause for these cracks was the use of taper lock fasteners throughout the forging." In September, Boeing came up with a repair and rework package to take care of the problem. The next month, engineers of Air Force System Command's Aeronautical Systems Division set up requirements to evaluate the impact of stress corrosion on all primary structural materials. Project Straight Pin, the modification package developed by Boeing, was not allowed to linger. Rework centers were immediately established at Moses Lake, Washington; Wichita, Kansas; and at the San Antonio Air Materiel Area's shops. There, maximum interference wing terminal fasteners were replaced with those having extremely low interference, and cracked fitting holes were "cleaned up" by oversize reaming. Although SAC suspended diversion of its airplanes to the modification centers during the Cuban Crisis, Straight Pin was virtually completed by the end of 1962.

Continued Problems   1962–1964

An older stress corrosion problem came to life again in August 1962. Two main landing gear outer cylinders failed on B–52D and B–52F aircraft, the latest in a series of similar incidents with B–52Gs and B–52Hs since the end of 1959. While SAC asked for redesigned cylinders, Air Force engineers noted that a quicker and safer alternative would be to make use of another alloy, one that would be less susceptible to stress corrosion. This gave way to a new study and test program to further investigate current and potential stress corrosion problems. Meanwhile, to prevent other incidents, anti-corrosion coating was applied to all components of the landing gear. Progress was also made to cure most of the B–52H's other early ills. By mid-1962, failure of the aircraft's Sunstrand constant speed drive was becoming a problem of the past. During the same period, a long-standing SAC requirement, only endorsed for the B–52Hs, was finally extended to all B–52s. Started in January 1963 and completed in March of the following year, this retrofit project put 2 cartridge starters in every B–52.[76] The modification was expensive, which accounted for SAC's difficulties in

---

[76] The installation of cartridge starters was not simple. The aircraft's electrical system had to be modified to accommodate the new starters and new valves. In addition, duct covers had to be redesigned and nickel cadmium batteries had to be added.

getting it approved for the entire B–52 force, but it was important. Besides giving crews the means to start their engines faster, it would allow dispersed or post-strike B–52s to take off from airfields lacking certain ground support equipment, electrical power carts in particular.

Structural and Other Improvements   1964–On

As already noted, all B–52G structural modifications were extended to the B–52Hs. These aircraft were also included in the many B–52G modernization programs of the early seventies. Like the Gs, the B–52Hs were being equipped to carry the new SRAMs; they were being fitted with electro-optical viewing systems, low-light television cameras, and forward-looking infrared scanners. Finally, they were due to receive better electronics and more sophisticated components to improve both their offensive and defensive systems. A new project, initially triggered by the relatively slow start of the B–52H's TF–33 engines, was also underway. Despite the cartridge starter retrofit that had been accomplished between 1963 and 1964, SAC was still dissatisfied with the time it took for the B–52 to take off. The recently approved Quick Start project, now only concerned with the B–52G and H bombers, would make the ground alert force far less vulnerable to surprise attacks. Quick Start specifically consisted of putting a quick start device on each of the aircraft's 8 engines, thereby ensuring take-off in almost no time.

End of Production   1962

Production ended in the fall of 1962,[77] SAC receiving on 26 October the last B–52H (Serial #61–040). This plane went to the 4137th Strategic Bomb Wing at Minot AFB, North Dakota.

Total B–52Hs Accepted   102

The 102 B–52Hs accepted by the Air Force, like the B–52Gs, were built in Wichita.

---

[77] This marked the end of a production run which had begun some 9 years before. Wanting to keep the production door ajar, at least for a while, the Air Force negotiated with Boeing a supplemental agreement to the final B–52H production contract—AF33(600)–41961. Signed on 17 October 1962, this $770,283 agreement ensured that Boeing, the prime contractor, would store the Wichita B–52H tooling until July 1963. Selected B–52 subcontractors, using government-owned facilities, would do the same.

Acceptance Rates

The Air Force accepted 20 B–52Hs in FY 61 (from March through June 1961); 68 in FY 62 (between July 1961 and June 1962); and 14 in FY 63 (the last 5 during October 1962).

Flyaway Cost Per Production Aircraft $9.28 million

Airframe, $6,076,157; engines (installed), $1,640,373; electronics, $61,020; ordnance, $6,804; armament (and others), $1,501,422.

Average Maintenance Cost Per Flying Hour $1,182.00

Subsequent Model Series   None

Other Configurations   None

Operational Status   Mid-1973

The Air Force inventory in July 1973 still counted 99 B–52Hs—against an initial contingent of 102. Like the B–52Gs, B–52Hs were undergoing modifications to extend their service-life as well as their efficiency.

Record Flights   January 1962

On 10–11 January, a B–52H of the 4136th Strategic Wing, Minot AFB, North Dakota, completed a record-breaking 12,532.28-mile unrefueled flight from Kadena Air Base, Okinawa, to Torrejon Air Base, Spain. This flight broke the old "distance in a straight line" world record of 11,235.6 miles held by the U.S. Navy's propeller-driven "Truculent Turtle." Weighing 488,000 pounds at takeoff, the B–52H flew at altitudes between 40,000 and 50,000 feet with a top speed of 662 miles per hour on the Kadena-Torrejon flight route.

June 1962

On 7 June, a B–52H of the 19th Bomb Wing, Homestead AFB, Florida, broke the world record for distance in a closed course without landing or refueling. The closed course began and ended at Seymour Johnson AFB, North Carolina, with a validated distance of 11,336.92 miles. The old record of 10,078.84 miles had been held by a B–52G of the 5th Bomb Wing since 1960.

Program Recap

The Air Force bought 744 B-52s—prototype, test, and reconnaissance configurations included. Precisely, the B-52 program counted 1 XB-52, 1 YB-52 (first flown on 15 April 1952, almost 6 months ahead of the experimental B-52), 3 B-52As (restricted to testing), 50 B-52Bs (27 of which could also be used for reconnaissance), 35 B/RB-52Cs, 170 B-52Ds, 100 B-52Es, 89 B-52Fs, 193 B-52Gs, and 102 B-52Hs. Six years of development preceded the beginning of production which, after a slow start around 1953, did not end until October 1962.

TECHNICAL AND BASIC MISSION PERFORMANCE DATA

B-52 AIRCRAFT

		B-52B	B-52C/D	B-52E	B-52F	B-52G	B-52H
Manufacturer (Airframe)	Boeing Airplane Co., Seattle, Wash., and Wichita, Kans.						
(Engines)	The Pratt & Whitney Aircraft Division of United Aircraft Corp., East Hartford, Conn.						
Nomenclature	Strategic Heavy Bomber						
Popular Name	Stratofortress						
Length/Span (ft)		156.6/185	156.5/185	156.5/185	156.5/185	157.6/185	156/185
Wing Area (sq ft)		4,000	4,000	4,000	4,000	4,000	4,000
Weights (lb)							
Empty		164,081	177,816	174,782	173,599	168,445	172,740
Combat		272,000	293,100	292,460	291,570	302,634	306,358
Takeoff[a]		420,000	450,000	450,000	450,000	488,000	488,000
Engine: Number, Rated Power per Engine, & Designation		(8) 11,400-lb st (max) J57-P-1WA	(8) 12,100-lb st (max) J57-P-19W	(8) 12,100-lb st (max) J57-P-19W or -29WA	(8) 13,750-lb st (max) J57-P-43 -WA, or -WB	(8) 13,750-lb st (max) J57-P-43WB	(8) 17,000-lb st (max) TF-33-P-3
Takeoff Ground Run (ft)							
at Seat Level[b]		8,200	8,000	8,000	7,000	8,150	7,420
Over 50-ft Obstacle		10,500	10,300	10,300	9,100	10,400	9,580
Rate of Climb (fpm)							
at Sea Level		2,110	2,225	2,225	2,300	2,150	3,000
Combat Rate of Climb[c] (fpm) at Sea Level		4,760	5,125	5,125	5,600	5,450	6,270
Service Ceiling at Combat Weight (100 fpm Rate of Climb to Altitude)		47,300	46,200	46,200	46,700	47,000	47,700

Combat Ceiling[c] (ft) (500 fpm Rate of Climb to Altitude)	46,550	45,800	45,800	46,000	46,000	46,200
Average Cruise Speed (kn)	453	453	453	453	453	453
Max Speed at Optimum[a c] Altitude (kn/ft)	546/19,800	551/20,200	551/20,200	553/21,000	551/20,800	547/23,800
Combat Radius (nm)	3,110	3,012	3,027	3,163	3,550	4,176
Total Mission Time (hr)	13.50	13.22	13.27	14.03	15.7	17.50
Armament	4 20-mm M24A1s or 4 50-mm M-3s	4 50-mm M-3 guns	4 50-mm M-3 guns	4 .50-cal M-3 guns	4 .50-cal M-3 guns	1 20-mm M-61 gun
Crew	6	6	6	6	6	6
Max Bombload (lb)	43,000[d]	50,000[e]	50,000[e]	50,000[e]	50,000[f]	50,000[f]

Abbreviations

cal = caliber
fpm = feet per minute
kn = knots
max = maximum
nm = nautical miles
st = static thrust

---

[a] Limited by structure.

[b] Takeoff power, i.e., maximum power of an airplane's engine or engines available for takeoff.

[c] Military power, i.e., maximum power or thrust specified for an engine by the manufacturer or by the Air Force as allowable in flight under specified operating conditions for periods of 30 minutes duration.

[d] Or 1 MK-6 and 2 MK-21 special weapons.

[e] For example, 27 1,000-lb bombs, 4 1,200-lb ADM-20 Quails, and 2 10,000-lb AGM-28 Hound Dog missiles, or MK-28, MK-41, MK-53, and MK-57 special weapons.

[f] For example, 27 1,000-lb bombs, 4 1,200-lb ADM-20 Quails, 2 10,000-lb AGM-28 Hound Dogs or up to 20 2,200-lb AGM-69A SRAM missiles. Bombload could also consist of MK-28, MD-41, MK-53, and MK-57 special weapons.

BASIC MISSION NOTE

All basic mission's performance data are based on maximum power, except as otherwise indicated.

Combat Radius Formula:

B–52B, B–52C, B–52D, and B–52E: Took off and climbed on course to optimum cruise altitude at normal power. Cruised out at long-range speed, increasing altitudes with decreasing weight (external tanks being dropped when empty). Climbed to reach cruise ceiling 15 minutes from target. Ran-in to target at normal power, dropped bombs, conducted 2-minute evasive action and 8-minute escape at normal power. Cruised back to base at long-range speed and optimum altitudes (as an alternate, a 45,000-foot ceiling could be maintained on the return leg with no radius penalty). Range-free allowances included fuel for 5 minutes at normal power for take-off allowance, fuel for 2 minutes at normal power for evasive action, and fuel for 30 minutes maximum endurance at sea level plus 5 per cent of the initial fuel load for landing reserve (the landing reserve range at optimum speed and altitude).

B–52F, B–52G, and B–52H: Took off and climbed on course to optimum cruise altitude at normal power. Cruised out at long-range speed (the long-range speed being maximum speed for 99 percent maximum miles per pound of fuel), increasing altitude with decreasing weight (external tanks being dropped when empty). Climbed to reach cruise ceiling 15 minutes from target. Ran-in to target at normal power, dropped bombs, conducted 2-minute evasive action and 8-minute escape at normal power. Cruised back to home base at long-range speeds, increasing altitude with decreasing airplane weight. Range-free allowances included 5-minute normal-power fuel consumption for starting engines and takeoff, 2-minute normal-power fuel consumption at combat altitude for evasive action, and 30 minutes of maximum endurance (4 engines) fuel consumption at sea level plus 5 percent of initial fuel for landing reserve. The prescribed fuel reserve for the basic mission was equivalent to the following reserve range at best range conditions: B–52F, 810 nautical miles; B–52G, 808 nautical miles (884 nautical miles, Alternate in-Flight); B–52H, 974 nautical miles (1,060 nautical miles, Alternate in-Flight).

B–57 Canberra

The Glenn L. Martin Company

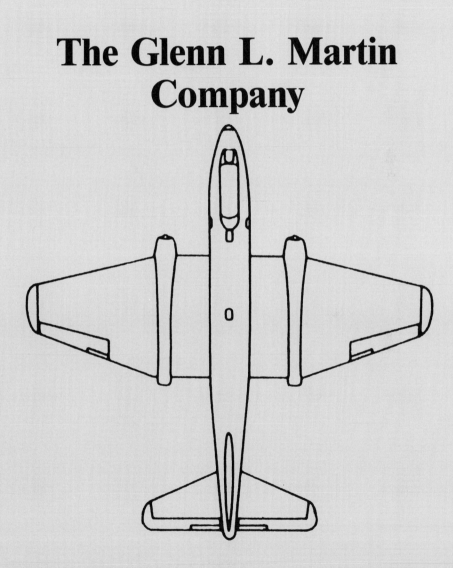

B-57 Canberra
Martin

Manufacturer's Model 272

Overview

The beginning of the Korean conflict on 25 June 1950 and the shortcomings of the weary Douglas B-26, a World War II production originally known as the A-26, accounted for the urgent procurement of a light tactical bomber. The new bomber became the Martin B-57, a by-product of the English Electric Canberra, the first British-built jet bomber, initially flown in 1949.

Adaptation of a foreign-made aircraft to American mass production methods, as well as the use of different materials and tools, could present many difficulties. Another problem, perhaps more critical, centered on the Wright J65 turbojets, due to replace the Canberra's 2 Rolls Royce Avon turbojet engines. The J65 was the U.S. version of the Sapphire, a British hand-tooled production currently scheduled for manufacturing by the U.S. Curtiss-Wright Corporation. The Air Force was fully aware of these potential pitfalls, but had no better option. It had an immediate requirement for a light jet bomber, with a 40,000-foot service ceiling, a 1,000-nautical mile range, and a maximum speed of 550 knots. The new bomber had to be capable of operating from unimproved airfields, at night and in every kind of weather, with conventional or atomic weapons. High altitude reconnaissance was another must. For such purposes, the B-45 was too heavy; the Navy AJ-1, too slow; and the Martin experimental B-51's range too short.

As a result of the outbreak in Korea, the Air Force reached a final decision. The desire for a night intruder was so strong that it took just a few days to set in motion the informal production endorsement of February 1951. Because of its experience with the XB-51, the Glenn L. Martin Company was recognized as the most qualified contractor to assume the domestic production of the British aircraft and to deal with the likely engineering difficulties involved in manufacturing a high-performance tactical bomber.

While the Air Force did not expect the B–57 venture to be free of problems, it did not foresee their magnitude. Testing of the 2 imported Canberras revealed design faults that could affect the safety, utility, and maintenance of the future B–57. Then, one of the British planes crashed; Martin's subcontractors could not meet their commitments; and the J65 prototype engines consistently failed to satisfy USAF requirements. In June 1952, further test flights had to be postponed for a year because of continuing engine and cockpit troubles. As a result, the Korea-bound B–57 did not fly before 20 July 1953, just 7 days before the conflict ended. Production of the crucial RB–57 was also delayed. The reconnaissance version entered service in mid-1954, after testing again confirmed that the more powerful J65 engines, added equipment, and other improvements had increased the aircraft's weight, in turn reducing the speed, distance, and altitude of both the B–57 and the RB–57.

Even though the Douglas B/RB–66s, on order since 1952, were expected to satisfy the tactical bombardment and reconnaissance requirements of the near future, the Air Force handled the disappointing B/RB–57 program with caution. The program was reduced, but there was no talk of cancellation. In keeping with procedures that unfortunately appeared to have become almost customary, steps were taken to ensure that the deficient B/RB–57s would be operational. This turned out to be expensive; later and considerably improved models still carried flaws, but in the long run the program's retention proved sound. In 1955, the B/RB–57s justified their costs when they served overseas pending the B/RB–66 deliveries which, as predicted, had fallen behind schedule. In 1956, much-needed RB–57Ds joined the Strategic Air Command, and various configurations of this model satisfied important special purposes.

Delivered too late for combat in Korea, the RB–57 in May 1963 and the B–57 in February 1965 began to demonstrate under fire in Southeast Asia the basic qualities justifying the Canberra's original selection. In 1970, other reactivated and newly equipped B–57s, known as Tropic Moon III B–57Gs, were deployed to Southeast Asia, where they made valuable contributions until April 1972. Finally, WB–57Fs, either modified RB–57Fs or former B–57Bs, were still flying high-altitude radiation sampling missions in 1973. Concurrently, EB–57Es, and related adaptations of the versatile B–57, continued to play significant roles, with no immediate phaseout in sight.

Basic Development   1945

The Glenn L. Martin Company's B–57 Canberra was derived from the first British-built jet bomber. This high-altitude radar bomber was developed by the English Electric Company, Limited, in answer to specifications B 3/45, as issued by the British Ministry of Supply in 1945.[1] The first 2-man prototype of the English Electric Canberra was flown in May 1949 at the Wharton airdrome. In September, it was revealed to the aeronautical world at the Farnborough flying display of the Society of British Aircraft Constructors. The plane, like the several variants subsequently developed from its basic design, demonstrated superior characteristics. Not only could the new bomber take off and land in combat configuration on short and easily constructed runways, but it maneuvered well at low and high speeds. The United States, through the Martin Company, eventually bought off-the-shelf 2 B.Mk.2s, English Electric's first true production of the Canberra. The B.Mk.2, in contrast to the May 1949 prototype, carried a crew of 3—a pilot, navigator/plotter, and observer.

Preliminary Requirements   16 September 1950

Soon after the outbreak of hostilities in Korea,[2] the USAF Board of Senior Officers began discussing how to replace quickly the weary Douglas B-26 Invader with a modern tactical bomber, specifically geared for night operations. To this end, the preliminary requirements of September 1950 called for a light jet bomber with a service ceiling of 40,000 feet, a cruising speed of about 400 knots, a maximum speed of 550 knots, and a range of almost 1,000 nautical miles. The needed aircraft also had to be capable of operating from unimproved airfields, of searching for targets at low speed and low altitude, and of destroying mobile or stationary targets at night or in bad weather, with conventional or atomic weapons. High-altitude reconnaissance was another requirement.

Initial Candidates   October 1950

Few aircraft, either under development or in operation, could be adapted to satisfy the requirements of September 1950 without excessive delay. Hence, the list of U.S. and foreign candidates was short. Specific possibilities were the Douglas B-26 (an improved version of World War II

---

[1] Britain's first jet bomber was actually conceived in 1944 by W. E. W. "Teddy" Petter, who later designed the Lightning and Gnat interceptors.

[2] The Korean conflict lasted from 25 June 1950 until 27 July 1953.

vintage), the Martin XB–51, the North American B–45 and AJ–1, the Canadair CF–100, and the English Electric Canberra. Much was already known about the new Canberra, but not quite enough. It had favorably impressed the USAF staff officers who had witnessed its first flight at Wharton airdrome in 1949.[3] In the summer of 1950, a committee headed by Brig. Gen. Albert Boyd, Commander of Edwards AFB, had given the plane an "expedited" and "limited evaluation." Therefore, the committee's report of 28 September was not conclusive. It deemed the Canberra suitable for all-weather fighter, tactical reconnaissance, and medium-altitude bomber operations. Yet, the report said the plane had little potential as a ground attack fighter-bomber because it was unstable during close support maneuvers. In the same cautious vein, the committee found that the British plane's tactical utility and ease of production warranted its "consideration" for the Mutual Defense Assistance Program.[4] On the other hand, the Canberra should not be used in the United States Air Force before "rigorous evaluation" of at least 1 aircraft and accelerated service testing of several prototypes. If eventually procured, the plane would require at least 25 changes. Even then, to benefit from the Canberra's design, the Air Force would have to accept the initial airframe, performance, and load capacity.

Subsequent to this appraisal, the Board of Senior Officers organized another committee. It was chaired by Brig. Gen. S. P. Wright, Deputy Commander of the Air Proving Ground, and included several representatives from Air Materiel Command (AMC) and Tactical Air Command (TAC).

Tentative Selection   December 1950

With the Boyd report on hand, the Wright Committee measured the Canberra's performance against that of the 4 remaining candidates, a

---

[3] The Canberra flight of 1949 underscored Great Britain's spectacular post–World War II advancements and her superiority in jet propulsion development. It gave credence to the British claim that production of thousands of Canberras was the factor which alone could best provide the tactical airpower necessary to counterbalance Soviet predominance in ground troops.

[4] W. Barton Leach, Special Consultant to Secretary of the Air Force W. Stuart Symington and to Secretary Thomas K. Finletter, Mr. Symington's successor, was among those who visited England in 1949 and 1950 for the primary purpose of reviewing the British jet propulsion accomplishments. Upon his return, Leach discussed the British Canberra proposal with John A. McCone, Under Secretary of the Air Force. While thinking that there might be disadvantages in diverting American production "heavily" to an aircraft of the Canberra type, Leach recognized that such a proposal could not be dismissed lightly, because the whole basic structure of strategic planning was involved. The discussion was to prove academic, since the Martin B–57 production never even reached the 500 mark.

comparison that did not help the North American B–45 and AJ–1. The B–45 was ruled out because it was too heavy; the Navy AJ–1, because it was too slow. While noting that neither the XB–51 nor the Canberra fully met the Air Force's night intruder requirements, the Wright Committee endorsed both. It proposed the immediate purchase of British Canberras for 2 light bombardment groups and future procurement of sufficient B–51s to equip 2 other groups. The Wright Committee's suggestion aroused scant enthusiasm among the Air Staff members. The Board of Senior Officers, after studying the Air Proving Ground Command's latest evaluations, found itself liking the Canberra's performance. In contrast, it seriously doubted that the B–51's range could ever match the Canberra's radius of action.[5] Although aware that the Canberra would need modification for the night intruder role, the board asked Lt. Gen. Kenneth B. Wolfe, Air Force Deputy Chief of Staff for Materiel, to ascertain if the British could furnish enough Canberras and still satisfy Royal Air Force orders. Nonetheless, as recommended by General Boyd, the board felt that no determination could be made until a borrowed Canberra became available. Going several steps further, the board then decided not only to await the plane's arrival, but to make on-the-spot comparisons with every initial aircraft candidate. This evaluation, it believed, together with a review of the night intruder's future role, should ensure the best solution to the present dilemma.

Final Endorsement   26 February 1951

After hinging for weeks on divergent opinions, the Air Force decision to get a facsimile of the English Electric Canberra was nearly unanimous. As negotiated with the British government, a Royal Air Force Canberra B. Mk.2, bearing USAF insignia, left Northern Ireland on 20 February for Gander Field, Newfoundland. It landed in Baltimore, Maryland, on 21 February—the first jet aircraft to complete an unrefueled flight across the Atlantic Ocean—and arrived at Andrews AFB 2 days later. Ensuing flight demonstrations and ground inspections of the Canberra sealed the fate of other candidates. On 26 February, the Senior Officers and USAF Weapons Boards picked the British plane as the best interim aircraft available for the night tactical intruder role. General Vandenberg, Air Force Chief of Staff,[6] and Secretary Finletter swiftly agreed.

---

[5] Martin's 2 XB–51s, under contract since May 1946, did not fly until October 1949. Costing a total of $12.6 million, both aircraft eventually crashed.

[6] General Vandenberg succeeded Gen. Carl Spaatz as Chief of Staff of the Air Force on 30 April 1948.

Program Go-Ahead   2 March 1951

The Air Force wanted a night intruder so badly that it took just a few days to set in motion the informal production decision of 26 February. Since General Wolfe had found out that the British could barely take care of their own Canberra needs, the Air Staff directed AMC on 2 March 1951 to arrange for the aircraft's domestic production. Martin became the chosen contractor. The Air Force was convinced that the XB-51 had given that company a sound background for dealing with the potential problems of a high-performance tactical bomber.

Production Restrictions   2 March 1951

Procurement Directive 51-135, issued by the Air Staff on 2 March, reflected the urgency of bringing into service an American version of the Canberra. The B-57, as the aircraft was to be known, was to go directly into production, a decision tantamount to buying an off-the-shelf airframe with an off-the-shelf engine and installed equipment. Even though the resulting aircraft, 250 of them to begin with, might not be exactly what was needed, configuration changes would be kept to a bare minimum—under the strict control of the Board of Senior Officers.

Testing Agreement   16 March 1951

The British Canberra, exhibited at Andrews AFB, reached the Martin Company on 10 March. This permanent assignment grew out of a Combined Test Project Agreement, formalized with the Royal Air Force on 16 March. Under the same agreement, Martin received a second British Canberra several months later. Although the 2 planes acquired USAF serial numbers (51-17352 and 51-17387), they were carried in the Air Force inventory as Canberras, not as B-57s.

Contractual Arrangements   24 March 1951

The informal production decision of 26 February 1951 was finalized on 24 March by Letter Contract AF 33(038)-22617. This production letter contract asked Martin to deliver 250 B-57s between November 1952 and October 1953. The schedule was predicated on Martin's attaining a peak production rate of 50 airplanes per month.

Other Negotiations   March/May 1951

The production letter contract of 24 March covered more than the procurement of 250 B–57s. It authorized Martin to acquire the Canberra manufacturing rights, and gave the company a $6 million advance payment to take care of its most pressing expenditures. The license agreement finally worked out by the British and American firms was signed on 8 May 1951. Martin eventually built 403 B–57s of one kind or another; the English Electric Company, Ltd., in time received royalties topping $3.5 million. Another $1 million was paid for the 2 Canberras secured by Martin during the spring and summer of 1951. The Air Force reimbursed Martin the full cost of the 2 imported planes.

B–57A

New Features

As an intended replica of the English Electric Canberra B. Mk.2, the B–57A featured no outstanding innovations. Nonetheless, because of the American mass production methods, standards, and uses of different materials, tools, gauges, wiring, and techniques, the plane differed from its British pattern in several aspects. The B–57A had a slightly modified cockpit and canopy that afforded better visibility and more room for the crew (reduced from 3 to 2). Two Wright Aeronautical J65 turbojet engines were substituted for the Canberra's 2 Rolls Royce Avon turbojets. Other changes included the addition of wing tip tanks (to increase loiter time) and replacement of the British "clam shell" type bomb-bay doors. Developed by Martin for the B–57A, the pre-loaded revolving bomb-bay door rotated 180 degrees and eliminated the drag caused by an opened bomb-bay compartment during the bombing run.

Pre-Production Planning   1 July 1951

Although the Wright J65 Sapphire engine,[7] due to power the B–57, and some equipment the Air Force wanted on the airplane would be furnished by the government, the urgent delivery schedules specified by the production letter contract of March 1951 presented difficult tasks. As a result, Martin began immediately to plan ahead and on 1 July subcontracted 60 percent of the actual production work. Its principal subcontractors were the Kaiser Products of Bristol, Pennsylvania, for the wings and special weapons bomb-bay doors; and the Hudson Motors Corporation of Detroit, Michigan, for the aft portions of the plane.

Pre-Production Testing   1951

Martin tested its first British Canberra from April to October 1951,

---

[7] The Sapphire was a hand-tooled production of the British firm Armstrong-Siddeley for which the Curtiss-Wright Corporation at Wood-Ridge, N. J., had acquired a manufacturing license. Production of the Wright YJ–65, as the Sapphire engine was redesignated, was not expected to begin before September 1951.

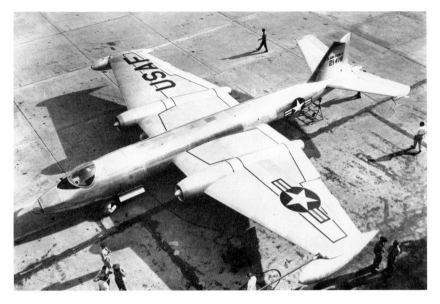

The B-57, an American version of the British Canberra, featured wing tip fuel tanks.

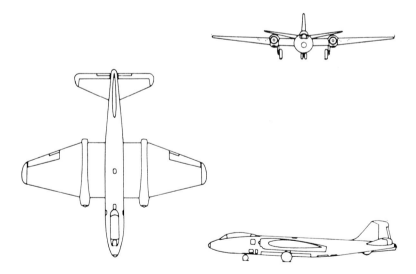

accumulating 41 hours of flying time in the process. The second imported plane reached Martin in September, was test flown not more than 4 hours, and disassembled. Appropriate sections of the plane were then shipped to Martin's main subcontractors.[8] USAF pilots began test flying the first Canberra in the fall of 1951. A 21 December accident, in which the plane was completely destroyed, accounted for some of the slippage that plagued the B–57 program from the start.

Mockup Inspection   20 July 1951

The Mockup Board's inspection of the B–57A was not an overwhelming success. The board approved the location of the eight .50-caliber forward-firing guns (placed in the wings instead of the fuselage nose), but noted numerous shortcomings. It also pointed out that the aircraft would have to be modified to carry special weapons, that a compatible bombing system was required, and that pylons were needed to support external stores. Particularly dissatisfied with the B–57A cockpit, the board insisted that it should be redesigned.

Other Initial Deficiencies   August 1951

The Aircraft Laboratory of the Wright Air Development Center examined Martin's first B–57 specifications in August 1951. The laboratory was well-prepared for its chores. In January, it had thoroughly evaluated the Canberra and indicated that an Americanized production from the British drawings and data would not satisfy USAF requirements. In August, the laboratory's criticism grew. Besides sharing the mockup board's concern, it found fault with the aircraft's landing gear, the brake actuating system, the absence of winterization, and many other items. Moreover, the laboratory concluded that, as currently planned, Martin's tip tank installation, engine mounting, and nose gear swivel angle would be inadequate.

Problems and Controversies   1952

In January 1952, Wright Air Development Center decided to challenge the B–57's production philosophy. So far, the center noted, the Board of

---

[8] Eventually reassembled, this Canberra went to the Sampson AFB Museum, Geneva, N.Y., on 2 June 1954. It was scrapped 2 years later.

Senior Officers had approved the correction of only 6 deficiencies. Yet, some of the 35 design faults uncovered by the center's engineers could affect the safety, utility, and maintenance of the future B–57. In fact, the Royal Air Force (RAF) had refused to accept the Canberra from the English Electric Company until many of the very same flaws were eliminated. It therefore appeared inconsistent to carry any of these deficiencies into the American production of the plane. At first, Wright Center's position was not well-received. Air Materiel Command was quick to point out that the center previously had made no attempt to integrate its list of deficiencies into the production schedule of the plane, even though it made no sense to discuss one without the other. Any configuration changes adopted at this late date, AMC emphasized, would cause unacceptable production delays. Moreover, in the command's opinion, several of the corrections suggested by the air development center were superfluous, at least for the B–57A. The Air Materiel Command agreed, however, that the B–57 production guidelines ran counter to the USAF regulations calling for technical excellence. Another month of debate failed to alter the production restrictions of March 1951, but it did bring AMC around to support Wright Air Development Center's position. And, as events soon proved, the center's effort would have significant impact on the program.

Program Changes   11 August 1952

On 11 August 1952, production of the B–57A's reconnaissance version, ordered earlier in the year, was reduced by one-third. More importantly, and to Wright Air Development Center's great satisfaction, procurement of the B–57A was virtually canceled. Only 8 B–57As would be built. Despite slight alterations, these aircraft would be recognized as direct copies of the Canberra. As actually recommended 2 years before by the Boyd Committee, the B–57A would be used for testing, thereby paving the way for production of a similar but better aircraft.

Production Slippages   1951–1953

The unexplained Canberra loss of late 1951 and ensuing testing setback undoubtedly accounted for part of Martin's production slippage. But a major initial delay was caused by the government-furnished Sapphire jet engines that were due to power all B–57s. The Sapphire was a hand-tooled production of the British firm Armstrong-Siddeley for which the Curtiss-Wright Aeronautical Division at Wood-Ridge N.J., had acquired a manufacturing license. However, the J65, as the Air Force version of the Sapphire was designated, was perhaps more difficult to adapt to American specifications and manufacturing methods than the British plane. Although the Wright production had been set to begin in September 1951, the J65 prototype engines consistently failed to meet USAF requirements.[9] In June 1952, when the Air Force finally accepted the first 2 YJ65–W–1 engines, neither had yet completed the required 150-hour qualification test. Still, there were other problems of equal consequence. In April of the same year, a technical status report could only state that the B–57 manufacturer and subcontractors had begun the fabrication of "bits and pieces." In June 1952, while the B–57A basic engineering seemed to be completed, projected test flights were postponed to mid-1953 because of continuing engine and cockpit troubles.

First Flight (Production Aircraft)   20 July 1953

The Martin twin-jet B–57A night intruder bomber at long last took to the air on 20 July. Company officials described the 46-minute flight as entirely successful. On 20 August, the plane underwent its official Air Force flight acceptance test at the Martin airfield at Middle River, Maryland. In attendance, among high-ranking Air Force officials, were General Twining, Air Force Chief of Staff since 30 June 1953; Lt. Gen. Edwin W. Rawlings, Commander of Air Materiel Command; and Lt. Gen. Donald L. Putt, Commander of Air Research and Development Command. Newspaper accounts of the B–57A performance were enthusiastic, more so than subsequent USAF appraisals.

Enters Operational Service

Relegated to the testing status, none of the B–57A productions entered operational service. Yet, 1 or 2 eventually participated in a few special projects.

Testing   December 1953

The Air Force accepted the first B–57A on 20 August, but lent it

---

[9] The new engine was also earmarked for the Republic F–84F. Due to the urgent need for improved fighter-bombers since the outbreak of the Korean War, the Air Force in December 1950 selected the Buick Division of the General Motors Corporation as the second source for the Sapphire engine.

immediately to Martin and never took delivery of the plane.[10] Hence, USAF testing did not start until December 1953, when all other B–57As were delivered. Once underway, however, testing was extensive. USAF pilots test flew the second B–57A (Serial No. 52–1419) for no less than 101 hours, reached in 80 flights. While testing would go on for years, by late 1954 the Air Force knew without doubt that the B–57A was somewhat superior to the original Canberra. Yet the overall improvement carried a price. Added equipment and the more powerful J65 engines had increased the aircraft's empty weight by 3,700 pounds, in turn reducing speed, distance, and altitude.

Total B–57As Accepted   8

Acceptance Rates

All B–57As were received in FY 54. The Air Force accepted—but never physically possessed—the first B–57A in August 1953. It took delivery of the remaining 7 in December.

End of Production   December 1953

Flyaway Cost Per Production Aircraft $9.3 million

Airframe, $8,937,886; engines (installed), $349,357; electronics, $20,780; ordnance, $7,442; armament and others, $33,704.[11]

Subsequent Model Series   B–57B

---

[10] This plane (Serial No. 52–1418) remained with the Martin Company from its completion until 19 June 1957, when it was transferred to the National Advisory Committee for Aeronautics. The contractor received the airplane under Bailment Contracts AF 33 (038)–32001 and AF 33 (600)–2407 of 6 August 1953 and 21 February 1956. Martin test pilots flew the plane 292 hours in 284 flights.

[11] The high cost of the B–57A was explained by the fact that only 8 of them were built, and that Martin's initial and one-time manufacturing costs were prorated among those first few aircraft. But for rare exceptions, the higher the production, the lower the cost. Although only 67 RB–57As entered the inventory, the reconnaissance B–57A showed a significant price decrease. And despite important improvements, the unit cost of the subsequent and more numerous B–57B was still cheaper.

Other Configurations   RB–57A

Phaseout   1961

Attrition, conversions, and special projects gradually absorbed the few B–57As. By mid-1961, the aircraft no longer appeared in the Air Force inventory.

Other Uses   1957

Early in 1957, the Air Force lent the second B–57A to the Weather Bureau of the Department of Commerce. Following modification, the plane participated in the National Hurricane Project.

RB–57A

Manufacturer's Model 272A

Weapon System 307L

New Features

Cameras, installed aft of the bomb-bay, constituted the main difference between the reconnaissance B–57A and the B–57A test-bomber. The cameras—P–2s, K–17s, K–37s, K–38s, or T–17s—could be interchanged, according to the aircraft's missions, which were many and included day and night, high and low, and visual and photographic reconnaissance besides day combat mapping. Unlike the B–57A, the RB–57A was totally unarmed and painted with a high gloss black paint that minimized detection by searchlights. In common with the B–57A, the plane carried only a 2-man crew—1 pilot and 1 photo-navigator, the latter replacing the B–57A's navigator-bombardier.

Basic Development   October 1951

As in the B–57A's case, the decision to develop a reconnaissance version was prompted by the Korean conflict. Increasingly effective enemy air defenses underscored USAF reconnaissance shortcomings. Hence, in an October meeting, the Air Staff and representatives of AMC and Wright Air Development Center defined the RB–57A configuration. So few changes were outlined that it would only take a minimum of effort to return the future RB–57A to service as a bomber—an occurrence that never came to pass in view of the B–57A's fate.

Program Reduction   1952

The Air Force at no time seriously considered canceling the B–57, but nearly deleted the reconnaissance counterpart. Early in January 1952, as a result of the past October meeting, AMC prepared to order 99 RB–57As.

Within a few weeks, however, a whole new situation arose. The Air Staff not only spoke of procuring only 87 RB-57As, but also ventured that eliminating the entire order might be best. Assuming the RB-26s could somehow be equipped with night photographic equipment and made to work until the Douglas RB-66 became available, about $30 million could be saved in doing away with the RB-57s. Because delivery of the first RB-66 could not be expected before 1954, and successful modernization of the RB-26s was questionable, the Air Staff finally decided against any drastic change. Nevertheless, after dropping the requirement to 87 planes, the RB-57A procurement underwent a final cut on 11 August 1952, when it was reduced to 67. Despite ensuing RB-57A problems, the decision proved wise. In the midst of the Korean War, the RB-26s steadfastly demonstrated the difficulty and occasional futility of fitting old planes with modern, sometimes unproven, components. Also, consistent with almost traditional production patterns, delivery schedules for the RB-66 slipped significantly.

Production Slippage   1952-1953

On 24 April 1952, the Air Research and Development Command asked Martin to give priority to the RB-57A at the expense of the B-57A program—officially still practically intact at the time. The RB-57A production nonetheless slipped. But the command's directive served its purpose and worked in favor of the B-57B—Martin's first true Canberra bomber. Meanwhile, the contractor's problems kept on growing. Part of Martin's Baltimore plant remained occupied by the Army Signal Corps, and the late delivery of machine tools hampered reactivation of available facilities. To make things worse, in addition to avowed engine difficulties, Kaiser production of wing panels and nacelles had also begun to fall behind.

First Flight (Production Aircraft)   October 1953

Flight of the first RB-57A came about 3 months after that of the first B-57A. Both flights were made from the Martin airfield at Middle River, and, ironically, the RB-57A flight occurred close to the date initially set for delivery of the 250th B/RB-57. By that time, the Air Force had reached several perplexing conclusions. First, the B/RB-57As would not meet USAF requirements; therefore, relatively small quantities would be built. On the other hand, regardless of their known shortcomings, the RB-57As remained urgently needed. However, speeding up Martin's new delivery schedules would be extremely costly. The Air Force, after weighing such conflicting factors, adopted what were most likely the best solutions. Testing was cut short, and most RB–57As were produced without benefiting from the usual "debugging" period that normally preceded operational use. But a major effort was made to improve subsequent models in the series—the B–57Bs and the unique RB–57Ds.

Enters Operational Service   July 1954

The RB–57As came into operational use in mid-1954. The Tactical Air Command earmarked the first few for transition training with the 345th Light Bomb Wing, Langley AFB, Virginia, and sent the next 22 to the 363d Tactical Reconnaissance Wing at Shaw AFB, South Carolina. The 363d reached an initial operational capability (IOC) in July.

Operational Problems   1954–1955

The 363d's initial operational readiness was short-lived. Subsequent RB–57A deliveries were held up because the J65–BW–5 engines started burning oil and filled the cockpit with smoke. This matter taken care of, all 67 RB–57As were accepted by September 1954. However, the entire Canberra fleet was grounded in January 1955, this time for engine compressor failure. And while this problem was being solved, new deficiencies were uncovered. The RB–57A's control system required adjustment, and the wing-fuselage attachment fitting needed reinforcement.

Structural Modifications   1954–1955

Modifications, referred to as Garden Gate,[12] strengthened the connection of the wings to the fuselage. All RB–57As had received the Garden Gate changes by November 1954, and these modifications later were incorporated into Martin's production line. However, new structural deficiencies came to light as cracks developed around the aircraft's nose cap.[13] Repair of the cracks limited the operation of the aircraft.

---

[12] The term came from the "garden gate" shape of the fittings that linked the wings to the fuselage.

[13] Martin had already canceled a Hudson subcontract involving the manufacture of RB–57A nose sections.

Overseas Deployments   1955

The engine malfunctions, structural deficiencies, and many other ills that afflicted the RB–57As were compounded by the lack of equipment and spare parts to support the new planes. Hence, at home or overseas, the aircraft assignments were delayed, and the first 2 USAF wings in West Germany which transitioned from RB–26s to RB–57As did not keep their new planes very long. Both the 10th Tactical Reconnaissance Wing at Spangdahlem AB and the 66th at Sembach AB started converting to more efficient RB–66s in late 1957.

End of Production   August 1954

Production ended with the August delivery of the last 5 aircraft.

Total RB–57As Accepted   67

Acceptance Rates

The Air Force accepted 49 RB–57As in FY 54—from December 1953 through June 1954. The last 18 were accepted in FY 55—13 in July 1954 and 5 in August.

Flyaway Cost Per Production Aircraft $1.66 million

Airframe, $1,240,051; engines (installed), $349,357; electronics, $4,096; ordnance, $9,324; special equipment, $58,485.

Average Maintenance Cost Per Flying Hour $191.00

Subsequent Model Series   B–57B

Other Configurations   RB–57A–1, RB–57A–2, and EB–57A

RB–57A–1s—Ten RB–57As, after elimination of their most serious deficiencies, were converted for high-altitude reconnaissance. The project, known as "Lightweight" and later renamed "Heartthrob," was handled by the Wright Air Development Center and Martin. Under Heartthrob, all equipment and items not absolutely essential for daylight photography were removed from the basic RB-57A. The plane's J65-BW-5s were replaced by higher thrust J65-W-7 engines, and the crew was reduced from 2 to 1. The RB-57A-1 was 5,665 pounds lighter than the RB-57A (43,182 to 48,847), and its altitude was increased by 5,000 feet. The Heartthrob modifications were successfully completed in August 1955. Six RB-57A-1s went to the 7499th Composite Squadron in United States Air Force in Europe; 4 to the 6007th Composite Squadron in Far East Air Forces.

RB-57A-2s—Two RB-57A-1s were modified under Hardtack, a project also referred to as Heartthrob, Jr. The modification removed some equipment from the airplanes to make room for the Convair-developed AN/APS-60 Startrack, a high-altitude radar that had been briefly tested on a B-57B. Martin undertook the project with reluctance, because the non-standard AN/APS-60 was highly sophisticated and its installation promised to be difficult—which in fact it was. The 2 Startrack-equipped RB-57A-2s were delivered in September 1957—a 9-month delay.

EB-57As—In the mid-sixties, the Air Force endorsed the modification of 32 RB-57As. The work, done by Martin, essentially consisted of fitting a compartment, full of electronic countermeasures equipment, in the aircraft bomb bay. The first EB-57A (Manufacturer's Model 272R) flew in April 1966 and was immediately accepted by the Air Force. Martin completed the fairly complicated project in less than a year and the Air Defense Command[14] continued to use the EB-57As for electronic counter-measures training until the early seventies.

Phaseout   1970–1971

The original RB-57A received little praise. By 1958 ten RB-57As had already been lost in flying accidents. At the end of 1970 only 2 remained on the active USAF rolls. But the RB-57A, although scarcely satisfactory from the start, did pay its own way. The aircraft's numerous special configurations proved invaluable for many years. Twelve EB-57As were still in the operational forces in late 1971.

---

[14] The Air Defense Command became the Aerospace Defense Command on 15 January 1968.

Other Uses

In early 1956 one RB–57A satisfied the special photographic requirements of the United States Air Forces in Europe. Known as the Sharp Cut RB–57A, the aircraft did not materialize as soon as expected. Revisions to the bomb-bay and instrument panels and the installation of special purpose photographic equipment (the F–11 camera in particular), took time. In 1957 the Air Research and Development Command lent an RB–57A to Northrop Aircraft, Inc., to study laminar-flow boundary layer control, a topic of crucial USAF interest. In the spring of 1958 the Air Force prepared a number of RB–57As for atmospheric sampler missions. The modification added special equipment to the aircraft, which were temporarily designated B/20 airplanes.

Other Countries

Two RB–57As, after modification, were turned over to the Republic of China under Project Large Charge.

B-57B

Manufacturer's Model 272

Weapon System 307A

Previous Model Series RB-57A

The RB-57A preceded the B-57B in the USAF inventory, but the B-model was the B-57's first production bomber as well as the major inventory model.

New Features

The most significant change featured by the B-57B was an entirely new design of the cockpit area. The reconfiguration placed the navigator-bombardier behind the pilot under a large bubble canopy similar to that of the T-33.[15] This arrangement improved visibility, afforded more space for the installation of equipment, and conformed to the Air Force-preferred tandem type of seating. Specifically, the B-57B pilot's seat was on the fuselage centerline. The navigator's back seat was slightly offset left of the center line to provide room for the Shoran receiver-indicator and the Swedish-designed M-1 toss-bomb computer unit. The B-57B also introduced a flatplate wind-shield allowing the installation of a gun sight, external wing pylons, improved defrosting, and fuselage dive brakes. The wing pylons mounted high-velocity aircraft rockets or bombs. Beginning with the 91st B-57B production, the eight .50-caliber forward-firing wing guns, first seen on the B-57A test aircraft, were replaced by 4 M-39 20-millimeter guns.

---

[15] The Lockheed T-33 Shooting Star was an all-metal, full cantilever low-wing, 2-seat, high-performance aircraft used by the Air Force for the training of flight personnel.

Basic Development   1952

The B–57B development took shape in early 1952, when Air Materiel Command and Air Research and Development Command acknowledged the unacceptable deficiencies of the B–57A configuration. In March, they jointly presented the current problems to Air Force Headquarters. And as early as 17 April, the 2 commands gave the Air Council a list of minimum but mandatory changes for ensuring production of a sound airplane. Although not relinquishing production control, the Board of Senior Officers did endorse most of the proposed modifications.

Production Decision   11 August 1952

The B–57B production became official on 11 August, concurrent with the B–57A's virtual demise.

Mockup Inspection   2 October 1952

The B–57B mockup was officially inspected on 2 October. Of primary interest was the new cockpit arrangement and the single blister canopy. Deletion of the Shoran equipment, to provide space for a new type of radar, was discussed but not adopted.

Additional Procurement   September/December 1952

Letter Contract AF 32(038)–22617 of March 1951 called for the production of 250 B–57s but was amended several times. In August of the same year, the number of B–57s on order stood at 209; in February 1952, at 177. On 11 August 1952, total procurement remained at 177, but 102 B–57Bs were substituted for 70 B–57As and for 32 RB–57As. The first follow-on fiscal year 1953 contract began with Letter Contract AF 33(600)–22208, which was issued 19 September 1952 and covered the additional procurement of 119 B–57Bs. An amendment on 18 December raised the FY 53 B–57B procurement to 191, bringing the cumulative B–57B future production to 293. This total, however, did not materialize. Affected by changes almost from the start, the B–57 program was revamped many times over. In some cases, obsolescence was the governing factor. On other occasions, special or ever-increasing operational requirements were the cause.

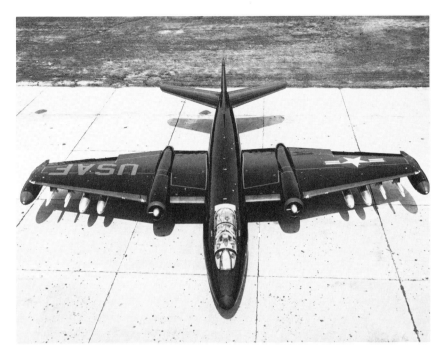

An armed B–57B, displaying the reconfigured cockpit which placed the pilot in front of the navigator-bombardier.

Revised Production Schedules   1952

Although frowned upon, the revision of production schedules was seldom avoidable. In August 1952, completion of the 177 B/RB–57s then on order was pushed back to August 1954, a date which proved highly optimistic. Also, Martin's production peak rate was reduced from 50 to 17 airplanes per month. The Air Force thought the B–57B would benefit from a slower production tempo. Still, it did not expect to wait until May 1956 for its full complement of new bombers—almost 3 years past the deadline set by the Board of Senior Officers back in 1951. Such complications, the program changes occurring during the interim years, and the new production schedules generated by such changes all proved costly. In the end, the B–57B's average unit price was double that first negotiated.

First Definitive Contract   1 August 1953

The Air Force finalized Letter Contract AF–33(038)–22617 in August

1953. Changes in quantity, type of airplane, and configuration explained the protracted negotiation period, and the contractor's hard bargaining played a part. Besides higher profits, Martin wanted to be amply protected against subcontractor failure and cost increase. The definitive contract was a fixed price incentive type, with reset. Martin received a 7.5 percent profit, with 80/20 sharing of increase or decrease of target cost, and a 120 percent ceiling independent of the subcontract costs. It took another year for the Air Force and Martin to agree on the amounts of firm target cost. By then, major subcontractor failings had upped the billing for the first 75 aircraft by $63 million. The target cost negotiations for the remainder of the aircraft under the same contract dragged on until April 1955. It was 1958 before the contract was completely closed out.

Production Slippages   1953–1954

Change-over to the B–57B cockpit set back production several months. Replacements of the aircraft's .50-caliber machine guns with better guns entailed airframe alteration and considerable wing modification, for which new tools were needed. Nevertheless, from the start, the most far-reaching production problem was Kaiser's failure to deliver B–57 wings on schedule. Martin asked for permission to cancel the Kaiser contract but was allowed to withdraw only part of it. The Air Force pointed to the exorbitant cost of dropping Kaiser, in money as well as time. In any case, Kaiser's difficulties could be traced to poor management, but the subcontractor still remained well-qualified to do the work. For that matter, Martin also posted a good record manufacturing the special bomb-bay doors pulled back from Kaiser. Yet, later events showed that the Martin engineering capacity could be overtaxed. In the long run, the price increase of the first 90 aircraft was chiefly due to the Kaiser muddle. Still, other alternatives undoubtedly would have been more expensive.

Program Changes   1954

The B–57B program, set at 293 aircraft, was reduced by 91. In early 1954, the Air Force pared the FY 53 B–57B procurement to 158 (a 33-aircraft cutback) and dropped the tentative purchase of 50 more B–57Bs. In the spring, 38 B–57Bs were canceled in favor of producing an equal number of B–57 dual-control trainers. A final change, a few months later, diverted 20 B–57Bs to the B–57D program of 1953. These aircraft were subsequently redesignated RB–57Ds.

First Flight (Production Aircraft)   18 June 1954

Following the B–57B's first flight, a few aircraft were delivered to the flight test center at Edwards AFB.

Enters Operational Service   1954–1955

B–57Bs were assigned to 2 Tactical Air Command light bombardment wings in late 1954 and early 1955. The 3-squadron wings in time received 18 aircraft per squadron—16 B–57Bs and 2 B–57 dual-control trainers. The initial recipient was the 424th Bomb Wing, Light, at Langley AFB. The 461st Wing, Blytheville AFB, Arkansas, acquired its first B–57B on 5 January 1955.

Operational Problems   1954–1955

Like the RB–57As, the B–57Bs prior to delivery suffered from engine malfunctions that filled the cockpit with toxic fumes. Following delivery, new engine problems required the grounding of B/RB–57s. Inspection of the engine compressor (the culprit) and lifting of the grounding order afforded short relief. Difficulties with the aircraft's stabilizer control system triggered another grounding in February 1955. The B–57Bs were released for flight the following month, but were restricted to a maximum speed of 250 knots pending modification of the horizontal stabilizer and the installation of a different stabilizer trim switch—yet to be accomplished by mid-year.

Testing   1954–1955

Fourteen of the first B–57Bs accepted by the Air Force never received the Garden Gate modification that was implemented on the production line. These planes were assigned permanently to testing, a program that started inauspiciously. Already delayed by Martin's production slippages, testing was continuously interrupted because the 14 test-bombers shared the deficiencies, groundings, and flight restrictions of other B–57Bs. Hence, an operational suitability test, conducted by the Air Proving Ground Command, was not completed on schedule. To make things worse, in February 1955 the command's interim test report generally confirmed TAC's expectations. After incomplete investigation, Air Proving Ground Command pointed out that the B–57B appeared in no way to satisfy the night intruder and close support requirements that had generated its production. The command gave several good reasons for its pessimism. The B-57B's target acquisition system was inadequate, the navigational range was too short, and the radio navigation could not recover the aircraft after strikes. The new bomber's armament also was deficient, the gun-bomb-rocket sight, the gun charging systems, and the external stores release being unreliable. Even the long-awaited M-39 guns could not be fired safely because the cartridge links hit the wing undersides. Moreover, the B-57Bs so far received still had no anti-icing and de-icing equipment. Nonetheless, the proving ground command tentatively concluded that the B-57B showed the potential of becoming an effective fighting machine. However, besides correction of the aircraft's present flaws, this would require the addition of proper internal equipment. Another obvious must was to increase range, which had shrunk in proportion to the aircraft's weight increase.[16]

Overseas Deployments   1955

Once underway, B-57B deliveries were almost uninterrupted. Thus, in 1955 two oversea light bombardment wings were equipped with B-57Bs. The 38th Bomb Wing, Light, at Laon AB, France, was the first, beginning in June. The other, the 3d Bomb Wing, Light, at Johnson AB in Japan, followed late in the year.

Improvement Postponement   1955

B-57B deployments, whether at home or overseas, did not signify that the Air Force was unaware of or accepted the aircraft's shortcomings underlined in the Air Proving Ground·Command's interim operational suitability test report. In fact, these deficiencies were amply confirmed in the spring of 1955, when the AMC's Inspector General rated the new bomber nearly as low as the obsolete B-26 it was to replace. But the B-57B as received was quite flyable. The Air Force knew that, unlike the B-47, the aircraft could go directly to the tactical units and not make an immediate turn-around to a modification center. Moreover, money was scarce. The Air

---

[16] It would cost too much to modify the B-57 for air refueling, but there were other means to extend range. In principle, this had been taken care of in June 1954, with a purchase order for 54 external fuel tanks of the kind used by the old B-26s. Years later, however, TAC still experienced difficulties in getting enough long-range ferry tanks for the B-57s of its Composite Air Strike Force.

Force wanted to see how the faster B–66 fared, before endorsing a costly B–57 improvement program. Also, new equipment (radar, navigational, and other electronic systems) was either in short supply or still in the development or early production stages. In any event, the B–57's longitudinal control and stabilizer systems would be modified. But this could be postponed temporarily because, should the Air Force decide on other improvements, it would be cheaper to do all the work at once. Meanwhile, enforced (and not so unusual) flight restrictions would continue to ensure the aircraft's safety.

Post-Production Modifications   1955–1957

In September 1955 the Air Force decided to bring the B–57 to tactical standards. To this end, it organized a 3-phase combat readiness program. Phase I installed the low-altitude bombing system (LABS), the AN/APS–54 Radar Search, and the ALE–2 Chaff Dispenser. Phase II added the M–1 Toss Bomb Computer as well as the AN/APG–31 Tie-in-Equipment. This phase also involved so-called Class IV and V modifications to the longitudinal control and stabilizer systems and to the fuel control panels and special weapon bomb-bay doors. Phase III dealt with the AN/APN–59 Radar Beacon and a number of tentative engineering change proposals. Planning its 3-phase program carefully, the Air Force directed that it should be carried out by USAF personnel and contractor teams during the normal inspection and repair of each plane, as necessary. Some of the work was to be done at the Martin plant and some at the Warner Robins Air Materiel Area in Georgia. Like most planning, these arrangements were affected by circumstances. For example, modification schedules were altered by changes in programming and B–57 utilization. On occasion, Phases I and II were lumped together. Sometimes there were delays. The AN/APN–59's Phase III installation did not materialize. A Martin subcontract with the Swedish Airlines Services in Copenhagen, covering the modification of 55 United States Air Forces in Europe (USAFE) B–57s, was amended. The change decreased the number of aircraft involved by 20. Late in 1956, special USAFE requirements prompted TAC to part with 15 reworked B–57Bs. These aircraft, no longer under flying restrictions, remained on loan overseas while an equivalent number of USAFE B–57Bs underwent similar modifications. As for the Pacific Air Forces (PACAF) B–57s, they were modified at the Kawasaki plant at Gifu in Japan. Air Force personnel and teams from Land-Air, Inc. (another Martin subcontractor) handled the modification. The same Land-Air teams also helped in the United States. Even so, a great deal remained to be done in late 1957, as the aircraft's phaseout already appeared on the horizon.

End of Production   May 1956

Delivery of 2 last B–57Bs marked the end of production.

Total B–57Bs Accepted   202

The Air Force accepted a peak number of 27 B–57s in June 1955—18 B–57Bs and 9 B–57Cs.

Acceptance Rates

The Air Force accepted 123 B–57Bs in FY 55, and 79 in FY 56.

Flyaway Cost Per Production Aircraft $1.26 million

Airframe, $852,973; engines (installed), $257,529; electronics, $49,032; ordnance, $16,090; armament and others, $88,738.

Average Cost Per Flying Hour $511.00

Subsequent Model Series   B–57C

Other Configurations   B–57G

Night strike operational problems in Southeast Asia led to a major reconfiguration of the plane that had been ordered many years before for another conflict. The B–57 night intruder, too late for combat in Korea and never totally successful in Southeast Asia, at least demonstrated under fire the basic qualities justifying its original selection. In 1967, after several trial projects involving the special equipping of different planes were delayed or proved unsuccessful,[17] the Air Force looked to the B–57 to begin satisfying

---

[17] Included in these many projects were the testing of a forward-looking infrared sensor, installed in an old B–26, and of a fairly similar but more sophisticated system, in a Fairchild C–123. These projects carried exotic names. One of them, Tropic Moon I, put low-light-level

increasingly tough requirements. As successively published in the late sixties, Southeast Asia Operational Requirements 35, 64, 77, and 117 called for a self-contained night attack jet aircraft. The plane had to carry every device needed to acquire and attack mobile ground targets and fixed anti-aircraft artillery sites, in any kind of weather and without any ground or airborne assistance.

The Air Force thought General Dynamics F–111D, as ordered in May 1967, would be the ultimate answer. Yet, production of such a high-performance, avionics-loaded weapon system would not be an easy task. For that matter, the less-ambitious reconfiguration of the already-proven B–57 would also be difficult, again because of the components earmarked for it. Pressed for time, the Air Force in March 1967 decided to equip 3 PACAF B–57Bs with an improved version of the Tropic Moon I low-light-level television already fitted in 1 A–1E. Referred to as Tropic Moon II, the new project was not allowed to linger. The Air Force notified all concerned commands on 12 April, and soon thereafter the Westinghouse Electric Corporation received the modification contract for the 3 aircraft that PACAF chose and ferried from Southeast Asia to Baltimore. Once modified, the Tropic Moon II planes were returned to Southeast Asia without delay. They actually reached Phan Rang AB in South Vietnam on 12 December 1967.

Meanwhile, the B–57's final reconfiguration was approved. Initially labeled Night Rider, this project centered on a General Dynamics proposal to equip 15 B–57s with low-light-level television, forward-looking radar, and infrared sensors. The B–57 appeared well suited for the Night Rider role. The aircraft was available, had room for several sensors, and could carry 9,000 pounds of bombs at speeds of 160 to 500 knots. TAC and PACAF supported the Night Rider project, but in May 1967 the Air Staff rejected it as somewhat risky and far too costly. Rising difficulties in Southeast Asia, where enemy night movement of troops and supplies continued unabated, caused the Air Staff to reconsider its disapproval. In mid-year, the Air Force not only decided to endorse the Night Rider concept, but also to speed it up. This gave way to Tropic Moon III, the conversion of B–57s to self-contained night attack configuration. Tropic Moon III received added impetus in August, when the Air Staff told the Air Force Systems Command[18] to skip usual managerial procedures, to develop a B–57G prototype "immediately," and to plan for simultaneous procurement of a full B–57G squadron. The

---

television in a McDonnell-Douglas A–1E Skyraider, but the plane was not expected to reach South Vietnam until the end of 1967.

[18] The Air Force Systems Command came into being on 17 March 1961, replacing the Air Research and Development Command that had been established in 1950.

Air Force wanted the Tropic Moon III prototype to be ready for testing by September 1968. It also wanted the 15 B–57Gs "to be deployed as soon as possible" to Southeast Asia.

Notwithstanding Tropic Moon III's urgency, money had to be found before anything could be done about it. By late 1967, the skimpiest Air Force estimates showed that it would take some $50 million to accomplish the project. But in early 1968, the problem seemed to be solved. Funds from lower priority programs had been shifted, $25 million had been added to the overall budget for fleet modification, and the Air Force was ready to inform industry of its requirements. Hence, on 8 March, Air Force Systems Command's Aeronautical Systems Division advertised for bids to modify government-furnished B–57Bs to a new "G" configuration by integrating government- and contractor-furnished equipment. The contractor guidelines, offered by the Aeronautical Systems Division, were quite explicit. Besides the basic airframe, the Air Force would furnish engines, electronic countermeasures equipment, and communications sets. The contractor would provide the weapons delivery and navigation systems as well as modify the airframes. Specific yardsticks were established for the B–57G's avionics. The Tropic Moon III forward-looking radar had to be highly sophisticated, certainly as efficient as the AN/APQ–126 of the Ling-Temco-Vought A–7D (the Air Force's forthcoming version of the Navy A–7 Corsair). The Tropic Moon III weapons delivery computer and navigation system were to be particularly accurate. Additional armor plate and new

Deployed to Southeast Asia, this B–57 Canberra completed a mission against Viet Cong troops in the province of Tay Ninh.

ejection seats had to be provided to increase crew protection. Also, other changes were required in order to enhance safety, including the mounting of self-sealing fuel tanks in the aircraft fuselage.

The Air Force's 1968 financial bliss did not last long. Bids submitted in April by General Dynamics, Ling-Temco-Vought, North American Rockwell, and Westinghouse topped the highest USAF estimate by $30 million or more. In May and June, the extra money actually needed could not be secured. It therefore became clear that the Air Force had only 3 choices, one of which was to forget the whole project, a possibility considered for a while. Less drastic second and third alternatives were to reduce the number of B–57Gs, or to trim some of the weapon system's costly requirements. Well acquainted with the state-of-the-art limits and the pitfalls of new components of the forward-looking radar type, the Aeronautical Systems Division fought for the third solution. The division[19] won its case, as Wright Air Development Center had years before when challenging the wisdom of the B–57A production. Reconfiguration of 16 lower-performance Tropic Moon III B–57Gs (prototype included) was officially approved on 29 June. The selected prime contractor, the Westinghouse Defense and Space Center of Baltimore, agreed on 15 July to do the work for $78.3 million—an amount still higher than hoped for. Two major subcontractors were involved. Westinghouse counted on Martin-Marietta to inspect and repair the elderly B–57Bs picked for reconfiguration. Texas Instruments was made responsible for the forward-looking infrared radar and laser ranger.

When dealing with new technology, the best plans could go astray. The Air Force wanted to put the Tropic Moon III B–57s into combat by April 1969, but this soon was changed to December. And this more realistic deployment date was not met, even though the modification at first proceeded smoothly. There were many reasons for every delay. In early 1969, Westinghouse category I tests fell behind schedule because the Air Force was late with the shipments of necessary ground equipment. To compound the problem, in August Texas Instruments' deliveries of forward-looking infrared sensors began to slip significantly, and the Air Force failed to deliver the electronic countermeasures equipment on time. In late 1969 investigation of recent crash of a B–57G, still being tested by Martin pilots, indicated that the aircraft's minimum speed was too slow for safety. Ensuing flying incidents, in February and May 1970, uncovered mechanical flaws which, although minor, had to be corrected.

Meanwhile, there were other setbacks. In 1968, the Tropic Moon II B–57's performance had proved disappointing, mainly because the low-light-level television system did not live up to expectations and the aircraft's

---

[19] Aeronautical Systems Division was established on 1 April 1961, replacing WADC.

navigation system remained unreliable. In mid-1969, Westinghouse announced that the Tropic Moon III project would cost at least an extra $3.5 million. This additional expense was troublesome, but the Air Force was more disturbed by other events. Foremost were difficulties experienced with the weapon system's most crucial components which, besides delaying the program further, affected crew training and testing of new devices and munitions. As a result, the Air Force no longer thought of Tropic Moon III as a partial solution to a most urgent Southeast Asian problem. Rather, it had begun to consider the B–57G and F–111D as evolutionary steps toward the development of a high-speed, fully integrated, self-contained night and all-weather weapon system of the future.

In line with its new Tropic Moon III appraisal, the Air Staff in early 1970 insisted that the latest September deployment date would be met. The B–57G's category III tests, conducted by the Tactical Air Warfare Center between 29 April and 27 July, did not alter the Air Staff's decision. Overall, the results of category III testing indicated that, except for the forward-looking infrared radar, the aircraft's avionics equipment satisfied basic requirements. Concluding that the aircraft performance was nearing that originally specified, Gen. John D. Ryan,[20] Air Force Chief of Staff, ordered the 13th Bombardment Squadron to move to Ubon Air Base, Thailand, on 15 September. Only 11 of the remaining 15 B–57Gs were assigned to the squadron, leaving 3 aircraft at MacDill AFB to train replacement crews. A last B–57G also stayed behind to serve as a "test bed" for future improvements.

The Tropic Moon III B–57Gs were returned to the United States in April 1972. Despite the combined efforts of Texas Instruments and Westinghouse, the forward-looking radar proved deficient. Improved sets updated at a cost of $2 million and first combat tested in September 1971, also never worked completely well. But the B–57G airframe, with its new J65–W–5D engines, measured up to the planning criteria. The aircraft also got involved successfully in such projects as Pave Gat, which showed that sensor-slued guns could function effectively in a jet bomber.

Phaseout   1958–1973

As programmed, TAC phaseout of its B–57B/C aircraft was fast. Started in April 1958, it was completed on 23 June 1959. To some extent, TAC deplored its loss. Despite limited speed, short range, and other

---

[20] General Ryan replaced Gen. John P. McConnell as Chief of Staff of the United States Air Force on 1 August 1969, and served in that position through 31 July 1973.

deficiencies, the B–57B had become a proven weapon system presenting few maintenance problems. A PACAF request for retention of its own B–57s fared better, and 2 squadrons remained at Johnson AFB, Japan, until 1965. These B–57 units, the 8th and 13th Bomber Squadrons, Tactical, then moved to Clark AB, in the Philippines for possible action in Southeast Asia. Small numbers of the aircraft soon flew missions from Bien Hoa and Da Nang Air Bases in South Vietnam. Combat attrition, accidents, and old age took their toll of the aircraft. Forthcoming Tropic Moon requirements also did not help, forcing PACAF to inactivate its last squadron in 1968. But this did not really spell the B–57B's end. As already noted, TAC reactivated the 13th Bombardment Squadron, Tactical, to fly reconfigured B–57B and B–57C aircraft. Known as B–57Gs, these planes stayed in Southeast Asia until 12 April 1972. Having been stripped of most of their Tropic Moon components, the B–57Gs went to the Air National Guard—like many of TAC's B–57Bs in the late fifties. The Guard flew the B–57Bs, that had been modified for reconnaissance, until 1966. However, its newly acquired B–57s were scheduled for storage at Davis-Monthan AFB in early 1974.

Other Uses   1956–1957

One B–57B was extensively modified for Operation Red Wing, a special weapons test held in the Pacific in 1956. To save time and money, the plane was modified while on the production line. Martin later restored this Red Wing B–57B to its regular configuration.

Six B–57Bs were modified during August and September 1956 to perform sampler roles in the Red Wing tests. In December 1957 four additional B–57Bs were also modified to monitor the type and rate of radioactive fallout in the upper atmosphere after a nuclear blast. Following completion of the Red Wing tests, these planes were all allocated to the Air Force Special Weapons Center at Kirtland AFB, New Mexico.

In late 1957, ten B–57Bs were modified under Project Stardust. This modification removed all armament equipment from the aircraft, but put in the latest flying instruments. These modified B–57Bs were used by high-ranking officers for proficiency flying and transportation.

Other Countries   1960

More than 50 B–57Bs, re-fitted with less-sophisticated components, were delivered to Pakistan under the auspices of the Military Assistance Program.

B-57C

Manufacturer's Model 272

Weapon System   307A

Previous Model Series   B-57B

New Features

Rear cockpit flight controls and instruments were the only new features of the B-57C.

Basic Development   1953-1954

Development of a dual-control B-57B was spurred by an Air Training Command request in February 1953. In the ensuing months, TAC also insisted that a new trainer was needed to replace the T-33. Even the most seasoned pilots, TAC argued, needed to learn how to handle multi-engine jet bombers skillfully.

Go-Ahead Decision   April 1954

Reduction of the B-57B program in favor of production of a dual-control version of the aircraft was officially approved in April 1954. At first, 34 B-57Bs on the fiscal year 1953 program were to be modified on the production line, but this number was almost immediately raised to 38. The modification, consisting mostly of installing government-furnished equipment in the aircraft's rear cockpit, was expected to cost less than $50,000 per aircraft. Although low cost was a factor, the Air Staff's decision stemmed primarily from Martin's assurance that the B-57B could be brought to the dual-control configuration without compromising its combat performance. In other words, no extra B-57Bs would be needed to replace those converted into trainers since the latter could still be used as bombers.

Additional Procurement   August 1954

Purchase of an additional 26 dual-control B–57s was included in the fiscal year 1955 program, in connection with the production of another B–57 type. In August 1954, however, the 26-aircraft order was canceled and the dual-control planes, formerly known as TB–57Bs, were redesignated B–57Cs.

Prototype Inspection   November 1954

The November inspection of the first B–57B modified for dual-control revealed no discrepancies.

First Flight   30 December 1954

The B–57C made its first flight on 30 December 1954 and its second one on 3 January 1955. The Martin pilots who flight tested the plane were impressed by its performance and pointed out that they encountered no handling difficulties.

Enters Operational Service   1955

Four B–57Cs, purchased to take care of attrition, were initially allocated to Air Training Command to support the B–57B transition training program. All other B–57Cs immediately went to tactical units. In fact, in the United States or overseas, 2 out of every 18 aircraft in a B/RB–57 squadron were B–57Cs.

Problems and Modifications   1955–1957

Being practically identical, the B–57Bs and B–57Cs shared the same operational problems. Hence, most B–57B modifications were applied to the B–57Cs.

End of Production   May 1956

Delivery of 1 last B–57C in May 1956 marked the end of the dual-control production line modification.

Total B–57Cs Accepted   38

Acceptance Rates

The Air Force accepted 18 B–57Cs in FY 55, and 20 in FY 56.

Flyaway Cost Per Production Aircraft $1.21 million

Airframe, $916,279; engines (installed), $144,523; electronics, $46,128; ordnance, $20,340; armament and others, $84,685.

Subsequent Model Series   RB–57D

Other Configurations   None

Phaseout   1958–1959

Phaseout of the small B–57C contingent followed the B–57B's pattern. Like the B–57Bs of the Tactical Air Command, most B–57Cs were brought up to the reconnaissance configuration in 1958, when they began reaching the Air National Guard. Three RB–57Cs were still listed on the Guard inventory in mid-1973.

RB–57D

Manufacturer's Model 294

Weapon System 307L

Previous Model Series   **B–57C**

New Features

The single-seat RB–57D featured a substantially altered B–57B fuse-lage, new wings, more powerful engines, and components that varied, according to the aircraft's many specialized roles. Specifically, the fuselage bomb-bay was permanently closed off, the fuselage fuel tanks were re-moved, and 4 camera windows were installed forward of the nose wheel well. The RB–57D's large nose and tail radomes further lengthened the fuselage. The aircraft empennage incorporated a power-driven rudder and yaw damper. Fuel cells were integral with the RB–57D wing, which was of honeycomb construction—the first time that such a structural feature had been used in a piloted aircraft. The new wings, with their 105-foot span and their 1,500 square-foot area (replacing the 64-foot span and 960 square-foot area of the regular B–57), completely changed the appearance of the airplane. Two 1,000-pound thrust J57–P–9 engines (that took the place of the 7,200-pound static thrust J65s) had anti-icing equipment and could be used at altitudes over 70,000 feet. To increase range, all but the first 6 RB–57Ds were equipped for air refueling.

Basic Development   **1952–1953**

Martin's Model 294, which ultimately became the RB–57D, developed from a study concluded in December 1952 by the Wright Air Development Center. This study showed that it should be possible to develop "in a relatively short time period" a turbojet-powered special reconnaissance aircraft, with a radius of 2,000 nautical miles at altitudes of 65,000 feet. Anticipating a formal requirement for such an aircraft, the center established design Project MX–2147, which also specified that subsonic speed would be acceptable and that no defense armament would be required.

Requests for Proposals   April 1953

The advertisement of Project MX–2147 in April 1953 was followed by the award of 3 design contracts—to Bell, Fairchild, and Martin. The Martin study contract was initiated by a 29 June letter contract, amounting to $31,406. This document, as revised in October, bound Martin to submit reports on its design study by 11 December 1953 and allowed a $2,784 cost increase.

Production Decision   21 June 1954

The Air Force decided in June that 6 of the B–57Bs currently on order would be built in the configuration of Model 294. The decision was based on several factors. Martin's high altitude design offered "relatively good performance, an operational date 12 to 18 months earlier, and lower costs" than Bell's X–16.[21] Martin's new planes, designated B–57Ds in August 1954, became RB–57Ds in April 1955—after the Air Force made it known that the airplanes would be used exclusively for strategic reconnaissance.

Additional Procurement   3 January 1955

The Air Force increased the specialized reconnaissance B–57D program to 20 airplanes—the final total—and attached an overriding priority to the whole project. The forthcoming RB–57Ds, all destined for the Strategic Air Command, were ordered in 3 versions. The original 6, plus 6 of the additional 14, would be 1-man RB–57Ds carrying among other components 2 K–38 and 2 KC–1 split vertical cameras. One RB–57D, singled out as the RB–57D–1, would be equipped with the AN/APG–56 high-resolution, side-looking radar for day or night radar mapping reconnaissance. The RB–57D–1 would also carry a crew of 1. The remaining 6 RB–57Ds,

---

[21] This did not mean the end of the X–16 Bald Eagle. The Bell design had actually been judged the best proposal and the Air Force endorsed the aircraft development concurrent with production of the Martin model. Just the same, the X–16 never reached the fabrication stage. Even though a significant number of Bald Eagles were ordered, the project was canceled in mid-1955 after Lockheed flew a U–2 which had been designed and built with company funds.

identified as RB–57D–2s, would be fitted with ferret electronic countermeasures equipment and would have a crew of 2—pilot and electronic countermeasures operator. All but the first 6 airplanes would be equipped for in-flight refueling by KC–97 tankers. Air-refueling would be done via a boom slipway door, aft of the canopy. The 20 RB–57Ds would have an autopilot and the D–1 and D–2s would feature the AN/APN–59 navigational equipment.

Contractual Arrangements   1954–1955

The Air Force intended to carry Martin's high-altitude B–57 on Contract AF 33(600)–22208, which followed the first definitive contract—AF 33(038)–22617—initiated by the letter contract of March 1951. However, negotiations for this second contract, like those of its predecessor, were complicated by the many changes that kept on afflicting the whole B–57 program. After discovering that less than 20 percent of the new aircraft's parts matched those of the B–57B, the Air Force had to alter its plans. The programmed quantity of B–57Bs was reduced by 20, and the 20 airframes (completed to the extent components were common to both B and D airplanes) were booked against contract AF 33(600)–25825, even though this document had been designed to cover nothing more than a pure development study. The stripped-down airplanes, transferred on paper as government-furnished equipment, were valued at $6 million. This sum, like subsequent costs for the D airplanes, was charged to the AF 33(600)–25825 development contract. This cost-plus-fixed fee agreement was allowed a high fixed fee rate of 7 percent, because of the program's urgency and the many imponderables faced by Martin in undertaking such a project. In early 1958 the total estimated cost of the entire D program was about $60 million—$1 million short of the final amount.

First Flight   3 November 1955

The high-altitude, daylight photo-reconnaissance RB–57D was first flown on 3 November. The flight lasted 50 minutes and the results were satisfactory.

Testing   1955–1956

Because of the urgency of the program for which the RB–57Ds were built, flight testing had to be limited and all tests ended in 1956. To begin with, Category II testing (a joint contractor-USAF effort) was not allowed to linger. Started on 29 November 1955, these tests were completed on 7 December. Just the same, RB-57D deliveries slipped to the spring of 1956.

Enters Operational Service   1956

It took until May 1956 for Strategic Air Command (SAC) to get its first RB-57Ds, even though the aircraft had been scheduled for delivery in late 1955. Strikes at Lear, Incorporated, which supplied the radars, caused delays in equipping the aircraft. Westinghouse, another main subcontractor, also had labor problems that created a shortage of autopilots. But the overall situation improved. By the end of September, SAC's inventory counted 11 RB-57Ds. Four B-57C trainers, brought up to the reconnaissance configuration, accompanied the new aircraft.

Operational Problems   1957–1958

Materiel deficiencies accounted for 20 of 22 unsatisfactory sorties, flown during June 1957 by the specialized RB-57Ds of the 4025th Strategic Reconnaissance Squadron. The Pratt and Whitney J57-P-9 engines, Westinghouse autopilots, and some of the more complicated electronic countermeasures systems did not function properly. In addition, it was difficult to obtain parts for the new electronic countermeasures components. The greatly enlarged wing also kept causing problems. First, the main wing spar had to be strengthened as did sections of the wing panels. Then, the Martin-developed "honey-comb" wing surfaces were subject to water seepage and wing stress. These shortcomings taken care of, the RB-57Ds served SAC's purposes well for several years.

End of Production   December 1956

The RB-57D production ended in December 1956, but the Air Force did not take delivery of the last plane before March 1957.

Total RB-57Ds Accepted   20

Acceptance Rates

The Air Force accepted 12 RB-57Ds in FY 56 and 8 in FY 57.

Flyaway Cost Per Production Aircraft $3.05 million

Airframe, $2,531,437; engines (installed), $313,974; electronics, $171,271; others, $39,750.

Subsequent Model Series B-57E

Other Configurations RB-57F and WB-57F

RB-57F—Most RB-57Fs were modified RB-57Ds even though a few B-57Bs were brought up to the same configuration. The modification, endorsed in the early sixties, was accomplished by the General Dynamics Corporation in Fort Worth, Texas. The first RB-57F flew in April 1964 and was accepted by the Air Force 2 months later. Still, it took until March 1967 to complete the last aircraft—a 2-year delay. The 16-aircraft project also proved to be much more expensive than expected. Each modified plane carried a price tag of $9 million—airframe, $5,958,530; engines (installed), $562,500; electronics, 1,573,750 others, $925,000. Moreover, some RB-57Fs, equipped for long-range oblique photography, cost an additional $1.5 million—for a unit cost close to $10.6 million. But the RB-57F, funded under a very special project, turned out to be an exceptional plane. Equipped with 2 Pratt & Whitney TF33-P-11A engines and 2 auxiliary J60-P-9s, the 2-seat (pilot, plus navigator or special equipment operator) RB-57F had a service ceiling of 68,500 feet, a cruising range of 3,690 nautical miles, a cruise endurance of 9.7 hours, and a cruising speed of 420 knots. Yet, the RB-57F's average cost per flying hour was only $886; the average maintenance cost, $407. Two RB-57Fs were allocated to the United States Air Forces in Europe and 2 others went to the Pacific Air Forces. The remaining 12 RB-57Fs were at Kirtland AFB, New Mexico, where they served with the 58th Weather Reconnaissance Squadron of the Military Air Transport Service.[22] These RB-57Fs were used to support Atomic Energy Commission and the Air Force Technical Applications Center's requirements until they were redesignated as WB-57Fs.

WB-57F—General Dynamics modified a few additional B-57Bs to give Military Airlift Command's Air Weather Service its 17 WB-57F contingent.

---

[22] The Military Air Transport Service, responsible for furnishing rapid airlift for the armed forces of the United States and its allies throughout the world since June 1948, was renamed the Military Airlift Command on 1 January 1966.

The WB–57Fs, former RB–57Fs as well as newly reconfigured B–57Bs, retained the RB–57F's price—$9 million each. The redesignated aircraft stayed at Kirtland AFB, with the same squadron, for very similar purposes. Among other duties, the 58th Squadron for years continued to fly high-altitude radiation sampling missions to furnish data to the Defense Atomic Support Agency. In mid-1973, however, both the aircraft and the squadron neared their end. The Air Force planned to inactivate the 58th and to put all WB–57Fs out of the active inventory in mid-1974. Two of the aircraft were scheduled to go to the National Aeronautics and Space Administration, where they were expected to support further high-altitude sampling projects and the development of satellite systems.

Phaseout   1959–1960

SAC did not retain its RB–57Ds and few RB–57Cs very long. Only 6 of the aircraft remained with the command by December 1959. On 22 April 1960 SAC disposed of the last one, an RB–57C (Serial No. 53–3838) assigned to the 4080th Strategic Wing, Laughlin AFB, Texas. Four years before, the 4080th, then located at Turner AFB, Georgia, had received the command's first RB–57C (Serial No. 53–3842).

B–57E

Manufacturer's Model 272E

Previous Model Series   RB–57D

New Features

The 2-man (pilot and tow-target operator) B–57E featured a hydraulic power-boosted rudder (to improve directional stability) and target launching equipment. The B–57E differed externally from the dual-control B–57C in that it carried 2 target canisters (located on the lower rear fuselage), a modified tail cone, 2 rotating beacons, and a larger tail skid. The E-model had no armament and no bombing equipment, but either could be added without difficulty. The tow-target B–57E could easily be brought to the configuration of the B–57B bomber, because its target containers, internal cable reels and fittings, as well as cockpit towing controls were removable.

Initial Requirement   16 March 1954

The Air Force asked the AMC to issue requirements for a modified B–57 that would be capable of acting as a tow-target aircraft and, like its predecessors, be suitable for rapid conversion to an operational bomber. The dual-control tow-target B–57 was expected to carry 4 tow reels and 4 banner targets per mission.

Go-Ahead Decision   January 1955

Although the Air Force was eager to replace its tow-target versions of the B–26 and B–45 airplanes, a firm decision on the B–57E program was not reached until January 1955. A number of factors accounted for the delay. Martin was slow in submitting specifications for the new configuration, and protracted program decisions as to quantities and types of airplanes did not help.

Contractual Arrangements   February–December 1955

The last major B-57 contract—AF 33(600)-29645—was initiated under the fiscal year 1955 procurement program by a letter contract, signed on 21 February 1955. Contract negotiations started with a requirement for 68 B-57Es and 26 B-57Cs, but this order was subsequently canceled. This prompted a new round of negotiations and postponed signature of the definitive contract to 8 December—half-way through fiscal year 1956. To avoid a costly break in production scheduling (estimated at $16 million), previous programs were stretched. This raised the cost of the fiscal year 1955 program by $1.5 million (a comparatively low-cost alternative) and lowered Kaiser's workload, giving the wing subcontractor a chance to finally catch up.

First Flight (Production Aircraft)   16 May 1956

Martin first flew successfully a production B-57E with tow targets on 16 May—the first aircraft built for the Air Force specifically for this type of duty. The target launchers of 2 modified dual-control B-57Cs, used by Martin as B-57E prototypes, failed to work during earlier flights in April of the same year. But eventually, these problems were solved, and the 2 aircraft joined the B-57E fleet.

Program Change   10 July 1956

The Air Force canceled Strategic Air Command's requirement for conversion of 7 B-57E aircraft to the TRB-57E configuration. The Air Staff decided that, as planned, all but 4 of the 68 B-57Es would go to the Air Defense Command. The 4 exceptions, B-57Es without tow-target equipment, were allocated to the Air Force Flight Test School.

Enters Operational Service   August 1956

A few B-57Es began reaching Air Defense Command in August and 18 more were delivered in September. However, Air Force Flight Test School did not receive its first aircraft until 24 October, and additional deliveries lagged behind schedule.

Program Slippage   March 1957

Because it started late, the B-57E program was accompanied by short deadlines and hurried production orders, all of which could spell trouble. But the program actually benefited from an odd combination of events. Already engrossed in the RB-57D program in February 1955, when the B-57E letter contract started, Martin found itself short of 600 engineers and of necessity subcontracted a good bit of the B-57E engineering. This turned out well. Hudson Motors was made responsible for the tow-target installation; Kaiser received an extension of its subcontract for the E wings; and excess parts, built by Martin for the high priority RB-57Ds, were transferred to the B-57E program. Nonetheless, there were a few setbacks. Late deliveries of government-furnished equipment, difficulties in getting the tow reel system to work with the B-57E without excessive airframe modifications, and other equipment problems held up the program for a time. Yet, much of the backlog was eliminated by the end of 1956. In the long run, the B-57E program's overall slippage did not exceed 1 month—a most rewarding accomplishment.

End of Production   1957

Production ended in early 1957, and the last B-57E was delivered in March.

Total B-57Es Accepted   68

Acceptance Rates

The Air Force accepted 2 B-57Es in FY 56—both in May 1956. All others were accepted in FY 57—beginning in August 1956 and ending in March 1957.

Flyaway Cost Per Production Aircraft $1.01 million

Airframe, $847,534; engines (installed), $125,756; electronics, $22,377; others, $21,433.

Subsequent Model Series   None

Additional Procurement   None

Rather than buying more B–57Es, the Air Force converted B–57Bs to the tow-target configuration. Some of these B–57Bs (such as those allocated in 1958 to TAC's lst Tow Target Squadron) came from USAFE, where they had received so-called "hard usage" modifications. Before undertaking their towing missions, these aircraft needed much more than modification. Fortunately, Warner Robins Air Materiel Area was able to do most of this work. The lst Tow Target Squadron flew its newly acquired aircraft for several years, transferring the last 14 to Air Defense Command on 1 July 1962. This marked the end of the B–57 weapon system in the TAC inventory.

Modernization   1965

In the mid-sixties, all B–57Es (converted B–57Bs included) were equipped with the external AF/A372–1 tow-target system.

Other Configurations   EB–57E, RB–57E, and TB–57E

B–57E productions as well as B–57Bs converted to the E configuration underwent changes throughout the years. The Air Force at times used a few of these aircraft for training—modifying, adding equipment, and referring to the planes as TB–57Es. Many B–57Es, regardless of their origin, became RB–57Es after modification and the addition of reconnaissance equipment. Some of these planes still served in Southeast Asia in mid-1966, even though they were beginning to show signs of fatigue. The most gratifying change (from the economical standpoint) put electronic countermeasures equipment in the planes, which were redesignated EB–57Es. The sophisticated but relatively inexpensive EB–57Es, with a unit price of $2.02 million (electronic counter-measures equipment and modification costs included), provided electronic countermeasures targets to ground and airborne radar systems. In mid-1973, the Air Force active inventory counted an almost equal number of reconnais-sance or electronic countermeasures-equipped B–57Es (19 RB–57Es and 23 EB–57Es), but the EB–57Es were expected to outlast every B–57 version.

Operational Status   Mid-1973

Air Force rolls only listed 9 B–57Es by the end of June 1973, but various configurations of the versatile airplane continued to play significant roles, with no immediate phaseout in sight.

Program Recap

The Air Force accepted a grand total of 403 B–57s, all of which were produced in Baltimore, Maryland, by the Glenn L. Martin Co. Specifically, the B–57 program comprised 8 B–57As, 202 B–57Bs, 38 B–57Cs, 68 B–57Es, 67 RB–57As, and 20 RB–57Ds. Other B–57s, such as the B–57Gs, RB–57Fs and WB–57Fs, were the result of extensive post-production modifications. Production ended in early 1957, but at the close of the year USAF records showed that 47 of the 403 aircraft had been destroyed in major accidents. This came as no great surprise. Overall, the B–57 was not easy to fly. Moreover, prior to modification of its longitudinal control and stabilizer systems, the B–57 was uncontrollable if 1 of its 2 engines failed during takeoff or landing. In 1958, after completion of all possible modifications, the Air Force ascertained that 50 percent of the major accidents resulted from pilot errors, with 38 percent of the accidents occurring upon landing. Yet, while the number of B–57 accidents was high—129 major and minor accidents as of 1958, the rate compared favorably with that of the B–47 and some other aircraft.

TECHNICAL AND BASIC MISSION PERFORMANCE DATA

B/RB-57 AIRCRAFT

	B-57B	B-57C	B-57E	RB-57A	RB-57F
Manufacturer (Airframe)	The Glenn L. Martin Co., Baltimore, Md.				
(Engines)	Wright Aeronautical Division of The Curtiss-Wright Corporation, Wood-Ridge, N.J., and Buick Division of The General Motors Corp.				
Nomenclature	Light Tactical Bomber, Trainer, Target Tug, and Reconnaissance Aircraft.				
Popular Name	Canberra				
Length/Span (ft)	65.5/64	65.5/64	65.5/64	65.5/64	68.3/122.5
Wing Area (sq ft)	960	960	960	960	2,000
Weights (lb)					
Empty	28,793	28,793	34,789	26,380	37,020
Combat	38,689	38,689	37,300	32,448	49,500
Takeoff	56,965[a]	56,965[a]	54,072	57,000	61,500[b]
Engine: Number, Rated Power per Engine, & Designation	(2) 7,220-lb st (max) J65-W-5 or (2) 7,220 lb st (max) J65-BW-5	(2) 7,220-lb st (max) J65-W-5 or (2) 7,220-lb st (max) J65-BW-5	(2) 7,220-lb st (max) J65-W-5 or (2) 7,220-lb st (max) J65-BW-5	(2) 7,220-lb st (max) J65-W-5 or (2) 7,220-lb st (max) J65-BW-5	(2) 16,000-lb st (mil) TF33-P-11A & (2) 2,900-lb st (mil) J60-P-9
Takeoff Ground Run (ft)					
at Sea Level	5,000	5,000	5,050	3,400	2,600
Over 50-ft Obstacle	6,200	6,200	6,250	4,300	2,800
Rate of Climb (fpm) at Sea Level	4,320	4,320	3,825	4,800	2,725
Combat Rate of Climb (fpm) at Sea Level	6,180	6,180	370 (with target deployed)	7,100	7,600

Service Ceiling (100 fpm Rate of Climb to Altitude)	40,100	40,100	28,600 (with target deployed)	44,500	60,800
Combat Ceiling (ft) (500 fpm Rate of Climb to Altitude)	45,100	45,100	36,950 (with target deployed) at final towing weight	49,000	60,650
Average Cruise Speed (kn)	414	414	342 (initial towing speed)	355	411
Max Speed at Optimum Altitude (kn/ft)	520/2,500	520/2,500	403/25,000 (limited by banner shredding)	499/9,000	420/63,500
Combat Radius (nm)	824	824	2.50 hr (towing time)	250	1,280
Total Mission Time (hr)	4.13	4.13	2.68	3.12	6.12
Armament	4 20-mm M39[c]	4 20-mm M39[c]	Not Applicable	None	None
Crew	2	2	2	2	2
Max Bombload (lb)	6,000[d]	6,000[d]	N.A.	None[e]	None[f]

---

[a] Limited by space.
[b] Limited by wheel loading.
[c] Plus 16 underwing rockets.
[d] Bombloads could be made of various combinations—M117s MK82s, MK81s, CBU/SUU–30s, M14A frag clusters, fire bombs, flares, and the like.
[e] Several cameras (P–2s, K–37s, T–11s, K–17s, K–38s), plus flash bombs and photo flash cartridges.
[f] High-altitude weather photo reconnaissance equipment and special components for atmosphere sampling operations.

Abbreviations

fpm = feet per minute
kn = knots
max = maximum
mil = military
nm = nautical miles
st = static thrust

Basic Mission Note

All basic mission's performance data based on maximum power, except as otherwise indicated.

Combat Radius Formula:

B–57B and B–57C—Warmed up, took off, and climbed on course at maximum power. Cruised out at long-range speeds, increasing altitude with decreasing weight (external tanks being dropped when empty). Over target, descended to sea level and dropped bombs; external stores also, if carried. Remained in combat area for 5 minutes and climbed on course to cruise ceiling at maximum power. Cruised back to home base at long-range speeds, increased altitude with decreasing weight. Range-free allowances included 5-minute normal-power fuel consumption for starting engine and take-off; 5-minute sea level fuel consumption at power required for maximum structural limit speed; 20 minutes of maximum-endurance fuel consumption at sea level, plus 5 percent of initial fuel load for landing reserve.

Formula: Radius Mission II (High Speed)

Same profile and fuel reserve as for basic mission (Mission I), except all cruising was at normal-rated power.

Formula: Range Mission V (Ferry Range)

Warmed up, took off and climbed on course to cruise ceiling at maximum power. Cruised out at long-range speeds, increasing altitude with decreasing weight (external tanks being retained when empty). Range-free allowances included 5 minutes of normal-power fuel consumption for starting engines and take-off, 30 minutes of maximum-endurance fuel consumption at sea level plus 5 percent of initial fuel load for landing reserve.

B–57E—Formula: Towing Mission I

Took off and climbed on course at military power to normal-power service ceiling for banner extended configuration. Extended banner and cruise-climbed at speeds for maximum mile per pound in a race track pattern until only fuel for landing reserve remained. Cut banner and landed. Time-free allowances included 5-minute normal-power fuel consumption for starting engine and take-off, and 30 minutes of maximum-endurance fuel consumption at sea level plus 5 percent of initial fuel load for landing reserve.

B–57E—Formula: Towing Mission II

Same as Mission I, except towing was conducted at a constant altitude of 30,000 feet.

B–57E—Formula: Range Mission III

Took off and climbed on course to optimum cruise altitude at military power. Cruised out at maximum-range speeds, increasing altitude with decreasing weight, until all useable fuel (less reserve fuel) was consumed. Range-free allowances similar to time-free allowances of Mission I.

RB–57A—Formula: Radius Mission I

From sea level, took off and climbed on course to 24,000 feet with military thrust. Cruised at 24,000 feet at recommended cruise speed. Made an on-course normal descent to 5,000 feet. Flew at 5,000 feet, at 300 knots true airspeed, with no distance credit. Climbed on return course to 24,000 feet with military thrust. Cruise back at 24,000 feet at recommended cruise speed. Made normal descent to sea level on return course. Mission reserve fuel was 2,500 pounds.

RB–57F—Formula: Radius Mission

Took off and climbed on course at maximum allowable power to initial altitude of 60,000 feet. Cruised out at long-range speeds and at maximum altitudes to target at 63,200 feet. Returned to base at long-range speeds and maximum altitudes. Range-free allowances were fuel for 5 minutes at take-off power (70 percent of military-rated power) and 20 minutes at maximum-endurance speeds at sea level, plus 5 percent of initial fuel for landing reserve.

RB–57F—Formula: Ferry Range Mission

Took off and climbed on course at maximum allowable power to optimum cruise altitude. Cruised out at long-range speeds at optimum altitudes. Range-free allowances were fuel for 5 minutes at take-off power (70 percent of military-rated power) and 20 minutes at maximum-endurance speeds at sea level, plus 5 percent of initial fuel for landing reserve.

B–58 Hustler

Convair Division of General Dynamics Corporation

B–58 Hustler
General Dynamics

Manufacturer's Model 4

Weapon System 102A

Overview

Future aircraft "will move with speeds far beyond the velocity of sound," said renowned Hungarian-born aerodynamicist Theodore von Karman in 1945. Highly regarded by Henry "Hap" Arnold, Commanding General of the Army Air Forces (AAF), and by Maj. Gen. Curtis LeMay, the first Deputy Chief of Staff for Research and Development, von Karman, as the AAF's chief scientific advisor, most likely influenced LeMay's vigorous and diverse research and development program. Part of the program prompted the impressive 14 October 1947 test flight of the Bell X–1 rocket airplane, a flight which shattered both the sound barrier and the speculation that aerodynamic forces became infinite at Mach 1.

Development in the late 1940s of the single-place, air-launched X–1 was a major achievement. Nevertheless, as time would show, production of a 3-seater aircraft, capable of sustained speeds approaching the muzzle velocity of a 30-caliber bullet and of functioning effectively as a strategic bomber, would be a challenge of monumental proportions. The controversial B–58 program that ensued was to illustrate the dangers of untried technology versus the necessity of pioneering state-of-the-art developments. Where to draw the line between the two would remain open to question long after the costly B–58 ceased to exist.

A 1946 study by Consolidated Vultee Aircraft Corporation (Convair), a contractor noted for interest in the delta-wing configuration, marked the beginning of the B–58. The project was so complex, however, that a new study was requested and a second contractor, Boeing, became involved. Proposed in 1951, the initial Convair design, as recommended by Dr.

Alexander M. Lippisch, an eminent German scientist, foretold a delta-configured, 100,000-pound bomber; the Boeing design, a conventional, 200,000-pounder. Suggestive of the future B–58's tumultuous history, the 2 contractors followed totally different development approaches, and drastically opposed concepts emerged within the newly independent Air Force. USAF engineers kept asking for realistic military requirements, but the Air Staff decided that instead of accepting technology as the determining factor against which a mission could be fitted, mission objectives would come first and technology would be developed to satisfy them.

In late 1952, believing it promised the best means of achieving supersonic speeds with a weapon system of minimum size, the Convair design, already altered several times, was selected over that of Boeing. The choice was not unexpected. In a recent study, the Rand Corporation had clearly stated that by minimizing size, one reduced the radar reflectivity of a vehicle and, therefore, the probabilities of interception by surface-to-air missiles. Also, the Air Force's latest development directive had reemphasized the importance of minimum size, of high-speed and high-altitude performances and, finally, of the weapon system development technique, an objective with which Convair was familiar.

General LeMay, who by the fall of 1952 had been heading the Strategic Air Command (SAC) for 4 years, and who would remain in that position until promoted to Vice Chief of Staff in mid-1957, did not like the Air Staff's selection. Among other arguments, he pointed out that instead of fostering economy and reliability, combining unconventional design and operational techniques made "it entirely possible that the system might prove operationally unsuitable." General LeMay's objections did not prevail, which was unusual. Rejection of the more conventional, longer-range, supersonic bomber, proposed by Boeing and preferred by General LeMay, also was ironic, since it was LeMay who, back in early 1948, ensured that a new strategic jet bomber would be developed on the heels of the B–52.

Throughout the years, money had a great deal to do with the B–58's retention. By 1954, for example, after an investment of some $200 million, the B–58 project could show no tangible achievements. Cancellation at this stage, the Air Staff reasoned, would mean an unacceptable financial loss. Hence, despite production slippages, soaring costs, and General LeMay's continued opposition, the B–58 survived. Yet, the program that finally emerged was emaciated, in terms of numbers as well as military capabilities.

The Air Force bought 116 B–58s, less than half of the minimum initially planned. At long last operational in 1961, the B–58 still harbored deficiencies of varying importance. Its bombing and navigation system was unreliable, and the aircraft was unable to carry several kinds of new weapons. Although expensive, necessary modifications were accomplished between 1962 and 1964. However, significant problems remained. In the early 1960s, technological advances had radically altered the antiair defenses that the B-58 was expected to challenge. Defensive nuclear-tipped air-to-air and surface-to-air missiles appeared to preclude penetration of enemy airspace at high altitude. Since the B-58 structure incurred significant fatigue damage when flying at low level, and since the new bomber had no terrain-following radar, extensive modifications would be needed to permit effective low-level penetration. Such modifications did not materialize because of their prohibitive cost, and all B-58s were phased out of the Air Force inventory by early 1970, less than 8 years after the last ones rolled off the assembly line.

While the $3 billion price tag of the B-58 program did not help the manned bomber's cause, the aircraft did represent an important technological achievement. In its day the B-58 broke 12 world speed records and won almost every major aviation award in existence. The aircraft marked the first major departure from the monocoque riveted metal construction techniques of the 1930s and prompted the investigation of non-metallic composite structural methods. It brought about major technical advances, entailing technical uncertainties which remained until such an aircraft was flown. The Air Force took the risk, and the results may not have been cost-effective. Nonetheless, similar developmental risks again would have to be taken to assure progress in aerospace technology.

Basic Development   October 1946

Development of a long-range supersonic bombardment aircraft was officially initiated by a generalized bomber study (GEBO),[1] begun in October 1946 by Convair.[2] In requesting GEBO, the AAF called for determination of which design trends would be necessary to achieve unspecified, yet ambitious supersonic performances. Of necessity, the scope of the study was very broad, but "investigation of low aspect wings in general and Delta Wings in particular" was emphasized. Although already acquainted with the delta wing and, therefore, well suited for the work, Convair had to investigate countless configurations to determine the effects of wing area, aspect ratio, thickness and sweep, as well as the impacts of type (turbojet and turboprop), size, and number of engines on airplane speed, range, and gross weight. The GEBO findings were described in 3 reports,

---

[1] Identified as GEBO I in June 1949, after the Air Force issued a contract for a second GEBO.

[2] The corporation subsequently became a division of the General Dynamics Corp. For details, see B-36, p 5.

which were completed in June 1948. Yet, this was only a beginning. Indicative of the magnitude of the project, in late 1948 the Air Materiel Command (AMC) Engineering Division of the now independent Air Force asked for a continuation of the GEBO study. The USAF engineers presented many valid reasons for their request, but their most telling arguments were that the findings so far obtained be used to show the "feasibility of military characteristics," and to assist in establishing "balanced characteristics and desirable design compromises." Meanwhile, pre-GEBO studies, conducted by Convair, had formed the basis of the winning interceptor design submitted by the company in 1946. Forerunner of the F–102, the ensuing rocket-propelled, XF–92 interceptor was extremely costly and highly impractical. Though the aircraft failed to earn a production contract, it proved to be an important step in the development of the delta wing, one of the future B–58's most striking features.

The delta wing itself, like many other aerodynamic innovations, had its inception in the German wind tunnels of World War II.[3] Although the National Advisory Committee on Aeronautics, independent of the German research, by 1945 had explained many of the delta configuration's theoretical advantages, the delta wing concept remained credited to Dr. Alexander M. Lippisch, leader of the German program.[4] In postwar years, U.S. governmental agencies and many of the American aircraft corporations studied extensively Dr. Lippisch's captured reports, with data on his never-flown, rocket-powered DM–1 glider and his spectacular, if not very successful, Messerschmitt-built Me–163B (the first operational liquid rocket-

---

[3] While the word "delta" is inextricably linked to the work of Alexander Lippisch, a brillant aeronautical scientist, his work followed a path first taken by John Dunne, who developed such aircraft in Great Britain prior to the First World War. Actually, Dr. Lippisch's efforts paralleled those of G. T. R. Hill and the Westland company in Great Britain and that of John K. Northrop in the United States. For details, see Richard P. Hallion, *Lippisch, Gluhareff, and Jones: The Emergence of the Delta Planform and the Origins of the Sweptwing in the United States, Aerospace Historian,* Volume 26, No. 1 Spring, March 1979. Dr. Hallion, a former curator of science and technology at the National Air and Space Museum, joined the Air Force History Program in January 1982, becoming Chief of the Office of History of the Air Force Systems Command's Flight Test Center at Edwards AFB, Calif. He is currently an historian at Headquarters Air Force System Command, Andrews AFB, Md.

[4] Reportedly, Dr. Lippisch's scientific curiosity was first stimulated by observing Orville Wright's flight at Templehof Airfield in 1909. Eventually, Lippisch became assistant aerodynamicist with Zeppelin-Werke, which later became the Dornier organization. His interest in gliders, which had its roots in the Rhone Mountain glider movement of 1920, brought him in 1927 to the Forschungs Institut der Rhone-Rossitten Gesellschaft, an institute for the study of gliders, where he became technical director of the design section. Although he designed the "Fafnir," a high-performance glider, as well as numerous others, his primary interest lay in proving his assumption that aircraft could have the appearance of a "flying wing" and still be practical—a delta-wing aircraft from which came the modern delta supersonic design.

propelled interceptor), introduced by the Germans in August 1944. Yet, while Dr. Lippisch was not the inspiration that caused Convair to continue working on the 60-degree delta, his comments reinforced and encouraged Convair engineers to believe that the delta wing could solve most of the problems of supersonic flight.[5]

Initial Requirements   1947

The initial requirements for a new bomber were emphasized in 1947 by Maj. Gen. Curtis E. LeMay, Deputy Chief of Air Staff for Research and Development.[6] In May, General LeMay wrote directly to Lt. Gen. Nathan F. Twining, AMC Commander, to urge that studies be undertaken of a new jet bomber that could become operational in the late 1950s. This airplane, General LeMay stated, should have a combat radius of 2,500 miles, a cruising speed of at least 500 miles per hour, and a gross weight of about 170,000 pounds. No amount of modification to the B-50 or B-36 would bring these airplanes within the desired characteristics, General LeMay added. A completely new medium bomber was needed, and development and procurement of such an airplane could well follow the B-52's development. That the B-58, generated by the post–World War II enthusiasm for the unconventional delta-wing configuration, evolved from requirements advocated by General LeMay was to prove ironic. Meanwhile, General LeMay's insistence prompted the Air Staff to solicit ideas about a new bomber from the Boeing Airplane Company of Seattle, Washington. Yet, several years would pass and many changes would occur before any specific projects started taking shape.

---

[5] Nature, Dr. Lippisch wrote, had designed the flying wing thousands of years before man even thought of flight. The flying wing was the Zanonia seed, a seed from a large vine of the cucumber family. It grew in the dense, moist jungles of Indonesia and adapted its reproductive processes to a region in which there was no wind to distribute the seeds. The vine climbed 150-foot trees, and from the top, the seed—a kidney-shaped platform—began its glide, rising on thermals from the jungle heat, and finally landing at considerable distance from its point of departure. The aerodynamic qualities of the seed attracted attention. Two Austrian engineers, Etrich and Wels, analysed its stability. Etrich eventually combined the Zanonia wing with a conventional monoplane configuration, known as the Etrich "Dove." The Dove became famous in the days before World War I, as the first German military aircraft. Its demise followed the onset of war, when it was abandoned in favor of the more maneuverable Fokker-designed aircraft.

[6] In spite of the declining post-war budget, General LeMay directed improvements in research and development. He also asked for more money. Appearing often before congressional committees, he pointed out on one occasion that the entire annual budget of the propeller division at Wright Field, "wouldn't buy one set of B-29 propellers."

Research Intensification   1949

As suggested by AMC, Headquarters USAF asked Convair to begin a second generalized bomber study for the development of future long-range supersonic bombers. This study, GEBO II, was formalized on 6 June 1949 by contract AF33(038)–2664 and, like GEBO I, ended covering a myriad of configurations. There were many justifications, besides AMC insistence, for the Air Staff's continued interest in the Convair research. To begin with, the shortage of funds forced the Air Force to make difficult decisions. Boeing's XB–55, a design initiated as an immediate result of General LeMay's 1947 request,[7] had been canceled in January 1949 for lack of money, as well as the following reasons. First, there no longer seemed to be an immediate need to originate a design to meet the medium bomber requirements, in view of the currently projected B–47 growth. Also, since the XB–55's development promised to take longer than anticipated, the Air Force thought its design should have been predicated on greater aerodynamic achievements and an improved propulsion system. Finally, and most importantly, continued testing of the delta wing XF–92, first flown in June 1948, was starting to attract wide attention. Even though the Board of Senior Officers in early 1949 had rejected an unconventional strategic bomber proposed by the Fairchild Aircraft Corporation, it was obvious by mid-year that the Senior Officers, with Secretary of the Air Force Symington's full support, were searching for new and imaginative solutions to the strategic bombing problem.

Conventional Alternatives   1949–1950

While looking for novel ideas, the Air Force remained cautious and did not lose sight of Boeing's extensive experience in bomber design.[8] As already noted, the contractor had been encouraged to investigate the development of higher-performance aircraft, long before its XB–55 was canceled. Boeing, therefore, had worked on a series of new turbojet designs in order to compare them with its original turboprop studies and with the XB–55 in particular. Aware of these facts, the Air Force issued termination orders for the XB–55 in such a way as to allow maximum benefit from the studies which Boeing had in progress. Mockup and detailed engineering on the XB–55 were stopped, but the study reports and tunnel tests then underway

---

[7] Requirements for a new medium bomber, submitted to industry in October 1947, proved Boeing the undisputed winner of the ensuing competition.

[8] The experimental B–47 earned a first development contract in December 1945; the XB–52, in July 1948.

were to be completed. Moreover, the Air Force soon increased the scope of the Boeing tunnel tests and asked for firm study results.

Competitive Proposals   February 1951

On 26 January 1951, following completion of GEBO II, Convair offered to develop and manufacture a long-range supersonic reconnaissance bomber.[9] The proposal, named Project MX–1626 by AMC, was accepted promptly by the Air Force. However, this did not spell the end of Boeing's related work. In fact, the Air Force endorsed in February the Phase I development of 2 reconnaissance bombers through wind tunnel testing, engineering design, and mockup. The Boeing project was designated MX–1712 and was initiated on 26 February by Letter Contract AF33(038)–21388. A similar document, Letter Contract AF33(038)–21250, had been signed by Convair on the 17th. It called for a 107,000-pound reconnaissance bomber, with a delta configuration and 2-stage system (release and retrieval) based on the parasite principle, using the B–36 as the carrier. The MX–1626's basic difference from the other Convair configurations studied in GEBO II lay in the use of 3 engines, 2 in wing nacelles and the third in a droppable bomb pod. In contrast, the Boeing MX–1712 project proposed a conventional, 200,000-pound medium-range reconnaissance bomber, capable of supersonic flight over a limited portion of its mission. The Boeing design objective involved a 2,000-nautical mile radius, 200 miles of which would be flown at Mach 1.3 or more, and the balance at Mach 0.9. For shorter missions, the supersonic radius would increase, while range extension devices such as refueling or extended wing tips would lengthen the range for longer missions. Power was to come from 4 J67-type engines with afterburners, and the aircraft as projected was to be capable of delivering atomic or conventional bombs from altitudes of 45,000 to 50,000 feet. Sea-level missions were another possibility being considered.

Radical Change   December 1951

The parasite-carrier combination, proposed by Convair in early 1951, did not last long. As conceived, Project MX–1626's primary appeal

---

[9] Reconnaissance had not been mentioned before. Most likely, the Heavy Bomber Committee's year-old decision that the heavy bomber program be expanded to include reconnaissance, accounted for the Convair suggestion. As far as Boeing was concerned, reconnaissance, as an adjunct to bombing, was almost routine, the RB–47B being already on the drawing board in March 1951.

stemmed largely from the stringent fiscal restrictions of the post–World War II period.[10] Since money was lacking, the parasite-carrier concept appeared to be the most economical method for tackling the unconventional approach to the long-range, strategic bombing problem. During 1951, however, the Air Force started to view MX–1626 from a different angle. Both the B–36 carrier and parasite aircraft (officially designated B–58 in December 1952) would require complete navigation equipment; the 2 might not locate one another on the return course of the mission; and once rejoined, the composite aircraft would be more vulnerable to attack. Finally, the 2-aircraft attack system would be far more expensive to build and maintain than would a single bomber. Hence, in December 1951, the MX–1626 configuration was altered drastically. The parasite mode of range extension was dropped in favor of air refueling; the third and expendable engine in the bomb pod of the original configuration was eliminated, while afterburners were added to the aircraft's remaining 2 engines. Moreover, a landing gear was provided to allow take-off at a gross weight of about 126,000 pounds, and the number of crewmen was increased from 2 to 3 (1 pilot, 1 navigator-bombardier, and 1 defense-systems operator).

General Operational Requirements   1 February 1952

Concurrent with the elimination of flaws from the initial MX–1626 configuration, the Air Force further defined what would be generally expected of the future Supersonic Aircraft Bomber (SAB). USAF planning culminated on 1 February 1952 with the publication of General Operational Requirement (GOR) SAB–51.[11] This highly ambitious document called for a versatile, multi-mission strategic reconnaissance bomber capable of carrying 10,000 pounds of bombs, and of operating in daylight or darkness under "all-weather" conditions. Production should take place within 5 years. There were many other sophisticated requirements. The aircraft had to be able to cover almost 5,000 miles (4,000 nautical miles) both ways, with a single outbound inflight refueling; about half that distance without refueling. It also needed supersonic speed at altitudes of 50,000 feet or more, and high subsonic speeds when flying at low levels. It was to be easy to fly, highly reliable, and should require few personnel for operation and maintenance. Although due to feature the best electronic countermeasures systems,

---

[10] Like the Glenn L. Martin Company, Convair at one point was also working on a Navy proposal for a money-saving carrier-based medium-range bomber.

[11] This actually was GOR No. 8 (SAB–51). It added reconnaissance to the requirements embodied in a December 1951 GOR, which only called for a strategic bombardment system.

"economy from the standpoint of cost to our national resources" was a must. The GOR also emphasized that the future aircraft should be small, a specification apparently suggested in a recent Rand Corporation study which stressed that by minimizing size, one reduced the radar reflectivity of the vehicle and the probabilities of interception by surface-to-air missiles. As it turned out, this "small size" requirement was to influence greatly subsequent decisions.

Revised Requirements   26 February 1952

As customary, the GOR of February 1952 led to a development directive. Also, detailed military characteristics were issued for the benefit of interested contractors. There was a significant change, however. The directive (No. 34, published on 26 February 1952) created a precedent in that it sharply curtailed the general requirements formulated earlier in the month. The revision, formalized on 1 September 1952 by GOR No. 1 (SAB-52-l), stood to reason. As pointed out by Gen. Donald N. Yates, Director of Research and Development, Office of the Deputy Chief of Staff for Development, it was unrealistic to expect the rapid development of a high-altitude, long-range, supersonic reconnaissance bomber that could also be used for low-level missions requiring high subsonic speeds. Some aeronautical engineers argued this could be done with the proper technological efforts and plenty of money, but many in the Air Staff were not convinced. Following discussions with members of the Air Council and representatives of Air Research and Development Command (ARDC), SAC, the Rand Corporation, and the Scientific Advisory Board, the Air Force endorsed General Yates' recommendation. Directive No. 34, as finally worded, only called for the development of a high-altitude, long-range supersonic strategic reconnaissance bomber. However, a low-altitude strategic bomber was still needed. Even though this would be costly, the Air Force issued a separate directive for development of such an aircraft,[12] insisting in both cases that the 2 airplanes should be available by 1957.

Early Problems   1952

If refining and slimming down requirements were not an easy matter,

---

[12] The Martin Company won the competition that ensued with a design featuring a delta-wing planform, but the Air Force canceled the project in 1957. SAC's confidence that the B-47 was rugged enough for low-level bombing accounted in part for the cancellation. Another factor was the Air Force's anticipation that modified B-52s would eventually fulfill the requirements wanted in a low-altitude bomber.

The delta-wing B–58 Hustler was powered by 4 General Electric J79 turbojet engines.

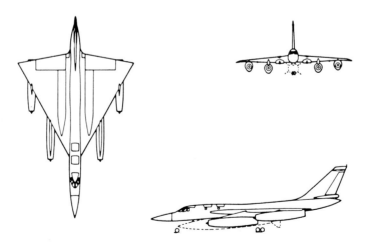

financing the Phase I development of 2 parallel projects was even more difficult during a period of austerity. Boeing's MX-1712 benefited to some extent from the XB-55 cancellation and did not seem to face a serious money problem, but the financial support of Convair's MX-1626 was another story. To begin with, although the 2 letter contracts of February 1951 were fairly similar, Convair's document failed to provide sufficient funds to carry the MX-1626 through the mockup stage. Complicating the situation further, confusing events began to emerge in early 1952. In January, the Air Staff asked Convair to prepare package program costs for specific numbers of airplanes (25, 50, and 100). Estimates were to cover all development and production costs, except for the engines which were to be furnished by the government. Tentative delivery schedules also were required. In late February, however, the MX-1626 project was nearly canceled. The emergency transfer of $100,000 provided some relief, but the MX-1626 status remained precarious until 15 May, when a supplemental agreement to the deficient letter contract assured the MX-1626's General Phase I Development Program of $2,800,000. Meanwhile, the Air Force faced another dilemma. Back in 1951, although reasonably sure that Convair and Boeing offered the best hopes to secure quickly the urgently needed supersonic bomber, AMC had requested informal proposals from other aircraft producers including Douglas, Lockheed, Martin, and North American. The field narrowed, when only 2 of the last 4 contractors submitted proposals. Moreover, the problem was resolving itself since these last proposals did not arouse any special interest. Nevertheless, now that the requirements were changed, the Air Force considered whether the entire aeronautical industry should again be queried.

Preliminary Conclusions   1952

Early in 1952, the Air Force agreed with Brig. Gen. John W. Sessums, ARDC Deputy for Development, that it would be better to forego additional competition along traditional lines. Time and money would be saved in selecting contractors on the basis of experience, facilities, and the intrinsic value of the proposals already submitted. Shortly thereafter, the Wright Air Development Center was given permission to eliminate or reorient current projects. In short, Boeing and Convair were instructed to stop their present investigations and to begin new Phase I designs of their respective projects (MX-1712 and MX-1626), as dictated by Directive 34. Maj. Gen. Donald L. Putt, the newly appointed Wright Air Development Center Commander, also informed the 2 contractors that contracts would be issued in the fall of 1952 for the detailed design and mockup of each supersonic bomber. Evaluation and selection of the winning design would follow in February or

March 1953, which clearly indicated that obtaining production aircraft by 1957 would never be feasible.[13]

Meanwhile, events were determining the shape of the program. To begin with, Development Directive 34 strongly reemphasized the Supersonic Aircraft Bomber design priorities of minimum size and high performance (altitude and speed), already specified by the GOR of February 1952. Secondly, both GOR and the directive called for the application of the weapon system concept, an objective with which Convair was familiar.[14] This concept, in essence, acknowledged that the increasing complexity of weapons no longer permitted the isolated and compartmented development of equipment and components which, when put together in a structural shell, formed an aircraft or a missile. It integrated the design of the entire weapon system, making each component compatible with the others, and put heavy responsibilities on the prime contractor. The weapon system concept coincided with a significant deviation from previous practices. Instead of accepting technology as the determining factor against which a mission could be fitted, the Air Force had decided that mission objectives now should come first and technology could be made to satisfy them. In any case, other events occurred in mid-1952, which also seemed to favor the delta-wing configuration. By that time, the 2 contractors had made considerable progress in their efforts to conform with the requirements set forth in Directive 34. In the process, Convair's former MX-1626 had become project MX-1964, while Boeing's MX-1712 was now known as the MX-1965. Wright Air Development Center's analysis of both designs in the summer of 1952 yielded no startling discoveries. The center tentatively concluded that the 2 designs appeared to meet performance and size requirements, but that extensive development work would be needed to give either configuration the necessary engines and the required integrated electronic system. Soon afterwards, the center's Weapons Systems Division proposed that recent plans be changed. The division's officials felt that selecting 1 of the 2 contractors before design and mockup completion would be advantageous to the Air Force. It would eliminate the many problems created by simultaneous development programs, as well as the need to develop costly electronic and control systems for 2 aircraft. Moreover, an earlier selection would save additional time and money, thereby allowing a more extensive

---

[13] Assuming all went well, Wright Air Development Center officials speculated, a prototype might perhaps fly in 1957.

[14] The so-called "1954 Interceptor," an upshot of the Convair XF-92, soon symbolized the difficulties involved. It marked the first attempt to apply the weapon system concept, and the concept's practical defeat. Yet, it eventually led to Convair's production of the F-102 and F-106, 2 most-effective and long-lasting fighter-interceptors.

development of the selected system. Since Project MX–1965 was lagging slightly behind the Convair MX–1964, such recommendations could hardly be expected to help Boeing's prospects.

Contractor Selection   18 November 1952

In September final evaluation of the competing designs by the Wright Air Development Center left little doubt about the forthcoming decision. The center thought that the Boeing MX–1965 design would produce either an aircraft of small size with mediocre supersonic speeds or one so large as to almost preclude any supersonic capability.[15] On the other hand, the MX–1964 design, already nicknamed the "Hustler" by Convair, provided the more promising means of achieving supersonic speeds with a weapon system of minimum size. In addition, the center felt that the Convair approach best satisfied the "spirit" of the Development Planning Objective for Strategic Air Operations during the period 1956–1960. This objective, issued by the Air Force on 29 May 1952, favored a small bomber and underlined that future strategic aerial warfare could be most economically and effectively accomplished by a "combination system that incorporates a tanker cargo airplane for refueling in flight the combat zone airplane." The small bomber concept, embodied by the Development Planning Objective of May 1952, reflected the opinion of Col. Bernard A. Schriever, the USAF Assistant for Development Planning in the Office of the Deputy Chief of Staff for Development,[16] and had been endorsed by the Air Force Council and Gen. Hoyt S. Vandenberg, Chief of Staff of the Air Force. But this Development Planning Objective of May 1952 also ran counter to many established principles. SAC officials and particularly General LeMay, who by 1952 had been heading the command for several years, generally favored large bombers, capable of greater ranges. "Even though the best intercontinental bomber available requires some refueling," SAC insisted, "it does not follow necessarily that the optimum system requires a bomber which has no intercontinental capability without refueling." The command argued that "high performance alone" could "never insure mission success"

---

[15] The Boeing supersonic bomber design was conventional. It featured wings swept at 35 degrees, an internal bomb bay, a fore and aft bicycle landing gear which, like that of the B–52, retracted into the fuselage. It called for 4 engines, similar to those proposed for the Convair bomber, but integral with the wing, 2 on each side, tucked inboard against the fuselage. It projected a supersonic speed of Mach 1.8 at 55,000, but promised plenty of room for its 3-man crew. Maximum take-off weight was about 156,000 pounds.

[16] Colonel Schriever was promoted to lieutenant general in 1959 and to full general on 1 July 1961, when he headed the newly organized Air Force Systems Command.

against targets defended by modern interceptors and surface-to-air missiles, and pointed out that the small supersonic bomber's lack of range would prevent it from operating without refueling from most forward operating bases. Also, crew members would be very confined in such a small bomber. Finally, instead of fostering economy and reliability, combining unconventional design and operational techniques made "it entirely possible that the system might prove operationally unsuitable." SAC's arguments notwithstanding, a decision was near. In an unusual step, the decision makers would totally disregard SAC's concern. In late October, following ARDC's thorough review of the Wright Air Development Center's conclusions, Lt. Gen. Earle E. Partridge, the ARDC Commander, recommended to Headquarters USAF that the competition between Boeing and Convair be stopped immediately. General Partridge noted that the MX–1964 supersonic drag and gross weight figures appeared optimistic, and if true, this would further limit the aircraft's range. Also, costs had not been considered properly, and the forecast operational date would inevitably slip, perhaps to 1959. Nevertheless, the ARDC Commander endorsed prompt selection of the Convair project and asked that accelerated development of General Electric's J53 engine (from which the J79 derived) be authorized without delay. This was approved by the Weapons Board, the Air Force Council, and by General Vandenberg on 18 November 1952. Soon informed that the design competition was ended, Boeing reportedly took the bad news well.

Design Refinement   1952–1953

The Air Force selection of Convair over Boeing was not a blanket endorsement of the MX–1964 design. It took several months and many consultations between Convair, National Advisory Committee on Aeronautics, AMC, ARDC, and Wright Air Development Center personnel to settle on a definite configuration which, as it turned out, was subjected to many later revisions. These initial delays were not unfounded. Development problems with the Convair F–102 interceptor were confirming the Air Force's suspicion that the contractor had failed to make proper allowance for the aerodynamic drag of a delta-wing aircraft, be it a fighter or a bomber. Moreover, the area-rule concept of aircraft design,[17] discovered by National Advisory Committee on Aeronautics researcher Richard T. Whitcomb, had been verified during December 1952 in the agency's new transonic wind tunnels. This concept held that interference drag at transonic

---

[17] A prescribed method of design for obtaining minimum zero-lift drag for a given aerodynamic configuration, such as a wing-body configuration, at a given speed.

speed depended almost entirely on the distribution of the aircraft's total cross sectional area along the direction of flight. The solution was to indent the fuselage over the wing to equalize the cross section areas (and thus the volume) at all stations, thereby producing the so-called "coke bottle" or "wasp waist" configuration. Yet, as in the F–102's case, Convair did not accept the Whitcomb findings until its own engineers had confirmed their validity. Another delaying factor was the absence of military characteristics, which were deferred until the fall of 1953.

Specific Planning   1952–1953

Although the MX–1964 design was yet to be finalized, the Air Force proceeded with specific plans. In December 1952, the Deputy Chief of Staff for Development endorsed a production schedule developed by the Wright Center. This schedule was based on the 4-year procurement of 244 B/RB–58s (more than twice the final total). Thirty of these aircraft, with the first one due for delivery in January 1956, would be used for testing, while preparations would be made for full scale production of a version incorporating all test-dictated changes. The 30 initial planes would then be reworked on the production line into the approved configuration. This plan, drawn from the "Cook-Craigie production policy," was expected to eliminate the faults in a basic design before many aircraft had been built and to speed the acquisition of operationally effective weapon systems.[18] Recent experiences seemed to justify such an approach. Building aircraft prototypes before selecting one of them, as occasionally done, had proved costly and time consuming. Moreover, the selected prototype, once produced, has often still been found to have design flaws that needed correction. In any case, the Cook-Craigie philosophy, if not an integral part of the weapon system concept, fitted it perfectly. The weapon system concept itself promoted significant changes and therefore more planning.

In early 1953, General Putt, ARDC's new Vice Commander, announced the Air Force's revised management tasks. The B–58 weapon system would require a minimum of government-furnished equipment since the prime contractor would be responsible for system design and engineering

---

[18] The Cook-Craigie production plan was actually a mere concept, developed in the late forties by USAF Major Generals Laurence C. Craigie, Deputy Chief of Staff for Development, and Orval R. Cook, Deputy Chief of Staff for Materiel. They both knew this concept could be expensive and thought "it was only applicable where you had a high degree of confidence that you were going to go into production." The F–102, a by-product of the "1954 Interceptor," bared some of the pitfalls of the Cook-Craigie plan for early tooling. In October 1953, when testing established unequivocally that important changes had to be made in the F–102's design, 20,000 of the 30,000 tools already purchased by Convair had to be discarded.

and would deal directly with subcontractors to acquire major components. The Wright Air Development Center, now headed by Maj. Gen. Albert Boyd, would contract for major components "only when limitations of industry, operations, or logistic considerations force the USAF to control source and/or methodology." Even then, such components would have to be designed, built, and tested to Convair's specifications. In short, the Air Force's role was to monitor the prime contractor's plans and progress; to approve specifications as well as subcontractors, and to supply the money. It also retained the right to veto any developments that could cause operational or logistical problems. The Air Force management of the B–58 weapon system would be exercised at the Wright Air Development Center by a 20-man joint project office, made up of ARDC and AMC representatives.

Contractual Arrangements   1953

Contracting proved to be a difficult endeavor, far more complex than usual. Limited experience with the weapon system concept prolonged negotiations, as the Air Force and Convair worked out specific provisions to define each party's prerogatives and responsibilities. These clauses became part of Convair's letter contract on 12 February 1953, when a supplemental agreement was signed.[19] This was an important turning point, indicating the B/RB–58 program was getting under way, with the B–58 mockup scheduled for the end of the summer, while that of the reconnaissance version would follow in the fall of 1953. The amendment also gave Convair $22 million to cover pre-production planning costs and the acquisition of long-lead time tools and equipment. Yet, it failed to resolve immediately a few basic problems. As single manager, Convair believed that compensation for its additional managerial efforts should be incorporated in the program's direct cost. The Air Materiel Command disagreed, contending that such payments should be added to the overhead administrative costs of present and future contracts, on a yearly pro-rated basis. AMC also postponed total approval of the funds requested by Convair to expand its Fort Worth facilities, causing the contractor to spend $500,000 of its own to secure extra office space.

Design Approval   20 March 1953

The Air Force selected a firm configuration for the B/RB–58 and

---

[19] This was the fifth and so far most significant amendment to Letter Contract AF33(038)–21250. The contract itself was not finalized until the end of 1955, even though the letter contract dated back to February 1951.

authorized Convair to begin work on each full-scale mockup version. The approved design incorporated the changes dictated by the National Advisory Committee for Aeronautics's transonic area rule. Specifically, the airplane cross-sectional area was redistributed longitudinally to minimize the compressibility drag rise encountered at transonic speeds. This had been accomplished by fuselage redesign, housing the engines in 4 staggered nacelles, and adding a 10-degree trailing edge angle to the wing, which also increased the wing area to 1,542 square feet. In addition, the wing's leading edge had been cambered and twisted to reduce drag at lift.

Immediate Problems   May 1953

Approval of Convair's new design did not ease the Air Force's concern about the engine of the future aircraft. As summed up by General Partridge, every effort had to be made to safeguard the successful development of the J79 upon which the "vitally important B–58 and other projects will be so heavily dependent."[20] Equally concerned, General Putt informed the General Electric Company that the J79 project controlled "to a very major degree, this country's ability to defend itself during the 1958-1965 period." "This responsibility," General Putt wrote, "should not be treated lightly." The fact remained that the development histories of American and British turbojets showed that 4 to 5 years were needed from the beginning of design to completion of the 150-hour engine test. This was confirmed by the General Electric engineers, who insisted that delivery of the J79 engine could not be scheduled until July 1957. Based on experience, the Air Force thought this schedule might still be unrealistic. The solution therefore was to equip early B–58s with a version of the already-tested Pratt and Whitney J57, but this temporary expedient also would pose problems.

Development Engineering Inspection   17–18 August 1953

This first development engineering inspection replaced the formal mockup inspection which, obviously, had been scheduled to occur too soon for major subsystems to be available.[21] Nevertheless, except for the missing

---

[20] The J79 turbojet became the world's first production Mach 2 engine. In addition to the B–58, it eventually powered the Lockheed F–104, the McDonnell F–4, and the North American Aviation A–5.

[21] A second development engineering inspection took place on 29 September 1953. It covered portions of the RB–58 that differed from the B–58. Also held in Fort Worth, the inspection did not cover major subsystems, most of them still remaining a long way off.

components (for which space was provided), the B–58 mockup was complete. Air Force inspectors, including representatives from SAC, were able to get a good idea of the new weapon system, by then known as Configuration II. The inspection group, and General LeMay in particular, asked for many changes, but none appeared vital. Just the same, as the inspection neared its end, General Boyd most likely expressed everyone's opinion in stating: "It is a radical design, and we must be careful in following through with these technical developments." He added, however, that Convair seemed to have done a very good job.

Military Characteristics ll   September 1953

Military characteristics (No. 345) for the B–58 high-altitude bombardment system, at long last issued in September 1953, did not bring any great surprises. The requirements fairly matched the specifications proposed by Convair in August 1952, and the lesser USAF demands embodied in the September GOR of the same year. Yet the new characteristics required the carrying of payloads in addition to the warheads originally specified. While this requirement had been anticipated, it implied that greater performance standards would have to be achieved in order to preserve the aircraft's range, which was unchanged.[22] There were a few other changes, most of which stemmed from SAC's criticism. For instance, the side-by-side seating that General LeMay preferred to the tandem seating arrangement of most Air Force planes was not provided, but the B–58 would at least contain a jump seat[23] for one of the crew members to sit alongside of the pilot during take-off and landing. The new characteristics also included some concessions. Maximum dash speeds at altitudes of 55,000 feet were reduced slightly, and the B–58's operational date was postponed from 1957 to 1958 or later.

Increasing Difficulties   1953

Much to the disappointment of ARDC, and despite application of the area rule, on-going wind tunnel tests of Configuration II continued to

---

[22] The B–58 would carry 20,000 pounds of munitions, a 13,000-pound increase. This could be expected to entail a reduction of the aircraft's fuel load and, therefore, a significant loss of range.

[23] Subsequently omitted, for lack of space.

produce high-speed drag figures. Stability test results also caused concern. The elevons and rudder were not inherently balanced and depended on the rigidity of their actuating systems to prevent flutter. The engine positions and the anticipated Mach 2.1 speed similarly produced some qualms. In addition, as first identified by the development engineering inspection of August 1953, it had become obvious that the compartmented pod, housing the bomb and fuel, needed to be entirely redesigned.[24] Finally, other changes had to be made to satisfy the anticipated new requirements of the September military characteristics. Meanwhile, other problems loomed ahead. Subsystem development, never considered to be easy, promised to be especially difficult in the B-58's case.[25]

The future aircraft had already been acknowledged as a most complex, highly integrated, and mutually interdependent weapon system. The Air Force, consequently, kept a close watch on every component's progress. In December 1953, it asked for studies to determine if the Arma Company's A-3A Fire Control System could serve as a back-up for the Emerson Company's Active Defense System earmarked for the B-58. The Air Force also wanted to know if a modified M-2 Bombing System, built by the International Business Machine Corporation, could possibly substitute for the sophisticated Navigation-Bombing and Missile Guidance System, being developed by the Sperry Gyroscope Company. Aware of the state-of-the-art's current and foreseeable limits, the Air Force attached great importance to the B-58's forthcoming bombing and navigation system. How a B-58 would find and hit its targets, given its speed and altitude design characteristics, was a difficult question to answer.[26] The problem was serious enough to justify organizing a special committee to monitor the development of B-58 bombing and navigation procedures.[27]

---

[24] This was confirmed in October 1953, when the Air Force authorized Convair to shorten the B-58 pod and to sling it on a pylon under the fuselage.

[25] As early as 1951, the Air Material Command stressed that it took much more time to design, develop, and produce new equipment such as guns, engines, and fire-control systems than it did to produce new airframes.

[26] Worrisome comparisons came to mind. For example, in order to obtain a 3-minute bomb run for a B-17 operating at 25,000 feet, the bombardier would have to get on his target about ll miles away; in the same vein, with a B-58 operating at 40,000 feet at an airspeed of 450 knots, the bombardier would have to spot and track his target from at least 25 miles away. But to have a 3-minute bomb run at the B-58's designed speed of Mach 2 and at an altitude higher than 50,000 feet, the bombardier would have to be on target some 66 to 70 miles away.

[27] This committee consisted of representatives from the Air Staff, ARDC, SAC, Air Training Command, and the contractors. In early 1954, the B-58 Joint Project Office considered the adoption of the monitoring committee idea for other component systems as well.

New Setbacks 1953-1954

Configuration III, as devised by Convair, did not fare as well as expected. The reconfigured B/RB-58 featured a new bomb and fuel pod that had been shortened from 89 feet to 30 feet, and was now detached from the fuselage and suspended on a pylon. To compensate for the smaller amount of fuel carried by the pod, external fuel tanks had been added to the wing tips. The search radar had also been removed from the pod and placed into the fuselage nose. There were other alterations and deletions. The droppable nose gear was eliminated, and the positions of the bombardier-navigator and the defensive systems operator were reversed. For lack of space, Configuration III omitted a jump seat, a new requirement of the military characteristics. In any case, the Air Force did not share Convair's confidence that the reconfigured B/RB-58 would achieve better performance. Early 1954 tests in the tunnels of the Wright Air Development Center and National Advisory Committee on Aeronautics soon confirmed that the contractor's estimates once again were wrong. In addition, a problem thought to be solved had reappeared. In 1953, the contractor and the Air Force had decided to abandon the previously endorsed split nacelle engine arrangement in favor of 2 strut-mounted Siamese nacelles. The change would save weight, ease engine maintenance, and facilitate retrofit of J57-powered aircraft with new J79s.[28] Recent tests, however, indicated that Siamese nacelles induced extra drag on the composite (pod- or missile-carrying) B-58, although the airframe itself was affected almost equally by either type of nacelles. In practical terms, this meant a return to split nacelles, more testing, more delays, and postponement of the Configuration III's mockup inspection from the initially scheduled May date to September 1954.

Program Reorientation 30 April 1954

Based on a preliminary review of the B/RB-58's third configuration, the Wright Air Development Center finally agreed on 4 December 1953 that Convair could begin the construction of airframe components. Yet, subsequent testing of Configuration III qualified this hopeful decision. In March, the B-58 program underwent a drastic change; research and development came to the fore at the expense of production, and the number of B-58s originally contemplated was reduced from 244 to 30, with the latter quota

---

[28] Unknown to all at the time, this last advantage would have been of no value since the B-58 schedule slipped and production of the J79 engine caught up with the Convair program.

emphatically referred to as "test vehicles." Moreover, long lead time items such as ground training devices and maintenance and test equipment were canceled. Secretary of the Air Force Harold E. Talbott approved the redirected program on 30 April 1954, and authorized release of the procurement funds necessary to support it.[29] Yet, as illustrated by the June procurement directive that followed, the Air Force again qualified its authorization. The directive freed about $190 million of fiscal year 1955 money for 13 test aircraft, but no procurement of any kind could be initiated prior to determining a firm configuration. As it happened, these 13 aircraft were the only B-58s covered by the first definitive contract, at long last signed in December 1955.[30]

Fourth Configuration   September 1954

Crucial events preceded Convair's achievement of its fourth B/RB-58 configuration. A development engineering inspection of Configuration III, held in mid-May, was a near fiasco. Not only did it endorse the poor results of past and concurrent wind tunnel tests, but SAC representatives insisted that the width of the configuration be altered to allow side-by-side seating of the pilot and the navigator-bombardier, a change considered totally impossible. But as the future of the B-58 appeared at its gloomiest, important research progressed. National Advisory Committee on Aeronautics aerodynamicist R. T. Jones at first had been mystified by the problems of airframes designed to the transonic area rule and tested at supersonic speeds. However, by the summer of 1954, he had ascertained that the position and the extent of the fuselage indentation was indicated by the aircraft's designed speed. This time, the Convair engineers did not question Jones' discovery. In August, Configuration III's fuselage was aligned to the modified transonic area rule for supersonic speeds.[31]

---

[29] Secretary Talbott succeeded Thomas K. Finletter as Secretary of the Air Force on 4 February 1953. Mr. Finletter had replaced Mr. Symington, the first Secretary of the Air Force, on 24 April 1950.

[30] The remaining 17 test vehicles were carried on another procurement contract, finally initiated by a mid-1956 letter contract. Indicative of the uncertainties that surrounded the costly B-58 program, it took 5 definitive contracts to get less than half of the number of B-58s first ordered. Furthermore, most letter contracts ended with an unusually large number of supplements and amendments. The whole procedure eventually resulted in substantial amounts of termination costs.

[31] For a transonic body, the area rule is applied by subtracting from or adding to its cross-sectional area distribution normal to the airstream at various stations so as to make its cross-sectional area distribution approach that of an ideal body of minimum drag; for a

Officially referred to as the B/RB–58A configuration, the new design featured other innovations. External wing fuel tanks were eliminated, the tail area was extended to 160 square feet, and the 4 engines were suspended by separate pylons, 2 under each wing. Convair was sure that the new B/RB–58A configuration would satisfy the performance requirements of the military characteristics of September 1953, but conceded that minor refinements might still be needed. The contractor also asserted that its new configuration was "the best design supportable by the current state-of-the-art." However, delivery of the first test aircraft, already delayed by the program reorientation, would slip further if production was not authorized soon. Still in a quandary, the Air Force doubted that the new configuration would meet Convair's expectations, and refused to approve the model specifications. Even so, the Air Force in November asked ARDC to develop 2 important back-up systems, one for the Sperry bombing and navigation system, the other for the Emerson tail defense armament. That same month, after learning that Convair was about to reduce its labor force, the Air Force finally authorized limited fabrication of the new airframe.

Near-Cancellation   1954–1955

After seeming to improve, the B/RB–58A's future once again appeared on the brink of disaster. A chief factor in the new crisis was SAC's dislike of the proposed aircraft. True to character, General LeMay had not changed his mind.[32] In fact, based on the command's arguments of November 1952, a mid-1954 staff study, prepared by Maj. Gen. John P. McConnell, SAC's Director of Plans,[33] had excluded the B–58 from the 51-wing bomber force proposed for the period 1958-1965. At first unimpressed by the SAC

---

supersonic body, the sectional areas are frontal projections of areas intercepted by planes inclined at the Mach angle.

[32] At the urging of General LeMay, the Air Force in July 1954 instructed ARDC to initiate the research and development of an intercontinental bomber to succeed the B–52. This eventually promoted North American's ill-fated B–70, a bomber which had its origin in May 1953. Boeing was the recipient of the May 1953 study contract for a nuclear- or chemical-powered weapon system of intercontinental range. In 1955, the Air Force Council agreed that development of a nuclear-powered aircraft would not negate the requirement for a bomber using conventional fuel, and weapon systems 125 (nuclear-powered aircraft) and 110A (B–70) assumed their individual identities. Reminiscent of the B–58's case, North American in 1957 won the B–70 design competition over Boeing.

[33] Promoted to four-star rank in 1962, General McConnell served as Chief of Staff of the United States Air Force from 1 February 1965 through 31 July 1969.

omission, the Air Staff in late 1954 was having second thoughts. In early 1955, after General LeMay had directly confirmed to Gen. Nathan F. Twining (Air Force Chief of Staff since 30 June 1953), that SAC wanted no B–58 aircraft for its operational inventory, the Air Force endorsed a thorough review of the program. A B–58 review board was appointed in February and chaired by Maj. Gen. Clarence S. Irvine, AMC Deputy for Production. The board faced the difficult task of recommending whether the B–58 program should be continued, modified, or canceled. General Boyd, one of the board's members, admitted that Convair's latest configuration might again not meet all requirements of the military characteristics, but still believed, that the B–58 should be built, even if the Air Force could not use it as originally intended. The B–58, the Wright Air Development Center Commander argued, represented major technical advances and, therefore, entailed technical uncertainties and the risk of high costs. These uncertainties would remain until "we have flown such an aircraft," and "we must accept such a risk sooner or later."

The board studied anew other valued opinions that had been discussed in previous months. As already stated by Lt. Gen. Thomas S. Power, in charge of ARDC since April 1954,[34] the B–58 was the first attempt to build a supersonic bomber (making in retrospect the production of supersonic fighters look relatively simple), and this task demanded extensive knowledge of aircraft materials and aerodynamic heating. The board's chairman agreed that from this standpoint the program was probably worth the money it had already consumed. Nevertheless, after an investment of 2 years and almost $200 million, no tangible achievements could be claimed. If the B–58 should now be canceled, the money would actually be lost, whereas another $300 million might suffice to build the 13 test-aircraft included in the reoriented program of April 1954. There were other pro-B–58 arguments. In his testimony before the review board, Convair's chief engineer maintained that, if allowed, the B–58 effort would produce the earliest and most inexpensive integrated weapon system, as well as a very outstanding bomber. At worst, he added, the B–58 would be superior to the existing B–47 medium bomber, a contention fully supported by General Power, who also noted that the aircraft might fulfill Tactical Air Command's requirements for a short-range attack bomber.

On 10 March 1955, the review board submitted its recommendations to the Air Force Council and to the Secretary of the Air Force. Aware that whatever suggestion was adopted could have far-reaching effects for years to

---

[34] Deputy Commander of SAC between 1948 and 1954, General Power left ARDC after 3 years. He acquired his fourth star in mid-1957 and returned to SAC, this time as General LeMay's successor.

come, the board took no chances. First, it emphatically recommended that the reoriented program be continued on a modified basis. Only 13 test-vehicles would be ordered; they would be equipped from the start with J79 engines; and all back-up subsystems would be eliminated in order to reduce costs. The board observed that Convair could be asked to submit several new design proposals, one for a B-58 tactical bomber, one for special reconnaissance aircraft, and one for a long range B-58 interceptor. Finally, to complete developments vital to the design and operation of future strategic bomber weapon systems, the board did not exclude another possibility. Instead of limiting the program to 13 test-vehicles, it might be wise to buy also a number of B-58s for the operational inventory.

Development Reendorsement   June 1955

Development of 13 B-58 test aircraft, and nothing more, was approved by Secretary Talbott on 2 June 1955. The Secretary's approval carried stern, if not unexpected conditions. The Air Force wanted the program's costs to be reduced, and it wanted the aircraft to begin flying before November 1956. Furthermore, ARDC was to plan the aircraft's utilization in light of the Air Force's new objectives. In short, there no longer was any question of producing a high-altitude, manned strategic bomber and reconnaissance weapon system out of the B-58 test-aircraft. The program's only purpose was to promote research and development.[35] The Air Force needed to learn more about the aerodynamic problems of sustained supersonic flights at high altitudes, and it needed to test subsystems and components for future weapon systems. There were no delays in satisfying most of Secretary Talbott's demands. AMC had been studying the aircraft's cost problem for several months. An April estimate showed that $554 million would cover 13 B-58s, 31 pods, all engines, other government-furnished equipment and support, as well as Convair's fee. With the aircraft now strictly earmarked for research and development, various items could be deleted. This would save about $50 million and bring total costs close to the Air Force's tentative maximum. Convair seemed unabashed by the cut of its program, believing time would work in its favor. Hence, it went all out to match AMC's cost reductions, while projecting costs for the production of up to 500 aircraft. In mid-June, AMC authorized Convair to resume work on development engineering, tool fabrication, airframe parts, and the like. At month's end, the contractor felt confident it could fly a B-58 by November 1956, which

---

[35] SAC was pleased with the decision, but thought a 13-aircraft research and development program was larger than necessary.

it did. Meanwhile, personnel of the B-58 project office coordinated with representatives of various offices to identify non-essential B-58 subsystems and components, while preserving the development of any B-58 hardware that could benefit other projects.[36]

Decision Reversal   22 August 1955

Scheduled for production in December 1952, an object of indecision in April 1954, practically canceled 10 months later, and relegated to research and development in June 1955, the B-58 project was yet to undergo another major change. Abruptly, on 22 August 1955, the B-58 weapon system once again emerged as a production candidate. The decision, approved personally by General Twining, climaxed weeks of debates.[37] General Putt, now Deputy Chief of Staff for Development, had helped to initiate the program and still professed the B-58 could be "a useful SAC tool." General Irvine, the new Deputy Chief of Staff for Materiel, and others on the Air Force Council shared General Putt's opinion. However, attempts to sway General LeMay failed. This failure most probably accounted for the production directive's unusual wording. The directive of 22 August 1955, calling for a wing of B-58s by mid-1960, was most specific in stressing the need for economy but made no mention of the wing's recipient or of SAC in particular.

Contractual Arrangements   1955-1956

Convair's Letter Contract AF33(038)-21250 of February 1951 was superseded in December 1955 by a definitive contract of the cost-plus-incentive-fee type. This gave Convair an additional $340 million for 13 aircraft, 31 pods, and all contractor-furnished equipment, bringing the contract's total value to about $540 million. The incentive fees depended on technical performance, weight control, and contractor adherence to cost and to delivery schedule. A second letter contract, AF33(600)-32841, issued on 25 May 1956, provided another $13.6 million to buy long-lead items and to maintain B-58 production at a minimum sustaining rate through October

---

[36] Included in such projects were the B-70, the nuclear-powered aircraft, and a tactical bomber logged as Weapon System 302A.

[37] Secretary Talbott did not participate in the debates. He resigned his position on 1 August 1955 and was succeeded two weeks later by Donald A. Quarles, who served as Secretary of the Air Force until 30 April 1957.

1956. The Air Force planned to decide in the fall of 1956,[38] if it should buy 17 more upper components (B–58 airframes), 17 powered bomb pods, 12 free fall bomb pods, 3 photo pods, and 3 electromagnetic data (ferret) pods. If it did, an extra $14.9 million of pre-production funds would be needed.

First Flight   11 November 1956

The initial B/RB–58 made its first flight on ll November 1956, taking off from the Convair Fort Worth facilities at Carswell AFB, Texas. A second flight on 14 November lasted one hour and was also described as successful. On both occasions, the maximum altitude reached was 30,000 feet, while the maximum speed did not exceed Mach 0.9. Supersonic speeds of Mach 1.6 and Mach 1.35, at altitudes of 35,000 feet, were first reached in a third flight on 4 December. The 3 flights were made by the same plane which, like several subsequent ones, was temporarily identified as a prototype (YB–58). In another departure from the usual, a characteristic that typified the B–58 program from the start, the YB–58 flights of late 1956 and early 1957 proved extremely important. Although testing had just begun, they undoubtedly influenced the Air Force's ensuing decisions.

Initial Testing   November 1956

By virtue of the weapon system concept adopted for the highly complex B/RB–58, the core of the testing program was altered. Also, the Air Force's insistence in 1952 that technological developments fit requirements inevitably affected testing.[39] As a result of such innovations, the flight testing program, an always thorough undertaking, acquired a new, time-consuming, and occasionally frustrating dimension.[40] The Category I tests, begun by the

---

[38] This planning was in line with the August 1955 decision to buy a wing of B–58s. As all along understood, this could only be done if there was sufficient evidence that the project was viable.

[39] The Air Force decision of 1952 was one of the many difficulties and momentary contradictions that plagued the B–58. A few years before, when the GEBO study was initiated, USAF engineers asked for more realistic military characteristics and advocated state-of-the-art design compromises.

[40] By chance, this coincided with the end of the 8-phase concept of testing, under which a new aircraft was designed, built, and tested first by the contractor, then at various ARDC centers, and finally transferred to a major Air Force command for operational utilization. The new testing program, although counting only 3 categories, did not degrade in any way the former program's scope (see B–52, p 225).

contractor in November 1956, accounted for almost 3,000 hours of flight tests by March 1962, and the destruction of 1 aircraft (the fifth YB-58, Serial No. 55–664) in November 1959. Furthermore, pod drops, aerial refueling, and a few other special tests, properly part of Category I, were completed under the Category II program, which did not officially start before March 1959.

New Controversy   1957

While the production decision of 22 August 1955 failed to indicate which command would use the new aircraft, it soon again became obvious that the B-58 lay in SAC's future.[41] As technological difficulties increasingly impaired the B-70 development, the command became more involved with the B-58. Willing to believe in the B-58's potential for improvement, SAC in late 1956 was actually preparing to participate in the aircraft's forthcoming test program. In the spring of 1957, imminent budget decisions affecting SAC aircraft nearly shattered the command's fragile cooperation. By that time, the B-58 had established itself as the world's fastest jet bomber. The Mach 2 speed success of the B-58, cited as one of the reasons for decreasing the B-52 production rate, did not satisfy General LeMay. He quickly reasserted his early 1955 position that no B-58s were needed. New studies, General LeMay explained, showed that the B-52G with its programmed penetration aids would be superior to the production-improved B-58 and to any "better" B-58, such as the new B-58B configuration proposed by Convair. This was particularly true from the standpoints of cost effectiveness and availability. As for the B-70, General LeMay added, there was no doubt that it would provide substantial improvements over the B-52G. Therefore, "the B-58 should be limited to a test program. Funding for procurement or model improvement testing should not be provided." The Air Staff bluntly disagreed with General LeMay, stating that it was "most desirable" that SAC get a supersonic bomber at an early date and that the decision had been made to buy a limited quantity of B-58s for the SAC inventory. In a mollifying gesture, the Air Staff underlined that the United States had to protect its technological lead over the Soviets as well as the

---

[41] General LeMay's lack of enthusiasm for the B-58 put the aircraft within the reach of the Tactical Air Command. It was a fact, however, that the Convair project had been geared from the start to meet SAC's performance criteria, that the recently flown YB-58 basically remained a SAC-configured aircraft, one that would require the time-consuming incorporation of many costly changes if it were to fulfill the Tactical Air Command mission. In early 1957, Gen. Otto P. Weyland, who headed the command, wanted a minimum of 2 B-58 wings, but the Air Staff disagreed.

money already invested in the B–58 program. Also, the B–58 would improve through normal growth, and the program's funding requirements would not affect the B–70's prospects.[42]

Critical Shortcomings   1957

Flight testing of the first 3 YB–58s, while accounting for some spectacular achievements,[43] brought to light several problems. The J79–GE–1 prototype engines, installed on the YB–58s pending certification of the J79–GE–5s,[44] had a number of flaws. Malfunctions in the fuel system sloshed the fuel around when the YB–58 accelerated or slowed down, impairing the aircraft's stability. Afterburner problems caused intermittent yawing at supersonic speeds. Of greater concern were already noted acoustical and sonic fatigue problems as well as excess vibration in the YJ79–GE–1 engines. The acoustical and sonic fatigue difficulties affected the aft area of the fuselage and would cause testing restrictions unless promptly solved. Fatigue created cracks along the rivet lines in the forward section of the fuselage. Since the cracks appeared after less than 50 hours of flight, replacing the YJ79–1 engine by the J79–5 would worsen the problem because the more powerful J79–5 would increase the sound level 10 decibels above the level induced by the YJ79–1. The engine vibrations also might affect components of the electronic equipment, installed in the fuselage's aft section and in the aft portion of the various droppable pods that were programmed for the aircraft. There were other difficulties of varying importance. The brake system was not satisfactory. Because of inadequate heat dissipation after braking, tire failures were frequent following landing at high gross weights and high-speed taxi runs. The upward-type of ejection seat put in the aircraft was unsafe at high speed, due to insufficient thrust. Convair tests of a more powerful, rocket-type catapult seat identified problems of another kind. Other sorts of ejection seats were being consid-

---

[42] Indeed, the proposed B–70 fell under a different time period. Nevertheless, by focusing attention on cost, the enormously expensive B–58 program did not help the cause of future high-performance manned bombers.

[43] By the end of 1957, the YB–58s had attained a maximum speed of Mach 2.11 at altitudes over 50,000 feet; made 2 successful pod drops from 42,000 feet at Mach 2 speeds; maintained a speed of more than Mach 1.15 during 91 minutes, and zoomed without pod from a speed of Mach 2 at 50,000 feet to a speed of Mach 1.13 at 68,000 feet.

[44] Even though General Electric's progress had negated the temporary use of Pratt & Whitney J57s, the J79–5's 150-hour preliminary flight rating test was not expected before year's end.

ered, with misgivings. The Air Force and the B–58 contractor greatly favored a capsule-type escape system, under development by both the Martin Company and the Goodyear Tire and Rubber Company, but time was of the essence. Finally, slippage in the bombing-navigation subsystem development program portended a serious delay in the delivery of the initial equipment. This would retard the B–58 flight-test program, as would shortages of spares for both the YJ79-1 and -5 engines.

Another Near-Cancellation   1958

In 1958, the B–58 program came under renewed scrutiny. The YB–58 could fly fast and high, but its range remained poor. With 1 refueling, the aircraft had a radius of 3,800 nautical miles; without refueling, the distance dropped by almost 40 percent. In addition, limited testing had already uncovered far too many problems. Configuration changes worked out between Convair and an 85-man team from ARDC, AMC, and SAC, would probably help a lot. Yet, changes were always costly. In August 1958, General Power, who had been heading SAC for over a year,[45] told the Air Staff that the B–58's deficiencies were exaggerated, a common occurrence, he remarked, when a program was expensive and it became difficult to obtain financial support. Believing that a mixed force of B–52s and B–58s was the best way to replace the B–47s,[46] General Power pointed out that the B–58's bombing and navigation system, already late, might become available sooner than expected since performance of the system's doppler radar was getting better. Agreeing with General Power that the B–58's early difficulties had been taken out of perspective, General White nevertheless cautioned that, should the program survive, the quantity of aircraft to be purchased in fiscal year 1959 would have to be reduced. The money thereby saved would pay for the most important changes and inevitable cost increases. By the end of December, photo reconnaissance, one of the B–58 program's initial requirements, was deleted. ME-1 pods and ground photo

---

[45] General Power acquired his fourth star and succeeded General LeMay as SAC's Commander-in-Chief in July 1957. General LeMay moved to Headquarters USAF as Vice Chief of Staff, under Gen. Thomas D. White, becoming Chief of Staff of the Air Force on 1 July 1961, when General White retired.

[46] General LeMay, although acknowledging in November 1957 that the mixed force concept was apparently in the offing, continued to question the wisdom of the proposed combination. The cost, from the standpoint of refueling operations alone, did not favor the B–58. It would take 1 tanker to refuel 1 of the new bombers, while 2 tankers could take care of 3 B–52s. Among the members of the Air Force Council, General LeMay stood alone in his opinion.

processing equipment, under contracts but yet to be delivered, were canceled, as were 45 ALD–4 ferret pods. On the positive side, the MB–l free fall bomb pod was exchanged for a 2-component bomb and fuel pod.[47] Other approved changes included improved communications equipment (single-side band/high frequency and emergency ultra-high frequency radios), encapsulated crew ejection seats (another new development), tactical air navigation (TACAN) electronics, and various minor improvements. However, as indicated by General White, one-third of the fiscal year 1959 B–58 procurement was canceled.[48]

Category II Testing   March 1959–30 June 1960

Officially initiated in March 1959, but actually started on 15 February 1958, the Category II tests first assumed some of the flight testing normally conducted under Category I. This variance was primarily due to the November 1957 decision to consolidate the B–58 flight test program under the direction of the weapon system office. While the ARDC testing role was not changed significantly, the proposed using command (SAC, as already confirmed) was to participate in all testing, which was unusual. In another departure from past procedures, testing would be carried out as close as possible to the contractor facilities, which made Carswell AFB the obvious location. The Air Force believed that, among other advantages, this arrangement should reduce costs for logistical training and for support of the Convair technicians. As to the consolidated testing program, it should help to discover and solve development problems quicker. SAC's 3958th Operational Employment Testing and Evaluation Squadron was activated on 1 March 1958, too late to monitor the beginning of the Category I tests. Nevertheless, the 3958th, its ARDC counterpart (the 6592d Test Squadron), and representatives from AMC and Convair soon were in place, constituting the test force that took care effectively of the Air Force Category II and III tests.[49] The Category II tests were completed on 30 June 1960, after

---

[47] The new 2-component bomb and fuel pod had special merits. After the fuel had been used, the bomb and integral tankage would be dropped on a target, making the aircraft lighter for its return flight.

[48] Letter Contract AF33(600)–36700, issued on 1 November 1957, called for 47 B–58s, bringing forecast procurement to a total of 77—30 so-called prototypes and 47 aircraft for the operational inventory. But the letter contract of November 1957 remained to be finalized, and its 47 aircraft were reduced to 33 on 26 September 1958.

[49] The bulk of the responsibility for the Category I tests did remain with the contractor; Category II proved the airplane's subsystems and was carried out mainly by ARDC's 6592d

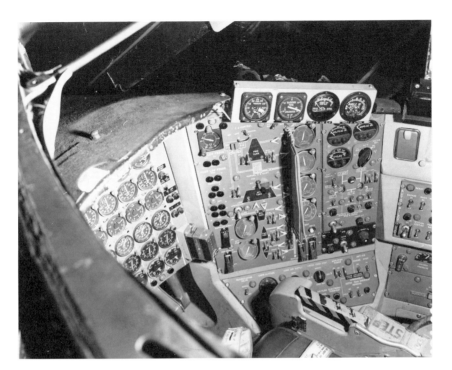

A control panel in the B-58.

accumulating 1,216 flight hours that were reached in 256 sorties. Except for a few authorized deviations and some unexpected delays, the Category II testing progressed as planned. Two YB–58As, undergoing stability and control evaluation, were flight tested from Edwards AFB, California, and from Convair's Fort Worth airfield. Another test-aircraft, earmarked for climatic hangar evaluation, went directly from Fort Worth to Eglin AFB, Florida. Finally, the accelerated service test of the J79–GE–5 engine, after 330 flight hours under Category II, was completed under Category III, when SAC crews accumulated 170 additional hours of flight. From the practical standpoint, the Category II tests proved invaluable. Yet, they probably accounted in part for the program's last near-cancellation and final reduction. Seven test-aircraft were lost between December 1958 and June 1960, including 1 which disintegrated in flight on 7 November 1959.

Squadron; the Category III operational tests (always accomplished by the using command) were conducted by the 43d Bomb Wing with the technical assistance of the Test Force.

Program Finalization   1959–1960

While testing was going on, the B–58's fate once again appeared uncertain. A Rand Corporation study, requested by the Air Staff, proved disappointing. Rand thought that the B–52 was superior to the B–58 because the Boeing aircraft could carry heavier payloads and had a longer range than the B–58. Of course, the corporation agreed that air refueling was a means to extend range, but pointed out that such recourse could be unreliable and expensive. Instead, the cheapest way to solve the dilemma would be to equip the B–47s with improved engines. Penetration was another factor to be considered in assessing the bombers. However, in Rand's opinion, the aircraft's penetrative ability was unimportant since enemy defenses of the near future would be so sophisticated that bomber losses would be high, regardless of speed. While these observations appeared valid, the Air Force did not want to alleviate its financial difficulties through retention of an improved but still obsolescing B–47 fleet. The Air Staff, therefore, asked Rand to review its original conclusions. This second round of deliberations served no purpose. Rand returned its study unaltered and without any further solution.

Meanwhile, dissatisfaction with the B–58 program grew. The correction of obvious combat deficiencies was slow, and it seemed almost certain that early inventory aircraft would be short of components and would have no high frequency radio or identification equipment. Some SAC officials were beginning to think that 2 wings of B–58s would be plenty since the aircraft would require greater tanker support than the B–52s. Also, the B–58s would not be able to fly at low level without extensive and costly modifications. Others at SAC wanted more B–58s, having faith in the follow-on B–58B that could be expected to materialize after production of the first 105 B–58As (test-aircraft included).

In May 1959, after reendorsing continued production of the B–52s, as well as support of the B–70 and of the nuclear aircraft program, General White refused to discuss the B–58's future. Just the same, the Air Force on 11 June 1959 began to plan the production and delivery schedules of 185 B–58Bs which, counting the B–58As, would increase the total to 290 aircraft, or enough to equip 5 wings. While at SAC, General LeMay had not liked the B–58A, and as Vice Chief of Staff, he did not change his opinion. The new model would be too expensive, its automatic equipment for low-level flight too complex.[50]

On 7 July, the Air Staff eliminated the B–58B from the program and the

---

[50] The B–58B was also due to provide increased range, speed, altitude, and external stores such as multiple free fall bomb pods, fuel tanks, and air-to-surface missiles.

B-58A itself again appeared to be in serious jeopardy. The 60 B-58As, under Letter Contract AF33(600)-38975 and due to be funded in fiscal year 1960, were first reduced to 32, then to 20. General Power tried to justify retaining the 290-aircraft program, but the Air Staff retorted that budgetary considerations were sometimes overriding and Secretary of the Air Force James H. Douglas confirmed that the B-58B was a dead issue.[51] The B-58A came very close to following the B-58B's path. A saving factor again proved to be the money already invested in its development. Also, as noted by Secretary of Defense Thomas S. Gates, a redeeming virtue of the B-58A was its availability in the near term. Yet, even the latter justification was weakening. Time had been catching up with the B-58 weapon system, originally designed to perform against enemy targets of the 1958-1965 period. It was now obvious that the B-58A would not be available in quantity before 1962. Once at the top of the Air Force's priority list, the B-58A program had lost its urgency. In July 1960 (FY 61), Letter Contract AF33(600)-41891 was initiated, but the 30 aircraft and 96 BLU-2/B pods covered by the document were subject to cancellation. The Air Force reached a final decision in December 1960. The fiscal year 1961 purchase was retained, but the fiscal year 1962 procurement was deleted. SAC would receive 2 wings of B-58As and no more.

Category III Testing   August 1960–July 1961

Category II test results and several accidents postponed Category III testing to August 1960, a 6-month slippage. SAC did not want to start the Category III tests before correction of certain B-58 deficiencies. Electrical malfunctions, tire failures, difficulties with the flight control system, and possible structural weaknesses appeared responsible for a rash of recent crashes. Accident findings did not indicate any consistency in the causes, but the B-58 remained under flight restrictions and SAC would not accept the aircraft pending further investigation.[52] Also, modifications required by SAC had to be made to improve safety. By mid-1960, some structural improvements were completed. The aircraft tail had been strengthened, critical side panels had been reinforced, and an ARDC ad hoc committee report was given to SAC. The report emphasized that there were no design deficiencies in either the aircraft or the flight control system, and that when

---

[51] Secretary Douglas succeeded Secretary of the Air Force Donald A. Quarles on 1 May 1957.

[52] Supersonic speed restrictions were raised to Mach 1.5 in March 1960, but only for the aircraft equipped with modified flight controls.

all functioned, the systems met the specifications. The report also noted that SAC pilots had verified the B-58's good handling characteristics, but pilot training and high proficiency were necessary. In addition, maintenance and control personnel should be highly skilled since those areas could greatly affect B-58 operations.

Obviously satisfied with the committee's report, SAC on 1 August 1960 assumed executive management of the B-58, a function previously vested in ARDC. This marked the beginning of Category III testing, which was accompanied by a number of changes. For example, ARDC's 6592d Test Squadron was inactivated, and the squadron's aircraft and personnel were transferred to the 65th Bombardment Squadron (Medium) of SAC's 43d Bomb Wing. The B-58 Test Force was formally dissolved, although a small nucleus of ARDC people stayed at Carswell AFB to assist the 43d Wing through completion of the Category III tests.

SAC's 3958th Operational Employment Testing and Evaluation Squadron had been a most important member of the now extinct test force. The 3958th was responsible for the proper development of a combat crew training program. It had to select and educate B-58 maintenance personnel and to create a cadre of flight crews that would serve as instructors in forthcoming combat crew training classes. In addition, the 3958th put together standard operating procedures for the future B-58 wings. When it took over, SAC's 65th Bombardment Squadron (Medium) found no fault in the 3958th's performance. Formal 3-month classes for combat air crews, started in mid-1960, encountered no personnel difficulties. Selected students, former B-47 pilots and regular officers for the most part, were highly qualified, with a minimum 1,000 hours of jet flying experience. Student navigators, with 500 hours of flying time on multi-jet aircraft, and defense system operators, with a minimum of 200 hours, were also excellent candidates. The 65th Combat Crew Training Squadron used Convair 2-place TF-102As to start training B-58 pilots and welcomed the August 1960 delivery of the first TB-58A trainer. As a rule, 3 TB-58 flights were made before a pilot could solo in a B-58A.

Even though nearly 1,879 combat crew training hours were flown as part of the Category III tests, the program had little to do with the 43d Bomb Wing's combat crew training. The Category III task was to evaluate the overall operational performance of the B-58A. Since the aircraft was a highly integrated, complex weapon system, the scope of the Category III tests was unusually broad. The tests covered all aircraft systems, passive defense, electronics, communications and the like, but also aerospace ground equipment and supply, for all these factors played a part. Still, because of its critical importance, a great portion of the Category III tests was devoted to the ASQ-42V Bombing-Navigation Electronic System. Ended on 31 July 1961, after the loss of 1 more B-58, Category III testing was credited with some 5,265 hours of flying time, of which about 945 hours were used strictly for testing. The rest was accumulated in various ways. A subtotal of 1,878 hours was flown to meet various Category III combat crew training objectives. The remaining hours, approximately 2,439 of them, encompassed maintenance test flights, the acceptance and delivery flights of new and retrofitted B–58As, airshows and record-breaking flights, and the hours flown for ferry missions.

Enters Operational Service   1961

B–58As, a first lot of 12, began reaching the 43d Bomb Wing at Carswell AFB in August 1960, but the 43d did not gain an initial operational capability until 1961, and waited until May of that year to get its full complement of 36 B–58s.[53] An unreliable bombing and navigation system, maintenance difficulties, shortages of ground equipment, and continuous involvement in the Category III tests combined to delay the 43d Bomb Wing's combat readiness. A second SAC wing, the 305th[54] at Bunker Hill AFB, Indiana,[55] received its first new bombers in May 1961 to start converting from subsonic B–47s to supersonic B–58s. SAC expected that the 305th would have its full allocation of B–58s by May 1962. Twenty KC–135 tankers were already in place at Bunker Hill.[56]

Initial Shortcomings   1960–1961

The first 47 B–58As did not have tactical air navigation (TACAN) electronics. The system, developed by the Hoffman Laboratories, was provided

---

[53] In later years, this number was increased to 45, a total which included 4 of SAC's 8 TB–58As. The other 4 trainers went to SAC's second wing of B–58s.

[54] SAC had earmarked the 305th as the first B–58 recipient. Initially, this was changed as a result of the new testing arrangement. Later, the 43d Bomb Wing's proximity to Fort Worth remained an important factor in view of the B–58's early operational problems.

[55] Bunker Hill was renamed as Grissom AFB on 12 May 1968, in honor of Lt. Col. Virgil Ivan ("Gus") Grissom (1926–1967). Colonel Grissom, one of the original 7 United States astronauts, made the second Project Mercury flight and a Project Gemini flight in July 1961. He died on 27 January 1967 in a fire aboard an Apollo spacecraft under test at the Kennedy Space Center, Fla.

[56] Aerial tests, completed in October 1959, showed that Boeing KC–135 tankers could refuel the B–58s. However, air refueling training and operations were limited at first because the B–58 search radar was not compatible with the refueling rendezvous equipment installed in the KC–135.

as government-furnished equipment and due to be retrofitted in most of these early planes. Also, the B–58As could not fly at low levels. Design changes to give the aircraft this added performance were being worked out. Prompt results could not be expected since the changes had only been authorized in mid-1959, when Convair's subsequent model series, the improved, low-level flying B–58B, was canceled. There were many other deficiencies of varying importance. The aircraft's ejection seats were still unsatisfactory. Development of a capsule-type of escape system for a single crewman, now handled by the Stanley Aviation Corporation, was progressing well. However, the capsule's stability remained marginal after ejection, thereby preventing Convair from incorporating the capsule during production. This meant that all B–58s would have to be retrofitted, a task started in late 1962.[57] Meanwhile, another retrofit project was taking place. B–58As were re-equipped with sturdier wheels and new tires, marking the end of at least one long-standing problem.[58] But this was just a beginning. In mid-1961, following completion of a 6-month study, the Air Staff decided that much more would have to be done to enhance the B–58A's performance. It also approved modification of existing B–58s (about 70 of them) to allow the aircraft to carry a greater variety of weapons, 4 of which would be transported externally. Subsequent B–58As would be so equipped on the production line.

Post-Production Modifications   1962–1964

Significant modifications were initiated in November 1962, under the code name of Hustle Up, a 2-phase project accomplished in Fort Worth by the prime contractor, and in San Antonio, Texas, by technicians of one of the Air Force Logistics Command's air materiel areas. The first phase of Hustle Up covered 59 B–58As; the second phase, only 36. However, Phase II also modified 76 pods of various configurations. Modification kits, including aircraft kits, pod kits, training kits and kit spares, were acquired through special contract at a cost of $6.1 million and used by both the Convair people and personnel of the San Antonio Air Materiel Area. Retrofitting the escape capsules and installing

---

[57] The B–58 was the first aircraft with individual escape capsules for emergency use at any speeds. This escape system could rocket the crew to safety from anywhere between ground level at 120 knots and 70,000 feet at Mach 2.2. The capsule, fitted with clam-shell doors, was pressurized. Once sealed and ejected, it stabilized itself and descended by parachute. It was equipped with a flotation system that deployed automatically in the event of a landing on water. The capsule was not large, restricting the size of the crew. Even so, the capsule consumed space and made the B–58's small crew compartments more cramped.

[58] The loss of a B–58A on 16 September 1959 (totally destroyed by fire after an aborted take-off from Carswell) was directly attributed to tire failure, followed by disintegration of the wheel.

multiple weapons proved to be the most extensive modifications covered by Hustle Up, which was completed in May 1964. Meanwhile, contrary to SAC's hope that the development program would yield a trouble-free aircraft, the B–58A weapon system was again encountering more than its share of difficulties. Two fatal accidents and 30 in-flight "incidents" between March and September 1962 imposed new flight restrictions and generated another major modification program. This program, centering essentially on the aircraft's flight control system, was also conducted in several phases. Phase I put a gang bar on yaw damper switches, but provided minimal improvements. Phase II (redesignated Phase I, following the May 1963 completion of the program's initial phase) modified the mach altitude repeater and improved the unreliable amplifier computer assembly circuitry, thereby allowing the B–58As to fly again at speeds up to Mach 1.65. Started in April 1964, the new Phase I closed before year's end, as scheduled, with 13 B–58s of the 305th Bomb Wing being so improved while undergoing the last part of the Hustle Up modification program. The next phase (Phase III, now known as Phase II) did not fare as well. It was due to further improve the flight control system, which in turn would allow the B–58A to use its desired Mach 2 speed. Many costly changes were involved, totaling $30 million. Furthermore, this phase was not intended to take place before the fall of 1966.

Crewmen dash for their B–58 during alert training at Carswell AFB, Texas, July 1961.

Unrelenting Problem   1965

Besides its obvious shortcomings, the B–58A was plagued from the start by a very serious problem. Its bombing and navigation system (the AN/ASQ–42) was far less reliable than that of the B–52 and the B–47. The problem, confirmed during Category III testing, did not lend itself to easy solutions. The AN/ASQ–42 was extremely complex. Its electronic signal loops were generated and circulated within several interconnected electronic "black boxes." Thus, malfunctions were hard to track down, since it was difficult to identify which black box was primarily responsible for the failure. By 1965, the AN/ASQ–42 had become an old problem, with no remedy in sight. Occasionally, malfunction causes were identified, but more often, they were merely suspected or totally undetermined. That the AN/ASQ–42 system had to be made to work well was obvious. To begin with, it was SAC's most sophisticated bombing system. Also, once fully operational, the AN/ASQ–42 would allow the B–58A to find and bomb any target, be it at high-altitude/supersonic or low-altitude/subsonic speeds. Yet, improvement proposals, submitted by various contractors in September 1965, were found unacceptable. They did not meet requirements, carried no guarantees, and fluctuated around $70 million, twice the anticipated cost. In any case, circumstances beyond SAC's control raised doubts about the AN/ASQ–42's potential performance.

Phaseout Decision   1965

In December 1965, Secretary of Defense Robert S. McNamara directed phaseout of the entire B–58 force by the end of June 1970.[59] Secretary McNamara also publicly announced that the FB–111A would be built.[60] The new bombers, along with improvement of the Minuteman and Polaris missiles and modernization of the B–52, would enhance strategic deterrence and make longer retention of the B–58s superfluous. In addition, Defense officials deemed necessary budget cuts another valid factor. Appalled by the decision, SAC pointed out that the B–58A, after coming off production with

---

[59] The decision followed completion of a study of the comparative costs and performance of a proposed bomber (the FB–lllA) and existing B–52 and B–58 strategic aircraft.

[60] The FB–lllA medium-range strategic bomber, like the B–58, was built in Fort Worth by the Convair Aerospace Division of the General Dynamics Corporation. The FB–lllA, a modified version of the F–lllA tactical fighter, was part of an interrelated and highly controversial program. As such, the FB–lllA coverage was included in Marcelle S. Knaack, *Encyclopedia of U.S. Air Force Aircraft and Missile Systems, Vol 1: Post-World War II Fighters, 1945–1973* (Washington: Office of Air Force History, 1978).

many weaknesses, was well on its way to becoming a sound, effective weapon system. Stressing the declining number of manned bombers, SAC in the ensuing 2 years kept pressing for retention of the B-58s, at least until June 1974. But the decision of 1965 was to prove unshakable.[61] And while it did not spell the end of the modifications programmed at the time, the overall B-58 improvement program was immediately affected.

Reduced Improvements   1965–1969

Modifying the B-58A for low-level flying would be a meager improvement if the aircraft were not properly equipped. SAC insisted from the start that the B-58A, to be truly effective at low levels, needed a terrain-following radar to penetrate increasingly fierce enemy defenses. Prototype development of the radar, approved with misgiving in view of the entire venture's cost and technical hazards, was the first casualty of the B-58's early phaseout. It was canceled in late 1965, when SAC settled for a reliable radio altimeter and a forward-looking visual sensor (day/night television) system. This much less expensive project, installation and modification included, was completed in early 1969. Another modernization project had an even more disappointing fate. The B-58A's electronics countermeasures systems, never updated since the aircraft's production, were nearly obsolete. Should the high-altitude B-58A be committed to combat, it would be extremely vulnerable to surface-to-air missiles, such as the SA-2s. Several contemplated modifications had been held in abeyance pending the development of better techniques. One of them, modification 1180, had been approved in mid-1966 and would give the B-58A a new version of the ALQ-16 trackbreaker. However, when flight tested in 1968, this component did not work. As to other penetration aid improvements, they had not even reached the testing stage. Ongoing talks that the B-58s might, after all, be retained through 1974 kept the electronic countermeasures improvement projects alive until the end of 1969. When the B-58's longer retention did not materialize, all penetration aid modifications were canceled.

Retained Modifications   1965–1969

Retirement of the B-58 by mid-1970 meant that modifications, even if approved, would be deleted if not funded by mid-1968. Aware that several

---

[61] On 21 February 1968, General McConnell, Air Force Chief of Staff since 1 February 1965, reaffirmed before the Senate Armed Services Committee that the entire B-58 fleet would be phased out before June 1970.

B–58 problems would take a long time to solve, SAC asked for a waiver of the so-called 2-year utilization rule, but the request was denied. Nevertheless, many of the modifications, pursued all along by SAC, came to fruition. After numerous setbacks, a solution was found for the B–58A's erratic flight control by adding a redundant yaw damper to the system. Retrofit kits were purchased in 1967, and the installation undertaken in May 1968 progressed smoothly. During the same period, an improved version of the AN/ASQ–42, flight tested in mid-1967, proved successful. Production of the improved system, approved on 27 September 1967 and funded within prescribed time limits, foretold no problem. Technical data and the delivery of spare parts had been included in the necessary contract. Moreover, installation of the system, as started in May 1968, was not expected to disrupt significantly SAC's operational plans. Another modification had also been sought by SAC, almost since the aircraft had become operational. The command wanted the B–58A crew to be capable of starting their engines without having to depend on pneumatic ground starting carts. Equipping the aircraft with a cartridge self-starter would allow it in an emergency to take off from dispersal, post-strike, and other remote bases. Yet the project had been handicapped from the start. It was approved, canceled, reapproved, modified, and constantly hampered by technical difficulties. SAC, nonetheless, won its case and the B–58 was equipped with a cartridge self-starter. The installation began on 7 May 1968, approximately 6 months after all B–58s had exchanged their J79–5B engines for improved J79–5Cs.

Inspections and Repairs   1966–1969

In mid-1965, the San Antonio Air Materiel Area recommended a program of inspect and repair as necessary (IRAN) for a scheduled, comprehensive depot-level inspection of the B–58. So far, San Antonio and SAC had taken care of the aircraft's difficulties as they arose. However, increasingly serious problems were being uncovered. The plumbing and wiring of the B–58As and TB–58As were deteriorating, and the aircraft were also showing signs of structural fatigue and corrosion. SAC had no objections to the IRAN program proposed for the B–58, a routine procedure for most aircraft. Nor did it object to the 36-month cycle favored by the materiel area. However, the command qualified its approval. Since fuel leaks indicated that corrosion was further along than estimated, corrective action could not await the January 1966 implementation of the IRAN program. Also, B–58s of the 43d Bomb Wing should be treated first, which they were. Initially conducted from Convair's Fort Worth facilities, the IRAN program was moved in mid-1967 to James Connally AFB, near Waco, Texas. There were no other changes. The B–58 modification/IRAN program was thorough. Major tasks included removal of all releasable panels; inspection and repair of the aircraft's primary and secondary structures; and inspection and repair of all wire bundles and cables, hydraulic lines and fittings, and air conditioning and pressurization duct components. The program also included bench testing and calibration of all electronic units, removal and overhaul of landing gear assemblies, and repair and treatment of corroded areas. This work consumed 16,000 manhours. In 1967, the cost per aircraft totaled $181,000; $201,000 in 1968.

End of Production   1962

Production ended in the fall of 1962, with the last 3 B–58s being delivered on 26 October, 1 month ahead of schedule.

Total B–58s Accepted   116

All B–58s were built at the contractor's Fort Worth plant.

Acceptance Rates

The Air Force accepted 3 B–58s in FY 57; 8 in FY 58; 16 in FY 59; 11 in FY 60; 30 in FY 61; 33 in FY 62; 15 in FY 63 (the last 3 in October 1962).

Research, Development, Test, $1.4 billion
    and Evaluation

The Air Force estimated the B–58 weapon system program's research, development, test, and evaluation at $1,408.6 million.[62]

---

[62] Air Force records reflecting appropriations for fiscal years 1954 through 1961 showed that a total of $3,174.4 million was approved for the B–58 program. This was reduced to $3,026.2 million in fiscal year 1962, after total procurement was set at 116. Prorated, this brought the cost of every B–58 weapon system to $26.9 million. However, additional costs were later incurred. In 1967 SAC estimated that each B–58 cost about $30 million.

Flyaway Cost Per Production Aircraft   **$12.44 million**

Airframe, $6,447,702; engines (installed), $1,117,120; electronics, $1,294,791; ordnance, $26,674; armament (and others), $3,555,573.[63]

Average Cost Per Flying Hour   **$2,139.00**

Average Maintenance Cost Per Flying Hour   **$1,440.00**

Subsequent Model Series   **None**

Other Configurations   **B-58C, RB-58A, and TB-58A**

B-58C—This model of the B-58, designated B-J/58 by Convair, but known unofficially by the Air Force as the B-58C, incorporated significant airframe modifications, including a new wing leading edge, more tail area, a 5-foot fuselage extension, and 4 Pratt & Whitney J58 engines without afterburners. In 1960 Convair estimated that its all-supersonic, Mach 2.4 B-58C would be as efficient and much cheaper than the B-70. The Air Force did not test these propositions for several reasons. Even if the proposed airplane approached the B-70's anticipated performance, it had neither the payload nor the growth potential of the latter. The B-70 was the beginning of a design, the B-58C would be the ultimate product of an old configuration. Further study of the Convair proposal practically closed the case. In April, ARDC reported that the contractor's estimate of a 5,200-nautical-mile unrefueled range was probably 25 percent too optimistic. Also, extensive use of aluminum in the B-58C could create problems since the effects of this metal's exposure to high temperatures (aerodynamic heat) was not known. Lack of funds prompted the final decision. Greatly concerned with the B-70, recently confined to development status,[64] the Air Staff as well as SAC did not want to risk the financial interference of a new project.

---

[63] Excluding prorated research, development, test, and evaluation costs and the expenses of modifications and engineering changes, added on after approval of a basic contract.

[64] In early 1961, the Kennedy Administration asked the Congress to cancel production of the "unnecessary and economically unjustifiable" B-70 Valkyrie. Thereupon, the B-70 funds were reduced and the program was limited to 3 experimental planes.

In late April, Convair was informed that the Air Force had no interest in the B–58C.

RB–58A—The early photo reconnaissance pod program, due to transform the B–58 into a high-altitude and speedy reconnaissance weapon system had been canceled, reinstated, and again canceled by December 1958. One pod, delivered in June 1958, was lost as the plane it equipped crashed in June 1960. The electromagnetic reconnaissance program followed the same pattern, being canceled in October 1957, then reendorsed, and finally abandoned in May 1958, after delivery of two pods. In 1963, another change took place. As a result of the October 1962 Cuban Crisis, SAC decided the B–58A could be used to great advantage for low-level, high-speed photographic reconnaissance. This was based on the assumption that the extra task could be carried out without making a reconnaissance aircraft out of the few available B–58As. After rejection of several unsatisfactory proposals, a solution was found. It simply involved the incorporation of a KA–56 panoramic camera into the nose fairing of the MB–1 pod. Approved by the Air Staff in mid-1963, the modification was successfully flight tested on 30 October and 10 cameras and associated equipment were purchased. Known as Project Mainline, the modification of 44 B–58As and 10 MB–1 pods was completed on 6 December at a cost of approximately $1 million.

TB–58A—The flight characteristics peculiar to delta-wing planforms and the B–58's unmatched high speed called for a trainer version of the new bomber. The Air Force first authorized the conversion of 4 early test B–58As to the training configuration on 25 February 1959. The modification, done under production contract AF33(600)–36200, provided side-by-side seating for pilot training, with the instructor placed aft and 10 degrees right of the student. The Air Force took delivery of the first TB–58A in August 1960, and subsequently ordered the conversion of 4 additional test B–58As to a similar configuration. This last lot was modified under special contract, but the costs were lumped together for a total of almost $16 million.

Phaseout   1969–1970

Phaseout of the entire B–58 force by the end of fiscal year 1971 (June 1970) was directed in December 1965. This schedule was a change from Secretary McNamara's earlier plans and gave the aircraft an extra year of operational life. However, once underway, the B–58 retirement program moved fast, actually ending 6 months ahead of time. It was completed on 16 January 1970, when the 305th Bomb Wing's last 2 B–58s (Serial Numbers 55–662 and 61–0278) were flown to Davis-Monthan AFB, Arizona. The planes joined 82 other B–58As, including the 8 converted trainers, retired since 3 November 1969. Two B–58As, responsible for record-breaking flights in 1962 and 1963, escaped retirement at Davis-Monthan and were placed in museums.

Record Flights   1961–1963

If the B–58 established itself at home as one of the most expensive and controversial weapon systems, it also attracted the world's attention as one of the most extraordinary airplanes. Actually, the B–58 broke a great many speed records (some still standing 10 years later) and won almost every major aviation award.

The aircraft's historical achievements commenced on 12 January 1961, when a B–58 of the 43d Bomb Wing set 6 international speed and payload records on a single flight, in the process breaking 5 previous records held by the Soviet Union. Two days later, another B–58 of the 43d Bomb Wing broke 3 of the records set on 12 January. The plane flew over a 620-mile closed course with similar payloads of 4,409.2 or 2,208.6 pounds and no payload at all, at an average speed of 1,284.73 miles per hour—an increase of 222.9 miles per hour. On 28 February, the crew was awarded the Thompson Trophy for 1961. This was the first time in 31 years that the trophy was awarded to a medium bomber. On 10 May, a new record for sustained speed was set by a B–58, flying 669.4 miles in 30 minutes and 45 seconds at an average speed of 1,302 miles per hour. This earned the aircraft's pilot, Maj. Elmer E. Murphy, the Aero Club of France's Bleriot Cup, a trophy named for Louis Bleriot, famous for his pre-World War I flight across the British Channel.[65] The B–58 continued its record-setting pace on 26 May when it flew the 4,612 miles from New York to Paris in 3 hours, 19 minutes and 41 seconds. The time was almost one-tenth that taken by Charles Lindbergh in his famous solo flight of 1927. The flight of 26 May 1961 earned the B–58's 3-man crew the Mackay Trophy, a trophy first won on 9 October 1912 by Gen. "Hap" Arnold, then a young lieutenant flying a reconnaissance mission with an early version of the Wright biplane.

The B–58 had another notable year in 1962. On 5 March, a 43d Bomb Wing B–58 broke 3 speed records in a round-trip flight between New York and Los Angeles. The B–58 made the entire trip in 4 hours, 41 minutes and 14.98 seconds while averaging 1,044.46 miles per hour. Three in-flight refuelings by KC–135s were required. The entire flight earned the crew the

---

[65] One of the first warplanes employed by the allies during World War I bore the name of France's aviation pioneer, Louis Bleriot. The Bleriot Cup, established in 1931, was badly damaged during World War II, while in Italy's possession. Subsequently remade by the Italians, the 1,600-pound trophy had been awarded before, but only provisionally. Not until the required speed and duration marks were reached by the B–58 could the trophy be won permanently.

Mackay Trophy. A part of the same flight was particularly impressive. The B-58 flew from Los Angeles to New York in 2 hours and 58.71 seconds, for an average speed of 1,214.65 miles per hour. For this the crew received the Bendix Trophy, first awarded in 1931 to Jimmy Doolittle for his 9-hour and 10-minute flight from Los Angeles to Cleveland. The B-58 closed 1962 with 2 altitude records, acquired on 18 September and worthy of the Harmon Trophy.

The B-58 set its last 5 records in 1963, all of them on 16 October. On that date, a B-58 of the 305th Bomb Wing set an official world speed record by flying 8,028 miles from Tokyo to London in 8 hours, 35 minutes and 20.4 seconds, averaging about 938 miles per hours.[66] Another B-58 established speed records, flying from Tokyo to Anchorage, Alaska, and from Anchorage to London.

---

[66] At retirement, this B-58 (Serial Number 61-2059) went to the SAC Aerospace Museum, Offutt AFB, Neb. The B-58 (Serial Number 59-2458) which set the speed and altitude records of March 1962 went to the Air Force Museum, Wright-Patterson AFB, Ohio.

Program Recap

The Air Force bought 116 B-58As, including 30 early planes identified as prototypes or test-aircraft. In 1959, the Air Force decided that 15 of the first YB-58As would be brought up to the production configuration's latest standards. Eight TB-58As, acquired through production modifications, were also part of the total contingent. The B-58 program proved costly, reaching over $3 billion, and its acquisition process was complex. It took 5 contracts (AF33(038)-21250, and AF33(600)-32841, -36200, -38975, -418911), all of the cost-plus-incentive-fee type, to acquire the aircraft, and each contract carried an unusual number of amendments and supplements. The Air Force also entered in almost a dozen miscellaneous contracts to secure B-58 modification kits, multiple weapon kits, mobile training units, flight simulators, and various items of lesser importance.

TECHNICAL AND BASIC MISSION PERFORMANCE DATA

B-58A AIRCRAFT

Manufacturer (Airframe)	Convair Division of General Dynamics Corporation, Fort Worth, Tex.
(Engines)	General Electric Company, Evandale, Ohio.
Nomenclature	Strategic Medium Bomber
Popular Name	Hustler

Length/Span (ft)	96.8/56.8
Wing Area (sq ft)	1,542.5
Engine: Number, Rated Power per Engine, & Designation	(4) 15,000 lb st J79–GE–5B (with afterburner)
Armament	1 M–61 Gatling gun
Crew	3

Basic, High-Altitude, Refueled Mission[a]

Weights (lb)	
Empty	55,560
Combat	82,595
Takeoff	163,000
Takeoff Ground Run (ft)	
At Sea Level	7,850
Over 50-ft Obstacle	13,700
Rate of Climb (fpm) at Sea Level[b] (Takeoff Weight/Maximum Power)	
With MB–1C Pod	17,830
With MB–1C Pod & 2 small weapons	16,805
Service Ceiling at Combat Weight (100 fpm Rate of Climb to Altitude)	63,500
Combat Ceiling with Max Power (500 fpm Rate of Climb to Altitude)	
With MB–1C Pod	63,080
With MB–1C Pod & 2 small weapons	62,900
Average Cruise Speed Outside Combat Zone (kn)	503
Max Speed at Combat Service Ceiling (kn/ft)[b]	
With MB–1C Pod	1,147/63,500
With MB–1C Pod & 2 small weapons[c]	1,147/62,500
Initial Cruise Altitude with MB–1C Pod (ft)	22,500
Target Altitude with MB–1C Pod (ft)	55,650
Final Cruise Altitude with MB–1C Pod (ft)	46,880
Combat Distance with MB–1C Pod (nm)	4,275
Combat Zone Distance with MB–1C Pod at Combat Zone Speed (nm/kn)[d]	500/1,147
Total Mission Time With MB–1C Pod (hr)	11

Basic, High-Altitude, None-Refueled Mission[d]

Weights (lb)	
Empty	55,560
Combat	81,345
Takeoff	163,000
Takeoff Ground Run (ft)	
At Sea Level	7,850
Over 50-ft Obstacle	13,700
Rate of Climb (fpm) at Sea Level[d]	
(Takeoff Weight/Max Power)	17,830
Service Ceiling at Combat Weight (ft)	
(100 fpm Rate of Climb to Altitude)	63,850
Combat Ceiling with Max Power (ft)	
(500 fpm Rate of Climb to Altitude)	63,400
Average Cruise Speed Outside Combat Zone (kn)	531
Max Speed at Combat Service Ceiling (kn/ft)[d]	1,147/63,400
Initial Cruise Altitude (ft)	28,200
Target Altitude (ft)	55,900
Final Cruise Altitude (ft)	46,900
Combat Radius (nm)	1,400
Combat Zone Distance at Combat Zone Speed (nm/kn)[d]	500/1,147
Total Mission Time (hr)	5.09

Abbreviations	
fpm	= feet per minute
kn	= knots
max	= maximum
nm	= nautical miles

[a] Under so-called "Post-Strike" conditions, which actually meant that all performance data were based on the assumption that the plane would have to fly 1,500 nm from the target to a recovery base.

[b] High speed restricted by engine and airframe structural limits.

[c] Altitude limited by physical load limits.

[d] All data based on airplane carrying MB–1C pod and no small weapons.

Basic Mission Note

Refueled mission's range data were based on refueling the B–58 with a Boeing KC–135 tanker having a 1,000-nautical mile post-refuel stage. The B–58 took off, climbed on course with military power,* then buddy-cruised with the tanker at Mach 0.8 to point of hookup for refueling. Range-free allowances included: 10 minutes for rendezvous after climb-out, additional fuel equal to 5 percent of fuel burned prior to hookup, and service tolerances amounting to an additional 5 percent increase in fuel consumption for both pre-refuel and post-refuel stages. Refueling was conducted at an altitude of 25,000 feet, at a Mach number of 0.8, and with the high-speed boom.

Formula: Basic Mission's Post-Strike Stage
After refueling, accelerated with military power to the speed for maximum range, cruised at maximum-range speeds and altitudes until initiating the maximum-power acceleration and climb to supersonic zones. The supersonic zone distance was 500 nautical miles and consisted of flying in at Mach 2.0 and dropping the MB–1C pod. After dropping the pod, cruised 1,500 nautical miles to complete mission at Mach number and altitudes for maximum range. Range-free allowances included: 5 minutes of normal-power and 1 minute of maximum-power fuel consumption for warm-up and take-off, 10-minute fuel consumption to cruise on Mach 0.8 flight path for buddy-refueling, 5 percent of fuel burned prior to refueling, and service tolerances amounting to an additional 5 percent increase in fuel consumption for the pre-refuel and post-refuel stages. A reserve fuel allowance sufficient to fly 8 percent of the creditable mission range after refuel, plus the amount of fuel required for 1 ground-controlled approach (GCA) go-around, was also included.

B/RB–66 Destroyer

Douglas
Aircraft Company

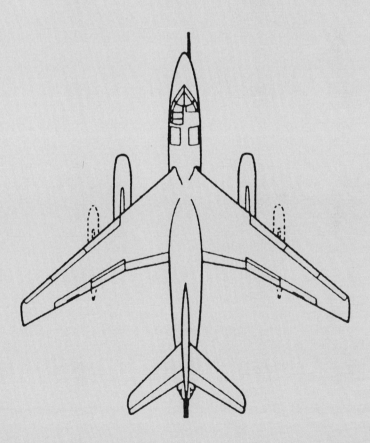

B/RB-66 Destroyer
Douglas

Navy Equivalent: A3D-1

Overview

As in the B-57's case, the Air Force bought the B/RB-66 for lack of any better choice. The analogy did not stop there. Like the stopgap B-57, which it was due to replace, the B/RB-66 was to be an interim weapon, primarily earmarked for tactical reconnaissance, until the subsequently canceled B-68 came into being. Similar misjudgments occurred: the difficulty of Americanizing a British aircraft was underestimated and, while not overlooked, the complexity of turning a Navy plane into an efficient land-based system was improperly assessed. On both occasions, the Air Force requirements proved too ambitious, too hasty, and the 2 programs fell behind schedule. Finally, it took years, and particularly the conflict in Southeast Asia, to justify the costs involved, a conclusion actually far more applicable to the B/RB-66 than to the B-57.

Based on a year-old proposal by Douglas, the Air Force in 1952 bought the Navy's yet-to-be-flown A3D-1 Sky Warrior. Hurriedly, and in keeping with the mood of the time, exacting requirements were levied which, in view of the program's urgency, proved totally unrealistic. The future B/RB-66 Destroyers, as the Air Force versions of the Navy aircraft were designated, had to be fast, highly maneuverable, and able to perform in all types of weather, at very high or low altitudes, and from makeshift or short runways. The B/RB-66s also had to have a 1,000-nautical mile radius and be large enough to accommodate a 10,000-pound payload of either atomic, conventional, or photographic flash bombs. The bomber and reconnaissance versions were to be kept closely alike. Finally, and of great importance, all versions were to be fitted with sophisticated electronic countermeasures components to deal with enemy radars.

As a necessary start, Douglas deleted the folding wings, catapult capability, and arresting gear from the Navy A3D configuration. In keeping with Air Force instructions, adaptations were kept to a minimum in order to expedite matters. The next major steps, therefore, were addition of upward ejection seats, a must when flying low at high speeds, and reinforcement of the aircraft structure to compensate for the greater stresses of low-altitude, high-speed operation. To the Air Force's dismay, once these changes were made, new requirements emerged, as did design and layout deficiencies. Hence, larger tires were provided, as were emergency air brakes, wing spoilers, and improved lateral controls. The wing's angle of incidence was altered to minimize dutch roll, the cockpit pressurization was improved, and a number of other development modifications took place. Just the same, problems remained. A more serious handicap was the need for better jet engines, still at a premium.

The RB-66's first flight in June 1954, 6 months behind the Air Force's deadline, was not a success. The aircraft did not handle well, it pitched up unexpectedly, the wings vibrated excessively, the vision from the canopy was poor, and the landing gear doors did not function properly. Ensuing efforts were hardly rewarding. In 1955, reminiscent of yet another aircraft, the B-58, the Air Staff pondered whether the B/RB-66 should be canceled, for a cold loss of perhaps up to $600 million. No substitute aircraft were available, and this fact also had to be considered. The dilemma was solved in familiar fashion; the program was retained, but reduced.

Improved RB-66s entered operational service in 1956, permitting the long overdue replacement of the obsolete RB-26s, and allowing phaseout in early 1957 of the problem-ridden RB-57As. While the bulk of the small contingent of B/RB-66s, 294 instead of the 342 aircraft initially pro-grammed, was earmarked for the Tactical Air Command (TAC), some of the badly needed reconnaissance models promptly joined the Pacific Air Forces in the fall of 1956. Others went to the United States Air Forces in Europe in late 1957. Whether at home or overseas, every version of the aircraft remained troublesome. Their successive engines, Allison J71-A-9s and J71-A-11s were better, but not good enough, and the subsequent retrofit of more powerful J71-A-13s caused other problems.

In the long run, the B/RB-66s were made to work, and the aircraft became a main asset of the Air Force intelligence gathering and electronic warfare forces. Even though lack of money precluded numerous special modifications and most modernization projects, many changes were ef-fected as the aircraft's specialized roles accrued. Because of the United States involvement in Southeast Asia, the aircraft's life-span was extended far beyond expectation. Some B-66Bs were phased out in 1963, only to be reactivated within a few years. After refurbishing, the aircraft, now known as the EB-66, headed for the war theater. Other B/RB-66s, although earmarked for retirement, were kept active, re-equipped, redesignated, and committed to combat as early as 1965.

In 1966, press accounts began to give the EB-66s credit for neutralizing surface-to-air missile radars as well as much of the enemy's radar-controlled but conventional anti-aircraft weaponry. As the war escalated and enemy defenses grew, the old aircraft, with their upgraded electronic devices and despite their worn-out engines, became invaluable and so remained until the end of the conflict. Thus, a difficult decision, made nearly 20 years before by a greatly concerned and cautious Air Staff, proved correct.

Basic Development   1951

The B/RB-66 Destroyer grew out of the Douglas Aircraft Company's XA3D-1, a high-altitude, light bombardment airplane developed for the U.S. Navy. The A3D-1 Skywarrior, the production version of the experimental carrier-based bomber, was first flown on 16 September 1953.

Initial Requirements   14 June 1951

The beginning of the Korean conflict caught the Air Force with a tactical inventory of light bombers and reconnaissance aircraft consisting essentially of World War II B/RB-26s. This was supplemented by a few B-45s, acquired between 1948 and 1950. However, 50 of the B-45 Tornadoes had been modified to carry atomic weapons, and another 60 were unable to meet the projected need for tactical bombers designed to carry conventional munitions. This predicament accounted for the March 1951 production order for the B-57 light bomber (too small to carry current atomic weapons). Yet the Air Force harbored no great illusions. Although it thought erroneously that the B-57 Canberra would be available between 1952 and 1953, it never overestimated the new aircraft's potential. The Air Force also knew that, realistically, the ideal weapon system for tactical bombing and reconnaissance—Weapon System 302A—remained a long way off.[1] The solution, therefore, was to seek a more satisfactory interim airplane that

---

[1] Design studies for Weapon System 302A were submitted by the Glenn L. Martin Co. and Douglas Aircraft Co. in 1952 and again in 1954, along with an entry from North American Aviation, Inc. A proposal by Boeing Airplane Co., presented after the competition deadline, was automatically rejected, and Martin ended being the winner. Unfortunately, the proposed B-68's inertial guidance bombing and navigation system ran into serious difficulties. This meant that production quantities of the B-68, should they be approved, would be postponed to at least 1963. This problem soon became immaterial. In early 1957, citing stringent budget limitations and the higher priorities of other weapon systems, Air Force Headquarters canceled the B-68 program.

would become operational around 1954. While the Air Force's June 1951 objective centered on a reconnaissance vehicle, this requirement was extended in August to include tactical bombing.[2]

Potential Candidates   Fall 1951

Defining a requirement was usually easy; finding the best aircraft for the task was always difficult. An improved B-45 might satisfy the Tactical Air Command's demands of the mid-fifties. However, the Tornado's relatively slow speed and inferior defense armament were not encouraging. The Air Research and Development Command (ARDC) believed the B-47 would be a preferable choice, even though the Boeing medium bomber was a Strategic Air Command airplane and rather costly. It also called for more maintenance than practical for tactical theatre operation. In any case, ARDC was the first to recognize that the B-47 would not be the absolute answer. TAC could put the aircraft to good use for high-altitude bombing, but the command's close air support missions would probably be better served by the Martin B-51. The latter, still in the experimental stage, was a 3-engine all-weather airplane designed primarily for low-level bombing. On the other hand, the XB-51 was far from perfect. First flown in October 1949, it had a short radius of action and could not carry more than 4,000 pounds of bombs. A fourth candidate, the Navy's Douglas XA3D-1, was the most promising on paper; however, as the plane was not expected to fly before another year, there was no knowledge of this plane's stability and control characteristics.[3] Finally, to make matters worse, whatever plane was chosen would suffer at first from a probable shortage of engines and a lack of reconnaissance equipment.

Tentative Selection   29 November 1951

Based on a Douglas proposal of 29 August, the USAF Aircraft and Weapons Board opted in November for an Air Force version of the future A3D-1. Inasmuch as the adaptation suggested by Douglas would require such major changes as deletion of naval aircraft carrier provisions; addition

---

[2] Tactical bombing is the bombing conducted, usually by tactical air units, in support of surface forces. Bombing to achieve air superiority or to carry out interdiction is a part of tactical bombing, although the term tends to be restricted to battle area operations.

[3] The XA3D-1 flew for the first time on 28 October 1952.

of ejection seats, of a larger search antenna, and an increase of the aircraft's load capacity, the board wanted to start with a few service test aircraft. The board also recommended procurement of modified RB-57s to fill the gap until Air Force A3Ds could be purchased in significant quantities, planning centering at the time on a fleet of about 350 interim aircraft. The Air Materiel Command (AMC) took exception, and actually did prevail, after arguing that such an arrangement would be wasteful, since the new aircraft most likely would be available only 8 months later than the additional RB-57s proposed by the board.

Definite Endorsement   12 January 1952

On 12 January 1952, AMC was informed by USAF Headquarters that the USAF Aircraft and Weapons Board selection had been fully endorsed, because the adapted A3D came closest to fulfilling the interim tactical requirements than other candidates, and that the Air Force version of the Navy aircraft would be designated B-66. Although brief, the Air Staff message carried specific instructions. Reconnaissance would have priority, the RB-66 would be immediately equipped for night photography, and electronic reconnaissance equipment, as well as electronic countermeasures components, would be added at the earliest possible date. AMC notified Douglas of the Air Force production decision on 15 January.

General Operational Requirements   1952

The Air Force issued the general operational requirement (GOR) for the future RB-66A, RB-66B, and RB-66C on 21 January 1952. A second GOR, strictly concerned with the B-66B, was published in April. In essence, these documents were basically alike. They asked for a fast, highly maneuverable tactical reconnaissance bomber that could perform in all types of weather, at very high or low altitudes. Nevertheless, the requirements were quite explicit. A 1,000-nautical mile radius was needed, and the planes had to be capable of carrying large amounts of equipment (radio, radar, electronics) without affecting their normal performance. The B/RB-66s had to be large enough to accommodate a 10,000 pound payload of either atomic, conventional, or photographic flash bombs. They had to be fitted with defensive armament, and would require sophisticated electronic countermeasures components to deal with enemy radars. Finally, the Air Force wanted every model of the new aircraft to be able to use makeshift or short runways. It also insisted that the B/RB-66's maintenance and logistic support be fairly simple.

Contractual Arrangements   1952

On 12 February 1952 letter contract AF 33(600)–9646 initiated the procurement of a test quantity of 5 RB–66As. The purchase of 2 Navy A3Ds, also directed by the Air Staff, was canceled after AMC pointed out that the testing value of the 2 would be negligible in view of the anticipated differences in the Air Force version. The February letter contract gave way to a definitive contract, which was signed on 4 December 1952. In spite of the configuration changes that were to be expected, the Air Force originally thought that the urgently needed RB–66As would be more or less off-the-shelf copies of the A3D. Hence, there would be no experimental or prototype B/RB–66s. Moreover, the December contract already called for production tooling for a peak rate of 12 airplanes per month by March 1955, and for a total of 342 airplanes. The Air Materiel Command warned, however,that since no A3Ds had been produced it could not properly assess the cost of changes necessary to satisfy USAF requirements. This precluded the usual fixed-price-firm (FPF) type of agreement then favored by the Air Force. Instead, the December contract covered cost, plus a guaranteed profit of 6 percent. In the meantime, Letter Contract AF 33(600)–16314 had been signed on 24 April 1952. This contract, providing for the fiscal year 1953 procurement of 127 RB–66As, also did not follow the standard procurement pattern. It was first negotiated as a FPF contract with a renegotiable clause, but reverted to the terms of the preceding letter contract in August of the same year, when the FY 53 procurement of the B/RB–66s was significantly altered.

Basic Configuration   May 1952

While the Air Force seemed to believe—or perhaps, hope—that the eagerly awaited B/RB–66 would partly replicate the A3D, the new aircraft's basic configuration was being worked out. Not yet incorporated were a few major changes proposed by Douglas back in August 1951, and subsequently approved by the Aircraft and Weapons Board. The difficulty of these basic alterations could be disputed. What was termed "major" appeared almost routine. The first step was to delete from the Navy A3D the various inherent features of a carrier-based aircraft, such as folding wings, catapult capability, and arresting gear. Satisfying the stated Air Force requirements came next, keeping in mind that only a minimum of adaptations could be tolerated in view of the program's urgency. Essentially, this meant that upward crew ejection seats had to be installed, since one of the aircraft's many roles would be to fly at low altitudes and at fairly high speeds. In the same vein, the airframe structure had to be strengthened to compensate for the greater stresses of low-altitude, high-speed operation. Finally, a 45-inch search radar antenna needed to be substituted for the 30-inch antenna of the A3D. These changes were the salient points of the basic configuration approved by the Air Force in May 1952. While they brought the airplane closer to the Air Force's tactical requirement, they reduced range from 1,325 to 1,070 nautical miles.

Additional Alterations   1952

That the May approval of the B/RB-66's basic configuration proved to be a mere beginning came as a surprise. The Air Force from the start had planned to define further the actual configuration of the new aircraft's bomber version.[4] And, while going along with the so-called major changes of the approved configuration, it had been busy identifying necessary minor improvements. Under this category fell the exchange of Navy- for Air Force-designed equipment, a substitution which would simplify the airplane's logistic support. An unexpected jolt, however, was the snowball effect of the changes introduced in the approved basic configuration.

Also, new requirements kept showing up, as did design or layout deficiencies. By mid-1952, the quasi A3D that the Air Force hoped to rush into production had acquired a long list of innovations. To decrease footprint pressures[5] and permit landing on runways designed for fighter aircraft, the B/RB-66 required larger tires. It also needed new emergency air brakes, wing spoilers, improved lateral controls, changes to the wing's angle of incidence to minimize dutch roll,[6] better cockpit pressurization, and a number of other improvements. The Air Force did not like the A3D's hydraulic system and wanted the system to be completely revised. It wanted the aircraft's fuel system to be redesigned and insisted that the B/RB-66 should carry a fuel purge system, a feature missing from the A3D. Finally, all B/RB-66s were to be fitted for in-flight refueling, the photo/navigator station had to be relocated, and better engines were needed.

---

[4] The Air Force nevertheless wanted the aircraft to be interchangeable, and every effort was to be made to keep the bomber and reconnaissance versions closely alike.

[5] Footprint pressure is the pressure of an aircraft's wheels (with tires inflated) upon the unyielding contact surface of a runway, expressed in terms of pounds per square inch, as determined by a ratio of static gross takeoff weight to the contact area.

[6] Dutch roll is the colloquial expression used to describe the combined yawing and rolling motion of an airplane. Dutch roll is usually caused by rough air, but it can occur even in still air.

Engine Problems   1952

As anticipated in late 1951, engine difficulties materialized. Development of the Westinghouse J40–WE–5, due to equip the Navy A3D, was not progressing well. This confirmed the Air Force's suspicion that such an engine would be unable to give the B/RB–66s the radius of action and overall performance required of the airplanes. An engine competition, initiated by AMC on 17 May, yielded several possibilities. Westinghouse offered a new version of the J40, which was turned down because of excessive fuel consumption and because the engine's 7,250-pound thrust was minimal, when compared to the 9,750 pounds of the J71 engine proposed by Allison, a division of the General Motors Corporation. The General Electric J73 failed because of its cost and the fact that its development lagged behind the J71. In addition, and perhaps of greater significance, General Electric at the time was fully occupied with the J47 engine program. Douglas Aircraft favored the Pratt and Whitney J57, but because it was earmarked for several weapon systems of higher priority than the B/RB–66, the Air Force, did not feel the manufacturer could produce enough J57s to satisfy all demands.[7] This left Allison's J71 as the undisputed winner of the competition. Yet, even though Allison had guaranteed the development status of its engine, problems in getting the J71–A–9 engine through its 50-hour test held back the Air Force production order until 5 August 1952, 2 months later than required in order to maintain the aircraft's schedule lead time. In fact, AMC authorized the engine's production before completion of the 50-hour test, a risk frowned upon by the Wright Air Development Center.

Mockup Inspection   June–July 1952

The RB–66A's official mockup inspection was held at the Douglas Long Beach Plant, California, from 27 June through 2 July. Sixty-three of 83 changes requested by the board members were approved. Most of the endorsed alterations were minor, a main exception concerning the aircraft's landing gear. The Mockup Board determined that the landing apparatus of the RB–66A, now stressed to the 70,000 pounds of the configuration first sought by the Air Force, would be altered in order to accept the 83,000-pound limit of the B–66. The decision confirmed the Air Force's intent to keep reconnaissance and bomber versions as similar as possible. Obviously, it also promised to simplify production.

---

[7] The J75 was subsequently selected by the Navy to replace the A3D's J40s.

A drawing of the Douglas B–66 in flight.

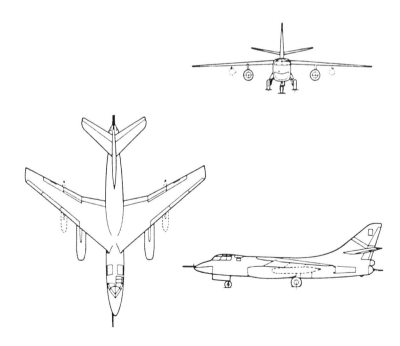

Program Revision   August 1952

Instead of producing radical changes, the RB–66A mockup inspection merely verified the basic configuration that had evolved since February 1952, when the first technical inspection of the aircraft had taken place. This configuration had become quite different from the slightly modified A3D aircraft envisioned by the Air Force. Hence there would be only 5 RB–66As; these aircraft would be used for testing, and subsequent productions would be known as RB–66Bs. Finally, the letter contract of April 1952 that had called for 127 RB–66s would be immediately amended. The amendment would reduce the fiscal year 1953 procurement to 99 aircraft—73 RB–66Bs and 26 B–66Bs.

Other Immediate Planning   1952–1953

If the configuration changes, program revisions, and procurement amendments deriving from such changes seemed confusing, they were not particularly unusual. The Air Force was prepared to cope with these factors, its task greatly eased because selection of the basic A3D design had been unanimous, a rather extraordinary occurrence. Actually, the Air Force's essential concern was to ensure that no configuration changes would preclude the urgently needed program from proceeding as scheduled. To that effect, a conference held in August paved the way for prompt approval of the B–66B configuration. In the same month, the Air Force directed a review of available and forthcoming electronic countermeasures components that could possibly be installed in the entire B/RB–66 fleet. Early in 1953, the Air Force ordered procurement of the RB–66C, the RB–66's ferret version,[8] and decided that the future B–66B would carry only atomic or modern conventional bombs, and not the bulkier high explosives from World War II. Late in the year, as the Allison J71 successfully completed its 50-hour test, AMC ended its search for an alternate engine, which until then had been considered an unavoidable form of insurance.

First Flight (RB–66A)   28 June 1954

The RB–66A's initial flight on 28 June 1954 was 6 months behind schedule and could hardly be called a success. Engineering flaws appeared

---

[8] The term "ferret" denotes an aircraft specifically equipped to detect, locate, record, and analyze electromagnetic radiation.

that required immediate attention. The aircraft did not handle well, the landing gear doors did not function properly, and vision from the canopy was poor. Although the Air Force officially accepted the initial RB-66A (Serial No. 52-2828) in June, it did not take possession of the plane, leaving it with Douglas for correction of the most obvious defects, prior to the beginning of the usual contractor flight tests. Douglas pilots flew the plane thoroughly, accumulating by mid-1956 300 hours of flying time in 192 flights.[9]

Increasing Difficulties   1954–1955

Flight of the first RB-66A was promptly followed by delivery of the 4 other RB-66As ordered from Douglas. The Air Force accepted these planes between August and December 1954, gaining nothing but problems in the process. Speed and load restrictions placed in effect in August hampered testing, actually preventing the early detection of many additional deficiencies. Yet, the restrictions could not be avoided. As suspected, even before the RB-66A's initial flight, the aircraft's flight control system was unreliable, and flying the plane using emergency manual control had proven hazardous. Besides, the RB-66A was unstable because its wings vibrated excessively, and the aircraft had the dangerous habit of pitching-up unexpectedly.

Near-Cancellation   1954–1955

The Air Force knew that an improved cockpit, giving the pilot better visibility, might not appear on the B/RB-66s before production of the 100th aircraft, but it did not anticipate the many aerodynamic shortcomings that came to light as soon as the RB-66As were flown. AMC's San Bernardino Air Materiel Area, responsible for the new weapon system, faced a difficult situation in the fall of 1954. TAC thought the first aircraft would be forthcoming in February 1955; Douglas admitted this could not be done, but insisted that deliveries could start no later than July—which was still unrealistic. The contractor, naturally enough, contended that the B/RB-66 was a good aircraft, which could be improved in several stages. Yet, Douglas

---

[9] Completion of the contractor's Phase I and Phase III tests in June 1956 marked the beginning of additional special modifications. When these changes were completed in October 1957, the plane was loaned to the Hughes Aircraft Company to participate in various experimental programs. However, Hughes pilots did not fly the plane, and it was returned to the Air Force in March 1958.

413

was unable to estimate the impact of the future modification work, since not enough was then known to define the number and types of changes needed. To the contractor's credit, Douglas at the time was also asking for an accelerated and intensified flight-test program. Meanwhile, the Air Force plant representative had reported that the contractor, to prevent further slippage of its original production schedule, was excessively resorting to expensive overtime. In late December, as recommended by the Air Materiel Command, Headquarters USAF cut off all overtime at the Douglas Plant and asked AMC to consider stopping or at least limiting production. In early 1955, the Air Staff began to investigate which aircraft could be substituted for the B/RB–66s, should this program be canceled. No rash decision had to be made, but the Air Staff wanted AMC and Air Research and Development Command to complete as soon as practicable their on-going evaluation of the new aircraft's many problems.

Final Decision   17 May 1955

Even though AMC and ARDC gave the Air Staff their appraisal of the Douglas program in February 1955, the B/RB–66's fate was not immediately determined. There were valid reasons for the delay. Phase II flight-test results were an essential part of the combined review. However, because of the flying restrictions still imposed on the RB–66As, the Air Force tests, like those conducted by the contractor, were not totally conclusive. For example, the airplane's high-speed limitations were still unknown. A great deal remained to be done. The static test program was incomplete, and the majority of the aircraft's equipment and subsystems had yet to be tested. Finally, the modifications needed to correct most of the aircraft's problems had been identified, but not verified. In essence, the 2-command evaluation of February 1955 pointed out that immediate termination of the program would cost the Air Force $300 million, a total that would double by mid-May. If the potential loss of $600 million influenced the Air Force to retain the program, the lack of suitable replacement aircraft undoubtedly was an equally important factor. At a meeting held in Washington on 17 May, General Nathan F. Twining, Air Force Chief of Staff, Lt. Gen. Clarence S. Irvine, Deputy Chief of Staff for Materiel, Lt. Gen. Frank F. Everest, Deputy Chief of Staff for Operations, and Mr. Roger Lewis, Assistant Secretary of the Air Force for Materiel, all agreed to stay with the program. However, this was not a blanket endorsement of the B/RB–66 aircraft, and several conditions, listed by the Air Materiel Command, qualified the decision, which in the long run would prove to be sound. As so often the case with many of the Air Force's new aircraft, the B/RB–66s had a shaky beginning, underwent many changes, but ended paying dividends.

Program Reduction   1955

Retention of the B/RB-66 was accompanied by a significant reduction of the program. Yet, it took several months to study the cost and logistic aspects of various possible changes. The Air Staff's goal, as related to AMC in late May, was to "reduce the B-66 program by the most economical and feasible method and still retain an RB-66B/C capabilty." By mid-August, a revised program, developed by AMC and Douglas, was approved by Headquarters USAF. The revision reflected an overall decrease of 48 aircraft from the total once approved for procurement. As directed, the brunt of the decrease fell on the B-66Bs.

Other Changes   1955

Engineering changes, as worked out between the Air Force and the prime contractor, were many. Forty-seven of them had been approved by the end of March, and additional ones most likely would be necessary in time. As a start, the Air Force wanted the B/RB-66 aircraft to be equipped with

An artist's conception of the B-66A taking off.

a parachute brake and an anti-skid device; it also desired immediate revision of the cockpit enclosure and relocation of the cockpit instruments. In addition, the aircraft's 2 J71–A–9 engines had to be replaced by more efficient J71–A–11s. Of course, these changes did not exempt Douglas from correcting the many problems already uncovered during the aircraft's flight tests. Moreover, none of the aircraft thus far produced by Douglas would be accepted by the Air Force before completion of so-called "turnaround" modifications.[10] Set on preventing further costly mistakes, the Air Force by June 1955 had also imposed various administrative adjustments on the contractor. To begin with, production would not exceed 7 aircraft per month until the fall of the year. All fiscal year 1955 subcontracts, not related to the RB–66C, had to be canceled. Finally, Douglas had to stabilize its labor force at the June 1955 level and keep overtime at or below 7 percent of the total labor effort.

Engineering Improvements   Mid-1955

By mid-1955, Douglas had significantly modified 1 RB–66A. The reworked plane featured an improved control system, a reconfigured tail turret, and heavier wing tips. Better engine pylons had been installed, and the J71–A–9 engines had been replaced by production articles of the Allison J71–A–11. In short, all modifications, recently identified but yet to be verified, had been incorporated into the plane. As directed by the Air Staff in late April, AMC began testing the aircraft's performance in July, which was very soon considering the RB–66A's many changes. Even more rewarding were the test results. Buffet appeared to have been reduced to an acceptable level, the control system worked fairly well, and the aircraft's speed had been increased to 550 knots. AMC was sufficiently impressed to predict that TAC could now expect delivery of its first RB–66s by year's end.

Flyaway Cost Per Test Aircraft $15.5 million

Airframe, $14,547,896; engines (installed), $719,500; electronics, $122,215; ordnance, $1,557; armament (and others), $125,043.[11]

---

[10] The "turnaround" modifications brought such aircraft to the level of the reworked RB–66A of mid-1955.

[11] Only 5 RB–66As came into being. As in the case of the B–57A and other aircraft, this limited production resulted in a high cost per aircraft.

416

Subsequent Model Series   **RB-66B**

Ultimate Use

None of the 5 RB–66As ever joined the Air Force's combat forces. Use of the aircraft exclusively for testing led to improved B/RB–66s and acquisition of considerable technical knowledge.

RB–66B

Manufacturer's Model 1329

Weapon System 308

New Features

The RB–66B at first closely resembled the improved RB–66A. Differences emerged over the years, as the B-model received better cameras and electronic countermeasures equipment. Some changes were made on the production lines; others, long after completion of the entire program. The J71–A–13 engine, an important feature of the aircraft, appeared on the last 17 RB–66Bs, earlier productions acquiring the higher-thrust engines through retrofit.

Special Testing   1955

Even though the improved RB–66A had been thoroughly tested, the Air Force Flight Test Center conducted extensive qualifying flight tests on one of the initial RB–66Bs. In contrast to the reworked RB–66A, which had been refitted with J71–A–11s,[12] this plane and 19 other early RB–66Bs carried the less powerful –9 engines. Nevertheless, the flight center's tests and subsequent RB–66B acceptance flights were generally successful. Electronic interference disturbed the image on the aircraft's AN/ARC–21 radar receiver, but Air Research and Development Command engineers soon found out that the ionization of particles in the jet engine exhaust caused the problem. This helped the contractor to swiftly devise an effective production modification.

First Flight (Production Aircraft)   29 October 1955

The first truly official flight of the RB–66B occurred on 29 October,

---

[12] This model powered most of the aircraft until the –13 engine became available.

after 8 of the aircraft had already been accepted by the Air Force. The flight, which was considered satisfactory, confirmed earlier test-flight results.

Enters Operational Service   January 1956

The first RB-66Bs joined the 9th Tactical Reconnaissance Squadron of the 363d Tactical Reconnaissance Wing (TRW), at Shaw AFB, South Carolina. Although the aircraft's initial all-weather capability was limited, arrival of the RB-66Bs permitted the long overdue replacement of the obsolescent RB-26s, and speeded phaseout in early 1957 of the problem-ridden RB-57As. The RB-66B program was a year behind schedule, but by the end of 1956 two-thirds of the RB-66Bs on order had been delivered, allowing activation of 2 other squadrons within the 363d TRW, the 41st and 43d, both located at Shaw AFB. The RB-66B in time became the primary night photographic weapon system of the Tactical Air Command.

Development Engineering Inspection   26–29 June 1956

A special development engineering inspection verified the proper installation of active defense electronic countermeasures equipment in forthcoming RB-66Bs. Several new devices were involved, most of which were intended to jam hostile radars. The 2-day development engineering inspection also covered retrofit of the 46 RB-66Bs, already accepted from Douglas. Even though attendees submitted 32 requests for alteration, the inspection board only approved 22 of them. The endorsed changes represented no extra expenses for the Air Force, since they all fell under the purview of Douglas's contract.

Overseas Deployments   1956–1957

While the bulk of the B/RB-66 contingent was earmarked for TAC, the Air Force originally wanted some of the delivered aircraft to be deployed overseas immediately. Slippage of the program changed this planning. Still, the 12th Tactical Reconnaissance Squadron, at Itami, Japan, a unit of the Pacific Air Forces (PACAF), received its RB-66Bs in late 1956, at about the same time that TAC activated 2 additional RB-66B squadrons. The United States Air Forces in Europe (USAFE), however, did not get any of the new aircraft until the fall of 1957. The 2 RB-66B squadrons, first assigned to the USAFE's 66th Wing, were later transferred to the 10th Tactical Reconnaissance Wing, another USAFE unit.

Operational Difficulties   1956–1957

The fact that the RB–66Bs were operational, at home and overseas, did not mean that all was well with the aircraft. To begin with, the program's near-cancellation and subsequent indefinite slippage, combined with overall financial restrictions, had created troublesome setbacks. TAC's 363d TRW was ill-prepared to support its first aircraft. The wing did not have enough MA–3 all-purpose servicing units and had too few of the MA–1 air conditioners that were necessary to preflight the RB–66s. There were also serious shortages of personal equipment, helmets in particular. The RB–66Bs themselves were encountering some of the problems often experienced during the early operational life of a new aircraft. Cautious, the Air Force grounded all RB–66Bs in mid-1956 after an incident at Shaw in which an aircraft suffered engine failure because bolts or screws either worked loose or sheared from the alternator. The grounding did not last, but similar restrictions were imposed in September, following the discovery of cracks on the horizontal stabilizer of a B–66B. The grounding this time affected both the B–66Bs and the RB–66Bs and remained in effect until all aircraft had been inspected and repaired, as necessary.

Engine Problems   1956–1957

Slow acceleration, flameout, stall, and surge were malfunctions that characterized the performance of the J71–A–9 engines that originally equipped 20 RB–66Bs and 17 B–66Bs. Allison improved the engine's bleed air system (reduced from the 16th to the 8th stage), and this with other minor changes led to the production of the J71–A–11. The new engine reached the Douglas plants promptly, equipping most B/RB–66s from the start. But the J71–A–14, despite its 9,700 pounds of thrust, proved disappointing. To begin with, the engine was still underpowered. In addition, like its predecessor, the J71–A–11 often stalled under high acceleration because of sticking compressor bleed valves and poorly designed electrical relays. Even though the most serious stall problems were solved without delay, TAC kept on insisting that better engines were needed. The command had in mind still another version of the Allison J71, namely, the 10,200-pound thrust J71–A–13, which could be injected with a mixture of water and alcohol. TAC believed, rightly as it turned out, that the higher-thrust engines would decrease takeoff roll by nearly 40 percent, would ensure a range increase of 10 percent, and would guarantee a 5-percent improvement of the aircraft's maximum speed. The Air Staff, in the fall of 1956, finally endorsed TAC's request. This meant that nearly 200 aircraft had to be retrofitted with J71–A–13s, while the B/RB–66s that had yet to clear the Douglas production lines would receive the new engines directly. Unforeseen by all parties—the Air Force, Douglas, as well as Allison— were the many difficulties that the new engines would soon create.

Significant Achievements   Mid-1957

Operational difficulties and forthcoming engine changes notwithstanding, the RB–66B by mid-1957 seemed to have shed most of its developmental flaws, and for all practical purposes the incorporation of production fixes had ceased. The aircraft, in addition, contributed to the successful development of a rain removal system that would serve the entire program, and other Air Force jet bombers. This system used a stream of engine bleed air, which was blown over the aircraft's windshield. Tested by the Wright Air Development Center under both artificial and natural conditions, the new development appeared to be the most effective and reliable means thus far devised to control a visibility problem of long standing. Indicative of the system's importance, the Air Force by mid-1957 had already initiated the procurement of retrofit kits for installing the new rain removal system on all B/RB–66s. The kits were geared to the J71–A–13s, since these engines were now due to appear on every B/RB–66 aircraft.

Unexpected Setbacks   1957–1958

Unforeseen problems were caused by the J71–A–13s, whether production installed or retrofitted on the B/RB–66s, because the new engines' higher thrust was accompanied by greater noise. Evidences of acoustically induced sonic fatigue were immediately noted, as skin cracks and stress breaks increasingly appeared in the ailerons, flaps, dive brakes, elevators, stabilizers, and rudders of the J71–A–13-equipped aircraft. Remedial procedures, undertaken without delay, consisted of pouring a powdered substance, known as Sta-Foam, into the aircraft's control surfaces that were subject to stresses. The powdered Sta-Foam, subsequently combined with chemicals causing it to foam up and solidify, promised to be a counteracting stress agent in the aircraft's most vulnerable surfaces.[13] TAC was greatly concerned by the stress problems besetting its new aircraft, particularly because the Sta-Foaming program, as initiated in 1957, would be lengthy. In effect, the most exacting work was assigned to Douglas, while tactical units

---

[13] The B/RB–66s predated metallic honeycombing, an industrial technique used to absorb the higher acoustical disturbances caused by the higher thrusts of later engines.

would accomplish the simpler tasks. Yet TAC insisted that whether the B/RB–66s were flown to the manufacturer for rework, or whether Douglas shipped Sta-Foamed surfaces to the tactical units, its new aircraft would be kept out of operation for an excessive period. In mid-1957, TAC again protested the program's pace, and suggested to save time that its RB–66s be flown to the San Bernardino Air Materiel Area where reworked surfaces would be exchanged for damaged and unmodified surfaces. Once flight tested, the modified planes would fly back to their bases. The Air Staff endorsed the TAC proposal, but new problems arose within a month. In August 1957, the command was informed that the B/RB–66 overall modernization program had to be curtailed for lack of money. The cut would be drastic, up to 80 percent if possible, and the entire inspect-and-repair-as-necessary (IRAN) program was eliminated. However, neither the aircraft conversion to J71–A–13 engines, nor the Sta-Foaming of fixed and movable surfaces were affected. The irony of the latter exemption came to light in February 1958, when the Sta-Foaming program was stopped. To some degree, 98 percent of the TAC B/RB–66s carried Sta-Foamed surfaces. Unfortunately, there was now clear evidence that the Sta-Foaming technique was a failure. The compound promoted corrosion and could eventually absorb up to 180 percent of its own weight in moisture, thus affecting aircraft balance. Although Douglas estimated that it would take some 8 months to fabricate new B/RB–66 control surfaces, the Air Force stated categorically that the work had to be done in little more than half that time.

Post-Production Improvements 1957–1958

Not only was the so-called all-weather RB–66B incapable of performing under adverse weather conditions, but it could not take photographs at night from high altitudes. Obvious from the start, the lack of proper tactical reconnaissance equipment was an increasingly crucial problem. To remedy the deficiency, Headquarters USAF in mid-1957 approved a TAC request for replacement of the aircraft's 12-inch cone K–37 camera by two 24-inch K–47s. However, the funding restrictions of the new fiscal year (FY 1958) postponed procurement of the more efficient cameras until mid-1958—fiscal year 1959. This would be in time to prevent Fairchild from shutting down its K–47 production lines, thereby saving the expense of re-establishing production, a financial burden that Air Force would have had to bear. Just the same, while this timing was a plus, the postponed camera procurement presented TAC with another delay, since the installation of K–47 cameras on all RB–66Bs would require nearly 1 year. Meanwhile, the acquisition of a high-resolution radar, to give the aircraft the capability to navigate in all types of weather, was almost at standstill. In late 1957, various radars were being considered and some testing was being done, but no solution was in sight.

Modernization   1958–1960

The B/RB–66 overall modernization program, postponed because of the FY 58 funding restrictions, finally got under way in May 1958. Tagged as "Little Barney," the $29 million project encompassed a myriad of technical order compliances, which had been delayed for lack of money. It covered the installation of J71–A–13 engines in the aircraft still equipped with J71–A–11s and the improvement of all PACAF and USAFE B/RB–66s which, in contrast to the TAC aircraft, had never benefitted from any type of modification. Of necessity, Little Barney also had to deal with the metal fatigue and corrosion problems encountered in all varieties of the B/RB–66s. Although Douglas provided sufficient newly designed control surfaces to allow all needed substitutions, Little Barney was not completed until August 1959, a slippage of several months. The delay was caused by a contractor-labor dispute, which prevented Douglas from sending field teams to the Air Force as soon as expected. Still, the project's results were satisfactory, and "Big Tom," which succeeded Little Barney at the Mobile Air Materiel Area in Alabama, also proved successful.[14] The 2 projects were closely related, since both centered on the yearly IRAN program of the weapon system. TAC delivered 5 percent of its RB–66s to Mobile each month and, as a rule, received its aircraft back within 30 days. The arrangement, while it lasted, worked well. Meanwhile, there were other problems, and frustrating incertitudes would soon follow.

Flaws and Frustrations   1959–1961

TAC grounded all its RB–66s in February 1959, after discovering cracks in the aircraft's nose gear attaching lugs. The repair of this flaw as well as other design deficiencies was guaranteed to be corrected by the contractor. The Air Force returned all available spares to Douglas for rework, and modifications to strengthen the nose gear strut assemblies were done at field and depot levels. Three Douglas teams arrived at Shaw, where they worked on 24-hour schedules so that all aircraft resumed flying before March. But another vexatious problem arose in mid-year, putting a new burden on the

---

[14] The managerial logistics support of the B/RB–66 program was transferred from the San Bernardino to the Mobile Air Materiel Area on 31 July 1959.

Big Tom project. The fuel tanks of all B/RB-66s had to be inspected, and most of them resealed, to prevent fuel leaks attributed to deterioration of the original sealant. When another sealant was applied, a different problem developed. Various areas of the resealed tanks started leaking under pressurization, which tended to indicate that the tanks were nearing the end of their useful lives.

In 1960, the long-awaited installation of K-47 cameras, having been canceled for lack of money, was reinstated.[15] However, the RB-66B's new K-47 camera system again became a cause of concern in early 1961. Camera magazines did not function properly. They could be fixed for $178,000 or replaced for $268,000, two expensive propositions considering the Air Force's continuing penury. In addition, while efficient for night photography, the cameras still needed to be upgraded for daytime operation, a modification finally approved in October.

Unrelenting Problems   1961–1963

Since its introduction into the TAC inventory, the RB-66B had failed to achieve the desired level of operational readiness, often due to maintenance and supply shortcomings. In fact, the same failings were experienced Air Force-wide by every version of the plane and persistent funding limitations did not help. While unwelcome by any command, support deficiencies made the Tactical Air Command's many tasks especially onerous. In the last months of 1961, TAC possessed an average of 20 RB-66s for combat crew training, but only 12 of them were flyable. Similar conditions compounded the difficulty of training replacement aircrews for all USAF RB-66 units, another responsibility of the command. Furthermore, B/RB-66 support problems might restrict TAC's ability to reinforce other major command units during contingencies. Although great improvements were realized in early 1962, the general support outlook was not optimistic. Subsystems of the RB-66 aircraft were past their normal life expectancy and were almost certain to cause further unexpected maintenance.

Planning changes, again intricately related to tight budgets, aggravated the overall situation. Previous phaseout schedules had spurred the end of the aircraft's IRAN program, but retention of the RB-66s was now programmed to extend through fiscal year 1965, because there was no replace-

---

[15] On the other hand, Headquarters USAF in 1960 also recommended that TAC drop its requirement for putting a high resolution radar on the RB-66Bs. The cost involved, about $100,000 per aircraft, seemed no longer justifiable in view of the RB-66B's near phaseout, then programmed to take place in fiscal year 1964.

ment. In 1962, this meant bringing back some kind of IRAN program, on a one-time basis, in view of the aircraft's forthcoming retirement. As approved by the Air Force, this $7.1 million project (About Time) covered 145 RB–66s, 32 of them belonging to TAC. The project was at once affected by fund shortages. To make sure that as many aircraft as possible would be repaired, without reducing the scope of the work to be performed, TAC agreed to a sizable commitment of its own resources.

In January 1963, a corrosion-induced failure of one aircraft's nose struts engendered a complete retrofit of the fleet by the Mobile Air Materiel Area. During the same period, overhaul of the RB–66's J71–A13 engines began. Done under contract at the Naval Air Station at Quonset Point, Rhode Island, this crucial task proved time-consuming, prompting TAC to wonder if some kind of arrangement enabling engine repair at Shaw AFB would not be more effective. On the other hand, Shaw had retained its full share of problems. Despite every effort, the overall maintenance of the RB–66s remained difficult. Parts shortages did not abate throughout the year, contributing to high cannibalization rates within the 363d Wing and 4411th Combat Crew Training Group of the Tactical Air Command.

Planning Changes   1964–1965

As of 30 June 1964, only 100 RB–66Bs remained in the Air Force inventory and within 12 months, this total had dipped to 79. Still, phaseout of the entire B/RB–66 fleet was becoming less likely. The Air Force's increasing involvement in Southeast Asia affected all planning. The primary question no longer seemed to be how long a given model's retirement would be postponed, but rather to assess how retained aircraft would cope with their extended commitments. Obviously, some modifications would be needed. Yet, experience showed that the best modifications would not necessarily work from the start. For example, 3 RB–66Bs had been equipped in 1963 with infrared sensors, electronic strobes, and side-looking radars, but the performance of the strobes and infrared sensors, as demonstrated during a 1964 exercise, did not satisfy TAC. In any case, retention of the RB–66s, however probable, could not be taken for granted. This posed another dilemma by preventing reinstatment of a formal IRAN program. Wanting to be ready for an early IRAN program, should the Department of Defense approve the aircraft's retention, Headquarters USAF in April 1965 directed a "minimum prudent work package for IRAN of RB–66 aircraft during FY 66." Developed by TAC and endorsed by Air Force Logistics Command, this program made allowances for the fact that previous work on the RB–66 consisted of a series of short-term actions, none intended to keep the plane in service for more than 2 additional years.

End of Production   1957

The October 1957 delivery of the last RB-66B reflected the end of the aircraft's production.

Total RB-66Bs Accepted   145

Acceptance Rates

The Air Force accepted 4 RB-66Bs in FY 55, 46 in FY 56, 87 in FY 57, and 8 in FY 58.

Flyaway Cost Per Production Aircraft $2.55 million

Airframe, $1,563,671; engines (installed), $696,034; electronics, $155,000; ordnance, $10,081; armament (and others), $166,137.[16]

Average Cost Per Flying Hour $715.00

Average Maintenance Cost Per Flying Hour $323.00

Subsequent Model Series   B-66B

Other Configurations   EB-66B and EB-66E

The EB-66Bs and EB-66Es came into being in the spring of 1966, when the prefix E was assigned to all versions of the B/RB-66s intended for electronic warfare.[17] However, neither of the 2 models was new. The Air

---

[16] Including the costs of research and development and in-production engineering changes, but excluding the expenses of all-post production modifications.

[17] The prefix E symbolized a modified mission. It was given to all aircraft equipped with special electronic devices for employment in 1 or more of the following roles: electronic countermeasures; airborne early warning radar; airborne command and control, including

Force contingent of EB–66Bs comprised both modernized and re-equipped B–66Bs and RB–66Bs, with no distinction made between the 2 types. In both cases, original electronic countermeasures gear (electronic devices and chaff dispensers) had been upgraded, and sophisticated pieces of equipment added. Similarly, EB–66Es, the first of which did not reach Southeast Asia before August 1967, could be converted B–66Bs or RB–66Bs.[18] The EB–66E did, however, represent an improvement over the EB–66B. Although the "E" carried fewer jamming devices, its new tuneable transmitters enabled the electronic warfare operator to change frequencies during flight in order to jam several kinds of radar.

Southeast Asian Deployment   April 1965

First committed to the war in April 1965, long before the Department of Defense decided to postpone the entire program's phaseout, the RB–66Bs quickly demonstrated the limitations of their equipment which, in view of existing retirement plans, had never been modernized. There was an exception, however. Three of the early RB–66Bs, deployed to Southeast Asia, had been equipped with infrared sensors, an important asset to meet growing night reconnaissance requirements. Nevertheless, the 3 planes were old and were replaced in 1966 by modern infrared-equipped RF–4Cs. Meanwhile, a great many RB–66Bs were being modified to update nearly obsolete electronic countermeasures (ECM) equipment. Improved support also was being worked out, in order to raise the aircraft's safety and efficiency. In 1966, most active RB–66Bs became EB–66s,[19] but this did not spell the end of the aircraft modernization.

Modernization Efforts   1966–1969

In mid-1966, the Air Staff directed that 26 RB–66Bs be fitted with

---

communications relay; and tactical data communications link for all non-autonomous modes of flight.

[18] This lack of specific identification was actually logical, since all B/RB–66s were basically alike. Initial differences had reflected the aircraft's individual roles. In practical terms, the Air Force intended all along that the aircraft's makeup and load be adjustable to mission requirements.

[19] Throughout the years, small numbers of RB–66s remained or were brought back in the active inventory. In 1968, for instance, the war's demands and the redistribution of electronic warfare assets caused TAC to use 20 RB–66s for training worldwide replacement crews.

passive and active ECM systems. The first of the 26 modified aircraft (EB-66Es) reached the war theater on 30 August 1967, but did not perform as well as expected, forcing PACAF to defer plans to make similar improvements to another 13 EB-66Bs. When money became available, 6 additional RB-66Bs, withdrawn from storage, were brought to an upgraded EB-66E configuration. At the same time, the problems of the first 26 EB-66Es were corrected. In 1968, confronted by increasingly sophisticated enemy defenses, the Air Force began using all EB-66s in the jamming role. This pinpointed the need for further improvements, such as steerable antennas and modification of the aircraft's new communication jammer. The wisdom of spending extra money on such an aged aircraft was debatable. TAC's new Commander, Gen. William M. Momyer, arriving from Southeast Asia in mid-1968, also had strong reservations about the modernized EB-66's effectiveness as a standoff jammer. Because no sound alternative could then be worked out,[20] General Momyer concurred in the extended modernization of the EB-66s, even though the entire project was fraught with difficulties since no single electronic-countermeasures configuration would meet the specific goals of all contingencies.[21] Continued EB-66 improvement reinforced TAC's argument that the aircraft's engines had to be replaced, a change sought by the command since 1966. TAC's belief, fully shared by PACAF and USAFE, was not unfounded.[22] The J71-A-13 engine was limited in power and had become extremely expensive to operate because of the short time between overhauls. Air Staff support notwithstanding, the Department of Defense had disapproved TAC's first request on the ground that the limited number of EB-66s remaining in the inventory did not warrant the purchase of better engines. Although TAC subsequently underlined that additional electronic systems could not be fitted in the EB-66s because the J71s and the associated generator banks could not supply enough electrical power, the Department of Defense did not alter its decision.

---

[20] In the fall of 1968, the Air Force Systems Command suggested that all EB-66 modernization programs be revalidated and that selection of an electronic warfare vehicle other than the EB-66 be reconsidered.

[21] The Air Staff had already told PACAF, TAC, and USAFE to review current planning and to develop alternate electronic countermeasures configurations to satisfy their individual requirements.

[22] The improved B/RB-66s (EB-66s) with their many new components had grown from some 70,000 to about 81,000 pounds. But the thrust of their engines had not changed. Obviously, the overworked J71 engines of the EB-66s soon began to consume fuel at a disturbing rate.

Modernization Reversal   1969

In May 1969, Gen. John P. McConnell, Chief of Staff of the Air Force, stopped the EB–66 modernization. Three of the primary factors accounting for the decision were cost, time involved, and Defense Department's denial of a new engine. The Air Staff made it known that remaining EB–66s would have to be maintained through normal processes for perhaps 5 more years.

Support Problems   1969–1972

Fatigue cracks in the compressor of the J71 engine became a problem of major importance. Since flight safety was at stake, most of the available funds went for engine repair, and little was left to invest in airframes and electronics. In these circumstances, maintenance of the EB–66s proved increasingly difficult. Reduction of the EB–66 inventory in late 1969 brought relief by allowing a realignment of the modification programs to match available funds. Nonetheless, critically needed alterations often could not be done.

Operational Status   Mid-1973

By mid-1973, the EB–66 had truly become an old, underpowered aircraft that had been extended repeatedly beyond its programmed life span. Because of the small fleet's approaching phaseout, no IRAN program supported the aircraft, and a contract team performed substitute inspections of the EB–66s. TAC had planned all along to get rid of its EB–66s as soon as the aircraft's Southeast Asian commitments were over. Yet, no other electronic countermeasures aircraft was available. In mid-1972, the Air Staff had recommended that the EB–66s be replaced by ECM-equipped F–111s, a solution actively pursued by TAC. But the Department of Defense had yet to reach a decision in mid-1973, and TAC had to retain a minimum number of EB–66s, as did PACAF and USAFE.[23]

Perilous Incident   10 March 1964

One year before the first RB–66Bs were sent to Southeast Asia, one of the aircraft was involved in a potentially very dangerous situation. On 10

---

[23] The EB–66s left the Air Force inventory the following year.

March 1964, an RB–66B of the 10th Tactical Reconnaissance Wing, a unit of USAFE's Third Air Force, took off from Toul-Rosieres Air Base, France, on a flight scheduled to carry it into West Germany. Malfunction of the RB–66B's compass and the crew's failure to recognize the problem brought the aircraft over East Germany, where it was shot down. After seeing the enemy interceptors, the crew ejected, landed, and was taken prisoner. No one was seriously injured, and the 3 crewmen were released before the end of March. The RB–66B loss, however, because it closely followed a far more tragic incident,[24] took on added importance. Hence, on 10 March, within hours of the airplane's crash, Gen. Gabriel P. Disosway, USAFE Commander-in-Chief, informed his staff of the President's deep concern and of the crucial necessity of preventing such incidents in the future. On 14 March, General Disosway imposed a buffer zone which extended and widened the existing Air Defense Identification Zone in central Europe. Special permanent procedures, known as Wind Drift, were established for positive control of every type of aircraft in the buffer zone. General Disosway also demanded that crew responsibilities and air discipline be "hammered home" to all aircrews during pre-flight briefings. The Wind Drift rules became even more stringent in 1965, when Gen. Bruce K. Holloway assumed command of USAFE.

---

[24] On 28 January, a T–39 straying over East Germany had been shot down, resulting in the death of the 3 crew members.

B-66B

Manufacturer's Model 1327

Previous Model Series   RB-66B

New Features

Increased design gross weight and the Western Electric K-5 bombing system were the most significant new features of the conventional swept-back wing, all-metal B-66B. Like the RB-66B, the B-66B carried a 3-man crew.

Basic Development   August 1952

The bomber configuration, endorsed by the Air Staff in August 1952, occasioned further changes to the initial Air Force version of the experimental A3D. The airplane's design gross weight was raised to 78,000 pounds (8,000 pounds more than the RB-66B's), the bomb bay was lengthened 17.5 inches, the capacity of the aft fuselage fuel tanks was increased, and pylons were provided to support extra 500-gallon fuel tanks. The approved B-66B configuration also involved the installation of a bombing system and of bomb dropping devices. Finally, a detachable probe-drogue in-flight refueling system was added, and a further revision of the XA3D's hydraulic system was directed. Of necessity, since every effort was to be made to keep the bomber and reconnaissance versions as close to each other as possible, most B-66B requirements were incorporated into the RB-66As. Ensuing problems, resulting modifications, and reduction of the B-66B procurement did not alter the program's policy on interchangeability.

Contractual Arrangements   1952-1956

The B-66B procurement was initiated in August 1952, when Letter Contract AF 33(600)-16341 was amended to cover the purchase of 26 B-66Bs. The amendment in addition changed the terms of the letter contract

431

of April 1952, which reverted to the cost-plus-fixed-fee type of agreement endorsed for the RB–66As. The amended contract of August 1952, like the initial RB–66A document, assured Douglas of a profit amounting to 6 percent of the aggregate contract cost. A similar contract, AF 33(600)–25669, started by an October 1953 letter contract, called for 75 B–66Bs, but was amended many times as a result of a program reduction in mid-1955. For the same reason, contract AF 33(600)–28368, the fourth and last procurement order signed on 24 September 1954 also underwent many changes.[25] By the end of 1955, only 55 B–66Bs were to be bought, but General Twining agreed in early 1956 that the single authorized wing of B–66Bs should acquire more planes to take care of normal attrition. The Air Force held the B/RB–66 program on a tight financial rein. The program's ceiling had been settled once and for all. Hence, the approved extra 17 B–66Bs were diverted from the RB–66B total. The Air Force also specified that any cost increases generated by the directed substitution would have to be absorbed by deleting additional RB–66Bs.

First Flight (Production Aircraft)   4 January 1955

The first official B–66B flight was accomplished on 4 January 1955, 7 other B–66Bs being accepted by the Air Force before the new tactical bomber was cleared for operational assignment. Besides participating in the usual testing program, the early B–66Bs were involved from the start in the crucial development of their future sophisticated components. For instance, flight testing of a prototype K–5 bombing system, tailored for the B–66B, was pursued actively during the early part of 1955.[26] These tests entered a new phase in March 1955, when high-altitude and high-speed trials began.

---

[25] Contract AF 33(600)–25569 and AF 33(600)–28368 were renegotiated during 1956, the Air Force being convinced that the cost-plus-fixed-fee type of agreements, dictated by circumstances, had worked even more poorly than expected. Nothing could be done to revamp the early B/RB–66 procurement, since deliveries on the first 2 contracts were nearly complete. The Air Force nevertheless intended to straighten out the 2 remaining orders. The service believed that frequent and onerous cost overruns in any given program could be avoided, or at least minimized, if all parties were affected by the program's financial outcome. This was reflected in the 2 supplemental agreements signed in March 1957 by Douglas and the Air Force. Douglas exchanged its fixed fee for a target fee of about 5 percent (the incentive was plus or minus 10 percent on sums falling within 115 and 85 percent of each contract's target cost).

[26] The K–5 was greatly altered for its use with the B–66, but it was not a weapon system development. The system had to be fitted into the already established airframe configuration, not developed parallel with it. The equipment was procured by the contractor rather than furnished by the government. Douglas spent about $100 million in subcontracts with Western Electric, manufacturer of the K–5, and with Bell Telephone Laboratories, which took care of the developmental engineering.

The functional testing of a production model of the bombing system soon followed. As fully expected by the Air Research and Development Command's Armament Laboratory in mid-1955, the K–5 promised to give the Air Force ". . . an all-weather tactical bombing capabilty compatible with the mission requirements of the B–66."

Enters Operational Service   March 1956

The B–66Bs began reaching the Tactical Air Command in March 1956, about 1 year later than originally scheduled. However, once under way, deliveries were reasonably steady, 64 of the 72 B–66Bs on order being accepted by mid-1957. The Ninth Air Force's 17th Light Bombardment Wing, at Hurlburt Field,[27] Florida, remained sole recipient of the B–66Bs until September 1957, when TAC began to transfer its total contingent to the United States Air Forces in Europe.

Development Engineering Inspections   Fall 1956

Despite the importance of the electronic countermeasures program, nothing could be done about it when the B/RB–66 configuration started taking shape. Electronic countermeasures components were in early developmental stages, and technological incertitudes prevented the establishment of firm operational requirements. Nevertheless, after many tentative plans, the Air Force in October 1954 decided the process should be accelerated to acquire at least an interim electronic countermeasures capability. Hence, a multi-phase interim ECM program was set up early in 1955. Briefly stated, the program called for installation (during the aircraft production) of available parts of the APS–54 radar warning receiver and ALE–2 chaff dispensers. Three interchangeable types of jamming equipment were ordered, and interchangeable ECM tail cones were to be fashioned to carry some of the chaff equipment and antennas. Finally, provisions for ECM cradles were to be made in the bomb bay of the B–66B. Yet, even though some B–66Bs had already begun to reach TAC, configuration changes were still under consideration in the fall of 1956. Procurement of the B–66B had been reduced in mid-1955, but the aircraft had not been exempted from the ambitious electronic countermeasures program planned for the entire B/RB–66B fleet. During the second half of 1956, 2 development engineering inspections were held a few weeks apart. The first, in late September, covered

---

[27] An auxiliary field of Eglin AFB.

The B-66B featured the new K-5 bombing system and increased fuel capacity.

all-chaff and half-chaff electronic countermeasures cradle configurations of the B-66B. The second, held in early October, was concerned with the B-66B's entire electronic countermeasures installation. The 2 development engineering inspections were successful, the Air Force being satisfied by the apparent completeness and flexibility of the selected arrangements. However, the whole project was soon to encounter problems.

ECM Program Changes   1956–1957

Soon after the development engineering inspections of September and October 1956, the electronic countermeasures program ran into trouble. Major alterations would be needed to fit the required pieces of ECM equipment into the B/RB-66 airframes. Even if the Douglas production lines expedited the necessary modifications, full transfer of the B-66Bs to Europe and deployment of the several RB-66Bs destined for the Far East would have to be postponed. By the end of the year, it became clear that more unexpected changes would be needed, all of which affected tail cones and cradles. Included were substitution of various components, addition of some kind of apparatus to permit selective switching among jammers (a requirement previously overlooked), more powerful jamming signals, and new tail cone antennas.[28] Moreover, just the interim ECM program pro-

---

[28] The antenna changes eventually delayed the beginning of tail cone deliveries to March 1958, a slippage of about 1 year.

posed in March 1955 would be extremely costly—$40 million for a partial installation. In July 1957, Headquarters USAF decided that no B/RB–66Bs would be ECM-equipped during production. The Air Staff also cut down the procurement of cradles by one-third, to a total of 12, and reduced the tail cone purchase to 113, a decrease of 25. At the same time, the Air Force indicated that a modernization/IRAN program would catch the B/RB–66Bs that had not been modified to accommodate needed ECM equipment. In late 1957, 13 B–66Bs and 31 RB–66Bs were scheduled for such preparation.

Flight Testing   1955–1957

For all practical purposes, flight testing of the B–66B ended in January 1957, for the few tests yet to be completed were of minor importance. Overall test results were satisfactory, and the engineering improvements prompted by the testing program either had been or were being incorporated into the aircraft. The B–66B nearly met the Air Force procurement specifications. Noted performance decreases (10 percent in altitude, 12 percent in range, and 7 percent in low-altitude speed) might not be correctable, but the aircraft's flying characteristics were good. Thorough testing had demonstrated that the B–66B was especially well-adapted to low-level flight, could handle a variety of special weapons, and could be aerially refueled to 96,000 pounds.

Operational Problems   1956–1958

The positive qualities of the B–66B, flown by the 17th Bombardment Wing, were not in doubt, testing having ascertained the aircraft's basic soundness. Nevertheless, being practically identical to the RB–66B, the new tactical bomber shared the engine problems, Sta-Foam vicissitudes, and other early difficulties of the reconnaissance aircraft. The B–66B in addition had a few flaws of its own, which also remained uncorrected prior to the aircraft's overseas deployment.

Overseas Deployment   1958

Early in 1958, after a period of training, the squadrons of TAC's 17th Bombardment Wing were transferred to the 47th Bomb Wing (Tactical), a unit of USAFE's Third Air Force, with stations at Sculthorpe and Alconbury in the United Kingdom. While the 47th Wing's conversion from the obsolescent B–45[29] was a major operational gain, the B–66B's arrival was accompanied by serious maintenance difficulties. The flow of spare parts from the United States remained inadequate until August 1958, and shortages of electronic equipment and of such critical items as hydraulic pumps and oxygen regulators persisted throughout much of the year. In addition, the bomb shackles initially installed on the B–66B did not have a lock secure enough to prevent inadvertent bomb releases. This problem, though addressed from the start by TAC, was not being solved as fast as the Air Force would have liked. To save time, personnel of the 47th Wing installed the first new shackles developed by Douglas. Other B–66Bs were due to receive the improved shackles during the B/RB–66 overall modernization program. However, even the simplest plans could be affected by circumstances beyond USAF control. Although started as scheduled on 1 May 1958, the "Little Barney" overseas program taking place at the AMC's Air Depot at Chateauroux, France, was hindered significantly by French labor unrest. The B–66Bs shipped to Chateauroux for modernization (elimination of Sta-Foaming damages, engine retrofits, and the like) were often held for 52 days, almost twice the work time authorized for every aircraft. To speed up the B–66B's operational readiness, the Air Force decided to ship new shackles directly to the 47th Bomb Wing, which would enable the unit to install them promptly on the modified aircraft, finally back from Chateauroux.

End of Production   1957

The October 1957 delivery of the last B–66B marked the end of production.

Total B–66Bs Accepted   72

The 72 B–66Bs accepted by the Air Force reflected a reduction of nearly 50 percent from the maximum procurement once considered.

Acceptance Rates

The Air Force accepted 1 B–66B in FY 55, 27 in FY 56, 36 in FY 57, and

---

[29] The B–45s were taken out of the combat inventory and transferred to USAFE bases in Europe and North Africa, where they were used for fire fighting training.

the last 8 in FY 58 (3 in July 1957, 1 in August, 3 in September, and 1 in October).

Flyaway Cost Per Production Aircraft $3.68 million

Airframe, $2,515,511; engines (installed), $664,034; electronics, $400,000; ordnance, $10,625; armament (and others), $95,300.[30]

Average Maintenance Cost Per Flying Hour $280.00

Subsequent Model Series RB–66C

Other Configurations EB–66B and EB–66E

The EB–66Bs and EB–66Es were reconfigured B–66Bs, identical to modified and similarly redesignated RB–66Bs. Like the former RB–66Bs, converted B–66Bs began to acquire "E" prefixes early in 1966.

Initial Phaseout Mid-1963

The Air Staff finally agreed to let USAFE retain its B–66Bs beyond the FY 61 inactivation date that had been established originally. Still, except for 13 specially equipped B–66Bs, the entire contingent was out of the operational inventory by mid-1963.

Special Modifications 1964–1965

From the start of the B/RB–66 program, the Air Force thought the B–66 light tactical bomber would also be used for ECM jamming. Hence, a pallet (or cradle), carrying jammers, chaff dispensers and other necessary gear, could be fitted in the aircraft's bomb bay, once the latter was stripped

------

[30] Including the costs of research and development and in-production engineering changes, but excluding the expenses of modifications added on after approval of a basic contract.

of its bombload and shackles.[31] Nevertheless, retention of 13 ECM-equipped B-66Bs would entail some work since the aircraft were not new. In April 1964, the Air Force Logistics Command began to develop a working agreement between USAFE's 42d Tactical Reconnaissance Squadron, the Mobile Air Materiel Area, and a Lear-Siegler contract team. The project, as settled, covered the IRAN program for each aircraft, including removal and inspection of all fuel cells and updating of the electronic countermeasures system of the aircraft, referred to as Brown Cradle. The Air Force estimated that to do the overall task properly would require some 3,400 manhours for each of the 13 Brown Cradle B-66Bs. Since USAFE did not want to part with more than 2 of the aircraft at one time, the B-66B's renovation and Brown Cradle modification extended well into 1965.

Southeast Asian Deployment   1965–1966

USAFE retention of its updated Brown Cradle aircraft was short.[32] In late 1965, 5 of the modernized B-66Bs were deployed to Southeast Asia. In May 1966, the 42d Tactical Reconnaissance Squadron's remaining 8 Brown Cradle aircraft also departed for the war theater.

Reactivation   1967

Eleven B-66Bs were reactivated early in 1967 and, after modification, were sent to Southeast Asia. Meanwhile, on-going testing to determine the aircraft's life expectancy proved satisfactory enough. Even though the B-66B shared the engine problems of the entire RB-66 fleet, additional B-66Bs were soon withdrawn from storage and modified for war service.

Operational Status   Mid-1973

Reactivated and modernized B-66Bs followed the operational pattern

---

[31] Similarly, the RB-66's bomb bay, minus cameras and related equipment, could accommodate a cradle. In fact, by mid-1959 ECM tail cones had been authorized for USAFE's entire B/RB-66 contingent and for all of the PACAF RB-66Bs.

[32] The B-66Bs had no electronic intelligence capability, when configured as ECM aircraft. The USAFE Brown Cradle aircraft's intended role was to support the strike force by actively jamming enemy radars. The command recognized that its ECM B-66Bs might be vulnerable to enemy interceptors, but bitterly deplored deployment of the 13 aircraft to Southeast Asia.

of the RB–66Bs. Also known as EB–66s since early 1966, a few of the aircraft still lingered in the active inventory in mid-1973.

Milestones   1956–1957

On 12 August 1956, one of the Air Force's new subsonic B–66 jet bombers flew from Hawaii to California in 4 hours and 27 minutes, covering a distance of 2,690 miles at an average speed of more than 600 miles per hour.

In the fall of 1957, only 17 hours after being alerted in the United States, several B–66Bs, after crossing the Pacific as elements of a Composite Air Strike Force, were flying simulated bombing missions over the Philippines.

RB-66C

Manufacturer's Model 1328

Previous Model Series   B-66B

New Features

The RB-66C featured a reconfigured bomb bay, which housed electronic components and provided space for 4 additional crew members (electronic countermeasures operators or observers). The aircraft's design weight was 75,000 pounds (5,000 more than the RB-66B's and 3,000 pounds less than the B-66B's). Wingtip radar pods and a radome containing antennas for the various radars were the other significant new features of the RB-66C. As in the case of every B/RB-66 version, the basic 3-man crew of the RB-66C (pilot, navigator, and gunner) used upward ejection seats, the 4 additional ECM operators, downward ones.

Basic Development   1953

Development of the RB-66's electronic intelligence version, although anticipated as early as 1952, did not begin until 1953. The aircraft's overall configuration was submitted to USAF Headquarters in early March and approved the following month. A more specific design was initiated in June, but the Air Force knew that the equipment required by the future aircraft's electronic reconnaissance role was not readily available. Production schedules, therefore, forecast an operational date of late 1956. Thus, despite the many problems that soon beset the entire program, the RB-66C practically escaped the production slippages of other and less sophisticated B/RB-66s.

Production Go-Ahead   15 April 1953

On record, the Air Force endorsed production of the ferret RB-66C in mid-April. In actuality, the production decision was only firmed up several months later. And like preceding models, the RB-66C was nearly canceled

440

in 1955, when the whole B/RB–66 program came under review. The RB–66C's initial procurement document was a purely developmental letter contract calling for "necessary implementation planning and design for the electronic reconnaissance version of the RB–66." This document, AF 33(600)–25669, was issued on 12 June 1953, but it took until August, when the fiscal year 1954 airplane program was released, for the Air Force to indicate a first requirement for 65 RB–66Cs.

Mockup Inspection   14 January 1954

Inspection of the RB–66C mockup generated 31 change requests. The 14 January mockup inspection, held at Douglas's plant in Tulsa, Oklahoma, reflected a change of plan. Originally, all B/RB–66s (RB–66Cs, included) were to be produced in Long Beach, a sensible decision since 60 percent of the airframe parts were expected to be alike, and a similar commonality percentage would apply to tooling. However, the Douglas Long Beach plant was already manufacturing C–124s. Despite its 3,320,000 square feet of space, the plant was not large enough, nor did it have the engineering capability to accommodate the whole B/RB–66 program. By necessity, Tulsa was selected in 1953 to build all RB–66Cs, but this decision, like most long-range plans, was revised. The Tulsa plant ended manufacturing a great many wings for other B/RB–66 models, while Douglas eventually found it more economical and convenient to produce certain portions of the RB–66Cs in Long Beach.[33]

Program Change   July 1955

In mid-1955, the Air Force confirmed a heretofore tentative decision to reduce the RB–66C program of 72 aircraft by half. The 36 deleted RB–66Cs would be produced in the synoptic weather configuration.

First Flight (Production Aircraft)   29 October 1955

The RB–66C's first official flight took place on 29 October 1955, TAC getting one of the new aircraft soon afterwards.

---

[33] The Long Beach plant had been built during World War II to manufacture such airplanes as the A–20, A–26, C–47, C–74, and B–17. The United States government only owned 52 percent of the plant. In contrast, the Tulsa plant was totally owned by the government. It was also not as large as the Long Beach plant and was expected to stop manufacturing and modifying B–47s sometime in 1955.

Contractual Arrangements   1955–1956

Procurement of the RB–66C mirrored the turbulent history of the entire program. An October 1953 amendment to the letter contract of June 1953 became the prelude to several unusual arrangements. Again, because Douglas could not possibly come up with realistic fixed-price estimates, the contract, finalized in December 1953, covered Douglas's costs, plus a fixed fee of 6 percent. In another departure from preferred procurement methods, contract AF 33(600)–25669 covered 3 different models of the B/RB–66s. The rationale for this procedure was that 1 contract would be cheaper than 3, because it would permit co-mingling of common parts and the use of common tooling. In any case, as a result of the mid-1955 program reduction, the contract was altered in August 1956. The changes, however, did not specifically affect the RB–66Cs. Meanwhile, another RB–66C order had been processed in fiscal year 1955, when the fourth and last B/RB–66 contract was negotiated.[34] This contract, AF (33(600)–28386, was signed on 24 September 1954. It was another cost-plus-fixed-fee contract, carrying the same fee of 6 percent, as well as several types of B/RB–66s. This contract also underwent changes. In January 1956, the contract's total was reduced; in August, the procurement of some models was altered in favor of others, and the 36 RB–66Cs canceled in mid-1955 were formally deleted in December. Finally, as already noted, the terms of both contracts (the last 2 of a total of 4) were renegotiated, 2 new supplemental agreements being signed in early 1957.

Enters Operational Service   1956

TAC's initial RB–66C, received at Shaw AFB on February 1956, was assigned to the 9th Tactical Reconnaissance Squadron. Only a few more of the aircraft were delivered before mid-year, but by the end of December, more than half of the RB–66C contingent had reached the Air Force. The ferret RB–66C was the first weapon system of its kind. Its assignment also proved unique, as TAC from the start planned to equip certain squadrons with a mixture of RB–66Cs and of forthcoming and equally novel WB–66Ds.

---

[34] At the time, only 1 RB–66A had been delivered, only 1 B–66B was partially shop-completed, and no work had been done on the RB–66C. Therefore, as far as prices were concerned, Douglas knew little more than it had the previous year. And obviously, the forthcoming production correction of airframe deficiencies was bound to complicate all cost estimates.

Engine Deficiencies   1956

As in the case of most B/RB–66s, some RB–66Cs were equipped originally with J71–A–11 engines. Hence, they too were hindered by engine malfunctions and demonstrated disappointing operational performance until retrofitted with more powerful J71–13s.

Grounding   June 1956

The Air Force grounded on 14 June the 6 RB–66Cs it had already accepted from Douglas. The grounding was necessary because the aircraft's center of gravity was affected by the fuel level. The retrofit installation of a boost pump in the aircraft's forward tank solved the problem, but it took until mid-August to flight test the modification. The change was incorporated during the production of subsequent RB–66Cs.

Engineering Problem   July 1956

An engineering difficulty, peculiar to the RB–66C, received special attention. The instability demonstrated by the first RB–66A had been corrected, but the wingtip radar pods featured by the RB–66C had created a new buffeting problem. In July, the Air Force Flight Test Center checked the effectiveness of a Douglas-devised modification, which attached a vane to the wingtip pod. The Air Force determined that the new device was fairly effective. Yet, it wanted a "buffet free airplane," not one so fitted as to bring buffeting to an "acceptable level." In late July, representatives from Air Research and Development Command, AMC, and the Wright Air Development Center met with Douglas and decided that the contractor's modification would do for a while, but that the root of the problem had to be eliminated. In short, better shaped pods had to be designed and tested. Following selection and production of a reconfigured pod, all 36 RB–66Cs would be retrofitted, which they were.

Overseas Deployments   1956–1957

The RB–66Cs arrived overseas shortly after TAC received its first aircraft. USAFE got most of its RB–66C quota in 1956. The 12 aircraft, one-third of the total procurement, went to the newly activated 42d Tactical Reconnaissance Squadron at Spangdahlem Air Base, West Germany.

PACAF in 1957 received 12 RB–66C electronic intelligence (ELINT) aircraft, which it assigned to the 67th Tactical Reconnaissance Wing's 11th Tactical Reconnaissance Squadron at Yokota Air Base, Japan. To various extents and regardless of location, the delivered RB–66Cs were to participate in the Little Barney and other modification programs, still to be applied to the preceding RB–66Bs and B–66Bs.

Special Testing   1957

Testing of the electronic reconnaissance RB–66C was completed in November 1957. The employment and suitability tests, conducted by the Air Proving Ground Command, showed that the aircraft was capable of performing "peripheral reconnaissance during peacetime" without equipment modifications. However, major engineering changes would be needed, should the RB–66C be used in a combat environment.

End of Production   1957

Delivery of 2 last RB–66Cs in June 1957 marked the end of the aircraft's production.

Total RB–66Cs Accepted   36

Acceptance Rates

The Air Force accepted 6 RB–66Cs in FY 56, and 30 more in FY 57.

Flyaway Cost Per Production Aircraft $3.06 million

Airframe, $2,138,445; engines (installed), $664,034; electronics, $155,000; ordnance, $13,722; armament (and others), $95,300.[35]

Subsequent Model Series   WB–66D

---

[35] The cost formula of previous B/RB–66s applied to the RB–66C and subsequent WB–66D.

Other Configurations   EB-66C

The EB-66C, so designated in 1966, when all B/RB-66 aircraft engaged in electronic warfare acquired the E prefix, was a modernized RB-66C. Even though the former RB-66C at the time was the only tactical electronic warfare vehicle in the Air Force, further improvement of the EB-66C was stopped in 1969. In short, all models redesignated as EB-66s underwent special modifications to improve their electronic warfare capabilities, but they needed additional changes which were not approved.

Canceled Modifications   1959–1961

While the RB-66C participated, as needed, in the B/RB-66 program's overall improvement, proposals for special modifications were often denied. As equipped in 1959, the RB-66C could not provide a rapid count and location of enemy radars. The addition of a Baird Remote Control Sextant[36] would help, but TAC's request was turned down by the Modification Review Board of the Mobile Air Materiel Area, because of fund shortages. Also, the expensive equipment was not readily available. If approved, it would have reached the aircraft too late to justify its cost, since the RB-66C was expected to begin leaving the inventory about mid-1963. In 1961, TAC again pointed out that the airborne system of the RB-66C had never been modernized,[37] and that manually operated equipment produced data which required hours of processing.

Cuban Crisis   October 1962

Operational deficiencies, observed during the Cuban missile crisis of 1962, vindicated TAC. In the next years, continuing reconnaissance operations around Cuba further demonstrated the validity of the modifications that had been sought by the command. Meanwhile, during the first months of the crisis, TAC's RB-66s (a mixture of RB-66Bs and RB-66Cs) flew many extra hours, and soon began to participate in numerous exercises.[38]

---

[36] An instrument that would provide a look-down altitude capability.

[37] TAC's deep concern led it to suggest that perhaps a single USAF organization, properly equipped, should provide electronic intelligence for the entire Air Force.

[38] The Tactical Air Command had been engaged in RB-66 electronic warfare since 1956, but emphasis had been on electronic reconnaissance. It took until 1960 for TAC to begin sending RB-66 crews to Europe to gain experience in electronic warfare operations.

New facts came to light. The RB–66C required more maintenance. Electronic countermeasures were most important during contingency operations, and the reconnaissance wing did not have enough trained personnel to maintain the system and to take care of the problem-ridden APD–4 antenna. TAC believed a pure training program was not required; instead technical support was needed to better indoctrinate a minimum of personnel on corrosion, interference, and other problems with the RB–66C's antenna. Activities prompted by the October crisis also served the useful purpose of testing a special RB–66B. The aircraft's recently installed infrared and KA–18 components were expected to provide reconnaissance information on troop and heavy equipment in forested areas.

Planning Changes   1963–1964

The Air Force's decision to retain its electronic intelligence gathering force, pending availability of ELINT RF–4Cs,[39] caused a first postponement of the RB–66C phaseout. The recent Cuban Crisis and its on-going impact, the growing threat in Southeast Asia, and the confirmed RB–66C shortcomings induced other changes. To begin with, TAC organized the USAF Tactical Air Reconnaissance Center (TARC). Located at Shaw AFB and due to serve as a worldwide focal point for tactical reconnaissance programs, TARC swiftly proved its worth. Although partially manned, TARC, in 1963 alone, tested an in-flight film processing magazine; the RS–7 infrared sensor; the KA–18A Sonne or continuous strip camera, and the KA–52A panoramic camera. The new center also ascertained how quickly electronic intelligence signals could be located and fixed. Finally, it tested a special navigation system for the Army; a portable film processor, and a TACAN antenna for the RF–101.[40] During the same period, minimum but significant modifications of the RB–66C were being devised.

Urgent Modifications   October 1964

Several RB–66Cs were modified, beginning in October 1964. The

---

[39] Slippage of a sensor being tested by the Navy was a primary problem. TAC attached great importance to the new ELINT sensor, which the RF–4C was expected to carry in a pod.

[40] The RF–101 was due to remain the principal intelligence gathering weapon system until replaced by the RF–4C, another McDonnell production. The RF–101 went through several modernization programs between 1962 and 1967, while the RB–66C asserted itself as the only USAF electronic warfare vehicle.

changes attempted to upgrade the aircraft's electronic countermeasures equipment, so it could cope with various types of enemy missiles. A subsequent but related modification, tested under Project Sea Fast, seemed to work fairly well, which meant that the RB–66Cs were at least prepared to enter the war.

Southeast Asian Deployment   1965

Like the RB–66Bs, TAC's RB–66Cs first went to Southeast Asia in April 1965. Soon the command's entire meager RB–66C contingent was committed to the war effort, leaving the command no other immediate alternative than to request 5 RB–66Bs for training aircrews. Of necessity, TAC's temporary duty RB–66C personnel carried out most electronic warfare operations in Southeast Asia during the whole of 1965.[41]

Other Modifications   1965–1968

As the Vietnam War escalated and enemy defenses grew, more modifications, the improvement of old and new components, and additional EB–66Cs (so redesignated in 1966) were needed. Big Sail, a priority modification started in 1965, hoped to reduce fighter losses by raising the EB–66C's efficiency against increasingly sophisticated enemy radars. Soon all USAFE EB–66Cs were included as backup for additional so-called Big Sail types of commitments. But the war demands did not abate. Although the Big Sail modification did work, TAC and USAFE asked the Air Staff that the EB–66C fleet be further updated for electronic warfare. Other modifications were made as unexpected problems arose. For instance, electromagnetic interferences with other aircraft systems demonstrated before long that the EB–66C needed a different jammer. TARC tested the new modification as part of the tactical electronic warfare system improvement.

Towards the end of 1966, the Center again got involved in a crucial task. The EB–66Cs in Southeast Asia often had to mask electronically the strike aircraft entering and leaving areas defended by deadly SA–2 surface-to-air missiles. Two jamming techniques could be used by the EB–66Cs, too few in number and increasingly vulnerable. Borrowing a B–52 from the Strategic Air Command, TARC helped determine which of the 2 B–66C techniques

---

[41] Electronic warfare officer training was started at Shaw AFB in March 1966.

was the safer and more efficient. In mid-1967, Secretary of Defense Robert S. McNamara explained to members of the 90th Congress that the RB/EB-66s, although not new, could satisfy adequately the Air Force's interim electronic countermeasures requirements. Mr. McNamara admitted that significant modifications would be needed to update the aircraft currently operational, as well as those being reactivated. While all of the Secretary's tentative plans did not materialize, the EB-66Cs were further improved. Among many important aircraft modifications, most noteworthy was the installation of steerable antennas in the EB-66Cs.[42] This change, begun in the spring of 1968, enabled electronic warfare officers to focus a plane's jamming energy against a specific radar transmitter.

Additional Commitments   1968-1969

Seizure of the USS *Pueblo* by North Korea prompted the immediate deployment of USAF forces. As part of the buildup, TAC had to send 6 EB-66s (4 EB-66Es and 2 EB-66Cs) to provide standoff ECM support to the strike units in the event of hostilities. The EB-66s departed the United States on 29 January 1968 and reached Kunsan, South Korea, on the 31st. However, before the end of February, priority requirements in Southeast Asia dictated relocation of the Kunsan EB-66s to Itazuke Air Base, a development TAC did not like. The command, during the previous year, had already pointed out to the Air Staff that any plan to replace Southeast Asian EB-66C losses with assets from the Shaw training pool would seriously affect the training of electronic warfare officer replacements. Nonetheless, TAC's predicament was to get worse. Early in 1968, crew training began to falter, as did the testing of ECM equipment and concepts, and TAC asked that all RB-66s be retrieved from storage and modified. In July, when most ECM modification programs neared completion, Secretary McNamara designated all EB-66s for dual-basing,[43] but TAC's reactivation request again proved futile. Meanwhile, since the total requirement for EB-66s far exceeded the number of aircraft available, other major air commands had problems. Because PACAF desperately needed a continuous flow of crew replacements, this command was the first to recommend in March 1968 that

---

[42] The EB-66E never carried this device, probably because the modification would have required the further installation of direction-finding equipment to tell the operators where to aim the new antenna.

[43] Dual-basing basically meant that a tactical combat unit, at a tenant location separated from its area of responsibilty and parent command, would deploy to a predesignated base within its area of responsibility, prior to or during hostilities.

8 EB–66s, programmed for Southeast Asia, be temporarily diverted to TAC. As for USAFE, after losing all its EB–66 resources to the Vietnam War, it flew inferior EB–57s pending activation of the 39th Tactical Electronic Warfare Squadron at Spangdahlem Air Base, West Germany. This interim arrangement lasted until April 1969, when 16 EB–66s finally became available to equip the new squadron.

Program Extension   1970–1974

Scheduled to phase out around 1970, the EB–66C's operational life was again extended. Still, like other EB–66s, the aircraft would no longer be modernized and would have to be maintained through normal processes. In 1969, decreased air activities in Southeast Asia promised relief and TAC expected the return of some of its resources. Meanwhile, the command found it difficult to support the new Spangdahlem squadron of EB–66s. During the same period, preliminary results of on-going structural tests showed that the B/RB–66 or EB–66 airframe could accumulate safely perhaps as many as 13,000 hours of flying time.[44] Hence, TAC once more asked that additional aircraft be removed from storage. Since its request again was turned down, the command reiterated that contingency support commitments would have to be scaled down. In mid-1971, the overall EB–66 program called for TAC to reduce combat crew training and to end it 1 year later. In the meantime, PACAF would handle the training of EB–66C crews until TAC received the EB–66s, due to leave Spangdahlem. Then, TAC would resume training of EB–66C and EB–66E personnel, while continuing to take care of all contingency operations. Clearly, both the Air Staff and TAC trusted that additional EB–66s would not have to be sent to Southeast Asia. However, B–52 support needs in November 1971, and problems with some of the war theater aircraft required the commitment of 2 TAC EB–66Cs. Moreover, a new contingent of EB–66s had to be deployed in mid-1972, when the enemy drive intensified and Strategic Air Command B–52Gs entered the war. Nevertheless, the B/RB–66 saga of nearly 2 decades was coming to an end.

Operational Status   Mid-1973

In mid-1973, few EB–66Cs remained in the inventory. As foreseen by

---

[44] The flight loads and analytical study phases of the aircraft's fatigue life program were practically completed in May 1969, when testing of the aircraft's components began. The thrust-deficient and worn-out J71 engine obviously was excluded from the testing program.

TAC, without enough money for proper support, many EB–66s had been lost to attrition. Deactivation of Shaw AFB's 39th Tactical Electronic Warfare Training Squadron, the last Air Force unit to use any type of the old B/RB–66 aircraft, would take place in early 1974. While in Southeast Asia, the 39th had received the Outstanding Unit Award for its contributions during the Linebacker II operations of December 1972.[45]

---

[45] See B-52, p 278.

WB-66D

Manufacturer's Model 1365

Previous Model Series   RB-66C

New Features

The WB-66D was identical to the RB-66C, except that the bomb bay housed electronic weather equipment in lieu of ECM components. The pressurized crew compartments also were alike, but the WB-66D only required a crew of 5—pilot, navigator, gunner, and 2 weather observers. In contrast to other B/RB-66s, all WB-66Ds were equipped from the start with J71-A-13 engines.

Production Decision   1 August 1955

Production of the WB-66D was made official on 1 August 1955, soon after the procurement deletion of 36 RB-66Cs had been confirmed. Contract AF 33(600)-28368, the fourth and last B/RB-66 contract, was amended accordingly on 12 December 1956.

Mockup Inspection   21 June 1956

The inspection team was actually confronted by a dual task, because Douglas displayed 2 configurations of the WB-66D synoptic weather reconnaissance aircraft. The first of the 2, referred to as the interim WB-66D, contained the weather equipment of the time; the second configuration, or best model, provided for and described the more sophisticated equipment expected for use within 2 or 3 years. The inspection prompted 47 change requests, 27 of which were considered of priority importance. Yet the AMC mockup board did not seem excessively concerned. Confirming this optimistic appraisal, the Air Force announced in November that both the interim and ultimate WB-66Ds would be purchased, with the understanding that the interim aircraft would be retrofitted with more modern weather equipment as soon as feasible.

Testing   1957

Douglas testing of the WB–66D ended with satisfactory results in late September 1957. Ensuing functional testing by the Air Force failed to uncover any significant problems and was practically completed before the end of the year.

Enters Operational Service   16 June 1957

The spring delivery of 3 interim WB–66Ds to Shaw AFB's 9th Tactical Reconnaissance Squadron was an important milestone for the Tactical Air Command. The synoptic weather mission, which covered a large geographical area simultaneously, was a relatively new development within the command. Theoretically, a few modified T–33 trainers (produced by Lockheed and commonly known as T–Birds) constituted TAC's weather reconnaissance fleet. In reality, these planes awaited delayed equipment kits. Because of the obsolescence of the WB–26s, TAC flew the partially equipped T–33s to gather high-altitude weather information, relying essentially on the data observed by the aircraft's back-seat weatherman. Although the early WB–66Ds did not meet all of TAC's needs, their arrival did signify a long overdue operational improvement.

Overseas Deployments   1957–1958

Except for 4 aircraft delivered in FY 1957, all WB–66Ds were accepted by the Air Force during FY–58. While the first deliveries went to the Tactical Air Command, WB–66D deployments to PACAF and USAFE closely followed. PACAF's 12 WB–66Ds were assigned to the 67th Tactical Reconnaissance Wing; USAFE's equal lot, to the 66th.

Program Shortcomings   1957–on

The WB–66Ds received by 3 of the Air Force's major air commands fell short of meeting the requirements set up for either the interim or ultimate version of the aircraft. Little more than a year had elapsed since the

WB–66D mockup inspection, but many events had taken place. Unexpected developmental setbacks, the procurement slippage of weather components much simpler than those under preliminary development, fiscal restrictions, and the high cost of on-going B/RB–66 modifications, all had caused the Air Force to lessen its weather reconnaissance objectives. In March 1957, while realizing that the ideal weather airplane would not materialize in the foreseeable future, the Air Force still hoped that the so-called interim WB–66D could gain, through post-production modifications, a few of the ultimate features that had been planned for the aircraft. In August 1957, even this more modest planning became uncertain, as deliveries of the proposed components could no longer be assured before 1960, or later. As feared, the Air Force on 30 October 1957, had to cancel the purchase of 5 future components. In their place, the Air Materiel Command would attempt to expedite the procurement of radiosonde sets,[46] MG–3 data computers, and AMQ–7 temperature and humidity devices. As time would show, this still remained a tall order.

Operational Deficiencies   1958–1959

TAC quickly took advantage of the eagerly awaited WB–66Ds. First received in late June 1957, the aircraft began flying regularly scheduled weather reconnaissance tracks on 1 September. Despite equipment problems, the superiority of the WB–66D over reciprocating engine aircraft or the T–33s was immediately apparent. To some extent, the WB–66D could determine weather conditions regardless of surroundings, and it soon started probing vast areas of hitherto unsampled overwater skies. This meant that weather briefings became more accurate, and that overseas deployments would face fewer weather hazards. Nevertheless, the WB–66D was still unable to transmit meteorological data automatically by radio. In mid-1959, the retrofit of key components kept slipping. For example, testing of the dropsonde receptors and dispensers was unsatisfactory. Ensuing live tests, conducted at Shaw AFB, only confirmed that the WB–60D's radiosonde system needed further improvement. In several drops, the dropsonde struck the aircraft on ejection and failed to transmit.

End of Production   1958

The Air Force took delivery of the last 2 WB–66Ds in January 1958, marking the end of the aircraft's production.

---

[46] Radiosonde sets are airborne meteorographs, with associated components, that automatically transmit meteorological data by radio.

Total WB–66Ds Accepted   36

Acceptance Rates

The Air Force accepted 4 WB–66Ds in FY 57, and all others in FY 58 (5 each month from July 1957 through December 1957, and 2 in January 1958).

Flyaway Cost Per Production Aircraft $1.91 million

Airframe, $1,313,373; engines (installed), $270,000; electronics, $138,784; ordnance, $15,160; armament (and others), $174,983.

Average Maintenance Cost Per Flying Hour $448.00

Subsequent Model Series   None

Other Configurations   X–21A and EB–66C

X–21A. In the late fifties, the Air Force gave Northrop a contract to convert 2 WB–66Ds. The purpose of the conversion was to test a new laminar flow control system developed by Northrop. Design of the conversion was started in August 1960, and modification of the Douglas-built aircraft began in 1961. Designated X–21A, the first modified WB–66D flew in April 1963, and testing of the laminar flow control system over sections of the wings was underway by 20 May 1963. Conversion of the second WB–66D was completed in August of the same year.

EB–66C. A number of WB–66Ds, withdrawn from storage after 1966, were brought up to the EB–66C configuration.

Phaseout   1960–1964

The WB–66D phaseout started in 1960, when USAFE and PACAF got rid of their weather reconnaissance aircraft. At the time, the Air Staff endorsed TAC's request to retain its small WB–66D contingent for a few more years. Nonetheless, by July 1965, all WB–66Ds were out of the Air Force's active inventory.

Reactivation   1966

In October 1966, press accounts began to give the EB–66s credit for neutralizing surface-to-air missile radars as well as much of the enemy's radar-controlled but conventional anti-aircraft weaponry. Less publicized throughout the years were the Air Force's difficulties in satisfying recurring or unforeseen demands with too few aircraft. Late in 1966, Secretary McNamara at long last approved the reactivation of 9 WB–66Ds and the modification of each aircraft to the EB–66C configuration. Even though some of the reactivated and modernized planes acquired slightly different components, all EB–66Cs remained basically alike and all played important roles. For that matter, the entire fleet of EB–66Bs, EB–66Es, and EB–66Cs, as well as their heroic crews, were highly praised for their combat contributions.[47]

---

[47] Like most other aspects of the electronic warfare effort, the EB–66's effectiveness could not be evaluated in terms of missions flown and fighter-bombers lost. There were no valid supporting statistics, but the aircraft became quickly known for its outstanding usefulness. Despite unrelenting engine problems, its performance was also well rated.

Program Recap

The Air Force accepted a grand total of 294 B/RB–66s—5 RB–66As, 145 RB–66Bs, 72 B–66Bs, 36 RB–66Cs, and 36 WB–66Ds. Early production difficulties, and deficiencies identified late in 1954, accounted for the program's reduction—48 aircraft less than initially ordered. The same reasons delayed deliveries to the using commands by about 1 year, and TAC did not receive its first RB–66B until January 1956. Still only 4 years elapsed between the production go-ahead and the aircraft's service introduction. And once in the inventory, the often-modified aircraft earned their keep far longer than anticipated.

TECHNICAL AND BASIC MISSION PERFORMANCE DATA

B/RB–66 AIRCRAFT

Manufacturer (Airframe)	Douglas Aircraft Company, Long Beach, Calif., and Tulsa, Okla.
Manufacturer (Engines)	Allison Division of The General Motors Corporation, Detroit, Mich.
Nomenclature	All-weather Night Photographic Aircraft; Light Tactical Bomber; Electronic Reconnaissance Aircraft.
Popular Name	Destroyer

	RB–66B	B–66B	RB–66C
Length/Span (ft)	75.2/72.5	75.2/72.5	75.2/72.5
Wing Area (sq ft)	780	780	780
Weights (lb)			
Empty	43,476	42,549	44,771
Combat	49,440	57,800	65,360
Takeoff[a]	83,000	83,000	83,000
Engine: Number, Rated Power per Engine, & Designation	(2) 10,200-lb st J71–A–13	(2) 10,200-lb st J71–A–13	(2) 10,200-lb st J71–A–13
Takeoff Ground Run (ft)			
At Sea Level[b]	6,750	6,750	6,750
Over 50-ft Obstacle[b]	9,350	9,350	9,350
Rate of Climb (fpm)	3,260	3,260	3,180
Combat Rate of Climb (fpm) at Sea Level	4,840	5,000	4,320
Service Ceiling (ft) at Combat Weight (100 fpm Rate of Climb to Altitude)	40,900	41,500	37,700
Combat Ceiling (ft) (500 fpm Rate of Climb to Altitude)	38,900	39,400	35,500
Average Cruise Speed (kn)	456	456	436
Maximum Speed at Optimum Altitude (kn/ft)	548/6,000	548/6,000	533/8,000
Basic Speed at Altitude (kn/ft)	496/36,089	498/36,089	477/35,000
Combat Radius (nm)	805	794	947
Total Mission Time (hr)	3.57	3.49	4.38
Armament	2 20-mm M–24A–1	2 20-mm M–24A–1	2 20-mm M–24A–1
Crew	3[c]	3[d]	7[e]
Maximum Bombload (lb)	4,084 (photoflash bombs & photoflash cartridges)	15,000 (E–53s, T–36s T–54E2s T–55E5 bombs)	Not Applicable

```
┌─────────────────────────────────┐
│ Abbreviations                   │
│                                 │
│ fpm   = feet per minute         │
│ kn    = knots                   │
│ nm    = nautical miles          │
│ st    = static thrust           │
└─────────────────────────────────┘
```

---

[a] Limited by gear strength.

[b] Using maximum takeoff power.

[c] Pilot, photo-navigator, and gunner.

[d] Pilot, bombardier-navigator, and gunner.

[e] Pilot, navigator, gunner, and 4 electronic countermeasures operators

Basic Mission Note

All basic mission's performance data based on military-rated power, except as otherwise indicated.

Combat Formula: Radius and Electronic Countermeasures Basic Missions
RB–66B and B–66B—Warmed up, took off and climbed on course to optimum cruise altitude at military power. Cruised out at maximum-range speeds increasing altitude with decreasing airplane weight to a point 15 minutes from target. Dropped external fuel tanks when empty. Ran-in to target at normal power, dropped bombload, conducted 2-minute evasive action and 8-minute escape to normal power. Climb to cruise altitude was conducted during the 8-minute escape operation. Cruised back to base at maximum-range speeds, increasing altitude with decreasing airplane weight. Range-free allowances included 5-minute normal-power fuel consumption for starting engines and take-off, 2-minute normal-power fuel consumption at combat altitude for evasive action, and 30 minutes of maximum-endurance fuel consumption at sea level plus 5 percent of initial fuel load for landing reserve

Formula: Ferry Mission
RB–66B and B–66B—Warmed up, took off and climbed on course to optimum cruise altitude at maximum power (military power in the B–66's case). Cruised out at maximum-range speeds increasing altitude with decreasing airplane weight until all usable fuel was consumed. External tanks were dropped when empty. Range-free allowances included 5-minute normal-power fuel consumption for starting engines and take-off and 30 minutes of maximum-endurance fuel consumption at sea level, plus 5 percent of initial fuel load for landing reserve.

Combat Formula: Radius and Electronic Countermeasures Basic Missions
RB–66C—Warmed up, took off, and climbed on course to optimum cruise altitude at military power. Cruised out to turn-around and cruised back at maximum-range speeds, increasing cruise altitude as airplane weight decreased. Dropped external tanks when empty. Range-free allowances included 5-minute normal-power fuel consumption for starting engines and take-off, and 30 minutes of maximum-fuel consumption at sea level, plus 5 percent of initial fuel load for holding and landing reserve.

Formula: Range Mission

Warmed up, took off, and climbed on course to optimum cruise altitude at military power. Cruised at maximum-range speeds, increasing cruise altitude as airplane weight decreased, until all usable fuel less reserve was consumed. Dropped external tanks when empty. Range-free allowances included 5-minute normal-power fuel consumption for starting engines and take-off, and 30 minutes of maximum-endurance fuel consumption at sea level plus 5 percent of initial fuel load for holding and landing reserve.

Appendices

Appendix I

World War II Bombers in the Postwar Period

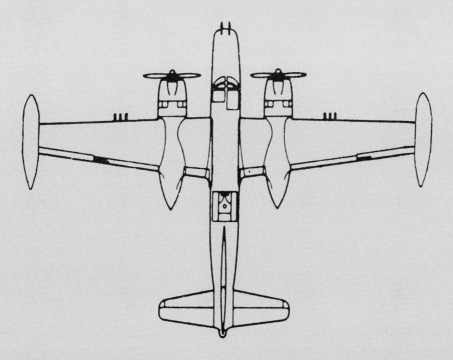

Appendix I
World War II Bombers in the Postwar Period

In 1945, the Army Air Forces had a fair selection of bombers in its operational inventory. But after World War II came to a close, only a few types were retained. Included were the Boeing B–17 Flying Fortress, the Consolidated B–24 Liberator, the Douglas A–24 dive bomber, the North American B–25 light bomber, the Douglas A–26 Invader, and the Superfortress—Boeing's new B–29.

Retention, however, did not necessarily entail significant post-war activity, be it in an aircraft's original configuration or any other mode. The handful of famed B–17s flown by the Strategic Air Command, when it was formed in 1946, were only used for reconnaissance, and no longer appeared on the command's rolls after 1949. The few B–24s, converted to train B–29 gunners, saw little service after the end of the war. Some of the Douglas A–24 dive bombers, redesignated F–24s in 1948 when the attack designation was officially dropped, remained active until 1950. Yet, their sole purpose was to test dive-bombing tactics for fighter-bombers. Similarly, after 1945 hundreds of B–25s served merely as trainers or staff transports, most of them having left the Air Force inventory by late 1959. The Douglas A–26 (redesignated as the B–26 in 1948) and Boeing B–29 fell in a different category. Both returned to combat. The B–29, in addition, briefly served as an instrument of deterrence—a post-World War II role of major importance.

B-26 Invader
Douglas Airplane Company

Navy Equivalent: JD-1

Basic Development   November 1940

Development of the B-26 Invader, initially known as the A-26, originated in November 1940, when the Army Air Corps's Experimental Engineering Section at Wright Field, Ohio, gave first priority to the Douglas Airplane Company for designing and developing a new plane. But, as evidenced by official requirements, the so-called new design drew a great deal from the A-20 Havoc.[1] The A-20 was a Douglas production, developed in 1937 from Model A-7: a 1936 original design for a high-performance attack bomber.

Initial Requirements   1940

Official Army requirements, as spelled out by the Air Corps, called for a new plane that would be faster and structurally stronger than the A-20. Additional defensive armament over the A-20 and shorter takeoff and landing distances, were also part of the requirements. The Air Corps wanted the new plane eventually to replace the A-20, the Martin B-26 Marauder, and the North American B-25 Mitchell.

Contractor Proposal   1941

In early 1941, Douglas proposed to manufacture 2 XA-26s, one a night-fighter adaptation of the other, and to schedule such a thorough series

---

[1] The A-20 was put into production for foreign air forces in 1938 and became the most-produced of all the "attack" aircraft procured by the United States Army Air Corps. The A-20 was the first type of aircraft flown by American crews in the European theater during World War II.

of wind tunnel tests of the experimental planes that mass production could follow almost immediately. Mockup inspections would take place during the spring.

Contractual Arrangement   1941

The Chief of the Army's Materiel Division did not endorse the developmental contract, submitted in March 1941, because overall costs seemed unreasonable. At Douglas's request, the contract was rewritten to cover costs, plus a fixed fee. Finally signed on 2 June 1941, the revised contract (W535 ac–17946) covered 1 XA–26 and 1 XA–26A (the XA–26's night fighter version) at an estimated price of $2.08 million. Excluded from this sum was Douglas's fixed fee, which was set at $125,000. Soon afterwards, a change order provided for an additional experimental plane. Designated the XA–26B, this third configuration would incorporate a 75-millimeter cannon.

Mockup Inspections   April 1941

As planned by Douglas, inspections of the XA–26 mockups were held in April 1941. Representatives of the Wright Field Production Engineering Section were particularly impressed by the apparent versatility of the future plane.

Production Decision   31 October 1941

The decision to go ahead with mass production of the A–26 became official on 31 October 1941, when Contract V535 ac–21393 was approved. Even though none of the experimental planes had been flown, the production contract covered 500 A–26s for a total cost of $78.2 million.

First Flight (XA–26)   10 July 1942

The first of the 3 XA–26s, ordered in the summer of 1941, was not initially flown until 10 July 1942. The other 2 experimental planes were flown on the heels of the first one.

Program Refinement   August 1942

Testing of the 3 XA–26s, as well as the experience already gained from combat in Europe and the Pacific area, prompted the Army Air Forces to decide that the 500 aircraft, covered by the production contract of June 1941, would be patterned on the third experimental plane: the XB–26B ground attack configuration that featured a 75-mm cannon nose, primarily intended to destroy tanks. In short, a heretofore uncertain Army Air Forces gave priority to ground attack over the multi-purpose light bomber requirements of 1940. Yet, the aircraft's versatility was not overlooked. Two hundred additional noses, each with six .50-caliber guns, would also be procured. Each of the latter noses could be installed in about 24 hours by field personnel.

Production Delay   1943

Delay of the XA–26's first flight clearly indicated that, at best, mass production would not begin before July 1943, a significant slippage from the original time estimate. Lack of tooling was a primary factor, but shortages of engineers were equally damaging. Hence, the Wright Field Production Division directed Douglas to transfer at least two-thirds of the personnel listed on the C–74[2] project to the A–26. Also, no engineers were to be utilized for the improvement of crew comfort, or any other endeavors, unless specifically authorized by Wright Field. Finally, no other armament studies were to be made until the A–26 production's stage was more advanced. In January 1943, despite these stringent directives, Douglas informed the Army Air Forces that the new production schedule would not be met. The contractor indicated that October appeared to be a more likely date for production to begin.

Additional Procurement   17 March 1943

A second production contract, W535 ac–34433, covering the procurement of 500 additional A–26s was approved on 17 March 1943. Total cost was $109.1 million. Included in this total was the purchase of 167 bombardier-observer nose sections that could also be quickly substituted for

---

[2] The Army Air Forces recognized that it needed a long-range heavy transport aircraft during the early days of World War II. However, the first C–74 (Model 415A, a development of the Douglas DC–4) was not delivered before October 1945. Hence, 36 of the 50 C–74s on order were canceled.

The B-26, originally developed as an attack bomber during World War II, served in both the Korean War and the Southeast Asian conflict.

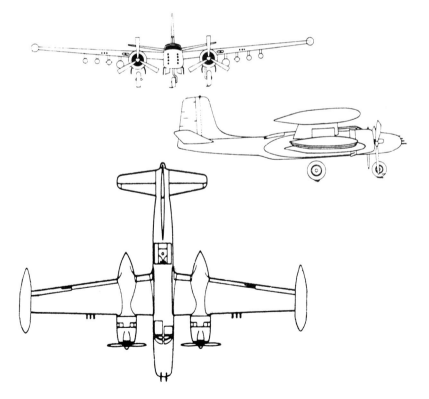

the A–26's 75-millimeter cannon nose. While the first 500 A–26Bs would come from the Douglas Long Beach plant in California, the new order was to be manufactured in Tulsa, Oklahoma. Obviously, time was important.

New Production Slippages   1943–1944

Although the Army Air Forces took delivery of a few A–26Bs in the fall of 1943, production again slipped. In early 1944, production was practically at a standstill, a situation which did not satisfy Gen. Henry H. Arnold, Commanding General of the Army Air Forces. Various excuses were offered, such as the shortage of machinery for making wing spars. Another valid reason was the number of modification requests, which was clearly excessive.

In March 1944, when only 21 A–26s had been delivered, General Arnold bluntly expressed his increasing dissatisfaction. "One thing is sure," said General Arnold, "I want the A–26s for use in this war and not the next war." Maj. Gen. Oliver P. Echols, Assistant Chief of Air Staff for Materiel, Maintenance, and Distribution, blamed the continuing delays on Douglas's apparent lack of interest or "little desire to manufacture the plane," and explained that the Materiel Command all along had urged the contractor to place orders for tools and to find qualified subcontractors. In defense of Douglas, the Western Procurement District, Los Angeles, California, stressed that the A–26 wing was entirely different from that of any other airplane; that delivery schedules were set before design and tooling problems were solved; and that there had been on occasions as many as 35 change orders a day on the A–26.

The divergence of opinion did not deter General Arnold. He insisted that something drastic had to be done to ensure that, as initially intended, B–25s, B–26s, and A–20s would be replaced by A–26s. As a first step, he placed additional A–26 orders.

New Production Orders   29 March 1944

Existing production problems were not allowed to affect the programmed procurement of additional A–26s. On 29 March 1944, the Under Secretary of War approved 2 supplemental agreements to the production contracts already in force. The extra A–26s, 2,700 of them, were expected to cost about $300 million.

Special Features

The A–26 had a 70-foot wing span, compared to the 61-foot span of the

30-percent-lighter A–20. Greater care had been applied to simplify the manufacturing and maintenance of the A–26 structure. Moreover, the fuselage of the all-metal, semi-monocoque A–26 allowed the 3 crewmen to exchange positions, an advantage the A–20 did not offer.

A most unusual feature of the A–26 was the aluminum alloy monocoque engine mount, which was a combination of structure and cowling, thereby reducing weight and easing engine installation. Another special feature was the Douglas-devised slotted wing flap, which had a lower pitching movement for a given lift coefficient than the Fowler flap. Finally, the engines were cooled with a new type of high entrance velocity cowling.[3] This cowl induced less aerodynamic resistance and lowered the temperatures of the engines.

Unexpected Setback   May 1944

Improvement of the A–26 production flow, recently achieved, did not last long. New complications arose in May 1944, when the A–26 wing failed during the static tests of one of the aircraft. Douglas was told to redesign the wing, if necessary, and was required to increase its strength by 10 percent.

Combat Testing   1944

The A–26 entered combat testing in mid-1944, when 4 of the aircraft assigned to the Fifth Air Force began operating in the Southwest Pacific. Lt. Gen. George C. Kenney, Commanding General of the Far East Air Forces, grounded the planes after less than 175 hours of total flying time and stated shortly afterwards, "We do not want the A–26 under any circumstances as a replacement for anything." Ironically, about 4 years before, as a colonel in charge of the Wright Field Production Division and a strong proponent of attack aviation, Kenney had strongly urged the aircraft's development. General Kenney's statement and his mid-1944 decision to ground the planes appeared justified. A–26 production had slipped badly; the B–25s and A–20s that the A–26s would replace had proven satisfactory; and the canopy of available A–26s was poorly designed. A new canopy was needed to improve visibility. Without it, pilots could not safely fly the formations required for low-level tactics. While the Wright Field Production Division agreed that the A–26 could not replace current types of light and medium

---

[3] The new cowl had been developed by the National Advisory Committee for Aeronautics and the Douglas Airplane Company.

bombers, Maj. Gen. Hoyt S. Vandenberg, Commanding General of the Ninth Air Force, was much less critical than General Kenney. The few A–26s introduced in the European theater towards the end of the summer were performing well. Undoubtedly, the aircraft's marginal visibility needed attention. But new productions were seldom free of problems, and General Vandenberg thought the A–26 was a satisfactory replacement for the B–26s and A–20s in Europe.

Final Procurement   1944–1945

Regardless of the mixed reports generated by the performance of the early A–26 (A–26As or A–26Bs), the Army Air Forces' plans to re-equip all B–25, B–26, and A–20 units with A–26s were reaffirmed in November 1944. In December, 2 more contracts were approved, and in April 1945 both of the new agreements were supplemented, bringing to 4,000 the total of new A–26s ordered since mid-1944. However, the German surrender on 8 May 1945 prompted a re-evaluation of military requirements. Production which had been scheduled to increase to 400 A–26s per month was cut to 150. The procurement orders of 1944 and 1945 were canceled.

Modifications and Appraisals   1944–1945

Douglas adopted several long-standing suggestions by General Arnold: engineering personnel at Long Beach established closer liaison with the Tulsa plant; extra well-qualified personnel were placed in the 2 plants; and the number of stations in the production lines was raised. These production changes facilitated modifications of the aircraft, which were designed to improve its effectiveness. An all-purpose gun nose was devised and the faulty nose landing gear redesigned. A–26s (redesignated as A–26Cs) that came off the production lines after January 1945 featured an enlarged, raised canopy which provided increased visibility.

The Ninth Bombardment Division was first in pointing out that once pilots were familiar with the A–26, they liked it better than any other plane they had flown. Even General Kenney eventually agreed that improved A–26s—particularly the A–26 with the 8-gun nose—were proving to be highly satisfactory replacements for the A–20s and B–25s. Deficiencies such as canopy frosting, faulty brakes, and the like were still being corrected. However, substantial progress was achieved swiftly.

End of Production   1945

The A–26 production was completed in 1945, but the last aircraft was delivered in early 1946.

Total A–26s Accepted   2,451

The Army Air Forces accepted a grand total of 2,451 A–26s. More than 4,000 A–26s, ordered before the end of World War II, were canceled. The first 9 of the 2,451 produced by Douglas were built in El Segundo, California. The remainder, consisting of A–26Bs and A–26Cs, was manufactured in Long Beach and Tulsa. The Tulsa plant produced 1,086 of the 1,091 A–26Cs.

Flyaway Cost Per Production Aircraft $242,595

Airframe, $143,747; engines (installed), $47,302; propeller, $14,583; electronics, $11,045; ordnance, $4,740; armament (and others), $21,178.[4]

Subsequent Model Series   None

The A–26C turned out to be the last A–26 model and was practically identical to the A–26B, except for its Plexiglass "bombardier" nose, which permitted more accurate bombing from medium levels. Initially delivered in 1945, the A–26C joined the A–26B in combat service during the last stages of the war in the Pacific.

The A–26D, a development of the A–26B, was designed with more engine power and more guns. But the 350 A–26Ds, ordered in April 1945, were included in the mass cancellation that followed the end of hostilities in the European theater.

Redesignation   June 1948

In June 1948, after the Martin B–26 Marauder was withdrawn from service, the Douglas A–26 dropped its prefix ("A" for attack) and became the B–26, a designation more representative of its actual role as a standard light bomber for the new United States Air Force and the Tactical Air Command in particular.[5]

---

[4] All modification costs included. No cost breakdown was available. The figure applied to the A-, B-, and C-models alike, being most likely an average of the total cost and the overall number of aircraft.

[5] The Air Force gained its independence in September 1947; the Tactical Air Command had been created in March 1946 from the wartime Ninth and Twelfth Air Forces.

New War Commitments   1950–1953

The outbreak of the Korean conflict on 25 June 1950 catapulted the Douglas B–26 back into combat. Initial targets, selected to prevent reinforcement of the enemy forces, included North Korean troop concentrations, tanks, guns, supply elements, railway yards and bridges south of the 38th parallel. Immediate results were disappointing because bad weather and darkness curtailed the B–26's effectiveness. Engine failures and various mechanical deficiencies were additional handicaps. Moreover, as the war continued, other problems became obvious.

The World War II B–26 was limited in radius of fire and its speed could no longer cope with the air and ground fire of the enemy's modern equipment. The B–26 had no electronic countermeasures capability and could not carry many types of new armament and control and guidance systems.

Almost from the very beginning of hostilities, the Far East Air Forces gained air superiority against an enemy offering little or no daylight air opposition to strategic or tactical operations. But the night hours presented a different situation. Commanders were forced to utilize a part of their available day force for night operations, and the 3d Bombardment Wing's B–26s, more readily usable for night duty, acquired new importance.

Refurbished B–26s sustained significant losses during the war as their tasks increased. Yet, despite their limitations, the obsolete B–26s compiled a distinguished combat record. The first combat strike into North Korea was flown in 1950 by a B–26 crew. On the evening of 26 July 1953, 1 day before the Korean armistice agreement was signed, a B–26 dropped the last Air Force bombs of the Korean conflict in a ground-radar-directed close support mission.

Special Modifications   1952–1954

The B–26's ineffectiveness in Korea, especially during night attacks directed by radar, prompted special modifications. In 1952, the Air Staff decided that several B–26s of the Tactical Air Command would be fitted with more sophisticated electronic equipment. In 1953, some B–26s, already brought up to the reconnaissance configuration, were given additional components to perform electronic reconnaissance and weather reconnaissance missions. Nevertheless, the usefulness of the outmoded B–26 was declining. Too many configurations—16 different ones in the United States, and about 14 in the Far East and Europe—had created supply and maintenance problems of terrific proportions. In mid-1953 the Air Staff approved a last modification to attempt standardizing most B–26s into a few basic configurations.

Phaseout   1954–1958

With the advent of the Martin B–57, B–26s began leaving the Air Force's active inventory in late 1954. The last of the B–26s were withdrawn from service in Air Force Reserve and Air National Guard units in 1958.

Reactivation   1961

President John F. Kennedy's policy that the major task of U.S. advisors in Southeast Asia was to prepare the Republic of Vietnam Armed Forces for combat raised the tempo of training and resulted in the delivery of additional equipment to the South Vietnamese. Fixed-wing aircraft were in short supply, so B–26s were taken out of storage and modified for special combat missions in Southeast Asia.

Return to Combat   1961–1969

Reactivated B–26s began reaching South Vietnam in the fall of 1961. Once in the theater, they accomplished a variety of tasks ranging from standard bombing operations and close air support attacks to visual and photo reconnaissance missions. In mid-1962, the B–26's role in the conflict was further expanded. Several of the aircraft, already equipped for reconnaissance, received additional modifications in order to perform night photo operations and some intelligence gathering duties.

Specially modified for service in Vietnam, the B–26K featured permanent wing tip fuel tanks and various bomb and rocket pods.

Keeping the weary B/RB–26s flying was a challenge. Despite changes and improvements, the aircraft actually belonged to a type that had been declared obsolete during the Korean War, 10 years earlier. The combination of old age, hard usage, and the operating conditions of Southeast Asia made maintenance of the B–26 force increasingly difficult. The aircraft were becoming more vulnerable to enemy ground fire, and most B/RB–26s were subject to flight restrictions to avoid undue wing stress. Just the same, losses occurred that were directly attributable to structural fatigue. In August 1963, a B–26 crashed after 1 of its wings broke off. Then, a B–26 wing failed during a combat flight in February 1964. All B/RB–26s were immediately grounded and withdrawn from Southeast Asia soon afterwards. Yet, this action did not end the aircraft's war involvement.

Forty B–26s returned to the war zone in mid-1966 as B–26Ks. The modifications for the K-model, accomplished by the On-Mark Engineering Company, Van Nuys, California, were extensive. The $16 million On-Mark contract, initiated in 1962, involved much more than a facelifting of the old aircraft—nearly a complete transformation. The B–26K differed from the basic aircraft in that both turrets had been removed; R–2800–52W engines replaced the B–26's R–2800–79s; the wings had been reinforced by the addition of steel straps both on the top and bottom of the spars; the propellers, wheels, brakes, and rudder had been changed; permanent wing tip tanks had been added; instrument panel and electronics were new; 8 wing pylons had been included; and a myriad of minor changes incorporated.

In short, the B–26K was a tactical bomber for special environments, mounted with rocket pods, guns pods, or bomblet dispensers, and capable of being readily fitted with photographic reconnaissance components and other sensors. The B–26K was redesignated A–26A soon after it reached the war theater.[6] The rejuvenated aircraft promptly proved to be an effective hunter and destroyer of trucks and other vehicles, its loitering capability enabling it to locate and attack an enemy often concealed by jungle or weather. Most A–26As stayed in Southeast Asia for nearly 3 years, the last combat mission being flown in November 1969.

Final Phaseout   1970–1972

In 1970, regardless of designations, none of the old B–26s remained in the Air Force's active inventory; and none remained with the Air National Guard after 1972.

---

[6] The attack category, dropped some 20 years earlier, was re-endorsed in the early sixties, when some aircraft were specifically earmarked for the attack role during limited war and counterinsurgency operations.

TECHNICAL AND BASIC MISSION PERFORMANCE DATA

B-26 AIRCRAFT

Manufacturer (Airframe)	Douglas Aircraft Co., El Segundo, Long Beach, Calif., and Tulsa, Okla.		
Manufacturer (Engines)	The Pratt and Whitney Aircraft Div. of United Aircraft Corp., East Hartford, Conn.		
Nomenclature	Light Bomber		
Popular Name	Invader		

	B-26B	B-26C	B-26K[a]
Length/Span (ft)	50.8/70.0	51.3/70.0	52.1/71.5
Wing Area (sq ft)	540	540	540
Weights (lb)			
Empty	22,362 (actual)	22,690 (estimate)	25,130 (actual)
Combat	31,775	29,920	30,809
Takeoff	41,811	39,416	37,000
Engine: Number,			
Rated Power per Engine,	(2) 2,000-hp	(2) 2,000-hp	2 2,500-hp
& Designation	R-2800-79	R-2800-79	R-2800-52W
Takeoff Ground Run (ft)			
At Sea Level	3,900	3,390	4,075
Over 50-ft Obstacle	4,820	4,180	4,800
Rate of Climb at Sea Level	1,060	1,220	1,380
Combat Rate of Climb (fpm) at Sea Level	2,515	2,745	2,050
Service Ceiling at Combat Weight (100 fpm Rate of Climb to Altitude)	19,200	20,450	28,600
Combat Ceiling (500 fpm Rate of Climb to Altitude)	21,800	23,100	24,400
Average Cruise Speed (kn)	200	196	147
Max Speed at Optimum Altitude (kn/ft)	322/10,000	323/10,000	281/15,000
Combat Radius (nm)	839	775	606
Combat Target Altitude (ft)	Sea Level	Sea Level	Sea Level
Total Mission Time (hr)	8:8	8:23	8:48
Crew	3[b]	3[c]	[d]
Armament	16 .50-cal guns & 14 5-in HVAR	12 .50-cal guns & 14 5-in HVAR	8[e] .50-cal M3 guns & 18 rockets (LAU-3A, -32A/A, -59A)
Maximum Bombload (lb)	6,000	6,000	6,000 (various types, M1A2, MK-82, BLU-10A/B, -27B, CBU-14A, -22A, -25A, etc.)

Abbreviations	
fpm	= feet per minute
hp	= horsepower

---

[a] The B–26K, a modified B–26B or B–26C, was redesignated A–26A in 1968. The aircraft was used primarily for special air warfare and reconnaissance. In the latter role, the B–26K/A–26A carried the F–492 camera, including a split-vertical F–477, a panoramic KA–56, and a K–38A reconnaissance camera.

[b] Pilot-radio-operator, gun-loader-navigator, and gunner.

[c] Pilot-radio-operator, bombardier-navigator, and gunner.

[d] The normal crew included pilot and navigator or flight mechanic. For reconnaissance, the aircraft carried a pilot, navigator, and photo systems operator.

[e] Some of the aircraft had 14 guns: 8 in the nose and 6 in the wing leading edge.

B-29 Superfortress
Boeing Airplane Company

Manufacturer's Model 345

Basic Development   1937

The B-29's development stemmed from the Boeing XB-15, a long-range bomber first flown on 15 October 1937,[7] and from a March 1938 design study of a pressurized version of the B-17 with a tricycle undercarriage. Since the Army had little money to purchase the existing B-17, Boeing developed the new pressurized model on its own. This was Model 334A, the B-29's direct ancestor. A mockup of Model 334A, also built at Boeing's expense, was completed in December 1939.

Initial Requirements   1938-1939

By September 1938, Nazi Germany had incorporated Austria into the Third Reich and seized part of Czechoslovakia. President Franklin D. Roosevelt therefore ordered a survey of the manufacturing capacity of the United States aircraft industry. According to Maj. Gen. Henry H. Arnold, then acting head of the Army Air Corps, the President believed that an air force was "the only thing that Hitler understands" and was determined to build up America's air power so it could defend the nation and the Western Hemisphere against any aggressors. On 4 January 1939 (still prior to the outbreak of World War II), President Roosevelt asked the Congress for $300 million to buy several types of military aircraft. On 3 April, Congress authorized the Army to purchase 3,000 new aircraft and raised the Air Corps authorized ceiling to 5,500. The Air Corps used some of the appropriated funds to finance subsequent work on the B-29. Later in the year, it specified that the future B-29 would need a range of 4,000 miles.

---

[7] Plans for the 5,000-mile range bomber were drawn up at Wright Field, Ohio, in 1933. In 1943, following modification, the single XB-15 was briefly used as an experimental transport.

Revised Requirements   February 1940

Boeing first thought it could satisfy the Army Air Corps's slightly altered requirements with design 341, an 85,000-pound bomber with the specified 4,000-mile range. But events had been moving swiftly. Although the United States would not enter World War II before 11 December 1941, the war in Europe was already raging, bringing to light new requirements. According to the revised requirements of February 1940, the new bomber visualized by the Army Air Corps would need armor plate, fuel tank sealing, and greater fire power than anticipated. Boeing consequently altered its plans. Competing with other contractors,[8] it answered the Army's revised requirements on 11 May 1940, with design 345, a still larger bomber with a gross weight between 100,000 and 120,000 pounds. Approved by a board of officers headed by Col. Oliver P. Echols, Chief of the Army Air Corps's Materiel Division, Model 345 became the experimental B-29—so designated on 24 August.

Initial Procurement   1940

Procurement of the XB-29 started in June 1940, when some of the aviation money that had been appropriated by the Congress was used to pay for further study and wind tunnel tests of Model 345. Satisfactory results quickly assured the experimental project of more than $3.6 million to cover the construction of 2 XB-29s and 1 static test article. The development contract (W535 ac-15429) that necessarily ensued was signed on 6 September and amended on 14 December. The amendment provided extra funds to increase the number of flyable XB-29s to 3.

Production Decision   1941

Although the experimental B-29 was yet to be flown, the Army in May 1941 notified Boeing of a forthcoming order for 14 service test B-29 prototypes and 250 B-29s that would be built in new government-owned facilities at the Boeing Wichita plant. Robert A. Lovett, Assistant Secretary of War for Air, confirmed the May decision in September, when the production contract was signed. In February 1942, the Army informed Boeing that the urgently needed B-29s would also be built in several new

---

[8] See B-50, pp 162-163.

plants by other manufacturers, namely the Bell Aircraft Corporation and the Glenn L. Martin Company. By September, 1,000 additional B-29s were under contract, and total production nearly reached 4,000.[9] The end of the war, in August 1945, prompted the cancellation of over 5,000 extra B-29s, still on order in September of the same year.

First Flight (XB-29)   21 September 1942

The first experimental B-29 (Serial No. 41-002) made its initial flight on 21 September 1942; the second XB-29 (Serial No. 41-003), on 30 December.

Testing   1942-1948

Boeing pilots test flew the first XB-29 for a total of more than 559 hours, accumulated in 417 flights. Army Air Forces (AAF) pilots completed more than 16 hours, but the number of flights they made was not recorded. On 18 December 1942, upon completion of its 19th flight, the first XB-29 encountered some difficulties. Two tires blew during landing, causing slight damage to the landing gear doors and to some wing flaps. A more significant incident ensued. On 28 December the Boeing test crew had to stop an altitude performance flight as soon as the plane reached 6,000 feet. Failure of the number 1 engine's reduction gear proved to be the problem. To correct this condition, Boeing replaced the nose section of all engines with noses having floating bushings which had passed 150-hour tests.

No accidents marred the first XB-29's operational life. The plane was sent to the 58th Bombardment Group, Wichita, Kansas, for accelerated testing and was loaned to Boeing in November 1943 to undergo the various flight tests required by the basic development contract. Testing ended in the spring of 1948, the first XB-29 being returned on 11 May.

The second XB-29 did not fare well, having flown only 7 hours in 10 flights when it was entirely destroyed on 18 February 1943. The plane was descending for an emergency landing at Boeing Field, Seattle, Washington,

---

[9] Development, plant exchanges, and the many problems inherent to the production of a revolutionary bomber in the midst of a world war have been well documented. Informative accounts may be found in Peter M. Bowers, *Boeing Aircraft Since 1916* (Fallbrook, Calif., 1966), pp 275-293; Gordon Swanborough and Peter M. Bowers, *United States Aircraft Since 1908*, rev ed (London, 1971), pp 97-108; and *Wings* 3 (Oct 73), 10-39. For a more comprehensive treatment of the new bomber, see Carl Berger, *B-29: The Superfortress* (New York and Toronto, Canada, 1970). Mr. Berger was a former Senior Historian of the Office of Air Force History.

but crashed into the Frye Meat Packing Plant, located 3 miles from the end of the Boeing Field runway, killing the 11-man crew,[10] 19 employees of the packing plant, and a Seattle fireman, and seriously injuring 12 persons. The accident, caused by fire which spread throughout the plane, was not attributed to any mechanical failure. Leakage of gasoline and a backfire were the likely factors.

Special Features   1944

Construction of the B-29 was thoroughly conventional. As standardized by Boeing and the aircraft industry during the pre-World War II decade, the new bomber had an all-metal fuselage with fabric-covered control surfaces. On the other hand, and in spite of being a further development of the B-17, the B-29 was a radically different airplane, featuring significant aerodynamic innovations. Included were a high-aspect ratio wing mid-mounted on the circular-section fuselage; huge Fowler flaps that increased the wing area by 19 percent when extended,[11] and also raised the lift coeficient; a dual wheel retractable tricycle landing gear; flush riveting and butt jointing to reduce drag (the landing gear lowered contributed 50 percent of the resistance); and pressurized compartments for the usual crew of 10.

For defensive armament, the B-29 was equipped with non-retractable turrets mounting ten .50-caliber machine guns and one 20-millimeter cannon (which was dropped from later models). All turrets were remotely operated by a General Electric central fire-control system. The B-29 also had an extensive radio and radar equipment that included a liaison set, radio compass, marker beacon, glide path receiver, localizer receiver, IFF (identification friend or foe) transformer, emergency rescue transmitter, blind bombing radar (on many aircraft), radio countermeasures, and static dischargers.

Another special—and for a while greatly troublesome—feature of the B-29 was the brand new, but fire-prone, 18-cylinder Wright R-3350-23 engine. The 4 engines were mounted by 4-bladed Hamilton constant-speed, full-feathering propellers, 16 feet, 7 inches in diameter. In addition, instead of the traditional single unit, each engine made use of 2 turbo-superchargers.

---

[10] Included in the crew casualties was Eddie Allen, America's most distinguished test pilot at the time.

[11] This arrangement reduced takeoff and landing distances to correspond to those of the B-17 and B-24 bombers. Nevertheless, the heavy B-29 generated extensive construction, as existing landing strips could not be used unless reinforced.

A Boeing B-29, equipped with 4 Wright engines.

Production Problems   1942–1944

The cumulative effect of the B–29's many new features caused more than the normal quota of "bugs" attendant to the production of a new plane. This was compounded by several factors. First, the B–29 was urgently needed. Secondly, troubles with the R–3350 engine hampered testing to the point that all flight operations were suspended until September 1943,[12] even though production models of the already greatly modified B–29 kept on rolling off the line. Also, the many subcontracts for equipment and sub-assemblies, generated by the rushed B–29 procurement, could not keep pace with the aircraft production. Many components, as they became available, did not fit the aircraft coming off the production line without having been modified to accommodate them.

Such a multitude of difficulties called for drastic action. The AAF's solution was to set up centers where the B–29s would be fitted with their indispensable components. But the AAF's lack of experience with the new bomber, as well as the shortage of ground equipment and tools, defeated the centers' initial efforts. The AAF then requested the assistance of Boeing and other contractors. Production personnel, mostly Boeing technicians from Wichita and Seattle, were brought to the centers to reorganize the AAF's modification programs and to help with the work. A first lot of 150 B–29s was successfully modified between 10 March and 15 April 1944, in a record period of time later referred to as the "Battle of Kansas."

War Commitments   1944–1945

B–29s of the Twentieth Air Force entered the war in June 1944 (less than 3 years after the experimental plane's first flight) with a "shakedown" raid on Bangkok, Thailand. The real air offensive against the Japanese Empire started in the same month, when 60 B–29s bombed steel mills and shipping facilities at Yowata in Japan proper. In the months that followed, XX Bomber Command B–29s from bases in China and India struck some of the enemy's most important targets in such major industrial cities as Nagasaki, Palembang, Singapore, Rangoon, Bangkok, and Tokyo. By November 1944, Tokyo was being raided regularly by the XXI Bomber Command, based at Isley Field, Saipan.

Early B–29 raids were hardly effective, their intensity being held down by inclement weather, logistical problems, and technical difficulties—espe-

---

[12] By mid-1943, 2,000 engineering changes had been made to the R–3350 engine, first tested in early 1937. Approximately 500 of these changes required tooling modifications.

cially engine troubles. Despite the progress in resolving these problems, overall results of the high-altitude precision attacks conducted by the new B–29s throughout 1944 were disappointing.[13] Aircraft losses, due to enemy defenses, high fuel consumption, or engine failures, remained excessive.

In January 1945, replacing Maj. Gen. Haywood S. Hansell, Jr., Maj. Gen. Curtis E. LeMay was put in charge of the XXI Bomber Command. The new Commanding General, under pressure from General Arnold and Brig. Gen. Lauris Norstad, Chief of Staff of the Twentieth, became convinced within a few months that low-altitude incendiary bombing was feasible and would be more productive, since the B–29s at low altitude would not have to carry so much fuel and, therefore, would be able to carry more bombs. Ensuing events demonstrated the validity of the low-level bombing tactics initiated by General LeMay. In a single raid on 9–10 March 1945, B–29s loaded with incendiary bombs destroyed one-fourth of Tokyo. By June, Japan's 6 most important industrial cities were in ruins, paving the way for a forthcoming planned invasion of the enemy territory—an endeavor which, even under the best circumstances, would cause a great many U.S. casualties. But the costly invasion of Japan proved unnecessary.

On 6 August 1945, the Enola Gay, a B–29 that had been secretly modified to carry a weapon also developed with the utmost secrecy, dropped the world's first atomic bomb on Hiroshima. Bock's Car, another modified B–29, dropped a second bomb on Nagasaki 3 days later. Being, at the time, the most terrifying weapon ever devised, the atomic bomb made its point. The use of only 2, Little Boy and Fat Man, as the bombs were named, in addition perhaps to the Soviet entry into the war, compelled the Japanese Emperor to accept the Postdam requirement for unconditional surrender, which was signed on 2 September 1945.

End of Production   10 June 1946

The end of World War II prompted the cancellation of over 5,000 B–29s, still on order in September 1945. However, several B–29s well along in production were completed. For all practical purposes, production did not end before June 1946, the last B–29 being delivered on the 10th.

Total B–29s Accepted   3,960

The AAF accepted a grand total of 3,960 B–29s: 3,943 B–29s, 3 XB–29s

---

[13] High winds over Japan adversely affected bombing; occasionally, operational activities were reduced to only a few days during an entire month.

(including the experimental plane which crashed before delivery), and 14 B–29 prototypes.[14] Actually, B–29s, B–29As, and B–29Bs made up the production total. The B–29 and B–29A were alike and barely differed from the B–29B. The B-model was about 2,000 pounds lighter than the A, had an extra 150 feet in service ceiling, and a slightly longer range.

Flyaway Cost per Production Aircraft $639,188

Airframe, $399,541; engines (installed), $98,657; propellers, $10,537; electronics, $34,738; ordnance, $3,977; armament (and others), $91,738.[15]

Subsequent Model Series   None

The B–29C designation was intended for a later model, due to use improved R–3350 engines, but the project was canceled. Featuring many improvements, including new Pratt & Whitney R–4360 engines, the B–29D was redesignated before procurement.[16]

New Planning   1945–1946

The end of the war did not diminish the importance of the atomic-capable B–29. The 509th Composite Group, activated in December 1944 and to which Enola Gay and Bock's Car belonged, was brought back intact to the United States. The group was then assigned to the 58th Wing of the Fourth Air Force of the Continental Air Forces, which became the Strategic Air Command (SAC) in March 1946.[17] Just the same, immediate post-World War II efforts to create a full-scale atomic program were entangled in the confusion of demobilization, the transition from a 2- to a 3-service

---

[14] The post-World War II records of the Army Air Forces and those of the prime contractor did not match, Boeing reporting that 3,974 B–29s were delivered: a discrepancy of 14 aircraft.

[15] Available records failed to reveal if the cost of modifying some B–29s to carry and deliver the first atomic bombs was prorated in the final figure.

[16] See B–50.

[17] Actually, the Headquarters, Continental Air Forces, was redesignated Headquarters, SAC. Some of the air forces under Continental Air Forces went to the Tactical Air Command and to the Air Defense Command.

military system, the question of atomic custody, and the belief that atomic bombs would not be extensively used in the future.

Despite the generally conservative attitude toward the atomic bomb in late 1945 and much of 1946, the AAF remained aware of the need to keep delivery capability up to date. A first step in that direction was the creation of a 3-squadron atomic striking force as part of the 58th Bombardment Wing. Other early plans were affected by various opinions. Shortly after the Nagasaki raid, Gen. Carl Spaatz, Commanding General of the U.S. Strategic Air Forces in the Pacific, pointed out that the atomic bomb had such a wide range of destruction that its use should primarily be intended against industrial areas. Smaller areas could be handled better, and at a much cheaper cost, by the normal type of bomb. In short, General Spaatz believed that wasting atomic bombs on small targets would be "like using an elephant gun on a rabbit." The words of General Spaatz, who was to become in September, 1947, the first Chief of Staff of the new United States Air Force, were not to be forgotten. In the meantime, however, they brought to mind another troublesome factor.

As early as 1945, it was obvious that any major war in the forseeable future would be against Russia. Using the atomic bomb as a weapon of psychological terror was one thing; the atomic strategic doctrine advocated by General Spaatz was another. Since the Soviet Union's industry was scattered in the Soviet Union's heartland, the general's strategy called for bombers capable of covering immense distances. Even from bases in Europe, the range would be very great. To further this strategy,[18] the AAF decided in January 1946 that atomic-capable B-29s would be equipped with new Pratt & Whitney R-435-57 engines. This change should improve reliability, while increasing range and speed.

Special Modifications   1946–1947

Modification of the original lot of B-29s, earmarked to carry the first atomic bombs, had been a slow and difficult task, even though most of the work centered on the aircraft bomb bay. At first, several of the designated aircraft were modified by hand. Changes in specifications were frequent, since scientists continued to improve their own designs for the new atomic bombs; the modification process grew more complex as new technological developments swiftly accrued.

Early in 1946, 22 of the 509th Composite Group's B-29s were at the Oklahoma City Air Materiel Depot for installation of the MX-344 radar

---

[18] See B-36, pp 11–14.

computer, more easily removable engine cowlings, and other miscellaneous items, which would further improve the performance of the newly, or soon to be, re-engined planes. By April 1947, 46 atomic-capable B–29s had received the latest special modifications, and work had begun on 19 others. However, only 24 of the 46 modified planes were operational, 20 being flown by the 509th and 4 by the testing section. Four of the other remodified B–29s had been destroyed, 1 was used as a mockup for further standardization of past modifications, and the remainder were being stripped of the equipment previously added to allow the aircraft to carry the original bombs.

Because of the advent of the B–50 (an improved B–29 known as the B–29D until December 1945), no additional modifications were programmed after May 1947. Yet, the atomic-capable B–29s would not immediately become obsolete. They were capable of carrying some of the latest atomic bombs and could be used for combat in an emergency. They undoubtedly could ferry atomic weapons from the United States to forward bases, as called for by the latest plans. In any case, obsolete or not, as growing international tensions were aggravated by the Korean conflict and the production of new atomic-capable aircraft slipped, 180 of the thousands of B–29s left from World War II had to be reactivated and modified for the atomic task.[19]

Overseas Deployments   1946–1952

While a handful of B–29s were earmarked for the atomic role, and various kinds of reconfigured B–29s became directly involved in the support of these special aircraft, a great many B–29s, left over from the war, remained the mainstay of the medium bombardment force until 1952.[20] There were good reasons for the aircraft's retention. The postwar period witnessed drastic budgetary restrictions; developing and producing any aircraft was a time-consuming task, and the impact of new technology was bound to lengthen this task.[21]

In 1946, SAC's only bomber was the B–29—148 of them. Despite the shortage, B–29 rotational tours of duty in Europe and the Far East were

---

[19] See B–50, pp 173–174.

[20] The heavy B–29 was reclassified as a medium bomber on 17 September 1947. For details, see B–36, p. 21.

[21] As aircraft systems became increasingly more complex, their production time rose by several orders of magnitude. Thus, while it took 200,000 manhours to assemble the B–17, the B–29 and B–36 required approximately 3 million manhours each. With the advent of the jet-powered B–52, production time again rose dramatically, to more than 7 million manhours.

started in that year. By 1948, the SAC B–29 fleet had been increased to 486 aircraft, and the oversea rotation of B–29 units had been intensified. In late June, when the Berlin Blockade began, extra B–29s were immediately deployed to England and Germany. The rest of the SAC force was put on 24-hour alert.

New War Commitments   1950–1953

On 25 June 1950, when the North Korean armies crossed the 38th parallel, the 19th Bombardment Group, the only Far East bombardment unit available for the air counter-offensive was immediately moved from Guam to the more strategically favorable location of Okinawa. Reinforcement, obviously needed, was provided swiftly. On 3 July, Gen. Hoyt S. Vandenberg, USAF Chief of Staff, ordered the 22d and 92d Bomb Groups to deploy their B–29s to the Far East to carry out conventional bombing operations north of the 38th parallel. Once in the Far East, SAC's 22d and 92d Bomb Groups joined the 19th Bomb Group of the Far East Air Forces (FEAF) to form the FEAF Bomber Command (Provisional), which was organized on 8 July. The bomber command's first strike took place on 13 July, when 50 B–29s hit Wonsan, an important North Korean port. But additional B–29s were still needed, and SAC again quickly managed to comply.

By late September 1950, the strategic bombardment offensive was finished. The FEAF Bomber Command had destroyed all significant strategic targets and enemy airfields in North Korea, establishing in the process that the Strategic Air Command's mobility concept was valid and practicable. This was an important lesson of the Korean War. Another, of a controversial nature, was demonstration of the strategic bomber's versatility. Because the early ground situation was desperate, many B–29s were initially diverted from the strategic mission to direct support of the ground forces. Despite adverse weather conditions, the B–29s blasted successfully such tactical targets as trucks, tanks, troop bivouacs, supply dumps, and the like.

The Air Force met the immediate demand for additional bombers in Korea in large part by withdrawing B–29s from storage. While commercial contractors removed the planes and made them combat ready, Air Materiel Command depots overhauled engines and accessories. The command also set up a production line at the Sacramento Air Depot, California, to recondition B–29s returned from the Far East for necessary repairs.

Late in 1950, 2 bomb groups were allowed to return to the United States. Other SAC B–29s, plus 1 squadron of B–29s that had been converted for the reconnaissance role, remained in the Far East, under the operational control of the FEAF Bomber Command, until the fighting ended on 27 July

1953. Except for FEAF's own B–29s, which had been raised to wing level, the FEAF Bomber Command was composed entirely of SAC units and was commanded by SAC personnel. Of course, combat losses occurred.[22] Yet, they were relatively low when compared to the bomber command's achievements. Through the 3-year conflict, B–29s flew 21,328 effective combat sorties, including 1,995 reconnaissance sorties and 797 psychological warfare sorties. The B–29s dropped 167,000 tons of bombs on various targets, ranging from front-line enemy troop emplacements to airfields on the banks of the Yalu River. The 98th and 307th Bomb Wings, also elevated from group level, and the 91st Strategic Reconnaissance Squadron were included in the South Korean Presidential Unit Citation that was bestowed upon the FEAF Bomber Command (Provisional).

Immediate Phaseout   1954

The increasing availability of B–36s, B–47s, and B–50s, spelled the B–29's end. On 4 November 1954, SAC's last B–29 bomber, an A-model, which had been assigned to the 307th Bomb Wing, Kadena Air Base, Okinawa, was retired to the Air Force aircraft storage facility at Davis-Monthan AFB, Arizona.

Other Configurations   KB–29M, KB–29P, RB–29, TB–29, VB–29, and WB–29[23]

KB–29M: In 1948, 92 B–29s were sent to the newly reopened Boeing Wichita Plant for conversion to hose-type tankers, subsequently known as KB–29Ms. This project was urgent, being directly associated with the build-up of the atomic forces. The bomber's serious range limitations had called for special arrangements. There was an extensive forward base network, encompassing airfields in Alaska, Canada, England, West Germany, Spain, North Africa, Okinawa, and Guam. But the use of overseas staging bases was a troublesome expedient.[24] A better solution was to

---

[22] The B–29 was exceptionally vulnerable to the MiG–15, even at night.

[23] Other designations were applied or allocated to reconfigured or due to be reconfigured B–29s, but such designations were dropped, as the reconfigured aircraft (usually a single model) fulfilled their special purposes, or were not used because the projects for which they had been designed were canceled.

[24] See B–50, p 11 and p 15.

develop inflight refueling systems that would give to the SAC bombers the intercontinental striking range they still lacked.

The first such system was featured by the K–29M, which was fitted with British-developed hose refueling equipment. The British system involved trailing a hose from the tanker to the receiver and transferring fuel practically by means of gravity. The receiver aircraft (listed as B–29MR, in the B–29's case) also required modifications, but they were relatively minor. In contrast, the tanker modifications were extensive. Each bomb bay was fitted with a separate jettisonable tank holding approximately 2,300 gallons of fuel. These tanks were connected to the aircraft's normal fuel system so that fuel from it could also be transferred to the receiver bomber. The KB–29M's inflight refueling system required that the tanker and receiver fly in formation, with the tanker above and ahead trailing a cable referred to as the hauling line. The receiver trailed a line of its own from its refueling receptacle. Called the contact line, this line was so equipped that it could hook the tanker's trailing line and lock the two lines together. The receiver operator then caught the lines, separated them, secured them, pulled the tanker's refueling hose and put it into the receptacle of his bomber. The

The forward compartment of the B–29 housed the bombardier (front), pilot (left), and co-pilot (right).

whole procedure, obviously, was perilous from the start, and the KB–29Ms, after reaching the inventory in late 1948, were replaced within a few years.

KB–29P: The hose refueling system had many disadvantages, especially in the lengthy time required to make contact, the slow rate of fuel transfer, and the very limited airspeed imposed by the hoses. Boeing therefore soon developed on its own an aerodynamically controlled swivelling and telescoping arm, known as the "Flying Boom." Essentially, this system consisted of a telescopic pipe, which was lowered from the tanker, and connected to a socket in the receiver aircraft. The system was entirely controlled by an operator in the tanker, and the fuel transfer was made with the aid of a pump. B–29s so equipped were designated KB–29Ps. The first of 116 KB–29Ps reached SAC's 97th Air Refueling Squadron on 1 September 1950, the total contingent being delivered by the end of 1951. In spite of the increasing availability of the much faster KC–97,[25] SAC retained many of its KB–29Ps until 1957. The Tactical Air Command gave up its last KB–29s in the middle of that year.[26]

RB–29: Nearly 120 B–29s were converted to the reconnaissance configuration and redesignated as RB–29s. Some of these aircraft, known as F–13s during World War II, were first fitted with fairly primitive photographic equipment: 3 K–17Bs, 2 K–22s, and 1 K–18 camera. After 1948, when the RB–29 designation came into being, the converted bombers began acquiring more sophisticated components. The RB–29s were assigned to the 91st Strategic Reconnaissance Squadron, which like other SAC units played a crucial role during the Korean conflict. The RB–29s followed the phaseout pattern of the bombers from which they derived. The same reasons prompted their retirement.

TB–29: Some B–29s, fitted with additional trainee or instructor stations, recording equipment, and related types of apparatus, were used for training and identified as TB–29s.

VB–29: A few B–29s, after being internally refurbished, were used for the transportation of key personnel.

WB–29: Some B–29s were modified to carry meteorological equipment

---

[25] Outfitted with an improved version of the flying boom and additional air-refuelable tanks, the 4-engine, propeller-driven KC–97 could fly fast enough to match the B–47's minimum speed. Manufactured by Boeing, the KC–97s began reaching SAC in July 1951.

[26] The urgent conversion of B–29s to the tanker configuration had been dictated by the initial deficiencies of the growing atomic forces. When more efficient, atomic-capable bombers and better tankers became available, the KB–29P's flying boom system was adapted to fighters and other bombers, which had their receptacle fitted in a variety of positions. This allowed other forces to make use of the KB–29Ps, when the allocation of improved tankers was still at a premium.

and used on weather-reconnaissance flights. Designated as WB–29s in1948, these aircraft were the last B–29s to phase out of the regular Air Force.

Final Phaseout   1959

Regardless of configuration, no B–29s appeared on any Air Force roll after 1959.

Milestones   1951

On 6 July 1951, despite its rudimentary equipment, a KB–29M refueled 4 RF–80 aircraft flying a reconnaissance mission over North Korea. On 14 July, a KB–29P, outfitted with the boom-type system, refueled 1 RB–45C on a combat mission over North Korea. These were the first air refueling operations conducted over enemy territory under combat conditions.

Items of Special Interest   Mid-1944

Early engine problems delayed the B–29's entrance into World War II. The much-needed and initially few bombers were piloted by some of the WASPs (Women's Air Force Service Pilots),[27] themselves a new phenomenon of the war and restricted to non-combat operations.

The technological importance of the American-made B–29 was quickly confirmed. One of the bombers, after crash-landing in Soviet territory during World War II, was not returned, even though Russian authorities promptly returned the unharmed crew. The reason soon became obvious, as Russia developed her own version of the B–29, known as the TU–4. In 1951, foreign observers in Russia saw a derivative version of the TU–4 with turboprop engines.

---

[27] The title WASP was the designation for the women pilots of the Army Air Forces.

TECHNICAL AND BASIC MISSION PERFORMANCE DATA

B–29 AIRCRAFT

Manufacturer (Airframe)	Boeing Airplane Co., Seattle and Renton, Wash., plus Wichita, Kans.
Manufacturer (Engines)	The Wright Aeronautical Corp. (a division of the Curtiss-Wright Corp.), Wood-Ridge, N.J.
Nomenclature	Medium Bomber
Popular Name	Superfortress

	B–29
Length/Span (ft)	99.0/141.2
Wing Area (sq ft)	1,736
Weights (lb)	
Empty	71,500 (actual)
Combat	101,082
Takeoff	140,000
Engine: Number, Rated Power per Engine & Designation	(4) 2,200-hp R–3350–57 or –57A
Takeoff Ground Run (ft)	
At Sea Level	5,230
Over 50-ft Obstacle	7,825
Rate at Climb (fpm) at Sea Level	500
Combat Rate of Climb (fpm) at Sea Level	1,630
Service Ceiling at Combat Weight (100 fpm Rate of Climb to Altitude)	39,650
Combat Ceiling (500 fpm Rate of Climb to Altitude)	36,250
Average Cruise Speed (kn)	220
Max Speed at Optimum Altitude (kn/ft)	347/30,000
Combat Radius (nm)	1,717 (with max bombload)
Combat Target Altitude (ft)	30,000
Total Mission Time (hr)	15:35
Crew	11[a]
Armament	5 turrets (mounting 12 .50-cal guns)
Maximum Bombload (lb)	20,000

Abbreviations			
cal	= caliber	kn	= knots
fpm	= feet per minute	max	= maximum
hp	= horsepower	nm	= nautical miles

[a]The crew of 11 were in 3 pressurized compartments linked by crawl-spaces. The standard crew had 5 officers: a pilot, co-pilot, flight engineer, bombardier, and navigator. These, plus the radio operator, normally worked in the forward compartment, while the one aft housed gunner-mechanics, and a radar operator. The tail gunner was alone in the smallest compartment.

Appendix II

Post–World War II Experimental and Prototype Bombers

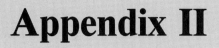

XB–35
Northrop
Aircraft, Incorporated

Manufacturer's Model N–9M

Basic Development   1923

The origin of the B–35 may be traced as far back as 1923, when John K. Northrop, then an engineer with the Douglas Aircraft Company, became interested in the possibilities of a "flying wing" design. However, more than a decade would pass before the young engineer's efforts showed tangible results. In August 1939, John Northrop became President and Chief Engineer of Northrop Aircraft, Incorporated, a totally independent concern primarily interested in the manufacture of military aircraft. Less than a year later, the N–1M, as Northrop called his initial "flying wing," took to the air.[1] It was the world's first pure all-wing airplane, and high-ranking officials of the Army Air Corps were soon impressed by the flight characteristics of the spectacular research vehicle. The Army Air Forces (established in June 1941) applied the designation XB–35 to the N–1M's military variant, which was subsequently ordered.

Military Characteristics   1941

On 27 May 1941, the Army Air Forces (AAF) asked Northrop to provide studies of the flying wing as it related to requirements for a bomber with a range of 8,000 miles, a minimum cruising speed of 250 miles per

---

[1] The N–1M's first flight occurred on 3 July 1940. In 1945, following completion of its test program, Northrop sent the airplane to the Army Air Forces for display in the Wright-Patterson Museum, Dayton, Ohio. The Air Force eventually transferred the N–1M to the Smithsonian Institution, which stored it at Silver Hill, Maryland.

hour, a service ceiling of 40,000 feet, and a bombload of 10,000 pounds. Such characteristics were far less demanding than the preliminary ones of April 1941, which led to production of the Convair B-36.[2] The revised characteristics of August 1941, slightly more ambitious than the May characteristics, were again submitted to Northrop and other potential manufacturers of conventional, long-range bombers. Contrary to expectations, by year's end only 2 models were contemplated for production before the Boeing B-29: the Northrop XB-35 and the Convair XB-36. The first was extremely unconventional, aerodynamically; the second was unconventional, but strictly from the weight, propulsion, and size standpoint. Although the AAF deplored the lack of choice offered by its experimental heavy bombardment program, several years would go by before comparable bombers would appear on the drawing boards.[3]

Initial Procurement   1941

The Northrop proposal submitted to the AAF in September 1941 was immediately followed by contractual negotiations. In a departure from standard practices, the initial procurement of the flying wing was preceded by a purchase order for engineering data, model tests, and evaluation of reports on the N-1M that had been flight-tested since June 1940. Also included was the purchase of the first N-9M, a 1/3-scale flying mockup of the future B-35. The entire order, approved by Secretary of War Henry L. Stimson on 3 October 1941, was covered by Contract W535 ac-21341 which was signed on the 30th.[4]

Procurement of the first full-scale flying wing, endorsed by Maj. Gen. Henry H. Arnold, Chief of the AAF, on 9 September 1941, came under Contract W535 ac-21920 on 22 November. At the contractor's request, the contract, estimated at $2.9 million, was of the cost-plus-fixed-fee type because, as pointed out by Northrop Incorporated, development of the XB-35 was a large project, involving funds in excess of those available to the company for experimental purposes. In addition, Northrop anticipated that materiel and labor costs would rise significantly before November 1943, when the XB-35 was scheduled for delivery. Besides providing for the first XB-35, Contract W535 ac-21920 included 1 XB-35 mockup, engineering

---

[2] See B-36, pp 5-7.

[3] See B-52, pp 205-211.

[4] Available records did not reveal the cost of Contract W535 ac-21341, an oversight which by the end of the costly flying wing program proved immaterial.

data, plus an option clause covering the purchase of 1 additional XB-35. This option was exercised on 2 January 1942. Northrop quoted a delivery date of April 1944 for the second XB-35, also known as the back-up article. Estimated extra costs were set at $1.5 million.

Additional Procurement   1942

Another cost-plus-fixed-fee contract (W535 ac-33920) was approved on 17 December 1942. It called for the construction and testing of 13 service test models of the XB-35, designated YB-35s. Counting spare parts and the contractor's fee, the contract's cost was expected to reach $22.7 million. The AAF's approval of this YB-35 prototype contract followed by a few months the purchase of 2 additional N-9Ms, a fourth and last N-9M being ordered in mid-1943.[5]

Special Features   1942

The huge XB-35's most noticeable features were its size and shape. Otherwise, the 4-engine aircraft was not so unusual. Its cantilever wings of aluminum-alloy were constructed in 1 piece, straight-tapered, and swept back. On the other hand, the XB-35 also featured some distinctive internal characteristics. It offered 8 spacious bomb bays, and the crew compartment and various systems bays were fully pressurized. In addition, the future B-35 would provide 6 beds and a small galley to allow 6 of the aircraft's 15 crewmen to rest during long missions.

First Flight (N-9M)   27 December 1942

As a military variant of the N-1M, the N-9M was similarly built and consisted primarily of a welded steel tube center section and an external covering of wood. As a research model of the XB-35, the 60-foot wing-span N-9M closely resembled the future full-size "flying wing." Two Menasco C654 engines aboard the N-9M, instead of the 4 Pratt & Whitney R-4360s earmarked for the XB-35, were the main difference between the 7,100-pound scaled-down model and the experimental bomber, originally planned. Actually, the N-9M was expected to allow Northrop to more accurately

---

[5] Retained records did not itemize the costs of the additional N-9Ms. However, such costs were included in the XB-35 program's total amount.

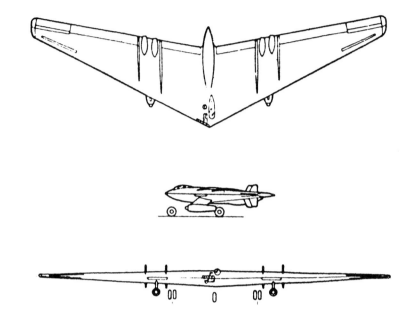

The Northrop XB–35, with its 4 engines at the rear.

predict the flight characteristics of the upcoming XB-35, a purpose which presumably would also save money and time. Nevertheless, the N-9M's first flight on 27 December 1942 was about 3 months behind schedule. Nearly all of the N-9M's ensuing flight tests were shortened by mechanical failures of one kind or another, most of them involving the Menasco engines that also equipped the next 2 N-9s.

The initial N-9M crashed on its 45th flight, killing its Northrop test pilot. The crash on 19 May 1943, after the model had only accumulated some 22 hours of flying time, was closely followed by the second N-9M's first flight. During the maiden flight of the second model, on 24 June 1943, the small aircraft's cockpit canopy was lost shortly after takeoff, but a successful landing was made.[6] Meanwhile, other difficulties had begun to compound the AAF's many problems.

Preliminary Difficulties   1942-1943

The multitude of requirements generated by World War II complicated from the start the Army Air Forces' many tasks. While all sorts of weapons were urgently needed, shortages of material and manpower resources could not be immediately resolved. National priorities, regardless of their careful selection, hampered the timely progression of some aircraft programs and nearly stopped the development of crucial experimental projects. Two cases in point were the Convair B-36 and the Northrop B-35, the latter presenting the AAF with a peculiar situation. Northrop, located in Hawthorne, California, while sharing the industry's shortage of engineers, also lacked adequate production facilities. The Materiel Command's efforts to borrow engineers from other West Coast manufacturers to assist the young corporation had been totally unsuccessful, and the possibility of enlarging the Hawthorne plant was non-existent.

By the end of 1942, it seemed that Northrop's problem was solved as negotiations, instigated by the AAF, were being concluded between Northrop, Incorporated, and the Glenn L. Martin Company. In short, Northrop had indicated that it would be satisfied to fabricate only the experimental and prototype B-35s. The Martin production contract for 400

---

[6] Slightly different N-9M's were still being tested late in 1945, even though a total of 150 flights had been accomplished. Flights of the remaining models averaged considerably less than 1 hour each. This time limit was shared by the N-9MB, the fourth N-9, bought to replace the lost N-9M and powered by 2 Franklin 0-540-5 air-cooled engines.

B–33s had been canceled on 25 November,[7] and this actually meant that the B–35 could be produced, in lieu of the deficient B–33, at Martin's spacious Baltimore plant in Maryland. This change would also allow Northrop and the AAF to benefit from Martin's engineering talent and experience in the design of large, long-range transport airplanes. But this optimistic outlook was to prove deceptive.

Other Problems   1943–1944

Hampered by mechanical failings, the N–9 flight test program prevented the acquisition of reliable flight data through 21 September 1943, when the N–9MB, last of the N–9s, initially flew. Engines excepted, the N–9MB included all latest design features of the XB–35, but the model's flight testing did not help the XB–35's cause. By the end of November, test results indicated that the XB–35's range would most likely be 1,600 miles shorter than anticipated and that the bomber's highest speed would be at least 24 miles per hour below previous estimates. Such disappointing prognostics were not overlooked. General Arnold[8] himself began to question the merits of the extensive B–35 production plans.

Production of 200 B–35s, as planned in November 1942, was formalized on 30 June 1943 by Contract W535 ac–24555, which called for delivery of the first "flying wing" by June 1945. But Martin had already begun to lose personnel to the draft before the contract was signed. In mid-1943, projected delivery rates were reduced by 50 percent, and Martin pointed out that changes requested by Northrop amplified the many risks shrouding the aircraft's manufacture. In August, Martin reiterated its concern for the shortage of engineers and the project's uncertainties, adding that perhaps further production expenditures should be postponed. By March 1944, the Baltimore plant still lacked tooling, and Martin had rescheduled delivery of the first B–35 to 1947. Not surprisingly, the AAF's headquarters canceled the Martin production contract on 24 May 1944. The decision, however, did not spell the end of the "flying wing." In November, the Air Technical Service Command's Engineering Division reported that the XB–35 project seemed worthwhile "even if the B–35 never becomes operational."

---

[7] By that time, Martin knew that a production contract for 200 B–35s was forthcoming. Furthermore, the company had many other commitments. In fact, it had to refuse to make a study of the long-range, heavy bombardment airplane, as suggested by the AAF in October 1942.

[8] General Arnold had received his fourth star in March 1944.

Program Changes   1944–1945

In December 1944, some 6 months after the Martin production contract was nullified, modification requests began to alter the B–35 development contract. The AAF decided that Northrop would build the first 6 B–35 prototypes (YB–35s) on the XB–35's pattern, with certain exceptions affecting individual aircraft. Soon afterward, Northrop was authorized to build 2 of those 6 prototypes as all-jet models, a change so important that it actually marked the beginning of a new program.[9] In 1945, after 2 YB–35s had been added to the first YB–35 lot to replace the 2 earmarked for jet-conversion, the AAF told Northrop to manufacture the remaining 5 airplanes to more advanced specifications, a directive that automatically entailed the aircraft's redesignation as YB–35A.

In the meantime, Northrop, like Martin, had its share of problems. The poor showing of the N–9 and the impact of the war had not helped the experimental program. In 1941, Northrop believed the first XB–35 could be delivered in November 1943. But by May 1944, the best estimate for the XB–35's first flight was August 1945, another optimistic prediction that would not materialize.

First Flight (XB–35)   25 June 1946

The initial flight of the first XB–35, from Hawthorne to Muroc Army Airfield, California, took place at long last on 25 June 1946 and lasted 45 minutes. Two AAF test pilots, after maneuvering the first XB–35 during its initial and second flights, termed the experimental flying wing "satisfactory, trouble-free." Yet, once again, this encouraging appraisal was to prove wrong.

Grounding   1946–1948

Gear box malfunctions and propeller control difficulties prompted the XB–35's grounding on 11 September 1946, less than 3 months after the aircraft's first flight. Flying was not resumed until February 1948, after many modifications had taken place that affected the aircraft's engineering as well as the entire experimental program.

---

[9] See YB–49, this appendix, p 536.

The all-jet prototype YB–35A.

Testing   1946–1948

The first XB–35 underwent only about 24 hours of testing, all of which were accumulated in 19 contractor flights. The second XB–35, also covered by Contract W–535–ac–21920 of November 1941, fared even worse. First flown on 26 June 1947 (a slippage of 3 years), the plane was tested for approximately 12 hours. As in the first XB–35's case, Northrop pilots did the testing. Only 8 flights were accomplished.

Modifications   1947–1948

Since most of the serious troubles encountered during testing were attributed to the XB–35's dual-rotation propellers and gear boxes, significant modifications were undertaken. In February 1948, flights of the first XB–35 were resumed, this time with single-rotation propellers and simpler gear boxes installed. The new installation began to operate without exhibiting any particular mechanical difficulties, but test pilots immediately reported considerable vibration and reduced performance. Moreover, the modified XB–35's landing gear doors still failed to close after gear retraction, a malfunction that had plagued the 1947 tests.

Cost Overruns   1947–1948

The cost of the first XB–35 had initially leaped from an estimated $2.9 million to a substantial $14 million, and other financial setbacks were on the way. In February 1947, Northrop reported that the 2 all-jet prototypes

(YB–49s) and the first 6 YB–35s (built to XB–35 specifications) were either complete or nearing completion. However, the originally allocated $23 million would cover construction of only 3 or 4 of these aircraft. An additional $8 million would probably finance completion of these 8 planes, and $16 million would make it possible to complete all 13 (counting the 5 YB–35As included in the program changes of 1945). On 28 May 1947, $12 million was approved for cost overruns—$4 million below Northrop's estimate. At the end of January 1948, Northrop again reported that an additional $4.4 million would be required to complete all 13 aircraft.

Program Review   June 1948

By mid-1948, the XB/RB–35 program had started to show definite signs of an approaching demise. To begin with, a propeller-driven bomber could not match the performance of jet bombers already in development and nearing the production stage. In addition, the "flying wing" in its mid-1948 configuration was less stable than a conventional wing-fuselage aircraft, and thus made an inferior bombing or camera platform. The factor that kept the program alive was the multi-million dollar investment in the aircraft's development, with no tangible gain for the operational forces. Such failing most likely accounted for the Air Force's decision to get a reconnaissance version of the jet-equipped YB–35s, first ordered in 1945. The decision, as formalized in June 1948, called for the production of 30 aircraft, due to be known as RB–49As.[10] As it turned out, the RB–49 project, like other "flying wing" ventures, proved unsuccessful. In the meantime, and again because of the money involved, the Air Force continued to attempt rescuing the original XB–35 program. For example, a study was underway in mid-1948 to determine the feasibility of producing the B–35 for the air-refueling role.

Other Proposals   July–December 1948

Proposals for conversions and modifications of the experimental B–35s increased during the second half of 1948. Both contractor and Air Force still hoped that a tactical or strategic mission could be found for the aircraft. Yet, the odds were not encouraging. In August, Northrop indicated that existing experimental contracts could be completed with the funds already allotted if no further changes were made, but Air Materiel Command promptly

---

[10] See this appendix, pp 541–542.

pointed out that such a procedure would be self-defeating. Changes were necessary, the command insisted, to solve the vibration problems created by the single-rotation propellers. Also, the XB–35's intricate exhaust system caused tremendous maintenance difficulties, and the cooling fans of the R–4360 engines were beginning to fail due to metal fatigue. The only solution, the Air Materiel Command believed, was to convert every B–35 prototype to a 6-jet configuration.

By the end of 1948, modification plans had evolved further. Five YB–35s and 4 YB–35As were to be equipped with Allison J35–A–17 jet engines (6 per aircraft), fitted with cameras, redesignated RB–35Bs, and used for reconnaissance. In addition, 1 YB–35A was earmarked for static tests, a second YB–35B, after being re-engined with 6 Allison jets, was to serve as a reconnaissance prototype for the B–49 program, and a third jet-converted YB–35A would be fitted to serve as a test bed for the T–37 turboprop engine being developed by the Turbodyne Corporation, a Northrop subsidiary. Referred to as the EB–35B, the test-bed aircraft (last of the 13 prototypes included in the B–35 experimental program) would be capable of carrying 2 T–37 engines, although only 1 would be initially installed. Finally, a flexible-mount gear box would be fitted in the second XB–35 to try stopping the vibrations caused by the aircraft's single-rotation propellers. All this, the Air Materiel Command calculated, could probably be done with an additional $13 million.

Total Development Costs $66 million

By the end of fiscal year 1948, development costs of the experimental B–35 had reached $66,050,506.[11] More than one-third of this amount had been spent on the first contract (535-ac–21920). This cost-plus-fixed-fee contract, as amended in January 1942, gave the Air Force 2 XB–35s for a final sum of $25,632,859, some $21 million more than originally estimated by the AAF. The remaining $40,417,647 covered the second and last cost-plus-fixed fee contract (535–ac–33930) which, as supplemented by Change Order No. 11, totalled $24,417,647, excluding cost overruns of $12 and $4 million, approved respectively in April 1947 and April 1948.

Program Cancellation November 1949

Faced with a $13 million modification proposal at a time when money

---

[11] Including $1,644,603, which paid for conversion of 2 YB–35s to 6-jet-equipped B–49 prototypes.

was especially scarce, Air Force enthusiasm for the B–35 conversion program fell sharply. In August 1949, the 2 XB–35s and the first 2 YB–35s were scrapped. And while the decision did not signify the official end of the program, its fate was determined soon afterward. In November, the Air Staff canceled plans to convert remaining YB–35s and YB–35As, pointing out that no requirements existed that a "flying wing" could fulfill as efficiently as more conventional aircraft.

Total XB/YB–35s Accepted   15

Two XB–35s and 13 YB–35s were paid for and also accepted, in theory. In actuality, the Air Force hardly took possession of the B–35 lot. Some of the aircraft were diverted to the B–49 program, and most others, although finally completed, were immediately scrapped.

Final Disposition   1950

Scrapping of the remaining YB–35 types started in December 1949 and ended in March 1950, when the disassembling of the EB–35B test-bed began.

TECHNICAL AND BASIC MISSION PERFORMANCE DATA

YB–35B AIRCRAFT[a]

Manufacturer (Airframe)	Northrop Aircraft, Inc., Hawthrone, Calif.
Manufacturer (Engines)	Designed by the General Electric Co.; built by the Allison Div. of the General Motors Corp.
Nomenclature	Long-Range Bomber
Popular Name	Flying Wing
Length/Span (ft)	53.1/172
Wing Area (sq ft)	4,000
Weights (lb)	
Empty	82,807
Combat	125,715
Takeoff	175,000 (limited by structural strength)
Engine: Number,	
Rated Powers per Engine,	(6) 4,900-lb st
& Designation	J35–A–19
Takeoff Ground Run (ft)	
At Sea Level	4,280
Over 50-ft Obstacle	5,380
Rate of Climb (fpm) At Sea Level	1,500 (at takeoff weight, with max power)
Combat Rate of Climb	
(fpm) at Sea Level	3,050 (with max power)
Service Ceiling (100 fpm	
Rate of Climb to Altitude)	30,200 (takeoff weight/normal power)
Combat Ceiling (500 fpm	
Rate of Climb to Altitude)	36,200 (with max power)
Max Speed at Optimum Altitude (kn/ft)	381/35,322 (max power)
Combat Radius (nm)	1,300 with no payload, at 337 kn
Total Mission Time (hr)	7:9
Crew	4
Armament (provisions for)	(20) .50-cal guns
Max Bombload (lb)	40,000

Abbreviations	
cal	= caliber
fpm	= feet per minute
kn	= knots
max	= maximum
nm	= nautical miles
st	= static thrust

[a]Estimates only.

XB–42 and XB–42A Mixmaster
Douglas
Airplane Company,
Incorporated

Basic Development   1943

Studies made by Douglas in early 1943 marked the start of the official development of the XB–42, first known as the XA–42.[12] The radically new design was another example of the evolutionary process, although it incorporated features of the slightly smaller A–20 and A–26 airplanes, also manufactured by Douglas.

Requirements   1943

Requirements for the XA–42 (formally redesignated as the XB–42 on 25 November) stemmed from the Army Air Forces's recurring need during the war years for smaller, more efficient, more economical, speedier, and longer-range tactical bombardment aircraft. Acquisition of the XA–42 was related to that of the B–29. The Army Air Forces (AAF) wanted modern light bombers to avoid using costly strategic bombers in strictly tactical applications.[13]

Initial Procurement   25 June 1943

The design proposal, submitted by Douglas in April 1943, impressed

---

[12] In 1939, the "attack aviation" category was replaced by a "light bombardment" one, even though the "A" designation was kept throughout the war. One reason for the change came from Gen. H. H. Arnold's belief that it was more efficient and safer to fight the enemy with light bombers, and their carefully selected bombloads, than to rely on the machine guns of the attack-type aircraft.

[13] A few B–29s were flyable in June 1943, but the aircraft would not be ready for combat before 1944. Moreover, even though production was stopped in late 1945, the average unit cost of the B–29 reached over $600,000 (a high price in 1940–1945 dollars).

the AAF favorably, and Letter Contract W535–ac–40188 was approved on 25 June. This document, calling for 2 experimental models and a static test article, was logged by the Materiel Command[14] under Project MX–392 as a purely experimental endeavor. And, as it turned out, plans for manufacturing production models of the airplane did not go beyond the discussion stage.

Additional Requirements   September 1943

In September 1943, just a few months after approval of the XB–42 project, the AAF asked if jet engines could be added to 1 of the experimental aircraft covered by the contract of June 25th. In October, the Materiel Command recommended that jet engines be installed in the XB–42 static test article, if the contractor thought that a satisfactory all-jet airplane would result. Douglas quickly pointed out that development of a practically new aircraft would take time and that modifying 1 of the XB–42s would be much faster. But the AAF's interest in jet propulsion was increasing, and the development and production of new jet bombers were strongly favored. Hence, the XB–42 modification devised by Douglas, although approved by the AAF in December 1943, would not get underway before 1945, 1 year after the aircraft's first flight.

Special Features   1944

Clean aeronautical lines and the novel engine-propeller arrangement were the most striking features of the all-metal, cantilever, mid-wing XB–42 monoplane. The 2 Allison liquid-cooled, reciprocating engines were mounted inside the fuselage in order to eliminate the drag of large nacelles. Pusher-type propellers were located in the empennage to do away with thrust disturbances. Twin shafts, similar to those in the Bell P–39 fighter, connected the propellers to the forward-located engines.

First Flight (XB–42)   6 May 1944

Designed and constructed in the record time of less than a year, the XB–42 was first flown by Douglas on 6 May 1944. As a safety measure, the

---

[14] Soon to be discontinued, as AAF Air Technical Service Command came into being.

aircraft's initial flight originated from and was conducted over Palm Springs Army Air Base, California. Even though the XB–42 was the first AAF bomber during World War II to substitute pusher for the conventional tractor-propulsion, a change requiring the development of radically different propellers,[15] the 22-minute flight proved uneventful.

Contract Changes   1944–1945

In routine fashion, the letter contract of June 1943 was replaced on 11 February 1944 by a definitive contract carrying the same identification (W535 ac–40188). The definitive contract, however, included a new provision covering the development of an all-jet version of the XB–42, later identified as the XB–43.[16] On the other hand, no official mention was made of the approved XB–42 modification until 23 April 1945, when a contract change notification authorized conversion of the first XB–42 to the XB–42A configuration.

Testing   1945–1947

Flight testing of the first XB–42 proved, on the whole, disappointing. In test flights, conducted between May 1944 and March 1946, stability of the airplane was satisfactory, but controls were inadequate. During development, the XB–42 had taken on considerable extra weight over that foreseen in the design proposal and, as a result, did not meet the Douglas guarantees either for maximum speed at altitude, or for range. Even more frustrating was the excessive vibration from the engines and propellers and from the bomb-bay doors when open.

Testing of the second XB–42, first flown on 1 August 1944, was another disappointment, mainly because its combat capability was no better than that of the first model. The plane did have slightly improved speed and range, however, as demonstrated in a coast-to-coast flight in November 1945 in which it covered 2,295 miles in 5 hours and 17 minutes. In any case, testing ended abruptly. The second XB–42 was completely destroyed on 16

---

[15] Built by Curtiss-Wright, the 13-foot propellers needed perfecting. However, further development was stopped when it became obvious that production of the XB–42 was out of the question.

[16] See this appendix, p 516.

December 1945, in an accident near Bolling Field, D.C. Failure of the landing gear and fuel starvation were the accident's major causes.

The XB-42 flight testing program was extensive, but the second aircraft's premature loss prevented completion of a number of special tests. Douglas tested the first XB-42 for some 129 hours, accumulated in 154 flights. The contractor test-flew the second, short-lived aircraft for more than 65 hours, accrued in 57 flights. The Air Force put in 14 hours of flight tests on the first XB-42, and 51 hours on the second one. The modified XB-42 (XB-42A) was flight tested by Douglas for approximately 17 hours that were reached in 22 flights. The Air Force test-flew the XB-42A only once, for 1 hour. The flight met the contractual acceptance requirements.

Modifications   1946–1948

Douglas was authorized to begin work on the XB-42 conversion in April 1945, but the modifications were immediately postponed because the Bureau of Aeronautics could not speed delivery of the Westinghouse 19XB-2A Navy-type jets due to be fitted on the aircraft (1 unit under each wing). Testing therefore went on until March 1946, when the aircraft's left engine failed in flight. The XB-42 was then returned to the Douglas plant in Santa Monica, California, where a new landing gear, plus internal and external fuel tanks were to be installed in addition to the auxiliary turbojet engines.

During the latter part of 1946 and early in 1947, after the forging problems of the Westinghouse turbojets were solved, Douglas advanced the factory completion date of the programmed modifications several times, consequently delaying the important vibration tests.

The first flight of the XB-42A on 27 May 1947, from Santa Monica to Muroc Army Airfield, California, was marred by the obvious drag of the XB-42A's new turbojets. In ensuing flight tests at Muroc, both the Allison engines and added jets proved unsatisfactory. To make matters worse, the vibration tests, only started in mid-1947, were stopped on 15 August, when the XB-42A made a hard landing in the tail-low position, damaging the lower vertical stabilizer and lower rudder. The contractor wanted to resume testing as soon as possible, but the Air Materiel Command[17] decided that the new jet nacelles also needed modifications, and the aircraft was flown back to Santa Monica late in 1947. In the ensuing months, although it appeared that the Air Force still wanted a perfected XB-42A, Douglas

---

[17] The Air Materiel Command replaced the Air Technical Service Command on 9 March 1946. For details, see B-36, p 13.

The XB–42 featured a novel engine-propeller arrangement.

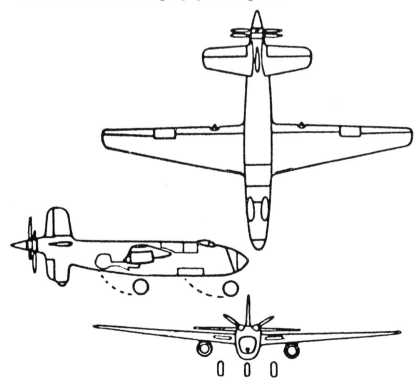

became increasingly convinced that further studies and engineering to reduce weight, eliminate vibration, and bring the modified plane up to guaranteed performance would not be economical.

Program Cancellation   August 1948

Convinced by the Douglas argument, the Air Force in August 1948 decided to cancel the remainder of the XB–42A modification program, and to accept the aircraft "as is." The decision also marked the end of the entire B–42 experimental project.

Total XB–42s Accepted   2

The first XB–42, after being conditionally accepted on 24 September 1946, became the XB–42A which was finally accepted on 19 August 1948. The second, ill-fated XB–42 was accepted and delivered on 8 December 1945.

Total Development Cost

Both the XB–42 and XB–43 (also developed by Douglas) were procured under the same contract (W535 ac–40188) at a total cost of $13,682,095, including the contractor's fixed fee of $227,775. The $13.7 million settlement figure, recorded by the Air Force Contract Audit Office on 30 November 1947, did not provide a breakdown of the amount expended on each project. A portion of the XB–42A modifications was the object of another contract (W33–038–ac–14525), signed on 31 March 1947. The contract's relatively small amount (about $300,000) was most likely covered by the audit of November 1947.

Final Disposition   November 1948

The Air Force thought the modified XB–42A, with its clean aeronautical lines and other novel features, was a true museum piece and kept it at the National Air Museum Storage Activity in Park Ridge, Illinois, pending completion of additional space at the Smithsonian Institution in Washington, D.C. In April 1959, the fuselage of the XB–42A was moved to the Smithsonian's Suitland Annex, in Silver Hill, Maryland.

TECHNICAL AND BASIC MISSION PERFORMANCE DATA

XB–42 AND XB–42A AIRCRAFT[a]

Manufacturer (Airframe)	The Douglas Aircraft Company, Inc., Santa Monica, Calif.
Manufacturer (Engines)	Allison Division of General Motors Corp. (V–1710–129); Westinghouse Electric and Manufacturing Co. (XJ–30).
Nomenclature	Light Bombers
Popular Name	Mixmaster

	XB–42	XB–42A
Length/Span (ft)	53.6/70.6	53.6/70.6
Wing Area (sq ft)	555	555
Weights (lb)		
Empty	20,888	Not Available
Combat	Not Available	33,000
Takeoff	35,702	35,000
Engine: Number, Rated Power per Engine, & Designation	(2) 1,460-lb st V–1710–129	(2) 1,460/lb st V–1710–137 & (2) 1,600-lb st XJ–30
Takeoff Ground Run (ft) Over 50-ft Obstacle	6,415	3,540
Rate of Climb (fpm) at Sea Level	1,050 (mil power)	Not Available
Service Ceiling (ft)	29,400 (takeoff weight/normal power)	35,500 (takeoff weight/normal power)
Maximum Speed	386 mph	385 knots (estimate)
Combat Range	1,800 miles	Not Available
Combat Cruising Radius (nm)	Not Available	495
Crew	3	5
Armament	6 .50-cal guns	None
Maximum Bombload (lb)	8,000	4,000[b]
Maximum Bomb Size (lb)	2,000	4,000

Abbreviations	
cal	= caliber
fpm	= feet per minute
mil	= military
mph	= miles per hour
st	= static thrust

---

[a]From Flight Test Reports only.
[b]Space and structural provisions for 8,000 lb.

XB–43
Douglas
Aircraft Company,
Incorporated

Basic Development   September 1943

The XB–43 was essentially a jet version of the unconventional XB–42, officially developed by Douglas in early 1943. The XB–43 did not reach the drawing board before 1944, but the project's development started in September 1943.

Requirements   1943–1944

General requirements for a jet bomber of the XB–43 type arose during World War II, as a result of the development of German jet fighters. Also, the Air Corps needed an aircraft that could destroy military targets on land and sea in support of air, ground, or naval forces. Specific requirements were defined in 1944. The Army Air Forces (AAF) wanted the XB–43 to have a gross weight of 40,000 pounds; a maximum speed of 420 miles per hour at an altitude of 40,700 feet; and a range of 1,445 miles, at the same high altitude, with an 8,000-pound bombload.

Initial Procurement   1944

A letter supplement to the XB–42 contract (W535 ac–40188) authorized on 14 January 1944 the initial procurement of 2 XB–43s. A formal supplemental agreement, approved on 31 March, set the estimated cost of the 2 experimental planes at $2.7 million and the contractor's fixed fee at about $107,000. The reason for such hurried transactions was to introduce tactical jet bombers swiftly into the operational inventory. As early as December 1944, the AAF seriously considered placing the XB–43 in production. Accordingly, the Air Technical Service Command asked Douglas on 30 December to submit a production proposal without delay.

516

Special Features   1944-1945

The XB-43 was the first American bombardment airplane to be powered exclusively by jet engines: TG-180 turbojets (later J35s), designed by the General Electric Company. Otherwise, except for the absence of the dual-rotating propeller at the rear of the empannage, the XB-43 had retained the XB-42's appearance and structural design.

Development Slippage   1944-1945

Early engineering problems with the pioneer J35 power plant hampered the XB-43's development. To begin with, General Electric only shipped the first J35 engine to Douglas in December 1944. Then, numerous changes in piping, wiring, and sheet metal work were necessary to make the engine suitable for flight. By March 1945, and in spite of the assistance of General Electric technicians, Douglas had spent more than 3,000 manhours to solve problems connected with the first engine. Moreover, subsequent engine deliveries, due since October 1944, were delayed until July 1945.

Program Change   1945

While the B-43 experimental program was assured from the start, the production program, which once appeared very promising, did not materialize. The Air Technical Service Command recommended in March 1945 the immediate procurement of 50 B-43s, but the Douglas production schedule for a preliminary lot of 13 test service airplanes proved unsatisfactory. Contrary to expectation, the planes would not be available for testing ahead of the B-45 and B-46 prototypes.[18] In addition, and probably of greater import, the proposed B-43 test aircraft would not meet the performance requirements that had been previously established. The AAF therefore opted to cancel all B-43 production plans. Air Technical Service Command notified Douglas of the AAF decision on 18 August 1945, specifying that the projected procurement of the 13 test aircraft was also nullified.

First Flight   17 May 1946

The XB-43 made its first flight on 17 May 1946. As in the XB-42's

---

[18] As it turned out the XB-43 flew almost 1 year before the XB-45. In any case, the small XB-43 could hardly be compared to the much heavier B-45 and B-46 experimental aircraft, except for the fact that all such projects centered on jet propulsion.

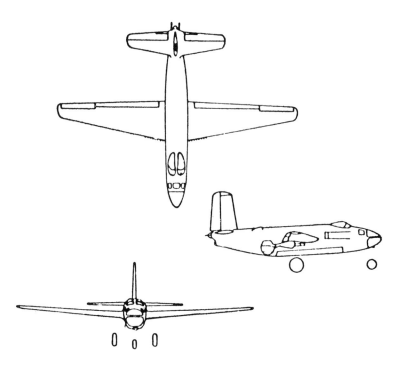

A Douglas XB–43, the first American jet-propelled bomber.

518

case, because of the experimental status of the aircraft, the 8-minute flight was made from a military installation. The XB–43 had been dismantled at the contractor's plant in Santa Monica, California, and moved to Muroc Army Airfield, where it was reassembled. The AAF had invoked the War Powers Act to override the state's objections to having the disassembled airplane trucked over the public highway.

The first official flight of the second XB–43, on 15 May 1947, lasted 20 minutes and took place between Hughes Field in Culver City, California, and Muroc. After being fitted with special instruments, the second XB–43 had been trucked to Hughes Field where Douglas tested its ground handling and flight characteristics. To control costs, the AAF had informed Douglas that the second XB–43's flight test time was not to exceed 5 hours, without special authorization.

Continuing Problems   1946–1947

General Electric's labor difficulties and similar problems at the General Motors Corporation's Chevrolet Division, where most J35 engines were being built, continued to slow Douglas's progress. For example, in January 1946, no one knew with any certainty when the J35s earmarked for the second XB–43 would be available.

However, Douglas's engineering setbacks were not confined to the XB–43's power plant. One early problem, stemming from the difficulty encountered in obtaining positive nose wheel door operation, involved the pressurization of the entire nose section and nose wheel well. This problem was solved, but only by default. In January 1946 Douglas requested, and the AAF granted, permission to eliminate this pressurized area because the original requirement which called for the installation of a nose cone had been deleted. A second serious engineering problem was the tendency of the XB–43's plexiglass nose to crack under temperature extremes. The substitution of costly metal units, $5,000 each, was first considered. In November 1947, however, the Air Force decided that the difficulty could be corrected by installing wooden noses, much cheaper and adequate for a plane earmarked for testing, but no longer due to reach production.

Testing   1946–1948

While both XB–43s were used extensively for testing purposes, flight testing of each aircraft was relatively short. Douglas test-flew the first XB–43 for over 9 hours, accumulated in 28 flights; the AAF only test-flew it for about 4 hours, reached in 3 flights. Testing of the second XB–43 was even shorter. Douglas flew it for less than 8 hours, gained in 17 flights; the Air Force test-flew it once, for 1 hour.

Total XB–43s Accepted   2

The first XB–43 was accepted on 27 February 1947; the second, on 27 April 1948.

Total Development Costs

The Air Force Contract Audit Office on 30 November 1947 recorded the cost of the XB–42, XB–42A, and XB–43 programs at $13.7 million, and did not provide a breakdown of the amount spent on each program.[19] However, retained data on the XB–43 project set the program's tentative cost at $6.5 million. Although estimated, the figure appeared creditable.

Final Disposition   1951–1953

ARDC used the first XB–43 for a variety of tests until February 1951, when an accident ended the aircraft's testing career, which by then had reached almost 400 hours in flight. The second XB–43, after being assigned to the Air Materiel Command's Power Plant Laboratory, went to Muroc where it served as a test-bed for the General Electric J47 (TG–190) engine. Supported by the spare parts retrieved from the first XB–43, the second model also paid back its investment, totaling more than 300 hours of flight time before leaving the Air Force inventory in December 1953. The second XB–43 then went to the National Air Museum of the Smithsonian Institution.

---

[19] See XB–42, this appendix, p 514.

TECHNICAL AND BASIC MISSION PERFORMANCE DATA

XB-43 AIRCRAFT

Manufacturer (Airframe)	The Douglas Aircraft Company, Inc., Santa Monica, Calif.
Manufacturer (Engines)	Designed by the General Electric Co.; built by Chevrolet Div. of General Motors Corporation
Nomenclature	Light Bomber
Popular Name	None

Length/Span (ft)	51.4/71.2
Wing Area (sq ft)	563
Weights (lb)	
Empty	22,600
Combat	35,900
Takeoff	40,000
Engine: Number, Rated Power per Engine, & Designation	(2) 3,820-lb st J35
Takeoff Ground Run (ft)	
Over 50-ft Obstacle	7,080 (contractor's guarantee)
Rate of Climb (fpm) at Sea Level (mil power)	2,470 (contractor's est)
Service Ceiling (ft)	41,800 (combat weight/mil power)
Average Cruise Speed	365 kn
Maximum Speed (mil power)	437 kn (contractor's est)
Combat Cruising Radius	470 nm
Crew	3
Armament	None
Maximum Bombload (lb)	8,000[a]
Maximum Bomb Size (lb)	4,000[a]

Abbreviations	
cal	= caliber
fpm	= feet per minute
kn	= knots
max	= maximum
nm	= nautical miles
st	= static thrust

---

[a]Space and structural provisions only.

XB-46
Consolidated Vultee
Aircraft (Convair)
Corporation

Manufacturer's Model 109

Basic Development   1944

The XB-46's development originated in 1944, when the War Department called for bids and proposals on an entire family of jet bombers, with gross weight ranging from 80,000 to more than 200,000 pounds.[20] Consolidated Vultee Aircraft (Convair) Corporation answered the War Department's requirements with the design study of a 90,000-pound, jet-propelled bomber. The design, submitted and accepted in November 1944, was labeled by the Army Air Forces (AAF) as the XB-46.

Initial Procurement   17 January 1945

The AAF initiated the XB-46's procurement with Letter Contract W33-038 ac-7674, which was approved on 17 January 1945. This first document covered preliminary engineering, wind tunnel, model, tests, mockup, and data that were to be based on the contractor's proposal of November 1944.

Definitive Development Contract   12 February 1945

The letter contract of January was supplemented on 12 February by a definitive contract of the standard cost-plus-fixed-fee type. This contract followed by 1 week completion of the XB-46's first mockup inspection. As was usually the case, the contract satisfied the inspection board's essential

---

[20] See B-45, pp 62-65, and B-47, pp 101-102.

Long, thin wings and a teadrop canopy were special design characteristics of the XB–46.

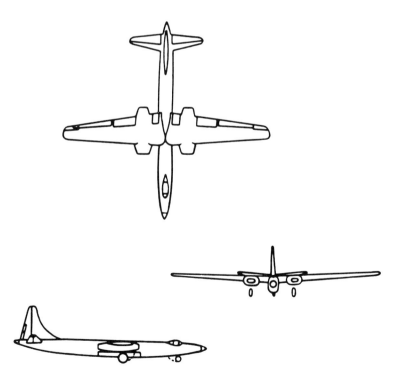

recommendations. In short, 3 experimental B-46s were ordered and required to incorporate the necessary changes identified by the board. A supplemental agreement on 3 March provided for data and spare parts for the 3 XB-46s. Because of fiscal restrictions, the AAF also altered the terms of the basic contract, changing it to the fixed-price type.

Near-Cancellation   November 1945

By the fall of 1945, the AAF had become particularly interested in a Convair jet attack design, identified as the XA-44. The AAF actually considered canceling the XB-46 in favor of the XA-44, since there was not enough money for both projects. The contractor, however, firmly believed a better solution would be to complete 1 XB-46 in a stripped but flyable condition and to develop 2 XA-44s in lieu of the 2 other XB-46s remaining under contract. Although the AAF ratified the suggested substitution in June 1946, the XA-44 program did not materialize.[21] Similarly, the special testing of a TG-180 engine, due to be installed in a B-24J airplane as an added requirement related to the XB-46 development, was also subsequently abandoned.

Special Features   1947

A distinguishing feature of the XB-46 was the tail turret, designed by the Emerson Electric Company Also, the pilot rode in a fighter-style cockpit with a teardrop canopy.[22] In other respects, despite its extremely thin wings and long, oval fuselage, the graceful airplane did display a few conventional features. Its wings were straight, and it was powered by 4 J35 axial flow engines, which were paired in low-slung nacelles, 1 on each side of the fuselage, a typical arrangement.

First Flight   2 April 1947

The XB-46's first flight on 2 April 1947, from San Diego, California,

---

[21] AAF support of the XA-44 did not last long. The program was ended in December 1946, when the design was converted to a light bomber design and redesignated the XB-53. The XB-53 project was given up soon afterwards. The XA-44 program was reinstated in February 1949, but only for a short while.

[22] The XB-46's cockpit design was selected for study by other aircraft manufacturers.

to Muroc Army Airfield lasted over 1 hour and a half. The contractor's test pilot praised the functioning and handling of the airplane which, as completed, contained only the equipment considered necessary to prove its air-worthiness and handling characteristics.

Testing   1947

The basic flight tests (Phases I and II) of the single XB–46 (Serial No. 45–59582) were concluded in September 1947, within 5 months of the aircraft's first flight. Convair test pilots accumulated more than 26 hours of testing in 16 flights; the AAF's pilots, about 101 hours in 46 flights. Although stability and control were for the most part excellent, engineering problems included engine troubles as well as difficulties with the spoiler clutch installation and with the lateral control surfaces when the aircraft flew at high speeds. All in all, the XB–46 appeared to meet the contractor's only guarantee—that it would be safe for experimental test purposes.

Total XB–46s Accepted   1

The Air Force accepted the sole XB–46 on 7 November 1947 and took delivery of the aircraft on the 12th.

Program Cancellation   August 1947

The B–46 program was officially canceled in August 1947, several months before the experimental aircraft was formally accepted and exactly 1 year after the AAF had endorsed the immediate production of the North American XB–45. Still, only a small quantity of B–45s would be bought because, in the final analysis, the performance characteristics of the XB–47, being developed by the Boeing Airplane Company, were sure to exceed those of the future B–45 and of the unfortunate B–46. The AAF selected the XB–45 over the XB–46 for a number of reasons. Weight was one of them. Being at the time slightly heavier than the XB–45, the XB–46 could not be expected to match the future B–45's performance. Another factor against the XB–46 was the size of the necessary radar equipment. Most likely, the installation of such equipment would have required an extensive modification of the aircraft's thin fuselage.

APPENDIX II

Total Development Costs $4.9 million

As agreed upon in mid-1946, completion of only 1 stripped version of the XB–46 was intended to provide "a very realistic approach to the problem of development with relatively low cost." Just the same, when completed 1 year later, the experimental program nearly reached the $5 million mark.

Final Disposition February 1952

Like most strictly experimental airplanes, once accepted by the Air Force, the XB–46 participated in a variety of extra tests such as noise measurements, tail vibration investigations, and the like. Additional stability and control tests were also conducted at West Palm Beach AFB, Florida, between August 1948 and August 1949. However, after 44 hours of flight, these tests were stopped because "maintenance difficulties, aggravated by lack of spare parts, required a prohibitive number of manhours to keep the aircraft in flying condition." Actually, no additional testing was done on the airplane for almost a year. The XB–46 was flown to nearby Eglin AFB in July 1950, where its pneumatic system was tested at low temperatures in the base's climatic hangar. Completion of the climatic tests in November 1950 marked the bomber's end, since the Air Force had no more use for it. Except for its nose section, which was sent to the Air Force Museum at Wright-Patterson AFB, Ohio, on 13 January 1951, the XB–46 was scrapped on 28 February 1952.

TECHNICAL AND BASIC MISSION PERFORMANCE DATA

XB–46 AIRCRAFT

Manufacturer (Airframe)	Consolidated Vultee Aircraft Corp., Fort Worth, Tex.
Manufacturer (Engines)	Designed by the General Electric Co.; built by the Chevrolet Div. of the General Motors Corp.
Nomenclature	Medium Bomber
Popular Name	None
Length/Span (ft)	105.8/113
Wing Area (sq ft)	1,285
Weights (lb)	
Empty	48,000
Combat	75,200
Takeoff	94,400
Engine: Number, Rated Powers per Engine, & Designation	(4) 3,820-lb st J35–C3 (axial flow-11 stage)
Takeoff Ground Run (ft)	
At Sea Level	2,000[a]
Over 50-ft Obstacle	4,000[a]
Rate of Climb (fpm) at Sea Level	2,400 (at design takeoff of 91,000 lb)[a]
Combat Rate of Climb (fpm) at Sea Level	3,000 (at target weight of 75,200 lb)[a]
Service Ceiling (ft)	40,000 (guaranteed by contractor)
Combat Ceiling (ft)	36,500[a]
Average Cruise Speed (kn)	381
Max Speed at Optimum Altitude (kn/ft)	425/40,000[a]
Combat Radius (nm)	603
Total Mission Time (hr)	Not Available
Crew	3 (pilot, co-pilot, & bombardier-navigator)
Armament	2 .50-cal machine guns (space and structural provisions for APG–27 remote control with optics & radar sighting)
Maximum Bombload (lb)	22,000 (in various loads)
Maximum Bomb Size (lb)	22,000

Abbreviations	
cal	= caliber
fpm	= feet per minute
kn	= knots
nm	= nautical miles
st	= static thrust

---

[a]Contractor's estimates only.

XB-48
Glenn L. Martin
Company

Manufacturer's Model 223

Basic Development   1944

The XB-48, like the more fortunate XB-45, originated in 1944, when the War Department concluded that jet propulsion was promising enough to warrant extension of the program, thus far centered on fighters and light bombers, to heavier aircraft with gross weights ranging from 80,000 to more than 200,000 pounds.[23] Realizing that such an ambitious project could be fraught with difficulties, Army Air Forces (AAF) headquarters informed the Materiel Command and Air Services Command on 10 August[24] that in the beginning contracts for jet bombers of the medium and heavy categories would have to be let on a phased basis so that they could be readily terminated upon completion of any one stage of development. This cautious procedure was formalized on 15 August.

Military Characteristics   1944–1945

On 17 November 1944, the AAF issued military characteristics calling for a bomber with a range of 3,000 miles (minimum acceptable, 2,500); a service ceiling of 45,000 feet and a tactical operating altitude of 40,000 feet (minimums acceptable, 40,000 and 35,000 feet, respectively); and an average speed of 450 miles per hour with a high speed of 550. These characteristics were amended on 29 January 1945 to reemphasize that such aircraft needed

---

[23] See B-45, pp 353–363.

[24] About 2 weeks later the 2 commands merged to form the AAF Technical Service Command, which was redesignated Air Technical Service Command on 1 July 1945. This organization became the Air Materiel Command on 9 March 1946.

to carry specific types of bombs, including the conventional M–121, a 10,000-pound "dam-buster" developed during World War II.[25]

Initial Procurement   1944–1945

In accordance with the AAF's endorsement of "phase" contracts and based on the military characteristics of November 1944, a Martin proposal, submitted to the Air Technical Service Command on 9 December 1944, led to Letter Contract W33–038 ac–7675. Approved on 29 December, this initial document covered certain engineering services and completion by 1 May 1945 of 1 mockup of Martin's Model 223, designated XB–48 by the Air Technical Service Command. Tentative costs were set at $574,826. The letter contract of December 1944 was replaced on 27 March 1945 by a definitive contract, which reduced estimated costs to $569,252, including Martin's fixed-fee of $16,500.

Final Procurement   13 December 1946

Procurement of the XB–48 overcame many vicissitudes. In June 1945, 2 months after inspection of the XB–48 mockup, Martin submitted a proposal for 1 stripped and 1, 2, or 3 complete XB–48s. Accompanying cost figures, however, were immediately questioned. To Air Technical Service Command's surprise, it was soon ascertained that the estimated cost of $80.09 per pound for the XB–48 compared favorably to the $105.68 for the XB–45, but the AAF remained dissatisfied because the XB–48's engineering lagged behind the XB–45 and XB–46. Despite these concerns, the XB–48 project survived, and the initial contract was supplemented many times while negotiations went on. In March 1946, the contractor introduced a new proposal and offered to furnish 1 stripped and 1 complete XB–48 for about $10 million. This proposal was made on a fixed-price rather than a cost-plus-fixed-fee basis in order to conform to the policy set forth by the Air Technical Service Command in December 1945 on the procurement of

---

[25] The M–121, sometimes called the "Earthquake" bomb, was more often referred to as the "Grand Slam" bomb, a totally misleading nickname. Actually "Grand Slam" was the code name of a highly classified modification project strictly concerned with atomic matters. The "Grand Slam" modifications would allow the Convair B–36 to carry atomic bombs, which the Air Force believed might weigh more than 40,000 pounds. Since the 10,000-pound M–121, when properly dropped, could inflict the damage of a 40,000-pound bomb, curiosity and rumors most likely explained the ensuing confusion. As a matter of fact, the "Grand Slam" designation was also loosely applied to other conventional bombs of the M–121 category.

experimental airplanes. Just the same, the Martin proposal of March 1946 had to be revised, and negotiations were not consummated until the end of the year. The final contract (W33–038 ac–13492), approved on 13 December 1946, superseded Contract W33–038 ac–7675 which, as amended, had reached an estimated future cost of $10.9 million.[26] For the same amount, the new contract promised 2 XB–48s, spare parts, and a bomb-bay mockup. Also, the first XB–48 was to be flight tested and delivered by 30 September 1947; the second one, by 30 June 1948. Finally, all wind tunnel tests were to be completed by 1 January 1947.

Program Slippage   1947–1948

Development and testing of the 2 XB–48s were delayed by engine difficulties. General Electric turbojet engines were installed, the first XB–48 being powered by 6 J35–GE–7 (TG–180–B1) engines; the second, by 6 J35–GE–9s (TG–180–C1s). Since the engines were in an even more experimental stage than the airplanes, it took time to get them to operate properly. Also, like every new engine, the J35s were in short supply. Still, the first XB–48 would go through 14 engines during its first 44 flights.

Special Features   1947–1948

The sleek, all-metal, high-wing XB–48 presented many special features, the most outstanding one being the tandem bicycle landing gear necessitated by the airplane's wings, too thin to house conventional landing gear with bulky retracting mechanisms.[27] Other novel features were the number of engines, 6 as compared to 4 on the other proposed medium bombers; the turbojet engine's installation, encased in pods (3 under each wing) in a lift section with air ducts between the pods; and also adjustable tail pipes on the engines. The 3-crew arrangement was also unusual. The pilot and co-pilot were seated in tandem under a canopy-type inclosure, similar to that found in high-speed fighter planes, while the bombardier-navigator was seated in the aircraft's nose. The XB–48 had retractable bomb-bay doors, a feature that sprang from the fact that all new medium and heavy bombers had to be

---

[26] Only some $500,000, covered by the initial letter contract, were unaffected.

[27] Martin had experimented with a 4-wheel bicycle landing gear on an XB–26H and concluded that such an arrrangement was feasible. Bicycle-type landing gears were later used by other jet bombers, including the B–47.

The XB–48, developed by Glenn L. Martin Company.

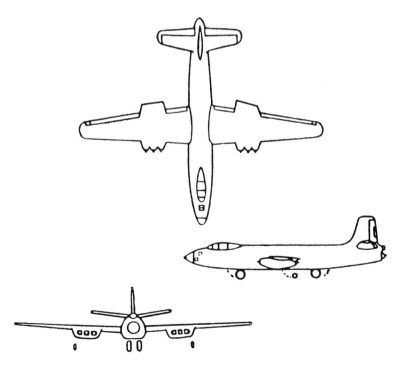

capable of carrying the so-called "Grand Slam" bombs, as well as the cumbersome atomic bombs of the period.

First Flight   22 June 1947

The XB-48, the first U.S. 6-jet bomber to fly, made its initial flight on 22 June 1947. The experimental plane took off from Martin's airfield at Baltimore and landed some 80 miles away at the Patuxent Naval Air Station, also in Maryland. The 38-minute flight was not a great success. At 10,000 feet, the Martin pilot discovered that the right spoiler aileron snapped up too rapidly. On landing, the XB-48 drifted across the runway. Rudder steering was attempted, but the rudder was ineffective with the full use of brakes. In addition, the brakes overheated and stopped working. The aircraft finally came to a halt off the runway with no damage, even though both tires were worn through.

The second XB-48 did not fly until 16 October 1948, some 3 months behind schedule. The 30-minute flight was satisfactory, but of relative unimportance since the future of the experimental program had already been decided.[28]

Testing   1947–1949

Martin pilots tested the first XB-48 52 times, for a total of 41 hours; the Air Force, 50 times for a total of 64 hours. The second XB-48 was also thoroughly tested. The contractor put in 14 hours, accumulated in 15 flights; the Air Force, 49 hours, reached in 25 flights. Results of the first XB-48's flight test program revealed that the aircraft did not meet the Martin guarantees. The XB-48 was 14,000 pounds overweight; the nose wheel was too sensitive; turbulence occurred in the bomb bay when the doors were open; and metal chips, deposited by disintegrated test stand hydraulic pumps, shattered the hydraulic system.[29]

Program Cancellation   1948

The experimental B-48 program agreed upon in December 1946 was not

---

[28] See B-45, pp 64-65, and B-47A, p 107.

[29] The Air Force gave the contractor the option to eliminate all flaws or to pay a lump-sum penalty of $25,000. In January 1950, Martin agreed to pay the penalty.

curtailed. Yet, in spite of the contractor's efforts, no production program followed. Although no firm commitment would be made before many months, planning for the procurement of B–47 production models began in December 1947, right after the XB–47's first flight—a poor omen for the B–48, initially flown in June of the same year.

In the spring of 1948, after early experimental flight information had been obtained for both the XB–47 and the XB–48, the Air Force conducted an evaluation to determine which of the 2 planes could best satisfy the urgent need for a high-speed, high-altitude medium bomber. The evaluation confirmed that the performance of the XB–47 was appreciably better than that of the XB–48. It was also apparent that the XB–47 design provided possibilities for growth which surpassed those of the XB–48. The XB–47's swept-back wing would enable it to attain higher speeds, and its simpler pod-nacelle arrangement minimized the problem of incorporating newer and more efficient jet engines as they became available.[30]

Early in 1949 Martin attempted to rescue the B–48 production program and proposed to modify the second XB–48 by removing the J35 engines and nacelles and installing 4 XT–40A propeller turbines in new and repositioned nacelles, at an estimated cost of $1.5 million. Actually, the reconfigured XB–48 would become a prototype of the Martin Model 247–1, an airplane, the contractor insisted, capable of competing with the B–47, B–50, and B–54. On paper, Model 247–1's performance looked good, but the Air Force did not believe the proposed reconfiguration could be accomplished for the amount of money estimated by the contractor. In addition, since the XT–40A turboprop was a Navy-developed engine, it was doubtful that Martin could obtain enough engines to complete the reconfiguration on schedule. Finally, and of overriding importance, senior Air Force officials believed that turbojet aircraft "currently offered greater promise than turboprop installations." Thus, on 31 March 1949, Martin was formally told that the Model 247–1, like the original XB–48, was a dead issue.

Total XB–48s Accepted   2

The Air Force accepted the first XB–48 on 26 October 1948, but only conditionally. The acceptance became final in 1950, when Martin paid the $25,000 penalty assessed by the Air Force because of the aircraft's several defects. The second XB–48, also conditionally accepted on 26 October 1948,

---

[30] The end of the B–48 production program became official in September 1948, when the Air Force ordered the first lot of 10 B–47s.

was finally accepted on 23 February 1949, after the contractor completed various modifications.

Total Development Costs $11.5 million

The total cost of the XB–48 development program reached $11.5 million. Of this amount, less than $500,000 pertained to the letter contract of December 1944. The rest covered the final contract of December 1946 and represented an increase of about $100,000, justified by various changes ordered by the Air Force.

Final Disposition   1949–1951

In the fall of 1949, the first XB–48 was cannibalized to provide parts for the second XB–48. The latter aircraft was scheduled for many tests, including tests on the F–1 autopilot, jet engine cooling system, and a hydraulic system for jet engines. The proposed tests, however, were canceled. The Air Force decided to use the second XB–48 as a test-bed for "bad-weather" flight items, including a badly needed deicing system. Completion of the thermal anti-icing survey test program in mid-1951 paved the way for the second XB–48's end. In September, the aircraft was flown to Phillips Field, Aberdeen Proving Ground, Maryland, where the strength of the XB–48 structure was tested until the aircraft was totally destroyed.

TECHNICAL AND BASIC MISSION PERFORMANCE DATA

XB-48 AIRCRAFT

Manufacturer (Airframe)	The Glenn L. Martin Co., Baltimore, Md.
Manufacturer (Engines)	Developed by General Electric; built by the Allison Div. of General Motors Corp., Kansas City, Mo.
Nomenclature	Medium Bomber
Popular Name	None
Length/Span (ft)	85.8/108.3
Wing Area (sq ft)	1,330
Weights (lb)	58,500
Empty	92,600 (max)
Combat	102,600 (4,968 gal of fuel, included)
Engine: Number, Rated Power per Engine, & Designation	(6) 3,820-lb st J35–B–1 (1st XB–48)[a] (6) 3,820-lb st J35–D–1 (2d XB–48)[a]
Takeoff Ground Run (ft)	
At Sea Level	7,900 (at 102,600-lb takeoff)[b]
Over 50-ft Obstacle	5,200 (at 102,600-lb takeoff)[b]
Rate of Climb (fpm)	
at Sea Level	3,250 at design takeoff of 102,000 lb)[b]
Combat Rate of Climb (fpm) at Sea Level	4,200 (at combat takeoff of 86,000 lb)[b]
Service Ceiling (ft) (100 fpm Rate of Climb to Altitude)	39,400[b]
Combat Ceiling (ft) (500 fpm Rate of Climb to Altitude)	43,000[b]
Average Cruise Speed (kn)	360[b]
Max Speed at Optimum Altitude (kn/ft)	454/35,000[b]
Combat Radius (nm)	433 (with max bombload)[b]
Cruising Radius (nm)	783[b]
Total Mission Time	Not Available
Crew	3 (pilot, co-pilot, & bombardier-navigator)
Armament	None (provided for 2 .50-cal machine guns to be controlled by AN/APG-27 Radar)
Maximum Bombload (lb)	22,000 (in various loads)
Maximum Bombload (lb)	22,000

Abbreviations			
cal	= caliber	max	= maximum
fpm	= feet per minute	nm	= nautical miles
kn	= knots	st	= static thrust

[a]First known as Allison TG-180s, the initial J35s were axial flow gas-turbine engines, grouped in threes under each wing. The J35-B-1s were later replaced by J35-GE-7s; the J35-D-1s, by J35-GE-9s.

[b]Contractor's estimates only.

YB–49 and YRB–49A
Northrop Aircraft,
Incorporated

Basic Development   1944

The YB–49 evolved from the unconventional XB–35 "flying wing,"[31] its development being prompted by a 1944 study of the possibilities of converting the propeller-driven XB–35 to turbojet engines. Actually, the YB–49 project and its reconnaissance counterpart represented the continuing effort of the Army Air Forces (AAF) and Northrop to establish a tactical use for the original "flying wing," yet to be flown but already plagued by virtually insurmountable problems.

Initial Procurement   1 June 1945

On 1 June 1945, Change Order 11 to Contract W535 ac–33920, a December 1942 document calling for 13 B–35 prototypes, confirmed earlier verbal decisions and authorized Northrop to convert 2 future YB–35s to the YB–49 configuration.

Conversion Slippage   1947

Conversion of the YB–35 to the YB–49 configuration, due to be completed by June 1946, slipped more than a year. The delay was caused by unforeseen problems, encountered in adding fins to the wings to provide the stabilizing effect that the propellers and propeller shaft housings gave to the basic XB–35.

Special Features   1947

The YB–49 featured eight 4,000-pound-thrust J35 engines, 2 more than

---

[31] See this appendix, pp 497–516.

planned; 4 small trailing edge fins, to replace the XB–35's yaw dampening prop shaft housings; 4 large wing fences; and a reconfigured leading edge ahead of and between each pair of fences that provided a low drag intake slot for each of the 2 sets of jet engines. In most other respects, since the all-metal XB–35 airframe was used for the conversion, the YB–49 was identical to the YB–35.

First Flight   21 October 1947

The initial flight of the first YB–49 occurred on 21 October 1947, from the contractor's plant in Hawthorne to Muroc Army Airfield, both in California. The new prototype's first flight lasted 34 minutes without incident. The second YB–49 was first flown on 13 January 1948, from and to the same places and also without special difficulties.

Testing   1947–1950

Testing of the first YB–49 was extensive. Northrop test-flew it for almost 200 hours, accumulated in some 120 flights; the Air Force completed about 70 hours, totaled in some 20 flights.[32] Early in 1948, Northrop began test-flying the second YB–49. Some 24 flights were made by the contractor's pilots for a near-total of 50 hours. The Air Force test-flew the second YB–49 5 times, for perhaps 13 hours. In the YB–49's case, early test results acquired special significance. Tragically, just after being officially accepted by the Air Force, the second YB–49 crashed, killing its entire 5-man crew.[33]

Investigations of the second YB–49's crash could assign no specific cause for the accident, but determined that a major structural failure had taken place in flight. An eyewitness described the plane as tumbling uncontrollably about its lateral axis just before hitting the ground. Project officers later verified that under certain conditions a "flying wing" would indeed "somersault" through the air. The loss of the aircraft and further wind tunnel work perpetuated doubts concerning the flying wing's aerodynamic stability and revealed the need for additional flight testing.

---

[32] Conflicting information did not allow the computation of absolute figures. However, extensive research by various Air Force historians confirmed the stated estimates.

[33] Capt. Glen Edwards, from the Air Materiel Command Flight Test Division, was co-pilot on this fatal trip. Muroc Army Air Base, after becoming Muroc AFB on 12 February 1948, was renamed Edwards AFB on 5 December 1949, in honor of Captain Edwards.

The Northrop YB–49 was a converted YB–35, with jet engines instead of propellers.

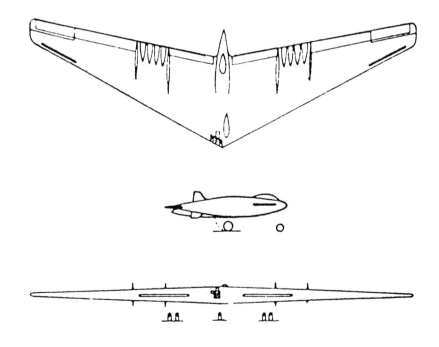

Program Re-Appraisal   1948-1949

By 1948, progress in range-extension had relegated the YB-49 to the status of a medium bomber. Actually, the YB-49 was the largest of the medium bombers under consideration, but it faced stiff competition from the B-45 (already in production), and from the XB-46, XB-47, and XB-48 (all in flight test). Soon afterward, and although the project would not be firmed up for another year or so, the Aircraft and Weapons Board decided to use flight test results to evaluate the B-47 and B-49 as possible "special piloted atomic" carriers.[34] The YB-49 program also profited from the Air Materiel Command's decision to de-emphasize turboprop propulsion and push turbojet development. Yet, other aspects of the program were not so favorable.

The first YB-49 made a significant flight on 26 April 1948, a test of the aircraft's range which proved quite successful. The aircraft was aloft 9 hours, of which 6 hours were flown at an altitude of 40,000 feet. Both accomplishments were believed to set records for that period. Only 1 engine and 1 auxiliary power unit failure marred the otherwise excellent performance. But the second YB-49's fatal crash in June prompted the contractor and the Air Force to decide that the remaining prototype would be flight tested an extra 125 hours, and the testing that ensued gave mixed results.

Meanwhile, Lt. Gen. Benjamin W. Chidlaw, Deputy Commander of the Air Materiel Command, had ordered that determination of the YB-49's stability as a bombing platform be given first priority. Evaluated against a B-29 on comparable mission tests, the YB-49 (without an autopilot) performed poorly. Pilots concluded that the jet-equipped "flying wing" was "extremely unstable" and found it "impossible to hold a steady course or a constant airspeed and altitude." The YB-49's circular average error and range error were twice those of the B-29. Finally, the B-29 invariably acquired bomb-run stability in under 45 seconds, while the YB-49's best time was over 4 minutes. Clearly, the B-49 program was doomed unless sweeping improvements were made to correct the performance defects demonstrated by the prototype.

Total YB-49s Accepted   2

The first YB-49 was not accepted by the Air Force until 15 March 1950

---

[34] See B-47, pp 125-126.

(after being extensively tested by the contractor). The second, ill-fated B–49 prototype was transferred to the Air Force on 28 May 1948. Northrop considered the airplane officially accepted on 5 June, when it crashed.

Subsequent Model Series   YRB–49

Program Cancellation   15 March 1950

The October 1948 conclusion of the primary evaluation tests comparing the YB–49 and the B–29, and the YB–49's poor showing most likely determined the outcome of the B–49 program. Just the same, the YB–49 testing was extended, and even though remote, the possibility remained that the program might survive its initial calamities. This did not prove to be the case. Between May 1948 and the spring of 1949, the B–49 prototype was involved in 5 incidents, most of them due or related to engine problems. On 26 April 1949, a fire occurred in 1 of the aircraft's engine bays, necessitating $19,000 worth of repairs. Cancellation of the B–49 program became official on 15 March 1950—the day the sole XB–49 crashed and testing came to an abrupt end. There were no fatalities, but crewmen were injured and the airplane was completely destroyed. Failure of the nose gear was the accident's basic cause. Contributing factors were excessive shimmy of the nose wheel and final collapse of the gear, resulting from the unsatisfactory center of gravity.

Total Development Costs

After 1948, the additions and withdrawals of funds made a separate appraisal of any one aircraft's cost impractical, especially since the Air Force found it difficult to secure anything but an overall "flying wing" program cost estimate from Northrop.[35]

Final Disposition   1948–1950

The second YB–49 was totally destroyed on 5 June 1948; the first, on 15 March 1950.

---

[35] See XB–35, this appendix, p 506.

YRB-49A

Basic Development   March 1948

Like the canceled B–49, the RB–49 grew out of the unconventional
XB–35, under development by Northrop since 1941. However, the aircraft's
basic development did not take shape until March 1948 when the contractor,
after canvassing possible uses for the "flying wing," submitted to the Air
Force proposals for a photographic reconnaissance version of the aircraft.
Referred to as the RB–49A and the FB–49A, the proposed aircraft would be
essentially a YB–49, stripped of items required only for bombardment
missions and incorporating necessary photographic apparatus. The formal
nomenclature of the prototype became YRB–49A.

Early Planning   April 1948

In April 1948, the Air Staff and high-ranking officers of the Air
Materiel Command, after comparing reconnaissance versions of the F–12,[36]
B–35, B–47, and B–50, concluded that perhaps the eventual RB–49A could
"realistically" perform a portion of the strategic reconnaissance mission.
Undoubtedly, this optimistic appraisal stemmed from the testing already
accomplished on the Northrop aircraft, as well as from the aircraft's range,
speed, altitude, and growth potential with combinations of turbojet and
turboprop engines. Therefore, 3 versions of an ever-improving RB–49A were
planned—an initial aircraft with 8 TB–190A (General Electric J47) turbojets, an interim model powered by 6 Westinghouse J40 engines (when they
became available), and an ultimate configuration, which would achieve
greater range and economy with 2 Turbodyne T–37 turboprops and 2
TG–190A engines. The ultimate model was not an immediate possibility,
since the T–37 engines would not be available until October 1951 or later.

Initial Procurement   12 June 1948

Believing that the planned RB–49A configuration truly had merits, and

---

[36] The F–12 was developed by the Republic Aviation Corporation. Only 2 prototypes came
into being.

still eager to salvage its costly investment in the unfortunate XB–35 program, the Air Force promptly decided to endorse the YRB–49A development. Following notice of the decision in May 1948, Northrop received a letter contract on 12 June for preliminary engineering work looking toward an eventual production contract for 30 reconnaissance aircraft, at a cost of $86,800,420,—this total to include aircraft, engineering data, and flight testing.

Production Contract 12 August 1948

Signed on 12 August 1948, Contract W33–038–ac–21721 covered the production of 30 RB–49As and a static test shell. One of the aircraft was to be built by Northrop, the remaining 29 by Consolidated Vultee, at the latter's government-leased plant in Fort Worth, Texas. The agreement had been preceded by difficult negotiations, the 2 contractors being unwilling from the start to accept the Air Force's contention that the nation would benefit from a pooling of Northrop's engineering skill and Consolidated's experience in quantity production of large aircraft.

Program Re-Appraisal Fall 1948

Support of the RB–49A production program was short lived. Less than 2 months after the contract's signature, several Air Materiel Command officials concluded that the program's initial 8-jet version would only be "satisfactory as an interim installation." In late September, the Air Force also began to encounter difficulties in pinning down the 2 contractors' future delivery dates for the 30 RB–49As. Just as disturbing was the continuing indecision over which prototype Northrop would use to develop the YRB–49A. At first, the remaining YB–49 was chosen. Then, various versions of the 13 YB–35s ordered in 1942 were reviewed, before settling on modification of the third B–35 prototype—a YB–35A featuring specific reconfiguration changes dictated early in 1945.

Against this clouded background, a board representing numerous Air Staff offices met in November to review the requirements for reconnaissance aircraft. All 3 versions of the future RB–49As came under fire. The 8-jet RB–49A, it appeared, would not be available until January 1950 and would have an inadequate operating radius; the 6-jet model, planned for 1951, would be much slower than the B–47; finally, Northrop could not promise the ultimate turboprop-turbojet version until 1953, at which time that particular RB–49A would be in competition with (and outclassed by) the

B–52. The Air Staff Board, therefore, recommended elimination of the RB–49A.

Program Cancellation   1948–1949

The RB–49A production program was irrevocably canceled in late December 1948, as the new USAF Board of Senior Officers[37] supported the Air Staff Board's recommendation, deciding also soon afterward to substitute the procurement of additional B–36s for the deleted RB–49As.[38] The RB–49 cancellation became official in mid-January 1949, when the Air Materiel Command directed Northrop to stop work on all phases of the reconnaissance version except for completion and test of the 1 YRB–49A.

First Flight   4 May 1950

Conversion of the third YB–35A was "shop completed" by February 1950, shortly after the Northrop project was totally cut back to the level of a low-budget, state-of-the-art research and development endeavor. Yet, despite the contractor's continuing attempts to revive its program, the April delivery deadline set by the Air Force was not met. The YRB–49A's first flight occurred on 4 May, a 1-month slippage due to the time consumed in installing additional instrumentation. Like the YB–49, the reconnaissance prototype's first flight was from Hawthorne to Edwards AFB, California.

Special Features   1950

The YRB–49A differed significantly from the third YB–35A by featuring 6 engines instead of 8. Four of the YRB–49's 6 J35s were internally-mounted; 2 were outside of the airframe. The removal of 2 engines and the relocation of an additional 2, allowed the YRB–49A to carry much more fuel, a configuration change designed to extend the aircraft's range.

Testing   1950–1952

The YRB–49A's test program was quickly marred by a potentially fatal

---

[37] See B–52, p 216.

[38] See B–36, p 26.

accident. On 10 August 1950, during its tenth test flight, the reconnaissance prototype was in a climb at approximately 35,000 feet, at a speed of about 225 miles per hour, when the canopy failed and blew off, tearing away the pilot's oxygen mask and injuring him slightly. Only because the alert flight engineer supplied emergency oxygen was the pilot able to land the aircraft without further incident. The test program was resumed after a replacement canopy was provided and various aircraft modifications were made. No test flights were recorded after 10 September 1950, even though the aircraft was probably still test-flown on and off. In any case, on 6 May 1952, the Air Materiel Command indicated that there was "no future flying time scheduled" for the YRB–49A.

Final Disposition   1953

The YRB–49A, the last of the "flying wings," was flown to Northrop's Ontario International Airport facility, and it most likely remained in storage for 18 months. The Air Force reclaimed and scrapped the aircraft in November 1953.

TECHNICAL AND BASIC MISSION PERFORMANCE DATA

YB–49 AIRCRAFT[a]

Manufacturer (Airframe)	Northrop Aircraft, Inc., Hawthorne, Calif.
Manufacturer (Engines)	Designed by the General Electric Co.; built by the Allison Div. of the General Motors Corp.
Nomenclature	High-Altitude, Long-Range Bomber
Popular Name	Flying Wing

Length/Span (ft)	53.1/172
Wing Area (sq ft)	4,000
Weights (lb)	
Empty	88,442
Combat	133,569
Takeoff	193,938
Engine: Number, Rated Power per Engine, & Designation	(8) 3,750-lb st J35–A–15
Takeoff Ground Run (ft)	
at Sea Level	4,850
over 50-ft Obstacle	5,850
Rate of Climb (fpm) at Sea Level	1,780
Combat Rate of Climb (fpm) at Sea Level	3,785
Service Ceiling (ft) (100 fpm Rate of Climb to Altitude)	35,400
Combat Ceiling (ft) (500 fpm Rate of Climb to Altitude)	40,700
Max Speed with max power at Altitudes (kn/ft)	403/35,000—428/20,800
Combat Radius (nm)	1,403 with 10,000-lb payload at 365 knots in 8:27 hours
Armament	None
Crew	6
Max Bombload (lb)	16,000

Abbreviations	
fpm	= feet per minute
kn	= knots
nm	= nautical miles

[a]Based on manufacturer's flight test and wind tunnel data.

XB–51
Glenn L. Martin
Company

Manufacturer's Model 234

Basic Development   1945

Development of the XB–51 was initiated in 1945, when the Army Air Forces (AAF) issued military characteristics for a light bomber aircraft. The AAF's requirements led to a design competition, held in February 1946. The Glenn L. Martin Company won the competition with a design for an airplane containing a composite power plant and promising a maximum speed of 505 miles per hour (438 knots), a cruise speed of 325 miles per hour (282 knots), and an 800-mile combat radius. The Martin design, then labeled the XA–45, also provided for a 6-man crew, all-around armament, and high-altitude bombing equipment.

Revised Characteristics   Spring 1946

The AAF military characteristics of 1945 were revised in the spring of 1946. The new requirements called for an aircraft with better performance for all-weather, close support bombing. In line with Gen. H. H. Arnold's deletion of the requirement for "attack" aircraft,[39] the revised characteristics also called for a redesignation of the Martin design, subsequently known as the XB–51.

Initial Procurement   23 May 1946

Procurement of the experimental B–51 was initiated by a fixed-price letter contract, issued on 23 May 1946. This agreement gave Martin $9.5

---

[39] See this appendix, p 509.

546

million to produce 2 XB–51s, to be preceded by the usual wind-tunnel models and mockups. Special tools, spare parts, drawings, technical data, armament reports, and the like were also required.

Additional Revisions   1947

The military characteristics of 1945 and 1946 were revised again in 1947 to satisfy officials of AAF Headquarters, who doubted that the XB–51, as then envisioned, would become a satisfactory light bomber. The possibility of seeking 1 or 2 new production sources was considered but given up after the Air Materiel Command pointed out that to stay with the XB–51 and use funds already obligated for this purpose was probably the surest way to acquire a light bomber that would not be obsolete before reaching the inventory.

Concurrent studies by Martin resulted in the design of an XB–51 aircraft with a top speed of 620 knots, a cruise speed of 463 knots, and a 378-mile radius of action. The revamped XB–51 was to be equipped with eight 20-millimeter cannon, be capable of carrying a 4,000-pound bomb load, and would require a 2-man crew, 4 men less than originally planned. Further design studies, conducted by Martin at the request of the Air Materiel Command, brought additional changes. More realistically, the revised XB–51's top speed was set at 521 knots and its cruising speed at 434. Since the XB–51 was intended essentially as a low-altitude weapon, the radius requirement was decreased, bearing in mind that the Shoran (*short-ra*nge *n*avigation) system earmarked for the plane was limited to less than 200 nautical miles. These final characteristics were approved by AAF Headquarters in early 1947. Shortly thereafter, the aircraft's development, in limbo for over a year, was re-instated.

Special Features   1949

Martin decided that a turbojet version of the basic XB–51 was the best configuration to satisfy the military characteristics that had been finally approved. Hence, the all-metal, mid-wing monoplane was fitted with 3 J47 engines. Two of the engines were in nacelles mounted on pylons on the lower forward sides of the fuselage, while the third engine was carried internally in the rear fuselage, with a top air inlet and a jet exit in the aircraft's tail.

First Flight   28 October 1949

The experimental XB–51 made its first flight on 28 October 1949. It was

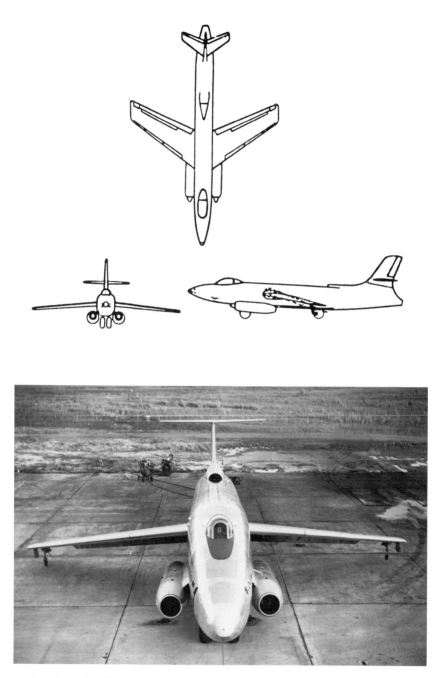

Two of the XB–51's turbojets were mounted on the fuselage. The third was inside the rear fuselage.

548

the Air Force's first high-speed, jet-propelled, ground support bomber, and was one of the first post-war airplanes designed to destroy surface targets in close cooperation with Army ground forces.

Definitive Development Contract   1 November 1949

Martin's letter contract of May 1946 was superseded on 1 November 1949 by a formal contract of the cost-plus-fixed-fee type. This contract (W33–038 ac–14806), carrying the same number as the 3-year-old letter contract, increased the amount initially obligated by $500,000 to cover the contractor's fixed fee.

Subsequently, change orders were to raise the cost of the ill-fated, $10.2 million development contract. Meanwhile, the procurement requirements of 1946 remained unaltered. Martin was required to provide mockups, spare parts, technical data, and 2 XB–51s.

Testing   1949–1952

Testing of the first XB–51 was extensive. The Phase I tests, which lasted until the end of March 1951, indicated that relatively few modifications were needed and attested to the serviceability and excellent functional design of the experimental aircraft. Results of the Phase II tests, that had been conducted from 4 April to 10 November 1950, corroborated these findings. Martin pilots flew the first XB–51 (Serial No. 46–685) for 211 hours, accumulated in 233 flights. Air Force pilots totaled 221 hours on the same aircraft. The number of Air Force test flights was not accurately recorded, but did exceed 200. Flight testing of the second XB–51 (Serial No. 46–686), first flown on 17 April 1950, although thorough, was relatively brief. Martin test pilots flew the aircraft 125 hours, accumulated in 168 flights; the Air Force put in 26 hours, presumably reached in 25 flights. The second XB–51 was destroyed on 9 May 1952, during low-level aerobatics over Edwards AFB, California. The pilot was killed as the aircraft exploded and burned upon striking the ground.

Total XB–51s Accepted   2

The Air Force accepted the 2 XB–51s built by Martin. The first one was accepted and delivered on 22 January 1952;[40] the other during the previous month, on 8 December 1951.

Program Cancellation   November 1951

The Air Force canceled production of the B–51 before the 2 experimental aircraft were formally accepted. Air Force records offered various reasons for the decision. For example, the XB–51 had received a second-best rating in comparison with other aircraft designed to fulfill similar mission roles. Yet, these records failed to identify the aircraft which were compared and the factors that established the XB–51's disappointing rating. Considering the time invested in the XB–51's development (about 5 years), the Air Research and Development Command offered a more specific explanation. The command stated that termination of the XB–51 contract in November 1951 was due to the fact that the plane, in its existing configuration, did not meet the requirements, particularly the range requirement, of the Tactical Air Command.

Total Development Costs $12.6 million

Although Martin was informed in November 1951 that the XB–51 program was ended, the light-bomber contract was not closed out until 7 October 1953, when a last change order was issued. This document had several important purposes. It instructed the contractor to repair the first of the 2 experimental aircraft which, though significantly damaged in February 1952, was the only remaining XB–51. The Air Force also instructed Martin to prepare the plane for bomb-dropping tests and to send 2 field service representatives to participate in a 3-month bomb-dropping program to be conducted at Edwards AFB. The final change order, in addition, determined the last sums owed to Martin. Included were $381,439 for the aircraft's repair, some $90,000 for the required special work and the field representatives' services, plus 2 fixed-fees. Added to the expenses previously incurred for minor repairs and unexpected modifications, this brought the total cost of the experimental program to $12.6 million, a $2.4 million increase in about 4 years.

---

[40] Delivery of the first XB–51 was delayed because of the extensive testing conducted by the contractor—a routine procedure.

Final Disposition   **24 March 1956**

The Air Force did not determine the final disposition of the repaired and much improved XB-51. The aircraft was totally destroyed on 25 March 1956 in a crash at Biggs Field, Texas. In the meantime, however, a great deal was learned from the experimental program. The work performed by the 2 XB-51s in the high-speed bomb-release program contributed much to advancing the state-of-the-art in that field. Also, the tail configuration, variable incidence wing, and bicycle-type landing gear of the XB-51 provided useful design data.

TECHNICAL AND BASIC MISSION PERFORMANCE DATA

XB-51 AIRCRAFT

Manufacturer (Airframe)	The Glenn L. Martin Co., Baltimore, Md.
Manufacturer (Engines)	The General Electric Co.; Schenectady, N.Y.
Nomenclature	Light Bomber
Popular Name	None

Length/Span (ft)	85.1/53.1
Wing Area (sq ft)	548
Weights (lb)	
Empty	29,584
Combat	41,547
Takeoff	55,923[a]
Engine: Number, Rated Power	
per Engine, & Designation	(3) 5,200-lb st J47–GE–13
Takeoff Ground Run (ft)	
At Sea Level	4,340[a] (no assist)
Over 50-ft Obstacle	5,590[a]
Rate of Climb (fpm) at Sea Level	3,720 (normal power)
Combat Rate of Climb	
(fpm) at Sea Level	6,980 (max power)
Service Ceiling (ft)	
(500 fpm Rate of Climb to Altitude)	32,400 (takeoff weight/normal power)
Combat Ceiling (ft)	
(500 fpm Rate of Climb to Altitude)	38,900 (combat weight/max power)
Average Cruise Speed (kn)	434
Max Speed at Optimum Altitude (kn/ft)	500/35,000 (combat/max power)
Combat Radius (nm)	378 with 4,000-lb payload
	at 463 kn average in 1.82 hr
Total Mission Time (hr)	2.07
Crew	2 (pilot and Shoran operator)
Armament	8 20-mm guns with total
	ammunition of 1280 rounds
Maximum Bombload (lb)	4 internal bombs (1,600 lb ea)
	or 2 external bombs (2,000 lb ea)
Maximum Bomb Size (lb)	4,000
Rockets	Provisions only for (8) 6-in HVAR[b]

Abbreviations			
cal	= caliber	max	= maximum
fpm	= feet per minute	nm	= nautical miles
kn	= knots	st	= static thrust

[a]Including 1,275 lb water/alcohol.
[b]High-Velocity Aircraft Rockets.

552

YB-60

Consolidated Vultee
Aircraft (Convair)
Corporation

Basic Development   25 August 1950

The YB-60 originated in August 1950, when the Consolidated Vultee Aircraft (Convair) Corporation offered to develop the B-36G, a swept-wing, all-jet version of the B-36F—fourth model of the basic B-36, initiated in 1941. The design, covered by the contractor's formal proposal, could eventually be converted into a turboprop bomber. Moreover, existing B-36s could later be brought up to the new configuration's standards.

Military Characteristics   November 1945

The first in a series of post-World War II military characteristics for heavy bombardment aircraft was issued on 23 November 1945. These characteristics were revised many times, but by 1950 the experimental aircraft thus far favored still fell short of satisfying the overall performance and long-range requirements expected of an atomic-capable, strategic bomber, due to be operational around 1955.[41]

Initial Procurement   15 March 1951

A letter, rather than a formal agreement, supplemented the basic B-36 contract and authorized Convair to convert 2 B-36Fs into prototype B-36Gs, entirely equipped with turbojets but capable of accepting turboprop engines. The first YB-36G was to be ready for flight testing in December 1951; the second, in February 1952.

---

[41] See B-52, pp 207-218.

Redesignation   Mid-1951

The proposed B–36G had little in common with the B–36F. The Air Force therefore determined that the B–60 designation would be assigned to the plane, because of the striking change in physical appearance and improvement in performance over that of the conventional B–36 airplane.

Program Change   August 1951

A misunderstanding concerning the configuration of the B–60 prototypes compelled Convair to recommend in August 1951 that at first only 2 stripped aircraft be developed. Accepting responsibility for the error, the contractor also proposed that the second YB–60 later be completed as a full tactical model. The Convair solution meant that separate specifications would have to be developed for each prototype. The Air Force agreed, after a 2-day conference during which the basic tactical configuration was set.

Special Features   1951–1952

The B–60 prototype differed significantly from the B–36 by featuring swept-back wings and swept-back tail surfaces, a new needle-nose radome, a new type of auxiliary power system, and 8 Pratt & Whitney J57–P–3 jet engines, installed in pairs inside "pods" suspended below and forward of the leading edge of the wings. Another special feature of the YB–60 was its extended tail, which enabled the aircraft to remain in a level position for a considerable period of time during takeoff and to become airborne, with a gross weight of 280,000 pounds, after only 4,000 feet of ground roll.

Engine Shortages   1951–1952

The J57–P–3, earmarked for the YB–60, was primarily scheduled for the B–52. Thus, while Convair would be able to use the Boeing-designed nacelles and engine pods, which seemed to be a distinct advantage, engine shortages were to be expected. This was particularly true, since the J57 engine was itself the product of an intensive effort to develop a high-thrust turbojet with a low fuel consumption. By the beginning of 1951, engine prototypes had accrued only 550 hours of full-scale testing. In 1952, even though production was already started, the engines were likely to remain in very short supply for quite a while.

First Flight   18 April 1952

The YB-60 flew for the first time on 18 April 1952—only 12 days after the prototype's eighth J57-P-3 engine finally arrived at the Convair's Fort Worth plant. The 66-minute flight was hampered by bad weather, but 2 subsequent flights in the same month were entirely successful, the YB-60 actually displaying excellent handling charaterics. This encouraging trend, however, did not prevail.

Flight Testing   1952–1953

Flight testing of the YB-60 officially ended on 20 January 1953, when the Air Force canceled the second phase of the test program. Convair test-flew the first YB-60 for 66 hours, accumulated in 20 flights; the Air Force, some 15 hours, in 4 flights. The second YB-60, although 93 percent complete, was not flown at all. By and large, test results were worrisome, because the stripped YB-60 displayed a number of deficiencies. Among them were engine surge, control system buffet, rudder flutter, and problems with the electrical engine-control system.

Program Cancellation   14 August 1952

The Air Force canceled the B-60 program several months before the prototype testing was officially terminated. The decision was inevitable. From the start, the project's sole purpose had been to help the Air Force in its quest for a B-36 successor. In this capacity, the B-60 competed all along with the B-52. There was no official competition, but test results were irrefutable. The YB-52 demonstrated better performance and greater improvement potential than the YB-60.[42] The latter was handicapped by the speed limitation imposed by structural considerations at low altitude and buffet at high altitudes. Also, the Convair prototype's stability was unsatisfactory because of the high aerodynamic forces acting upon the control surfaces and the low aileron effectiveness of the plane.

Total YB-60s Accepted   2

The B-60 program was canceled in the summer of 1952, and testing of

---

[42] The YB-52's first flight on 15 April 1952—3 days ahead of the YB-60's—was an impressive success and generated great enthusiasm for the Boeing airplane.

The prototype YB–60, a reconfigured B–36 with jet engines and swept-back wings.

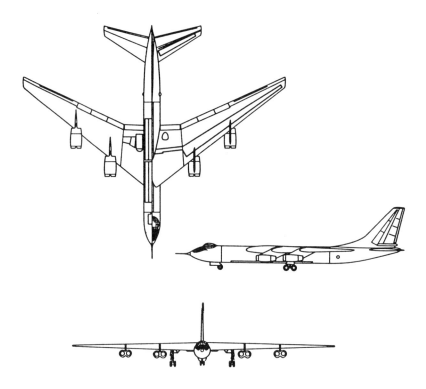

the stripped prototype ended in January 1953. Even so, the Air Force did not accept the 2 YB-60s before 24 June 1954. There were valid reasons for the delay. Convair truly believed, and tried to convince the Air Force, that the YB-60s should be used as experimental test-beds for turbopropeller engines. Shortage of money and the YB-60's several unsafe characteristics accounted for the Air Force's decision to turn down Convair's tempting proposal.

Total Development Costs $14.3 million

The final cost of the 2 B-60 prototypes was set at $14,366,022. This figure, agreed upon by both the Air Force and the contractor on 13 October 1954, included Convair's fee, the contract termination cost, and the amount spent on the necessary minimum of spare parts.

Final Disposition   June 1954

The Air Force scrapped the 2 YB-60s before the end of June 1954.

TECHNICAL AND BASIC MISSION PERFORMANCE DATA

YB-60 AIRCRAFT[a]

Manufacturer (Airframe)	Consolidated Vultee Aircraft (Convair) Corporation, Fort Worth, Tex.
Manufacturer (Engines)	The Pratt & Whitney Aircraft Division of United Aircraft Corporation
Nomenclature	Strategic Heavy Bomber
Popular Name	None

Length/Span[b] (ft)	171/206
Wing Area (sq ft)	Not Available
Weights (lb)	
Empty	150,000
Takeoff	410,000 (contractor design)
Engine: Number, Rated Power per Engine, & Designation	(8) 9,000-lb st J57-P-3
Service Ceiling (ft)	45,000
Maximum Speed (kn)	451
Combat Speed (kn)	440
Range (nm)	8,000
Combat Radius (nm)	2,910 with 10,000-lb payload at average speed of 400 kn
Crew	10

Abbreviations	
kn	= knots
nm	= nautical miles
st	= static thrust

---

[a]Based on contractor's estimates and flight-test results.

[b]The new swept wing reduced the overall span to 206 ft as compared with 230 ft for the B-36.

XB-70A
North American
Aviation, Incorporated

Manufacturer's Model NA-278

Weapon System 110A

Basic Development   1954

The XB-70A had its genesis in Boeing Aircraft Corporation's Project
MX-2145, in which the contractor conducted studies relating to the type of
weapon system required to deliver high-yield special weapons. The contractor, along with the Rand Corporation, considered various types of weapon
system carriers. Among them were manned intercontinental bombers,
delivering both gravity bombs and pilotless parasite bombers; manned
bombers, air-refueled by tankers to extend their ranges and cover round-trip
intercontinental distances; manned aircraft and drone bomber combinations; and unmanned bombers. During these studies Air Force Headquarters requested enlargement of the study program to include possible
trade-off information; for example, the potential results of trading weight
for speed, weight for range, or speed for range.

Boeing presented the requested information on 22 January 1954,
pointing out the possibilities of a bomber aircraft powered by chemically
augmented nuclear powerplants. For the first time, it appeared feasible to
develop a weapon system of a reasonable size possessing the unlimited range
characteristics of nuclear propulsion,[43] plus a high-altitude, supersonic dash
capability. In March 1954, Boeing presented promising data on a chemically
augmented, nuclear-powered aircraft. At the same time, both the Convair

---

[43] The development of nuclear propulsion for aircraft or missiles originated in 1945. In
May 1946, the Army Air Forces signed a "letter of intent" with the Fairchild Engine and
Airplane Corporation, thereby conferring on the highly classified NEPA (Nuclear Energy for
the Propulsion of Aircraft) program a legal right to exist. While favoring the program, General
LeMay, then Deputy Chief of Air Staff for Research and Development, said the work to be
performed under NEPA would be somewhat speculative.

Corporation and Lockheed Aircraft Corporation, under contracts with the Office of Aircraft Nuclear Propulsion, submitted similar data.

Developmental Changes   Fall of 1954

In the fall of 1954, the Air Force Council endorsed 2 independent but simultaneous development programs, one for a nuclear bomber capable of short bursts of supersonic speed;[44] the other, for a subsonic, chemically powered, conventional bomber. The Air Force Council's announcement closely followed the October publication of General Operational Requirement No. 38. The document was brief. It simply called for an intercontinental bombardment weapon (a piloted bomber) that would replace the B–52 and stay in service during the decade beginning in 1965.

General Operational Requirement   1955

The Air Force, on 22 March 1955, put out a second general operational requirement, No. 82, which superseded No. 38. Like its predecessor, the new general operational requirement was short. It called for a piloted strategic intercontinental bombardment weapon system that would be capable of carrying a 20,000-pound load of high-yield nuclear weapons, a requirement increased to 25,000 pounds by a September amendment. But the task of defining the Air Force's new project fell to the Air Research and Development Command. The command, therefore, had issued a study requirement, designated No. 22, which identified the Air Force's future new bomber as "Weapon System 110A" and established 1963 as the target date for the first wing of 30 operational vehicles.

Study Requirement 22's performance objectives were mach .9 for cruise speed and "maximum possible" speed during a 1,000-nautical mile penetration. Still, high speed was of less importance than the penetration altitude and radius. A revision of Study Requirement 22 on 15 April stipulated that the new weapon system's cruise speed should not be less than mach .9, unless a lower speed would result in a significant range increase. There were other important changes. Instead of the subsonic requirement covered by General Operational Requirement 38, maximum possible "supersonic"

---

[44] General Operational Requirement No. 81, issued in March 1955, specifically called for the development of a nuclear-powered weapon system that would be capable of performing a strategic mission of 11,000 nautical miles in radius, of which 1,000 miles were to be traveled at speeds in excess of mach 2, at an altitude of more than 60,000 feet.

speed within the combat zone was desired. On 11 October, Air Research and Development Command amended the revised Study Requirement 22. The amendment set July 1964 as the target date for the first operational wing of B–70s—so designated in February 1958. The purpose of the delay was to avoid financial and overall weapon system risks, if at all possible.[45]

Other Requirements   1955–1956

In early 1955, the Air Force released another general operational requirement (No. 96) for an intercontinental reconnaissance system having similar objectives as the previously established bombardment system, known as Weapon System 110A. In July, the Air Research and Development Command issued a study requirement of General Operational Requirement 96 that validated a reconnaissance version of the B–70. The reconnaissance system was identified as Weapon System 110L. The 2 systems were combined soon afterward, becoming in the process Weapon System 110A/L.

Program Implementation   June 1955

In June 1955, the Air Staff directed that development of Weapon System 110A/L be initiated as soon as possible with a multiple, competitive "Phase I" program.[46] Although 6 eligible contractors were contacted, only the Boeing Airplane Company and North American Aviation, Incorporated chose to submit proposals.

Contractual Arrangements   1955–1956

On 8 November 1955, the Air Force awarded letter contracts to both Boeing and North American for the Phase I development of Weapon System 110A/L. Boeing's letter contract amounted to $2.6 million; that of North

---

[45] In 1955, the Air Research and Development Command estimated the weapon system's costs through fiscal year 1962 at $2.5 billion. The estimate covered development, test aircraft, and 30 operational bombers, but assumed that a nuclear bomber would also be developed, that a new engine for the chemically powered bomber would be created, and that the price of certain subsystems, earmarked for the B–70, would be borne by the nuclear aircraft program.

[46] The use of "phase" contracts was not new, having been approved as early as 1944 by the Army Air Forces to facilitate the termination of contracts dealing with highly experimental and, therefore, very uncertain programs.

American, to $1.8 million. Each contractor had to furnish a design for the required weapon system; provide models, drawings, specifications, reports, and other data; conduct studies and wind tunnel tests, and construct a mockup. The mockup was to be completed and ready for Air Force inspection within 2 years of the date on which the contractor accepted the contract. Contractor fees could not exceed $450,000.

The 2 letter contracts became definitive in 1956. The Boeing contract, AF33(600)–31802, signed on 15 March, specified a total estimated cost of $19.9 million; the North American contract, AF33(600)–31801, signed on 16 April, $9.9 million, subject to renegotiation. The Air Force, in its definitive contracts, allotted originally $4.5 million to Boeing and $1.8 million to North American.

Military Characteristics   1956

Concurrent with the letter contracts of 1955, the Air Force established specific requirements that were included in the final documents signed in 1956. To begin with, each contract emphasized that the purpose of the entire program was to develop, test, and produce for wing strength by 1963 (much sooner than decided in October 1955) a chemically powered weapon system which, in conjunction with the nuclear-powered bomber, would replace the B/RB–52 as a "first line operational weapon."

With regard to operational characteristics, the new weapon system was to rely primarily on nuclear weapons to accomplish its mission, and the origin and termination of its operations were to be within the limits of the North American continent. The Air Force specified that weapon system 110A/L would have to be capable of performing during the day, at night, and in any kind of weather. A minimum unrefueled radius of 4,000 nautical miles, and a desirable extended radius of 5,500 nautical miles were required, with aerial refueling allowed in the latter case. Finally, the minimum target altitude was to be 60,000 feet, and the contracts reiterated that cruise speed could not be less than mach .9, with maximum supersonic dash speed in the combat zone.

These were exacting characteristics. Studies of conventional aircraft had shown that no such performance could be obtained with proven design techniques. The Air Force acknowledged that the ability to satisfy its demands, particularly the radius-of-action and speed requirements, would depend on the use of high-energy fuels, new engines, new design techniques, and some other break-through in the state-of-the-art by the operational date of 1963. The Air Force also made sure that the contractors knew that while range and speed trade-offs would be acceptable in order to assure maximum supersonic dash at a "practical" gross weight, every reduction would have to be minimal. Finally, the new weapon system's configuration would have to allow for the easy addition of state-of-the-art improved subsystems and components, not initially incorporated.

Design Proposals   Mid-1956

Naturally enough, the preliminary design proposals submitted in mid-1956 by Boeing and North American were quite different. Boeing utilized a conventional swept-wing configuration; North American, a canard-type, resembling a scaled-up Navaho missile.[47] Still, in order to attempt meeting the payload requirements and ranges stipulated in the spring of the year, the contractors had incorporated similar features in their respective designs. The aircraft envisioned by both would weigh some 750,000 pounds and require the use of cumbersome floating wing panels. These panels would carry fuel for the outgoing trip and be jettisoned when empty. Maximum speed might then exceed mach 2 by a significant margin.

The Boeing and North American preliminary designs had another common factor: both were unsatisfactory. The gross weights were excessive. The proposed fuel devices, whether fuel panels or straight floating wing tips, while promising to extend the aircraft's subsonic range, seemed impractical. To begin with, the enormous expendable panels (or non-folding floating wing tips) would create logistical problems and runway difficulties because of the total width of any airplane so equipped. In September, a disappointed Air Staff recommended that both contractors "return to the drawing board." And money being short, a more drastic decision followed that nearly spelled the program's cancellation. On 18 October, the Air Force discontinued the weapon system's Phase I development. Boeing and North American were allowed to resume their studies, but solely on a reduced research and development basis.

Concerned that the contractors might construe their contract's reorientation as resulting from lack of funds—an interpretation not far from the truth—and would merely mark time while refining their current designs, the Air Force promptly minimized the impact of its October decision. First, new work statements were issued, underscoring the necessity of achieving acceptable, but less exacting, performance characteristics. Then on 20 December, the Air Force sent identical letters to the presidents of Boeing and

---

[47] The North American SM-64A Navaho (System 104A) was a vertically launched, air-breathing, intercontinental surface-to-surface, delta-wing missile, with a length of 87 feet and a diameter of 6½ feet. Production was canceled in July 1957 because of budgetary and technical problems. The Navaho development cost over $600 million, but the work expended on the canceled program was not a loss and benefited other projects significantly.

North American, asking that every possible means be explored to improve the aircraft's range "through complete redesign if necessary."

Contractor Selection   23 December 1957

After the delay induced by the rejected proposals, events moved swiftly. By March 1957, it seemed almost certain that the new weapon system could be an all-supersonic cruise air vehicle as opposed to a "split-mission" (subsonic cruise-supersonic dash) aircraft.[48] In other words, aircraft designers had discovered that, if the entire design (especially engines, air induction system, and airframe) was geared for a single flight condition such as mach 3, the range of the supersonic system would compare favorably with that of a subsonic vehicle. Both contractors, independently, had also concluded that, as suggested by the Air Force, high-energy fuel would be needed and that its use should be extended to the engine afterburner.

In mid-1957, believing their re-oriented contractual commitments had been fulfilled, Boeing and North American asked for an early competitive selection of 1 contractor over the other. Dual contracting and dual funding made extra work and was costly. Moreover, the Air Research and Development Command was convinced that state-of-the-art advances had been fully exploited by both contractors. Further study of the project would mean more delay and be self-defeating. Hence, the tempo of activities quickened. On 30 August, the Air Force directed a 45-day competitive design period, ending with the onsite inspection of each contractor's facilities. On 18 September, the Air Force gave Boeing and North American the new system characteristics established for the competition. These characteristics called for a speed of mach 3 to mach 3.2, a target altitude of 70,000 to 75,000 feet, a range of 6,100 to 10,500 miles, and a gross weight between 475,000 and 490,000 pounds.

Meanwhile, a source selection evaluation group had been organized. It comprised 3 teams: representatives from the Air Research and Development Command, the Air Materiel Command, and, for the first time, a using command—the Strategic Air Command, in this case. The evaluation group, numbering about 60 members, reviewed the North American proposal during the last week of October; that of Boeing, during the first week of November.[49] The 3-team evaluations were presented to the Air Force Council

---

[48] Theoretical research on the "supersonic wedge principle," conducted by the National Advisory Committee for Aerononautics in 1956, actually had much to do with the "graduation" to an all-supersonic flight pattern.

[49] Due to the success of the 3-team evaluation group, the Air Force changed its source selection procedures, the using command becoming an integral part of the selecting process.

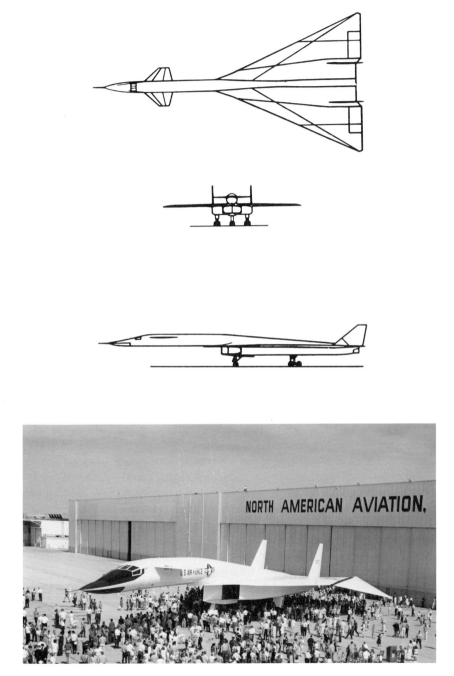

The striking XB-70A was "rolled out" at the contractor's plant.

on 15 December. The North American proposal was found unaminously to be substantially superior to that of Boeing. The Air Force formally announced North American's selection on 23 December.

New Planning   1958

As winner of the 1957 competition, North American on 24 January 1958 signed contract AF33(600)-36599. Strictly speaking, this document again covered only the new weapon system's Phase I development. Just the same, availability of the first operational wing (30 planes and 15 test vehicles) was already planned for late 1965. In February 1958, believing that by late 1965 or thereabouts, when the RB-70 would become operational, other systems could better satisfy the reconnaissance requirements, the Air Force canceled the development of Weapon System 110L (part of WS 110A since 1956).

While the reconnaissance requirement was being deleted, an 18-month acceleration of the B-70 program was planned. This change, endorsed by the Air Research and Development Command and Air Materiel Command, scheduled the aircraft's first flight for December 1961 and formation of the first operational wing for August 1964. No performance decrease would result, and the increase in costs would not exceed $165 million. The Air Staff approved the accelerated plan in principle on 19 March 1958. In the same month, a revised general operational requirement was issued, updating such matters as the speed specification. In April, a preliminary operational concept was published.

In the fall of 1958, the Air Force's apparent optimism had a severe jolt. Gen. Thomas D. White, Air Force Chief of Staff since August 1957, announced that the B-70 program's planned acceleration was no longer viable because of funding limitations. A first flight, therefore, should not be expected before January 1962; an operational wing, in August 1965, at the earliest. This reversal damaged the program, particularly the weapon system's components. General White wanted more judicious use of currently available equipment and flight test inventory. He further wished to reduce the overall complexity of the bombing-navigation and missile guidance subsystems. Of greater import, and a harbinger that worse might yet come, General White also told his staff that the Eisenhower Administration believed that no large sums of money should be committed to the program before the B-70 prototype had proven itself. General White's words reflected the Administration's determination to hold military expenditures for radically new or unproven weapon systems to a minimum, while taking advantage of technological advances. Deployment of the free world's first long-range ballistic missiles, and accelerating the operational readiness of additional weapons systems of this type, which appeared more cost-effective and less speculative, fell under the purview of such a philosophy.

Mockup Inspection   30 March 1959

A development engineering inspection and mockup review were conducted at North American's Inglewood plant on 2 and 30 March 1959, respectively. The mockup review differed from the inspection in that it was styled to present the operational characteristics and suitability of the weapon system's configuration, rather than to introduce detailed system analysis and theory. On both occasions, the Air Force requested a great many changes, some of which were considered of primary importance. Nevertheless, almost 95 percent of the work generated by the requested alterations was accomplished before the end of the year.

New Setbacks   1959

Decisions made in the second half of 1959 hampered Air Force aircraft development efforts, placing additional pressure on the B-70 program.[50] On 11 August, the Department of Defense canceled the high-energy fuel program. The use of this fuel had been counted on to extend the B-70's range substantially over its required radius. As it turned out, the high-energy fuel program cancellation had a lesser impact than anticipated because other jet fuels, JP-6 especially, were greatly improved. Just the same, as planning stood in mid-1959, elimination of the high-energy fuel program required additional configuration changes and, more specifically, a new engine for the B-70.

Termination on 24 September of the North American F-108 Rapier, a never-flown long-range interceptor under letter contract since 1957, was another blow. The B-70 program was directly affected. It would now be compelled to finance, at least partially, such development items as engines, escape capsules, and fuel systems that had been common to both aircraft systems and previously covered by F-108 funds. The loss was expected to boost B-70 program costs by at least $180 million.

---

[50] The nuclear-powered bomber, after overshadowing the chemically powered aircraft for years, began to suffer from financial malnutrition in 1956. By mid-1959, decisions at the highest executive level had put the program into almost total eclipse. The project's downfall was bound to impede the B-70 program since the cost of several B-70 subsystems were to be borne by the nuclear-powered bomber—officially canceled by the Kennedy Administration in March 1961.

Near-Cancellation 1959

General White's words of caution notwithstanding, more than 15 major subcontracts were let during the early part of 1959. In the ensuing months, after the high-energy fuel program and F-108 project were given up, money became increasingly scarce, and most B-70 activities were slowed down. But the program's new predicament was only a beginning.

In November 1959, during a meeting concerning the military programs of the coming year, President Eisenhower told the Air Force Chief of Staff that the "B-70 left him cold in terms of making military sense." General White conceded there were important questions involved and that the aircraft was very different from anything previously developed. He said the B-70 must overcome the terrific heat generated by high speed and high altitude and that the shape of the aircraft's wings and fuselage must be studied. However, to eliminate such unconventional aircraft would be going too fast and too far. Hardly impressed with the many pro-B-70 arguments put forth, the President stressed that the B-70, if allowed to reach production, would not be available for 8 or 10 years, when the major strategic retaliatory weapon would be the missile. The President finally agreed to take another look at the B-70 proposition, but in the same breath pointed out that speaking of bombers in the missile age was like talking about bows and arrows in the era of gunpowder.

The Air Force announced on 29 December that the B-70 program was reoriented to produce a prototype vehicle only and that the development of most sub-systems was canceled. The program's near demise was generally attributed to the Administration's budget.

Program Reendorsement 1960

The politics of the 1960 presidential campaign kindled the interest of both parties in the B-70. Thus, with the approval of the Defense Department, the Air Force in August 1960 directed that the XB-70 prototype program once again be changed to a development and test program. Twelve B-70 prototypes were added, and the program was designed to demonstrate the bomber's combat capability. This directive, coupled with a congressional appropriation of $265 million for fiscal year 1961, restored the B-70 to the status of a weapon system headed for production.

In September, North American was instructed to proceed with the design, development, fabrication, and testing of a number of YB-70s. Also, development of the major systems for an operational mach 3 bomber had to be ensured, which meant that many of the recently canceled subcontracts (let by the prime contractors early in 1959) had to be reopened. This exercise might be time-consuming as well as difficult, since some of the subcontractors might now be involved in other work. Even so, by mid-October the defensive subsystem contract with Westinghouse Electric Corporation had been reinstated. In November, North American reactivated the contract with Motorola, Incorporated for the mission and traffic control system of the B–70. In the same month, development of the B–70's bombing and navigation system, under the auspices of the International Business Machines Corporation and significantly reduced since the summer of 1959, regained the impetus normally afforded a system intended for production. Still, the B–70 program's recaptured importance was to be short lived.

Definite Cancellation   1961–1962

Once in office, it did not take long for President John F. Kennedy to take a critical look at the B–70 program. Like his predecessor, President Kennedy obviously doubted the aircraft's reason for being from the standpoint of future operations. On 28 March 1961, he recommended that the program be continued in order to explore the problems of flying at 3 times the speed of sound with an aircraft "potentially" useful as a bomber.[51] This, President Kennedy underscored, should only require the development of a small number of YB–70s and bombing and navigation systems. No more than $220 million should be needed in fiscal year 1963, and the program's total cost should not exceed $1.3 billion.

President Kennedy's words gave the Air Force no choice but to redirect the B–70 program from full weapon system status to that of a mere prototype aircraft development. Since the aircraft's eventual production appeared now most unlikely, the Air Force immediately began to consider various alternatives to the defunct B–70. In May 1961, there was talk of an improved B–58, armed with both bombs and air-launched missiles; of a specially designed, long-endurance, missile-launching aircraft; of transport planes modified to launch ballistic missiles; of the nuclear-powered aircraft, and again of a reconnaissance B–70, which would also be capable of striking the enemy.[52] In August, the U.S. Senate attempted once more to rescue the

---

[51] President Kennedy's recommendations were part of his special message on the Defense budget, as submitted to the Congress on 28 March. The President emphasized the importance of accelerating long-range missile programs and of increasing the armed forces' capability to handle limited wars.

[52] The Air Force's persistent search for a new manned bomber seemed unrealistic. On 25 May 1961, in an address to a joint session of the Congress, the President proposed to reinforce further the military establishment's capabilities in limited warfare and to expand substantially the Defense programs related to the newly accelerated national space effort. These specific

B–70 and asked that a production program be outlined for the purpose of introducing the aircraft into the operational inventory at the earliest possible date. Undaunted, Secretary of Defense Robert S. McNamara expressed his thorough dissatisfaction with North American Aviation's handling of the B–70 development.

The year 1962 did not resolve the B–70 predicament. The President insisted that only $171 million of FY 63 funds ($49 million less than proposed in 1961) be spent on the prototype program, instead of the $491 million requested by the Air Force and previously approved by Congress. In March, Congress indicated that the Air Force should use the $491 million for planning and procurement of a reconnaissance and strike B–70 (RSB–70), but later in the month reduced the amount to $362.6 million. In April, a group headed by Gen. Bernard A. Schriever, Commander of the Air Force Systems Command, developed several approaches to the proposed RSB–70 system. The development plan preferred by the group would cost $1.6 billion and it programmed the RSB–70's first flight within little more than 2 years. In June, this plan and others were disapproved by the Department of Defense. Nevertheless, on 23 November the President authorized the addition of $50 million to the currently approved $1.3 billion B–70 development program. The extra money was intended for the development of highly experimental sensor components, a requirement if the RSB–70 (as unlikely as it was) or any similar new weapons system should be considered later.

Technical Problems   1962

As explained to members of the Congress in January 1960 by Thomas S. Gates, Secretary of Defense during the last 2 years of the Eisenhower Administration, the B–70 program was hampered from the start by technical problems stemming from the "use of metal and components . . . still in the research stage." By 1962, although much progress had been made, severe problems remained. North American was still working on an automatic air induction control system for regulating the flow of air to the J93–3 jet engines, originally designed to power the canceled F–108 and, following the end of the high-energy fuel program, immediately earmarked for the B–70.

The secondary power generating subsystem, due to provide current to the pump that maintained hydraulic pressure, also was unsatisfactory.

---

goals clearly indicated that production of a costly new aircraft was excluded from President Kennedy's foreseeable planning.

Excessive vibration caused failures in the generator gear boxes, and the hydraulic pumps frequently broke down. Braces were added to steady the gear boxes, but the pumps had to be rebuilt with metals capable of withstanding the intense heat of supersonic operations as well as the extreme pressure generated within the hydraulic lines.

At the close of 1962, other serious problems still prevented completion of the first air vehicle, accounting for North American's continual revision of the XB-70's delivery schedule. Defective stainless steel honeycomb panels necessitated an unanticipated number of repairs. The panels of the air ducting system bay and the fuel tank areas had numerous examples of such defects. A nickel-plating process was sufficient to eliminate most imperfections, but repairs on the fuel tank areas had to be air-tight to prevent the escape of nitrogen gas. In December, North American was considering giving up the use of polyimide varnish in favor of vitron sealant. Another significant problem was that the wings did not fit properly to the wing stubs. Special adapters had been developed and were being manufactured, but again this took time and money.

Other Difficulties 1963–1964

In 1963 and 1964 frustrations with the B-70 increased. Almost 40 of the $50 million approved for the development of sensor components was diverted to the experimental bomber to allow continuation of the 3-plane program. In June 1963, the Air Force converted the XB-70 contract from the cost-plus-fixed-fee to the cost-plus-incentive-fee type. But no spectacular progress ensued. In September, North American suggested further delivery revisions. The first aircraft, North American said, would be completed in April 1964—4 months past the latest deadline assigned by the Air Force. In October, continued technical problems and rising expenses prompted the Air Force to request that the cost of a 2-vehicle program be defined. On 7 January 1964, Gen. Curtis E. LeMay, Air Force Chief of Staff since 30 June 1961, although a strong supporter of the B-70, endorsed the Air Force Council's recommendation favoring the 1-vehicle reduction. The decision was dictated by the compelling need to avoid exceeding the program's approved total cost of $1.5 billion. The decision also practically closed the case of the two-XB-70 program and definitely prevented the start of RSB-70 development.

First Flight   21 September 1964

The first flight of the XB-70A Valkyrie[53] occurred on 21 September 1964, nearly 4 years later than the date scheduled in 1958 (right after North American had won the contract). The experimental bomber flew for approximately 1 hour in the northeast-southwest corridor between Palmdale, California, and the Rogers Dry Lake at Edwards AFB, also in California. The 2-member crew—Alvin White, North American Chief Test Pilot, and Col. Joseph F. Cotton, USAF B-70 Chief Test Pilot—landed successfully at Edwards AFB. Nevertheless, the plane had to undergo additional ground tests before entering an extensive flight testing program at Edwards.

Special Features   1964

The striking features of the experimental B-70 centered on the configuration and composition of its airframe, with its semi-monocoque fuselage of steel and titanium. Also, the bomber's external skin was composed of brazed stainless steel honeycomb sandwich, wide use having been made of titanium alloys. The XB-70's flying controls comprised elevons on the trailing edges of the cantilever delta wings and twin vertical fins and rudders. The large canard foreplane was adjustable to achieve "trim" (balance in flight or landing, etc.). Its trailing edge flaps enabled it to droop the elevons to act as flaps, making it possible for the XB-70 to take off from and land on existing B-52 airstrips.

Unrelenting Problems   1965-1966

Continued technical difficulties delayed the XB-70's testing program. For the same reasons, completion of the second experimental B-70 took longer than expected, and the bomber did not fly before July 1965. Less than a year later, on 19 May 1966, the second XB-70A flew for 32 minutes at the sustained speed of mach 3. Unfortunately, tragedy closely followed this remarkable achievement. On 8 June, the plane was lost in a mid-air collision with a Lockheed F-104 fighter. The loss, occurring at approximately 25,000 feet, near Barstow, California, 43 miles east of Edwards AFB, reduced the XB-70A program to a single vehicle.

---

[53] The name Valkyrie resulted from a "name the B-70" contest, sponsored by the Strategic Air Command in the spring of 1958.

Total XB–70As Accepted **2**

Total Development Costs **$1.5 billion**

Final Disposition **1967**

In March 1967, the Air Force transferred the remaining XB–70A to the National Aeronautics and Space Administration, where the plane took part in an expanded flight research program. The program's main objective was to verify data applicable to a supersonic transport. The space agency's retention of the XB–70 was of short duration. Before the end of the year, the Valkyrie reached its final destination and was put on display at the Air Force Museum, Wright-Patterson AFB, Ohio.

TECHNICAL AND BASIC MISSION PERFORMANCE DATA

XB–70A AIRCRAFT[a]

Manufacturer (Airframe)	North American Aviation, Inc., Los Angeles, Calif.
Manufacturer (Engines)	General Electric Co., Flight Propulsion Division, Evendale, Ohio
Nomenclature	Supersonic Bomber
Popular Name	Valkyrie

Length/Span (ft)	185.8/105
Wing Area (sq ft)	6,297
Weights (lb)	
Empty	231,215
Combat	341,096
Takeoff	521,056 (273,063 lb of fuel, included[b])
Engine: Number, Rated Power per Engine, & Designation	(6) 28,000-lb st (max) YJ93-3 (axial turbojet)
Takeoff Ground Run (ft)	
At Sea Level	7,400 (with max power)
Over 50-ft Obstacle	10,550 (with max power)
Rate of Climb (fpm) at Sea Level	7,170 (with military power)
Combat Max Rate of Climb (fpm) at Sea Level	27,450 (with max power)
Service Ceiling (100 fpm Rate of Climb to Altitude)	28,100 ft (with military power)
Combat Service Ceiling (100 fpm Rate of Climb to Altitude)	75,500 ft (with max power)
Combat Ceiling (500 fpm Rate of Climb to Altitude)	75,250 ft (with max power)
Basic Speed at 35,000 ft (kn)	1,089 (with max power)
Average Cruise Speed (kn)	1,721
Max Speed at Optimum Altitude (kn/ft)	1,721/75,550 (with max power)
Combat Range (nm)	2,969
Total Mission Time (hr)	1.87
Crew	2 (pilot and co-pilot)
Armament	None
Maximum Bombload (lb)	65,000 (space provisions, only)
Maximum Bomb Size (lb)	25,000

Abbreviations	
fpm	= feet per minute
kn	= knots
max	= maximum
nm	= nautical miles
st	= static thrust

[a]Derived from flight-test results.
[b]Specifically, 43,646 gal of JP-6 fuel.

B–1A
Rockwell International
Corporation

Manufacturer's Model W/S 139A

Basic Development   1963

Known as the Advanced Manned Strategic Aircraft (AMSA) until April 1969, the B–1 had its beginning in July 1963, when a USAF program change proposal called for an extra $25 million in fiscal year 1965. The Air Force wanted to use this money to develop 1 or more of the various advanced strategic manned systems then under study in mid-1963. Unofficially, the B–1 dated back to 1961, when the Air Force began considering alternatives to the canceled B–70.

Developmental Planning   1961–1963

Budgetary restrictions and the Eisenhower and Kennedy Administrations' clear belief that missile systems[54] like the Minuteman[55] were the strategic weapons of the future generally explained why the XB–70 did not go to production. Gen. Thomas S. Power, Commander-in-Chief of the Strategic Air Command since 1 July 1957, offered another reason: the B–70 was really "killed" because it was designed for flight at very high altitudes —an advantage when the aircraft was first conceived, which lost most of its attraction when the Soviets developed effective, high-altitude antiaircraft missiles. Whatever the cause, several studies were undertaken to circumvent the B–70's deficiencies, while enhancing the manned bomber concept. The Air Force insisted that bombers would continue as a necessary dimension to the United States' strategic deterrent capability.

---

[54] See this appendix, p 569.

[55] The first Minuteman squadron was activated in late 1961, but the new intercontinental ballistic missile did not become operational until 11 December 1962.

The first of the bomber studies accomplished in the early sixties was finished in 1961. Known as SLAB (for *S*ubsonic *L*ow *A*ltitiude *B*omber), the study demonstrated that a fixed-wing aircraft of 500,000 pounds, with a payload of 12,000 pounds and an 11,000-nautical mile range, including 4,300 nautical miles at low altitude, was needed to replace the B–52. Next came ERSA (for *E*xtended *R*ange *S*trike *A*ircraft), a study which maintained that a 600,000-pound plane of variable swept wing with a payload of 10,000 pounds and a total range of 8,750 nautical miles (with 2,500 nautical miles at 500 feet) would suffice. Then in August 1963, a third study, LAMP (for *L*ow *A*ltitude *M*anned *P*enetrator), was completed. It recommended a 350,000-pound aircraft with a 6,200-nautical mile range (and 2,000 nautical miles at low altitude), carrying a 20,000-pound payload. As anticipated by the Air Force, these studies were not conclusive, and other planning was already in motion.

By mid-1963, a Manned Aircraft Studies Steering Group, headed by Lt. Gen. James Ferguson, Deputy Chief of Staff, Research and Development, examined various possibilities. Included were a long-endurance aircraft, a supersonic reconnaissance craft and, eventually, LAMP, which the steering group later recognized as most promising. In the meantime, another major Air Force effort to calculate its future needs had been making progress. Initiated in 1963 and known as "Forecast," the project was directed by Gen. Bernard A. Schriever, Commander of the Air Force Systems Command and an advocate of acquiring an advanced manned system.

In October 1963, Generals Schriever and Ferguson, accompanied by Lt. Gen. William H. Blanchard, Deputy Chief of Staff, Programs and Requirements since August 1963, met with other members of Project Forecast and the Manned Aircraft Studies Steering Group. The 2 organizations, after arguing over such factors as size and payload, eventually reached conclusions that were to provide the foundation for a new bomber, now termed the Advanced Manned Precision Strike System (AMPSS).

Requests for Proposals   November 1963

In November 1963, the Air Force gave 3 contractors—the Boeing Company, General Dynamics Corporation, and North American Rockwell Corporation[56]—requests for proposals for the AMPSS. However, as in the B–70's case, Secretary of Defense Robert S. McNamara had a tight hold on

---

[56] The North American Rockwell Corporation was formed on 22 September 1967, when North American Aviation, Incorporated, and Rockwell Standard Corporation merged, the 1967 designation being applied ahead of time for clarity's sake.

any money earmarked for a sophisticated new bomber. In addition, Mr. McNamara questioned the validity of the assumptions used by the Air Force to justify the AMPSS. Because of the Secretary's doubts, only $5 million became available, and the released requests for proposals were limited to the mere study of the bomber concept. Moreover, some of the tentative requirements outlined by the Air Force were promptly discredited by all contractors. One of the suggested USAF designs would have involved prohibitive costs; another, including a vertical and short takeoff and landing capability, was not feasible when dealing with the heavy gross weights envisioned by the Air Force. In any case, the industry's negative comments proved academic. By mid-1964, when the results of every study had been received, the requirements outlined in the requests for proposals of November 1963 had been substantially altered.

New Requirements   Mid-1964

By mid-1964 the bomber concept, illustrated by the proposed AMPSS, remained basically unchanged, but some of the tentative requirements previously identified had been redefined and the aircraft, expected to satisfy the new criteria, had been retitled as the Advanced Manned Strategic Aircraft (AMSA). Briefly stated, the AMSA system, while retaining the required takeoff and low altitude characteristics of the AMPSS, would also be capable of maintaining supersonic speeds at high altitudes. As a basis for further study, the Air Force in July 1964 gave the renamed, and now supersonic system, a projected gross weight of 375,000 pounds, and a range of 6,300 nautical miles, 2,000 of which would be flown at very low altitudes.

Project Slippage   1964–1968

Against odds which at first appeared highly favorable, the AMSA project was to remain unsettled for years to come. Gen. Curtis E. LeMay, Air Force Chief of Staff, after briefing President Lyndon B. Johnson in December 1963 on the program's importance, secured in 1964 the Joint Chiefs of Staff's approval of the USAF plans. In that year, as well as others, Congress approved all the AMSA money the Air Force wanted, be it for project definition,[57] or for the advanced development of engines and of an

---

[57] Project definition would produce data on probable costs, time needed for development, and technical risks. If the results were satisfactory, the Air Force would be in a position to contract for further work.

avionics system. Yet, Secretary McNamara again refused to commit any Department of Defense funds unless he was given a better justification for developing the new manned system and a clearer picture of what the projected AMSA could do.

Attempts to change Secretary McNamara's opinion of AMSA were futile. The Secretary thought surface-launched ballistic missiles could perform the "assured destruction" strategic mission better than manned bombers, and insisted that development of an expensive new system of the AMPSS/AMSA class was most unlikely. On the other hand, he believed the technological effort of avionics and propulsion research and development should go on to produce advances in the state-of-the-art applicable to future or existing manned systems. Thus, while only small sums would be released for preliminary AMSA studies, significant amounts would be allocated for research work on subsystems and components.

In late 1964, Boeing, General Dynamics, and North American Rockwell submitted initial reports on their study of AMSA. Concurrently, propulsion reports were received from Curtiss-Wright, General Electric, and Pratt & Whitney, while International Business Machines (IBM) and Hughes Aircraft sent in their avionics recommendations. In 1965, as the airframe contractors continued to study the AMSA system, General Electric and Pratt & Whitney were selected to construct 2 demonstrator engines that would meet the requirements of the AMSA mission. While this seemed encouraging, the uncertainty of the AMSA project would soon increase.

In December 1965, the Defense Department selected an elongated version of the General Dynamics F–111, known as the FB–111,[58] to replace the Strategic Air Command's B–58s, B–52Cs, and B–52Fs by fiscal year 1972. The Air Force had not requested the development of a bomber version of the controversial F–111, and opinion varied widely on its likely value. Still, the acquisition of a low-cost, interim bomber had merits. The Air Force endorsed production of the plane so long as it did not jeopardize AMSA development. As General Ferguson stated in 1966, the FB–111 was and would remain a "stopgap airplane," an assessment shared by the Strategic Air Command and the entire Air Staff even though Secretary McNamara continued to think otherwise.

By 1968, an advanced development program for avionics had been assigned to 2 contractors, IBM and the Autonetics Division of North American Rockwell. They were to determine if advanced avionics concepts were achievable and compatible to operational development. Ten sub-

---

[58] Development and production of the FB–111 proved to be closely interlaced with the whole F–111 program. The bomber's coverage was therefore included in the F–111 chapter of *Post-World War II Fighters*, Vol. 1 of the *Encyclopedia of U.S. Air Force Aircraft and Missile Systems*.

contractors, selected by the 2 firms, worked on various components, studied a wide range of components, including forward-looking radar, doppler radar, and infrared surveillance. Early in that same year, the Joint Chiefs of Staff recommended the immediate development of AMSA, and Secretary McNamara once more vetoed the proposal. He preferred instead to develop several subsystems and components for upgrading the performance of the FB-111s and the remaining B-52s with new technology that might be applied to AMSA.

Planning Changes   March 1969

The election of Richard M. Nixon in 1968 brought about a fundamental transition in strategic thinking, particularly with regard to the continued usefulness of the strategic bomber. In March 1969, Melvin R. Laird, the new Secretary of Defense, announced that the Defense Department's bomber plans were being changed. To begin with, the programmed acquisition of 253 FB-111s would be reduced to 76, because the FB-111 lacked the range and payload for strategic operations. Secretary Laird also directed the acceleration of the AMSA design studies, noting that despite the numerous and costly improvements earmarked for the last B-52 models (B-52Gs and B-52Hs), a new strategic bomber was "a more appropriate solution for a longer term bomber program."

New Designation   April 1969

In April 1969, Secretary of the Air Force Robert C. Seamans, Jr.,[59] redesignated the AMSA as the B-1A.[60]

New Requests for Proposals   3 November 1969

New requests for proposals were not issued before November 1969, even

---

[59] Secretary Seamans succeeded Harold Brown on 14 February 1969. Dr. Brown had replaced Eugene M. Zuckert as Secretary of the Air Force on 1 October 1965—a position held by Secretary Zuckert since 23 January 1961. Mr. Zuckert began serving the Air Force in 1947, when he was Assistant Secretary for Management and worked closely with W. Stuart Symington, the Air Force's first Secretary. Mr. Zuckert proved to be an earnest supporter of the AMPSS/AMSA bomber. Dr. Brown for a while became an advocate of the manned strategic aircraft, although not necessarily of AMSA.

[60] The B-1A designation was temporarily changed to B-1. Still, most of the time, the system continued to be referred to as B-1A.

though a competitive aircraft system design, coupled with an initial engine development program, had been approved in November 1968. The delay, oddly enough, was intended to speed up matters, which it did.

From the start, it had been clear that the design characteristics of the manned strategic bomber system would change as full-scale development proceeded. Because of the system's complexity, trade-offs that would affect performance were not only expected—they were considered as a future integral part of development. The Air Force was convinced that a continuation of the design competition would be fruitless and that, as agreed by Secretary Seamans, further studies would only add to the vast amount of paperwork already produced. Defense Secretary Laird's decision in March 1969 to revise the program in order to begin the B–1A's engineering development sooner confirmed the Air Force's conclusions that additional competitive designs would be time consuming and raise the program's cost without a commensurate return that could be measured by any tangible improvement of the system.

Thus, requests for proposals were issued in November 1969 that reflected an unequivocal departure from the temporizing motions of the past. The new requests were based on Defense Department approval of the USAF engineering plan and were meant to promote the prompt award of major contracts. The same airframe manufacturers, plus the Lockheed Aircraft Corporation, were in fact asked how they proposed to fabricate the B–1A airframe and to satisfy the integration requirements of the total system. In the same month, engine proposals were requested from the General Electric Company, and the Pratt & Whitney Corporation. Proposals for avionics design were again solicited, this time from 15 avionics companies. Only 5 of them chose to submit proposals to the B–1A program office.[61]

Contractor Selection   1969–1970

The avionics proposals received in December 1969 were swiftly disposed of, those of the Autonetics Division of North American Rockwell and the Federal Systems Division of IBM being selected on the 19th. In another positive departure from past procedures, the contracts awarded to the 2 companies no longer centered on feasibility but on advanced development studies. Yet, the overall avionics program was soon to experience serious setbacks.

---

[61] Established within the Aeronautical Systems Division as the AMSA program office on 13 March 1964 and redesignated in the spring of 1969.

Selection of the airframe and engine contractors started poorly, as Congress cut back on B–1A money for fiscal years 1970 and 1971. Such a decision was bound to increase development time which, in turn, would raise costs. Still, the Air Force had no recourse. Contractors had to revise airframe and engine proposals (received in January and February 1970) to fit under the program's immediate funding ceiling. The revision delay was short, but no effort could completely eradicate the impact of present and future financial restraints.

The Air Force Source Selection Evaluation Board, assembled initially on 8 December 1969 and numbering about 600 personnel at one time or another, began evaluating and scoring the revised proposals in the spring of 1970. On 5 June, following a presentation to the Defense Systems Acquisition Review Council, Deputy Secretary of Defense David Packard endorsed the Air Force's contractor selection. On the same date, Air Force Secretary Seamans announced that North American Rockwell and General Electric had been selected as the respective B–1A airframe and propulsion contractors. Secretary Seamans's announcement, wholly supported by the Air Force Chief of Staff and all the general officers in charge of the various Air Force commands concerned with the program, rested on 2 basic factors: superior technical proposals, as well as lower cost estimates.

Contractual Arrangements 5 June 1970

The Air Force negotiated 2 cost-plus-incentive-fee contracts for the B–1A development—a type of contract providing great incentive for technical innovations. Both contracts were awarded on 5 June 1970. The North American Rockwell contract (F33657–70–C–0800), with its 90/10 sharing basis,[62] had a target price of $1.3508 billion. If performance, cost, and time estimates were met, the contractor's incentive fee would amount to $115.75 million. The contract called for the development and delivery of 5 test aircraft, plus 2 structural test articles. It also covered system integration, which encompassed Total System Performance Responsibility, meaning that North American Rockwell would not be simply responsible for the B–1A airframe, but for the full-fledged weapon system.

The General Electric Company cost-plus-incentive contract (F33657–70–C–0801) had a sharing basis of 80/20 and a target price of

---

[62] The contract's sharing arrangement meant that 10 percent of any amount over the target ceiling of $1,350.8 million would be deducted from the contractor's incentive fee. But if the contractor fulfilled his commitments for less than targeted, 10 percent of the difference would be added to the incentive fee.

An artist's conception of the B-1 in flight.

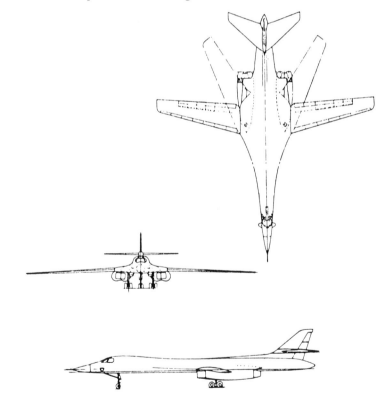

$406.7 million.[63] It covered the design, fabrication, and qualification testing of 40 engines, as well as a potential incentive fee of $30.2 million.

Immediate Setback   1970

As already noted, the Air Force knew that unexpected funding restrictions would cloud the beginning of the B–1 development. A possible palliative was to minimize management costs and to promote economy in the acquisition of the aircraft without affecting its future performance. To this aim, a special study—Project Focus—came into being. Sponsored by the B–1 project office and actively supported by the 2 major contractors, Focus did satisfy some of the Air Force's money-saving requirements. However, the Focus managerial achievements were not enough to prevent the entire project, as well as related studies, from infringing on other facets of the B–1A development program.

Most Focus recommendations were approved by Secretary Seamans before the end of 1970. One of them dealt with the assignment of a minimum of program office personnel in close proximity to the plants of principal contractors and subcontractors. The arrangement, not new but significantly extended, would reduce the voluminous, periodic paper reports that routinely plagued important development programs. It would also foster the detection and solution of many problems before they could affect cost, schedule, or performance. The Air Force believed a savings of about $60 million might ensue. Many other Focus recommendations were endorsed. Some of them, particularly those with long-range impact, were open to question.

The B–1A program was not an experimental or a prototype venture. Yet, without definitive financial support from the Congress, the Air Force did not know how many aircraft the ultimate B–1 force would include. A figure of 241 production aircraft was used for planning purposes, but this planning was doubly tentative in view of Deputy Secretary of Defense Packard's new concept of systems acquisition. "Fly-before-buy," as the concept was known, emphasized hardware demonstrations, at predetermined dates, prior to making such major program decisions as full-scale development and production. In addition, approval of the Department of Defense Systems Acquisition Review Council would be needed before the B–1A development program could enter a new phase.

All Project Focus decisions had been reached under the purview of

---

[63] The cost-sharing basis of the General Electric contract followed the formula used for North American Rockwell, except that percentages and amounts were different.

Deputy Secretary Packard's new acquisition concept. Among the most salient ones was the determination that efforts not directly contributing to a logical production decision would be deleted or deferred until such a decision had been made. Also, B-1A flight test hours would be reduced by combining the development, test, and evaluation phase (DT&E) with the initial operational test and evaluation phase (IOT&E). This was a fairly drastic departure from the established USAF testing cycle, in which the contractor took care of all initial tests (Category I) and the Air Force's participation began with the so-called Category II.[64] But the new procedure of having Air Force and contractor personnel fly together in test aircraft was expected to eliminate duplication that usually occurred during the categories I and II flights of the regular test program. In any case, the program's thoroughness was not to be undermined. The initial development flight test program was scheduled for 1,060 hours, 100 of which (later increased to 200) were to be completed prior to a production decision.

Project Focus did not overlook wind tunnel testing. Such testing would not be diminished, but the USAF facilities at the Arnold Engineering Development Center in Tennessee would be used to the maximum extent possible. Air Force program officials, after meeting with Arnold personnel, had estimated that the air vehicle would require over 18,000 hours of wind-tunnel testing; the engine, some 12,000. Other noteworthy recommendations, due to decrease costs by almost $180 million, were to be reflected in a forthcoming program reduction.

Program Reduction   18 January 1971

The B-1A development program, initiated under the procurement arrangement of June 1970, did not last long. As anticipated, Congress in the summer of 1970 had further restricted the B-1 funding to levels below $500 million for several fiscal years to come. And while Focus and additional B-1 innovation studies helped to save money, they could not totally prevent some undesirable changes. On 18 January 1971, Secretary Seamans approved a reduced program which cut the number of flight test aircraft from 5 to 3, decreased the airframe's amount of costly titanium, and slightly lowered some performance requirements. In addition, the procurement of engines was slashed from 40 to 27; selected major structural items would be tested to design-limit load levels to eliminate, if at all possible, the purchase of a static test aircraft; and the development program's pace would be slowed down.

---

[64] Until the late fifties, phases—instead of categories—delineated specific facets of the testing program. However, the program's streamlining and new terminology barely affected the test cycles and objectives. For details, see B-52, p 225.

In effect, as rescheduled, the B–1A's first flight would slide from March to April 1974, and a production go-ahead would not be considered before April 1975—a 1-year lapse between first flight and production decision, instead of the 6 months originally agreed upon. Finally, the initial operational capability (IOC) date was moved to December 1979, when the Strategic Air Command would receive its 65th B–1A. This was a long delay. Back in 1970, the Air Force had planned that the command would receive the 68th production aircraft by December 1977 and would reach IOC by that date.

Other Changes   Mid-1971

Early in 1970, IBM and North American Rockwell had participated in avionics studies, referred to as Junior Crown. This project analyzed the pros and cons of various avionics packages, taking into consideration size, performance, and cost. Junior Crown, in addition, identified equipment and development phases associated with the progression from the initial avionics subsystems to the standardized ones. But the period's budgetary limitations had also induced B–1 program officials to single out alternate design configurations. Five of those alternate combinations were based on the initial subsystems; 4, on the avionics equipment featured by several F–111 models.

In mid-1971, Secretary Seamans informed Gen. John D. Ryan, Air Force Chief of Staff since 1 August 1969, that because the B–1A production go-ahead had been postponed and only limited avionics would be needed for quite a while, earlier avionics plans could be shelved. All told, selection of an avionics subcontractor was no longer urgent; as required to accomplish the Category I tests, research and development, test and evaluation (RDT&E) B–1As would be fitted with FB–111A components and other off-the-shelf avionics; such equipment would be installed by North American Rockwell; and industry was being notified that the choosing of an avionics integrating contractor was deferred.

Secretary Seamans's decision did not negate the built-in growth factor approach that had been part of the Air Force's B–1A requirements from the start. This approach meant that technological advances could be incorporated into the aircraft design throughout the development period. In fact, while early B–1As would be equipped with available avionics, space would be provided to allow for the later installation of a more advanced network.

Unexpected Shift   September 1971

After stating in mid-1971 that selection of an avionics integrating contractor could wait, the Air Force changed its mind. On 29 September, requests for proposals that separated the avionics subsystems into offensive and defensive functions, were issued to 27 companies. Only 5 companies chose to submit proposals, but all were received before the end of November. Still, the evaluation of proposals was a time-consuming task, a factor that probably explained the Air Force's unexpected about-face. In any case, it would take until 13 April 1972 for the Boeing Company to receive the $62.4 million contract that was involved. This agreement, covering the development of offensive avionics and integration of avionics subsystems, like those of the 2 main contractors, was of the cost-plus-incentive-fee type. The contract's terms were different, however. It had a 90/10 sharing percentage arrangement, and a zero to 14 percent profit range, with a $1 million award fee provision.

In November 1971, requests for proposals for the B-1A's future defensive avionics also were issued to 23 companies. Only 2, Airborne Instrument Laboratory, a division of the Cutler-Hammer Corporation, and the Raytheon Company, responded. Evaluation of the 2 proposals was completed in February 1972, but no contract resulted because the Air Force decided that new requests for proposals were needed. The decision was prompted by the system's complexity. The Air Force believed that development of the advanced defensive avionics wanted for the B-1A could very well involve great technological risks. Therefore, it would be more sensible to divide the project into 2 phases. The first would be a 10-month attempt by 2 competing contractors, working under fixed-price contracts for a maximum combined price of $5 million. The second phase would cover engineering development, but only 1 cost-plus-fixed-fee contract would be finally awarded.

The revised requests for proposals were received by 23 firms on 17 May 1972. One year later, the same 2 contractors (Airborne Instrument Laboratory and Raytheon Company) were nearing completion of their Phase I contract—the 10-month risk reduction demonstration. Phase II, due to begin in mid-1973, was scheduled to run through December 1976. It would commence with proposal instructions for development of the radio frequency surveillance and electronic countermeasures subsystem. In the event that contractor proposals proved unacceptable, the Air Force planned to evaluate one of its own conventional subsystems.

Mockup Review   October 1971

The B-1A mockup review occurred at the North American Rockwell's Los Angeles Division in late October 1971, 2 months after the arrival of a full-scale mockup of the General Electric F101 engine. The review's primary objective was to determine if the USAF specifications were being met by the prime contractors, but some 200 Air Force representatives also examined the location of equipment in the mockup, ease of maintenance and operation being of great importance. The mockup review board and the contractors ended developing and processing 297 requests for alteration. Over 90 of those concerned the maintenance of the future aircraft; nearly 60 dealt chiefly with safety; and 10 with the aircraft's logistical support. The rest fell in the operational category. In addition, there were 21 requests for alterations to the engine, the most noteworthy one involving a change in the piping to make the engine handling mount more accessible.

Special Features   1971–1973

The future B–1A's most notable features were its variable swept wings, which could be fully retracted or totally extended in flight. The aircraft's body shape also was most unusual in that it tended to blend smoothly into the wing to enhance lift and reduce drag.[65] Finally, particularly in view of their length, the location of the 4 F101 supersonic turbofan engines, each in the 30,000-pound thrust class, was another very special feature. The engines (2 per pod) were mounted beneath the inboard wing, close to the aircraft's center of gravity, in order to improve stability when flying through the heavy turbulence often experienced at low altitudes.

The B–1A's special features promised to pay high dividends and put the new weapon system in a unique category. It differed radically from existing bombers,[66] particularly the B–52, the Air Force's highly praised but aging mainstay. Specifically, the B–1A's variable-geometry (swing) wing and high thrust-to-weight ratio would enable it to use short runways, a characteristic due to provide additional opportunities for aircraft dispersal throughout the United States. The new bomber would have a low turn-around and maintenance repair rate because of new methods for rapidly checking out and verifying subsystems. Although only two-thirds the size of the B–52, with aerial refueling the B–1A would be able to carry twice the weapons load over the same intercontinental distances. The future aircraft's supersonic fly-out speed would get it airborne faster, a vital asset in case of an alert warning. And with regard to a nuclear attack, hardening techniques would

---

[65] In accordance with the so-called blended-wing body concept.

[66] The relatively small FB–111A, the production of which ended in July 1971, basically was little more than a modified fighter. Its take-off weight was under 110,000 pounds and this interim bomber, as the Air Force regarded it, could not even be remotely compared to the future aircraft.

enable the B-1 bomber to withstand greater over-pressures and thermal radiation from nuclear weapons.

An automatic terrain-following radar and a near-sonic speed capability at low altitudes would permit the new weapon system to penetrate the sophisticated defenses expected to be used into the 21st century. The B-1A's low-altitude performance also would be a defensive advantage against enemy interceptor aircraft since the high aerodynamic stresses of low altitudes would nullify the interceptors' effectiveness. Moreover, the new bomber's small radar cross section would minimize its detection by enemy radars.

Development Problems   1971–1972

Development of any weapon system routinely entailed problems, and the Air Force did not expect the B-1A to deviate from this pattern. Yet, by the end of 1971, except for some weight increase, not an unusual occurrence, and difficulties with the crew escape system, problems were minor. For example, the aircraft's windshield, which included a thin polycarbon inner layer, had poor optical qualities and tended to shatter upon impact. However, 2 new windshields, incorporating different inner layers of stretched acrylic, were soon to be tested, and 1 of the 2 most likely would be satisfactory. The integrated semi-conductor of the Central Integrated Test System AP–2 computer also was deficient, but the technical problems of this major component were solvable.

The crew escape system was a different story. As developed (and eventually installed on the first 3 RDT&E B–1As), it resembled the F–111's crew module which ranked as a major advancement in aircraft design.[67] But when it came to the 4-crew B–1A, the new module's research and development costs could reach about $125 million; nearly half of that amount had already been spent, and test results thus far had been disappointing. Another alternative might be the development of standard, but greatly improved ejection seats—not the Air Force's preferred solution, but an option of last resort. Consequently, the B–1A program office in early 1972 planned to study once again the various options to the basic module system, knowing full well, however, that no clear answer was in sight. The B–1A's

---

[67] Developed by the McDonnell Aircraft Corporation and initially tested in 1966, the crew module of the General Dynamics F–111 was fully automated. When forced to abandon his aircraft, the pilot only had to press, squeeze, or pull 1 lever. This caused an explosive cutting cord to shear the module from the fuselage; a rocket motor ejected the module upward and it parachuted to the ground or sea. There, like the Mercury and Gemini capsules of the U.S. early space programs, the capsule could serve as a survival shelter for the F–111's 2 crewmen.

prototype F101 engines also were experiencing some of the problems common to all development programs in their early stages. Such difficulties centered on turbine blade failures, high speed compressor stalls, excessive oil consumption, and related deficiencies. But all problems were being taken care of or soon would be. And the propulsion outlook seemed even more rewarding, when USAF engineers commented in mid-1972 that the General Electric F101 had the potential to be the most durable high-performance engine the Air Force had yet procured.

Second Slippage   1973

An April 1972 review of the B–1A program at the Los Angeles Division of the Rockwell International Corporation[68] yielded encouraging results, leading the Air Force to conclude that the B–1A's first flight would occur,

---

[68] So designated on 16 February 1973, following merger of the North American Rockwell Corporation with the Rockwell Manufacturing Company.

Interior view of the cockpit in a B–1 full-scale mockup.

as scheduled, in April 1974. But the optimism of the spring of 1972 did not necessarily prevail 1 year later.

In July 1973, Secretary of the Air Force John L. McLucas, who had replaced Secretary Seamans in May, notified Senator John C. Stennis, Chairman of the Senate Armed Services Committee, that fabrication of the first RDT&E B–1A had fallen behind schedule. The start of the second one also had been delayed, because the effort involved in manufacturing and assembling the aircraft had been underestimated. The Air Force had become aware of such problems in early 1973 and had turned down the contractor's request for overtime work, since this expedient might increase the program's technical risks and would definitely raise costs. Slowing down the development program seemed to be safer. As now planned, the initial flight of the first B–1A would take place in mid-1974; fabrication, assembly, and flight testing of the second and third B–1As would be slightly delayed, and the production decision would be postponed from July 1975 to May 1976. The new schedule would increase the estimated total development cost from $2.71 billion to $2.79 billion—an $80 million solution, cheaper than attempting to adhere to the original timetable through the expensive use of overtime.

As a direct response to Secretary McLucas' news, the Senate Armed Services Committee's Research and Development Subcommittee held on 27 July a special hearing concerning the B–1A program. Senator Thomas J. McIntyre, Chairman of the subcommittee, expressed his concern about the state of the program. Senator Barry Goldwater commented on the Air Force's inability to adhere to schedule and cost estimates for the program and requested assurance that the Air Force would meet the new schedule. Secretary McLucas pointed out that the Air Force did not anticipate any major production problems. Except for increases caused by inflation, production cost estimates were not expected to rise excessively. Maj. Gen. Douglas T. Nelson, Director of the B–1 program since 13 August 1970, underlined the Air Force's own dissatisfaction, stating that Rockwell should have been better prepared either to prevent or to solve the problems that had come up.

Asked about the contractual provision which limited government obligation each fiscal year, General Nelson explained that this provision enabled the Air Force to develop a stable budget, based on the contractor's funding request for the coming year. The provision also precluded the possibility of a subsequent request by the contractor for additional funds to continue working. The obligation for fiscal year 1974 was $312 million. The contractor would have exceeded this amount by $134.8 million if the development program had not been restructured and if the original schedule had been allowed to continue.

Another Reduction

Restructure of the B–1A development required the amendment of the program's 2 major contracts, since both included very specific provisions. By supplemental agreement, signed before 15 July 1973, the first flight of the Rockwell International B–1A was moved from April to June 1974, and the initial flights of the second and third articles were scheduled for January 1976 and September 1975, respectively.[69] Selected static tests were to be completed by February 1976, while procurement of a full-scaled fatigue test B–1A was definitely deleted.

The General Electric contract, modified in the summer of 1973 like that of Rockwell International, involved more drastic changes. To save money, the number of experimental F101 engines was reduced from 3 to 2, the quantity of prototype F101s was cut from 27 to 23, and the option for 6 F101 qualification test engines was canceled. The modified contract provided for 4 F101 qualification test engines, and for an extended YF101 flight test program of 1,105 hours, due to end in September 1978. As in the airframe's case, engine deliveries were paced down.

The development program's entire funding also was spelled out in no uncertain terms. The total allotment for fiscal year 1970 through fiscal year 1974 was limited to $1.0238 billion, and the allotment for fiscal year 1975 was not to exceed $200 million. The allotment for subsequent years was established at $153.2 million per year, without restriction. Funds for the offensive avionics were included in such figures. The multi-year total for both offensive and defensive avionics was set at $71.8 million, but the money could be disbursed in a more flexible fashion. In other words, not more than $30 million could be spent in any given year through fiscal year 1974, but if only $11.8 million had been paid out by then, the remaining $60 million could be later disbursed in one lump sum.

The avionics funding flexibility was important in view of the fact that amendment of the B–1A weapon system's 2 major contracts dictated another significant change. Specifically, the Boeing offensive avionics integration contract, a $62.4 million deal, had to be revised to match Rockwell's new delivery schedules. Simply put, Boeing would have to postpone for 8 months the installation, check-out, and flight testing of the offensive avionics which, from the start, had been earmarked to be first integrated in the second B–1A.

---

[69] This apparently odd sequence made sense; since the second B–1A was to be fitted with the first set of offensive avionics, a trying as well as time-consuming task.

Total B-1A's Accepted   None

Total Development Costs $1.1338 billion

As of mid-1973, cumulative development costs reached over $1.13 billion. This total included the amount spent since 1963 on AMPSS/AMSA studies and other related projects. In 1970, when the program's first reduction occurred, Air Force budget analysts estimated that total development costs would reach $2.6283 billion; production costs (for the planned 241 B-1s), $8.4943 billion. Hence, the Air Force anticipated the entire program's cost would top $11 billion.

Program Status   1973

As 1973 came to a close, the future of the Air Force's new bomber, be it known as the AMSA or the B-1A, remained uncertain. In August, the Air Force Secretary asked Dr. Raymond L. Bisplinghoff, Deputy Director of the National Science Foundation, to conduct an independent review of the B-1A's status. Secretary McLucas' concern centered primarily on the restructured program's management and the adequacy of efforts to develop and produce the aircraft. The Secretary's request led to the formation of a review committee of 25, staffed with people from industry, the Air Force Scientific Advisory Board, other government agencies, and retired military and civilian federal employees. Members of the Bisplinghoff Committee, as it became known, worked quickly. On 4 October, Dr. Bisplinghoff and 3 committee members gave Secretary McLucas their findings.

Briefly stated, the committee did not foresee any technical problems that would prevent successful development or production, although the B-1 weapon system's complexity could not be overlooked. In this regard, except for wind tunnel testing and engine development,[70] the development program's new schedule was still unrealistic, and the program was insufficiently funded. There was no money to cope with possible problems. Moreover, 3 test aircraft were not enough in view of the redesign work that probably would be necessary prior to production. This was particularly crucial, since each test aircraft had a specific purpose. Should 1 of the 3 aircraft be destroyed during testing, the program's risks would be greatly increased.

---

[70] The propulsion system, the committee members confirmed, was the program's brightest spot; chances were good that cost, schedule, and most technical goals would be realized.

Dr. Bisplinghoff in his conclusion described the B-1A's structure as airworthy, but heavy and costly. The Bisplinghoff Committee questioned the accuracy of the USAF estimates of the aircraft's empty weight, range, take-off distance, and refueling altitude. Therefore, the program's cancellation should be seriously considered, in the event of a further funding reduction for an already "marginal" program. As time would show, lack of funds, technical difficulties, and other problems were to plague the B-1A program. Governmental policy changes obviously had the greatest impact. But while the B-1A was to become a dead issue under one administration, a subsequent one would champion an improved version of the aircraft, later known as the B-1B.

TECHNICAL AND BASIC MISSION PERFORMANCE DATA

B-1A AIRCRAFT[a]

Manufacturer (Airframe)	Rockwell International Corp., Los Angeles Div., Los Angeles, Calif.
Manufacturer (Engines)	General Electric Co., Evendale Plant, Evendale, Ohio
Nomenclature	Strategic Bomber
Popular Name	None

Length/Span (ft)	145.3/136.7
Wing Area (sq ft)	1,946
Weights (lb)	
Empty	143,000 (est)
Combat	200,102 (est)
Takeoff	360,000 (est)—limited by landing gear strength
Engine: Number,	(4) 29,850-lb st
Rated Power per Engine,	F101-GE-100 (max with afterburners)
& Designation	(axial turbofan)
Takeoff Ground Run (ft)	
At Sea Level	4,440 (with max afterburner thrust)
Over 50-ft Obstacle	6,135 (with max afterburner thrust)
Rate of Climb (fpm)	
at Sea Level	2,820 (intermediate thrust)
Combat Max Rate of Climb	
(fpm) at Sea Level	30,930 (with max afterburner thrust)
Service Ceiling (100 fpm	
Rate of Climb to Altitude)	27,000 (intermediate thrust)
Combat Service Ceiling	
(100 fpm Rate of Climb to Altitude)	39,300 (intermediate thrust)
Combat Ceiling (500 fpm	
Rate of Climb to Altitude)	58,800 (with max afterburner thrust)
Basic Speed at	
35,000 ft (kn)	1,092 (with max afterburner thrust)
Average Cruise Speed (kn)	
Outside Penetration Zone	420
Max Speed at Optimum	
Altitude (kn/ft)	1,262/59,000 (with max afterburner thrust)
Combat Range (nm)	6,103
Total Mission Time (hr)	14.0
Crew	4 (pilot, co-pilot, & 2 sub-systems operators)
Armament	
Internal	24 AGM-69A SRAMs[b]
External	8 AGM-69A SRAMs
Maximum Bombload (lb)	75,000

Abbreviations			
cal	= caliber	max	= maximum
fpm	= feet per minute	nm	= nautical miles
kn	= knots	st	= static thrust

[a]January 1972 estimates.
[b]Short Range Attack Missile (SRAM), produced by the Boeing Airplane Company.

594

Glossary

AAF	Army Air Forces
AFB	Air Force Base
AMC	Air Materiel Command
AMPSS	Advanced Manned Precision Strike System
AMSA	Advanced Manned Strategic Aircraft
ARDC	Air Research and Development Command
Convair	Consolidated Vultee Aircraft Corporation
DT&E	development, test, and evaluation
ECM	electronic countermeasures
ECP	engineering change proposal
ELINT	electronic intelligence
ERSA	Extended Range Strike Aircraft
FEAF	Far East Air Forces
FPF	fixed-price-firm (contract)
FPI	fixed-price-incentive (contract)
FPIR	fixed-price-incentive renegotiable
FY	fiscal year
GAM	guided air missile
GEBO	generalized bomber study
GOR	general operational requirement
IBM	International Business Machines, Inc.
IFF	identification friend or foe
IOC	initial operational capability
IOT&E	initial operational test and evaluation phase
IRAN	inspect and repair as necessary
LAMP	Low Altitude Manned Penetrator
LAMS	Load Alleviation and Mode Stabilization
MADREC	Malfunction Detection and Recording
NASA	National Aeronautics and Space Administration
PACAF	Pacific Air Forces
QRC	quick reaction capability
RAF	Royal Air Force
Rand	The Rand Corporation, Santa Monica, Calif.
RDT&E	research and development, test and evaluation phase

GLOSSARY

SAB	Supersonic Aircraft Bomber
SAC	Strategic Air Command
SHORAN	short-range navigation technology
SLAB	Subsonic Low Altitude Bomber
SRAM	short-range attack missile
TAC	Tactical Air Command
TARC	Tactical Air Reconnaissance Center
TRW	tactical reconnaissance wing
USAF	United States Air Force
USAFE	United States Air Forces in Europe
VDT	variable discharge turbine
WIBAC	Wichita Boeing Aircraft Company (Project)

Selected Bibliography

This volume, covering over 30 years of aviation technology in bomber aircraft, is a compilation of Air Force data from countless official documents. Secondary sources (commercial publications, newspapers, etc.) were used only to confirm data of minor importance. The most important source materials were the major command histories and the special studies of the Air Force Logistics Command, the Aerospace Defense Command, and the Strategic Air Command. Air Staff semiannual reports, technical summaries, and records of wing and squadron histories also provided valuable information. These documents are in the archives of the USAF Historical Research Center, Maxwell AFB, Alabama. Those of special interest are listed below.

Governmental Sources

Air Staff Directorate Histories

Development and Acquisition, DCS/Research and Development. 1 April 1970–on.
Maintenance, Supply and Services, DCS/Materiel. Until 10 April 1951.
Maintenance Engineering, DCS/Materiel. 10 April 1951 to 30 June 1961.
Maintenance Engineering, DCS/Systems and Logistics. 1 July 1961 to 14 March 1973.
Operational Requirements, DCS/Operations. 20 April 1959 to 31 January 1963.
Operational Requirements, DCS/Programs and Requirements. 1 February 1963 to 2 May 1965.
Operational Requirements and Development Plans, DCS/Research and Development. 3 May 1965–on.
Procurement and Production Engineering, DCS/Materiel. Until February 1955.
Procurement and Production, DCS/Materiel. 1 February 1955 to 30 June 1961.
Procurement Management, DCS/Systems and Logistics. 1 July 1961 to February 1963.
Procurement Policy, DCS/Systems and Logistics. February 1963–on.
Production, DCS/Systems and Logistics. 1 February 1963 to 14 January 1965.
Production and Programming, DCS/Systems and Logistics. 15 January 1964 to 14 February 1969.
Production and Programming, DCS/Research and Development. 15 February to 13 November 1969.
Production, DCS/Research and Development. 14 November 1969 to 31 March 1970.
Reconnaissance (Assistant for), DCS/Research and Development. 3 May 1965 to 14 April 1968.
Reconnaissance and Electronic Warfare, DCS/Research and Development. 15 April 1968–on.

BIBLIOGRAPHY

Historical Studies and Monographs

Alling, Frederick A. *History of the B-57 Airplane, July 1953–January 1958.* Wright-Patterson Air Force Base: Air Materiel Command, September 1958.

_____. *History of the B/RB-66 Weapon System, 1952–1959.* Wright-Patterson Air Force Base: Air Materiel Command, 1960.

Air Materiel Command Staff. *Case History of the B-36 Airplane.* Wright-Patterson Air Force Base, Ohio: Historical Office, Air Materiel Command, May 1948.

_____. *Case History of the B-36 Airplane.* Wright-Patterson Air Force Base, Ohio: Historical Office, Air Materiel Command, May 1949.

Air Research and Development Command Staff. *Air Force Developmental Aircraft.* Baltimore, Md.: Historical Office, Air Research and Development Command, April 1957.

Air Technical Service Command Staff. *A-26, November 1940–October 1945.* Wright Field, Ohio: Air Technical Service Command, 1945.

Bagwell, Margaret C. *XB-52, November 1945–November 1948.* Wright-Patterson Air Force Base, Ohio: Historical Office, Air Materiel Command, 1949.

_____. *XB-47, B-47, November 1943–February 1950.* Wright-Patterson Air Force Base, Ohio: Historical Office, Air Materiel Command, 1950.

_____. *Special Weapons Supplement to the History of the B-47, October 1945–May 1952.* Wright-Patterson Air Force Base, Ohio: Historical Office, Air Materiel Command, 1953.

_____. *B-47 Production Program, 1949–1953.* Wright-Patterson Air Force Base, Ohio: Historical Office, Air Materiel Command, 1954.

Caywood, Ron. *Major Problems in the B-52 Conversion Program, 1955–1958.* Offutt Air Force Base, Nebr.: Historical Office, Strategic Air Command, n.d.

Del Papa, Michael. *From Snark to Sram: A Pictorial History of Strategic Air Command Missiles.* Offutt Air Force Base, Nebr.: Historical Office, Strategic Air Command, March 1976.

Dubuque, Jean H., and Gleckner, Robert F. *The Development of the Heavy Bomber, 1918–1944.* Maxwell Air Force Base, Ala.: Air University, 1951.

Fenwick, Amy C. *Supplementary B-36 Study, Preliminary Negotiations for Long Range Bombardment Airplane.* Wright-Patterson Air Force Base, Ohio: Historical Office, Air Materiel Command, July 1949.

Goldberg, Alfred and Little, Robert D. *History of Headquarters USAF, 1 July 1949–30 June 1950.* Washington: USAF Historical Division Liaison Office, 1954.

Greene, Warren E. *The Development of the B-52 Aircraft, 1945–1953.* AFLC Historical Study. May 1956.

Greenhalgh, William H. *U.S. Air Force Reconnaissance in Southeast Asia, 1960–1975.* Washington: Office of Air Force History, 1977.

Hall, Cargill R. *Hustler: A History of the B-58 Bomber.* SAC Historical Study. Offutt Air Force Base, Nebr.: Historical Office, Strategic Air Command, November 1978.

James, Martin E. *Historical Highlights, United States Air Forces in Europe, 1945–1980.* Ramstein AB, Germany: United States Air Forces in Europe, May 1980.

Kipp, Robert M. *B-47 Procurement, Production and Modification, 1953–1956.* Wright-Patterson Air Force Base, Ohio: Historical Office, Air Materiel Command, 1957.

Loegering, J. R. *The B-36 Design, Procurement and Materiel Development through 1950.* Offutt Air Force Base, Nebr.: Historical Office, Strategic Air Command, 1951.

_____. *The B-47 Modification, Armament, Equipment, and Training, July–December 1951.* Offutt Air Force Base, Nebr.: Historical Office, Strategic Air Command, 1952.

Marmor, Arthur K., *The Search for New USAF Weapons, 1958–1959.* Washington: USAF Historical Division Liaison Office, April 1961.

Miller, Martin J. *XB-48, August 1944–January 1950*. Wright-Patterson Air Force Base, Ohio: Air Materiel Command, December 1950.

Moulton, Harland B. *The Evolution of the SAC Mobility Plan and Logistics Support Program through 1951*. SAC Historical Study. Offutt Air Force Base, Nebr.: Historical Office, Strategic Air Command, 1952.

Moulton, Harland B., and Caywood, E. Ron. *The History of the B-52: Background and Early Development, 1946–1954*. SAC Historical Study. Offutt Air Force Base, Nebr.: Strategic Air Command, n.d.

Mueller, Robert. *Air Force Bases. Vol 1. Active Air Force Bases within the United States of America on 1 January 1974*. Maxwell Air Force Base, Ala.: Albert F. Simpson Historical Research Center, 1982.

Nalty, Bernard C. *The Quest for an Advanced Manned Strategic Bomber, USAF Plans and Policies, 1961–1966*. Washington: USAF Historical Division Liaison Office, August 1966.

_____. *The Air Force in Southeast Asia, Tactics and Techniques of Electronic Warfare: Electronic Countermeasures in the Air War against North Vietnam*. Washington: Office of Air Force History, August 1977.

Neufeld, Jacob, *et al. Major Changes in Air Force Organization*. Washington: Office of Air Force History, January 1978.

_____. *USAF Turbojet and Turbofan Engines, A Brief History of Their Development*. Washington: Office of Air Force History, 1979.

Perry, Robert L. *A Brief Narrative History of the YB-49 and YRB-49A*. ASD Historical Study. 1961.

Pfau, Richard and Greenhalgh, William H. *The Air Force in Southeast Asia, The B-57G—Tropic Moon III, 1967–1972*. Washington: Office of Air Force History, 1978.

Strategic Air Command Historical Staff. *The Development of Strategic Air Command, 1946–1975*. Offutt Air Force Base, Nebr.: Historical Office, Strategic Air Command, September 1974.

_____. *The Development of Strategic Air Command, 1946–1976*. Offutt Air Force Base, Nebr.: Historical Office, Strategic Air Command, March 1976.

_____. *The Development of Strategic Air Command, 1946–1981*. Offutt Air Force Base, Nebr.: Historical Office, Strategic Air Command, July 1982.

Schulz, Helen H. *Case History of the B-57 (Canberra) Airplane, August 1950–June 1953*. Wright-Patterson Air Force Base, Ohio: Historical Office, Air Materiel Command, 1954.

Scott, Andrew W. *SAC Specialized Aircraft Maintenance: Early Development through July 1957*. Offutt Air Force Base, Nebr.: Historical Office, Strategic Air Command, 1958.

Scott, Jessie C. *Conclusion of the B-36 Phaseout, July 1957–May 1959*. Kelly Air Force Base, Tex.: Historical Office, San Antonio Air Logistics Center (AMC), 1960.

Stacy, Bill B., and Patchin, Kenneth L. *SEA Logistics Support, July 1961–March 1966*. Wright-Patterson Air Force Base, Ohio: Historical Office, Air Force Logistics Command, 1967.

Tarmena, Bernard J. *XB-35 and YB-49 Cost Data*. Wright-Patterson Air Force Base, Ohio: Historical Office, Air Force Logistics Command, February 1984.

Thomas, Richard D. *History of the Development of the B-58 Bomber*. Wright-Patterson Air Force Base, Ohio: Historical Office, Aeronautical Systems Division (AFSC), November 1965.

USAFE Historical Staff. *Aircrew Survival in the Cold War*. Lindsey Air Station, Germany: Historical Office, United States Air Forces in Europe, April 1964.

Van Staaveren, Jacob. *SAC Participation in the Missile Program, March–December 1957*. Offutt Air Force Base, Nebr.: Historical Office, Strategic Air Command, 1958.

BIBLIOGRAPHY

Air Force Major Command and Division Histories

Aerospace Defense Command, 15 January 1968–on.
Air Defense Command, until 15 January 1968.
Air Force Logistics Command, 1 April 1961–on.
Air Materiel Command, until 1 April 1961.
Air Force Systems Command (AFSC), 1 July 1961–on.
    Aeronautical Systems Division (AFSC), 1 July 1961–on.
Air Research and Development Command (ARDC), until 17 March 1961.
    Air Development Force (ARDC), 2 April 1951 to 6 June 1951.
    Wright Air Development Center (ARDC), 2 April 1951 to 6 June 1951.
    Wright Air Development Division (ARDC), 15 December 1959 to 31 March 1961.
Pacific Air Forces, 1 July 1957–on.
Strategic Air Command, 21 March 1946–on.
Tactical Air Command (TAC), 21 March 1946 to 1 December 1948; 1 December 1950–on. (TAC was subordinate to Continental Air Command between December 1948 and December 1950.)
United States Air Forces in Europe, 10 October 1947–on.

Reports and Recurring Publications

Air University Review. Air University, Maxwell Air Force Base, Ala. Bimonthly. 1975–on.
Annual Report of the Secretary of the Air Force in Annual Report of the Secretary of Defense. FY 1956 through FY 1970.
Army Air Forces Statistical Digest. World War II through 1946; 1947.
Prologue. National Archives Trust Fund, Washington, D.C. Quarterly. 1975–on.
Semiannual Report of the Secretary of the Air Force in Semiannual Report of the Secretary of Defense. January 1955 through June 1955.
USAF Aircraft and Missile Characteristics Summary (Black Book). 1948–on.
USAF Management Summary, Selected Acquisition Report. 30 September 1970.
USAF Production Digest. 1956 through 1971.
USAF Standard Aircraft Characteristics (Green Book). 1949–on.
United States Air Force Statistical Digest. 1947 through June 1950 and FY 51 through FY 74.

Orders, Manuals, and Other Publications

Department of Defense Model Designation of Military Aircraft, Rockets, and Guided Missiles. July 1967, January 1970, April 1974.
Air Force Pamphlet 190-2-2. Releasable Data on USAF Aerospace Craft. 1 June 1964.
Air Force Pamphlet 190-2-2. A Chronology of American Aerospace Events from 1903 through 1964. 1 September 1965.
Technical Manual (T.O. 00-25-30). Air Force Logistics Command. Unit Costs of Aircraft, Guided Missiles and Engines. 30 June 1971, 30 June 1972, and 30 June 1973.
Technical Order 00-25-30. Air Force Logistics Command. Unit Costs of Aircraft, Guided Missiles and Engines. 20 February 1962, 30 April 1968, 1 July 1969, and 30 June 1970.
Technical Order 00-25-30. Air Materiel Command. Unit Costs of Aircraft, Guided Missiles and Engines. 25 August 1958 and 20 February 1960.
USAF Research and Development Quarterly Review. 1950 through 1960.

Congress

House. Hearings before Subcommittee No. 2 of the Committee on Armed Services. *Department of Defense Decision to Reduce the Number and Types of Manned Bombers in the Strategic Air Command*. 89th Cong, 2d sess. Washington: Government Printing Office, 1966.

Senate. Hearings before the Committee on Armed Services. *Department of Defense Appropriations for 1967*. 90th Cong, 1st sess. Washington: Government Printing Office, 1967.

Senate. Report of the Preparedness Investigating Subcommittee of the Senate Committee on Armed Services. *Investigation of the Preparedness Program, The B-70 Program*. 89th Cong, 2d sess. Washington: Government Printing Office, 1960.

Books

Allen, William H., ed. *Dictionary of Technical Terms for Aerospace Use*. Washington: National Aeronautics and Space Administration, 1977.

Berger, Carl, ed. *The United States Air Force in Southeast Asia, 1961–1973*. Washington: Office of Air Force History, 1973.

Craven, W. F. and Cate, J. L., eds. *The Army Air Forces in World War II*. 7 vols. Chicago: University of Chicago Press, 1948. [Reprinted by the Office of Air Force History, 1984.]

Futrell, Robert Frank. *The United States Air Force in Korea, 1950–1953*. Washington: Office of Air Force History, 1983.

Heflin, Woodford A., ed. *The United States Air Force Dictionary*. Maxwell Air Force Base, Ala.: Air University Press, 1956.

Ravenstein, Charles A. The Organization and Lineage of the United States Air Force. Washington: Office of Air Force History, 1986.

Wolk, Herman S. *Planning and Organizing the Postwar Air Force, 1943–1947*. Washington: Office of Air Force History, 1984.

Non-Governmental Sources

Books

Borowski, Harry E. *A Hollow Threat, Strategic Air Power and Containment Before Korea*. Westport, Conn.: Greenwood Press, 1982.

Bowers, Peter M. *Boeing Aircraft Since 1916*. London and New York: Putnam and Company, Ltd, and Aero Publishers, Inc. 1966.

Bridgman, Leonard, ed. and compiler. *Jane's All the World's Aircraft*. London: Samson Low, Marston & Co., Ltd., 1946-on.

Jones, Lloyd S. *U.S. Bombers*. Fallbrook, Calif.: Aero Publishers, Inc., 1980. 3rd ed.

Munson, Kenneth and Swanborough, Gordon. *Boeing, An Aircraft Album No. 4*. New York: Arco Publishing Company, Inc., 1972.

Swanborough, Frederick G., and Bowers, Peter. *United States Military Aircraft Since 1909*. London and New York: G. P. Putnam's Sons, 1963 and 1971 Revised Edition.

BIBLIOGRAPHY

Periodicals

Aerophile. Aerophile, Inc., San Antonio, Tex. Bimonthly. May 78–on.

Aerospace Historian. Kansas State University, Manhattan, Kans. Quarterly. June 1975–on.

Air Force Magazine. Air Force Association, Washington, D.C. Monthly. August 1957–on.

Airpower. Sentry Books, Granada Hills, Calif. Bimonthly. September 73–on.

Armed Forces Journal. Army & Navy Journal, Inc., Washington, D.C. Monthly. 1960–on.

Aviation Week and Space Technology. McGraw-Hill, Inc., New York. Weekly. 1959–on.

Journal of the American Aviation Historical Society. American Aviation Historical Society, Santa Ana, Calif. Quarterly. 1978–on.

Index